# SPENDING ADVERTISING MONEY

Simon Broadbent

# SPENDING
# ADVERTISING
# MONEY

an introduction to media planning,
media buying and the uses of media research

THIRD EDITION

*Published in association with CAM
(Communication, Advertising and
Marketing Education Foundation)*

**BUSINESS BOOKS**
COMMUNICA - EUROPA

*First published in 1970*
*Second impression 1971*
*Second edition 1975*
*Third edition 1979*

© SIMON BROADBENT, 1970, 1975, 1979

ISBN 0 220 67024 2 (cased)
     0 220 67020 X (limp)

*This book has been set 10 on 12 pt Press Roman.*
*Printed in England by The Anchor Press Ltd*
*and bound by Wm Brendon & Son Ltd*
*both of Tiptree, Essex for the publishers,*
*Business Books Ltd, 24 Highbury Crescent, London N5*

# SPENDING ADVERTISING MONEY

*'The trade of advertising is now so near to perfection that it is not easy to propose any improvement.'*

DR JOHNSON, *The Idler,* No. 40 (1759)

*'The science of advertising is at the same stage of development that the physical sciences were in the 13th century – in the alchemist's cell, the four basic elements, secret potions and magical incantations.'*

PROFESSOR GENSCH in 'Computer models in advertising media selection', *Journal of Marketing Research* (November 1968)

# CONTENTS

# *INTRODUCTION*

# INTRODUCTION TO
# THE FIRST EDITION

This book is about money — the vast amount *[[£900 million in [1977]* spent each year by British advertising agencies on display advertising in the mass media.

It is the responsibility of these agencies to recommend where the money goes — to independent television, to newspapers and magazines, to outdoor advertising, to cinema or radio. One object of the book is to increase the efficiency of the decisions they make, to stretch the advertising pound. So this book is about advertising agencies and how they make their media choice. It is particularly about the large agencies, who set the pace. It is also about the media themselves, as vehicles for advertising.

## WHO THIS BOOK IS FOR

*For the agency*

I have written primarily for planners and buyers in agencies, showing the part they can play in the whole advertising process. I have tried to describe the methods and data developed to help them in their work. I hope it will be of some use in their training and that of other students (now those reading for the CAM Certificate or Media Diploma).

The media man is only one member of the team in the agency which makes media decisions. Many others work with him — account executives, creative groups and researchers. These people should not treat the media department merely as a storeroom for rate cards and a typing pool for schedules. I have indicated how they can get the best from a modern media department.

## For advertisers

Media decisions are concerned with how much should be spent on a campaign, when it should be spent, in what regions and in what media. Their value emerges only when their effects have been assessed. The principles and methods which I have attempted to explain may help advertisers — both in their own decisions and in supervising their agencies — at all stages of planning and evaluating a campaign.

## For media owners

Advertising revenue means life or death to most media. Their advertisement departments and representatives, who sell time or space to agencies, should know how the media choice is made. Only then can they properly direct their attempts to influence these decisions to their own advantage.

## For a wider public

Advertising attracts comment by government bodies, economists, journalists and other keepers of the national conscience. All these people express their views freely about the mass media and the spending of advertising money — which is as it should be. But they sometimes lack information about the objectives and criteria used in the industry. It has in fact been difficult for them to find out: the literature on advertising economics is remarkably obscure and tendentious. I have tried to describe for them, as clearly as I can, what in practice influences advertising expenditure.

# HOW TO USE THE BOOK

The book has been designed to be used selectively. The contents list shows in detail the ground covered; each chapter starts with a short summary; the index helps the reader to find the explanations of technical terms. An outline of the four parts of the book now follows:

*Part 1* is a simple introduction for non-specialists. It sets the scene in which media decisions are taken. It gives the common view on how advertising helps to sell products and describes the way advertising money moves from consumer to advertiser and thence to agency and to media owner.

*Part 2* is about the mass media — independent television, the national press and so on. It is intended particularly for agency people outside or just joining the media department and for advertisers. Media specialists require a more detailed and up-to-the-minute knowledge than this outline.

*Part 3* is for the media department and those who work closely with it, especially planners, account executives, brand managers and media owners. It sets down the steps by which the agency reaches its media choice. There is a discussion of agency structure and of the media brief. The jobs of the media planner and buyer are described. A check list, given in the Appendix, summarises in a practical form the decisions which have to be taken for each campaign and which are discussed in detail in this part of the book.

*Part 4* is to help those who want to get the most out of research data and the computer, for specialised users and producers of data. Interested non-specialists will find the descriptions have been kept as non-technical as possible.

The methods used to analyse research data, to select media and to construct advertising schedules are in a state of flux. Time-honoured techniques are still with us — over-simple measures of relative cost, inspired hunches on the suitability of different media, criteria whose appropriateness is untested. I do not suggest for a moment that the time has come to discard this experience and tradition. Where so little has yielded to the scientific approach, informed commonsense is

5

indispensable. But the influence of more modern techniques is beginning to be felt. As yet there is no science of advertising, but its foundations are at least being excavated. The researcher and computer programmer now sometimes work in the same building as the copywriter and the media buyer.

## THE BALANCE OF THEORY AND PRACTICE

Most text books concentrate on the theory of their subjects. People who learn from them are notoriously unable to cope with actual problems until they have had practical experience. What they then gain is an appreciation of the atmosphere of the real world. Media decisions are not reached in a leisurely laboratory. Time is always short and information always fallible.

Reading this book cannot be a substitute for experience. But I have covered a wider area than is usual in books on this subject. I have done so without going deeply into any one aspect because it seems more useful to indicate the general flavour and breadth of the motives and politics, the commercial pressures, the difficulties and fascination of media work. I have written this book in a busy media department where media decisions are being made every day, not in an ivory tower. I have tried to distil how this experience can be combined with the more disciplined approach of the researcher. Classically, case histories are the way to communicate this experience. I have given some examples; to provide more would be to add to an already long book; also, case histories tend to be confidential, untidy and to raise more problems than they elucidate.

The longest part of the book is about research and not only because this is an intriguing subject. It is because measuring the exposure and effects of media seems to me to lead to a better understanding of advertising itself. Research with all its limitations has contributed to the solution of real problems. The investigations and developments outlined here promise further improvements to come.

## SUBJECTS NOT COVERED

This is not a book about advertisements themselves. I am involved with getting them into the right medium, in front of as many of the right

6

people as possible, but not with their creation.

This is neither a text book on economics nor a defence of advertising. I am not concerned here whether advertising money should be spent — only why and how it is spent.

I do not discuss classified, financial, industrial or trade advertising. These are important sources of revenue to the media owner but pose different problems from the selling of branded goods and services in mass media.

Only British media are described in detail. To people outside this country these details are not of immediate interest. But advertising itself and agency practice are now so international that the principles of media planning and buying, and the handling of research data, could be of interest in many other countries.

# INTRODUCTION TO THE SECOND EDITION

Rewriting the book for this edition has been an opportunity in several ways. I have benefited from the criticisms made of the first edition: many of them I have acted on, two I comment on below. I have had to survey the whole field again in detail and this has made me appreciate how much has altered in these five years. This is not just a matter of decimalisation and of metrication but of real changes, both in the media and in agencies' beliefs and practices.

## TWO SIDES OF EVERY QUESTION

One of the complaints made about the first edition was that it gave both sides of every question rather than coming down firmly each time with one recommendation: 'It points out the advantages and disadvantages of an approach with such...balance that the reader is left uncertain and disappointed...One feels cheated!'.

Although people like simple solutions and often prefer being told what to do, I am quite unrepentant about this way of discussing media problems. I believe one way can be right for one problem but not necessarily for another. Sometimes bursting is better than continuous advertising; perhaps we should accept a creative man's insistence on a high-cost medium; it may be sensible to match a competitor's spending pattern. But these do not then become universal truths, only appropriate strategies. It is harder work to decide between the pros and cons but this is more likely to lead to the right answer. I therefore continue to list the points to be considered in each problem, but the reader must judge the relevance in each particular case.

## IS MEDIA SELECTION REALLY RESEARCH-BASED?

After five more years experience, how do I feel about the book's central point? According to one reviewer this is 'how the computer and media models help to sharpen concepts and improve media planning'. In contrast, another reviewer wrote, 'It is all very well to believe that media selection should be a wholly research-based function...but in fact at present it is nothing of the sort. And advertising people are by no means unanimous that it should be... The book's basic recommendation is the need for more research'.

Life is not as black nor as white as this. We should use research to keep our feet on the ground, to dispel myths, to demonstrate the astonishing variety of our subject matter, occasionally to teach us something new. I have not reduced the space given to this subject. But I do not claim it can solve all of the problems involved in media choice. Research can never take a decision. But 'it must be relevant to examine the purely physical distribution of advertising exposures for different media strategies — so that one is better informed as to the *objective* situation about which one is going to make subjective *judgements*'.

When research does not help, which is most of the time, of course we are thrown back onto the commonsense which good media men need in abundance. It is possible we shall have to do so in future more often. We need people with strong intuition and beliefs: 'Great things are not done by those who sit down and count the cost of every thought and act', was a contemporary comment on Brunel. But this flair cannot develop without experience, and measured results — which research provides — are the most relevant experience.

Bill Ambrose has written about his 'early days, when there was no research, that we know today, when hunch, expertise, the flair of the individual who had an idea, researched it in a very rough way then positively went forward to prove that his idea was right...I do not think that there is enough flair, there is enough hunch, enough expertise being used by marketing people today. Many men have got to sit back and can't make a decision without having research to support it, which is often too late, too inaccurate and incomplete.'

I am on the side of Brunel and of Ambrose's examples (Ford, Nuffield and Beecham were among them). I am not arguing 'the need for more research' but the need for judgement which feeds on and certainly does not neglect or contradict what we know from research.

It now seems to me that in the late 1960s we were over-optimistic about models and the coming triumph of media technology. We underestimated our ignorance of how advertising worked and our uncertainty about the effects of different factors. Some of the case histories called for then have been produced but there are still too few to generalise on, though they help our judgement. The analogy with physics has plagued social scientists. Experiments (they think) ought to be reproducible: we should (but have failed to) uncover the formulae that link advertising, beliefs and behaviour like those that link temperature, pressure and volume. The ultimate generalisation has eluded us and I now believe it always will: the situations we study are so diverse; the goals and criteria are perpetually shifting. What has just been seen to work may not do so for another product, nor for this product next year.

This has not prevented progress being made. We can in each situation set advertising a sensible task and carry it through consistently. We have at least broken away completely from pre-war ways of producing schedules: 'their design was deeply traditional; they were the result not of scientific experiment and design but of a progress of practical evolution characterised by lack of experimental enterprise and by technical conservation and they were constructed of materials which by modern standards were crude in the extreme'. This is actually a description of small, 19th century wooden merchant ships, but applies accurately to the standard publication lists kept in the top drawers of media directors' desks in the Dark Ages.

The ideals of explicit criteria for schedule construction, of experiments to evaluate media in practice, of improving measurements of advertisement exposure, of trying to understand how the whole apparatus works — all these may still be incomplete but they are recognised and striven for. They may be unattainable but they are recognised as directions for improvement and as standards against which practice is judged. With this background, the last section in this book is now less dogmatic but hopefully more practical.

10

## PLANNING

This is still a book about *media* planning, I recognise that good planners do other tasks as well. The advertisements themselves are not my subject, but the planner cannot as arbitrarily cut himself off from them. Working with the creative people is part of his job; a good campaign is not assembled from a number of unrelated decisions. Qualities matter as much as quantities.

## CHANGES

As well as these differences in emphasis, there are some important changes in detail from the first edition. Inflation has of course altered all the sums of money involved; 1973 has been taken here as the base year but room has been left in the Appendices for continual updating of the media expenditure figures.

There are new publications, some big movements in circulation and readership, longer hours for ITV, the new independent local radio stations, fewer people going to the cinema, new ways of buying outdoor and so on, all described in the appropriate places.

The Press now has single-source data, the Target Group Index, and is ahead of TV in this respect. It has also demonstrated a much higher probability than was previously thought to be the case that a reader is exposed to an advertisement.

But total television viewing and the amount of reading, the broad balance between media and the job done in agencies have all remained much as before. So the purposes of the book and its structure remain exactly as I wrote about them in the introduction to the first edition.

# INTRODUCTION TO
# THE THIRD EDITION

Although inflation has changed media numbers dramatically in the last few years, the business itself has not altered so much.

Increasing demand for our single commercial television channel, with its limited supply of time, has reduced the bargaining power of the buyer but not eliminated it; the need for planning is still as important. A second channel, recommended by the Annan Committee and accepted by Government, is still below our horizon.

The press suffers more from labour problems than in the past, but its basic structure is still the same.

Commercial radio has blossomed and it is used better than it used to be. Outdoor is now easier to buy.

Where examples in the last edition used 1973 or earlier data but conveyed a point which is still valid, they have not been updated just for the sake of it. But the main media facts have been given with 1977 as the base year.

Media and agencies have been more concerned with falling advertising revenue (in 1975 and 1976) and changes in consumers caused by the economic crisis than in launching new media or innovation in methodology. So there is no great difference today in the methods or preoccupations of media people, though some changes are worth mentioning.

The split between account planning agencies and a more traditional structure is widening; media buying specialists have increased; commission paid by media to agencies is now a normal practice rather than a restrictive practice. I am not concerned with structure or agency economics in this book but with the media job itself, which remains the same wherever it is done and whether the person responsible does other work or not.

Interest has increased in modelling applied to how advertising affects sales and so how advertising money should be allocated. This is controversial but a very welcome addition to our thinking and has affected several of the later chapters.

# ACKNOWLEDGEMENTS

While writing the 1970 and 1975 editions I was Media Director of Leo Burnett, where I still work. What I describe reflects the experience of this agency.

My debt remains to all those mentioned in previous editions. In revising this text I have been helped by the following, to whom I express my thanks.

Valerie Baker — Media Expenditure Analysis Limited
Richard Chilton — Rank Screen Advertising
Lynne Farrar — Leo Burnett Limited
Cecilia Garnett — Association of Independent Radio Contractors Limited
Tony Logie — Radio Luxembourg
Colin Macleod — Leo Burnett Limited
Judith Salinson — Leo Burnett Limited

The index demonstrates the importance of ADMAP as a forum for communication and controversy in media planning and research; I am particularly grateful to its publisher, Ross Harvey.

# Part 1
# THE BACKGROUND

# 1 A GAME FOR FOUR PLAYERS

*An elementary introduction to the four main
participants in spending advertising money —
the consumer, the manufacturer, the agency and
the media owner. A description of their
objectives and the way they relate to each other.*

Spending advertising money is a game for four players — the consumer, the manufacturer, the advertising agency and the media owner.

You are a consumer: you buy food and furniture, paint and petrol. Opposite you sits the manufacturer, watching every move you make. He designs, makes and offers you everything you buy. You exchange money for goods and services: each needs the other. These are the two principal players. Purchases over the counter far exceed the flow of advertising money.

There are two other partners in the game: the agency and the media owner. The media owner offers the consumer news and entertainment. Together, the agency and media owner produce and distribute advertising which maintains, guides and accelerates the exchange between consumer and the manufacturer. The press and the cinema also sell you a product: a newspaper, magazine or a visit to the cinema.

The manufacturer contacts the consumer directly — through the

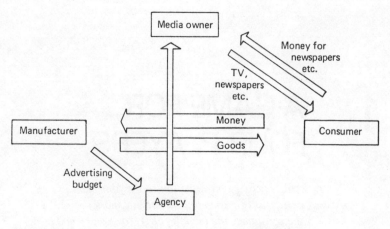

*Figure 1*

product itself and through the indispensable retailer. But he sometimes diverts part of his selling budget into advertising, both to the consumer and to the trade. The advertising budget is usually handed over to the agency; the agency passes it on to the media owner, meeting its own expenses from fees or its share of the budget as commission. The media owner uses his direct contact with the consumer to communicate the advertiser's message.

Sometimes it seems that the three other players have ganged up on the consumer: they are all in an alliance to extract his money. At other times the manufacturer sells directly to the consumer without the benefits of advertising. And if the media owner's link with the consumer should weaken, he gets little help from his partner the agency; he is then in danger of falling out of the game.

Figure 1 shows the main exchanges between the players. The actual sums of money involved are described in Chapter 3.

## THE CONSUMER

The consumer is concerned with only two of the other players: the manufacturer and the media owner. Figure 2 emphasises this. A woman out shopping has no one to answer to except her family at home.

The consumer sees media primarily as a source of information and entertainment. People watch TV or go to the cinema or read a magazine

18

to be amused and to pass the time. They read newspapers for the news, to get comments on the news, for the strip cartoons.

The consumer finds most advertisements rather irrelevant. It is like walking down a street — afterwards you could not describe most of the people you passed. But some advertisements catch the eye; these are looked at and read. You notice the pretty girl who crosses your path in the crowd — but to notice her you have to have glanced at everyone. Even the advertisements you pay no attention to, have to be rejected. 'Of course, I never look at the advertisements' is true at a certain level. Most men are uninterested in margarine and detergents. People who are not managing businesses pay no serious attention to advertisements for factory sites in Northern Ireland. The consumer's experience of most advertising is tangential. Exposure to media and to advertising is so casual it is a subject which is difficult to research. Total exposure to mass media is enormous. A TV set is on for five hours on average every day. About half of this time the set is tuned to ITV — which means that commercials are being received for a quarter of an hour in total. In the average household one national newspaper is bought every day, and two magazines each week. People also read publications outside their homes and they read local papers and specialist magazines. In towns, where four out of five people live, the average person passes over 90 posters a

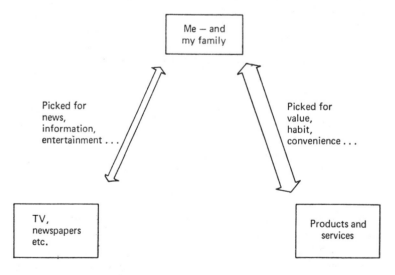

Figure 2    As seen by the consumer

19

day. Every day over 300,000 adults go to the cinema, nearly a million people listen to Radio Luxembourg and more to independent local radio.

An estimate that was made in the US [1.1] showed an average of around 200 advertisement exposures a day, but with some people confronted by up to 500. Asking how many were noticed reduced the number on average to 76, and only 12 'make any kind of impression'. Probably UK figures would be similar.

## THE ADVERTISER

There are no willing advertisers. There are only manufacturers who decide to advertise. Each time the decision is made to spend money on advertising it is only because the manufacturer does not know of a more efficient, more economical way to help the sale of his product. The manufacturer feels no responsibility to keep media or the advertising business going. His object is to make a profit by finding and satisfying a demand for his product. This objective can be taken as a definition of the marketing task. It is the location or stimulation of the market and the selling of goods to it which matter. Advertising competes with all the other ways by which products can be made attractive and available to the consumer. Advertising is only a part of the marketing mix, of the armoury available to the manufacturer.

So in Figure 3 the main elements are the manufacturer's product, the people who buy it and how he distributes it. Distribution and retailers do not figure largely in this book, though they are prominent in the manufacturer's mind. They are his ally – but can be treacherous, since they can squeeze his profit margin or favour their own-name products. He can reduce this danger by appealing over the heads of retailers to the consumer – by advertising.

The manufacturer's product may be something tangible, sold across the counter, but the man supplying a service – a banker for example – takes the same attitude to advertising. So does a Government department giving advice (for example, on road safety) or information (say, about Social Security).

All products and services compete with each other. Either they sit side by side on the supermarket shelf, or, less obviously, the consumer has to decide to spend on one rather than another: to put down a deposit on a car or on a washing machine; to go on a holiday abroad or buy a central heating system.

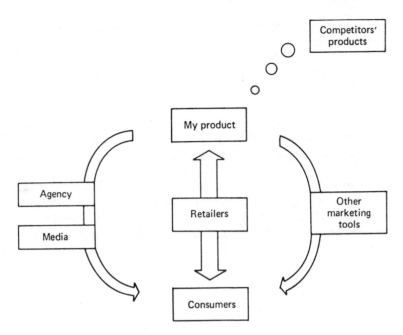

*Figure 3    As seen by the manufacturer*

*Board level*

The manufacturer's decision to advertise is usually taken at board level. The decision sometimes comes more from the heart than from the head: there is often less insistence on accountability than with other expenditure. This softness, when it occurs, does no good to the advertising business because it leaves the advertising budget unprotected against cost-cutting attacks. The true benefits of advertising are often unappreciated because they are so hard to measure reliably. But everyone has views on what is good or bad advertising – no experience of the results seems to be necessary.

Advertising is one of the ways a firm achieves an identity. It becomes known by its product, its personnel and its share price, but it is also advertising which shows the world what a firm is about. The board is rightly concerned with this public appearance. The top decision-makers are therefore consulted in the major advertising expenditure decisions: the appointment of an agency and the size of the budget. They are sometimes involved in the details of campaigns, especially in companies where advertising may be a major part — say 10 or 20 per cent — of total turnover.

## Marketing director

There are many different structures in a firm for controlling an agency and advertising. One way is described here. Direct responsibility for advertising is allocated to one person on, or just below, the board. He may be the marketing or the sales director. He sees the agency occasionally: monthly or weekly, say. No major decision is taken without his agreement. He approves campaigns in outline: both advertisements and the media schedule. It is his job to see that the agency is informed about all activities in the firm which may affect advertising — changed budgets, new products and so on. But he has many other responsibilities, principally the setting and the achievement of the sales target.

## Brand Manager

A marketing company with a variety of products usually gives a brand manager the job of making a profit from one or more products. Advertising then enters, as it should, as a part of his decision on the marketing mix. Without being a specialist in advertising, the brand manager knows enough about it to work with the agency day-to-day. His approval is required for each advertisement and for the media schedule. His view is often short-term and he rarely thinks it worth diverting money to work that might in the long run increase advertising effectiveness.

## Others concerned with advertising

Some companies replace this organisation by, or add to it, an advertising manager. His responsibilities vary widely, from genuine control to a clerical function. Again, at most it is policy and quality control that are his job, not execution. A few large advertisers do more than this. Procter & Gamble, Unilever marketing companies, Cadbury Schweppes and Beecham Products, for example, have media specialists. Unilever has its own media division and even an agency, Lintas. These specialists have frequent, direct contact with media and keep an eye on the detailed work done by the media department.

A few advertisers do wholly or partly without agencies, prepare their own advertising and buy themselves, though they do not save the full commission on which an agency operates. This may happen for example when the content of advertisements is decided at very short notice, as is the case with much work for stores or for newspapers themselves. It has long been predicted that more and more advertisers will buy the services they need in separate parts — from creative boutiques, media buying shops and so on — but the full-service agency continues to supply the vast majority of display advertisers.

Finally, the agency is occasionally in contact with others who have less to do with advertising: salesmen, accountants, consumer researchers and technicians developing new products.

Advertisers have their own association, The Incorporated Society of British Advertisers. Because of the reluctance already noted of advertisers to divert money to long-term work there is an anomaly here: the people with the purse-strings and the real power are in some ways less active than their agents, many of whom, nearly 300 in fact, belong to the Institute of Practitioners in Advertising. Advertisers keep agencies to bark for them.

*Agency selection*

Competition between agencies is encouraged by an advertiser. He changes agencies rather frequently, compared with his auditor or his lawyer. A large advertiser employs several agencies, each working on different products. He asks them all for advice on media or on new products and he compares their buying performance.

The commonest reason for changing agencies is simply a desire for change, though personal reasons also enter. Advertisers also like changes in campaigns. The suggestion that advertising works slowly prompts the suspicion that the agency is slacking. The advertiser likes seeing new commercials, new press advertisements; the concept of an inattentive consumer, unaware that the manufacturer has started a new financial year and who is still unable to recall this year's advertising, is difficult for the advertiser to grasp. 'Let's take this campaign off. They'll all be tired of it by now.' 'But it hasn't gone out yet. You've only seen it at internal meetings.'

The search for change for its own sake is almost always harmful. Good advertising can stand repeating. It needs repetition, considering how relatively seldom it is seen. Frequent changes of agency lead to great inefficiency. Not only has a new team to learn about the advertiser's business, agencies start to spend more time on getting new accounts than in servicing existing accounts.

The most successful advertisers are those who develop a stable, confident relation with their agency, based on mutual respect. A basically sound advertising idea is repeated year after year. The brand develops a consistent personality, though developed and modified. Fortunately, the large agency finds most of its clients are of this character.

While the advertiser is all for competition between agencies, he is worried by his own competitors. He fears that his agency might help these competitors if it had any contact with them. This has led to the convention that an agency shall not accept as clients two manufacturers in direct competition. An agency advertising a British Leyland car cannot accept Ford as a client; an agency with a Procter & Gamble detergent will not also handle a Unilever detergent.

In this form, the convention is reasonable. Commercial secrets are entrusted to agencies, such as the planning of new products, launch dates, profitability figures and so on. It is proper that security precautions should be taken. But some advertisers take the convention further. A manufacturer of a deodorant and a lipstick, who gives the deodorant to a particular agency, may feel that this agency should not take a competitor's lipstick. An agency handling a competitor in another country may be barred in this country. Sometimes the local company of an international advertiser is made to appoint the local branch of an international agency. At other times the local company is biased against the agency network his head office uses: he wants to retain independence. As agency international networks grow, as manufacturers diversify and merge, all these forms of restrictive practice become increasingly harmful.

The selection of an agency is a disturbing procedure — on both sides. The manufacturer is forced to review his own business in order to explain his requirements. Competing agencies overhaul their services and the people who provide them. The more logical elements in a manufacturer's choice of agency are:

1    A good opinion of creative work, always the primary reason.

2    Feeling the agency has people he can work happily with.

3    A good opinion of other agency services: planning, media, research, new product development, public relations, merchandising, etc.

Media efficiency is only one of these factors, and far from the most important. Accounts are rarely won or lost on the media front. The conventional belief — though it is open to debate — is that the difference between a good and bad media plan, or between good and bad media buying, is less than the difference between a good and a bad selling idea or a good and a bad advertisement.

Once an agency is appointed, there is traditionally an annual cycle of advertiser decisions. The company's accounting year generally determines when the cycle begins. The annual plan agreed between the agency and the advertiser covers marketing strategy and creative work as well as the media plan. The advertiser is much more involved with the first two of these three subjects. Some advertisers are not over-concerned with the detailed allocation of the budget to different media owners. Nevertheless a professional agency will always present a consistent and reasoned case for its media choice.

Media owners also try to sell their media directly to manufacturers. In fact media often feel it is they and the manufacturer who together form the more effective partnership. Advertisers who are interested can be just as well informed about media as agencies. But the agency will give way to a media-inspired suggestion by an advertiser only when it is convinced that it is an improvement on its own plan, or when the difference is not serious.

The advertiser treats media as he does any other supplier. He encourages those media developments which he sees to be in his own interest. He respects media as businesses in their own right. He likes to see them in competition.


## THE AGENCY

Historically, the agency's closest relations were with the media owner. Agencies developed from space brokers who sold in small quantities the advertising space they bought in bulk from newspapers. They still are paid by commission from the media owner. Legally the agency is a principal when it buys time or space: the agency and not the advertiser

25

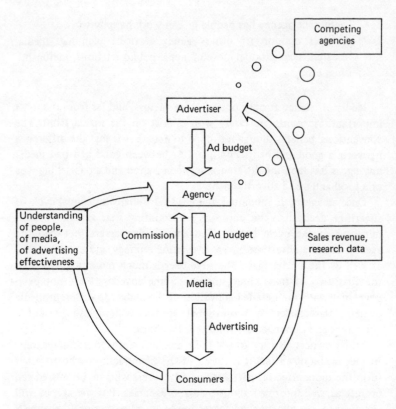

*Figure 4    As seen by the agency*

is responsible for the bill. In recent years bad debts borne by agencies who belong to the Institute of Practitioners in Advertising have averaged £½ million a year. The financial stability of agencies is important to media owners. But an agency is appointed by an advertiser. Its task is to help sell his product. Its fortunes are bound up with the success or failure of this product. If the advertiser makes satisfactory profits there are few difficulties in the agency's relations with him.

*Why an agency is appointed*

Anyone may buy advertising space or time, and write advertisements – if he keeps within the law. In fact you occasionally see display

26

advertisements placed by individuals — people who are making political protests or a statement of their religious beliefs. And as already noted, some manufacturers manage their own advertising.

Why then use an agency?

1   Above all, to get the best possible advertisements; the agency's existence depends essentially on its ability to turn a marketing objective into words and pictures which successfully persuade the consumer.
2   To get an independent but informed view of a marketing plan.
3   To avoid the chore of media buying, and use the agency's negotiating skill and weight.
4   To get access to other agency services.

The agency is only too well aware that competition between agencies is at least as fierce as between the products of rival manufacturers. Therefore when the agency thinks the advertiser is wrong in his policy, it is tempted to be obsequious, or 'If the client wants to waste his money, he may as well spend it with us'. But in the long term, these policies do not pay off. The advertiser does not really want yes-men; he probably has enough in his own business. He needs a detached view and usually expects it. Justly or unjustly, sales are the ultimate verdict on the agency's advice. To have agreed with the advertiser when he was wrong is no safeguard against being fired later. In any case, a far-sighted agency says to itself: 'We're now spending £100,000 a year; if we do a good job, it may be £200,000 next year'.


## The agency's attitude to media

The agency has a healthy scepticism about the value of media. A natural buyer's caution is a positive asset in the media department.

The agency recognises the need for editorial integrity, for a characteristic flavour in a medium which will attract and hold readers. The environment a publication provides for the advertising may matter and is considered in more detail later on. But it is less relevant to the agency than the number and type of readers it can deliver to the advertiser. The agency understands the TV contractor's need to find or invent attractive programmes. But it does not discuss the content of programmes in the dramatic language of the TV critic; it waits to see the TV ratings. Indeed the agency is prohibited by law from influencing the content of programmes.

The job of the media department is the subject of Part 3, but it can be stated here in outline. It must evaluate the different media available for a particular advertising campaign. This is partly quantitative (How many people will see the advertisements? How often? Who are these people?) and partly qualitative (Will the advertising message be delivered effectively?). Having selected media in the best interest of the advertiser, the agency buys them at the lowest possible cost. So although the agency sells for media owners to manufacturers, it sells only what it believes is the best.

The media owner depends on the agency's media decisions for his livelihood. He is therefore particularly concerned with how and why these decisions are taken. If he is rejected he is quite within his rights to ask why. He can then put his case better next time, or put a case that his medium be used for some more suitable product. So in a sense media decisions are made in public: the methods used are of interest to many people outside the agency. But the agencies usually do not tell all. The results of searches for the best buys, media research interpretation, deals achieved with media owners — these are not broadcast from one agency to another.

*The agency and research*

The agency should acquire and use an intimate knowledge of consumers. It does not have with them the direct commercial contact of the manufacturer, nor the actor-audience relationship of the media owner. But it should know more about the consumer's motives than any one manufacturer, drawing information from its work on a variety of products. It should know how to affect consumers and how to measure whether it has affected them.

The agency should certainly be expert in media research. It sits in judgement on the efforts of media owners to sell their wares; part of this sales effort is the interpretation of data on how media expose advertisements to people. The agency must evaluate and, in the long-term interest of advertisers, guide the collection of this data.

**THE MEDIA OWNER**

The media owner is schizophrenic. Nothing matters more to a publication than the relationship between its writers and the reader — it is for

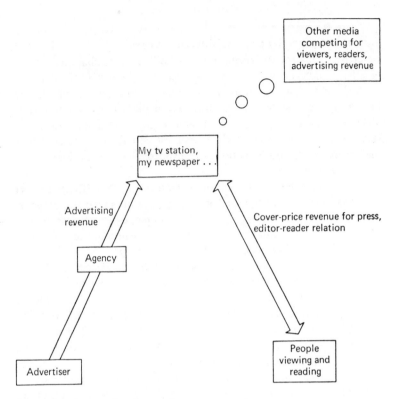

*Figure 5    As seen by the media owner*

this that the publication is bought and read. Nothing matters more to a TV contractor than to produce programmes which the viewer stays at home to watch. But the media owner also intends to deliver this audience to the advertiser. Much of his income comes from selling advertising space — between a quarter and three-quarters for most publications, virtually all for a TV contractor.

*Editorial and advertising in the press*

There is traditional hostility between the editorial department and the advertising department of a newspaper or magazine. If there is not, then the publication is in danger of losing its character — and its value to the advertiser. It is worth examining where the front lines are drawn.

There is a distinction to be made here between the different media. With a newspaper, columns of editorial run between banks or islands of advertising. Except for financial and classified advertising (you decide whether or not you want to read these sections) there is editorial matter throughout the paper. But most magazines have a specialist appeal. You look at a magazine because you like to read about fashion, motoring or amateur photography. The advertisements there are usually about the same subjects and are as likely to interest you as the editorial. There may therefore be thick sections of advertisements facing each other, without articles or stories between.

The subjects selected for editorial treatment — for both newspapers and magazines — are often picked with an eye on advertising revenue. The *Sunday Times Business News,* for example, exists because enough advertisers want to appear in this section. Here editorial and advertising depend on each other as do the chicken and the egg.

The editor of a newspaper does not like to see too much advertising. He recognises its commercial value. He sees that some of it interests some readers. But he fights to keep a recognisable character for his paper. The advertisements in most papers are similar: it is only *his* writers and *his* layout which make his paper distinctive. The magazine editor is less fussy. Advertisements — for fashion and food for example — can be as appealing as anything she can produce. The distinction here between an advertisement and an editorial article is less important. But there is the same possibility of character being overlaid by advertising which makes the editor cautious.

There is also the possibility of direct pressure from advertisers on editorial. 'I can give you two pages of advertising if you bring my name into this feature', or worse 'I shall withdraw my advertising unless you mention me — or stop running down my product'. These crude attempts are rare and properly resisted. It would not be in the advertiser's real interest if editorial comment were dictated by the advertiser.

Therefore both the following statements are true. The editor of *Vogue,* Miss Beatrix Miller, declared categorically: 'We have never, never put in a garment because the manufacturer has bought ten colour pages (of advertising). Once you start doing that, where do you stop?' The *Observer* commented: 'Of course, *Vogue*'s advertisers are represented on editorial pages, it would be unthinkable if they weren't. *Vogue* and its advertisers are doing the same job for the same people.'

Agencies also ask for special make-up. 'I'd really like four consecutive colour pages from page three,' or particular positions: 'Can't you get this opposite the cookery page?' or positions normally used for editorial: 'Can't I have your centre spread for this issue?' Again, it is the editor who must have the last word.

*Editorial and advertising in other media*

A TV contractor faces these problems in a less extreme form. The amount of advertising in ITV programmes and their separation are laid down by law. There is no overall make-up for an editor to approve. Some people resent the commercials and to this extent advertising presents a problem but programme controllers do not decide where each commercial will appear.

For the minor media these problems are even less acute. For outdoor they do not exist; there is no editorial. In the cinema, advertisements are limited even more than on television. Radio has in principle the same difficulties as television but lower listener interest in radio programme content reduces the tensions.

*Competition between media*

Media compete for readers. As a business, a publication has to sell enough copies to the right people to achieve two objects. First, to get revenue from its cover price. Second, to offer advertisers an audience of the kind they want to reach. Keeping circulation, production expenses, cover price and advertising rates in balance is a skilled juggling act which is analysed in Chapter 3.

Media also compete with each other for advertising money. This competition is the mechanism that controls advertising rates. Because so little is known about advertising effectiveness, competition is often fiercer between two similar publications (whose effectiveness cannot be very different) than between two dissimilar media (press and TV for example). But sometimes local competitors combine to fight larger battles.

The fact that many media have interlocking financial interests makes no difference to the vigour with which they are marketed. The representative of a TV contractor is interested only in getting advertising on to television. He is unconcerned that the publications he is competing with may be part-owners of his company — and this is as it should be.

31

# 2 HOW DOES ADVERTISING WORK?

*A simple description of the commonly held view about the part advertising plays in marketing. Advertising does not work in the same way in each particular situation. Its purposes are as varied as the different marketing problems it helps to solve. Consideration of the purchase of a product introduces the main points covered in this book.*

The question that starts this chapter is inevitable. We have to face it because the media decision cannot be taken without a belief in what advertising is doing.

Although the question has often been answered, the answers are usually different. We have to conclude that no one knows how advertising works. That is, that there is no convincing, universal theory of advertising.

This is not a cause for despair. How does politics work? Or the novel? Or marriage? In this context, the question even appears absurd. You can write an election manifesto, criticise *Sons and Lovers* or be married without being able to answer such questions. In other words, you can have a good general knowledge of a complex subject and you can explore individual cases in depth, but you should not therefore expect to be able to write a description that covers every individual case.

The truth is that advertising works in different ways in different situations. You should not look for a standard pattern in an announcement about a Government regulation, the claims made for a new car, a house for sale notice, a TV commercial for a well-known brand and a chairman's report. What we should do is decide in each case what advertising can reasonably do and then describe how it may achieve this particular result. We then get answers like the following: advertising informs about novelties; advertising adds value to products; advertising lifts products onto a plateau of acceptability; advertising changes consumer's images of products; advertising turns products in brands and so on. More specifically, we may say: advertising shows this product being used by young people because too many think of it as an old person's product; advertising shows why this product is of good quality; advertising reminds people this is a product that does X as well as Y. Of course, the variety of advertising tasks follows the fact that products face different situations in the market place. At one extreme are the major, well-known brands and products about which there is no new story to be told; take milk as an example. Others are little-known, struggling brands but which have something genuinely new to say. Some products, like a car or a holiday, are bought after deliberate consideration. Others are frequent, casual purchases. The people whom advertising tries to influence are all different too. Some already know and use the product; advertising has to reinforce their habits. Others may never have tried it, advertising has to encourage trial.

We conclude then that we need to define, and ideally to measure, in each case what advertising is to achieve. Otherwise it could not be agreed who is to be influenced, when, or how; there would be no criterion by which to judge a media plan; it would be impossible to decide after the event whether advertising did its job well or badly.


## STEP BY STEP MODELS, OR SALES?

There are two distinct approaches to the problem of measuring the way advertising works in particular cases: step-by-step models and the sales criterion. A useful summary of the controversy between these schools of thought is given in the report on the ESOMAR seminar on this subject [2.1]. The most recent review of the various theories is in Reference [2.2]. Examples are given in Chapters 12 and 16.

The first approach states that advertising works by pushing a

| AIDA | DAGMAR |
|---|---|
| *from the initial letters below* | *from the title of a book [2.3]* |
| Attention | Awareness |
| Interest | Comprehension |
| Desire | Conviction |
| Action | Action |

*Figure 6*

consumer through various steps up to the point of purchase. These steps are given different names. Two well-known formulations are shown in Figure 6.

Commonsense accepts that most consumers affected by advertising must be taken through some such stages. Much diagnostic research after a campaign is based on these steps. For example, it is often useful to measure whether the advertising got attention, whether awareness has increased, or whether people's intentions to buy have changed.

A less dogmatic view, still very applicable today, was expressed in the thirties [2.4] : that advertising may work in any of these five ways:

By familiarising
By reminding
By spreading news
By overcoming inertia
By adding a value not in the product

The ATR model has been proposed recently [2.5]. This is based on the analysis of purchase diary data, which shows patterns of great consistency and which does not support the conversion theory (that advertising, by a strong form of persuasion or manipulation, changes brand loyalties dramatically). Instead, it is suggested that first advertising helps to create *Awareness* of the product. Next, it makes *Trial* likely. Finally, the main determinant of sales volume is whether repeat buying develops and here advertising helps *Reinforcement* of the purchase habit. In this model, attitudes are more likely to be changed by behaviour than to cause alterations in behaviour. So advertising's main task, for frequently bought going brands, is 'to inform the rather experienced consumer that Brand X is as good as the others'. It is principally a defensive tool — the price the producer pays to stay in business.

The hesitancy of this last model (How much does the product do? How much does advertising contribute?) is typical of the current cautious approach. The old, simple steps have disappeared with the 'atoms are just billiard-balls' ideas of physics. We now recognise that the purposive, learning-theory view of consumers is inexact. They just do not bother to maximise their benefits in the way that some economists imagine. 'Reducing indifference' has been stated as the object of advertising and this is often closer to reality than we liked to think.

But it is also argued that advertising should be judged only by sales increases or at least by preventing a sales decline. The intermediate steps may be inapplicable or even misleading: there are examples of successful communication not followed by sales and of sales increases without more comprehension. Interest in the advertising may be caused by having bought the product rather than the reverse. In other words no one can be sure which intermediate measures are relevant. It is also said the models are too simple and mechanistic. The consumer is in fact not driven like a sheep through these stages, she does not always make considered, rational decisions. She has her own habits and experience with which advertising interacts. The relationship between advertising and the consumer's attitudes and behaviour is a two-way process.

In reply it is pointed out that sales are also a doubtful measure of advertising effectiveness: they are affected by so many other factors that advertising may be wrongly praised — or blamed. It is said that advertising has a communication function and should be judged by whether it communicates.

The media department gets little help from this controversy, though following the arguments guards us against some errors in interpreting research.


## THE PURCHASE OF A TYPICAL PACKAGED PRODUCT

Think of a housewife doing the shopping. She sees a pack in the supermarket, perhaps with some special offer. She decides to buy it. When she is at home, the product is used.

Those four short sentences describe baldly what marketing is all about. Without even mentioning advertising they also imply what problems are posed to the advertiser. From this description of a typical purchase in the product fields where most display advertising money is spent, can be deduced where the advertising agency is involved, including the media department.

## Who buys?

The description stated that 'a housewife' was doing the shopping but more detail is needed about who makes the purchase. It must next be settled which of these people should be influenced. Defining the target, i.e. the people we want to reach with advertising, is central in media planning. Of course there may be other people involved in the purchase decision besides those actually going into shops. The housewife may for example be following a suggestion from her family: 'Don't forget the fruit gums, Mum!' Some products bought for the household are a joint decision, talked through by several people. There is more on this in the description of the target in Chapter 14.


### The pack and the product

The pack is often the main link between the advertisement and the housewife's action in choosing it. The agency may be involved in pack design. Often the advertising has to emphasise the pack and show it as realistically as possible — which may mean an advantage to a medium offering mass coverage in colour, such as magazines.

The advertising for a familiar product may only have to remind the housewife that it is still there: reliable and trusted. In these cases advertisements may not have to be long or complicated. We may be able to use a simple reminder on posters or brief TV commercials — 7 or 15 seconds. In other cases the product is unfamiliar. The advertising may have to tell a complicated story. Media may be valued for their ability to make a difficult point. Press advertising can get across more details than TV, though it cannot always demonstrate as convincingly.

Advertising effectiveness — and other factors — are often tested in a single region or town. One of the media department's jobs is to set up such tests realistically. There is often difficulty in placing local advertising which is representative of national advertising. After test market, it may be necessary to extend sales in one or more regions at a time. Perhaps national distribution cannot be got at once or the risk of going national may be too high; perhaps some regions are expected to be better prospects for the product than others. When this happens, the media allocation obviously has to follow the overall plan. The regional use of media is easier with TV, posters, cinema and local publications than with the national press.

Sometimes consumers come into the shop asking for something they have seen advertised. This is the exception: most purchases are chosen only from what is visible. This means, obviously, that a product must get distribution and display in order to be sold. The advertising has to help persuade the retailer to stock and show it. In fact a major objective of some campaigns is simply to get or to improve distribution of the product in shops. Here advertising to the housewife has an important part to play.

At first sight the statement just made looks like a mistake. Advertising to the retailer must have a part to play. This is true, and advertising direct to the retailer is important. But advertising to the housewife also affects the retailer. In one way this is quite straight-forward: the retailer sees some of the advertising on TV or in the press simply because he watches TV and reads the papers. He is influenced by this advertising in much the same way as the housewife: he is more likely to buy for his shop what is familiar and what he trusts.

Even if he does not see the advertising in the ordinary way, it should be brought to his notice. The manufacturer's salesmen visit wholesalers and retailers. Their main jobs are to get stocks into the shops, to get payments, to negotiate deliveries, promotions and so on. The same salesmen often carry descriptions of the consumer advertising to show the retailer. 'You have to take our product: people will see our advertising and come in here asking for it.' A salesman who does not get worthwhile advertising support is likely to ask for it. A retailer who is not assured that advertising will persuade consumers may not stock the product and nowadays he wants to know in increasing detail what support is being given to the product. He accepts new products and continues to take existing products because he believes in the effectiveness of advertising. There is of course some circularity in this argument. He believes in advertising because he has seen the high turnover of advertised products; however, they may sell just because he displays them.

Both extremes can actually occur. Some products sell, not because of the direct effect of consumer advertising, but because of its indirect effect on the retailer. Other products sell because the advertising causes people to ask the retailer for them. For most products there is a mixture of these two mechanisms. Further, the salesman himself is also influenced by being exposed to the advertising. He works for much of the time away from his colleagues and his management. The advertising does not have any new information for him: he should know far more about his product than the advertisements tell him. But it reassures him that the product he is selling is important and that his efforts are being backed up.

## Special offers

When a manufacturer spends money through an agency on a medium which allows the agency commission, such expenditure is called 'above the line'. A line is imagined drawn in the budget list above which expenditure is commissionable, while below it is not. Largely, 'above the line' means the conventional media described in this book.

The manufacturer's expenditure on other ways of maintaining or increasing sales, promotions, competitions and so on is called 'below the line'. Most of the money is non-commissionable though the manufacturer may pay a fee to the agency for its advice. Promotions obviously form a major part of the appeal to the consumer and this appeal should be co-ordinated with the main advertising programme. Consumer promotions are themselves often advertised. This is called 'scheme' advertising in contrast to 'theme' advertising which is about the product itself. Scheme advertising should of course only appear at the times the promotion is running.

## The advertising influence

The actual decision to buy is affected by many factors, but there are four which are particularly relevant to media planning.

1  *Advertising effectiveness depends on the advertising idea and on the medium.* The crucial factors are what the advertising actually says and how this can be executed in the different media. TV may be more efficient for transmitting one message, magazines more efficient for another. The agency's judgement about the effectiveness of media for the purpose of a particular campaign is central in the choice of media.

2  *The more a person sees our advertising, the greater its effect.* Usually the advertising should be shown as often as possible: the more repetition of the message the better. If there are exceptions

to this rule they are very rare. Of course heavy repetition can be bought only at the expense of other desirable factors as is explained in Chapter 10.

3  *Competitors are there too.* The housewife should choose the brand advertised although competitors' products are available too. Competitors' activities are always relevant. What is their product like? What are they spending? What media are they using?

4  *When did the consumer see the advertising?* It is usually believed that the closer advertising is seen to the time of purchase, the more effective it is. Hence the case for posters seen on the way to the shops and for advertising at the end of the week near shopping days. But an image of a brand may be built up over years — hence the advantage of being seen near the time of purchase may be real but small.


*The product is used*

The product may be stored for some time before it is used. The timing of the advertising may have to be more appropriate to usage than to purchase or consideration of purchase. Usage also determines how soon the housewife is ready to buy again. This time interval may also matter to the media man.

# 3  MONEY-GO-ROUND

*The money spent on advertising is analysed in
this chapter. It is broken down by the main
product groups and the main media. Advertising
money is compared with other expenditures.*

Nine hundred million pounds a year was spent in 1977 on the advertising described in this book. In this chapter the money is followed on its
rounds. It starts as part of the cash paid over the shop counter by the
consumer and is passed on to the manufacturer. He in turn hands it to
the agency, which keeps its commission and pays the media owner the
rest. The media owner carries the advertisements; in many cases he
also sells a product to the consumer, such as a newspaper, making a
full circle.

A great deal has been spoken and written about the economics of
this process — so much and so ill-informed that it has been called
[3.1] 'a Niagara of bilge'. This chapter is not intended to contribute
to the dispute but attempts only to give a description.

The analysis in this book is restricted to the money paid for space
or time for 'display' advertising to consumers. This includes all
commercial TV, consumer newspapers and magazines (except for

40

financial, trade and technical and small classified advertising for jobs, cars and so on), posters and transport advertising, cinema and radio. At the end of this chapter the exclusions are explained in more detail.

It is expenditure in Great Britain that is described, though Ulster is shown separately in some of the TV figures. The data are difficult both to define and to collect; most of the figures are only approximate. All the figures given relate to 1977 unless otherwise stated. At the current rate of inflation (10 per cent a year) and of changes in advertising spending, this means that much of the detail will soon be out of date. The differences here from the first edition of this book (which took 1968 as the base year) are large. Some comments are made later in this chapter on the changes that have already taken place but I do not give any forecasts here.

## WHAT THE CONSUMER PAYS

There were 18.5 million households in the UK in 1977, containing 56 million individuals. Of these 43 million were over 15 — 'adults' to the advertiser — and 13 million were children. The 'average household' can be a misleading concept; for example, millions of people live alone or in institutions. Nevertheless there is an average household and it contains two adults and one child (actually 2.3 and 0.7). The household's average expendable income, i.e. after taxes, savings and national insurance, was £72 in 1977.

To show what kinds of product spend money on advertising an analysis of advertising expenditure is required by product group. This analysis is available only for TV, the majority of the press and outdoor advertising. It is calculated at card rates [3.2]. Table 1 breaks down the figure of about £900 million for 1977. This is about 93p per week for each household, or 1.3 per cent of total consumers' expenditure. This does not mean that advertising costs the consumer this amount in the sense that stopping advertising would save this much, as is shown later.

It is clear from Table 1 that foods, medicines and cosmetics take the largest share of the budget, both for the household and for display advertising. Household goods, leisure activities, drink and tobacco are the next biggest advertising spenders. Housing, which comes high in household expenditure, requires virtually no advertising because demand exceeds supply.

41

Advertising expenditure is about 40p per week for each adult. To put this figure into perspective, consider another way which might be used to persuade and inform: direct mail only. If it costs 14p to write and post each letter, the money spent on advertising is enough to send one letter to each adult three days a week.

In addition to advertising costs, it is useful to recall what people pay to media direct. Most households pay a TV and radio licence — £25 currently for colour. Their bill for papers and magazines is over 110p a week. Going to the cinema costs them over £4 a year — though much more is spent by young people. So, on average, a household paid over £1.60 a week in 1977.

## WHAT THE MANUFACTURER PAYS

The manufacturers who advertise do not receive all the money spent by consumers shown in the first column of Table 1. First, retailers and distributors take their share. Then a great deal of money crosses the counter for goods which are advertised little or not at all: own-label or small local manufacturers' products for example. Therefore ratios of advertising cost to turnover for manufacturers who do advertise are much larger than the percentages shown in the last column of the table; they may be 5 or 10 per cent or sometimes more.

The larger brands and advertisers set the pace, even though the share of any one brand or firm is small; 308 brands spent over £½ million (MEAL) in 1977, averaging £1 million each — and totalling only a third of all MEAL. The top twenty in 1977 spent only £220 million on TV and press — less than a quarter of the total. The first ten averaged £14 million each and were Unilever, Imperial, Cadbury Schweppes, Mars, the Government, Beecham Group, CWS, Reed International, Rowntree Mackintosh, Procter and Gamble. When it comes to brands the amounts are of course smaller. Nearly 80 brands spent over £1 million in 1977, 230 brands spent over £1½ million. The top ten averaged £3.3 million and were Boots, Co-op local and national, Woolworth, Tesco, Currys, MFI, Williams Furniture, Rothmans King Size and Allied Carpets [3.4]. Nine of these are retailers, whose advertising budgets are largely the result of requests to manufacturers which they cannot refuse.

An analysis of the way advertising for different types of product is

42

Table 1  ANALYSIS OF ADVERTISING EXPENDITURE BY PRODUCT GROUP

| Product group | Average household expenditure per week, £p | Advertising expenditure per household per week, p | Advertising as a percentage of household expenditure, % |
|---|---|---|---|
| Foods, medicines and cosmetics | 18.8 | 23 | 1.2 |
| Household and leisure | 13.5 | 16 | 1.2 |
| Housing | 10.3 | – | – |
| Drink and tobacco | 6.1 | 12 | 2.0 |
| Tourism and entertainment | 6.1 | 4 | 0.7 |
| Cars | 7.8 | 6 | 0.8 |
| Clothing | 5.8 | 2 | 0.3 |
| Publishing | 1.1 | 2 | 1.8 |
| Others, | 2.3 | – | – |
| | 71.8 | 93 | 1.3 |

Source: [3.3]

split between the media is published each year by MEAL. This must be treated with care because rate-card figures are used and the definitions of the product groups are wide. It is more practical, when it comes to studying a particular market, to have the figures re-worked for the particular brands which are considered to make up the part of the market we are interested in. Nevertheless the overall figures are of value to media owners, since they define *their* market for advertising revenue, and they are of general interest. In the television revenue, much the biggest item is Food, followed by Drink, Retail Stores, Toiletries and Cosmetics and Household Stores. The press display revenue is dominated by Retailers, approaching £100 million, followed by Finance, Motors, Tobacco and Holidays. Outdoor's heaviest advertisers are in Tobacco and Drinks.

The consumer, of course, eventually pays also for the manufacturer's total selling costs: packing and transporting goods to the shops, his sales force, promotions for retailers and for consumers, display material and so on.

## WHAT THE AGENCY TAKES

Advertising agencies are paid mainly by media owners – not by manufacturers. The agency receives commission – nearly always 15 per cent – of the gross cost of the space or time it buys. When an agency orders £100 worth of space the media owner invoices him £85, but the agency invoices the advertiser £100. This commission can also be stated as 17.65 per cent of the net £85. Agencies generally pay out their money to media owners more promptly than advertisers pay their bill to agencies, so an agency needs a relatively large amount of working capital.

Some publications and other media still pay only 10 per cent commission, but the advertiser then usually pays a fee to bring the agency's revenue up to 15 per cent of the gross or 17.65 per cent of the net. Outdoor is also an exception; most advertising agencies buy through a poster-buying specialist who charges a percentage for his services.

Agencies increasingly charge advertisers a fee in addition to commission. In some quarters the view is held that fees should completely replace commissions and some agencies work largely or completely on fees. This argument will doubtless rumble on for years to come. The commission system is at present the backbone of advertiser-agency-media owner economics. It is anachronistic, but no one has yet produced a more acceptable formula. Whatever the system, an agency [3.5] 'treads a narrow knife edge, poised between overserving its clients and going broke, or underserving them and getting fired'.

Out of the £900 million, agencies keep about £132 million. Their costs represent about £110 million, their profits from media commissions under £20 million. Agencies do other work for advertisers not included under the commission arrangement. The biggest items are the production of advertising films for TV, artwork and blocks for press. These cost £45 million for TV and £73 million for press in 1977. The agency may also plan and commission research, buy print and do other work on behalf of the advertiser. The agency's part in such work is traditionally paid at the same rate as space and time, i.e. for every £85 charged by the supplier, the agency adds £15 to the advertiser's bill. In total, about 30 per cent of an agency's revenue is earned from fees outside the commissions from media. It is common to 'gross up' fee revenue when agency turnovers are discussed; this means that an agency with £4 million media billings (£600,000 commission revenue) and £150,000 fee revenue is said to have a billings equivalent to £5 million. As with many other practices in this industry, the difference leads to confusion.

A development in this decade is advertisers buying piecemeal the services that agencies provide. Boutiques and hot shops, some staffed by moonlighters, can provide creative work; media buying shops can plan and buy and perhaps placed £50 million in 1977. The advertiser sometimes believes this saves him money though having such services from an agency, all under one roof and from teams used to working together, must normally take a much greater load off the advertiser and provide an operation of higher real effectiveness.

There are about 600 agencies in Great Britain, but the top 20 of these, with media billings of £11 million and over, handle half the business described in this book. The three hundred agencies in membership of the IPA handle about 90 per cent of display advertising. They have about 4500 accounts whose grossed-up billing totals £925 million: an average of fifteen accounts and £3 million.

In 1968 agencies employed about 20,000 people. By the end of 1977 this had fallen to 14,000; the services have reduced but the efficiency increased.

The range of size is very wide – the IPA average is 50 but a large agency employs 200 or more. Over half of an agency's revenue is paid out in salaries. An advertiser spending £1 million a year on media takes up the time equivalent of ten or more people in the agency. Of these, he never sees three or four − accountants, clerks, secretaries and so on. The media department whose work is described here absorbs less than 10 per cent of the payroll − one person for an account spending £1 million a year. Of course, the advertiser has many more people than this working part-time on his affairs, but they work also on other accounts. There are about four people in the media department of an average agency, between 20 and 50 in a large agency [3.6].

## THE MONEY TAKEN BY MEDIA OWNERS

We are left with £750 million as the income of media owners from display advertising, after they have allowed agencies their commission. This breaks down between the main media in round figures as shown in Table 2 [3.7]. Comments on the differences between the years shown in the table follow in the section on inflation. The share taken by each medium showed a considerable jump for regional newspapers in 1973, reflecting their growth in retail advertising. Radio is of course remarkable in 1977. The overall picture is, however, one of stability.

Thus, the press takes half the revenue from display advertising and television takes nearly 40 per cent. The three smaller media together take about 10 per cent of all display advertising. A large agency, however, tends to have a lot of TV advertisers and television accounts, not for 40, but 60 or 70 per cent of its total billing. There are a large number of smaller advertisers and agencies who make up the bulk of press advertising.

## PRESS

The economics of the national press have been frequently documented [5.4]. Taken as a whole, the nationals are hardly major profit-makers. Most papers require support from other parts of their groups so it is the economics of the whole group and the priorities of the proprietor that determine how it is run.

National newspapers can be divided into two groups. There are eight national daily and Sunday newspapers usually called popular,

46

Table 2  MEDIA OWNER DISPLAY REVENUE AFTER
AGENCY COMMISSION HAS BEEN DEDUCTED,
£MILLION

|  | 1968 | 1973 | 1977 |
|---|---|---|---|
| **Press:** | | | |
| National newspapers | 58 | 88 | 150 |
| Regional newspapers | 36 | 86 | 139 |
| Magazines, etc. | 42 | 59 | 92 |
| Total | 136 | 233 | 381 |
| TV | 99 | 161 | 300 |
| Outdoor | 17 | 26 | 46 |
| Cinema | 5 | 6 | 8 |
| Radio | 0.5 | 1 | 22 |
| Total | 258 | 427 | 757 |

e.g. the *Daily Mirror* and *Sunday People*, and seven called quality, e.g. the *Daily Telegraph* and *Sunday Times*. The division is mainly in the social grade of their readers and their age of leaving school or university.

The dependence of different types of publication on advertising varies widely.

Of national newspapers, the qualities get 70 to 80 per cent of their revenue from advertising; populars get only about 40 per cent. Weekly newspapers get over 80 per cent (more than half from classified — the sector which has grown most — but outside the scope of this book). Consumer periodicals get about a third of their revenue from advertising, trade and technical publications two-thirds, or even all their revenue when they are distributed free. Popular publications cannot charge proportionately as much for advertising, because advertisers are less anxious to reach their sort of reader. They also carry little classified advertising.

The publisher has to strike a delicate balance between his cover price and advertising policies. If he charges too much, his circulation will go down and the publication will become less attractive to the advertiser. If he charges too little, his costs of production will swamp

47

the benefit of higher sales and the additional readership he gains may not be the sort that advertisers are interested in.

The amount spent by consumers on newspapers and magazines has been increasing of course at current prices – more than doubling in the five years to 1977. However cover prices have risen faster than this and the actual numbers sold have dropped. The amount spent as a share of total consumers' expenditure has remained steady recently.

*Press advertising costs*

It is impossible to summarise in a few figures what it costs to advertise in the press. Even in the national press the range is very wide: from £19,656 for a full page in black and white in the *News of the World* to £64 for an advertisement 3 centimetres high in one column of the *Daily Mail*. A colour page in *Woman* costs £7550, in the *Sunday Times Magazine* £6,400.

These capital cost figures make more sense when they are related to the number of readers of each publication or the number of copies sold. The usual basis is a thousand readers, or a thousand copies. Costs per thousand readers, or per thousand copies, are much less variable. Allowing for the proportion of readers who see the average page, an advertisement in the popular nationals measuring 33 cm high across five columns costs about 61p for every thousand adults who will see it: sixteen for 1p. A colour page in the women's weekly magazines costs about 95p for every thousand housewives who will see it: more than ten a penny.

In 1977 MEAL monitored 700,000 press advertisements: four every three minutes. Their rate card cost totalled £406 million, an average of £580 each.

## TELEVISION

The ownership of the television companies overlaps to some extent with the press. It is not so unexpected that Associated Newspapers (which owns the *Daily Mail, Evening News* and so on) and D. C. Thomson (which owns the *Sunday Post, Annabel* and so on) are

## Table 3 ITCA REVENUE, £MILLION
## (before agency commission deducted)

| 1968 | 1970 | 1972 | 1974 | 1975 | 1976 | 1977 |
|------|------|------|------|------|------|------|
| 116  | 110  | 157  | 176  | 208  | 271  | 353  |

shareholders of Southern Television. It may be more surprising that the *Observer, Economist, Spectator* and *New Statesman* all own shares in London Weekend Television.

While the press relies more or less heavily on advertisement revenues, commercial television, of course, depends on it almost completely. All the television licence fee goes to the Government, and thence to the BBC after the deduction of costs of collection.

The net revenue of the TV contractors is published monthly. It has varied considerably over the years (see Table 3), falling in both 1969 and 1974. The ITV contractors have some other interests such as *TV Times*, the sale of programmes abroad and other diversifications. Of these, programme sales are the most important; ATV is the company most active in this respect. But the attention of contractors is concentrated on their UK interests and it is doubtful whether their revenue from all additional sources is much over £20 million.

The revenue received by the contractors is subject to a levy by the Government. Introduced in 1964, the levy was intended to reduce the level of profits, which are sometimes regarded as high; they have at times been about £20 million a year, but the NBPI report published in 1970 estimated them at £6.3 million and added that the rate of return on capital was 'substantially lower than that required'. The levy was up to 1974 drawn direct from revenue, i.e. before expenditure on programmes, but agreement has now been reached that it should come from profits. It has averaged about £20 million a year 1972-5 but has risen since then. Since ITV started in 1956 not less than £300 million has been paid as levies, in addition to Corporation tax and tax on dividends, which amount to a similar sum.

The contractors also pay the Independent Broadcasting Authority a rental which totalled £16 million in 1976/7. This pays for the transmission system and the Authority's control function. The Authority itself pays taxation and direct contributions to the Exchequer.

After the levy, taxation and the IBA rental the contractors were left with about £230 million in 1976. Of this about £140 million was spent on programmes; supporting departments and depreciation took about £46 million. This went to produce 2500 hours of networked programmes and 5000 of regional material. The total of programmes shown, including 14 per cent of imported films, etc., was 11,000 hours.

In comparison, the BBC in 1976/7 had an operating expenditure of £149 million and a capital expenditure of £14 million, both on television alone. They spent £85 million on production, artists and other people, £42 million on what are called 'recording and design materials, etc.'. They made 5000 hours for BBC1, 3,700 hours for BBC2 and 2,900 hours for regional services. (Incidentally their operating and capital costs on radio were £63 million and they made 24,000 hours excluding local radio production, which totalled 87,000 hours.)

The methods of operating ITV and BBC are not directly comparable. ITV has a greater regional variety; the BBC fills two channels but transmits for a shorter time. Each system spends about the same in total on programmes and transmission; in total, each costs very roughly £250 million a year at 1977 prices (for details see the ITV, IBA and BBC yearbooks).


*Television advertising costs*

The cost to the advertiser of a 30-sec spot (the most common length) transmitted in peak time in every region is currently about £21,500. At this rate, TV time is worth about 2½ million pounds an hour. But taking into account the number of people who will be present in the room when that spot is shown the cost is only 170p a thousand viewers, or six viewers a penny. To reach housewives costs about twice this, or three a penny. Altogether, just over three-quarters of a million spots are transmitted each year, at an average rate-card cost of £500 each (and £450 net). On London Weekend — the station with the highest basic rate — a 30-sec spot on Sunday costs £5590 but may be seen by 4¼ million people. On Channel Television — the lowest rate — the cost is only £40 and the audience might be 30,000.

The number of new commercials made in a year is about 8000 — excluding the 15,000 made for small local advertisers. The cost of making a 30-sec commercial can be £20 to 30,000, though many are made for much less. This is usually a small part of the total advertising budget but at a far higher cost per second than the programme material.

## OTHER MEDIA

Outdoor sites are owned by a number of independent contractors, e.g. Mills & Allen, London and Provincial Poster Group, none of whom are truly national. For selling purposes some groups of sites are available through a consortium called British Posters; another group, Independent Poster Sales, exists to sell sites and packages. British Transport Advertising, London Transport Advertising, Adshel (bus shelters) and More O'Ferrall (supersites) are, of course, all separate organisations.

Independent local radio, like ITV, consists of contractors who are awarded their contracts from the Independent Broadcasting Authority. There were usually two to half a dozen consortia competing for each contract during 1973/4. Nineteen companies were appointed by 1974; in October 1978 a further nine stations were announced. The consortia are generally of twenty to thirty individuals and firms – breweries, merchant banks, unions and so on. TV companies may and do hold shares but not a controlling interest; the press, especially the local press, are encouraged to participate. Associated Newspapers are major shareholders in the London Broadcasting Company; the *Evening Standard* and *Observer* have shares in Capital Radio; the *Evening Citizen* was the largest shareholder in Radio Clyde and so on. Radio Luxembourg is similarly supported entirely by advertising.

Cinema lies at the other extreme, advertising contributing only a small part of the turnover of the medium. Cinema admissions totalled about £90 million in 1977, the rise above 1972 being 70 per cent. Advertising contributes about 10 per cent of total revenue.

## DIFFICULTIES OF MEASUREMENT

The basic sources for media expenditure data have already been mentioned [3.2, 3.7]. Some of these analyses have to assume that the normal rate-card cost has been paid for each insertion. However, the same space or time may be sold at different prices dependent on the circumstances. Agencies negotiate privately with media owners what the actual price will be. A page of advertising may be offered at short notice at a much reduced rate. Every TV spot must be sold at a rate-card price, but the cards contain pre-empts and regulators explained in the next chapter. And all prices are subject to volume and other dis-

## Table 4  AVERAGE DISCOUNT FROM FULL RATE CARD FOR ITV

| 1968 | 1970 | 1972 | 1974 | 1975 | 1976 | 1977 |
|------|------|------|------|------|------|------|
| 19%  | 24%  | 24%  | 21%  | 27%  | 24%  | 17%  |

counts. As a result of regulators and discounts the rate-card take and costs based on rate cards can be misleading. Variation affects the figures year-to-year and even more month-to-month. As an example, Table 4 gives the average discounts for the last few years. They show the amounts that the average advertiser gets off the fully-paid rate; they are worked out by grossing-up the ITCA net revenue, i.e. adding 17.65 per cent to allow for agency commission, and expressing the result as a percentage of the MEAL figure. This gives the percentage of rate-card paid by the advertiser. The difference from 100 is the average discount.

An advertiser knows of course what net figure he has paid, but not his competitors'. To compare one agency's buying with another's, or to describe total expenditures and trends, is like trying to complete a jigsaw with many lost pieces.

## RESEARCH COSTS

The research that guides the expenditure of advertising money is described later in this book. Most of its cost falls on the media owner and is looked on as part of his selling expenses: he has to show what audience he delivers.

It has also been suggested that the research data would be better designed and underwritten by the advertiser (who would admit media owners to participation of both the cost and the output). In this way the buyer of media for advertising purposes would design his own quality control system and would overcome sectarian interests. The cost to the advertiser would not be any greater than now, since it is his money which pays for media research anyhow. Unfortunately this state of affairs is most unlikely to be reached, as too many sacred cows would have to be slain.

The total cost of the major media research projects is probably about £3 million a year — one-third of one per cent of total media turnover. The proportion is higher for television, lower for press. The amount is sometimes criticised as too large; it has been suggested that it would be better spent on research into advertisements themselves, since the selling power of a better advertisement may be much greater than that of a better media plan. The choice does not in fact lie between these alternative expenditures; the industry has to decide separately how much each is worth: it has been pointed out [3.8] that a car needs both an engine (the advertisements) *and* steering (the media plan).

## INFLATION – OR REAL GROWTH?

Has spending on display advertising really grown in the last decade? The figures as usually published make it appear so: £300 million in 1968 (the year taken as the base in the first edition of this book) £500 million in 1973 (second edition) and now £900 million.

To answer this question we must look at these figures after inflation has been removed. Using the Retail Price Index we can put these figures at 1970 consumer prices. They now hardly change: in millions of pounds 350 rises to 390 and falls to 360. So it appears that the amount spent on display advertising has actually been rather constant.

We also need an index of media inflation before we can interpret the growth in media money. It is one thing if advertisers are getting more exposure of their advertising and another thing if they are just paying more for the same. Since media owners are in business like other firms, buying labour and raw materials, it would be understandable if their effective rates went up at something like the Retail Price Index: this would just be part of the falling value of money. If their costs per advertisement exposed went up less than the Retail Price Index then their worth would be increasing and advertisers would get better value for their money. This could happen for example if ITV delivered more viewers than before, or magazines increased in circulation.

It is in fact possible to estimate whether the media are providing more or fewer opportunities to see advertisements and to compare the amount spent with what the money bought. The Advertising Association construct indices for ITV and groups of various publications.

Deflating the total spend on display advertising by the average index of media rates we get a slightly higher rise to 1973: plus 27 per cent from 1968 to 1973 and a fall by 11 per cent to 1977. Thus the amount of advertising rose a little up to 1973 but is currently slightly lower.

The relative prices of TV and print alter quite sharply from time. From 1968 to 1973 TV rose less than print. This has reversed recently and in 1977 the TV index (at 100 in 1968) was 277 while the press total was 210.

Real spending on display advertising has therefore not altered much though this is hard to see from the raw data. Naturally, the year taken as the base has a big effect on all these comparisons.

The broad pattern of changes in the last decade has been as follows.

From 1968 to 1973 the British economy enjoyed real growth at 2 or 3 per cent a year. Inflation then in retrospect looks moderate: in single figures. Advertising shared in this calm and prosperity; it grew slightly overall, mainly in 1972 and 1973.

The economic upheavals of 1974 and 1975 caused a real fall in our standard of living, with drops of 2 per cent a year. Inflation leapt to a maximum of plus 24 per cent in 1975. In 1977 and 1978 the results were still being felt, with inflation still above pre-crisis levels. By 1977 no real growth had occurred, though this appeared in 1978.

Advertising suffered during the crisis, especially TV advertising, which reacts quickly to demand pressures. It fell 14 per cent in 1974 and again, though not as severely, in 1975. By 1977 it had not altogether recovered, but is expected to break new records in real terms in 1978.

Tables in the Appendices show some of the detailed changes that have taken place between 1968 (the year taken as the base in the first edition of this book) and 1977. Space is left there for the reader who wants to keep the figures up to date.

## £900 MILLION OR £1,500 MILLION?

The Advertising Association reports already referred to give a larger figure, £1,499 million for total advertising expenditure, than the one used in this book. This is because they include both production costs and some advertising which is not display or not directed at consumers, whereas I am describing the work that flows through large agencies. The differences are explained in detail in Appendix 4.

When total promotion costs are considered the figures become much larger again. It is even harder to define and measure these expenditures below the line. They are currently estimated at about two to three times total advertising. The items that would be included are direct

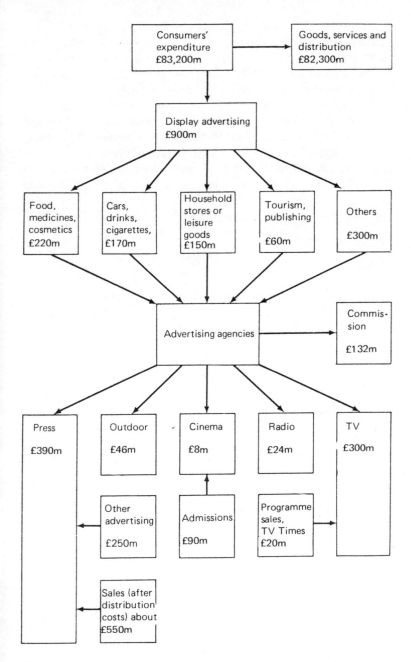

*Figure 7*

mail and sample distribution; catalogues, leaflets and calendars; exhibitions; window and interior display; point-of-sale aids; salesmen's and retailer incentives; trade deals, a fast-growing item in recent years; and the manufacturers' sales force itself might be counted.

Finally, there is a smaller figure even than the £900 million which I estimate goes to display advertising in the main media. This is also given by the AA. It is called Manufacturers' Consumer Advertising, which is defined as advertising from the private sector aimed at the general public and so it excludes all retail, industrial, government and financial advertising. In 1977 this was £613 million and had only doubled since 1968. Crudely, this is the amount spent on branded goods advertising; it is a declining share of the total.

## SUMMARY

The main figures estimated above are collected in Figure 7.

# Part 2
# THE MEDIA

TELEVISION
THE PRESS
OTHER MEDIA

# 4 TELEVISION

*A description of Independent Television as an advertising medium. The structure of the industry, technical details of transmissions and sets, the audience and the cost of reaching it with an outline of the research available.*

## THE EFFECTIVENESS OF TELEVISION ADVERTISING

This chapter is concerned with the facts about exposing TV commercials to people, with the control of Independent Television, with the technicalities of transmission and reception, TV ratings and other research matters. These details must not be allowed to obscure the central quality of the television medium: its power as a method of advertising.

TV commercials have some limitations. Many watch it in black and white (more on colour later). The screen is small and intimate, unsuited to appeals on the grand scale; the definition of the picture is often poor; the message cannot be re-examined at leisure. But agencies and advertisers have seen on sales graphs the effects of television advertising. Of course TV does not have in the home the impact it has when commercials are shown in the agency, with due preparation, on a big

59

screen, in the dark and in silence. Nevertheless TV commercials are hard to escape; some people leave the room during breaks or do not watch the commercials, but the majority of the audience cannot – indeed do not want to – close their eyes and ears. Those whó do pay attention are exposed to the sales message, frame by frame, in the order planned by the agency; the advertisement has movement and sound; the product can be demonstrated in action.

## THE STRUCTURE OF INDEPENDENT TELEVISION

### One contractor to each area

Commercial or advertisement-carrying television is currently controlled by the Independent Broadcasting Authority Acts of 1973 and 1974. These are administered by the Independent Broadcasting Authority (IBA, previously the Independent Television Authority) and the Home Office. The contractors currently hold contracts until 1981 but extensions are likely.

There have been many different opinions expressed about the future use of the potential broadcasting facilities in this country. The television contractors would naturally like a second channel controlled by the existing companies, advertisers and agencies would prefer a more independent but still commercial second channel. At the moment (1978) the whole structure is in doubt. The Annan Committee recommendations (1977) have not been translated into a new Act.

Regular TV transmissions started from the BBC in 1936. ITV first broadcast in London in 1955 and the network was completed in 1962. There has been a period of fifteen to twenty years of improvements and modifications to basically the same system; the contractors have been regrouped, BBC2 opened in 1964, colour started on BBC2 in 1967 and was used first by ITV and BBC1 in 1969, the transmission system has been modified and gaps have been filled in, hours of broadcasting have been gradually extended. Smaller developments and those to come are not dealt with here: cable TV, small local services, e.g. for hotels or experimental areas, or *Oracle* and *Prestel*, the transmission of 'pages' that the viewer or user can choose.

So ITV are essentially the current television contractors. Each covers a single area, except in London, since a single contractor here would be so much larger than the others; in London there is both a weekday and a weekend contractor. The IBA favours a single contractor in each area for three reasons. Each company is supposed to achieve identity with its area: regional loyalties are built up. To split transmissions between two contractors complicates the problems of balanced and continuous programme planning. And continuous seven-day working should be more economical.

The advertiser and agency see this structure rather differently. Programmes are made by many contractors and shared between all of them, so the viewer sees the emblems of many different regions on his screen. He is probably more aware of ITV as such, or of its channel number on his set, than of his local company. The advertiser is also concerned that in a seven-day area he is dealing with a monopoly holder. If you wish to advertise on television in Central Scotland you have to buy from Scottish Television. This lack of competition (except in London) may outweigh to the advertiser the economies of seven-day working, which in any case benefit the contractors, and not the advertiser directly.

In rejecting the view which has just been stated about regionality and monopolies, Lord Hill, when Chairman of the ITA, made the significant statement: 'While Independent Television is a system which supports itself from the sale of advertising time, it is – first and foremost – a public service of television and not just an advertising medium. This means that the arrangement of the service must be governed primarily by what is best for the viewers, rather than what members of the advertising profession might regard as better from their client's point of view.'

Despite this clash of opinion between the Authority and the advertising business, both sides agree that the regionality of transmission by ITV is one of its major advantages. Because it is possible to advertise in one area alone, a reasonably isolated advertising test or product launch can be mounted. Because it is possible to bring in other areas, one at a time, a launch can be phased to cover the country gradually, in step with production and distribution. A national advertiser can adjust his advertising pressure by area to suit his marketing situation. Local advertisers can use television.

So as well as persuading an advertiser to use television, the contractor has to get his own area selected. The contractors compete to be used as a test area, to come in early on an area-phased launch, to get a larger share of a national campaign, not to be dropped when a budget does not allow every area to be included. It has already been stated that there are large differences between the amounts of time sold, and so between the relative profitabilities of a popular and an unpopular area. The agency view of the choice between areas is given in Chapter 9.

There are fourteen ITV areas in the UK; since London is served by two companies there are fifteen contractors. The companies providing the services for each area are essentially separate and each has its own personality and characteristics. They fall into natural groups according to size. After London, there are three large areas, each with 11 to 16 per cent of the ITV homes. With London, these five contractors or four areas cover over 60 per cent of the country. There are five regional areas, each with 5 to 8 per cent of ITV homes. There remain three small areas, with only 1 to 3 per cent of ITV homes. Finally, there are Ulster and the Channel Islands, which an advertiser may or may not include in his definition of national cover. This data is given more fully in Table 5.

## Programmes

ITV is in another sense simply the programmes it outputs. These are hard to describe in a summary form. The reader — if he is a typical agency or marketing man — is likely to be rather ignorant about them as he watches so much less than the typical viewer. Attention to the set is the only way he will acquire real understanding. Nevertheless summaries can be given. The breakdown by type, for example, in the year ended March 1974, was:

| | |
|---|---|
| Plays, drama and serials | 24% |
| Entertainment and music | 13% |
| Feature films | 11% |
| Sport | 10% |
| Children's programmes | 10% |
| News and news magazines | 9% |
| Current affairs and documentaries | 9% |
| Others | 14% |

In the week ending 5 November 1978 the top ten programmes were:

Table 5

| ITV area | Contractor | ITV homes[1], % | |
| | | Including overlap | Net |
|---|---|---|---|
| London | Thames TV (Mon -Fri 7 pm) London Weekend TV (Fri 7 pm -Sun) | 22.6 | 21.1 |
| Midlands | ATV Network | 16.5 | 15.2 |
| Lancashire | Granada TV | 14.1 | 13.5 |
| Yorkshire | Yorkshire TV[2] | 11.3 | 10.8 |
| Southern | Southern TV | 8.7 | 7.5 |
| Wales and the West | Harlech TV | 7.6 | 7.1 |
| Central Scotland | Scottish TV[3] | 7.0 | 6.7 |
| East of England | Anglia TV | 5.8 | 4.8 |
| North Eastern | Tyne Tees TV[2] | 5.0 | 4.8 |
| South West | Westward TV | 3.0 | 2.6 |
| North East England | Grampian TV[3] | 1.9 | 1.6 |
| Border | Border TV | 1.0 | 0.9 |
| Ulster | Ulster TV | 2.2 | 2.2 |
| Channel Islands | Channel TV[4] | 0.2 | 0.2 |
| | | 107.8 | 100.0 |

*Notes*

1 ITV homes: households possessing a TV set that actually receives transmissions of acceptable quality; the data report the situation at April 1978 and are based on JICTAR Establishment Surveys.
2 These two sell jointly as Trident.
3 These two sell jointly as Stags.
4 Sold by Westward TV.

| | |
|---|---|
| Coronation Street (Mon) Granada | Coronation Street (Wed) Granada |
| This is Your Life Thames | Robin's Nest Thames |
| The Sweeney Thames | Crossroads (Wed) ATV |
| All Creatures Great and Small BBC | Top of the Pops BBC |
| Crossroads (Thu) ATV | Mixed Blessings LWT |

Each contractor is responsible for the programmes shown in his own region. But this does not mean he makes them all — that would be impossibly expensive. Most he buys from outside his region — especially from the other contractors. Some programmes are the responsibility of the contractors as a whole: the news for example. A Network Programme Committee works out the exchange of programmes.

The Television Act charges the IBA with detailed programme responsibilities: the Authority must ensure that programmes 'maintain a high general standard in all respects and in particular in respect of their content and quality, and a proper balance and wide range in their subject matter'. The IBA sees its function [4.1] in relation to programmes 'to encourage, stimulate and exhort far more that it is to repress, deter or ban'. At the same time, the Authority admits that it has to be 'a guardian in a negative sense. Except in a society which admitted no responsibility for the protection of its members in matters of truth and morals, this must be inescapable.'

Discussion about programmes inevitably polarises round 'give people what they want' and the elitest view of 'give them what they ought to have'. It is not easy to give working definitions of these concepts and it is unlikely that everyone means the same by the words 'quality' and 'balance'. The whole subject is controversial, and not only between the IBA and the contractors, but between and within contractors. A high rating may be pandering to the lowest common denominator; on the other hand, it may show that a lot of people are enjoying themselves — it certainly means that commercials are being shown at a low average cost per thousand viewers.

Both programme controllers and the advertiser view the BBC as the enemy. Total hours of viewing television are limited and relatively stable. The share of this viewing got by ITV, and so the value of television to the advertiser, is variable and depends essentially on which programmes people prefer to watch. The Chairman of the ITA said in 1968 [4.1] 'Our relationship with the BBC, happily friendly in personal terms, is nevertheless one of open and unremitting competition.

In the field of programmes, this is an obvious requirement and it has had incontrovertibly beneficial effects on both organisations.' This competitiveness does not, of course, prevent the considerable co-operation which takes place between ITV and the BBC on technical matters.

In practice, ITV programme policies are an uneasy compromise between:

1 What Parliament and other opinion leaders feel, especially as expressed through the IBA.
2 What the viewers think, as expressed in letters, through more organised bodies and as measured in surveys.
3 The pressure for high ratings applied by the advertiser and agency, who are pursuing value for money in terms of advertisement exposure.
4 The desire of contractors and their production teams to have good standing in their professional circles.
5 The money allotted by contractors for programme production.
6 What the BBC is doing.

The day-to-day practice of ITV programming, and agency discussions with contractors about the ratings they achieve, reflect this variegated background. The IBA has to approve all programme schedules; this influences and can delay contractors' policies. Because good standing with the IBA is politically important to them, contractors are encouraged (as well as sometimes being directed) to insert deliberately minority audience material. Also the ITV programme timetable is rigid compared with the BBC's because of the exchange of material between contractors, though the times allowed for production are usually shorter.

All these problems are exclusive to television; they arise from the same characteristic which makes it a powerful advertising medium: the viewer cannot skip and does not want to do so. There are discriminating viewers who turn on the set for occasional programmes but these are in the minority. In most homes TV is 'moving wallpaper' – the set is on practically all evening.

*Advertising on television*

The Independent Broadcasting Acts lay down that advertisements must be clearly distinguishable from the programmes. They must be inserted between programmes or at 'natural breaks'. Some types of programme may not contain advertising at all.

The final authority which approves commercials is the IBA, which excludes any likely to mislead or offend. Some products, for example cigarettes, may not be advertised on TV at all. Advertisers, agencies and contractors all subscribe to the British Code of Advertising Practice, which regulates advertising material. The IBA Code incorporates this code and adds further restrictions of its own. Generally, the rules for television advertising are more strict than for other media. This can influence the choice of medium (in addition to TV being barred for some products): 'We couldn't say that on TV.'

In practice, scripts are cleared before shooting, to avoid expensive re-makes. They are submitted by agencies to the contractors — first to the copy secretariat of the Independent Television Companies Association, who pass on problems to the Copy Clearance Committee. If the ITCA, with its experience of the case law built up, cannot decide, then the scripts are referred to Advertising Control at the ITA. Over 30 scripts are cleared every working day for nationally distributed goods and services; there are twice as many new advertisements for local products and shops.

The IBA sets the rules about hours of transmission and the amount of advertising permitted. These rules are complex; the main points are that not more than an average of six minutes advertising in any hour are allowed and not more than seven minutes in one clock hour. The actual amount of advertising carried varies with demand on the medium. It depends especially on the area and on the time of year. On average about 80 minutes of commercial time is carried each day. By adroit late selling and filling every break, this can be raised to about 100 minutes a day; in some areas it falls as low as 50 or 60 minutes a day. Typically, 15,000 or 16,000 spots are transmitted by the network each week, obviously depending on demand.

The shortest and simplest commercials are 7-second slides and longest are occasional 'specials' of two or three minutes. Most (71 per cent in 1977) are 30 seconds, but 15, 45 and 60 seconds are available. Currently, a move to multiples of 10 seconds is being discussed. Most commercials are made as films, but they can also be recorded on magnetic tape, and this method is growing. Copies of commercials should be with the contractor at least five clear working days before transmission, to allow the whole break to be laced up ready for showing. Orders may generally be cancelled up to eight weeks before transmission is due.


## THE TRANSMISSION AND RECEPTION OF ITV

Up to 1969, ITV signals were all in the VHF (very high frequency or 30 to 300 MHz) waveband and the picture was defined by 405 lines. VHF has the advantage that it can 'go round corners', i.e. it is not vital that the receiving and transmitting stations are in direct sight of each other. Only 47 such transmitters are required to give reasonable (in fact, 99 per cent) cover of the country. This system will continue as long as reasonably necessary, say until the 1980s.

As well as the VHF 405-line system, ITV and BBC1 have duplicated their broadcasts on the UHF (ultra high frequency or 300 to 3000 MHz) waveband. The picture standard used is 625 lines. The same programmes and commercials are transmitted under both systems. This decision was taken because of the band-width required for colour, because interference is lower in the UHF band, and because 625 lines gives a better defined picture. But the number of transmitters (and their cost) is considerably increased. By the end of 1973 UHF cover was only about 93 per cent from 116 transmitters in total because UHF can, approximately, go only in straight lines. But the cover is now effectively complete: the plan is for 50 main and 350 relay transmitters.

Transmissions in colour are also in UHF and 625 lines. Roughly, they share the same transmitters and opening dates. The first colour commercials were broadcast in November 1969.

BBC transmissions were also until a few years ago only on VHF 405 lines. BBC2 opened in London with UHF 625 lines in April 1964. This service has been extending gradually over the country. They started colour transmissions in July 1967.

Thus the choice of signals available to most viewers (ignoring the cable services) is:

| | |
|---|---|
| VHF 405-line monochrome: | ITV |
| | BBC1 |
| UHF 625-line colour: | ITV |
| | BBC1 |
| | BBC2 |

Originally, sets had to receive only VHF 405 lines. Then dual-standard sets became required to receive both types of transmission in monochrome, i.e. VHF 405 lines and UHF 625 lines. Next, colour sets were needed to receive BBC2 in colour as well as VHF 405 lines in black and white. The colour signal is of course shown in monochrome on a black and white set. Finally, makers have been able to revert to a single standard, i.e. UHF 625 lines, on which viewers receive all three services.

The household has also to possess a suitable set; in 1978 97 per cent of all homes in the ITV areas had a set receiving ITV. The acquisition of colour sets has grown faster here than it did in the US because of the British TV set rental services, the relative robustness of present-day sets and the negligible amount of monochrome in 'colour' programme transmissions. Colour was at first associated with up-grade, older, childless (and well-off) households but this has changed as penetration increased. It is the C1C2, younger households with children who are currently acquiring sets and the amount and character of viewing in colour homes (after an initial period of heavier viewing) is now not very different from the national average. The proportion of homes with colour has grown steadily and steeply: from 4 per cent in January 1971 to 29 per cent in January 1974, 40 per cent in January 1975 and 63 per cent in April 1978.

Since the overall proportion of households with ITV is now so high. their characteristics are almost the same as the national average. Exposure to commercials is neither as high nor as well balanced as actual viewing data shown later makes clear.

The fourteen ITV areas seem to present a tidy regional breakdown. But signal transmissions do not recognise lines on a map: there are pockets within areas which cannot receive signals, and signals go on beyond the area to create overlaps. In an overlap area households have a choice between channels, sometimes a choice made when the aerial is set up, sometimes only a matter of turning a dial on the set.

The definition of an ITV area is important to the contractor, since it affects the size of his audience and hence his revenue. More importantly, the advertiser wants to relate TV advertising to his own product's distribution and sales. Since ITV areas are not isolated (except for Ulster) analyses of sales and advertising relationships become fuzzy.

Several definitions of ITV area are in use. One is an engineer's definition of signal strength: at least 250 microvolts per metre of arc

68

for VHF and 70 dB for UHF. There is also a market research definition: at least 15 per cent of those households with adequate aerials and sets must get satisfactory reception from the home station. This requires time to establish itself, as setting up a new transmitter changes the acquisition of sets and aerial tuning. And there is a proposed, but not generally accepted, definition based not just on technical ability to receive a signal but on the preferences which people state in an interview.

The existence of overlap depresses ratings. This is a purely numerical point. The number of potential ITV homes in an area includes those which can receive two or more ITV channels. Naturally some of these view other stations. Thus the proportion viewing the home station is lower in an area with many dual-channel homes, even if ITV is just as popular there. There are about 7 per cent nationally in overlap areas but more in some areas: importantly, 31 per cent in Anglia, 28 per cent in South, are in dual and triple channel homes.


## RATINGS

An ITV homes rating is the percentage of sets in ITV homes which are on and switched to the ITV home station at any minute. An ITV adult rating is the percentage of adults in ITV homes who are viewing ITV. Similarly, there are housewife ratings and so on. These definitions call for two immediate comments. First, it is easy to forget that a rating is not among all adults or all housewives; there are always those not in ITV households to be considered (3 per cent of all adults). Second, to understand the detailed definitions of ratings requires a study of the research methods used and this is not a simple subject. For example, 'viewing' is not what it at first appears, as is discussed below.


*Switching the set on*

Viewing television (ITV or BBC) is a major part of the British way of life. The amount of time the set is on, in ITV homes, has been constant for several years: it averages 5 hours each afternoon and evening. Broadly speaking 5.30 p.m. to 10.30 p.m. are these hours. The set is turned on when people come back from work and it is turned off when they go to bed. On Saturday afternoon it is turned on earlier; on

Sundays earlier still. Of course, this varies with the time of year and, marginally, with the weather. In summer more people are away from the set: ratings in July and August are roughly 15 per cent below the annual average.

ITV contractors prefer to give homes or set data of this kind. The figures for individuals are of course more relevant to advertisers and are lower. For example, the average hours of viewing for an individual are not 5 hours but just over half this: 3 hours.

When ITV started in September 1955 it was more in tune with the wants of the British public than the BBC. It was livelier, it was 'us' and not 'them'. The commercials themselves were a revelation to people with more to spend who welcomed suggestions on what to buy. These factors are not so true today. The BBC has in many ways more programming liberty than ITV. It has two channels to ITV's one. In some fields — sport and official events for example — viewers traditionally prefer the BBC. Commercials are no longer news.

It is therefore not surprising that ITV's share of the audience has fallen since, say, 1965. It is rather surprising that it has kept above a half. The two major events in the last seven years which have disturbed the general 54:46 shares have been, first, the 1968 change in contractors which coincided with a brief disruption in transmissions and a different research method, and, second, the increase in ITV transmissions in the afternoons, or daytime, which started in October 1972.

ITV's set share since 1965 is given in Table 6. The reader should be warned that the BBC contest this; they regularly claim to have a share of audience 'a little larger than ITV's'; see the comments later on research methods. Whether the ITV share will fall again depends most on the effort and money it puts into its programmes, but its palmy days of audience domination, like those of high profits, are probably over.

*Light and heavy viewers*

The set in an ITV home is tuned to ITV for about 3 hours a day on

Table 6   ITV SHARE OF VIEWERS, %

| 1965 | 1968 | 1970 | 1972 | 1973 | 1974 | 1975 | 1976 | 1977 |
|------|------|------|------|------|------|------|------|------|
| 64   | 54   | 54   | 54   | 56   | 55   | 55   | 52   | 54   |

average. The average viewing of ITV by an individual in an ITV home is about 2 hours a day — which covers a very wide range. The causes of this variation and its effect on the audience to an actual schedule of TV spots are complicated. The earlier sections of this chapter may have made TV seem almost a commodity: a medium with a very high and therefore uniform cover. It is on the contrary a medium which contains infinite variety, exposed to individuals with very different requirements and who select from it by literally the turn of a switch. Further, we can know about this complexity only through research which itself serves a number of purposes: to sell the medium, to act as currency between buyer and seller, to help programme planners and so on. Inevitably our knowledge of how viewers use the medium is incomplete. It would be uneconomic to expect much more.

The most important variation in the audience is their weight of viewing: whether they view at all and then whether they are light, medium or heavy viewers. Within this there are differences in the amount of time given to ITV and to the two BBC channels. The normal description of this situation ignores the non-ITV viewer (who is too easily forgotten) and then divides the rest into light, medium and heavy (or in the case of the National Readership Survey, into five groups) by their ITV viewing only. Questions are asked in the industry about the amount of exposure a heavy viewer receives, whether this can all be really effective, whether the light viewer is reached enough, how to pick spots to reach her more often, whether to use another medium to do so and so on. These are difficult and worthwhile questions, but to give them a more general introduction I start by considering all viewing.

There are very few people who literally never view TV — under 3 per cent do not have a set at home. Of course some people have a set but never use it, others may see TV in friends' homes or pubs and clubs. It does little harm to our understanding to lump non-viewers and light viewers together. We then need to define non and light, medium and heavy viewing. This cannot be exact, since claimed viewing differs from actual, men's habits differ from women's and so on. But we can approximately divide people into:

*30 per cent non and light viewers of any channel* who view less than 2 hours a day and average 8 hours a week.

*30 per cent medium viewers of any channel* who view between 2 and 4 hours a day and average 20 hours a week.

*40 per cent heavy viewers of any channel* who view 4 hours or more a day and average 40 hours a week. (These are the

71

square-eyed people who can hardly be paying close or continuous attention to the set.)

When we consider ITV alone (and the two BBC channels together give a similar picture) we have approximately equal thirds at:

> *Non and light viewers of ITV* who view it less than 1 hour a day and average 4 hours a week.
> *Medium viewers of ITV* who view it between 1 and 2 hours a day and average 10 hours a week.
> *Heavy viewers of ITV* who view it 2 hours a day or more and average 23 hours a week.

These observations lead to an important conclusion which contains the key to much of the controversy about the medium. It is that the light viewer of ITV is very little exposed (and of course the non-viewer not at all) while the heavy viewer sees considerably more than the average which is what we usually see reported. The ratios of viewing are about 4:10:23; put more simply, when a series of spots totals 100 TVRs (reaching all ITV individuals once each on average) the light viewer accounts for only 6 per cent of all the impacts, the medium viewers 27 per cent and the heavy viewers 67 per cent. We can say roughly that at 100 TVRs in total we cover half all the viewers and so each of these has two OTS on average; but of the light viewers only 20 per cent are covered and have a frequency of one; of medium viewers 60 per cent are covered, with a frequency of 1½; of heavy viewers 90 per cent are covered with a frequency of 2. Even with a 500 TVR schedule the total cover of light viewers is only one half, while at 300 TVRs or more virtually all medium and heavy viewers are covered.

These analyses are based on four weeks' data, i.e. 'light viewers' are those who watch ITV least during this period. The same people are not necessarily all in the lightest third in another period, so 'light viewer' is a definition which can change with the weeks and the apparently very poor performance of ITV in one period is improved a little over time. The definitions used in a survey method (often necessary if we are looking at advertising effectiveness) are different again and depend on claimed viewing, a claim probably not made very exactly. Therefore light viewers in a survey tend to show a better effectiveness of ITV (e.g. higher recall) than we would expect from JICTAR schedule analyses.

I now turn to the relation between ITV viewing and total viewing, or peoples' relative exposure to ITV and BBC. The reasons why light viewers are so are of two sorts: either because of their general social habits and preferences they watch little TV of any kind, or they do watch TV but distinctly prefer BBC. The two reasons are of course crucially different to the programme companies: they have an easier job persuading the BBC viewer to switch than getting light viewers to stay at home and turn the set on. Table 7 indicates roughly how ITV and BBC viewing are related, as percentages of all adults.

If all heavy ITV viewers were also heavy BBC viewers and so on, this table would have entries only along the diagonal. Actually it is very well spread out, showing that people do choose apparently separately how much to watch and then they make a channel preference decision.

It is in fact possible to demonstrate general differences between the ITV viewers and the BBC viewer. For example the heavy ITV viewer tends when compared with the heavy BBC viewer not to be quite as old but to be more downscale and less well educated, to prefer also popular newspapers and to have a distinct Life Style (more gregarious, up to date, wanting to be amused, sexually tolerant but prurient, Labour-voting, living for today and dreamy) and to have clear programme preferences (in which *Coronation Street, Family at War, On the Buses* and other series about people or comedies score higher than news or current affairs).

The imbalance of the ITV audience leads to several proposed courses of action. The contractors claim they could carry more specialised and minority interest programmes on a second channel. They point out that selective and attentive viewers may anyway require less repetition of a message. The press say that a mixed media schedule can add to

Table 7  RELATIONSHIP OF ITV AND BBC VIEWING AS
A PERCENTAGE OF ALL ADULTS

| ITV viewers | BBC viewers | | | Total |
|---|---|---|---|---|
| | Non and light | Medium | Heavy | |
| Heavy | 9 | 12 | 12 | 33 |
| Medium | 8 | 13 | 11 | 32 |
| Non and light | 14 | 11 | 10 | 35 |
| Total | 31 | 36 | 33 | 100 |

Source: *Burnett Life Style*

73

advertising cover on the light viewers. The agencies try to redistribute their schedules to reach the lighter viewers but with little success; it is always possible after the event to see how a little more cover could have been attained, but very difficult in practice to do better than buy as many total ratings as possible and to get high ratings (since light viewers are bought more cheaply in popular programmes), though specialist times like sport, news and daytime have their place. The heavy viewers cannot be avoided: we have to reach them repeatedly. They will be exposed to our commercial again and again — and to competitors' commercials. They may be less affected by commercials — certainly by the twentieth or fortieth repetition — than people who see a smaller number. At low rating times these people form the majority of the audience. Therefore off-peak time is cheap but its real value is sometimes questioned.

*The effects of sex, social grade, age and education*

So people who are viewing ITV at any one moment are not typical of the whole population: they are more likely to be in a lower social grade and they are more likely to be 25 to 34 years old, to have young children or to be over 55. For every hour a housewife watches ITV, other adults watch for only 40 minutes. The average ABC1 views only 2 hours for every 3 spent viewing by a C2DE. ABs are more likely than average never to view and much more likely to be light viewers. DEs, when they do have a set, are the heaviest viewers. Differences in ITV viewing related to social grade are explained by the number of other interests enjoyed by the upper social grades. The better-off are more likely to have cars, to visit friends, to read books, and so on. They are also more likely to view BBC.

The AB or managerial grade are only 15|per cent of the population, but for some products they are an important target group. A campaign intended to reach them will do better in the later parts of the evening. Office workers come home and go to bed later than manual workers. There are also a few programmes a little more likely to appeal to them — *University Challenge* or *News at Ten*. But on the whole, as for lighter viewers generally, it is the high-rating times which reach ABs most economically.

The social grade bias also affects the different ITV areas. The Southern area and London contain more than their share of ABC1s.

Lancashire, Yorkshire and the Midlands contain more manual workers. This is one reason why ratings in London and the South are comparatively low.

The reasons for the differences in ITV viewing with age are equally obvious. The 16 to 24-year olds are more likely to be out of the house, to be listening to radio or doing homework. Young marrieds are tied to the house and children; they find in TV contact with the outside world. These people are an important target to many advertisers and their attachment to the set is a major advantage to ITV. From 35 to 54, people are more free to go out again, and over 55 they settle down once more in front of the set.

The age at which people finished full time education is also associated with ITV viewing (and of course with social grade). The better-educated (or, more accurately, the longer-educated) view less. About three-quarters of the adults in the UK left school at 15 or under; among heavy viewers the proportion rises to 80 per cent but among light viewers it falls to 60 per cent. Only 5 per cent of all adults were still being educated at 19; among heavy viewers this proportion is as low as 2 per cent but among light viewers it is as high as 10 per cent.

*The effects of time, day and programmes*

The most critical factors affecting ratings are the time of day, day of week and the programmes on ITV and BBC. These cause important fluctuations over the evening in the actual numbers of people reached by ITV and in the cost of reaching them.

The amount of sampling of other programmes that goes on during the evening is unknown. The overall effect is that people appear to be loyal to — or apathetic about — the channel they are viewing. An audience attracted early in the evening tends to stay with that channel. So programme planning by contractors requires skill. A rating is not achieved by a programme in isolation but depends on the total audience viewing at the time and on the programmes competing. We hear of 'hammocked' programmes — weak programmes supported at each end by strong ones. The TV buyer has to be aware of these patterns in detail in order to predict good times for his spots.

To demonstrate this, a simplified version is given in Figure 8 of a chart in the JICTAR Weekly Report showing sets switched on for part of a single day in London. On this day ITV maintained a clear lead up

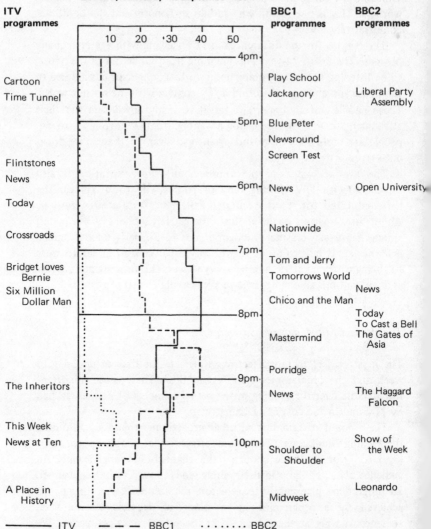

**EXAMPLE OF HOMES TV RATINGS**
**London, Thursday 12 September 1974**

| ITV programmes | | BBC1 programmes | BBC2 programmes |
|---|---|---|---|
| | 10  20  '30  40  50 | | |
| | —4pm— | | |
| Cartoon | | Play School | |
| Time Tunnel | | Jackanory | Liberal Party Assembly |
| | —5pm— | Blue Peter | |
| | | Newsround | |
| | | Screen Test | |
| Flintstones | | | |
| News | | | |
| | —6pm— | News | Open University |
| Today | | | |
| Crossroads | | Nationwide | |
| | —7pm— | | |
| Bridget loves Bernie | | Tom and Jerry | |
| | | Tomorrows World | |
| Six Million Dollar Man | | | News |
| | | Chico and the Man | |
| | —8pm— | | Today |
| | | | To Cast a Bell |
| | | Mastermind | The Gates of Asia |
| | | Porridge | |
| | —9pm— | | |
| The Inheritors | | News | The Haggard Falcon |
| This Week | | | |
| News at Ten | | | Show of the Week |
| | —10pm— | Shoulder to Shoulder | |
| A Place in History | | | Leonardo |
| | | Midweek | |

———— ITV  — — — BBC1  ········ BBC2

*Figure 8*

to 8.30 p.m. Its children's programmes were preferred by the majority though a few sets were switched away from *Flintstones* to John Craven's *Newsround*. *Today* and *Crossroads* beat the BBC's regional news programme *Nationwide*. *Tom and Jerry* brought the BBC a few extra

76

viewers, but a new SF series, *The Six Million Dollar Man,* retained ITV's lead over a comedy film series *Chico and the Man* and the quiz programme *Mastermind* which the BBC put out. A substantial proportion however turned away from ITV's series *The Inheritors* to watch Ronnie Barker's series *Porridge.* The BBC started to lose this audience at the *Nine O'Clock News* while ITV's current affairs programme *This Week* and *News at Ten* held the audience. BBC1 fell off severely when their play about suffragettes started, *Shoulder to Shoulder.* Most of them seem to have switched to BBC2's *Show of the Week* which got a rating of 11; otherwise BBC2 did not get above a rating of 5.

The buyer is, of course, concerned with individuals seeing his commercials, not with sets switched on. Broadly, the ratings for individuals follow the pattern shown for sets, but there are important variations in the adults-per-set and housewives-per-set figures through the evening. The industry's research gives individuals' ratings and it is these which agencies study most closely, though sets or homes ratings are still commonly used.

Ratings vary by day of week (lower on Sundays and lowest on Saturdays as the BBC is strong then), by audience definition (e.g. adults are lower than homes) and especially by time of year (e.g. low in summer, high when the weather is poor, such as in February).

## RATE CARDS

Rate cards are issued periodically; their form and content differ from one contractor to another and they contain many complexities. But basically a rate card gives the area's rates for a 30-second spot shown at different times. Spots of other lengths are charged at proportionate rates, except that a 15-second spot costs about 70 per cent and a 7-second costs about 40 per cent of a 30-second. In 'soft rate' periods, usually summer and post-Christmas, reduced rates may be charged.

The discrepancy noted in Chapter 3 between the gross or card-rate cost of TV and the net or actual cost can now be examined in more detail. It arises because rate cards contain two important kinds of discount.

### Bulk discounts

An advertiser spending a large sum with a contractor expects and gets a lower cost than a small advertiser. This reflects his value to the contractor, benefits of scale and so on. The discount may be given either as a reduction in the rate or as additional spots.

Discounts obviously encourage an advertiser to spend a little more with a contractor in order to qualify for the next discount level. Money may therefore be moved from one contractor to another in order to get the best overall value. This has to be done with care, as it is pointless to spend where value is low or where the marketing situation does not require it in order to achieve apparent but unreal efficiency.

It is important to note that it is the *advertiser* who is entitled to the bulk discount, not the *brand*. The agency therefore adds together the expenditure for all the brands it handles for one advertiser to calculate this discount. But brands placed with different agencies also qualify. The advertiser with several agencies co-ordinates his total expenditure with all agencies in order to achieve the maximum discount. He may do this himself or through one of his agencies. Local advertisers i.e. those who distribute their products largely within one TV area, may qualify for special discounts.

*Flexibility*

The rate card is usually written so that the contractor need not charge the full rate for every spot — and also so that he may charge more. The lower rates are called regulators. Some time is sold at run-of-week rates, allowing the contractor to choose when the spot will appear — perhaps at a high-rating time. Some spots are sold to produce GHIs (Guaranteed Home Impressions), so the commercial is repeated by the contractor until agreed total ratings are obtained. Some spots can be bought at a low rate unless the contractor finds someone to pay a higher; this auctioning method is known as pre-empting. Another special feature is a special rate for test markets. There are also packages — for example one spot at run-of-week rates may appear in peak time for every two fully paid peak spots bought. But if a spot has to appear in a break insisted on by the agency rather than at any time in the cost segment a fixing charge of 15 per cent is made. Position in break also carries an extra charge.

A last word on rate cards is that they were, in 1968 and 1969, voluntarily submitted by the contractors to the Prices and Incomes Board. Government has since then taken over control of all such selling prices and requires justification of all increases. The rate cards of

TV companies, however, properly allow for considerable flexibility and respond partly to demand, i.e. a rate card increase does not imply that real prices will rise exactly in proportion, nor does the volume of advertising drop in proportion to a fall in the available money. The mechanism is complex and both volume and cost are affected by changes in rates and by the actual take.


## TV VALUES

The value of time on television depends both on the ratings achieved and on the rate paid. The graphical example given above can be given in numerical form. The ratings are then transformed into costs per thousand. The example in Table 8 is for a Thursday four years later. The ratings were very similar. Three segments are shown, the peak period from 6.45 to 10.15 p.m., and one period either side. Peak has much the highest card rate cost, and higher ratings but not in proportion, so it has also higher cost per thousand. This is the price paid for higher cover.

Both ratings and values vary appreciably from one area to another, as well as by time of year, as Table 9 indicates. The values shown in such published figures are necessarily at rate card, while availability and demand affect the net costs which individual agencies or advertisers have to work out for themselves. Also, as already pointed out, adults or housewives are more relevant criteria than homes. Nevertheless, for the allocation of a TV budget over areas, discussed in Chapter 9, the crude values shown in such a table are usually adequate.


## CONTRACTORS' OTHER ACTIVITIES

As well as giving information about their areas, the contractors provide various kinds of marketing services. These are more common outside London, which does not have to compete so hard in this way. The most important service is the Television Consumer Audit, which describes the purchases made in product fields by some 5800 households representative of Great Britain. The service is sponsored by the contractors in London, the Midlands, Lancashire, Yorkshire, Tyne Tees and Southern. Manufacturers subscribing to it who also satisfy certain TV expenditure requirements get special rates.

Table 8   EXAMPLE OF RATE CARD COST AND BREAK
VALUES. THAMES, THURSDAY 14 SEPTEMBER
1978 (Part only)

| Segment, 30-sec rate, average c/000, p | Slot time | Housewives TVR | Cost per '000 housewives, p |
|---|---|---|---|
| 5.30–6.45 pm £2400 281 | 5.39 6.30 | 15 24 | 357 231 |
| 6.45– 10.15 pm £5100 409 | 6.46 6.58 7.17 7.36 7.55 8.11 etc. | 29 26 26 26 25 32 | 404 442 453 449 463 362 |
| 10.15– 10.45 pm £2900 296 | 10.16 10.29 | 24 21 | 273 316 |

As well as the TCA, the advertiser may get from contractors other free or subsidised research, retail audits and distribution checks. He can get sales and merchandising teams to supplement his own sales force, to make additional calls on retailers to publicise his product, to take orders and arrange point-of-sale material and promotions. He can hire studios and rooms for conferences. Thus area sales tests are made easier and more useful. The services allow the manufacturer to test products even in areas where he has no distribution at present. The small manufacturer

Table 9  EXAMPLES OF DIFFERENCES IN RATINGS AND VALUES BY AREAS AND BY MONTHS

| ITV area | Peak time, weekdays | | | |
| | March 1978 | | September 1977 | |
| | Homes TVR | Cost, p/1000 homes | Homes TVR | Cost, p/1000 homes |
|---|---|---|---|---|
| London | 34 | 300 | 29 | 350 |
| Midlands | 40 | 192 | 34 | 229 |
| Lancashire | 40 | 195 | 35 | 220 |
| Trident | 39 | 198 | 33 | 231 |
| Southern | 34 | 156 | 28 | 192 |
| Wales and the West | 39 | 201 | 35 | 223 |
| Scotland | 36 | 168 | 36 | 132 |
| East of England | 34 | 188 | 31 | 212 |
| Southwest | 37 | 199 | 32 | 233 |
| Border | 41 | 186 | 34 | 229 |
| Ulster | 46 | 152 | 41 | 173 |
| Network | 38 | 209 | 33 | 237 |

Source: AGB, *Directors' Report*

is encouraged to expand and the large manufacturer to increase his sales share.

The contractors' motives in setting up these services are clear. As well as making it more likely that the brand advertised does well – and so goes on advertising – contractors themselves learn more about the way consumer goods are currently marked. They get closer to the people who matter at the manufacturers. They collect case histories of successes to help sell the medium.

### TV Times

There is a single independent television programme journal with separate regional editions: the *TV Times*, published by Independent Television Publications Limited which is owned by fourteen contractors. *TV Times* is read by about 27 per cent of the people who ever view ITV. This publication has a triple role. Like any publication it is intended to make profits; its editorial function is 'to achieve the maximum possible viewer involvement with ITV'; finally it is so closely linked to ITV that a joint campaign in TV and the *TV Times* is sometimes very appropriate – and earns an additional discount. Thus it reinforces TV as entertainment to the viewer and as a medium to the advertiser.

### Television bureau

The contractors used to sponsor an organisation which produced data on the ITV system, case histories of TV successes, presentations about the TV medium and so on. This was the British Bureau of Television Advertising. As a result of the economic crisis of 1974, and ironically also because TV revenue has boomed since then, the Bureau no longer exists. As often with advertising itself, this selling operation was seen as too costly in poor times and unnecessary in good times.

# TV RESEARCH

## JICTAR

The initials JICTAR stand for the Joint Industry Committee for Television Advertising Research. The principal object of this committee is to run the industry's method of determining TV ratings. There has been a committee and a service of this type since 1955. The committee is made up of the contractors, the agencies and the advertisers, who share the total cost which is about £¾ million a year roughly in the ratio 4:2:1. Contractors pay the largest share because this data is part of their sales presentation and evidence of what they are selling. The logic behind the relatively large agency contribution is less clear.

Since July 1968 the research company operating the JICTAR service has been Audits of Great Britain Limited (AGB). This replaced Television Audience Measurement Limited (TAM) who ran the service for thirteen years.

Although there have been changes of detail in the technique and reports, and in panel sizes, the method of research has remained basically the same since it started. It is based on a panel of households — between 100 and 425 — in each area. There are 2580 over the UK and about 7500 individuals. These are net reporting figures: there is a reserve in each area of about 10 per cent, so that although some homes do not complete records in any one week, results can be produced from a selected, balanced panel.

## Establishment surveys

Ratings are flesh and blood in buying and selling television and programme planning, but they need a backbone: surveys which establish the basic data. The proportion of households in an area which have UHF sets, for example, cannot be obtained very accurately from the panel itself and the proportion with ITV cannot be obtained at all because obviously the proportion in the panel is 100 per cent. Further the panel itself must be recruited and its demographic representativeness assured. Establishment surveys are regularly carried out, using 24,000 households annually. They are partly integrated with the AGB Homes Audit. The national results are part of the JICTAR contract.

In each panel home there is a meter attached to the TV set. It is called a SETmeter and records when the set is switched on and to which channel. This information is marked on a paper tape which the housewife mails each week to the AGB production centre. From these records a computer calculates the number of homes viewing each channel during each minute.

In addition, diary records are filled in at each home. They are meant to be kept by the set and completed during viewing. Members of the household and any guests record whether they are in the viewing room during each quarter hour of viewing. The actual definition is 'for eight or more minutes out of the quarter hour'. The diaries are also mailed in each week. An interviewer calls on the home on average once every six weeks to renew the tape in the meter and leave a further supply of diaries. Diary information is also processed in the computer. It is checked against the SETmeter record to ensure, for example, that the set was on during the quarter hour in which viewing was claimed. From the diary can be deduced the individual audience during each quarter hour. The quarter hour audience is allocated for each minute to the channel shown by the SETmeter. In this way, for example, the number of adults viewing ITV in each minute is estimated. Other demographic breakdowns can be analysed — housewives, men, women, children and so on. Finer breakdowns than these are hardly feasible since the sample is so small in each area.

These records are used to produce the various ratings, values and so on given in the Weekly Report which covers the nine largest areas and reaches subscribers on Mondays, eight days after the end of the week to which it refers. Reports for the four smaller areas (excluding Channel Islands) are delivered to subscribers two days later with the Product Group Report, which is a rearrangement by product categories of the data on commercials given chronologically in the Weekly Report. More detailed audience breakdowns are given on cumulated data for one month in every four in the Audience Composition Report. Many different kinds of special analysis are also available: summaries by time and by product, trends and projections and so on. The data is also available as magnetic tapes, which are used by agencies to evaluate their individual schedules.

## TV frequency distributions

As well as the ratings for individual spots, occasional checks on whole schedules are required. The way a schedule is analysed is simple though laborious. A schedule is in this case a list of actual time of transmission in an area: 5.58 on Monday, 2 December, and so on. A panel of individuals who completed records for the whole of the analysis period is first compiled – perhaps of a special category, e.g. light viewers or housewives. The analysis then considers each person in turn. For the first individual, was she viewing ITV when the first spot was transmitted? If so, she is counted as being exposed once. Similarly, was she viewing for the second spot, for the third, and so on? In this way, her total number of exposures is counted. Similarly, all the individuals' records are processed. Naturally there are complications: the panel used is not identical with that used in the Weekly Report so the ratings produced differ slightly, for example.

The result is a *frequency distribution*. It shows how many people were exposed to none of the spots, how many to just one and so on. The use of such a distribution is discussed later but here its three most important aspects are listed:

1   *Cover*. This is the proportion of people exposed to at least one spot. Obviously the advertising cannot have any effect on those who saw no spots at all, i.e. those who were not covered, so cover is always an important consideration in evaluating a schedule.

2   *Four-plus*. This is the proportion of people exposed to at least four spots. The figure four is a conventional one, chosen because it corresponds to an average of one exposure a week when the analysis is carried out over four weeks of a campaign – which is usually the case.

3   *Total ratings*. The total number of rating points achieved by the schedule can be calculated directly, or from the frequency distribution. Since ratings are percentages, the total, when divided by 100, is the *average number of exposures* or opportunities-to-see produced by the schedule on the target audience. When this in turn is divided by cover the *average number of exposures* on those covered has been calculated. When the cost of the campaign is divided by the overall ratings and the size of potential audience and then multiplied by 1000, the *cost-per-thousand* of the schedule is obtained.

Take, as an example, a typical campaign of 14 spots transmitted in four weeks which achieved a cover of 86 per cent and accumulated 306 women ratings. This means each woman in the area was exposed on average 3.06 times. Among those covered the average number of exposures was 3.56, i.e. 3.06/0.86. In this particular case 34 per cent were exposed to at least four spots so 'cover and four-plus' would be reported as '86 and 34'. This schedule in fact cost (at rate card) £19,100 and was transmitted in London where at the time every woman rating point represented 48,200 people reached, i.e. the ITV woman universe was 4.82m. So the cost-per-thousand women was 129p, i.e. £19,100 x 100p x 1000/(48,000 x 306).

Schedule analyses take money and time. Because TV viewing has many regularities, an approximate method based on an inspection of many such analyses gives results close to the exact method.

Various guides have been produced to predict cover and four-plus and even to estimate the whole frequency distribution, [4.2]. The main differences are in the years covered by the basic data (patterns of viewing have changed since TAM produced the first guide), the representativeness of the schedules (some schedule analyses are deliberately on non-typical cases) and the entry variables used. For example, a method produced in 1974 was based on 458 schedules transmitted in 1972 and 1973 and requires for entry:

Total ratings for all the spots in the schedule.

The average rating (or equivalently, the number of spots).

Sections of the Guide appear as in Table 10.


## COMMENTS ON JICTAR

The scale, speed and attention to detail in the JICTAR service are impressive. It has been called the largest research contract in the world. Further, this type of data collection has been validated. The most accurate method of measuring TV viewing is to interview in a random sample of homes during actual viewing. The interviewer asks what the set was switched to and who was in the viewing room at the time just before she rang the doorbell. This 'coincidental' method is of course very expensive; it has been found to give results very close to the JICTAR method [4.3].

Criticisms can be made about the small size and representativeness

Table 10

| Total TVRs | Average TVR 17 or 18 | | Average TVR 23 or 24 | |
|---|---|---|---|---|
| | Cover | Frequency | Cover | Frequency |
| 300–319 | 76 | 4.0 | 78 | 3.9 |
| 320–339 | 77 | 4.2 | 78 | 4.1 |
| 340–359 | 78 | 4.4 | 79 | 4.3 |
| 360–379 | 79 | 4.6 | 80 | 4.5 |
| 380–399 | 80 | 4.8 | 81 | 4.7 |

of panels, the imprecision with which the diary is filled in, the assumptions involved in producing minute-by-minute individual data and so on. Portable sets are not covered (in 1978 12 per cent of homes had two or more sets), nor is viewing in pubs, clubs or hotels. Viewing at a transmitter other than the home station is not counted. But to remedy or even to measure the results of all these imperfections would be extremely costly. The system is more than adequate for the main purposes for which it is used — that is, to establish the general level of exposure to ITV commercials and the relative differences between times, areas, broad types of audience and so on.

The main criticisms come from opposite directions. The first was made forcefully and after a very detailed study commissioned by JICTAR from Aske Research. In brief, Ehrenberg [4.4] has argued that other methods of measurement are cheaper and may be sufficiently accurate; for example, set measurements multiplied by viewer-per-set averages or a panel without SETmeters, or diaries completed by informants who do not join a panel permanently, or interviews in which informants recall the past week's viewing. He states that short-term buying cannot use in any achievable way the detailed information now available, since viewing itself fluctuates too violently for predictions to be accurate. The evaluation of each spot apparently to the nearest penny is useful to agencies in negotiating with contractors and to advertisers in supervising agencies. Ehrenberg argues that this is self-deception, since ratings are not all that closely related to advertisement exposure. He says that only a fraction of the present data is used. The advertiser generally wants to look only at the average cost of a schedule

87

or the overall distribution it achieves. Long-term planning in television also does not require detailed figures but averages which could be obtained from larger, more reliable but also more economical samples giving less intense data. Buying, selling and post-campaign analysis expenses could also be reduced. The waterfall of data is made to turn a lot of costly grinding machinery.

The other direction of criticism is that we know very little else about the people whose viewing is so closely studied. We are unaware of what other advertising they see, in the press for example, or more seriously what they buy and use. JICTAR data is therefore very little used for planning and not at all for effectiveness measurement. SETmeters in households that complete purchase diaries have for example been suggested as more valuable. There is more on this viewpoint in Chapter 14.

While there may be major changes in data collection after 1981, at present the traditional approach looks very well established. It is hard to change a system which so many people are used to.

*Presence and attention*

Even if everyone were scrupulous in completing their diaries — which is unlikely — the present JICTAR system does not give an accurate figure for the audience to a commercial. Consider a person who leaves the room only during a 2- or 3- minute commercial break. She should still enter in the diary that she was in the viewing room for 8 or more minutes in each quarter hour. This is the simplest case: people may be asleep, making love, reading, talking or coming in and out of the room on various household errands.

What commonsense suggests is well established by research [4.5], that the audience to a spot is lower than the ratings show. This is true whether a rigorous definition is used such as 'the proportion paying full attention to the set' or a loose one like 'the proportion present in the room'. Estimates have ranged from about 40 per cent of normal ratings for the first definition to about 85 per cent for the second.

How is it that ratings can still be accepted which are known to be overestimates of the true audience? Contractors are obviously reluctant to admit to apparently lower figures, even if they are closer to reality and do not alter TV's real efficiency.

It is possible, of course, that the differences between being rated and being present or paying attention should not affect *buying* (though they should certainly be in our minds in planning or in evaluating the medium generally and considering how it works). For it is only if the differences themselves vary by time of day or by day or by programme that we would use them to change buying decisions. Is a 20 rating at 10 p.m. worth the same as getting twice a 10 rating at 5 p.m.? The answer to this question should contain some discussion on cover or the frequency distribution, but more fundamental is whether TV *works* better at 10 p.m. Are a higher proportion of those rated actually in the room? Paying attention? Affected by the commercials?

Similarly there is evidence that people pay greater attention to programmes which they say they view frequently |[4.6]. By and large, these are the programmes that they enjoy watching most and are also those shown at peak viewing times. There is therefore evidence which can be used to support three different statements. First, an advertisement is likely to be more effective if it is near a programme that viewers enjoy, because the set is more likely to be the focus of attention in the room when these programmes are on. Second, peak time is more valuable than the normal cost per thousand comparisons show because people have settled down to their evening's viewing at that time without the distractions that take place earlier in the evening.

A third possibility is that greater attention is simply the result of a greater proportion of the people watching at such times being light or selective viewers who anyway pay more attention. The evidence is not clear on whether or how presence and attention vary. The latest evidence in fact suggests that between 6 and 9 p.m. no variation exists. Therefore in practice the ratings are used for evaluating the worth of different times without modification. There is vague agreement that heavy viewers are likely to be inattentive, that high ratings mean more attention, that programmes which are liked are probably more efficient for advertising and that the ratings give an exaggerated idea of the real situation, for most people do not use TV in the way selective viewers and educated commentators like to think they themselves do. Further, no routine method of making presence measurements has been agreed. For these reasons it is again an open question whether or when the JICTAR method will be changed. But when TV media values are compared with those of other media it must always be kept in mind that 'being rated' does not mean 'seeing an advertisement' but only 'having a chance to see an advertisement'.

The most recent data [4.5] suggests that the best estimate of the proportion present (of those rated by JICTAR) is higher than the 75-85 per cent previously supposed. The latter may well be the proportion of those whose diaries claimed they were viewing. But the SET meter already reduces this number, by recording set switching to the nearest minute. The analysis is complex, but the most authoritative estimate is that 85 to 88 per cent of the JICTAR audience is present during the break. Some of those missing may be in audio range but some of those present may be virtually unaware of the advertising, so exactness will always escape us.

The conclusion is that the frequency of exposure to TV campaigns is a little less than the routine figures suggest. Cover is probably very little reduced. For example, 400 TVRs sound like a respectable weight (for three or four weeks' advertising). Conventionally, we would expect about 80 per cent cover and those covered to be reached on average five times. When presence is the criterion cover is probably about 78 per cent but these are reached only 4.4 times.

### Liking the programmes

A good rating for a programme does not necessarily mean that the audience liked it: they may be only mildly interested but want to have the set on and positively dislike what is showing on other channels. Therefore programme planners are interested in other ways of assessing the audience reaction to programmes. The agency is also interested, since liking the programmes may help in the prediction of ratings and may also be linked with the reaction to commercials appearing in or near particular programmes. However, such data is not in current use in agencies.

The ITA maintains a panel of 1000 viewers as well as carrying out other qualitative work [4.7]. The panel members record in a diary how much they enjoyed the programmes they chose to view. An average score or appreciation index is calculated and shows the kinds of people who like the different kinds of programme as well as giving trends over time for series. Both large and small audiences may have high or low appreciation indices. The data is available to contractors but not to agencies, who have of course no direct connection with programming. Nevertheless agencies have done work in this area. For example Burnett included the Segnit scale on TV programmes in their Life Style work (I really like to watch it/I watch it only because someone in my family likes it/I watch it when there's nothing better/I don't watch it) largely to help in understanding the informants, but the data also gives insight into programme liking. The TAPE system [4.8] was also developed in an agency (Masius, Wynne-Williams), though it is now sold separately to contractors. This was originally a ratings share predictor for the situation where two films competed on ITV and BBC1. It used in the prediction the type of film and the stars. In studying how the audience divides it also measures in a practical way how they like the programmes.


## BBC RESEARCH

The BBC do not subscribe to JICTAR but carry out independent research. This produces their own figures for ratings and share of audience. More than 800,000 interviews are completed every year, with six-year olds and over, by more than 150 interviewers, covering in each interview the previous day's viewing and listening. The BBC also maintains over 6000 people in panels which give qualitative opinions about programmes.

Unfortunately, but typically, the definitions used in the two approaches are different. The most serious result is that the 'share of audience' claimed by each system is consistently in conflict; when JICTAR says that ITV got a 50 per cent share the BBC may say that ITV got only 43 per cent — a discrepancy which monotonously makes headlines and throws research into disrepute. Unfortunately both figures can be criticised; the JICTAR figure is actually about sets and not people (JICTAR does not analyse individuals' BBC viewing); also the populations covered differ, for example an individual who can receive BBC TV only is excluded by JICTAR but included by the BBC.

The Annan report suggested the common sense solution to the discrepancy: a single source of audience measurement. This is (in 1978) under discussion, principally between the BBC and the contractors. It is likely that the present meter and diary system or something similar will be selected.

# 5 THE PRESS

*A description of the Press as an advertising medium. An outline of circulations and readerships. The research data available.*

## DIFFERENCES FROM TELEVISION

The Press is far more varied than television. There is little enough sense in talking of *the* viewer: there is none in talking of *the* reader. In September 1978, *British Rate and Data* [5.1] listed:

30 national dailies and Sundays
1600 local newspapers and groups
230 local free sheets
1200 other consumer publications
2500 trade, technical and professional publications

Anyone can start a newspaper or magazine. No contracts are awarded as for Independent Television. Births and deaths are familiar in Fleet Street, though major publications and the large publishing houses are remarkably stable. Only one major publication a year has on average been launched or withdrawn over the last decade.

An editor tries to make his publication strike a distinctive note. Publications have policies and not 'balance' like a TV programme. A good newspaper or magazine has a personality that attracts its own readers, though it may repel others. In the early days of advertising this aspect of a publication was the most important thing about it. The advertiser or agency man thought most naturally about the kind of audience he wanted to reach in terms of publications. For a person to be a reader of the *Daily Mail* or of *The Times* was a sufficient description of the advertising target. The medium was the market.

Not every reader has paid for his copy, but every issue sold has been bought. You do not look on your paper or magazine as free in the sense that television is often thought to be. Selling a publication to a reader is like selling him a car or some other durable. Though each day's purchase is a decision made lightly enough at traditional cover prices the overall relationship between reader and publication can become ingrained and the relationship between reader and editor or writer can be almost personal.

You decide for yourself the way in which you read a paper or magazine. With television, you have to sit through the material in the order which the producer dictates and at his speed. With the press, you can choose what to ignore, what to skim, and what to read thoroughly. This selection is necessary — the editorial matter alone in a quality daily or Sunday newspaper can run to over 50,000 words — more than half the length of this book — and the space taken by advertising can be as much again. Thus a publication can offer more internal variety than television: it can be simultaneously the equivalent of bingo and the National Theatre simply by carrying different items on different pages. You can ignore the pop star gossip if you want, and ready only the City news.

The advertising carried in the press repeats this variety and reflects the difference in the type of exposure. There can be several pages of classified advertising which is ignored by those not interested: they simply turn over these pages which therefore do not irritate them in the way the equivalent intrusion on TV would. When they *are* concerned with a subject — looking for a job or at second-hand car prices for example — they find the advertising practical and helpful. Similarly display advertising can be passed over except by those whose attention is caught and who choose to let themselves be involved. Therefore much of the space in press advertising is designed to signal to the minority who are in the target; the headline will be aimed to tell those with rheumatism or children who ask unanswerable questions that something can be done to help. People *use* advertising in the press. They study the cut of a dress, the ingredients in a recipe, the layout of a kitchen; advertisements may be torn out for reference; a coupon may be filled in. Like all such generalisations, these statements have to be applied with care to particular campaigns; they are however confirmed by the small amount of qualitative intermedia research available [5.2].

Another characteristic of the press is that colour is commonly available. The three classical reasons for using colour in advertising are:

1    The advertisement gets more attention; it is hard to put a figure on this, but noting and reading data suggests perhaps one and a half times or twice that of black and white.
2    It is more lifelike and appealing, particularly important for example for foods, fashions, cosmetics and paint.
3    Pack recognition is greater because the pack is shown more nearly as it really appears.

In magazines the same process is used for colour advertising as for editorial. In newspapers, the most common method at the moment is pre-print which means the colour page is printed first of all with advertising and then the back of the page is used to carry normal black and white production. There are over a thousand newspapers able to accept pre-printed colour advertising. But already, and at an increasing rate, offset lithography is being used for colour during normal production.

The press has a long history and many unique features; no other western country for example has our few newspapers distributed nationally with enormous circulations. Both the history and the structure of the industry have advantages — much advertising tradition draws on press experience, very high cover of an announcement can be reached very quickly — but also serious disadvantages. The unions with which the press has grown up are it has been said [5.3] in control rather than the management. Some proprietors, managers and editors have old-fashioned views, out of tune with the day. There is 'very considerable scope for improvements' in achieving more realistic manning levels, control of wastage and improvement in distribution [5.4]. The imported raw material has been rapidly increasing in price.

All these features have been the subject of constant comment and advice from outside the industry. Frequent committees examine the whole subject, for the Fourth Estate interests politicians intensely for obvious reasons. The phrase 'a free Press' has joined motherhood and equality of opportunity as unquestioned goods. But despite the prophets of doom the Press so far has survived the unions, the proprietors and Governments. The number of titles has increased over the last decade. The number of pages published has grown even faster. This is not to deny there are failures, only that the medium is if anything growing and remarkable for stability.

For a closer look at the Press — especially at its economics and management — a collection of papers which appeared in ADMAP [5.4] is strongly recommended.

While marketing people view less television, they read more than the average person — or at least skim through more publications. This means that some consumer publications are specially useful for reaching the trade; it also means that advertising people have more definite views and more prejudices about press schedules than those in other media.


## THE NATIONAL PRESS

In this book I do not attempt detailed descriptions of different groups or individual publications. Other sources are available [5.5] but there is no substitute for handling the papers and magazines themselves or for making use of circulations, readership research and rate-cards.


### National press circulations

The 105 publications included in the National Readership Survey in 1977/8 [5.6] are the most important to large, national advertisers. Table 11 classifies them by publication period, e.g. weekly, and gives circulations, i.e. the number of copies sold in a publication period. It also relates circulations to the number of households in the country.

Every publisher knows how many copies he printed and how many were returned unsold, though he rarely knows how to put these two together with precision. Even circulation figures are not exact. Most large publishers belong to the Audit Bureau of Circulations to which his auditors return these sales figures. The Bureau has the right to investigate them and random checks are in fact made. The Bureau

Table 11  CIRCULATION OF NRS PUBLICATIONS

| Publication | Number | Circulation, millions | Number of copies bought per household |
|---|---|---|---|
| Morning newspapers | 9 | 15 | 0.8 |
| Evening newspapers | 7 | 2 | - |
| Sunday newspapers | 9 | 21 | 1.1 |
| General weeklies and Weekend magazines | 19 | 14 | 0.8 |
| Women's weeklies | 13 | 8 | 0.4 |
| General monthlies | 16 | 5 | 0.3 |
| Women's monthlies and bi-monthlies | 32 | 8 | 0.4 |
| TOTAL | 105 | 73 | 3.8 |

Source: ABC January-June 1978 and July-December 1977.

issues an ABC Certificate which gives the ABC figure for the publication, published quarterly, showing the individual monthly figures, by the ABC in their *Circulation Review*. Publications that do not belong to the Bureau may issue their own unaudited circulation figures. Some publications do not issue figures at all but this is happily becoming rare. We must be careful to distinguish between circulation in the UK and circulation abroad, as the ABC has done formally from January 1975.

Distribution is a headache for publishers. Their product is bulky, needs display and must be moved quickly. Copies may be delivered to the home, or ordered at newsagents and picked up by the buyer, or they may be bought casually. The business is therefore in the hands of wholesalers and newsagents — but for many of them publications are not an important part of their business. Direct mail might seem to be the answer; subscription lists are the backbone of some magazines' sales. But a magazine costing the buyer 20p or more also costs almost as much to post, and this is becoming uneconomic.

New distribution methods have been developed in recent years. *Family Circle* and *Living* were successfully launched through supermarkets and groceries. The new evening papers started by the Thomson Organisation rely on home deliveries independent of the traditional outlets. In mid-1974 the average daily sale of the *Evening Post* in Luton was 57,000. The paper employs 900 'junior agents' who deliver 80 per cent of this sale – an average of 50 copies each – while traditional outlets account for only 20 per cent. The local weekly freesheets described later are home-delivered by battalions of housewives, pensioners and young people.

The agency would like to be able to buy advertising in a newspaper or magazine in separate areas – preferably TV areas since this is the commonest regional unit in marketing. However to sell advertising in one area only sets the publisher severe production and distribution problems. Unless he already has regional editions, e.g. to carry different sporting news, he has to stop the run and change cylinders in order to produce different editions. He may also have to alter the distribution of the publication as far as the network of wholesalers and newsagents allows him.

To offer full regional facilities would be in the long run of great importance to the national press. Agencies have learned from using television how beneficial it is to alter the weight of advertising from one region to another, or to use some regions and exclude others. The national press cannot match TV's flexibility yet (regional publications of course are excluded) and perhaps because of its production problems it never will, but it has begun to realise the marketing importance of regionality and some publications offer some regionality, though often at considerable extra cost and this facility is currently declining.

The production problems of the press make them particularly liable to last-minute selling. The size of the paper is dictated largely by the amount of advertising carried. The editor may decide to add another four or eight pages, then find that he is short of a half-page or quarter-page of advertising, or an advertisement may be cancelled suddenly. In these circumstances, rather than fill this space with editorial, the paper is obviously better off in the short-term if advertising is taken at a reduced rate. Chesterton pointed out that newspapers are written on the back of advertisements and this is still true. However unless the advertisements rates are high enough and the management of the paper juggle efficiently with all the variables it can happen that the reader is subsidising the advertiser. The cost of newsprint alone is currently between one-third and a half that of an advertisement and for some publications extra advertising is hardly profitable [5.7].

Now that the paging problem has been mentioned the size of the page requires discussion. This is currently an issue of importance to newspapers though not to magazines which are generally of course of a smaller size. A tabloid is more flexible than a broadsheet in two ways: adding four pages is less of a trauma and in addition the editor is freer to change the mood of the paper from spread to spread — with only two or three articles or stories on a page there is less clash than with four or six. The same actual size of advertisement (costing the same in newsprint, ink, labour and transport) is more dominant on the tabloid page. Hence the switch in recent years away from broadsheets.

Similar difficulties arise with seasonal demand. For some days or weeks there is little advertising booked, yet the readers expect a publication approaching normal size. More flexible rate-cards are the answer to this and they are gradually being introduced.

*National press readerships*

The great advantage that readership data has over circulation is that it tells us something about the type of person who reads the publication — as well as that he chose to read it. This is often critical in the choice of a medium for advertising. The 'profile' of a publication describes how many of its readers are in each age group, live in each area and so on. These figures confirm and quantify the character or editorial appeal of the different publications.

For example, the national dailies fall into three distinct groups when we examine their profile by social grade (there is more detail in Chapter 14 on the terms used here). The *Daily Express* and *Daily Mail*, which are usually classified as 'popular', have a clearly greater proportion of ABC1 readership than the *Sun* or *Mirror* (see Table 12). Note that one paper may have many more upgrade readers than another, but a lower percentage of upgrade people among its readers, e.g. the *Daily Express* compared with *The Times*. The result of this variety is that the advertiser has in the press neat packages of media

Table 12

| Publication | Per cent of readers who are ABC1 (profile) | Per cent of ABC1 who are readers (penetration) |
|---|---|---|
| *Sun* | 23 | 17 |
| *Daily Mirror and Daily Record* | 24 | 20 |
| *Daily Express* | 46 | 19 |
| *Daily Mail* | 51 | 17 |
| *The Guardian* | 80 | 4 |
| *Daily Telegraph* | 79 | 16 |
| *Financial Times* | 85 | 4 |
| *The Times* | 80 | 5 |

Source: *National Readership Survey* (July 1977 - June 1978)

Table 13  READERSHIP OF NRS PUBLICATIONS

| Type | Number | Average issue readership totals, millions | | |
|---|---|---|---|---|
| | | Adults | Men | Women |
| Morning newspapers | 9 | 44 | 25 | 19 |
| Evening newspapers | 7 | 6 | 3 | 3 |
| Sunday newspapers | 9 | 61 | 31 | 30 |
| General weeklies and Weekend magazines | 19 | 55 | 29 | 26 |
| Women's weeklies | 13 | 34 | 6 | 28 |
| General monthlies | 16 | 31 | 22 | 9 |
| Women's monthlies | 32 | 51 | 11 | 40 |
| TOTAL | 105 | 231 | 127 | 155 |

Source: *National Readership Survey* (July 1977 - June 1978)

that can deliver appropriate audiences.

Another example: only 2 per cent of the readers of *Titbits* were being educated at the age of 19, but of *Punch*'s readers the proportion was 27 per cent.

Another major use of readership data is to examine how much the readers of each publication are exposed to television, in order to plan the use of press to supplement a television campaign. The objective may be to expose the same people both to .TV commercials and to press advertising. For this we require publications whose readers are likely to be heavy ITV viewers; this is called duplicating heavily with television. On the other hand, the object may be to reach as many people as possible with either medium. Of the national Sundays, for example, the *News of the World* and *Sunday People* have over 25 per cent of readers who are heavy viewers. (Here the NRS definition of a heavy viewer is used: not a third of ITV viewers, as with TV analyses, but 22 per cent of all adults.) The *Sunday Times* and *Observer* on the other hand each have only 6 per cent.

Table 13 shows the same publications as above, but this time their readership is given in total and also broken down by sex.

Since the size of the population and the number of copies sold are both known, it is possible to work out two instructive figures, given in Table 14:

1    *Number of publications read per head.* This shows, for example, how many Sunday newspapers are claimed to be read by each adult on average. The figure is surprisingly high, 1.4, which raises doubts how thorough some of this reading can be. This point is gone into later.

2    *Number of readers per copy.* This gives the number of people who read a single copy, either in the same household as the person who originally bought it (the father brings a paper home from work, the daughter looks at her mother's magazine) or outside it. In some cases the latter accounts for the majority of readers. General monthlies for example average over nine readers a copy, three-quarters of whom must be outside the household: a woman takes her magazines to her sister or passes them to her neighbour; a man borrows the paper from the next desk in his office; some magazines may be seen by large numbers of people at hairdressers or in waiting rooms. The value of pass-on readership is disputable. Some of the reading must be cursory

Table 14   READERSHIP OF NRS PUBLICATIONS

| Type | Number of publications | Number read per head | Readers per copy | Single issue cover, % |
|---|---|---|---|---|
| Morning newspapers | 9 | 1.0 | 3.0 | 72 |
| Evening newspapers | 7 | – | 2.6 | – |
| Sunday newspapers | 9 | 1.4 | 2.9 | 81 |
| General weeklies and Weekend magazines | 19 | 1.3 | 3.9 | 52+ |
| Women's weeklies | 13 | 1.3* | 3.5* | 55* |
| General monthlies | 16 | 0.7 | 6.2 | 36 |
| Women's monthlies | 32 | 1.8* | 5.0* | 53* |

Source: *National Readership Survey* (July 1977 – June 1978)

*Women only; other figures are for adults.

+Excludes weekend magazines

and some of it takes place a considerable time after publication. There is evidence that these readers should be discounted but it is arguable what value should be attached to them: one half the value of the first reader has been suggested. It is also suggested that reading in a hairdresser's may be more intense than at home.

It is also possible to calculate the proportion of the population who will read at least one of the publications in a group when a single issue of each publications is considered. This is called *single-issue cover* and emphasises, for example, how widely read are the national Sundays.

The reader of this book may have assumed up to this point that for each publication a person is either a reader or not a reader. This was in fact commonly thought a decade or so ago. There are two views he might have held about the value to the advertiser of a reader actually going through a copy: either that he was bound to see the advertisement which the advertiser had placed there, or that many pages must be missed so only a proportion of readers saw the advertisement. We are now going beyond single-issue readership and raising the questions of reading frequency and reading intensity. It is not possible to discuss these without going into research techniques, which we do later in this chapter.

## ADVERTISING IN THE PRESS

As with television, the amount and the cost of advertising in the press are regulated only by economic forces. Editors are, however, chary of diluting editorial too far, and generally expand or contract it to match advertising. A typical ratio of editorial space to advertising is half-and-half, but there are extremes in both directions.

The British Code of Advertising Practice applies to press advertising. Decisions on whether advertisements are acceptable are made by individual publications, but they may refer cases to the Newspaper Publishers' Association's and Newspaper Society's joint advertisement committee.

Whether or not a publication should be included in a particular schedule depends on a complex of factors examined later in the book. Cost is of course one of the most critical factors. Every publication has its own rate-card for the sale of advertising space. This lists the costs of the different sizes available; often these are in proportion to the area covered. Costs are also given for special sizes, positions, bleed (printing of the advertisement to the edge of the page without a white margin), quantity and seasonal discounts.

Rate-card costs, ignoring discounts, are used in analyses of industry data. But in the buying and selling of space a free market operates. Deals may take the form of rate reductions, of free insertions, or of special positions not charged for.

A prosperous publication does not bargain or deal. Many advertisement directors refuse to countenance deviations from the rate-card in public though some of these are not averse to dealing in private. This is a sensitive subject since, once a rate-card is known to be soft, a great deal of pressure is put on to it — and it has been said that the short road between Fleet Street and Carey Street is paved with broken rate-cards.

## PRODUCTION

The complexities of printing and the production of advertising for the press are matters for specialists. The planner needs to assure himself that the ideas of the creative man are understood by the agency's production team. In turn the production people must know which publications will be used and what facilities they offer. Media, creative and production plans must be fully compatible, for it can be disastrous to send a paper a block of even slightly the wrong size, or to design artwork without taking into account the reproduction process. Mechanical details can be referred to on the rate-card and in *British Rate and Data*. Publications and their printers can give a great deal of assistance here. They will for example advise on the colours and type of artwork which will reproduce best.

A critical aspect of this part of advertising is timing. The buyer has to become familiar with copy dates. These vary by publication and are currently shortening. Typical dates are two days before publication for a daily, six days for a Sunday, eight weeks for colour in a weekly or monthly. Cancellation dates also vary; four to six weeks for monochrome and four to six months for colour are normal. The buyer must know how far he can go in getting concessions from publishers on both copy and cancellation dates — and, of course, he must also know the current availability situation, since some newspapers and magazines may be sold out for advertising months ahead.

Publication owners frequently complain that agencies do not design advertisements specifically for their publications. On the editorial pages they are careful to keep to a particular style and they are distressed to see this ignored by most advertisers. There is some evidence that advertising is more effective when it is close to the editorial style of the publication in which it appears. This is easily understood: it was this style which attracted these particular readers in the first place. The advertiser would however find it expensive to prepare special advertisements for each publication or group of publications and specially designed advertisements are therefore rare.


## OTHER SERVICES

Publications offer other services besides advertising space. These are neither as extensive nor as organised as those offered by TV contractors. The reason for this is the fragmentation of the press compared with television.

The most common facility offered is one that benefits the publication as well as the advertiser: notifying the trade about the advertising which is appearing. Reprints of advertisements, pre-prints before they have been published, point-of-sale material, editions with special overprints – these can be got from most newspapers and magazines. IPC Magazines publish a review for advertisers and agencies on the subject of advertising in women's magazines – *Women's Market*. There are also bulletins that describe to the trade the products being advertised in current issues. These are mailed to retailers to encourage them to display and stock the goods. They also draw attention to press advertising as such, for it would be optimistic to assume that every counter assistant or store manager is an avid reader of women's magazines.

Some publications offer to insert printed material or, in some cases, samples of products in their issues. The facility of inserting or tipping-in advertisements can be used to test advertising. IPC Magazines offer a mini-test market service using this method. An extra leaf or double leaf is added to a normal issue in such a way that it is undetectable to the normal reader. The treated copies are distributed in one or more of 24 special areas – a town like Dover, Swindon or Carlisle and the surrounding rural catchment area. In this way scheduling, creative and weight tests can be carried out or, with special distribution arrangements, new products can be tested.

IPC Magazines also promote to agencies the new advertisements appearing each month – like *Monday Newcomers* on TV. Most publications offer print technology advice so that the production processes are used in the best way by advertisers. Some media offer in-store merchandising. Others have research facilities they can put at the advertiser's disposal free or at reduced cost. Publications are usually ready to discuss special schemes provided the potential revenue is large enough.

Advertisers and agencies are frequently asked to take space in 'special supplements'. The idea from the publication's point of view is simple. Pick a subject in which a number of specialists are interested; collect a few writers on this subject; make the feature pay by arguing to the firms concerned that 'they have to be there' with advertising. This can help the advertiser to reach specialist audiences. For example a supplement on kitchens in *Ideal Home* is going to be studied with care by readers of the magazine who are planning changes in their kitchen equipment, and it will even be bought specially for this by non-regular readers. The idea of supplements in some newspapers or specialist trade magazines is less attractive and some advertisers rebel against the blackmailing element in the approach.

## OTHER PUBLICATIONS

Most of what has already been said applies also to publications other than those included in the National Readership Survey. These other publications are now briefly described.

### Nationals not in NRS

There are many national publications which do not appear in the National Readership Survey. The decision whether or not a publication is included is based on several factors; the NRS generally does not research publications whose circulation is less than 100,000. Examples of two such publications are given in Table 15, with their circulations and estimated readerships. These estimates are based on readers-per-copy estimates, a method which is often also appropriate for new publications until reliable readership data is produced.

Table 15

| Magazine | Circulation ABC, Jan - Jun 1978 | Estimated readers-per-copy | Estimated adult readership |
|---|---|---|---|
| *Motoring News* | 87,000 | 7.8 | 1.6% |
| *New Scientist* | 70,000 | 10.6 | 1.3% |

It might be thought that the advertising in such publications was small in quantity because they did not appear in the National Readership Survey. They might be forced to set low advertising rates in order to attract business and therefore might be exceptionally good buys. This is often the case, though some such publications succeed quite well in getting themselves known and in attracting business. The proportion of advertising in them is, however, often low and their cover price is often relatively high.

*Local Press*

The local or regional press can be divided into three groups:

*Mornings.* There are 19 papers with total sales of about 2 million copies, and 6 Sundays.

*Evenings.* There are 76 evenings selling over 7 million copies. This includes the two London evenings though they are more often counted among the nationals and were indeed included in the tables above. Some evenings have separate regional editions not counted separately here.

*Sundays, weeklies and fortnightlies.* There are 1200 of these selling over 11 million copies. There are also some publications sold less frequently, e.g. county magazines, and over 200 freesheets.

By their nature, local papers have much smaller circulations than nationals: whereas national newspapers measure their circulations in millions, a local or regional daily counts in hundreds of thousands and a local weekly in tens of thousands. Most of the advertising revenue for all these publications comes from local advertising, particularly local stores and classified advertising. Most local papers have no direct competitors in their own areas and are therefore able to charge rates that are relatively higher than those of the national publications — often four times as high per reader. In any case, they have to charge more because of the economics of small runs.

The local evening paper usually reaches a very high proportion of the households in the urban centre of its area — sometimes as much as 80 or 90 per cent. It is claimed that reading of the local paper is particularly thorough and that the reader's relationship with the publication is a stronger one than with national publications. The local newspaper's advertising is used as a shopping guide [5.8] and its atmosphere is quite different from that of a national paper. It is also true that 'all sales are local' but then so is all advertisement exposure.

'Local advertisers do not need complicated expensive research studies to know if advertising in the local paper works, because there is an absolutely accurate market research tool immediately available to prove its worth or otherwise. It is called a cash register. When the advertisement goes in, results appear; if not — look out, local advertisement manager or copywriter.' [5.9]

Most national advertisers place relatively little advertising in the local press. But in addition to local advertisers, small ads and recruitment, local papers offer a very useful medium to retail stores. There are also special cases where the national advertiser needs local advertising. Test marketing is the most important: if a manufacturer is launching a new product in a town or other small area and he intends later on to use national press advertising, the only way he can simulate this in his test is to use local papers. He has to accept the possibility of a different kind of readership and a higher cost for this test than he will pay when he goes national. Another classical way of using the local press is to tie in with local promotions or dealers. A car manufacturer, for example, may run advertisements that list local franchise holders. The same principle can be useful when local authorities or petrol stations require support. Using the local press to match the weight of advertising with the regional distribution or sales for the product is also possible: there are some weaknesses in the regional profiles of individual national publications. By using the local press it is possible to fill in these gaps or strengthen areas where this seems needed.

Regional publications have formed bureaux which do a valiant job in presenting the advantages of using local papers. They also allow the agency to buy a group of papers, such as those covering a TV area. It is possible to issue one order to the Evening Newspaper Advertising Bureau and buy space in half a dozen or more publications. ENAB also offers information about the local press in the form of an annotated atlas — *Where*. Similarly the weekly papers have formed the Weekly Newspaper Advertising Bureau (WNAB) with the reference book *Contact* and similar ordering facilities.

The yellow pages of telephone directories are a local advertising medium. Although each entry is small and cheap, there are so many of them that this is a big business. The Thomson Organisation, which holds the contract, has estimated that they could take eventually between £20 and £25 million a year. This medium is again not interesting to most packaged goods advertisers because the cost of a display advertisement would be relatively high for them. The medium becomes worthwhile to a firm only when it knows that its customers are likely to look in the directory for his type of product, e.g. airline ticket agencies or a central heating installer. Therefore, to most large agencies telephone directories are a sideline at present.

*Free sheets*

While there are isolated earlier examples, free sheets made a real impact only in the mid-1960s. The idea is simple: advertising can provide three-quarters or more of the revenue for some local publications. By reducing the editorial costs to nearly nothing and by cutting standards in printing and distribution (many are posted door-to-door by part-time housewives or schoolchildren) a publication can be profitable on advertising alone. This description covers more than 200 different newsprint-format sheets. They are essentially shopping guides, supported by local stores and traders. Very few are recommended by agencies to national advertisers because of their uncertain circulation data and absence of readership figures, their probably high cost and the environment they provide. Nevertheless (in and round London, and in Teeside and Tyneside particularly) well over a million circulation is claimed for free weekly papers. A few, in much more sophisticated magazine format, are produced for working girls and women, mainly round London.

There are few professions, industries or businesses which do not have their own journals — over 2000 publications cover such specialist fields, though only a quarter of these are supported substantially by advertising. Again, for packaged goods sales these journals are largely irrelevant except for two sorts: those in the particular product field and those concerned with its channels of distribution — *The Grocer* or *Motor Trader* for example.

These journals should provide details about their circulation and readership in a standardised way — on the Media Data Form. This was designed by advertisers, agencies and publishers. It asks 48 questions about the publication, from a detailed breakdown of how it is circulated to a statement about its editorial policy.

This area is much less researched than are consumer publications. This is inevitable because the development budgets available to individual publications are small or non-existent. The standard of some of the research published is so low that it can be positively misleading. Considerable care is needed in media planning in this area. It is a specialist's job which we will not describe here in detail [5.10]. However, one or two groups have accumulated considerable data. For example the businessman's readership has been frequently studied by such papers as the *Financial Times*, *The Times*, *Time*, *Newsweek* and so on (see, for example, [5.11]).

## PRESS ORGANISATIONS

Publishers, as already mentioned, tend to run groups of publications rather than singletons. The most notable groups are those of a single type, for example the divisions of the International Publishing Corporation, or national newspapers based on regionals. Many publications have minority shareholdings in television contractors. Others have diversified into the travel business or other publishing fields such as books. These other interests have very little effect on the selling of advertising space. Each publication's advertising director and his representatives are wedded solely to the interests of that publication. Publications within the same group compete fiercely, except where joint selling operations have been set up.

There are larger groupings in the press. The most important are the Newspaper Publishers' Association and the Periodical Publishers' Association. These have attempted to co-operate practically for their common interest in selling advertising — among other objectives. Competition between publications and their heterogeneity have so far prevented the formation of a Press Bureau which would sell press advertising in the same way as the British Bureau of Television Advertising sold TV. Traditional enmities die hard. Individuals have, of course, realised that the medium as a whole, e.g. newspapers as such, has to be sold before the case for an individual publication has any chance of success, but they have not been able to change their management's prejudices. An opportunity is certainly being missed. Bureaux exist, as already mentioned, for evening and weekly newspapers.

There are other organisations relevant to advertising in the press. One of these is the Press Council [5.12], which acts mainly as an umpire between the press and the people, and is meant to judge the press in the same way as the press sets itself up as a judge on anybody and anything.


## PRESS RESEARCH

*National Readership Survey*

For the national press, research means above all two sources: the National Readership Survey and the Target Group Index. In this chapter the NRS is briefly described, while in Chapter 14 the TGI gets more attention. The distinctions between the two are that the NRS is 'official' and controlled by an industry body but gives little description of readers beyond demographics; the TGI is a private survey (by the British Market Research Bureau) but bought by many publishing houses because it gives claimed product purchase and usage as well as media data, so it enables the media salesman to use target definitions that the agency and advertiser find more relevant than demographics. There is, of course, far more research done than in these two services; a recent review listed over seventy items since 1960 [5.13].

The National Readership Survey is the bible of the space salesman, the media planner and the media buyer. It is paid for largely by the publication owners, but also derives income from the sale of reports and data. It is controlled by the Joint Industry Committee for National Readership Surveys (JICNARS) on which media, advertisers and agencies are represented.

The survey has been carried out since 1956, with minor modifications in most years and a major face lift in 1968. Over 500 copies of the report are bought each year and the raw data is an essential part of every media model. The sample is 30,000 adults interviewed each year. This is large enough to make it feasible to carry out most analyses on six months' data. Reports are issued twice a year covering January to December and July to June.

The report of the NRS is a document useful in several ways additional to the readership data. It is the largest generally available random sample of the population; it is therefore consulted throughout the industry on such points as social grade distribution, household composition and so on. It contains information on other media besides national press: television, cinema, radio and regional papers. There are also questions about the purchase of certain products, quaintly called 'special interest questions'. The techniques used and the absence of qualitative data about reading are currently being debated. In other countries this return to basics is also evident. The most impressive example of re-thinking is by Wally Langschmidt [5.14]. Improvements are likely to be introduced, but not major changes as far as the user will see.


*Readership definition*

It is important to understand what 'readership' means. There is no test that any informant actually read a publication: only a series of questions that the informant answers. There is some evidence that the procedure produces reasonable results. Other, more careful techniques have been used to investigate readership and obtained similar figures for dailies, Sundays and weeklies. But for monthlies the NRS results are still subject to some reservations. Asking for recall of readership over a period as long as four weeks is demanding a lot from informants [5.14].

The definition of a reader of a daily newspaper is as follows. The interviewer shows the informant a set of cards. On each card is the masthead of a paper, i.e. its name in the same style as on the front page of the paper. There is also a scale on the card which reads:

111

'In an average week these days I read or look at this number of issues: 6, 5, 4, 3, 2, 1, less than one, none.'

The interviewer says 'I want you to go through this booklet with me, and tell me for each paper, roughly how many issues you have read or looked at recently – it doesn't matter where. As I show you each card, will you tell me which of the statements applies?' This is the *frequency* question. If a woman being interviewed says she sees no issues, the next question is not asked. But if she gives any answer other than 'none', she is asked the *readership* or *average issue* question: 'I would now like to go through some of the publications again and ask you to say, for each one, when you last read or looked at a copy'. If the informant answers 'Yesterday' (except in interviews on Monday, when the qualifying answer is Saturday) then she is classified as a reader of this daily paper.

Two points will be noticed about the readership question. First of all, it is not necessary to have read right through the publication – or even to have read it at all – in order to qualify. The informant only has to claim that she has 'read or looked at'. This definition includes some people who actually did not see anything of the publication yesterday, but who claim they did because they are confused or feel they should have read it. Also, very cursory 'reading' of the publication qualifies. It is quite possible to glance at the cover of a magazine which your neighbour in the train has on her knee and then answer truthfully in the interview next day that you have 'looked at' the publication. Secondly, the method seems to ignore any readership a publication accumulates after its day of publication. This should be compensated [5.15] by the reading of earlier issues which happens to take place 'yesterday'.

The form of the questions is slightly different for Sundays, weeklies and monthlies. The informant qualifies as a reader if she read or looked at an issue in the last week, or for monthlies in the last four weeks.


*Reading frequency*

The interviewer collects the informant's frequency of reading claim and whether she qualified as a reader yesterday. The relationship between these two pieces of information can be set out for the whole sample of 30,000. Table 16 gives as an example the *Daily Mail*.

112

While the average issue readership is 13 per cent, eventually the cover could approach 24 per cent since this is the percentage who 'ever read', i.e. who make a frequency claim other than 'none'.

It is clear that a high proportion of people making the highest frequency claim (read six issues out of six) were also 'readers': the actual figure is 92 per cent. The meaning of the claim to read every day is in fact taken to be a probability of 92 per cent of reading on any particular day.

Frequency of reading information given in table form in this way is difficult to grasp. A media model and computer are needed to draw out the full implications, as explained later, though suitable tables are given in the NRS.

Frequency information does not make a major difference to the value of individual publications. That is, the value to the advertiser of a publication is reasonably described by its readership in the target population. Therefore the basic tables in the National Readership Survey report about average issue readership are still the starting point for an examination of the national press. It is only when the cover of a schedule is very important that much attention need be paid to frequency; in this case a publication with many irregular readers has a slightly better case for inclusion in a schedule than its average issue readership indicates.

Table 16

| Claimed number of issues seen in average week | 6 | 5 | 4 | 3 | 2 | 1 | <1 | 0 |
|---|---|---|---|---|---|---|---|---|
| Percentage of adults making this claim | 10 | 1 | 1 | 2 | 3 | 4 | 3 | 76 |
| Percentage making this claim who are 'readers' | 92 | 65 | 45 | 31 | 19 | 11 | 7 | - |

Source: *National Readership Survey* (1973)

*Intensity of reading*

We now turn to the chance that these opportunities to see are actually taken, as far as a particular advertisement is concerned. Our understanding of this area has changed a lot since 1970, so the description I have to give is somewhat complex. The object is 'eyes open in front of the page', i.e. a research technique that selects from the average NRS reader (or if necessary using different methods for different sorts of reader) those who have faced the page on which our advertisement appeared. For example, we might say (as indeed the first edition of this book *did* say) that for the average publication in the NRS only between 60 and 70 per cent of the readers actually faced the average page.

Before getting into detail, we look first at some of the background.

1   *The readership definition.* This could be a very loose classification: as already pointed out, very little exposure is needed to qualify. As we shall see, most of those who qualify turn out actually to have high exposure.

2   *Many irregular readers.* The data above on the reading frequency of the *Daily Mail* can be looked at in two ways. Because nearly twice as many 'ever read' as are reached by a single issue, it may appear that the irregular readers are very important, equally important perhaps as those who say they read every issue. But because the irregular readers have such low probabilities of reading, they contribute little to the reading of an average issue. For example, those who claim to read four, five or six issues a week in fact make up 85 per cent of the readers of any issue. Those who say they read every issue form three-quarters of the readers of any issue. In general the regular readers are those we should take most into account: and they read regularly because they choose to, which has important implications on their intensity of reading.

3   *Time spent reading.* Research has been carried out by IPC Newspapers [5.16] and, for some magazines, into the time of day people read publications and for how long (see Table 17). While these claims are probably a little exaggerated (because the interviews concentrated on this activity) the order of magnitude must be about right. It is unlikely that half an hour or more is spent on a newspaper just to look at a proportion of the pages

## Table 17 TIME SPENT READING, MINUTES

|  | Adults | Men | Women |
|---|---|---|---|
| Popular morning newspaper, weekday, e.g. *Daily Mirror* | 33 | 38 | 29 |
| Popular Sunday newspaper, e.g. *Sunday People* | 37 | 42 | 32 |

and leave all the others completely unopened. We control the pace at which we go through a newspaper in order to take out of it all we expect to get in the time we allow. It has also been claimed that all the time spent reading is potential exposure to advertising.

4    *The reading process.* Without going into the mechanics of perception, we can agree from our own experience that much of our reading of newspapers and magazines is in two stages. The first stage is a general and rapid search of a large area, probably of the whole page, in order to decide whether to become involved and so whether to read anything in more detail. Habit plays a part here: we can tell very quickly that in certain places we will find the leaders or the sports results, in others classified advertising; according to our needs we pass over some and concentrate on others. We talk about 'our eye being caught' by a headline or picture; we know we linger over some items and read only a sentence or two of others. We scan the printed word selectively to suit our own requirements. The processes of perception and selection are complex. To add recollection in an interview later about what we did makes it all more complicated still: much of the casual glancing we have done escapes conscious attention and our long-term memory. Having decided we do not want to spend time on a page, we bother with it no longer.

Research has in fact investigated this process. A major step forward was taken by the British Market Research Bureau for the Agencies Research Consortium [5.17]; the method was developed at the Mannheim Institute for Market Psychology and is called DEMOS (Direct Eye Movement Observation System). It is obviously difficult to record what individuals actually saw in normal reading situations before we come to interview them. Therefore, in this method informants are invited into an office to take part in some other research. They are shown into a waiting room which contains a lectern in it and a chair. The informant sits down and, hopefully, looks through the publications placed on the lectern. Unknown to her at the time, a camera behind and above her records both the pages as she looks at them and also a reflection of her face in a mirror. It is possible to analyse the film afterwards to see which parts of the page her eye has passed over. The main purpose of the technique is to compare this record with what the informant states afterwards about her behaviour. Even in this laboratory situation, just after reading, there are considerable discrepancies. She was seen to glance at pages which later she denied looking at — perhaps those which she decided not to read. She is known not to have opened pages she later claimed to have read — perhaps the habits referred to above and confusion between similar items made her feel she must have read them: 'I'm sure I've seen that somewhere, it must have been here', or 'What an interesting picture: I always read about things like that'. There will be even greater problems in research carried out more than a day after normal reading.

So much for introducing the subject. I now describe in turn the stages through which research has recently taken us.

At one time it was assumed that all readers of a publication saw all the advertising it contained. In the days before television, with more time to read, and when publications were smaller, this could have been true.

But a service used by agencies to investigate the reactions of readers to individual advertisements seemed to tell a different story. This is the Noting and Reading service offered by Gallup, which was previously called the Field Readership Index, and which has been operating in this country continuously since 1947. In the US a similar service offered by Starch has run even longer. Checks are carried out on a number of issues of each of the dozen or so publications covered during the year — sometimes only one, sometimes half a dozen. On each individual issue check, which is carried out shortly after publication, between 120 and 250 adults are generally interviewed. The respondents qualify for interview by recalling one or more items in the issue being carried; they are therefore not typical NRS readers, but are more likely to be primary readers and may be more thorough readers.

The informant is taken through the publication page by page in the order in which she read it. She points out to the interviewer every item noted in the publication and every item read, including both editorial and advertisements. The results can be analysed to show the proportion of readers who say they have noted anything on a spread (spread traffic), anything on a page (page traffic), whether they have noted or read an individual advertisement, and even parts of individual advertisements.

In 1964 a group of agencies called the Agencies Research Consortium got together to collect their own data on reading and noting and, more importantly, to conduct validation work into this area. The method they used in their surveys was very like Gallup's. They covered a larger number of issues of each publication in a year, but with a smaller number of informants on each issue. The main object of the analysis was to produce averages for the amount of reading and noting over different types of advertisements for different types of people. Their overall findings are very similar to Gallup's.

Such data was the source of the estimate already quoted, that page traffic averaged 60 to 70 per cent. These scores were used to weight publications so as to favour those apparently read more thoroughly. When looked at in more detail, the findings also suggested rules of thumb which have entered into mythology in daily use. For example, to quote from the first edition of this book: 'Traffic is not constant throughout a publication and guidance is obtained on the value of different parts. Thus, traffic is higher in the first half of a magazine, and certain types of page attract different people, although as already stated the particular product and target affect the results. A value can for example be put on being on the sports page or the letters page. Advertisements on right-hand pages get higher noting than on the left. Larger publications or issues get less traffic per page. In Sunday newspapers, classified and financial pages have a lower readership than the rest; display advertisement page traffic is therefore higher than the average page traffic of the publication. In the class Sunday papers it is important to distinguish between the main paper, the review section and the colour supplement: the review section has a lower page traffic than the main paper.

'Because agencies press for advertisements to appear early in a magazine, and facing editorial matter, magazines have to fight to sell the rest of the space. They do this first by charging higher rates for popular positions. In general these rates reflect myths and common-

117

sense rather than higher values proved by research. The research-based decision will usually be that special positions are not worthwhile though there are exceptions where the editorial is likely to attract particularly the kind of reader we want. Publications of course argue that many readers are interested in advertisements for themselves; therefore an advertisement in any position is going to work. They also point out that editors are cunning enough to structure the magazine so that the reader is led right through it. Both these points are legitimate but do not seem as convincing as the page traffic evidence.

'Reading and noting data have also been used to assess the value of different sizes of advertisement. Analyses have suggested that the scores decrease as the square root or cube root of the area of the advertisement. This means that smaller advertisements are better value − provided the copywriter has room to make his point, for the scores of course fail to reflect the total impact of an advertisement and the 'square root rule' should not be taken seriously.

'Finally, the scores can be used to assess the value of colour − usually worthwhile in noting terms. They can also assess the value of repeated insertions − the wear-out of an advertisement over time is very slow by this measure.'

For many years it has been seen that there are snags in using the Noting and Reading data in this way. First, the product group advertised is known to affect the score for advertisements: shoes do well among women, cars among men. Whether the reader is in the target for the product also has a major effect. Both these factors can be summed up in the phrase used by Alan Smith and Norman Webb: 'Noting means involvement'. Second, the traditional use of the reading and noting technique is as a post-test for copy, when the score achieved is compared with scores for other similar advertisements, preferably among people who are in the target. However, this use of the technique also seems to put individual reading and noting scores beyond media planning use. A single score cannot measure 'eyes open in front of the advertisement' if it also measures copy effects. It cannot determine the contribution of the media buyer (in selecting the space) if it also evaluates the copywriter (who fills it). The use of these individual scores as a quality control measure by the advertiser should therefore apply at most to the creative department. Third, the rate-card and demand may already iron out any advantage that could exist. Perhaps the experience of direct-response advertisers has already uncovered whatever unevenness there is in reading behaviour. For example, an AID run carried out by Gallup on 263 advertisements in the *Daily Mirror* in 1971, when noting per £1000 cost was compared with size, position and so on, did *not* find left and right-hand pages to be important, or smaller and larger issues, or appearing early and later in the paper. Of course, these results cannot be confidently extrapolated to magazines.

A final word of warning is that the 'quality' of the advertising, to use a very ill-defined word, may be confounded with position, size, colour, etc. Suppose the larger, more successful and experienced advertisers who use the best creative talent also tend to use colour more. Then colour advertising may get exceptionally high scores at least partly because it is used for attractive products and striking advertising, rather than earning them all on its own account.

The position as I have described it continued until about 1969 to 1971 [5.18]. There were underlying rumbles. For example, the Agencies Research Consortium results were not accepted without question: 'the implications of this study were the subject of considerable divergence of view among members of the Consortium' [5.19].

Meanwhile the NRS experimented with a picture scale (from 1968 to 1972) which had been selected from several possible techniques to measure the reader's intensity or thoroughness of reading. The method required the informant to claim to read appropriate proportions of the pages. The method was to be calibrated by a postal technique, but difficulties were encountered and as a result an intensive piece of research took place, the Reader Categorisation Study [5.20]. This was designed by the Development Working Party of the National Readership Survey. It was carried out to investigate a number of variables which might divide readers by their reading behaviour, but its most significant result was the generally high level of exposure of the publication found among readers. The average spread traffic found among 'readers' was 91 per cent, varying between 88 per cent for dailies and 93 per cent for weeklies. The reason, for which convincing evidence was quoted and has since been separately provided, is that many of the people who say, for example, they did *not* glance at an advertisement, can in fact be persuaded to describe their behaviour in a way that makes clear they took in enough to decide they did not want to study it further. For example, they may give a reason connected with the page ('I didn't look at it because there was too much on one page' or 'It wasn't in colour') or with the advertisement ('I don't use that product' or 'I already know about it' or 'I use something else' or

119

even 'I've seen it before'). In another project, a quarter of informants said they had not glanced at an advertisement; 21 per cent of informants however, i.e. over three-quarters of these, implied they had taken in something. The conclusions we are invited to draw is that a magazine or newspaper has done its job for the advertiser with 90 per cent of the readers in leading them as far as glancing at a spread: beyond this is the job of the product or of the copywriter.

Admittedly the sample in the Reader Categorisation Study was small (510 housewives) and for some publications the amount of data was tiny (for the *Times*, *Telegraph* and *Guardian*, together, for example, only 19 page checks were made — so the data are hardly conclusive for the thicker, quality newspapers). Nevertheless the effect of the study has been major. Reading intensity measures have been dropped from the NRS, and it is now assumed that throughout the press virtually every reader (or more exactly, 90 per cent) are exposed to the average advertisement, rather than the 60 to 70 per cent which previous reading and noting work had indicated.

The almost subliminal exposure among the 20 to 30 per cent that makes up the difference is very reminiscent of the low attention sometimes paid by viewers to the TV set. An announcement like 'Mary Smith, there's £100 for you under your chair', might break through to Mary Smith. It is doubtful whether much advertising which the manufacturer hopes is relevant to her does actually get her involvement. Another analogy is that the noting score a press advertisement receives is like the share of audience a TV programme gets: a combination of viewing habits and programme effects.

A further effect of the study is that some commonsense views about readership now look doubtful. Infrequent readers do not seem to have a lower chance of seeing an advertisement; of course there always was the argument that the occasional reader would find an issue that much more interesting and would read it *more* thoroughly than the regular reader. Similarly, people who say they spend less time reading than average seem to be exposed to as many pages as the average reader, i.e. they are more likely to flick through the whole issue but more quickly, than to read less of it but as thoroughly.

The most recent research [5.21] has been to explore both the non-reader of an advertisement and the reader; the former to establish whether or not she did actually get a chance to receive an impression (and if she does not report one it could be the fault of a boring product or uninspired writer or the wear-out of the advertisement *or* her not glancing at the page), the latter to investigate what passed through her mind. At their best, the results show advertising working; they illuminate the way women relate stimuli to their own lives and needs, sometimes irrespective of the advertiser's intention. This is achieved by the question: 'At that time, when you first saw the advertisement, it must have made something cross your mind. It could have been what you just told me* or your first thoughts could have been different. They might even have been nothing to do with the advertisement. Can you tell me what crossed your mind as you looked at this advertisement at that first time?'

This question is from IPC Magazine's Evaluative Assessment service [5.22] carried out by Gallup. The answers can be encouraging and informative, for example, 'I wished that I had some for tea. On my way home I will look for a shop where they are sold', or 'I thought I might copy the idea for tea on Sunday — but I have no tall glasses. I'll make them in ordinary glass tumblers'. They can also be informative but worrying, for example, 'Fancy a whole family washing their hair at once, it's ridiculous. Where did they all wash it, one in the bathroom, one downstairs, what about the others?' or, about a cosmetic advertisement featuring a close-up of a girl talking on the telephone, 'It reminded me that I haven't paid the phone bill'.

## RESEARCH FOR PUBLISHERS

This section has concentrated on research that helps the media owner to sell and the agency to evaluate. It should not be forgotten that some research also helps proprietors and editors to design and improve publications. While it will never replace flair and integrity, there is evidence that research can and has been used to advantage in this area [5.23].

## CONCLUSION

Press research has changed in two major ways in the past decade. There

---

*This is in answer to a 'safety valve' question, which is meant to get rid of the superficial and 'professional' statements informants tend to give in order to create the impression they know what they are talking about.

is now more use of single-source data, more understanding that targets for advertising are often based on behavioural definitions and not just demographics. The traditional readership question, used in the NRS and other questionnaires, has proved remarkably robust. People choose their newspapers and magazines; the bulk of readers get involved with what they want and ignore the rest. Most display advertisements get a chance to be used by the readers: it is hardly surprising they are not all used — nor are all products.

# 6 OTHER MEDIA

*Brief descriptions of outdoor advertising,
cinema and radio, with outlines of research
available.*

The media in this chapter account for a tenth of all the money spent on display advertising. Outdoor gets about 6 per cent, cinema 1 per cent and radio currently less than 3 per cent. They are often used as supporting media in campaigns where TV or press take most of the money, which is not to say that they are unimportant, or should never be used on their own.

## OUTDOOR

To most agencies, outdoor advertising means principally posters and supersites. These take nearly twice the turnover of the next largest group agencies use — bus and underground advertising. There are roughly 160,000 poster sites throughout the country of which the smaller sizes are about 80 per cent. The total number of sites appears to be static. The smallest standard size of poster is the 4-sheet (60 by 40 inches); the number of these is increasing. A 12-sheet size is currently being introduced; there are also 16-sheets, a few 32-sheets and the popular 48-sheet (10 feet by 20 feet). Supersites, with much more elaborate surrounds, are isolated from other objects and some of them even have their own gardens. These are 9 feet 6 inches high and of various widths, from 27 to over 40 feet. They do not carry posters, but advertisements painted in oils. Most posters and supersites are located in towns and are concentrated both on the roads most used by traffic and, more recently, in shopping precincts. Bus shelters have recently appeared, put up by the contractor, Adshel, and offering illuminated sizes for 4-sheets. These are growing in number and currently total 11,000.

Outdoor also includes transport advertising of which the major groups are buses offering advertising space both inside and outside some 40,000 vehicles, main-line railways with a variety of spaces on about 2300 stations and further advertising opportunities in carriages, London Underground with a great variety of space in its 300 stations and 4000 carriages, advertising in taxis and the newscasters in some city centres. Facia signs, which are mostly simple announcements that a pub or shop or petrol station is there, take about a quarter of all outdoor expenditure and are not usually planned by an agency.

Outdoor advertising is subject to the local authorities' control and to a voluntary Code of Standards for Advertising on Business Premises. Good relations between local authorities and the industry require a compromise between good taste and aggressive selling.

## The use of outdoor

Posters are bought most often to increase the cover of a campaign on a major medium, to reinforce it by frequent reminders and to continue its effect by running when the main campaign has finished. They are generally used only when the advertising message can be reduced to a simple form.

Posters claim very high and rapid cover of the population, of which about 96 per cent may be reached. For example, 20 sites in a town with a population of 100,000 would provide 80 per cent of all adults with at least one opportunity to see a poster within a week. In fact, each of these people would receive on average 24 exposures during the week.

The type of advertiser using poster has changed in the last decade.

New methods of selling have attracted more packaged goods, e.g. foods, more cars, and a wide variety of new advertisers. Cigarettes are still major users but the proportion of drink advertising has declined. Local advertisers contribute only 3 per cent of the revenue.

The crux in evaluating posters as an advertising medium is that the unit used for calculating cover and opportunities-to-see figures is a passage past a site, i.e. a person is counted as being exposed or having an opportunity to see if he walks, drives or is driven along the road past the poster. Now turning a TV switch, opening a magazine or going to the cinema are deliberate, but exposure to posters is involuntary. Many journeys are routine; the same sites are passed again and again; it is arguable how much attention they get. There is some evidence from camera work that about a third of the people passing a site look in its direction — which is not to say that they notice it. There is however a great deal of evidence of the spontaneous awareness of posters since British Posters has been actively involved in this kind of research in conjunction with advertisers. The average aided recall of a poster design is normally between 40 and 50 per cent.

The figures for opportunities to see posters are therefore not easy to compare with those for other media. Posters look cheap — about 4p for a thousand opportunities to see — but this figure has to be discounted by an unknown factor. Exposure data is useful for deciding between types of campaign, for example how much to concentrate posters regionally or in time, but not for evaluating the medium itself.

To determine the worth of the medium more direct measures should be used: the most convincing is of course sales. There are advertisers who have used posters for many years and who have carried out regional tests. It is significant that they still use the medium — though this is not proof of its value for other products in other situations. Less directly, there is evidence, some of which is summarised below, that outdoor advertising can communicate a simple message to parts of the population. This should dissuade anyone from taking up the extreme position that 'no one notices outdoor advertising'.

*Structure of the industry*

In 1971-72 the industry underwent what the trade press [6.1] called 'private and public wrangling. . . . resignations, warnings, alignments, appointments and general politicking'.

There have been two sorts of change, in the ownership of the sites (mergers) and in their cooperative selling for short-term campaigns. The medium has become easier to use [6.2].

First, there are three main sorts of campaign. The largest part of poster sites, about 35 per cent but currently a declining share, are sold to advertisers who hold them till cancelled (TC), i.e. until they choose to give them up. Three months' notice is usually required. The TC sites naturally include many of those in the best positions which the advertiser will not lightly relinquish.

Another third of the sites are sold as pre-selected campaigns (PSCs). This means that an advertiser can buy a package consisting of an approximately representative cross-section of all such sites. Different weights and types of PSCs are available, depending on the target and type of area required. Currently a basic national campaign for a month consists of about 1,300 4-sheets and 3,000 16-sheets. This costs about £51,000 in January to March and £73,000 in October and November. It covers about 90 per cent of housewives with an average of 50 passages past a site. There are also packages in eight major conurbations, and near specific outlets, e.g. chemists and supermarkets or confectioners, tobacconists and newsagents.

The remaining poster sites are sold line-by-line, that is individually (or they are unsold but posters are allowed to stay up after the period bought has expired). It is common to thicken up and balance a PSC by adding sites bought this way.

Supersites are also sold in packages or individually; for example 200 sites might cost £60,000 for a month. Similarly Adshel sites may be bought both ways; the package called Superfours offers for £60,000 a month 2,000 sites, and TV area packages are also available.

About half of all sites become available during each year at a wide range of prices depending on a number of factors, from about £1500 per month for a 48-sheet site at the corner of Piccadilly Circus to less than £25 per month for an average provincial 4-sheet site.

Thus a poster campaign usually consists of hundreds or thousands of sites, each of which must have its poster despatched, put up and invoiced. PSCs of course simplify this process as far as advertiser and agency are concerned and this move to packages is welcome as long as quality does not suffer.

Individual posters are replaced on average every four to six weeks to maintain a good appearance after damage by weather etc., and this is the responsibility of the poster contractor. Damage to posters is always a worry; so is the possibility of mis-posting or late appearance. To check on these points the Poster Audit Bureau is supported by the contractors and agencies (the ratio of costs being about 2:1; agencies pay a levy of ½ per cent on all short-term campaigns and voluntarily on campaigns over four months; they may pass these charges on to advertisers). The Bureau is a monitoring service; inspectors examine in rotation all the sites in the scheme and regularly report whether the correct poster is up and in good condition.

## How Posters are bought and sold

Poster contractors (who own the sites) number about 60. In 1971, seven of the largest of these formed a sales consortium called British Posters to sell the medium through pre-selected campaigns. Together, these contractors own about 75 per cent of all poster sites and currently claim to sell a higher proportion still, although only half of the sites are at present included in the PSCs. A similar group called Independent Poster Sales covers a large part of the remaining sites. Since the contractors have different regional strengths, both groups — and some individually bought sites — must be used for a full national campaign. It is also necessary to deal individually with More O'Farral for supersites, Adshel for their sites, and with London Transport, British Transport Advertising for London buses, Smith and Mason for provincial buses, etc.

It is clear that the sale of posters has simplified but is still complex. In addition to planning and buying there is also relatively expensive production (often over ten per cent of space costs), warehousing and despatch to arrange. There is often argument about the detail to a greater extent than with other media. Therefore most agencies content themselves with buying packages which could be unbalanced, or leave the whole business to the advertiser to buy direct (common for tobacco and drink) or use a specialist poster agency. There are a half-dozen of these who work on fees or split commission.

The site classification system described below shows no signs yet of being detailed enough to replace one of the major functions of the specialist agency which is to employ a sufficiently large field force for regular quality control.

JICPAS, the Joint Industry Committee for Poster Audience Surveys, representing advertisers, agencies and the various associations of site owners, exercises some control over industry audience surveys although this is usually restricted to approving or modifying projects initiated and funded by site owners.

Although the unit used in poster research is a simple one — passing a poster location — basic research on posters is superficially more complex than in other media. This is partly because the opportunity to see is here so distantly related to advertisement exposure in the sense used for other media, partly because the industry is helpfully trying to measure *more* than in other media — not exposure to one advertisement but to a whole range of campaigns in towns of different sizes and at different densities.

The classical method of research [6.3] starts by drawing a sample of people living in a town of known population size. A number of locations are sampled from all the sites in the town. In an interview, each informant describes all the journeys made in the previous week and the interviewer notes the number of times the informant passed each location. It is then possible to work out whether or not the informant would have passed during the week at least one location when the campaign consisted of one, two...or twenty sites, hence the cover of campaigns of various numbers of sites. The total number of passages during the week is of course directly related to the number of sites used.

The cover just described applies to this size of town only. Obviously ten sites in Dunstable will provide high cover rapidly, but the same number of sites in Birmingham will never give high cover. The relation between the size of a town and the number of sites on one hand, cover and repetition on the other, have been expressed as formulae [6.4] whose derivation is necessarily technical but whose final results look like those for any other medium. Later studies have updated and validated these methods [6.5]. The earlier applications excluded conurbations. Indeed it was concluded from studies in Leeds and London [6.6] that conurbations behaved differently. However the latest work [6.7] successfully covers both types of area.

One variation on the recalled journey question is to ask the informant how often she has recently been past specific places in the town which are in fact poster sites. This differs little from the journey description method and still requires a long interview. Or the informant may be asked much less detailed questions about the number of times she goes out for various purposes, and what methods of transport are used. This takes only part of an interview; it gives no detailed information but successfully discriminates between those lightly and those heavily exposed to posters. This method has been validated [6.8].

Another technique is to count the number of people passing a few random site locations, which should give overall repetition figures equal to the survey method (except that visitors to the town are excluded from the latter). This method cannot describe cover or breakdown of the audience (other than men and women). There is also the photographic method, similar in principle to a traffic count, in which a photograph of the people passing the site is taken from the poster location. This has been adapted by London Transport [6.9] to moving locations: the outside of Central London buses. The results were shown to be of the same order as those for a journey recall method in which crossing or following bus routes was the definition of an opportunity to see. This showed, for example, that a campaign on 500 buses provided in a week 'bus encounters' with 84 per cent of adults living in London, with an average frequency of 21.

These results do not give what is often required: estimates for the exposure of a particular campaign to a particular target audience. However by adding together exposure estimates obtained from figures now provided for the New Districts (the new administrative unit for Great Britain) it is possible to obtain estimated cover levels and frequencies for any sized campaign in any area, region, or even the whole country. It is unusual to analyse the performance of a schedule on different demographic sub-groups although reasonable estimates can be made.

Attempts have been made to summarise site values in a formula. While this would simplify buying and selling it is a viable method only if there is agreement on the relative values of different types of site, which is not the case. All sites are classified by the contractors, the main variables being the type of location or road (which is related to traffic past the site), visibility and the amount of competitive advertising also visible. There are currently 96 different combinations but attempts are being made to simplify and standardise, thus leading to industry agreement on the quality of a campaign.

Various studies have been made of the effectiveness of outdoor campaigns. Here is one which has been used a great deal [6.10]. In

1967 in Bristol and in Exeter a sample of people was asked to identify from pictures various breeds of dog, and to guess their actual names. Thirteen per cent could identify the Basset Hound. Incidentally, people with a dog in their household were more than twice as likely as others to identify the breed, which shows the effect of interest in a product field.

Then for three weeks, at a space cost of £390, four bulletin boards were used in Bristol and one in Exeter. The cover of such a campaign is only one-third of the population with an average number of exposures of about 11. The boards showed a cut-out picture of the Basset and the message: 'This is a Basset Hound named BERTIE'.

In a subsequent, separate survey, 23 per cent could identify the breed and 14 per cent gave the correct name. It is legitimate to conclude that a good proportion of those covered could recall the message, and that this communication was due to the advertising. But the message was an unusual one — both because it was an announcement about a novelty (brand advertising has such an opportunity only rarely) and because it was not an advertisement for anything, which was striking in its context.

Since then many more relevant case histories have been collected and published by British Posters, who also started an awards scheme in 1977, based unusually but sensibly on evidence of posters' real effectiveness.


## CINEMA

About 2¼ million people pay to go to the cinema each week, in 1600 cinemas. This is a severe decline in the last ten years in admissions (240 million in 1968, 108 million in 1977) but interestingly the number of cinemas is about the same. There is of course no comparison with the 1600 million admissions and 5000 cinemas of just after the war, when there was no television and fewer other distractions. But the decline seems at the moment to be halted: admissions grew in 1977 and 1978; cinemas actually increased in numbers between 1971 and 1974. Films have become more relevant and more exciting than the formulas of the sixties. They are more intelligently distributed. Many cinemas have been modernised, the most important change being the conversion of a two-, three-, four- or even five-unit complex (there were 850 cinemas in multi-screen complexes in 1978, more than double the number in 1973).

Advertising films are usually shown for a maximum of 10 minutes, just before the main film, with the house lights down. The commercials have, of course, sound, movement and colour. The screen is more dominating than the TV set; the environment is more of an occasion. Not everyone admitted sees the commercials; it has been estimated that 80 per cent are present [6.11] but those present receive a greater impact than the TV audience. The normal length of a commercial is 60 seconds, which the rate card favours as we see later.

*The cinema audience*

The cinema audience tends to be the young and unmarried, who go regularly to the cinema. The young unmarrieds are a useful target for many advertisers, both because of the way they spend their money now and because they will soon be setting up their own households. Distribution by social grade in the audience is roughly similar to that in the whole population; there are rather more men in the audience than in the population. Half the population say they never go to the cinema. But among 15 to 24-year olds, 87 per cent say they go and 30 per cent go once a month or more often. About half the adults in a typical cinema audience fall into the ages 18 to 30 though they represent only 23 per cent of the population; about three-quarters of the audience are between 15 and 34, though these represent only a third of the population. Except for newly-weds, the cinema does not cover housewives adequately — more than half say they never go — but for the young adults it offers reasonable cover: an eight-week campaign can reach 47 per cent of the 15 to 24s with an average frequency of 2.2.

*How the cinema is sold*

Advertising rights in different cinemas are held by seven different contractors. Pearl and Dean have exclusive rights to the ABC, Star and Classic circuits, Rank Screen Advertising to the Odeon and Granada circuits. The share that a contractor can be said to have depends on the definitions used, but by any standard these two are much the largest contractors. Advertisers generally use both and occasionally all the contractors.

Cinemas are sold individually, although in some multi-cinema complexes two screens are sold together as one package. To have a 60-second film shown at the Leicester Square Odeon costs £131 a week. The cost at the Regal, Daventry, is £7. Costs are roughly related to the number of admissions to the cinema, but an advertiser cannot check this, since neither the admission nor the audience profile figures for individual cinemas are published. Rank will give cinema admissions in blocks of 20 or more on request. Therefore in a single week at one cinema the advertiser may get a bargain or he may reach very few people, but over a whole campaign he gets close to average value.

An advertiser trying to reach young children effectively can book a Disney film package. Alternatively, advertisers may have their commercials exhibited exclusively with X certificate films. The last few years have also seen a growing increase in the number of packages offered in specific films, e.g. *Star Wars*, which can provide a certain type of expected audience. There are also a number of regional packages available using defined marketing areas for test marketing or simply localised advertising. These packages may be booked by ITV areas, conurbations, seaside holiday resorts or even university towns.

It cost about £22,000 in 1978 to show a one-minute film for a week in every cinema in the country. The rate per thousand admittances (including children) was approximately £9. A 30-second film costs about two-thirds and a 15-second one-third that of a 60-second. For young people the cost of an opportunity to see is comparable with that of TV and it is arguable that the impact is greater.

Given the cost, regional and time specifications for a campaign, a cinema contractor will draw up a list of cinemas. ITV regions or conurbations are standard areas used, or the agency can also choose individual cinemas, selected on its knowledge of the locality and type of cinema. The regionality of the medium is one of its greatest attractions, for example cinemas near retail outlets can be picked. The exact weeks of showing can, of course, be chosen. It is possible to arrange displays and merchandising for some products in the cinema foyer in the same weeks as the commercial is shown.

As well as national campaigns, the cinema attracts local retailer advertising, sometimes linked with brand advertising. If the message is 'Get your X at Y' then the cost may be shared between the manufacturer X and the retailer Y.

The Screen Advertising Association represents the interests of the advertising contractors. The Association collects and publishes cinema statistics and case histories. It has also carried out interviews with

132

people leaving the cinema to establish that most of them can recall the commercials. It commissions an inspection service which verifies that advertising films are shown under specified conditions.

*Cinema research*

The National Readership Survey obtains adults' claims on how often they go to the cinema. These can be reconciled with total admission figures published by the Department of Industry, allowing for those under 15 who go to the cinema. The frequency claims can also be compared with their recent visits and in this way turned into probabilities of visiting a cinema, just as reading frequency claims are compared with average issue readerships (explained in the previous chapter). In this way the cover and frequency of a campaign can be predicted and the main contractors offer a service to do this, as well as publishing other data relevant to the medium.

## RADIO

BBC Radio is still the dominant force in this medium, with a long history, four national programmes, some regionality, and twenty local stations, soon to be increased.

Challenging the BBC we have had in turn Radio Luxembourg (which also has a respectable history), Radio Manx (which started in 1964 and covers basically the Isle of Man, population 50,000), the pirate stations (between 1964 and 1967 when they were outlawed) and, since October 1973, Independent Local Radio.

Virtually every home has at least one radio and the transistor has extended listening outside the home. Total radio listening has been constant for some years at about 1¼ hours a day. This is made up of a wide range — those who use radio very selectively, for example for news or while driving, and those for whom it is a constant background. Much listening takes place while doing other things.

*Radio Luxembourg*

Since 1967 the only national commercial radio station has been Radio

Luxembourg. Here commercial broadcasts started in 1935, principally for the Continent. The British hours vary with the season: 7 p.m. to 3 a.m. in winter. Peak listening hours are 9.30 p.m. to midnight.

The programme content is mainly popular or disco music: 'If they're buying it, we'll play it.' There are no needle-time restrictions; news is on the hour every hour. The audience is therefore highest among 15 to 24-year olds; but it is virtually classless.

There are eight million 15 to 24s in the country and 1.7 million listen at least once a week, 2.2 million in a fortnight. Cover builds up higher than this over a longer period, probably unlike the Independent local stations. There are, of course, listeners of other ages too: in total the weekly cover is three million and in a fortnight five million.

Advertising time is sold mostly in packages: 49 spots a week is the commonest. A 30-second total audience package costs about £4000 and is guaranteed to give (against the most recent, annual research data) a cost per thousand of 50p, or 76p on 15 to 24s. The cancellation notice required is eight weeks. It is also possible to sponsor say an hour and have appropriate DJ comments as well as commercials. In total, advertising can go up to 12 minutes an hour. An hour at peak time used this way again costs about £4000 a week.

A campaign on Radio Luxembourg – or on Independent Local Radio – is not usually thought of at the individual spot level, though the total cover and frequency of a package is obviously built up from these spots. This is because the spot as a unit is too small, costing here less than £100, and the individual ratings are also small (3 or 4 per cent, even among 15 to 24s, is a good rating). It is the overall result of a package, or of a Luxembourg package plus ILR packages, which matters.


*Independent Local Radio*

Britain is one of the last western countries where the Government permitted the commercial use of this medium. In March 1971 a White Paper forecast 60 independent stations. The first contracts were awarded by the IBA in 1973 and in the same year three stations went on the air, followed in succeeding years by six, seven and three stations. Thus in 1976 we had nineteen contractors. After a pause due to the economic crisis and to the rethinking delegated to the Annan Committee further expansion with nine more stations was announced. The award of these contracts starts in 1979 and the enlarged network should be complete in 1981. The description which follows is about the nineteen stations. These already cover the major areas: 65 per cent of the population live within their reception areas; only a further 5 per cent will be added by the next nine.

The nineteen are:

| | |
|---|---|
| London | London Broadcasting (news and information) |
| | Capital Radio (general) |
| Glasgow | Radio Clyde |
| Birmingham | Birmingham Broadcasting |
| Manchester | Piccadilly Radio |
| Tyne/Wear | Metropolitan Broadcasting |
| Swansea | Swansea Sound |
| Edinburgh | Radio Forth |
| Liverpool | Radio City |
| Plymouth | Plymouth Sound |
| Sheffield | Radio Hallam |
| Nottingham | Radio Trent |
| Teeside | Radio Tees |
| Bradford | Pennine Radio |
| Portsmouth | Radio Victory |
| Wolverhampton | Beacon Broadcasting |
| Ipswich | Radio Orwell |
| Reading | Thames Valley Broadcasting |
| Belfast | Downtown Radio |

The next nine are Aberdeen/Inverness, Bournemouth, Cardiff, Chelmsford/Southend, Coventry, Dundee/Perth, Exeter/Torbay, Gloucester and Peterborough.

ILR stations are genuinely local and have their own personalities and specialities. Some of them (Capital, Clyde and City for example) have an exuberance and confidence which has made them the most popular single station in their area, though the BBC total audience is larger. The programme content on each station is different; most include popular music, chat shows, phone-ins and news. London Broadcasting is however mainly talk, news and information.

This success with audiences has naturally been accompanied by rapid revenue growth, approximately doubling each year from 1974. Luxembourg has benefited in the long run from the renaissance of radio, probably taking about £2 million a year currently. All nineteen ILR stations were profitable for the first time in 1976/77, after some initial crises. Of the £23 million spent on ILR in 1977 about 60 per cent is from national advertisers. In the US, radio accounts for about 10 per cent of advertising expenditure. Even at 5 per cent as a ceiling we could see radio become twice as important here.

The rate cards give the costs of individual spots in each time segment, dependent on ratings and the area size.

Nine minutes of advertising are allowed each hour. Peak time is generally from early morning to noon. Agencies again buy packages much more than individual spots — for example 20 or 40 spots — the times of transmission being rotated by the contractor.

The three companies selling advertising time at present are Broadcast Marketing Services, Air Services and Radio Sales and Marketing; these act as agents for the stations in rather the same way as British Posters acts for a group of outdoor site owners.

The audience to radio is very diverse. Some people use it only for news or serious music. Others, probably the majority, want undemanding music or chat as a background or to reduce loneliness [6.12] :

'I get up in the morning and I switch the radio on. I don't actually listen to it but it's there as company. That's the thing — something that's making a noise while you're there working. You feel you're not alone because the radio is on.' (*Housewife*)

'I listen to Radio 1 while I'm studying. I'm used to working with sounds and I can't work in silence. I need something in the background to prevent me from feeling cut off.' (*Male student*)

'Without it I get upset driving. I'd be more annoyed by other people in their cars. Music allows me to let other people overtake me without feeling frustrated. I listen to chat. It goes in one ear and out the other.' (*Male motorist* — note that only a half of all cars here are fitted with a radio, far less than in the US.)

*Radio Research*

The amount of money available for radio research is small, the technical problems are formidable [6.13] and initially research was varied and confusing. There has however been improvement.

Although radio is covered in the National Readership Survey and in the Target Group Index, the principal current source is under the JICRAR (Joint Industry Committee for Radio Audience Research) specification, commissioned by the AIRC (Association of Independent Radio Contractors). There used to be separate pieces of research in each area, but in April–May 1977 the first simultaneous surveys were carried out in all 18 areas. Thus as well as having results within each area we can make statements about the audience in all the ILR areas together. For example, about half those living within earshot of an ILR transmitter, or 32 per cent of all adults, listen to ILR at least once a week. The cover within each area varies between 20 per cent (LBC) to about 60 per cent (Clyde and Downtown). The average listener is tuned in for nearly two hours a day, and has a slight tendency to be young, male and downgrade. Peak listening on weekdays is at 7.30–9 a.m. when ratings are typically 10 per cent; on Saturdays and Sundays the peak in the morning spreads over two or three hours. These audiences levels have grown since 1975-76 but now seem to be levelling off.

These data come from a diary kept by respondents over one week. This technique is becoming the standard. Its advantages are that cover and frequency analyses are possible and, to the contractors, that it gives higher audiences than recall methods. Radio Luxembourg has derived its data from diaries since 1971.

Radio listening is often unmemorable; station identification and remembering it correctly are not easy. The sample that misrepresents the number of people in-home and out-of-home is going to give unrepresentative results – and samples are very prone to this kind of bias. Prompting by a diary may produce results in favour of more radio listening and again throw the sample off balance.

As a guide to the relative values of different times and days the present method is acceptable, though the absolute values are unknown (i.e. there is no equivalent to presence research). The decision to use radio when compared with other media hardly compares costs per thousand so this omission is not serious. Cover and frequency figures are now available. A guide based on the analyses of 300 schedules is published by the AIRC [6.14]. This is clumsy to use; it requires input like the highest-rated spot in a schedule, which is in practice not available; it gives one-week cover only; it gives no indication of how many people 'heard' just two or three spots, giving only one or more. These are at present refinements which are hardly worth bothering

137

about for the normal use of radio.

Using the 1978 research we can assess for example a 49-spot 30-second Total Audience Package — one of the standard packages on all rate cards. This cost £22,000 (£24 per spot) over the nineteen stations — from nearly £5,000 on Capital to about £400 on the smaller stations. Its cover is about four-fifths of each station's weekly reach and those covered are reached on average five times. The weekly reach itself is variable: 60 per cent of adults is high, 30 per cent low and the network average is 50 per cent. Thus the national cover of the package, as a proportion of all adults, is about 0.65 (population) x 0.5 (weekly reach) x 0.8 (package) = 26 per cent. The average cost per thousand is about 40p.

## PERIPHERAL MEDIA

The conventional media have now been briefly described. There remains a host of other ways in which the advertiser can sell and promote his product. The media department does not often get involved in them, but they have definite uses.

Direct mail is the largest of these, in fact it has a greater turnover than any of the media in this chapter. It is used mostly in the professional, retail and industrial fields where names and addresses can be obtained which accurately pinpoint the target. It is not generally used for consumer advertising because of its high cost over broad targets, though the *Reader's Digest* successfully sells books and subscriptions this way and the National Coal Board has said [6.15] it produced inquiries about central heating more cheaply than any other method. Telegrams and even the telex are used in the same way.

Bingo halls are a medium that clearly resembles the cinema — slides can be shown with a recorded announcement. The audience is much older than the cinema's and the majority are working class housewives. This area was being promoted to agencies five or so years ago but is currently little used.

The distinctions between media, trade relations, public relations and product promotions are blurred. Probably most people would include as media launderettes, supermarkets and hotels where piped music or closed circuit TV are available for advertising [6.16], the sites round race tracks, football grounds, or even equipment like cabers, clothing, caravans at sports events, perhaps hot air balloons, sky divers and the like — some of these can get exposure on television | [6.17] — deck chairs at holiday resorts, matches, beer mats, ashtrays, bus tickets and directories.

It is less likely that the media department will get involved with calendars, carrier bags, stickers, playing cards, buttons, T-shirts, key rings, pens, records and so on | [6.18].

Finally, there are some important selling methods that the agency may advise on but which are not usually thought of as media — sports promotions, coupons, price offers, multi-packs, announcements on containers of other products, competitions, self-liquidators (the public buy an offer at a price which covers its cost to the promoter), demonstrators and so on. There are also exhibitions and the distribution through letter-boxes of samples, coupons and printed material.

# Part 3
# THE AGENCY AT WORK

# 7 BRIEFING THE MEDIA MAN

*A brief description of the different jobs in the agency. The procedure that ensures the situation facing the product is described to the media department. The headings in the media brief.*

## AGENCY STRUCTURE

The way the media job is carried out is different from agency to agency; it also changes from time to time within agencies. This happens for several reasons. The simplest cause is increasing pressure of work. While the number of brands handled in agencies is probably growing, the number employed has fallen rapidly. What three people did in 1966 (when IPA agencies employed 20,000), only two people worked on in 1975 (13,300); the numbers rose slightly in 1977-8 (about 14,000). 'It is most likely that this reduction in numbers has borne relatively heavily on those agency functions which lack an immediate pay-off, which nicely describes the long-term plodding of media researchers. It is also likely that the degree of senior executive involvement in this field has been reduced' [7.1]. It is not only the media research contribution which has diminished, it is the whole media department.

It has always been true that the media job has these two character-istics: it requires specialist knowledge and skills, but it also has very indeterminate frontiers with other functions such as campaign planning, creative work and consumer research. Different agencies have been experimenting with structures and job definitions in order to connect economically with the rest of the agency. Currently there is no general agreement on how best to specify the job. On the contrary, there is warm – though not always friendly – controversy about it [7.2].

Further, agencies have different styles or philosophies. Some are informal, others are disciplined and pass all the work through review committees which exercise central control. Some employ all-rounders and have only a few people working for each advertiser (small agencies have to run this way), others break the job into several specialised tasks.

Nevertheless the job requires certain things to be done, whatever the titles of the people doing them and however the work is shared. I describe a typical large agency organisation, where the different functions are carried out by separate people. But the account executive may be the traffic controller as well, the planner may also himself be the buyer.


*Three key functions*

There are three key jobs that, with the media department, are the heart of the agency.

1    *Account control.* The account director runs the whole agency team and is responsible for 'account control' or 'client service'. Here the day-to-day work is done by the account executive or manager. He represents the agency to the advertiser and is answerable for all its work. In particular, he agrees the advertising objectives with the advertiser and – for products where advertis-ing has major importance – the marketing objectives. He has assistants to help him.

    Direct contact often takes place between other agency people and the advertiser, but the account manager should know when this happens. The advertisers' decisions should come through the account executive to the rest of the agency team.

2    *Creative group.* The creative group is the factory or heart of the agency. The creative group head directs the people who make the

advertisements. This job may be divided into words under a copy chief, and pictures under an art director. Or one man may run a team which consists of writers, visualisers, TV producers, typographers and so on.

The creative group usually uses talent outside the agency to shoot films, take photographs and produce finished artwork. Creative people may have their own advertisement researchers or workshop to help them take into account the consumer's view of their work.

3   *Traffic control.* The traffic controller or administrator links the creative and media teams with the actual making of the advertisements: he is the route to mechanical production (for print material) and to film production. He ensures that an order for space or time is followed by the advertisement which is to appear there. He is also in charge of the rotation of TV commercials, i.e. deciding which of several films is shown at each time the buyer has bought. He keeps the timetable for the agency and chases the work in progress.

*Other agency functions*

1   *Research.* Advertising research has already been mentioned – this is basically concerned with creative briefing, advertisement development and advertisement pre-testing. Media research is discussed later. There is also the general area of consumer and trade research. The research executive collects and interprets consumer research data; he may commission it or do the work himself.

2   *Merchandising.* The merchandising executive advises on all the non-media aids which help to sell the product. Consumer and trade promotions, competitions, point-of-sale material may be his responsibility. The agency should advise at least on consumer promotion so that a single face is presented by the product to the public.

3   *Public relations.* The agency may advise on and carry out public relations work for the manufacturer.

4   *New products.* A new product executive may work with the manufacturer on the development, selection, testing and launching of new products. Currently the trend is towards giving this work

to existing teams or full-time venture groups. Packaging and other designers may be available.

## The media department

I write for simplicity 'the media department' and 'the media man' though some of the work described below may be separated between account planning and the media department itself and although women can do the work as well as any man and often play a major role in the department. When account planning exists it may also advise on market data and on research, i.e. the planner may take part in general strategy decisions, based on data about what is happening to the product in the market place. He may summarise and project sales, distribution and consumer research data. This book is about media, not broad strategy or campaign planning, so the wider aspects of the planner's job are not discussed here.

1   *Planner.* This job has various names: account planner, media planner, media group head and so on. It is done in very close co-operation with account control – or may even be done by the account executive. The work concerns media strategy, that is, the determination and broad split of the media budget and how it should be spent. The planner represents the media department to the advertiser and to the rest of the agency. He works with others in the agency to develop the media plan – the agency's recommendation on the media in which the advertising is to appear. He reports on the execution of the plan, that is budgetary control and on the efficiency of the buying of space and time. He is in touch directly but intermittently with media owners.

2   *Media buying.* The media buyer collaborates in the writing of the media plan. He ensures that the proposal is feasible. He then executes the agreed plan, negotiating the actual buys and issuing the orders. He is in touch directly and continuously with media owners.

Buyers are usually specialists – a TV buyer buying only TV time, a press buyer only press space. Outdoor buying (posters, transport advertising and so on) is nearly always specialised: so is direct mail. Cinema and radio benefit from specialisation but because of their relatively small turnover their buying is often combined with that of other media.

146

3   *Other media work.* The media department includes others who assist in the main tasks of planning and buying. There may be media researchers. Data processing may be in the hands of systems or computer specialists and requires its own clerical staff. There will be typists, secretaries and voucher clerks.

Invoice control may be carried out in the accounts department which, with other administrative work in the agency, is not described here. The work is complicated because of the large number of individual media orders and because changes from the original schedule can take place right up to the appearance of the advertisement. The advertiser receives a simple accounting statement but its accuracy is the result of tedious checking.


## THE MEDIA BRIEF – MAIN FACTORS

*The agency team*

The advertiser usually has a relatively large group of people working for him, and on other accounts, at the agency. Good advertisements are nearly always produced by individuals and not by committees, but a good advertising operation as a whole needs a team. The account manager is its leader, the agency paperwork system provides its discipline.

If the account manager issues separate instructions to each member of the team then the benefits of cross-fertilisation are lost. The planner in particular will not be able to incorporate in his plan what others in the agency can contribute. It is part of the planner's job to involve others in the team in media decisions.

The way the planner starts work is now explained by going through the brief on which the media plan is based. This sounds like a simple transaction, but it would be inefficient if orders came down to the planner and he simply returned a finished plan. There may indeed be a formal document sent to him from account control. But for a satisfactory campaign this written brief must be filled out by conversations within the team. The planner contributes positively when he questions and enlarges the brief. It is unnecessary to repeat at each subsequent heading that the brief is not so much a set of instructions as the starting point for a dialogue.

*Product*

The agency should record the history of the product group and of the brand they are advertising. The product situation report, brand book or other document in which this is done should be available to all the team so they work from the same base.

A brief description is needed of the product itself, its uses, the pack and price, the way it is distributed and so on. What sales movements are taking place among all the products of which this is one: is the market expanding or steady, and how do our brand's sales compare with competitors'? How have our brand and its competitors been advertised and promoted? It is an established brand or a new brand fighting for a beach-head?

The media plan should evolve from the more general marketing plan for the product, so the marketing objective should be stated as exactly as possible: not 'to increase sales' but 'to raise the market share from this percentage to that', or 'to persuade this percentage of housewives to try the new product'. Marketing strategy lays down the broad way the objective should be reached: by creating awareness of particular features or uses of the product, or by helping to get improved distribution, or by maintaining use among those who already know the product, or by increasing purchases among that group who now buy very little. The strategy statement will record what non-media marketing activities are being planned; media expenditure may have to be co-ordinated with these.

Previous experience with this product of different media also enters the discussion. It is helpful to say 'In view of its success in the past, television is a likely choice', or 'The advertiser is satisfied with the rate of coupon returns from weekly magazines'. The planner is thus given initial indications about the way account control and the advertiser are thinking.

*Budget*

How much there is to spend on a campaign is so critical that it gets the next chapter on its own. At the briefing stage the planner needs to know the media budget — after the costs of producing advertisements and other expenditure have been deducted. This may be broken down into theme advertising (long-term support) and scheme advertising (short-term announcements about promotions). Within each of these the amount for advertising direct to the trade should be set aside.

*Timetable*

The earlier the start of planning a campaign, the more thorough the plan will be and the better the buying. In practice detailed planning cannot begin more than six or at most twelve months before: market situations change and a great deal would have to be done again.

Six months before the campaign is a reasonable time to start detailed planning. Eight weeks at least should be allowed between briefing and presentation of the plan to the advertiser for approval. This brings us to four months before the campaign — and near the time when we must seriously consider copy dates (especially for colour work) and cancellation dates. If any of the media to be used are likely to be in short supply then planning should start earlier and options should be placed.

It is prudent to be clear, when briefing starts, about the dates on which the plan is to be ready for presentation, when client approval is to be obtained, when the campaign is to start and finish. If time is short, the whole team must be made aware of copy and cancellation dates. The buyer must know whether negotiations with media owners can be started, whether he has authority to make bookings and whether the campaign and product are particularly confidential. Freeze dates should then be agreed after which the broad strategy, commercial lengths and so on, will not be altered.

The timetable for the work done by the agency obviously involves more than the media department. In the creative department in particular proper scheduling can bring benefits. But the production of advertising ideas and of good advertisements are not mechanical processes, and competitive activity and other marketing problems produce crises of their own. Whilst plans can always be produced at short notice and media can be bought in the same way this makes good results harder to obtain.

*Target*

It is wasteful and often futile to aim advertising at everybody. In that way, the effort is diffused and no one thinks the advertisement is meant for him. There should be a precise definition of the people the advertising is to reach.

The definition of the target may be a simple, even an obvious, procedure. Ideally it should be based on research which demonstrates the value of different sorts of people. This may lead to a straightforward allocation of weights to different sexes, age groups, social grades, etc. It may, on the other hand, bring up complex and sometimes unanswerable questions. Is the object to reach present users of our product more than the non-users (who might be converted)? Is it only mothers with children who buy tinned baby food? (No, flat dwellers, old people and some cooks do too). The answers to such questions are important, since they affect the whole advertising strategy and creative approach as well as the media plan.

It may be that the classification used in laying down the target definition is not available in the data held in the media department. For example, the marketing and creative objectives may be to reach people already buying the product and to persuade them to buy more. But purchasers of this product may be a classification not in the media research data. For planning or buying purposes a criterion has to be agreed which is used as an approximation. For example, in this case the TV buyer may be told his objective is simply to reach housewives.

This subject is raised again in Chapter 14.

### Regionality

One part of the target definition is particularly important for media decisions: regionality, or the importance of the different regions. Chapter 9 expands on this. Present sales or usage of the product should be broken down by regions (usually TV area). This pattern may be followed in the allocation of advertising weight or it may be modified.

### Seasonality

When to advertise is not a simple decision and is also discussed in more detail in Chapter 9. But as a routine in briefing it is advisable to record when, by months, sales of the product are expected. If the purchase decision is considerably earlier than sales, as with holidays, information about this should be available. The allocation of advertising weight over time must then be agreed. The important of advertising on special days or at special times should be noted.

## Creative objective

The brief given to the creative group, and the way they set about meeting it, must be well understood by the planner. What proposition or benefits is the advertising putting forward? What are the advertisements going to say? This area is often a major factor in media choice.

The creative group head – or whoever produces the advertising idea which is the heart of the campaign – often thinks of the message in media terms. He 'sees' a television commercial, or a press advertisement, not an abstract statement.

His first thoughts are not the last word in media selection, they are the beginning of the discussion which is the media planning process.

In more detail, the media planner must take into account how the creative man at this early stage evaluates the different media. Does it matter whether colour is available? Is the product to be demonstrated in action? Is a detailed story to be told or is the treatment a simple one? The media considered feasible by the creative group should be listed, and so should their first thoughts about commercial lengths or advertisement sizes.

## Media objectives

Sometimes a separate heading on the brief states the 'media objectives' and here some nonsense is entered like 'maximum cover with optimum repetition'. It is difficult at this stage of planning a campaign to be precise about what media exposure achievements are possible, or about the characteristics required of the distribution of advertisement exposures, or on the most effective attitude to adopt about competitors. The media planner himself usually has to determine the media objectives, or at least has to put up alternatives from which account control and advertiser can choose. If it were easy to state the media objectives confidently and precisely, much of this book would not need to be written.

It is at the time when the marketing and creative objectives are being settled that the team should consider whether this is a campaign in which the advertisements should be seen by as many people as possible, if only a few times each, or a campaign which should concentrate on a limited audience, with heavy repetition. Response functions are a way of distinguishing these objectives and are discussed in Chapter 9, where this balance has to be determined in the media plan, and in Chapter 16, in a more technical way.

*Research*

Within a year or 18 months more should have been learned about how media work for this product. Research is often planned to investigate how the market has changed, and to see whether marketing and creative objectives have been reached. The planner should always initiate or be included in discussions about what tests or post-campaign research are being planned. He should try to get media performance assessments built into this research. This subject is raised again in Chapter 12.

*Trade advertising*

If the budget allows for direct advertising to the trade we should go again through the headings in the brief to clarify the requirements of the trade campaign.

# 8 HOW MUCH TO SPEND?

*A discussion of the advertising budget. Suggested questions that help to determine the economical amount to spend on advertising. Comments on some of the methods now used for fixing budgets.*

Deciding how much money to spend on advertising is not like the budget decisions on raw materials or labour. You cannot see so many tons in the warehouse or count so many man-hours worked. You are really defending your existing sales (in the jargon, 'protecting your franchise') which means preventing lost sales, or creating additional sales — but you can hardly ever point precisely to which these are. We are back at the conclusion of Chapter 2 — that it is rare to know how advertising works. From this uncertainty spring all the difficulties of determining the advertising budget — and many of the problems of the whole industry. Nevertheless, the decision is actually made for every brand every year, though often with little logic or faith in advertising effectiveness.

The decision how much to spend is the advertiser's alone. The agency may be asked for its recommendation, which it gives with reasonable disinterest, since it wants to keep its client next year and not just this year. It is usually account control or the planner who gives this advice. The media department picks up a budget someone else has laid down, though it advises on media costs and performance.

Even within the company several people influence or take part in the budget decision, with a variety of backgrounds and motives.

In reality the freedom with which the *Brand Manager* exercises his supposed budget-setting authority is normally quite limited. His recommendation will be primarily dependent on the brand's marketing requirement. But even the requirements of *other* brands within the company affect the decision and it will also be altered by overall company financial considerations and to these he is unlikely to have made a major contribution. It may also be geared to that outcome which will most assist his own personal advancement. It is not unknown for the brand's advertising budget to be reduced in the short-term, for immediate profit improvement, with too little understanding of possible harmful effects in the long-term. *Company Management* is heavily influenced by the trained accounting mind with its due emphasis on safety, stability, the share price and proven margins. When this attitude dominates, marketing expenditure is only that which will be (or sometimes has been) generated by sales in the short-term, i.e. the relevant accounting period.

Theory usually assumes that an entrepreneur allocates his capital on raw materials, labour, promotion, etc., for a specific period in advance. Actually, cash shortages usually ensure that budgets are determined on a rolling basis. From one point of view, advertising maintains or causes future sales; it is in practice equally true that past sales cause the advertising budget.

It is not surprising that a number of myths or rules of thumb on budget setting have emerged and are sold by *consultants* – 'missionaries and charlatans' [8.1] they have been called. These provide the necessary reassurance when difficult decisions have to be taken on inadequate data. Some of these myths were soundly based when they were fathered, some are mis-generalisations, others sadly fail even the most cursory examination. It is frustrating that the world in which the budget decision has to take effect is seldom the same as that in which the decision is taken; seemingly helpful historical relationships between marketing variables never have quite the same current meaning. Theoretical studies, based on mathematical models, are usually the least relevant because they deal less than convincingly with cause and effect, let alone subjective matters such as advertising content. A review of the literature reveals disappointingly little that is really helpful.

Only the media budget is discussed here — what is spent on TV, press advertising and so on. At the first stage, production costs are usually included, but they will be separated later on. The advertiser of course also has to fix the rest of his marketing budget, which includes expenditure on trade and consumer deals, promotions, door-to-door distribution of samples and so on — each with its own cost, efficiency, long-term effect, etc. These should be examined as carefully as the advertising expenditure.

## A HOMELY EXAMPLE

Suppose you have been over-enthusiastic in planting lettuces in your garden. You decide to write to your friends and relatives and ask them to buy your lettuces. You look at your address book and find there are 100 people you might write to. Some are friends who live near you and who are likely to buy, others live far away. You arrange them into groups of ten. The first ten are the most likely to buy; the last ten, the most unlikely.

You decide that after paying for stamps, paper and envelopes, and taking into account the trouble to you, ten letters are worth writing only if you sell at least £2 worth of lettuces between the ten recipients. How many letters should you write?

You start with the most likely ten. Three days later, you find that you have made £6 — a profitable exercise. If all your friends responded like this, you would make £60. You now realise that you have to estimate your break-even point. Which group of ten will buy £2 worth of lettuces — or just over — whereas the next group would buy less than £2? You should write letters to the first group and those more likely to buy — but not the second group, and those less likely. You have only one experimental fact: the first group brought in £6. You also check your size of stock, £50, which looks quite enough.

At a guess, you decide you will break-even at the sixth group. You write fifty more letters. After a hectic week you find you have made £24. And the sixth group brought in just £2: you estimated the break-even point accurately.

*Was this example realistic?*

In this story you are the manufacturer. Two pounds spent on direct mail is a unit of expenditure on advertising. Up to the break-even point expenditure produces economical sales. Beyond this point some sales are produced, but no longer economically. If you knew this point you would know exactly how much to spend on advertising.

You were worried at one stage whether demand would exceed your stock. This can happen in real life. Advertising sometimes has to be stopped while the manufacturer catches up on production. You had to guess the sales to expect from different expenditures not covered in the experiment. This is typical of our ignorance about the response to advertising. In fact we hardly ever know as much as you did in this example.

You were able to define your target as the 100 names in your address book. Normally it is impossible to identify your target so exactly, and then reach them so precisely (through direct mail). It is also most uncommon to know that you have reached every prospect with an equal weight of advertising.

This example started and finished with letter-writing and the sale of your lettuces. You were not concerned with next year's crop or the influence of your letter on next year's sales. The advertiser should not be so short-sighted. Advertising usually works over much longer than one year: the sales observed now are in part produced by last year's advertising; advertising this year will assist sales in future years.

## FOUR QUESTIONS TO DETERMINE THE BUDGET

I recommend asking four questions about the budget. These approach it from different directions and rarely lead to the same answer, but they enable you to bracket the area in which a sensible answer lies. One question usually dominates the others but it is wise to ensure that this aspect does not settle the point on its own.

1    What can the product afford?
2    What is the advertising task?
3    What are competitors spending?
4    What have we learned from previous years?

*What can the product afford?*

This is not simply the question asked by a naïve advertiser or by a cynical agency, eager to draw from the product the last drop of advertising money. It is a request for a frank discussion on the budget for the product.

Every product is under an obligation to make profits. Profits are what remains from the sales income of the product after all the costs have been accounted for: manufacturing and distribution costs, other selling expenses and an allowance for overheads. The brand manager has in effect bills to meet from his factory manager, transport manager and so on. Such a calculation must be based on a sales forecast. Here is a paradox in this problem: the advertising budget is often based on a sum which assumes that sales are fixed − yet the object of advertising is to affect this sales figure.

The supply of money for advertising may be further limited by the cash situation for the firm as a whole. Only so much is available: it may not be prudent − or possible − to borrow more. Most firms are run to produce annual accounts which should show a reasonable profit each year. There are exceptions both ways: some firms require profitability to be maintained by quarters − a rather short time in marketing − others take a longer view and, especially when establishing a brand, are prepared to invest over several years. An annual cycle, or shorter, can be very hard on a product. It may go through a bad patch which, with sufficient faith from the management and promotions to the public, it would weather. Some firms actually practise what most advertising men believe: that advertising causes sales. Such firms will spend their way out of depression. The alternative, under a pessimistic management, can be to spiral into the ground, as advertising cuts cause sales losses which result in further budget depression. Such cuts in the advertising budget can take place at short notice. This can cause considerable harm to buying efficiency in the media department.

Advertising and profit are too often left alone to share out the tail-end of the budget. When profit takes a fixed percentage of turnover then what is over is for advertising: the 'residual method'. More expenditure on advertising is anomalously thought of as lower profits. This attitude is the reverse of the more expansionist philosophy: more expenditure on advertising leads to more sales at marginal manufacturing cost which in turn lead to higher profits.

*What is the advertising task?*

Before any kind of work is started, it is usual to agree on its objectives.

Advertising management should be no exception to this practice. Agreement on the advertising task reduces confusion, gets the team all pulling the same way, prevents subsequent disappointment and incidentally helps to determine the advertising budget.

Statement of the objectives leads to three questions: What media are likely to be chosen? At what cost do they reach the target? What number of exposures to the target might achieve the specified effect?

It is far too early at this stage to make even the broad choice between media. Nor is this the time for refinements, such as the actual publications likely to be used. Nevertheless a tentative media choice must be made for this purpose — if it is changed later this will only increase effectiveness.

The cost question can be answered with moderate accuracy. For example, suppose TV is likely to be used with 30-second commercials. At rate-card costs it will take about £20,000 to transmit one commercial at peak time over the whole UK network. The average rating achieved among housewives living in homes with ITV will be about 30. Thus 3.3 spots must be transmitted — at a rate-card cost of £66,000 — to reach each ITV housewife once on average. To allow for our buying some cheaper off-peak time, for volume discounts and other deals, some 20 per cent is subtracted from the rate-card cost. Thus we reach ITV housewives once on average by spending £53,000. A complication is that 'once on average' means a range of opportunities to see. Some housewives may see two or three commercials, others none. This, and the many differences between people, mean that only approximations are possible.

We do not know how advertisement exposures affect changes in people, but it is reasonable to bracket the desirable numbers of opportunities to see. One exposure over a year, for example, would be too little for most objectives. Two a week throughout the year may be more than enough. These two rates of spending cover a range of 1:100. Obviously the rate can be narrowed down to finer limits than this. For example, suppose it is decided the task can be accomplished on one exposure a month. Multiplying by twelve the previous figure gives a budget of nearly £636,000.

Next, trade advertising needs have to be settled. And we must decide whether this amount of consumer advertising will make a convincing story for salesmen to tell the trade — 'We're spending £¼ million on television in the launch alone, and after that...'.

*What are competitors spending?*

Like the first question, this one looks very cynical. If the object were only to equal competitive advertising expenditure, without inquiring into its suitability or effectiveness, it would be a disappointing question. But its purpose goes rather deeper: it reminds us that we are not alone in the market. Usually our brand competes with two to ten major brands and many smaller brands. This means that consumers will be bombarded by the competition as well as wooed by us. We have to shout to be heard.

The advertiser should first define what market he is in. This is not as easy as it may at first appear. What does the consumer see as alternatives to our product? Perhaps not only those very similar products with different names (if such exist). There are other kinds of product which may be substitutes in the buyer's eyes.

Advertising expenditure data is measured by Media Expenditure Analysis Ltd, or MEAL. This company records what space or time each product buys and they extend this at card rates. This work also tells us which media competitors are using. Trend information is really needed — and a forecast of market development as a whole.

The share of market held by each manufacturer must also be known. This may be available from trade sources or from one of the services in this field — Nielsen, Attwood or TCA [8.2].

Several important conclusions can now be drawn. The first is the *share of advertising* (in expenditure terms). This can be seen at various possible expenditure levels, e.g. £100,000 will be 20 per cent and £150,000 will be 30 per cent if the total is £½ million. This admittedly ignores the media used, different efficiencies in buying and — most seriously — differences in the advertisements themselves.

A crude but useful rule of thumb is:

> The sales expected for our product are
> the same share of the market as our advertising share.

This rule follows from two lines of thought. Sales may reasonably be affected by advertising in proportion to the advertising seen. Or, suppose all manufacturers in the market operate in roughly the same way. The differences between them are mainly differences of scale — and we ignore here both the additional economies brought about by large-scale operation and also the share of market held by non-advertised brands. Each firm will have the same budget restraints and will allocate about the same proportion of its budget to advertising. Thus our share of advertising will turn out to be the same as our share of market.

A useful discovery from this analysis will be the advertising-sales ratio accepted as average in this product-group. For example 'In this market, advertising expenditure is usually 2 per cent of sales value at retail level'. If we depart from this average ratio it should be for good reasons. If we are below it, we should have a superior or cheaper product, a better image, better distribution, offer the trade a higher margin and so on. Or we must be deliberately risking under-expenditure. If we are above it, we must be compensating for some defects or attempting to expand our share of the market.

Nielsen [8.3] examined 17 brand leaders in grocers, of which 13 increased their share of market between 1965 and 1971, and four showed no significant change. On average, the first group increased considerably their share of advertising in their markets between these years, the second group also increased their share of advertising but less so. Those brand leaders that were declining had falling advertising shares. Such associations do not *prove* that positive sales changes followed the increased advertising expenditure, but are suggestive.

For example, the advertising-sales ratio was studied in my agency for a particular product group for several brands over several regions. A graph was plotted of the change in sales on the previous year against this ratio. These points were scattered about a line which indicated that an advertising-sales ratio of £10 per thousand pounds weight of product sold was associated with stable sales, whereas £20 per thousand pounds weight was associated with a sales increase of 10 per cent. This information was used to show that some levels of the advertising budget were too low and would probably result in the long-term decline of the brand.

Studying shares of market and shares of advertising and their changes in this way can sometimes disclose useful regularities. While it would be an overclaim to say that the sales resulting from advertising can be predicted, it may look like this. The relationship studied by Moroney at Unilever and which has since been widely tested [8.4] is the 'dynamic difference'. This is a plot of

Sales share in year 2 minus sales share in year 1

*against*

Advertising share in year 2 minus sales share in year 1.

In some markets the results indicate both the sales changes associated with advertising changes and the effect of other differences between brands in the market (better product, better image) which also push up sales.

Notice that when several large manufacturers are all jostling for increased market shares, and smaller manufacturers are trying to break into the big time, then more than one firm will try to advertise above its market share. The result is escalation of total advertising spending in this product group. This escalation can also result from deliberate policy. For example, when a competitor launches a new product we may deliberately overspend in order to depress his sales result and profit or at least distort them.

## What have we learned from previous years?

It used to be said that advertising budgets were most likely to be the same as last year. In the early 70s this was in fact so. Since the upheavals of 1975 and 1976 it is no longer true. But since we might return to such practice it is worth recording why.

In the second edition these reasons were given. First it is difficult to argue convincingly for departure from a previous budget pattern which has functioned satisfactorily. Second, established products are relatively unresponsive to changes in budget level; consequently experiments with higher budget levels tend to be disappointing in the short-term, and this is how they are normally judged.

If things are not stable then changes are indicated — usually in an obvious direction. Last year's budget may have to be cut, because of a market decline, for example. Perhaps a competitive product is growing and our brand has been allocated the task of producing more profit on a smaller advertising budget in order to finance the launch of another brand. Perhaps the market is growing or a positive reaction to advertising has been measured, and these may justify an increased budget this year.

The agency can learn also from the market's reaction to competitive brands. Major new introductions, including regional tests, in our product field should be monitored. Information over several years is more helpful than over one.

So much for the years of stability. Since 1973 many established brands have got by with much less advertising spend than they received traditionally (there are new advertisers who have caused the total spend to hold up and recently to increase). The share taken by advertising of their total market budget has dropped. The beneficiaries have been trade dealing, discounting, promotions, advertising allowances etc., in fact, the retailer. It is believed by many marketing directors that these payments are essential and can be shown to produce sales immediately — the longer-term losses when competitors promote are ignored. They can point to the turnover of price-cut packs and in the weeks of promotion. Retailers meanwhile have been in unprecedented competition with each other, not on quality or improved products or convenience or range or service, not even on their own-label brands, but almost entirely on price. To the housewife — and to the Government — 'inflation' means shopping prices, and retailers have seized on this as the arena. The cost of course falls on the manufacturer, whose margins fall and whose marketing budgets, which used to allocate 60 or 70 per cent to advertising, may now allow only 30 or 40 per cent. The short-term logic behind this shift is strong, but the effect is to move many markets back to commodities, where good value means low price, not high quality.

Inspection of recent years therefore often shows products retaining sales share, or perhaps falling only slowly, with reduced advertising. Budget determination requires that we look not only at recent sales but at the structure of the market. Is loyalty decreasing? Are brands less differentiated by consumers? Is the power of the retailer to give or withhold an order to the manufacturer going to be the main factor, rather than demand from the consumer? In a word, will branding continue to matter? The question is outside the scope of this book, but is raised at this point in budget determination.

In order to learn as much as possible, deliberate experiments may be made with different budget levels. This is more common in the US than in this country, since a large number of experimental markets are more easily isolated there. It is hard to follow here the advice given by du Pont: 'Have at least six experimental areas, three for each of two levels. One will probably go wrong and you have two left with which to estimate sampling error.'

The regional structure of ITV provides a reasonably good basis for testing alternative TV advertising levels. Provided that the experiments are planned, controlled and measured properly theory suggests there is a good chance that meaningful results will be achieved which can be part of the material in a subsequent national budget decision.

In planning area tests to determine the best budget level it is obviously important to pay considerable attention to the experimental design. The cardinal points to observe are:

1   There must be a means of accurately measuring the changes generated by the experiment.
2   There should be an agreed basis for projecting the experimental results to a wider area, and prior agreement that the test areas are reasonably typical.
3   There should be adequate controls. The same measurements made in the test areas should also be made in more than one other area.
4   Experience suggests that an advertising weight test is unlikely to produce measurable results if conducted for much less than a year or if the budget change is less than halving or doubling. However, this is a generalisation and there are markets, e.g. cakes, where results are visible much more quickly.

Most experimental work points more to the *direction* of the optimum advertising budget rather than its *precise level*. It can also provide a better understanding of the relationships between the various marketing factors such as advertising, consumer and trade promotions, price, distribution and profits so as to arrive at a better overall balance. There is further discussion on effectiveness measurements in Chapters 12 and 16.

In practice there are many problems, not the least of which is finding the right balance between the length of test needed to produce reliable evidence and the time by which this evidence can be used in still relevant circumstances. This problem will always in the end be a matter of judgement but two suggestions are made. First, that weight tests may be much more rewarding with brands that have not yet reached stability, when consumer knowledge and experience are still fairly sensitive to the amount of advertising exposure. Second, that budget planning should be sufficiently flexible to implement a favourable experiment promptly rather than waiting for the next financial period when circumstances have changed.

We have found that area tests do not automatically answer all the questions to which they are applied. In particular they may produce unreliable, slow and insensitive results. Even in such a numerical area, advertising resists the scientific method. Great care should be used in interpreting the findings especially from sales data for stable products. Area tests are of most use when diagnostic information is also collected, e.g. by consumer research, especially when this links media exposure with sales and intermediate measures. Often such research is helpful even without deliberate experimentation.

*Putting together the answers*

These four questions are likely to produce rather disparate answers. For example:

1    £350,000 is all that is allocated in the preliminary budget.
2    £260,000 would achieve the advertising exposures regarded as desirable.
3    £400,000 will buy a share of advertising equal to the product's share of market.
4    £300,000 was spent last year — but there are indications that brand share is responsive to the amount of advertising support.

You can imagine the discussions which take place around the range of £400,000 to £260,000. Ultimately the decision will lie in the character of the firm. The conservative firm will settle at a low figure; the thrusting, expansionist firm will invest in its future.

## THE USE OF A MARKETING MODEL

This description of practical budget-fixing has not included a search for a break-even point on the lines of the lettuce-selling example. Manufacturers would like to find such an optimum, but they hardly ever know enough about advertising effectiveness to set about looking for it.

The budget for the brand was treated above as if it were based on a single forecast sales figure. However a range of possible values could be considered. For each sales figure there will be a different production, distribution and overhead cost total. The cost per unit will come down as the amount sold goes up, because the fixed costs are spread over more units. A table can be drawn up to show the amount we expect to sell at different levels of advertising expenditure. For each amount we can enter the total costs of making, distributing and promoting the product. The profit at each level can be worked out. The level which gives the maximum total profit is the optimum.

This is the beginning of a description of how advertising, sales, profits and other factors are related. Such a model can be made more complicated in various ways. For example the amount spent on advertising in previous years can be credited to the brand in later years according to some mathematical formula.

The use of such a model to assist practical budget determination is very uncommon. The difficulty is lack of knowledge about the central mechanism: the relation between advertising expenditure and sales. While this is so uncertain, our arguments may look more rigorous without actually being so.

In the US, various models are used and opinion about them is divided. Some feel that with care they can be extremely helpful, others that they are only suggestive and that experiments must confirm their recommendations; most do not use them. In the UK, market modelling under the name of econometrics has attracted attention and can be used to estimate whether past budgets were too small or too large (see Chapter 15).

In my opinion the model approach can be worth experimenting with and using as an aid to decisions. But I would give this advice only to a sophisticated manufacturer who has research data on the various mechanisms he intends to build into the model. Most manufacturers have neither such data nor the staff to apply this technique. They are best served by such an empirical, commonsense method as the four questions.


## THREE TRADITIONAL METHODS

### Fixed ratios

In some firms, it is a tradition that advertising takes so much per case sold, or per ton or per pound sterling. These methods do determine a budget but it is not recommended that they be slavishly followed. To set the budget by weight sold for example does not allow correctly for changes in packaging. If the weight per pack is reduced, such a rule could lead to lower advertising expenditure at the time when advertising is most needed. The rule can lead to too much being spent on advertising − or too little.

The rule which states that advertising takes a certain proportion of the sterling value of sales is the best of a bad bunch. It results in a fixed advertising-sales ratio. If the ratio is one which is near average for the industry concerned, this method leads back to advertising share being approximately equal to market share.

A fixed advertising-sales ratio can lead to a neat logical trap, which more than one analyst has fallen into. This is particularly the case if the sales concerned are forecast for the coming year. For then advertising increases in years when sales are expected to be up, and decreases in years when sales are expected to be down. Looking at the advertising and sales figures after the event, we see that the two are associated. It is tempting to conclude that we are observing the effect of advertising on sales: 'Every time you increased the advertising by £$x$, the sales went up by £$y$. So each pound spent on advertising brought in £$y/x$ in sales.' Of course we are actually observing the effect of sales on advertising, and $x/y$ is simply the advertising-sales ratio used. Similarly, advertising may be spread over areas in proportion to expected sales. An analysis of advertising and sales by area will then uncover this relation — which the advertiser himself put there!

## Minimum campaigns

Another method of deciding on the advertising budget is particularly common when TV is used. It is simply a traditional budget size or threshold: 'It's not worth spending less than £$x$ on TV'. The amount £$x$ is curiously different from one advertiser to another: some say £200,000, others £500,000. The method is based on a feel for the way TV works, but on the whole I do not recommend it.

## Media inflation

As media costs change — and we have seen that the direction is continually upwards — there is an argument for spending 'the same as last year, plus inflation'. This has been called the 'inertial method'. However sterling budgets for individual brands have not generally risen as fast as inflation; hence the real advertising impact for most major brands has fallen over recent years. Experience therefore suggests that the inflationary argument has not been particularly successful in increasing advertising budgets, or perhaps that brands at a later stage in their lives need less advertising support. The effect of not allowing for this rising cost may however be serious where the total market therefore declines. If the total market is not sensitive to advertising pressure then a brand that maintains its share of a reduced total is of course more profitable. Manufacturers hope they are in the second situation — but some too late find they are in the first.

## SOME SPECIAL CASES

### Launching a product

It is more difficult to get a new product, or a major change in an existing product, accepted by the consumer than to sustain acceptance of a well-established product. At least, such is the common belief. There are examples of new products gaining sales rapidly with little advertising (marijuana, stainless razor blades, $33\frac{1}{3}$ rpm records) but these usually have obvious sales points that newspapers and magazines treat as news items or which are easily passed on from person to person in conversation. For most products we cannot rely on word-of-mouth because the claims made for the product are not normally the subject of conversation — even between technically minded houseproud housewives.

Usually advertising a launch is a deliberate investment, like buying new machinery to make the product. We do not normally expect to recover all our investment in one year — a two or three year period is more usual. Thus 'What can the product afford?' does not mean now 'What can be spent if a profit has to be made at the year-end?' It means 'What should be spent this year in order to make the highest profits in the long term?' This can mean an advertising rate at least 50 per cent or 100 per cent above the eventual going rate.

A launch is a highly artificial situation. Not only are the sales force and trade untypically concentrated on the product, hopefully the consumer is too, through product promotion and sampling as well as advertising. As a result sales are often artificially high to begin with, as the pipeline is filled and some consumers who will not later stay with the product are persuaded at least to try it. To monitor this situation carefully and compare it with previous new product experience is obviously sound advice. The majority of new products in fact fail and it is an economy to decide early and accurately how our product is doing. Generalisable experience and good case histories are hard to come by; in this respect the US is more fortunate [8.5].

167

## A dying brand

'Milking' a brand during the last years of its life means taking from it the maximum profit while allowing its sales to decline. This policy does not always mean stopping advertising — which might seem the obvious policy. Total profits may in fact be increased if sufficient advertising support is given to slow down the rate of decline. This objective often requires a special choice of target audience and copy policy. If there is no intention of increasing sales it will pay to appeal only to loyal product purchasers.

## Corporate advertising

So-called prestige advertising is intended to change or emphasise a company's image rather than that of any one of its individual brands directly. Three of the four questions asked above are now irrelevant. The question of what the company can afford would lead us to consider sums which are very much larger than the amounts which might realistically be spent. It may be difficult to define who the competitors are. Modern companies are often so diversified that the list of other companies in similar fields becomes extremely long. The amounts they are spending in image advertising give little guidance. Finally, the amount learned from experience may be negligible since the effects of company image advertising are exceptionally hard to measure, but case histories are now more common [8.6].

The advertising task is left as our only guide. Who do we want to reach, and how often? Luckily the people involved in decisions on this type of budget (for example, the company chairman) are also well situated to decide whom they want to affect. They can also speculate quite reasonably about the effect of six insertions a year or six a month.

## Products with measured results

There are some products for which the relation between advertising and sales can be measured. For instance, some advertisements ask people to write in or complete coupons. These leads can be analysed to show which produced sales. Some products are sold almost entirely in this way in such fields as central heating, camera film and garden sheds. Store advertising can also lead to results which are accurately measured. The merchandise advertised is either sold or not sold; traffic through the department advertised increases or does not increase. In such cases the advertising budget can be fixed with a precision unavailable to most advertisers.

For example [8.7]: 'Mail order companies have extensive records of the results obtained from various media. These results only change marginally year by year and so very accurate forecasts can be made of the profit that will be obtained from (say) a 10-inch triple in a Tuesday edition of the *Daily Mirror* early in January . . . One probably . . . arrives at within 2 or 3 per cent of optimum profit in this investment, i.e. advertising appropriation.'

This book is not about direct response, and the lessons learned in these fields [8.8] are oddly at variance with traditional practice in display advertising. For example, small spaces in black and white with frequent changes of copy seem to give the best value, but are seldom used for packaged goods. It is therefore unlikely that in the budgetting problem very much can be transferred from direct response. The following quotation [8.9] gives apt, if gloomy, advice:

> 'Generally, it is not considered reasonable to use sales results as a basis of measuring advertising effectiveness, except where advertising is the dominant sales force, where results of advertising are quickly reflected in shipments and billings. Where these conditions do not exist, other yardsticks must be used.'

# 9 WHEN — AND WHERE?

*Determining when the advertisements should appear. The spread of advertising over the year and whether it should be placed continuously or in bursts. The spread of advertising across different regions, particularly the problem of allocating money to the different TV stations.*

## WHEN?

Of course, we would like to dominate with our advertising all the year round — but this is the fortune of very few brands. There is rarely enough money. We may choose to spread what money there is evenly, if thinly, over the year. Or we may concentrate it in certain periods. Such timing decisions apply to all aspects of promotion. Point-of-sale material, special tasks for the salesmen, a consumer offer, a change in the product — all these have to be timed and the advertising must be in step with these decisions.

Usually the timing of advertisements is considered after other media decisions have been taken: the actual advertisements are spaced in a separate procedure from deciding which media to use. For example we first choose which publications to include in a press schedule and how many insertions will appear in each. Later a date plan gives the exact day or week of each insertion. Similarly money is first allocated to TV areas and the actual amount to be spent each month or week is settled last. It is impractical to build time into these procedures from the beginning, however desirable this may look in theory.


*Sales and media patterns*

When considering how much we should spend, I recommended examining the sales of our product and of others like it. The way their sales are spread over the year should also be looked at. Remember that even when sales are continuous you will not see exactly equal figures over calendar months. February will be low, for example, because it has only 20 or 21 weekdays. Similarly, much TV data is recorded by 4 or 5-week periods which are given the names of the months. Here a long month has 25 per cent more days than a short one.

When we look at the sales pattern we must remember that for some products the decision to buy may be considerably earlier. And the decision itself may be discussed in the family some time before it is actually taken. It is, of course, the decision we want to influence, not the recording of the sale.

The patterns of availability and cost in media should be borne in mind. Christmas and summer discounts can be used to advantage. Special days or issues may cost more and the real value, as opposed to fashionable appeal, of such extra costs needs careful evaluation. As a generalisation, media owners have to make unpopular times specially attractive, while advertisers wanting a particular time are ready to pay well over the odds for it. Thus discounts are usually worth it and surcharges are usually over-expensive, to the ordinary advertiser.


*Advertising effect*

When advertising schedules are matched to the selected timing it is usually assumed that each advertisement has its greatest effect just after it is seen. Later it still has influence, but this decreases as it is eroded by failing memory and competitors' advertising. A TV, cinema or radio commercial is counted as seen when the insertion appears. Outdoor is assumed to work throughout its exhibition. The press is more complicated. The date of publication is not necessarily the day the advertisement is seen — though this is virtually true for a daily newspaper. A monthly still attracts new readers long after publication. The value of later readers is sometimes disputed, but coupon return evidence shows that advertisements are still working later than is sometimes imagined. We must allow for press advertising to be still carrying out its task for two or even three times the publication period.

## Launches and sales peaks

For some products there is little dispute when the advertising should appear. Attention and interest have to be created at the launch or special promotion of a product: a concentrated burst is essential. Equally with products that have sharp seasonal sales peaks it is normal to advertise at or just before the peak.

We might follow exactly the majority of the market in its timing of advertising. However, this means that our share of advertising is consistent. It is possible that share of advertising is more influential than the actual amount. We might therefore try to dominate the advertising for at least part of the time. This can be achieved by concentrating at some other time than the obvious one — often before our competitors' peak. This will be chosen rather than after it because it is hoped there will be some effect remaining during the competitors' burst. And we may have succeeded in influencing some consumers to decide definitely in our favour before competitors reach them. It is for this reason that advertising and promotion often get so far in advance of the apparently appropriate time.

## Spreading the peak

The timing of advertising may also be an attempt to influence the shape of the sales curve. Rather than getting a higher share of the existing peak, we may want to move some sales to a different time, or to create additional sales at periods which are now troughs. These are two of the classical uses of advertising. The first is to influence demand to a pattern more suitable for mass production:

smaller stockholding or longer production runs can result from less peaked demand. The second is to bring about additional demand by educating consumers. The introduction of any new idea or habit will work only if consumers are ready to take it up. It is only latent demand that can be stimulated. It takes time to re-shape an habitual pattern.

*Continuous or burst advertising?*

The real problem is the timing decision for an established product without special promotions or sharp sales peaks. Advertising might be continuous — which does not mean every day, but fairly evenly spaced. Or it might be in bursts. There are no rules about this decision. There is however a list of factors to bear in mind when evaluating each particular case. The choice will be based on a balance of conflicting arguments.

Most campaigns in the press and minor media are continuous. They are rarely over all 52 weeks, because this cannot be afforded, but an even spacing is quite normal over the 10 or 20 weeks of the campaign. This may be influenced by the difficulty of buying an effective burst in the Press (except in dailies) because of the long life of publications. It may also be the result of tradition — when newsprint was rationed, products got an allocation which was evenly spaced.

Most TV campaigns, in contrast, are usually grouped into bursts. Traditionally rapid retailer and sales response encourage this. There is however no real reason why other media should not be treated in the same way. Since the argument about this policy arises more often with TV, and because a TV spot can be seen only when it is inserted, the discussion is continued here in TV terms.

*Modelling the timing decision*

Like the budgeting task already discussed, the timing decision can be assisted by a modelling approach. This can be made more complicated than below, but essentially depends on four factors. The first two are practical and familiar, the second two are abstractions but essential if the model is to be realistic.

1    The *value* of each period, let us say months. This means putting a

number or weight on each month which represents the return the advertiser expects from reaching an individual then. For example, where a product group has a seasonal pattern, past sales in each month indicate their relative values.

2   The *cost* of reaching an individual in that month. Since demand for advertising is usually highest in spring and autumn, costs are often higher then, though as demand rises the troughs are tending to fill up.

3   The *decay* of advertising's effect. This is a very controversial subject, but it is often the case that analyses assume advertising has a large effect in the month it appears and the subsequent month and then a smaller and diminishing effect in following months, and such analyses provide a better fit to data on consumer measures and sales than analyses which assume all the effect is immediate. Common sense agrees with this assumption. The main subject of controversy is whether in addition to this medium-term effect (e.g. over several months) there is also a long-term effect (e.g. over years). Such an effect is confused with the general image of the brand, with the memory of outstanding campaigns and so on. Long-term effects are extremely hard to measure numerically.

4   The *response* to advertising. This subject will be dealt with in more detail in Chapter 16, but here response is defined as the differing result, in consumer measures or sales, of different amounts of advertising. Usually 'advertising' is defined in models as the 'stock' of 'lagged' advertising from the current and earlier months.

The first two factors may be examined on their own. It is useful to *index* the values calculated for each month (i.e. divide each one by their average and then multiply by 100) and the costs. This may show for example that May is a good sales month with an index of 150 (i.e. sales are then 50 per cent above the average). May might also be expensive, with costs perhaps 25 per cent above the average. When we divide the value index by the cost index (and multiply by 100) we produce a value/cost index which sums up the return we expect from spending £1 in that month. Here 150 x 100/125 = 120; since this is above 100 we see that the sales value is more above average than the cost. Similarly some months may be cheap but still not as good to advertise in because value is even lower.

In addition, it is recommended that we examine competitors' spending patterns. There is no rule which tells us to be on at the same time or before them or how to balance 'share of voice', i.e. our proportion of all the spend expected, against good value or low cost. But all three should enter our decision when to advertise.

So much for practical advice. But it is also possible to combine all four factors (value, cost, decay and response — competition rarely being allowed for) into a mathematical formulation. The details will not be described here, nor the way historical data may be used to estimate the shape and size of the decay and response functions. At present there is no generally accepted way to model this process; there is a certain amount of heat generated among the small number of people working in the area. Andrew Roberts and Stephen Prentice [9.1] have published an investigation of the effect of the four factors on the choice of the best timing plan. Two turned out to be crucial: decay and cost. The other two were less sensitive: response and value.

As with the budget, I recommend that common sense should usually be the method to arrive at timing decisions, because few advertisers have the resources to emerge unscathed from meetings with specialists in this subject. Some advertisers will however benefit.

The models frequently find that continuous advertising looks more effective than bursts. This is because the response functions derived rarely show thresholds in the region of interest, but are convex curves with diminishing returns at high weights. It does not take any mathematics to see that when this is the case we should spread our advertising, since two OTS at once are less effective than one now, one later: 'let the grass grow before you mow again'. The industry's historical preference for bursts is nevertheless strong and is expressed in the next section.

*The arguments for bursts*

A million pounds seems a large budget to spend on TV. But it buys only 0.2 per cent of the spots available. This means that of every 500 spots seen by an individual (about three weeks' viewing) only one is ours.

Of course, most of the other advertising seen is not directly competitive but it may be a barrier of distraction and irrelevance that our advertising has to penetrate. Hence the idea of a threshold: unless advertising for a brand reaches a certain level it will be wasted. The logical conclusion is to concentrate. A rule of thumb is that one exposure a week *is* the threshold, though some would say two a week. In research language this means achieving 100 or 200 TV ratings a week. It is frequently said that these rates have been proved to be successful: this means that a number of well-known brands have been built on such intensities of advertising. Since hardly any brand can afford this rate throughout the year it is normal for them to work in bursts of three, four (very common) or six weeks.

The retail trade may act as another threshold. If TV advertising causes some housewives to ask for the products seen on the screen (and it often does), do we want them to come into the shop in a continuous but unremarkable stream? Or will the retailer pay more attention if he gets a relatively large demand in the space of two or three weeks? Retail ordering and display caused by such a demand are themselves the cause of more sales — a familiar gearing.

There is evidence [9.2] that a concentration of advertising does raise maximum response to a higher level than the same amount of advertising more widely spread. This supports the widely believed Napoleonic dictum — to concentrate and dominate. An extreme form of this strategy is to place two or more advertisements on the same evening. This certainly attracts attention, which is probably half the battle. When a campaign consists of several commercials which gain from being seen together, the same conclusion should be drawn.

Another frequently quoted study [9.3] concluded that 'two exposures (between purchases) seems to be an optimum number for stimulating a purchase change (to our brand). One exposure alone runs the risk of being beaten by the competition; three or over has no greater stimulating power than two.' Thus for a product bought monthly, two OTS a month is suggested. When we cannot afford to be continuous at this rate throughout the year, bursting is indicated. On the other hand, the size of the burst should not be too large. The research from which this finding emerged was small-scale (255 housewives) and has not been repeated since 1966 (though attempts are being made to fund a larger version in the US). It was unusual because diaries were used to measure brand purchases and detailed media exposure, the method of analysis was unusually thorough and thoughtful, and competitive advertising was taken into account. The finding is very suggestive, especially in its insistence on the purchase interval. Though not conclusive for any particular case it can guide us on timing and even on budget size.

A special case is the advertiser with several brands sharing the same house name. He can indulge in umbrella advertising, i.e. the name may receive a benefit from the advertising of each brand. Such an advertiser can burst on each brand while co-ordination ensures that the house name receives continuous advertising.

## Objections to burst advertising

We might expect the advantages of burst advertising to be proven by experimental evidence. The experiments are after all not difficult to organise, and have indeed been tried. Unfortunately two familiar problems arise. First, that conclusions for one brand in its particular situation may not apply to another brand with other problems and opportunities. Second, short-term and long-term results are difficult to disentangle; other factors confuse the findings. Timing experiments are therefore frequently inconclusive.

The argument that brands have been successful with a particular policy does not eliminate the possibility that other policies would have been as successful or more. The traditional level of expenditure for a number of brand leaders has in real terms been falling over the years. Therefore rules of thumb about minimum exposures or expenditure are useful but not mandatory.

The argument that advertising should be concentrated has a converse. The periods in which we are not advertising become longer as a result. If domination works in our favour while we advertise, it works equally in favour of our competitors when they advertise. For every week we double the annual rate of expenditure there is a week when none of our advertising appears.

## The arguments for continuity

Mass market products are bought frequently — once a week is a typical average. The advertising seen nearest the time of purchase is the most likely to influence the sale. If two advertisements for the same product are both close to a purchase decision then one is wasted.

Advertising often serves as a reminder or reinforcement. It is not announcing anything new, it says to the current or occasional user 'We're still here, we're reliable, trust us'. The existing image of the brand is being maintained from several sources — by actual usage of the product, by packaging and point-of-sale material (if its marketing is consistent) and by the advertising itself (if the theme and treatment are stable). The brand is adequately served by advertising which is occasionally and regularly seen. There is no barrier or threshold against what is familiar.

The effect on the viewer of successive advertising impacts is difficult to study but is investigated in Chapter 16. It is there suggested that the second impression within a fixed time period usually has less effect than the first. Each should therefore be widely separated from the others, when it has most chance of acting like the first. In other words, bursts lead to diminishing returns. 'Greenacre didn't sell so well as might have been expected, for such a diabolical out-and-out crime as he committed; but you see he came close after Pegsworth, and that took the beauty off him. Two murderers together is never no good to nobody'. So Mayhew recorded the view of a nineteenth century running patterer, describing the market for his broadsheets.

It is possible that irritating aspects of a commercial (for advertising does not have to be liked to be effective) may be more noticeable and even harmful when it is seen frequently over a short period. A few viewers have written to contractors objecting to commercials seen in very heavy bursts. Contractors may consider this as detrimental to their business of attracting an audience. Just as a TV performer rations his appearances and avoids over-exposure, so perhaps should advertising.

*A compromise*

Retailers may be persuaded to stock and display a product because of advertising. If the budget has been temporarily exhausted these retailers are left without support and with a product which perhaps moves only slowly without advertising. This causes resentment which the manufacturer can ill afford. It may be wiser to continue with at least some advertising than to stop abruptly at the end of a burst, in other words to compromise between burst and continuous advertising.

Equally, an inflexible policy of bursts leaves a manufacturer unprotected against the introduction of a new product or other competitive activity. It is in practice harder to introduce an unexpected campaign than to strengthen an existing one as self-defence in these circumstances.

A rigid pattern of bursts also harms buying efficiency measured by cost per thousand exposures. When the buyer is restricted to a heavy expenditure in a particular period he is unable to avoid some of the worst times then, or to take some of the better buys available in other weeks. His negotiating position is undermined. Of course, the same is true of an evenly spaced requirement too strictly interpreted.

The effects on cover and frequency of different degrees of concentration can be analysed theoretically. It is possible to buy a continuous schedule of low cover but high repetition by repeating spots at the same times each week. A burst often forces the buyer to use many different times and so achieves higher cover. These considerations have less practical importance than the improved negotiating power which flexibility provides.

### Summing up

This discussion is necessarily inconclusive. Any one of the factors listed might dominate in a particular case. But the case for bursting, when it exists at all, is usually a strong and obvious one. For a going brand, with reminder advertising, bursts should not be exaggerated and the buyer should be allowed some flexibility over time.

## WHERE?

Next comes the question of allocating the advertising budget geographically. This problem always arises in television and radio, when the amount of money which should go to each region has to be decided. It is therefore discussed here in TV terms. The same principles apply to other media, especially outdoor and cinema, whose regional distribution is closely controlled. The national press offers some regional flexibility and obviously regional papers and magazines have this facility.

### The importance of different regions

The first decision must be on the relative importance of the different regions for our campaigns. Sometimes this is easy. The campaign may be extending gradually over the country and we want to cover at present only certain regions. There may be no distribution of the product in some areas. There may be advertising weight tests which determine the regional allocation.

The importance of a region may be defined by existing sales there — either of our product or of the product group. The advertiser's area sales data may therefore be vital, though it is surprising how often this information cannot be recovered. Such a policy rewards success: it has been called feeding the fat pig, or putting money where the profit is. Where areas do well, they are reinforced; areas doing badly are starved. This has obvious dangers and may be mitigated by the demographic weighting suggested next. An alternative policy is to decide to plug gaps in order to prevent a bad situation becoming worse.

The target may also be defined demographically, for example as housewives in ITV homes. We use the word 'importance' to specify the value to the advertiser of a typical individual in the region. The importance of the area is then the number of individuals multiplied by a weight for their importance. There are many ways the 'value to the advertiser' can be defined. Usually it is proportional to the individual's purchases in the product field. However, general demographic or economic indices may be used.

It is reasonable to examine several definitions, and to compare for example the distribution of present sales with that of the target. A compromise can then be struck between the two.

Naturally TV contractors compete for their share of expenditure. Much of their promotion is intended to present their own region in a favourable light. Some claim that they are typical of the rest of the country and therefore suitable for test marketing, whereas they might have been thought unusual. Not many London-based agency men are familiar with actual conditions in the remoter areas: it is in fact untrue that the Border TV region is populated only by sheep. Of other regions it is claimed that they have above average value, so that they should not be dropped if the budget will not cover the whole country. Much of this promotion is emotional, showing at least that the advertising business takes its own medicine even in problems which should really be solved on completely rational grounds. Much area promotion turns on matters of definition:

'Housewives in the North West spend more on food than do housewives in any other area.' *(Granada, 1968)*

'Southern shoppers are big spenders – second only to London.'
*(Southern TV, 1968)*

It is this competition for advertising budget which encourages various kinds of non-media support, merchandising services, research and so on, described in Chapter 4. Rate discounts are also important. It is often worthwhile to disturb an allocation and move money to a particular area if by so doing we qualify for an extra quantity or other special discount. An agency will therefore monitor expenditure carefully during the year – as well as review the proposed allocation – with this objective.

An allocation may leave some areas with a very small budget. This brings us back to the possibility already mentioned, that there is a threshold level below which expenditure is ineffectual. Even if unproven at the consumer's level, this belief might operate within the trade, i.e. at the retailer-representative level. It could be dangerous to leave the trade with too little support, so we might increase the allocation to the minimum level in light areas. Or we might cover some areas only, withdrawing completely from other areas and rotating those covered year by year.

Finally, allocations may be modified to take account of competition, either to match competitive expenditure or to avoid it and concentrate on some limited, profitable areas. We may also react to a competitor entering or testing in a region by overwhelming his advertising there with transferred spending of our own.

## Working out the area allocation

The most frequently used method of allocating TV money is to arrange that each area receives impacts, i.e. opportunities to see or TV ratings, in proportion to its importance. A common special case is when the areas are thought to be of equal value and each is to receive the same number of TVRs (an equal-impacts allocation).

It is easy to get confused about how the arithmetic to achieve this should be done. Another hoary problem here is what to do about the overlap areas, which are double-counted in the standard industry data. Without going into this particular difficulty, the general principles are easily explained by the example at the end of the chapter.

The first step is to agree for each area the forecast cost of buying

100 TVRs on the agreed criterion. This may be taken from historic data or by converting a forecast cost-per-thousand (see Example 1). The next step is to write down the TVRs to be achieved in each area in the correct *ratios* but at an arbitrary convenient level. For equal impacts, take 100 TVRs in each area. The budget is also needed at this stage. See Example 2, which explains how to do the sums.

It is recommended that costs *are* taken into account in this way, rather than simply dividing the budget in proportion to the importance of each region, as in Example 3.

Either allocation is open to objections. To *ignore* costs means that some areas of high value to the advertiser can actually get fewer advertising impacts, because they are also areas where TV is more expensive. To *include* costs means that an expensive area gets a higher share of the budget (see Example 4). At first sight the latter seems sensible, but it does mean that areas giving the advertiser better value get less reward and an expensive area receives an unduly large share of the money.

A potential source of confusion is whether or not a TV area is credited with the total of its overlap areas, i.e. where ITV homes can receive signals from two or more contractors. When London Weekend says, 'London accounts for 26 per cent of the homes in the country, yet we regularly hold over 30 per cent sterling share in fast-moving package goods: product fields like fabric conditioners, yoghurts, instant coffee and toothpaste', then they are including all the overlap areas round the home area. When these are shared out equally between the contractors London has only 22 per cent of all the ITV homes. So the argument why the London contractors should get more than 22 per cent of ITV's revenue (as they do) has three parts. First, as just explained, Londoners buy relatively more of some nationally distributed products, so the area is more valuable to these national advertisers. This is true whether the overlap areas are included or not. Second, for some specialised products, e.g. airlines or financial advertising, the London market is so exceptional that some advertisers use TV only in London. Third, as a result of these demands, the London ITV contractors can set their rates higher than the national average; advertisers who require equal impacts over the country therefore have to pay relatively more for London.

So a contractor with exceptionally good ratings or a low rate card, trying to increase his revenue, may ask himself, 'Should I try to get the ratings down or my rate card costs up?' If this question baffles him —

and who can blame him — he tries other ways of getting his area selected or favoured by the advertiser [9.4].

The worst aspects of this anomaly can be partly corrected by the flexible system of strategic budgeting explained in Chapter 11 where buying is looked at in more detail. Meanwhile the method arouses natural indignation [9.5]:

'These stations (the four smallest) can deliver (in June 1968) at a minimum, 110 impacts for the average cost of 100 elsewhere, or something like 140 compared with London. Yet time and again manufacturers prefer to spend their money where they get less return for it. In some cases no doubt this may be due to the lack of area sales analyses, so that manufacturers simply do not know what these areas are worth to them. But for the most part the tendency can be ascribed to indifference, the result of ignorance.'

The full answer to this dilemma must come from an understanding of the sales return expected from different levels of advertising. Meanwhile it is worth looking at the additional impacts that can be bought in the cheaper areas at the cost of a little reduction in the expensive areas.

## Example 1

In the Midlands, the rate-card cost per thousand housewives in October 1973 was 114p. Since there are 2,868,000 housewives there in ITV households (Establishment Survey, January 1974, including overlap) the cost of buying 100 TVRs in the Midlands is £3270 (1.14 x 2868).

Similarly in the Southern area the cost per thousand was 122p; there are 1,508,000 ITV housewives there and the cost of 100 TVRs is £1840.

## Example 2

Suppose it has been agreed that a housewife in the Midlands has only 80 per cent of the importance of one in the South; this may for example be the conclusion from sales or distribution data. We therefore decide to allocate our impacts in the ratio 80:100. The budget is £25,000. We then tabulate as shown in Table 18. In column 3 of this table we enter the cost of achieving the TVRs in column 2, i.e. £2616 is 0.8 x £3270.

Table 18

| Region | TVRs in proportion | Cost | Final TVRs | Final budget |
|--------|--------------------|------|-----------|--------------|
| (1) | (2) | (3) | (4) | (5) |
| Midlands | 80 | £2616 | 449 | £14,677 |
| Southern | 100 | £1840 | 569 | £10,323 |
| | | TOTAL £4456 | TOTAL | £25,000 |

Table 19

| Region | Importance, weighted '000 | Importance, % | Final budget |
|--------|---------------------------|---------------|--------------|
| (1) | (2) | (3) | (4) |
| Midlands | 2294 | 60.3 | £15,075 |
| Southern | 1508 | 39.7 | £ 9,925 |
| TOTALS | 3802 | 100.0 | £25,000 |

The total of £4456 has to be multiplied by a factor of 5.61 to give the budget. We therefore multiply column 2 by this factor to give column 4, the actual TVRs we expect to buy; column 3, multiplied by the same factor, gives the allocation in column 5.

*Example 3*

We continue with the same data to show the effect of ignoring costs (see Table 19). In column 2 of this table, the importance of a single housewife in the Midlands, 80 per cent, multiplies the number of housewives to give the weighted importance of the area. These figures are given as percentages of the total to arrive at column 3 and hence the final budget.

*Example 4*

The second allocation gave Southern 539 TVRs (9925 x 100/1840), less than the first allocation.

The first allocation gave Southern 41.3 per cent of the budget, more than the second allocation.

## Modelling the area decision

Just as with timing, the area decision can be modelled. In fact here the models are simpler, since the areas are independent, whereas months are not. That is, adding money to the Southern area in the example just given affects sales in the Midlands only by reducing the budget there. But adding money to April by taking it from May has two effects: it reduces the budget in May but also benefits sales then in so far as April advertising has a lagged effect then. This is one reason why the regional allocation was the first to benefit from computerised systems. The second reason is that some routine methods already exist (ratings in proportion to value, equal ratings, budget in proportion to value) so planners are used to an allocation being calculated.

The various methods of modelling all start with the *value* indices and the *costs* which are defined in the same way for regions as they were above for months. The value index most commonly used is proportional to sales, but we can of course also allow for the strategy of building up weaker areas simply by giving them a higher value. It is then easy to work out the *value/cost* index as before, so we can sort out the areas into those where a pound looks like giving a good return and those where value is low or cost high or both.

We next need some criterion on which to make the allocation. As pointed out above, we need an assumption about the return or response to different weights of advertising. Various computer models are available, for example AASAM at Beecham and SORBA sponsored by Scottish Television [9.6], each of which differs from the others at this point. They may make other assumptions too, perhaps allowing for competitors' expected weight, the stock of advertising left over from the previous year, different costs of delivery to or profit from each area, a minimum level if we are to advertise at all and so on. In effect, the models put more money into the areas with a high value/cost index, and the assumption made about response determines how much more.

185

In my own agency we have had for a decade a computer program called BAR (Budget Allocation by Region) which calculates various allocations. Rather than making a single assumption about response, a number of assumptions are made so that the outputs can be compared. Standard allocations are also worked out (budget in proportion to importance, TVRs in proportion to importance, equal impacts). The alternatives can be inspected so that a choice is based on results as well as on the underlying assumptions; I personally find this preferable to choosing an assumption without knowing its implications.

These allocation models are more common than those which advise on allocation over time, but they are still rarely used. The reasons are the inconvenience of using a model at all, uncertainty about the response assumption — and, a more sophisticated comment, that the overall benefits calculated by the model itself seem to be small (5 per cent overall improvement is exceptional) while sometimes the recommended allocation is drastic, e.g. no advertising in London. Nevertheless I recommend that a model should be used if available. It does the arithmetic (not an entirely trivial advantage), it rewards cheaper areas, it forces us to be logical, it suggests improvements. But we do not have to accept the output uncritically — more on this in Chapter 15.

# 10 THE MEDIA PLAN

*A suggested procedure by which the planner takes into account all the relevant factors in his recommendations how advertising money should be spent. How media should be evaluated and whether more than one medium should be used. The drawing up of the media plan for approval by the advertiser.*

## APPROACH TO THE PLAN

We now come to the central point of this book: making the main media decisions and agreeing the criteria for detailed scheduling and buying. I draw together here the threads of some earlier discussions and anticipate the detail which follows later.

The verdict for which media owners have been anxiously waiting may be reached quickly, using conventional wisdom and with little real consideration. In the short run this is easiest for the agency. Many plans resemble the dinosaur: a pea-sized brain followed by yard upon yard of analysis, fake justification and arithmetic. But a conscientious agency will take trouble and time over their media choice, will methodically consider all the alternatives, will allow for innovation and will record their recommendation briefly but logically as described below.

The discussion in this chapter is summarised by checklists in the

Appendices, which should help as a practical tool to ensure that nothing is overlooked. It is a reminder – not a set of mandatory instructions. Each marketing situation is unique; each product has its own problems and its own objectives; so no one set of rules can cover every eventuality. Advertising is not so much a science as a branch of show business. Persuading people to buy is not always accomplished by repeating what has been done before.

Nor is the checklist a job definition for one person – the planner – but an outline of the work to be done by the whole team. It is divided into three parts. First, the briefing or discussion by the planner with the client, client service people and creatives on one hand, and with the buyer on the other hand. The second part is about media evaluation, when the planner and buyer turn over in their minds the reasonable alternatives. Third, the media plan itself, which records the agreement reached by the team. For simplicity, I write from now on as though the planner is working on his own, to avoid constant repetition of the need for teamwork.

A fuller checklist on one aspect of this process, selecting the main medium or mixture of media, has been published by the Media Circle [10.1].

Before settling down to write the media plan, the planner may well check with other people in the agency that the work he is doing is still consistent with theirs. He may write a *media strategy statement* which outlines his plan without going into details. This will record his understanding of the creative requirements, e.g. length of commercial, budget size, target definition, the analyses of media data he intends to have done and so on.

Media planning is more difficult even than deciding how much money to spend on advertising. There is little conclusive evidence about the effectiveness of different media, or about the best way of spreading money over areas or over time. Opinions differ how much the plan should be logical and numerate and how much it should depend on intuition. For example, the Institute of Practitioners in Advertising sponsored an excellent book on this subject [10.2]. Its Foreword, by the President of the IPA, states confidently that media planning 'has become a science over the past few years'. Its author calls it more modestly 'a fairly new art'.

Essentially, the classification of planning as a science assumes that we can express our knowledge about advertising, media and creative objectives as numbers. I believe we should try to do so but that we are bound, more or less, to fail. The classification of planning as an art assumes that we make an intuitive judgement about how advertising is to work in this particular case and that we allow creative people, who are after all doing the influencing or selling, a considerable though non-numerical part in the decisions. This whole subject has been debated frequently and in depth [10.3] and is discussed further below, particularly in Chapters 15 and 17.

## MEDIA EVALUATION

We start with a reasoned evaluation of the media available. At each stage of this checklist the medium is compared with the requirements of the brief. The objects of the evaluation are:

1    To see which media are feasible.
2    To pick the main medium.
3    To prepare for the decision on how it should be used.
4    To see whether there are suitable supporting media if required.

### Creative suitability

There may be obvious reasons why a particular medium is specially suitable for the campaign or another is unsuitable: a coupon has to be included or the absence of colour is critical. Often the preference of the creative group is not backed up by concrete evidence but they have strong views nevertheless about the media to use and those not to use. The media planner must not disregard these feelings. The agency is not in the business of reaching consumers with exposures of advertisements (which tends to be the media department's natural criterion), but in the business of selling the product. So if the creative choice looks at all reasonable in media terms, it is usually sensible for the planner to accept it. There is more on this point in Chapter 17.

Sometimes the creative choice is unreasonable and may have been reached without full consideration of the alternatives. So the planner should always go through the systematic search now described. If it throws up a case for other media, he should point this out. Even if he is overruled, he may succeed in getting experiments or other research carried out this year so that he can put forward a more substantial case next year.

*An idea*

Sometimes a media idea, or better an idea which involves media and creative content, is 'obviously' right or simply a novelty which is expected to attract attention and so work. A press advertisement in the shape of the product, using publications that have never before carried this type of advertising, a radio commercial announcing 'officially' there is now no shortage of the product, a TV commercial that starts with silence and a black screen, a poster that looks like a shop window and so on. Sometimes a change is as good as an increased budget.

*Proven effectiveness*

When there is evidence that a particular medium is the most efficient, the choice is obvious. This evidence may come from tests on our own product or from a study of competitors' activities.

The advertiser often insists on using the same medium as before, even without testing its effectiveness. The best predictor of an advertising schedule is the schedule for the previous year. This is not always laziness. It is partly because the media scene is not very different from year to year: media change is usually dictated by a major shift in the market place, a new medium, a new definition of the target, or a new advertising idea. Advertisers resist change because it involves more risk than to continue with a proven, viable strategy. Past success using a particular medium is not decisive — another policy might have done even better. This objection is facile. A profitable operation should usually be continued until a convincing case has been made for a better solution. On the other hand tests are quite likely not to produce conclusive results, and rather than waiting for evidence which might not arrive, we sometimes decide to switch boldly to another medium.

*Availability and timing*

The type of product or the copy claim may prevent the use of a medium — this is most likely to rule out TV, on which, for example cigarettes are not advertised. The flexibility required by the advertiser, for example being able to cancel or change advertising at a few days' notice, may also rule out a medium — for example it may make colour press impossible.

There are other constraints on the media used. It may not be feasible to spend all the money in a particular medium within the period of the campaign. Advertising for one medium cannot perhaps be got ready in time, even if the media owner were prepared to break his own rule for the latest date for receiving it.

*Regionality*

If regional flexibility is required, this will count against press — with its present facilities — and Radio Luxembourg.

*Competition*

'We can't come off the box, that's where our competitors are.'

'Look, there's no advertising for this product in women's magazines: let's dominate there'.

Of the two policies — match the competition or avoid it — the first is more common in media choice. This may be because the main purpose of the advertising is defensive — to reassure existing buyers and defuse competitors' attacks. It may also be a fear of leaving him to dominate a medium. Or the medium normally chosen is simply the most suitable for that product group. Or the consumer and the trade have come to expect the advertising to be in that medium and look for it there, so it works best there; on the same principle, shops often do better together in the High Street than scattered over the town.

These arguments apply to the large advertisers: McDougalls will not leave Spillers to be the only large flour manufacturer on TV, nor Cadburys leave TV to Mars. But for small budgets it could be inefficient to hit the competition at knee-level. A small advertiser might do better to dominate a less used medium.

*Effect on the trade*

It can be important that the advertising reaches the trade — in its widest sense. And, that the media plan makes a good story for representatives to tell retailers. Of course, advertising in the trade press may be run in parallel.

## Other aids from media

Some of the other services offered by media, such as merchandising support and research, were outlined in Chapters 4 to 6. These aids may fit into the agency's requirements and may be taken into account in the choice of medium. More often they do not affect broad media choice but are the equivalent of a cost reduction or promotion for the medium.

## Media representatives

It would be unfair to the representatives who sell media to agencies to leave them out here as a factor. A good representative should not be able to get a bad vehicle on to the schedule, but he may make the difference between two good vehicles. He does this by being aware of the product's needs and showing how his medium fulfils them.

## Cost per thousand and cover in the target

I have left to the last the cost of reaching the target. This is a complex subject which is dealt with in more detail in Chapter 11 and Part 4. It is often critical in choosing within a media group (for example, between newspapers) but difficult to use systematically in the much more important choice between media groups. This is because advertisement exposure is the criterion usually employed in quantifying cost effectiveness, whereas sales effectiveness, which should be the criterion, is elusive. The range of costs of exposing advertisements on TV or on posters is over 50 to 1, yet it is often right to use most the medium which appears on this basis to be the more expensive. If advertisement exposure were used strictly, colour advertisements in the press would rarely be bought, and the smaller space sizes would usually be preferred. Conventional measures of cost effectiveness are only one factor in the media decision: quality must be taken into account as well as quantity. For broad media decisions great precision in cost calculations would be out of place.

Average cost figures need revision before they can be applied in a particular plan. They are a good starting point but may be misleading. Three adjustments should be made to these crude costs per thousand:

*1   The effect of the target definition.* Costs over *all* adults or *all* housewives are irrelevant once a particular group has been selected as the target for advertising. All that matters is the cost of reaching this target. The number of other people reached is irrelevant; so is the idea that these are wasted, unless irritation is going to be caused by these exposures. An example of the effect of evaluating two publications on a target definition rather than on all housewives is given near the beginning of Chapter 14.

The figure for the number of readers or viewers in the target for each medium or publication is necessary not only for working out its cost effectiveness, it also shows how much of the target the medium covers. This is itself an important factor. It is common to pick the medium which covers a large part of the target on its own. For the same reason, press scheduling often starts by picking a 'banker' publication, i.e. one that has high cover of the target at a reasonable, but not necessarily minimum, cost.

*2   Realistic costs.* Average rate card costs may need adjustment. The actual commercial length or space size likely to be taken must of course be used. Fixing on TV or special positions in the press should be borne in mind. The discounts or deals the buyer expects to negotiate should be taken into account.

*3   Advertisement exposure factor.* The conventional units of media exposure are TV ratings, circulation, readership, passing a poster site and so on. It is better not to be content with these but to use units that are closer to 'open eyes in front of the advertisement'. This makes the comparison fairer between media groups and between vehicles, though it by no means removes all the differences. When such a factor is expressed as a number it is an example of a media weight, a concept that is dissected in Chapter 17.

The three factors just listed can be combined to obtain a more relevant measure of cost effectiveness than average cost per thousand. The index recommended is called VIP, or Valued Impressions per Pound. It is also called the score-cost ratio. We have already met its equivalent in Chapter 9 — value/cost:

$$\text{VIP} = \frac{\text{Readers (or viewers) in target x Media weight}}{\text{Cost}}$$

This calculation is described in more detail in Chapter 15. It is the inverse of cost-per-thousand, i.e. the *higher* it is, the *more* efficient the medium.

## ONE MEDIUM – OR SEVERAL?

When each medium-type has been compared with the requirements of the brief all the information has been collected on which the main medium can be selected. Often this choice is obvious: one of the factors just listed dominates the others. The first three are particularly likely to force the choice: availability, creative suitability or proven effectiveness. Even if the choice is not easy, it has to be made at this point.

We must not expect every plan to be reached in the same way. Sometimes a factor that plays no part in one plan, dominates the next. The checklist ensures that each element gets considered. Media planners can be trained; the advertiser can be reassured that the job has been done thoroughly; some uniformity of approach is possible; quality control is feasible. But the output of planning cannot be standardised.

When the decision requires real heart-searching or a confrontation between protagonists in the agency of two different media then it is likely that the choice is finely balanced. There may be nearly equal arguments on each side. The decisive factor is usually inspection of rough creative work in each medium, if necessary pre-tested. The planner can propose the numbers, 'Do we want *this* exposed five times or *that* three times?' The final decision should be the account director's. A test might be proposed of the medium which loses.

Media planning is always a compromise: to meet any one objective adequately is to fall short at another. Figure 9 indicates the tug of war – of which the media planner is at the centre.

The advertiser and creative group may call for longer commercials, or bigger spaces in the press. They often prefer colour to black and white, they may want bleed and special positions. In a word, they want impact. But the same advertiser is likely to say that he wants a longer campaign. He is not satisfied with 24 weeks, he wants 36. The bursts should last not three weeks at a time, but four weeks. At the same time it is important to get high cover. There is pressure to put more publications on a press schedule, to add a second medium. And there must not be too long between impressions. More insertions and domination are asked for in each medium used.

194

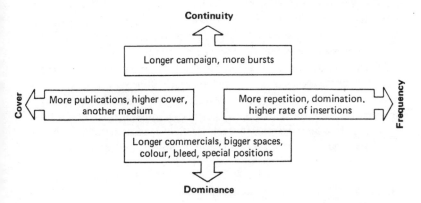

*Figure 9*

We have come back to the setting of media objectives, which was hard to do at the briefing stage. It is only when the choices available are seen as mutually exclusive, requiring reconciliation within a fixed budget, that repetition, a second medium, the extra cost of bled advertisements in the press and so on can be sensibly discussed. It is the planner's job to find the point of balance. Again, this has to be by judgement, just as the main medium was chosen. No model or calculation is going to provide more than illumination.

Finding equilibrium in this balance of forces is best done by trial and error. For example the buyer writes a schedule with the advertisement sizes first suggested. Then by analysis or experience its main characteristics are evaluated. The planner decides how near these come to meeting the campaign objectives and in which direction modification is most required. He gets a new schedule written. He attempts to satisfy his own feeling for the appropriate solution, and to meet the requirements of the rest of the team.

Once the main medium has been chosen we have to decide whether it should take the whole budget. To assist this decision the next step should be to estimate the media results of spending all the budget on the selected medium. Full precision here would require the writing and evaluation of a realistic schedule in the medium. This is not necessary at the broad planning stage: it is enough to make an estimate of the cover which will be produced in the target population (based on experience) and of the average number of impacts or impressions (based

195

on the VIP and budget size). This analysis may show that there is an important part of the target not covered; there may be long periods in the year advertising cannot be afforded; or the whole story cannot be told in this medium in the way the creative group want.

There are various conventional solutions to the choice of a second medium. Often magazines are used to reach upper social grades who watch less TV; cinema or radio are used to reach younger age groups; posters are used to extend a campaign over time; magazines are used to add colour and so on. In each particular case the disadvantages and advantages of a multi-media schedule must be evaluated as follows.

*Arguments against a second medium*

1    *Loss of domination.* A second medium should not be used unless there is a satisfactory campaign in the first. Concentration in the preferred medium gives the best chance of out-gunning the competition and building up a large number of repeated, effective exposures.

Any other medium which might be used will by definition have lower cost-effectiveness than the first. Only in the case of seriously decreasing returns in the first medium is there a case for switching money out of it. The planner should ask questions like 'Are you satisfied that someone should see her tenth TV commercial — or would you prefer that someone else, who would otherwise see no advertising, saw her first press advertisement?'

2    *Additional production costs.* To use a second medium requires the time, thought and cost of preparing additional advertisements.

*Arguments for a second medium*

1    *Wider cover.* Usually a single medium does not give everyone in the target an adequate exposure to advertising. There is heavy repetition on some people, while many of the others are at best lightly exposed though they could be reached adequately with the second medium. Consideration of the second medium could therefore involve a new target definition: those not yet properly exposed to our advertising, or those not sufficiently reached by a competitor. This point is currently a pre-occupation for television

campaigns, where a normal campaign reaches light viewers (30 per cent) seldom and of course does not reach non-viewers of the campaign (10 per cent) at all. These people account for more than 40 per cent of purchases in some product groups.

2 *Greater effect from two media.* In some cases the effect of two media reaching the consumer has creative benefits neither can give alone. For example, a TV commercial may demonstrate a product and tell the viewer to study the details and perhaps fill in the coupon in a press advertisement. Or a cheap poster may trigger off recall of the main point of a more expensive TV commercial. The use of two media may convey an impression of size and domination: 'They're everywhere: they must be important'. This effect could be particularly important with the trade.

3 *Wider media experience.* Using several media gives the opportunity to learn more about advertising for the product. The tests carried out with a second medium may lead to a case for a media switch being made next year. Media owners become more anxious to give service when they see other media being used, or their own being given a chance.


*Budget allocation to a second medium*

If a case is made for a second medium — or a third — the proportions of the budget to allocate to each have to be decided. Again, estimates of cover and of the average number of impressions produced at various sums of money are required. A compromise has to be found.


## THE MEDIA PLAN

Once the agency is agreed on its media policy, the decisions reached must be recorded. The media plan is a document which must convince the advertiser that a logical recommendation is being made; it must inform the buyers who are to execute the plan exactly what is required of them; it must be easily referred to by other users in the agency.

The plan may be either a part of the agency's overall documentation presented to the advertiser or may be put forward as a separate document. The contents of a media plan are now outlined when it is designed to be used on its own. It therefore summarises the relevant parts of the media brief. Since it is to be read by non-media people, details for specialists should be kept to appendices.

1   *Description.* The media plan should start by naming the advertiser, product and period of the campaign. It should give a brief description of the campaign itself: is this the consumer campaign only or is trade advertising included, for example. The author of the plan and its date of issue should not be omitted.

2   *Media brief.* The plan should recall in outline the marketing and creative strategies agreed, the budget allocated and any seasonal requirements. The target audience should be stated in media planning terms and the regional requirements should be recorded.

3   *Media recommendations.* The media objectives and strategy finally agreed should be described. This makes clear whether the campaign is to concentrate on a limited part of the target and achieve as many impressions as possible there, or whether high cover is intended at the expense of repetition, or what compromise is recommended between these two.

The plan reports the evaluation made of the media available. The reasons for recommending the main medium are given; this is the most important section of the plan. The choice of a second medium, if this is the decision, is argued through. Comments are made on the media rejected. The plan gives the allocation of the budget between media and analyses of expenditure by time and by region.

Within the media to be used, the objectives and criteria set for the buyers are laid down. Schedules are given; these may be in outline or in detail – the choice between these two is discussed in the next section.

Media tests, media research, post-campaign assessment and any development work proposed are described.

*Should schedules in the plan be detailed?*

It must be decided whether the schedule in the media plan should be in outline, and so leave some initiative to the buyer – or even a tactical budget left for him to spend – or detailed and so include the main buying decisions. The advantage of giving an outline schedule at this stage is that the agency has flexibility to meet the altered conditions which it encounters during the campaign. Publications become ready to deal; new publications appear; TV opportunities arise which could not be foreseen months in advance. Flexibility within an agreed framework keeps the buyer on his toes. In my opinion the advertiser therefore gets better buying when he allows flexibility — but he then needs a quality control system reporting to him. He should be given an estimate for the media exposure which the schedule will achieve, and he should be told after the event how near the buyers came to the objectives set. Further, a detailed schedule demands full consultation and disclosure to media owners, which may break the security which many campaigns require.

The advantage of a detailed schedule is its simplicity. The advertiser knows exactly when and where his advertisements will appear. He does not have to make further checks on the agency's buying performance. He may particularly require a detailed schedule when it has to be co-ordinated with other advertising, or for a launch, or when he wants to tell his own staff and the trade where to look for the advertisements. He can however always get these details from the media department nearer the time the advertisements are to appear.

1   *TV schedules.* The key facts in an outline TV schedule are:
    *(a)* The length of commercials, or the mixture of lengths, to be used.
    *(b)* The money to be spent in each area during each time period.
    *(c)* For convenience, totals of expenditure by area and by time period (and by commercial length if several are used).
    *(d)* Buying objective and predicted performance.

    A detailed schedule includes all of these and lists also the numbers of spots to be bought. This listing will be at least by week and by time-segment. It may show the day and actual break in which each spot is to appear. Midway between outline and detail is the 'peak-equivalent' schedule, showing the number of spots which would be bought by area and time period if only peak time segments were used.

2   *Press schedules.* An outline press schedule shows:
    *(a)* The publications which will certainly be used.
    *(b)* The publications which may be used, depending on negotia-tions.
    *(c)* The size and type of advertisement in each.

*(d)* The positions it is intended to buy.

*(e)* The minimum number of insertions expected to be bought in each.

*(f)* The approximate dates of appearance or overall timing of the expenditure.

A detailed schedule gives the actual dates of insertions and the firm number of insertions bought, with details of the positions negotiated.

3   *Schedules in other media.* In the media plan, schedules in other media should generally be in outline only. Expenditure should be broken down by area and time period. The sizes of posters and lengths of cinema or radio commercials should be recorded. The media performance expected (cover and number of repetitions on the target) should be indicated. But lists of cinemas or of poster sites are not generally required at this stage.

## MAINTENANCE OF THE MEDIA PLAN

The media planner's work does not end with the advertiser's approval of the media plan. The emphasis shifts to buying and quality control, which is described in the next chapter. Few plans survive the campaign unaltered: the market changes, media values rise or fall, sales figures come in, budgets are adjusted. Each change requested should be measured against the thinking behind the original plan: probably the most careful reader of the plan is its original writer, six months later. Major changes should be documented as carefully as the first plan.

# 11 BUYING

*How the agency can ensure that it buys time and space at the lowest possible cost. How schedules in the press and on television are drawn up. The criteria which buyers should be set. Quality control.*

## WHAT MAKES A SUCCESSFUL BUYER?

Planning and buying are two parts of a single operation: spending efficiently the advertiser's money. The two cannot in practice be separated. The obvious distinction between strategy and execution is too simple. The information which the buyer provides about forecast costs and availabilities enters into strategic decisions. Details such as the choice between individual publications may involve the planner.

The two jobs are often done by different people, as is assumed in this book. In career terms, young people often start in buying and then some of them become planners; moves the other way are rare. But the planner-buyer is also often found.

It has been argued that the buyer makes the greater contribution because he demonstrably saves money. A 10 per cent saving on a large budget is a very persuasive argument. The planner cannot quantify his expertise so easily. It has also been said that the buyer has wrongly been excluded from his share of the spotlight, that the case histories and papers are always about planning, never about buying. It is true that buying gets — even in this book — less discussion. Compared also with selling, on which there are so many books and courses, buying is rarely taught.

Arguments about the relative importance of planner and buyer are like two links in a chain disputing which is carrying the greater weight: both are indispensable. But in this chapter, I try to give the buyer his proper due and to emphasise the great value he can contribute. In the UK — it is different in some other markets — he does not just look up the rate card and issue the order. He can stretch the advertising pound and make real money for the advertiser.

There are six factors that help the buyer to turn in good results:

1   *Size.* The large advertiser and the large agency get more attention from media owners. If each group of accounts in an agency is handled by buyers who remain separate, then the buying power of the agency is not concentrated and cannot be brought into play. There should be one person responsible for the whole of the agency's buying in a medium.

2   *Sharing information with the media owner.* The buyer should know the reasons behind the agency's strategy; he should understand the media objective, the target definition and the criteria he will be judged by. He should meet the advertiser and be involved in the team. He should see his work as part of the whole campaign. Any advertising man, no matter what his job, should be encouraged to contribute his ideas and comments. So he not only helps the agency, he can (where he is not breaking a confidence) help the media owner. It goes without saying that he understands thoroughly the media objectives, the target and the buying criteria. This information is vital to the media owner, who cannot make a case for his medium without it — and the case for the medium may often include further helpful ideas for the advertiser. So the buyer does the best job for the advertiser when the media owner looks on the agency as his partner: 'How can we get together to sell this product?'

3   *Authority.* The buyer should ideally have a real voice in media decisions, though few advertisers appreciate how this should be balanced against marketing considerations. The buyer should

be known to have the power to move money between media — on at least a part of the budget if not on the whole. Otherwise he cannot reward good value with further orders, so the media owner has no incentive to satisfy him. Unless he is in a position to give quick decisions, he does not get offered good time or space when these become available at short notice.

4   *Respect.* The buyer's paper-work should be faultless. His budgets, orders and invoice-checking must be accurate and up-to-date. The buyer's word has to be trustworthy. Without being a research expert or accountant he has to be happy with figures.

5   *Persistence.* The buyer must insist on getting good value: the best position, the highest rating slot, the lowest cost. He must never be satisfied. He must go on asking the medium for improvement, without being overbearing beyond the point of irritation.

6   *Follow-up.* Buying does not end when the order is issued and the advertisement has appeared. The buyer needs a quality control system which reports what media value was obtained — for example by cost-per-thousand on TV or position in the press. This provides him with the argument that he should get compensation if the media owner has not given his best value.

*The media owner's reaction*

Now suppose that this paragon of a buyer actually exists. The media owner tries to treat all his customers equally. But with this buyer he finds that:

1   The agency is a large source of his revenue.
2   The buyer gives him all the information he needs in order to sell.
3   The buyer genuinely influences how much money he gets, and gives quick decisions.
4   The figures used by the buyer are accurate and his word can be trusted.
5   The buyer does not give up until he gets good value.
6   The buyer is well aware what he has bought; bad value is inevitably followed by a complaint.

It is then simply easier for the media owner to give this buyer preferential treatment and better value. And this is the buyer's objective.

The buyer has two weapons in dealing with the media owner: whether or not he will place an order, and the timing of his order.

He normally does not reveal to the media owner exactly how much he intends to spend on the medium. He says only that he will spend so much provided he gets this or that price or concession. He must of course be able to carry out any promise he makes to spend more or any threat to spend less.

When the buyer believes a medium is likely to be oversold, he orders early. He may of course over-option and cancel some options later, but this practice soon becomes known to the seller who makes allowances accordingly. If he is correct in anticipating heavy demand on a medium, other buyers will have difficulty in getting the time or space he has prudently reserved; he will do relatively better than them. But when he believes the medium is going to be undersold, he delays his order. If he is correct, he will at the cost of some nervous strain get eleventh-hour concessions from the medium which would rather sell cheaply than not at all. If, however, he is wrong and the medium does not have time or space available, he will have difficulty in getting his money away. Underspending is not only failing to meet the advertiser's marketing plan but financially damaging to the agency because commission is lost.

## A PRESS SCHEDULE EXAMPLE

The buyer plays a major part in drawing up media schedules, whether in outline for the media plan or later in detail. There is no precise demarcation between planning and buying. The example now given uses real data [11.1] though the costs are well out of date; the principle remains the same. The tug of war between cover and repetition, one of the agency's main problems, emerges clearly.

Press scheduling should start with a list of candidate publications — those which are feasible and not ruled out by the restraints mentioned in Chapter 10. This list should next be evaluated for cost effectiveness in reaching the specified target, i.e. it should be put in order of VIPs. The problem of balance is, stated crudely, how far to go down this list when including publications in the schedule. Is a short schedule appropriate, with many insertions in each publication (low cover, high repetition) or a long one with fewer insertions (high cover, low repetition)?

Suppose the brief is to reach housewives with black and white advertisements, in a mixture of full pages, four columns, and 13 inches by five columns. Table 20 gives the first fourteen publications out of fifty listed in VIP order. In this example there is no allowance for advertisement exposure or qualitative factors.

The cost of taking one insertion in each publication was £14,000 in 1973. This schedule would cover 86 per cent of all housewives; the average number of issues read by a housewife covered would be 2.6. The same money could however be spent on only seven publications — or on four. Obviously many other combinations are possible but these three schedules indicate the range of alternatives available. Schedule analyses give the results shown in Table 21.

The buyer's job is to suggest candidate publications, draw up such schedules and get analyses done. He does not decide between these alternatives. Nor does the planner on his own — though he recommends

## Table 20

| Publication | Cost per insertion, £ | Housewife readership, % | VIP* |
|---|---|---|---|
| *True Story* | 204 | 6 | 5220 |
| *Daily Sketch* | 400 | 9 | 3940 |
| *Reveille* | 675 | 13 | 3460 |
| *Daily Mirror* | 1856 | 36 | 3420 |
| *True Romances* | 204 | 4 | 3210 |
| *Women's Weekly* | 875 | 16 | 3210 |
| *Woman's Realm* | 1340 | 23 | 3090 |
| *Titbits* | 360 | 6 | 3900 |
| *Sunday Post* | 600 | 10 | 2830 |
| *Weekend* | 668 | 10 | 2700 |
| *Woman and Home* | 720 | 10 | 2590 |
| *Reader's Digest* | 1080 | 15 | 2540 |
| *Woman's Own* | 2256 | 32 | 2500 |
| *The People* | 2795 | 37 | 2380 |

* Housewives reading, per pound

Table 21

| Number of publications in schedule | Housewife cover, % | Number of issues read by those covered |
|---|---|---|
| 4 | 46 | 6.1 |
| 7 | 65 | 4.2 |
| 14 | 86 | 2.6 |

the best compromise. One way is to set a minimum to the cover required: for example if this were 60 per cent the middle schedule might be chosen. Or the average number of issues read might have to be six at least, in which case the first schedule would be chosen.

This simple example has left out many of the complexities which in practice the buyer has to cope with. Qualitative and other research factors have to be taken into account, as discussed in Part 4. Different sizes of advertisement, whether bleed will be bought and so on, must be considered. And of course the prices used in the initial evaluation may be altered in negotiation. Practical schedule building is not simply picking from the top of an academic VIP list.

The press buyer also has to make sure he gets options in early if publications that are heavily under demand are likely to be on the schedule. He advises the planner on availability and on the time-table which restricts orders, copy dates and cancellations. He is not limited to the publications in the industry research data, but has to choose (and often provide readership estimates for) a bewilderingly wide range of publications. In my agency we used in 1973 a total of no less than 1,500 different publications.

*Press post-campaign evaluation*

The press has at least this simplicity — compared with television — that a schedule is evaluated and agreed in outline before it is finally bought. The press buyer does not usually have to justify his performance.

When voucher copies arrive after the campaign, voucher clerks check not only that the advertisement appeared as ordered, but evaluate its position. They monitor competitors' advertising. Press production experts check the reproduction quality.

It is not very common to report on buying efficiency in the press and certainly it is less of a preoccupation than with TV. When a detailed schedule has been previously evaluated and agreed there is little point in doing more than report that it appeared as planned. But when the buyer has some latitude, or the publications used have been changing in circulation, or position is of serious concern, then the buyer should report back the added value he has obtained. In addition, the agency as a whole should evaluate the effect of the campaign, as explained in Chapter 12.

## A TV SCHEDULE EXAMPLE

At the planning stage the TV buyer does not usually go into as much detail as the press buyer: he cannot because his medium is more dynamic. He can however also help to evaluate different types of schedule. For example, suppose that the agency is considering how much of the budget should be spent in daytime and off-peak television. The answer will depend on the marketing objectives, the target, the budget and so on, but also on the costs, cover, frequency, etc. Daytime is cheaper but tends to reach the same people, and some of these very infrequently.

The buyer might for example draw up three possible schedules, all to produce say about 250 TVRs. The first consists only of peak and shoulder peak time; the third is all daytime; in between is a schedule that spends 20 per cent of the budget on daytime and off-peak (but obtains 40 per cent of its total ratings in this time).

The three schedules have the characteristics shown in Table 22. Thus schedule 2 has an average rating between the high value of Schedule 1 and the low value of Schedule 3, with corresponding cost. A schedule analysis (Table 23) obtains the key performance figures. This shows how limited is the cover of a schedule transmitted only in daytime, obviously unlikely to reach many of those normally working. The average frequency on those covered is high, but their detailed analysis reveals a very different shape of frequency distribution from the peak schedule's, with a high proportion of those covered seeing only one or two spots and a small number of heavy viewers seeing a very large number of spots. However when only a reasonable part of the budget goes into low-rated time almost the same cover, frequency

207

and shape of distribution is obtained, but at lower cost than Schedule 1.

It is by this kind of analysis and discussion that the agency will reach a view about the buying criteria to use. It is not the buyer's job to choose between these alternatives. He produces and explains the figures. The planner then finds the compromise that most nearly satisfies the media brief.


## OTHER TV PLANNING WORK

The buyer similarly advises on the two other basic decisions on television: when and where. He provides cost forecasts and carries out the arithmetic work required, as discussed in Chapter 9.

Buyers should routinely agree on forecasts of average costs by area. These forecasts will never be completely accurate but they must nevertheless be attempted. They should not be used afterwards as a

Table 22

| Schedule number | 1 | 2 | 3 |
|---|---|---|---|
| TVRs | 246 | 252 | 243 |
| Number of spots | 10 | 16 | 25 |
| Average rating | 25 | 16 | 10 |
| C/000 | 130p | 105p | 50p |

Source: Midlands, June 1973, Housewives

Table 23

| Schedule number | 1 | 2 | 3 |
|---|---|---|---|
| Cover, % | 75 | 74 | 47 |
| Number of opportunities to see by those covered | 3.3 | 3.4 | 5.2 |
| See more than 4, % | 41 | 38 | 18 |

Source: Midlands, June 1973, Housewives

stick to beat the buyers who did not achieve them — or their next year's estimates will all be too high.

Ideally, the forecasts should be specific to the campaign in question. The factors which influence actual values are now listed, though the variation they cause is usually smaller than the inevitable errors of forecasting. It suffices for most purposes to take a convenient but relevant buying criterion, e.g. housewives, a standard spot length, e.g. 30 seconds, and a standard buying policy, e.g. peak time weekday.

*Factors influencing TV values*

1   The buying criterion, e.g. whether the buyer wants to reach adults or housewives.
2   The volume discount the advertiser is entitled to; whether seasonal or other discounts can be obtained.
3   The length of commercial, for a 15- or 30-second spot is easier to move, in order to take advantage of a good slot, than one of 45 seconds.
4   Availability at the time of the campaign, for if this is tight it will be difficult to avoid some poor values, and the contractor will have no incentive to deal. This factor alters dramatically month-to-month: traditionally late spring and early autumn are times of low availability and high cost.
5   The time between booking and transmission, because a booking made late cannot get into the slots reversed by earlier buyers, nor can they qualify for early-booking discounts when these are available. Similarly if a late cancellation has to be made it is only the good time which can be cancelled easily, since the contractor knows he can sell this again. Advertisers who are continually altering their budgets should not overlook the harm this can do to the value they get.
6   The type of product may affect costs, for example time for confectionery advertising is so short that it is in effect rationed and rotated between advertisers who all achieve similar values.
7   Any restriction on buying imposed for marketing reasons will result in lower value since the buyer loses some freedom to manœuvre.

It is good practice not to allocate all the budget to contractors immediately but to keep back a tactical budget. This can be used as an incentive to contractors to offer good value, or to take advantage of special buying opportunities, or for marketing reasons (to ward off a competitor or halt a sales decline), or to make up in an area where the ratings achieved have fallen below what was expected.

*TV tactics*

Once an outline TV plan has been agreed the buyer is left to achieve the best possible performance. Normally the criterion he will be judged by is simply total ratings. This is not the only objective which may be set. He may occasionally be told exactly what days and segments to use, or what type of programme to be near. He may be strictly limited to certain burst patterns, e.g. four weeks on, four off. He may be expected to apply weights for presence and attention factors. All these restrictions and modifications may be for good marketing reasons, but they can result in a rise in the overall cost per thousand achieved. This does not mean they should never be applied, but that if they are, then good cost per thousand by the conventional measurement should not be expected as well. No general rule can be given for the effect of such restrictions − they may increase costs by 1 or 2 per cent or by 20 per cent.

Another objective given the buyer may be cover or some other characteristic of the frequency distribution of opportunities to see. Hence phrases like '80 per cent cover, 30 per cent four plus', meaning that 80 per cent of housewives or adults in ITV homes should have at least one opportunity to see and 30 per cent should have at least four. He may also be told to spend at least $x$ per cent of the budget in peak time or not more than $y$ per cent in day-time. It is argued that the objective of a low cost per thousand may be achieved by buying only low-rating, cheap spots. It is possible that if all the money is spent in this way then the campaign might reach only very heavy viewers and so light viewers, an important part of the target, are left untouched. It is for this reason that a low average rating for the spots in a schedule is sometimes frowned on. In practice it is hard at present to buy only cheap time: buyers are forced into more expensive time by the general demand for off-peak time.

If cover is set as an objective then the buyer will usually spend a high proportion of his budget in peak time, even at relatively higher cost. He will of course in any case try to get the highest rating slots in any time segment he uses. He may try to vary the type of programme he is near, in order to reach a variety of people. He will certainly avoid repeating his spots at the same day and time each week, which would tend to reach the same people. He may consult analyses of light viewers' preferences, to see where he can reach them best. It is debatable how useful the criterion of cover is generally. There will always be special cases where cover is important. The pursuit of cover can divert the buyer from good cost per thousand — and the pursuit of cost per thousand often brings good cover with it.

Whatever the criteria by which he is judged, a good TV buyer:

1    Must forecast availability and costs adequately.
2    Must judge correctly how much money to place now and how much to hold back.
3    Must judge correctly how much he can risk placing at pre-empt rates, how much at full rates and how much he must fix in order to get into very desirable breaks.
4    Must know every hole and corner in the rate card.
5    Must understand the short-term effects of programmes on ratings, correctly anticipating which slots will get good ratings. It has been argued [11.2] that buyers are rather bad both at these short-term forecasts and at estimating the resulting frequency distributions; certainly forecasting can be more systematic than is usually the case.
6    Must continually assess and, if necessary, move his bookings, especially after detailed transmission times and BBC programmes become known.

*TV post-campaign evaluation*

After the campaign, every spot transmitted has two values: the one recorded in the JICTAR Weekly Report at rate card cost and its net value using the price actually paid, including fixing, discounts, special deals and so on. It is therefore possible to work out the rate card value for any schedule and the net value for our own schedules. In this evaluation 30-second costs are taken as the standard.

The advertiser uses the net figures to see what value the buyers actually got — and if he has several agencies he may well set them in competition with each other. He notes also what competitors' values were at rate card cost — admittedly an imperfect measure, though the industry average discount (explained in Chapter 3) can be allowed for. The published costs of television are always at rate card and most agencies beat them (which leads to the cynical comment that every agency in London buys better than every other agency). It is therefore possible with care to compare an agency's TV buying with the average, though the factors listed above that influence the values may make the comparison invalid. The advertiser can also compare his competitors' TV buying, this time at rate card only. Agency management uses these figures for quality control. Planners use them to check that ratings are being achieved as planned. They are also required for decisions on the deployment of the tactical budget.

Post-campaign assessment is therefore an important part of TV buying — and an arduous clerical task. It is necessary to total in each area the ratings achieved, and the cost paid, in order to calculate the average. A computer can do these sums though when the buyer does them himself he benefits from the detailed study this entails of his schedule's achievement.

## ADMINISTRATION

Copies of schedules and orders go to the traffic controller to ensure that blocks, artwork and films are dispatched in time to fill the space or time bought. Orders and cancellations must be summarised to ensure that future commitments are known and in order to control the budget. Similarly invoices have to be checked. There are formidable, though straightforward, procedural problems here. A mechanised system is essential in an agency of any size and the computer is in its element.

## INFORMATION SERVICE

As well as sharing its own information with media owners, the agency must collect information from them about their media. The buying units in the media department should keep up to date records about media values. Trend information, forecasts and media news should be circulated to the rest of the agency. Data on coupon returns and other direct effectiveness measures should be assessed and on file. When new media, new rate cards or other facilities are on the horizon, buyers should review the agency's accounts and advise planners whether a change of schedule should be considered.

The agency should deserve a reputation for understanding media. It should be knowledgeable about developments and sound in its long-term predictions. It is the buyer's discussions with media owners that form the basis of the agency's knowledge.

# Part 4
# THE USES OF RESEARCH

# 12 WAS IT WORTH IT?

*The subject of research is introduced by an outline of one of its most important applications – the evaluation of an advertising campaign after it has appeared. Case histories are given to demonstrate the kinds of data available and their use in evaluating media and advertising. Technical problems are not discussed.*

Part 3 dealt with how much should be spent on a campaign and when and where to spend it. The objectives and a media plan were agreed. Suppose now that the advertisements have duly appeared. The advertiser is entitled to ask whether his campaign was worth it. Was the right amount of money allocated to advertising? Was it spent in the right media? Can the media plan be improved next time? Who was reached and affected, who was missed? What else can be learned from this experience? These are questions to ask researchers, which is why this chapter starts the part of this book dealing with research.

While these questions seem natural, they are not often asked: 'The results expected from advertising expenditure are seldom spelled out, and in only a minority of instances is an effort made to find out what benefits have been derived'. This is as true in this country now as it was in the US in 1962, when it was the main conclusion of a study [12.1] carried out on advertisers.

One of the reasons why relatively little is done is that these questions are so hard. It must be admitted that, more often than not, research cannot provide the answers. There are two separate problems here. One is that our advertising is only one — and usually a small one at that — of the forces in the market place. When we do a test, or compare one year or area with another, can we be absolutely sure that none of the following have altered: our product, its price, pack, below the line promotion, sales force, trade acceptance, distribution or point of sale support? Were all our competitors also stationary in these respects? Did the advertising budgets or creative work alter? And were there no underlying shifts in consumer behavior or attitudes? It is rare that we can ignore or evaluate all these other forces.

The other problem is evaluating advertising is the time span involved. The major result of advertising is often that it lifts the product advertised, over the years, to a certain height of acceptability. This is associated with its distribution, use and sales. But evaluating a campaign is a short term operation. In Year 1 the advertising appears, in Year 2 its immediate results are studied and in Years 2 and 3 the conclusions reached are used to design a new campaign. This process improves advertising efficiency and may indicate in which direction advertising should move, but it is unlikely to reveal fundamental truths.

Despite these problems, I recommend that whenever possible advertising is made accountable by setting objectives and then seeing whether they are met. It is not only that budget and media decisions may be helped. We also stay up to date with whatever changes are taking place in the market and so can keep our product and advertising appropriate. And we get experience which may help us in other cases.

I give below some examples of learning about individual campaigns. But before doing so it is worth dwelling on the last point, that some generalisations are possible. A comprehensive review of this subject [12.1], by Ron Critchley, draws three main conclusions: that advertising effects can often be measured; in practice we very rarely do so; there is no clear superiority of one medium over another:

> 'If one wishes to distinguish the sales effects of TV commercials or campaigns from those of press ads or campaigns, the researchers now know how to avoid the various pitfalls which have reduced the value of many past attempts. The desired result (in *total*, without reasons) seems possible both through controlled experiments and through analytical methods where detailed media

exposure and product purchasing data are available covering a reasonable period of time.'

There has, however, been

'a lack of determination to define the needs and to pay for the necessary research. Perhaps there was an unconscious bias against facing up to the possibility of large scale research and confusion from trying to think of ways of "doing it on the cheap".'

He might have added that recently, when advertising has had its economic back to the wall, there is even less willingness to spend in order to justify further expenditure: it is as though advertising has lost its normal determined optimism. Finally,

'As far as *generalisable* results are concerned, only time will tell but, so far, the evidence suggests that (as between TV and press, for instance) a *mixture* of results is to be expected, with results varying from product to product and even between campaigns for the same product. A number of controlled tests would therefore be necessary before media decisions were much assisted.'

These conclusions seem to me justified, and I would add two more. I doubt whether even a very large number of tests, although reasonably comparable to the particular problem we may be facing, will ever indicate with certainty the action we should take. The circumstances will never be exactly the same: 'you never step in the same stream twice'. There is always the chance that this is the time it pays to break the rules. Campaign planning certainly benefits from experience but judgement will always be essential. The other finding I suggest is that familiar one that experiments can definitely disprove hypotheses even if they cannot prove them but only make them more likely. As Michael Bird has suggested [12.3], we rarely stand close enough to Occam's razor or have enough faith in our beliefs to test them in the accepted way: to be scientific a hypothesis must resist systematic attempts to falsify it. There are so many traditions and myths for which there is little sound foundation that it is a common experience to do a test 'just to check' and then find that the opposite is the case. We may not find through tests new unassailable positions but we do at least have to abandon untenable ones. This is the main reason I recommend post-campaign measurements: there is nearly always some surprise, something to learn, some improvement to make, although certainty in constructing the next plan is too much to expect.

Therefore no *rules* for campaign planning are to be expected from this chapter. The careful procedure through the checklist of Chapter 10 and the use of commonsense are still recommended.

## What should be measured?

Obviously advertising is undertaken to maintain or increase sales. Since this is the eventual objective advertising should be evaluated by relating it only to sales effects. The manufacturer should count the cases leaving his factory, or packs crossing the counter; he should observe the effect of advertising on these sales. This concept is logically impeccable. But it is also idealistic: it ignores the interference of other factors. And it gives no diagnostic help: it does not reveal *how* advertising is helping or how it might help more.

Therefore sales measures are often supplemented or even replaced by indirect measures. The indirect measures chosen should depend on what the advertising should be doing, in other words on the subjects of Chapter 2 (how advertising works) and of Chapter 7 (the brief). Post-campaign research starts by agreeing on the objectives of the campaign. Next, procedures must be agreed that determine whether these objectives have been reached. It would, of course, be foolish though unfortunately not rare to choose an objective or an indirect measure simply because a research tool exists which purports to report on it. Table 24 shows some of the objectives and corresponding measurements commonly used in post-campaign evaluation.

One general rule can however be given about what *not* to do when evaluating the contribution of different media: to ask in a survey, 'Where did you see the advertising?' Classically, the intrusive medium television gets high mention, even when not used [12.4]. Advertisement recognition also introduces pitfalls.

## Research costs

It is difficult to give guidance on the correct amount to spend on such work. The principle to apply is that we are dividing a total sum of money into the advertising budget and the research budget, and the cost of the research must not exceed the value of the long-term improve-

Table 24

|  | Objectives | Examples of measures |
|---|---|---|
| Direct | Sales | Audits, panels, claimed purchase or usage |
|  | Coupons | Returns, conversions |
| Indirect | Awareness change | Recall, recognition, saliency |
|  | Communication | Comprehension |
|  | Attitude change | Image, liking, believability, likelihood of purchase |

ment it is expected to cause in the advertising. From an annual budget of £100,000 less than £5000 would normally be spent on this type of research. This implies that the research is not expected to increase the efficiency of advertising by as much as 5 per cent. But to spend £10,000 from a total of £1 million seems moderate, as a 1 per cent gain is not over-ambitious.

The costs will, of course, also depend on the exact objectives, which are generally to describe, to diagnose and to predict — though as Donald Monk has said: 'The object of research is to predict trends; it is also to suggest action which proves the predictions wrong'.


*Observe — or experiment?*

Suppose it has been decided what to measure and how much to spend on doing so. The alternatives then are to carry out advertising in the normal way but to observe carefully what occurs, or to set up a deliberate experiment.

More work is in fact done through observation than through experiments. Existing standard audits are most commonly used but more or less elaborate special techniques may be set up. In either case the existing pattern of advertising expenditure need not be disturbed. This is the easier and cheaper method. It also seems to involve less risk, though this may be an illusion. The results may be disappointing, because they are more likely than not to be inconclusive. And though relationships may be observed, this does not prove that certain advertising caused certain sales.

The argument in favour of the experimental approach points out that it is only after an experiment that any evidence of causality can be expected. On the other hand, experiments are also often inconclusive, slow, artificial and risky, as was discussed in their application to the budget problem in Chapter 8.


## CASE HISTORIES

The surest way to learn what works in any market is to be close to that particular market. We should observe what other brands are doing as well as our own. What happened when there were changes in rates of expenditure, media choice, creative theme, promotions and so on? What changes took place in distribution, in image and in sales? The few examples given here are not meant to replace careful observation and deduction. More examples are briefly summarised in Chapter 16, since response functions are a refinement of general advertising effectiveness measurement. Many others will be found by following up the bibliographies given in the references. Reading case histories is a very efficient way of learning about advertising: in an hour we can relive months or years of other people's experience. Experience is the acid test which dissolves a hundred misconceived, untested theories.

There are many ways of collecting evidence on what happens when advertising reaches the market place. The eight methods which follow cover most cases.


### 1    Historical evidence on a market

The first example is observed non-experimental data on a whole market: total sales and advertising expenditure on frozen foods in the UK for the nineteen years 1955 to 1973. The data are shown in Figure 10. The

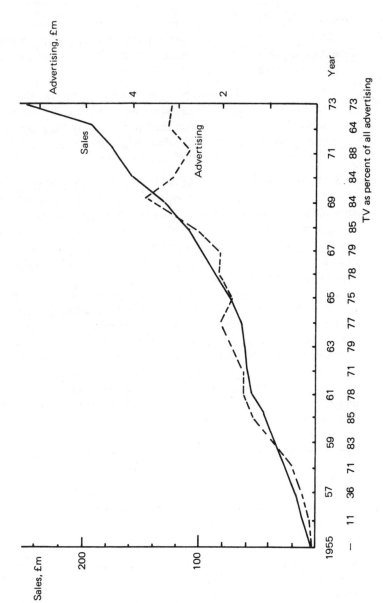

*Figure 10*

223

percentage of advertising which went to television is also shown.

Clearly the last few years provoke rather different thoughts from those that the data up to 1969 suggest. With only the earlier results it would be easy to draw conclusions of this kind:

> The amount of advertising has gone up year by year, and the total market has expanded. These sales have been caused by the advertising. Because the television share has been very high, generally over three-quarters of total advertising, and sales have gone up, the choice of television must have been right.

Such conclusions may be right or they may be wrong. They are not proved by this kind of data. It is equally possible that the advertising-sales ratio was fixed in advance. Sales may have gone up because the product was good and therefore the advertising has gone up, rather than the other way round. Because the television share has been high in a successful situation this is no proof that some other media mix might not have done better.

But it would be foolish to neglect such figures, and to say there is no real evidence here. It would be a foolhardy marketing director who looks at such data and says 'I'm going to change it all. I'm going to switch 100 per cent to press next year' — or 'I can do without advertising'. This is an example of the conservatism of media practice which was discussed in Chapter 10.

The most recent years divide conveniently into two pairs: in 1970 and 1971 the TV share remained high; in 1972 and 1973 it fell sharply (the money going into women's magazines and posters). For all four years advertising expenditure remained steady at about £3 million while sales increased more steeply than before, growing over 40 per cent.

It is easy to imagine these figures being used in the opposite argument from the previous one:

> Sales are clearly not related to advertising expenditure. The money spent in 1969 was wastefully high and further cuts should be made. Nor does the main media choice have any effect.

Again the conclusions are not proved by the data. They are certainly suggested but it is possible that other factors affected the results. Clearly the two sets of conclusions we would have drawn at different times cannot both be correct. It is also salutary to reflect what the findings might have been if the switch away from television had been made two years earlier.

This example is enough to prove the dangers of naive deductions from overall data. It is necessary to go into detailed investigations, both at the retail and consumer levels, before the mechanisms in this market have been made clear. For example, the following questions might be asked. What happened to other convenience foods and social habits from 1970 on? How did distribution and prices alter? What happened to the volume of purchases? Did the competitive situation change? Were new products still being launched or had we entered a period of product stability? Do we understand how housewives make their purchase decisions on frozen foods? Is £3 million a ceiling at which we are reaching them with adequate frequency? Did the creative objectives change so that advertising became more efficient?

Enough has been said to show the dangers of too shallow an investigation. On one point there is interesting evidence: the creative and media decisions. Birds Eye (who dominate this market) went into print [12.5] to explain the changes they made in 1972 and 1973:

'TV provided us with a very quick way to launch the many new lines we introduced in the 50's and 60's. In particular, the immediacy of the medium helped to put Fish Fingers on the map with a speed that made this product almost a national institution within a year or two of its introduction. But today's marketing situation is very different. We believe it calls for a much broader, more colourful, more thoughtful media approach, in which both posters and magazines have an equally important role to play.

'The new Birds Eye strategy involves a radical departure from the company's traditional policy of individual product campaigns. It was signalled by the growing realisation that women tend to plan their catering on a meal-time basis — main course, snacks, desserts and so on — rather than through buying individual products, such as vegetables, fish and meat.

'Our decision to rely much more on women's magazines — like that to put more emphasis on posters — grew naturally out of the requirements of our new "corporate" platform for the Birds Eye advertising/marketing strategy introduced in 1972. This strategy is aimed at projecting what we call "a total corporate image" of ourselves as a food company, catering for almost all eating requirements and all meal-time occasions.

'TV is used to project a single simple thematic message, linked

225

with any one of a variety of products. Posters sited on — or near to — high streets serve as a reminder to women shoppers who might have seen the TV commercial the night before.

'The policy of concentrating our advertising on solutions to specific meal-time problems offers us special scope for the promotion of new recipe ideas. And clearly here is where women's magazines have a unique plus. Indeed, their editorial environment surely makes them the ideal medium for this purpose.'

Studies of markets can be far more elaborate. Classical examples were published in 1970 and 1971 by the Television Consumer Audit [12.6]. These covered fruit squashes, toothpaste, heavy-duty washing powders, instant coffee and washing up liquids. The object was to study the relations between market size, branded products' sales and consumer loyalty on the one hand, media expenditure and below the line or promotional expenditure on the other. Various methods were used: time series, brand switching and regression analyses. The findings were complex: each market had a different history and structure. Broadly, it was concluded that price promotion could diffuse loyalty and end in the decline of major brands and of the total market. Price promotion could produce short-term gains for individual brands without increasing the market value, followed by individual losses subsequently. Advertising on the other hand defended brands and caused long-term improvement in the total market size.

## 2 Historical evidence on individuals

One approach is to track, by a diary, through individuals' actual purchases and to compare the brands bought on successive occasions with the advertising they have been exposed to meanwhile, also recorded in a diary. The results of this approach have proved positive; that is, it can be shown that people *do* buy more of the brand they have just seen advertised. The results of this method have already been referred to [9.3] as a help in the timing decision. It is also noteworthy as a method of demonstrating that individual behaviour really does alter after advertising exposure. The method is not easy to apply and indeed has been used once only as far as I am aware, so I am not recommending it for general use; but the findings can help to convince the advertising sceptic. They can also uncover the basic behaviour pattern which consumers follow and which advertising attempts to alter. For example, 'Although there are instances of housewives who remain totally loyal to one brand, brand loyalty seems more often to consist of loyalty to one or other of two, three or perhaps four brands, which have somehow got onto the housewife's list of brands that she is prepared to buy. One brand may, of course, be her favourite and she may shift her main preference between different brands 'on her list' over a period of time, but purchasing patterns of this kind are far more common than either complete loyalty to one brand or utter indifference between brands.'

Unfortunately, this method has not entered the normal repertoire of researchers and a really large syndicated study has not been carried out. Also, the method can measure only short-term effects and the cruder, overall measure is what counts.

## 3 Historical evidence on a change of method

Sometimes very convincing evidence of the effect of advertising can be obtained when it is employed for the first time, especially in a launch situation or using a new medium. The advertiser knows what else was happening and it is not too hard for him to decide whether it was worthwhile. Some agencies are currently, for example, using radio as a cheap test medium for products that have not been advertised before or for some time.

The BBTA have provided several examples, this one [12.7] being drawn from industry. A small foundry and engineering works in East Anglia, Elliott and Garood, was looking for subcontracting work. TV would not normally be thought of for this task and a sales force plus direct mail were tried first. The plan was next to take a half-page in the *Financial Times*, but for the same cost of £800 nine spots were taken instead in the local area over one weekend. Twenty-four enquiries were received, all but one from new contacts. Recruitment of staff was helped. And clinching a major contract was assisted, the buyer using the memorable words, 'I saw you on television, I didn't realise you were as big as that'.

## 4 Direct response

Before going into some detail on a press example (the medium where most direct response advertising appears) I give a brief TV example in recruitment advertising. This case history was also published by the British Bureau of Television Advertising [12.7] as part of the TV medium's drive to attract new types of advertising. Direct response is, of course, very powerful as a tool for evaluating many aspects of advertising. Recruitment advertising has recently expanded considerably into TV and radio because of this kind of data.

GEC-Elliott Automation employs some 15,000 people. In 1970 they were short of computer personnel and had decided to use as the main medium the national press, but this campaign was followed by six commercials in the London area. They were transmitted during *News at Ten* in order to reach the type of person likely to be watching at that time. A telephone number was given during the commercial; 600 interviews were arranged as a result: 'the standard of applicants was very high and the interviews are working out at a cost to us of £15 a head, and cheap at the price'. The campaign was followed in other areas and in 1971 by another for recruiting senior executives.

Here is an example of coupon analysis for a campaign which used five publications and ten different advertisements. The campaign was spread over nine weeks, finishing just before Christmas when the majority of purchases took place. The object was not solely to obtain coupon returns — which requested a catalogue — but to build up awareness of the range of products advertised. Other research methods were also used and effectiveness could not be judged from coupons alone. Nevertheless the results were a valuable guide in three areas:

1    As far as catalogue distribution was concerned, the value of insertions in different weeks was clearly demonstrated; this was not conclusive about the timing of the campaign as a whole,

Table 25    INDEX FOR COST PER REPLY
(AVERAGE 100)

| Variable | Low | High |
|----------|-----|------|
| Time | 71 | 426 |
| Advertisements | 54 | 263 |
| Publications | 71 | 164 |

because it is purchases rather than catalogue distribution which were the real objective.

2     The pulling power of particular advertisements was demonstrated; the coupon results were consistent with pre-tests and with Gallup reading and noting checks. This data was helpful in guiding future creative work.

3     The cost efficiency of the different publications used was estimated. Their value was then compared to readership profiles, which enabled the media man to judge the worth of an upper grade profile or of having a high proportion of women readers. This data guided future media choice.

4     Other factors also emerged as perhaps influencing the results: position in the publication, content of the issue and the weather.

The actual figures were dramatic. Clear conclusions emerged as shown in Table 25.

The analysis of such data presents few problems when a properly-balanced design is used, i.e. when each publication carries each advertisement at evenly spaced times. In practice this may not be possible and methods of analysing the data are required which are more complex than just finding the marginal totals in a large table.

Coupon analysis used to be regarded as the number one criterion for assessing advertising effectiveness. The principles and valuable insights learned from coupon returns were applied to all forms of advertising. Over the years, monitoring coupon returns has been badly neglected, which is regrettable because this form of analysis in many ways far outstrips the current research measurements.

A drawback to using coupon returns and other direct measures as a standard criterion for media planning is the security aspect. Despite valient attempts on the part of some publications, who wish to use them for promotion, many advertisers are unwilling to release return data. There are even advertisers who still do not sufficiently realise the benefits of keyed returns to make the data automatically available to their agencies. Thus there is no coherent volume of information on the subject.

Of course I do not imply that coupons are the only useful direct measure of effectiveness. Classified advertising, store advertising, entries for competitions, requests for salesmen to call, catalogue distribution — all these help to evaluate a publication's real worth to particular advertisers and guide other advertising decisions besides media choice.

229

Even if an advertisement is not intended for direct response, hidden offers can be used as a guide to media choice, creative approach, wear-out and so on. This means that in the body of the copy readers are invited to write in for a leaflet, sample pack etc. Only those who have go as far as this and been interested are expected to take up such an offer.

## 5   Area tests

The British Bureau of Television Advertising published case histories in its Bulletin. An example of an experiment with indirect measures is the following data [12.8] on the Woolmark, the symbol launched in 1964 by the International Wool Secretariat. This is evidence of advertising working, not a test of television versus press.

In 1966 the International Wool Secretariat spent £162,000 in the London, Northern, Southern and Central Scotland areas. Surveys were carried out before and after the campaign, measuring awareness, which increased from a range of 50 to 63 per cent before (the result of earlier promotions) to 70 to 80 per cent after. In regions without television advertising awareness increased over the same period from 19 to 24 per cent over the same period to 27 to 36 per cent.

Outdoor can also be used in tests of this kind. For example, British Posters claimed in a trade advertisement in October 1974:

> 'The International Wool Secretariat sought to increase advertising awareness and to project a theme of style for wool. With striking advertising featuring Mary Quant and Mohammed Ali, using a British Poster 16 and 4 sheet Super Seven Campaign, wool advertising awareness was increased by some 37 per cent in the posted areas whilst those areas not covered remained static. A totally successful operation which has resulted in a follow up poster campaign for wool this autumn.'

It is not necessary that TV areas be involved in this kind of test. Towns are often used (not of course for TV tests) and different parts of one area (where two different transmitters can be employed). The logical extension of this is to control the advertising exposure of individual homes. This can be done for example by tipping-in page advertisements into the magazines these homes normally receive: a very useful facility for cheap test marketing. So far there is here no TV test

230

system of this kind. In the US the 'advertising laboratory' approach has been carried out by splitting the transmissions to different homes through the cables which carry them. The Milwaukee AdLab claims some notable improvements in sales discovered by creative and scheduling tests through this method. In the UK there are problems of a legal nature and of financial support: similar systems have been proposed but are not off the ground. The cost is considerable and advertisers, who would have to pay, leave to their agencies the decisions which would be affected.

There are many more complex cases. One which incorporated a test of TV versus women's magazines – a common comparison – and which was particularly well written up, was United Biscuits [12.9]. In the US the most famous recent example of this type was supported by 50,000 interviews and *Life*, *Look* and *Reader's Digest* co-operated. The results were 'favourable to magazines but only just', which was taken to show that 'magazines are generally comparable with television'. The findings have been published with perceptive comment from four independent UK marketers [12.10].

## 6 *Pre- and post-campaign research*

The method used most often to evaluate advertising – after straightforward observation of sales – is to repeat a survey before and after the campaign. Of course, this timing ignores the decline which may take place when we are *not* advertising. Remember that the survey should be about the *product* more than about the *advertising.* At its simplest the advertising objective might be to increase awareness of some product attribute; before the campaign there were $x$ per cent aware, after the campaign $x + y$ per cent.

This simple approach can be extended in several ways. There will normally be more than one measure of interest, for example awareness of several points, comparisons with competitors and intention to purchase. It is in fact advisable to explore several different criteria: advertising sometimes has unintended affects. We must however remember that our measures are not usually independent; often they are all only slightly different ways of saying, 'I like it'. The analysis may be carried out on different groups of people: obviously those in the main target are of most interest. It is also desirable to identify people with different amounts of exposure to the advertising, for example by obtaining their media habits and in analysis separating the heavy, light and non-exposed (these relationships are further commented on in Chapters 14 and 16). The surveys may also be linked with an area test, as in the Example 5 above. Finally, do not ignore any other available source of information in interpreting the research. Sales data, representatives' reports, trade reactions – all these may help in forming the most accurate possible view of what is actually happening.

## 7    Continuous research

The cyclical nature of advertising planning has already been mentioned: campaign, evaluation, new campaign and so on. It is therefore natural to set up a series of surveys or continuous research which provides repeated and comparable data.

Sales data falls into this category. It is at the regular meetings where the latest sales share figure is considered that most marketing and advertising policies are determined and evaluated. Continuous studies of usage, recall and image can perform a similar function. Moreover, without qualitative research the regular sales data raise more questions than they answer. Of course sales are what advertising is for, but without research we cannot diagnose why the sales were made, who to and where the changes took place (see [12.11] for two major American advertisers' position statements on this subject).

An example in this country serves to illustrate pre and post work but particularly the development of a campaign when the planner was continually nourished by data on the consumer, including her media exposure. The example incidentally also shows area tests being used.

The product in this case history is Vapona fly-killer, a slow-release insecticide strip, initially marketed by Shellstar Limited, now Temana UK Limited, a subsidiary of Shell. The strip is hung up in a room and kills insects, especially flies, over a period of about six months. We are not concerned here with smaller versions for wardrobes and cupboards or later more sophisticated designs called Spirelle and Cassette also marketed by Temana.

Our story starts in 1969 which was only the third year Vapona was on the British market when it was still without competition. There was therefore little understanding among housewifes about what the product actually did: advertising had of course to sell Vapona – but by creating awareness of the product field. Awareness has to be stimulated each year since this country is relatively insect-free and the season when flies are a nuisance is a short one, say May to August, and of uncertain intensity and data of starting. Shellstar faced two further difficulties: the product cost about four times as much as an aerosol insecticide (aerosols are particularly cheap in this country) and was not sold directly by a sales force to retailers but through distributors.

The 1969 campaign plan [12.12] included pre and post measures of awareness and purchase as well as media habits; these were designed to evaluate a media test which involved three areas: in area A both TV and magazines were used; in B the same weight of advertising was spent in the press only; in C only a light weight was employed, all in the press. Taking as an index of 100 the awareness in the area where it was highest after the campaign, we found the overall results shown in Table 26. The simple conclusion from this data would be that television was clearly the medium to use in future. However, this would have been oversimple. The use of the media classifications allowed us to separate informants in area A into groups according to the amount and type of their exposure to the advertising. A reduced version of this data shows awareness on the same index basis — see Table 27. This was compared with the awareness of the same groups before the campaign

Table 26

| Area | Media | Awareness index |
|------|-------|-----------------|
| A | TV and Press | 100 |
| B | Press only | 40 |
| C | Press, lightweight | 21 |

Table 27

| | Not and lightly exposed to TV | Medium and heavy exposure to TV |
|---|---|---|
| Exposed to Press | 81 | 131 |
| Not exposed to Press | 48 | 108 |

233

and shows about twice the awareness created by TV compared with press — but at twice the expenditure. The numbers who were reached by press but only lightly or not at all by TV were substantial: nearly a quarter of the population. And the shape of the detailed response functions suggested that the first few exposures to advertising of either kind were relatively more valuable than later exposures. Not only this, but the small numbers of housewives who said they were using Vapona were actually more concentrated among those reached by Press, whether or not they were heavily exposed to TV, than those reached adequately by TV alone. For all these, and for creative reasons, the decision was made to use both Press and TV next year. Television was to be used to create fast awareness — and in the circumstances its timing was crucial — while press seemed more capable of creating sales and also reached the lighter viewers to improve awareness.

The 1970 media plan reflected these objectives: TV started with a heavy burst in May, continued in June and was followed by another burst in July-August. The press campaign appeared in June and early July. Research was repeated pre and post campaign. These results confirmed the complementary roles of the two media, but this time a demographic analysis revealed a new point. It is normal to include an urban/rural breakdown in analyses and this showed a far greater use of Vapona in rural areas. The reason was obvious once it had been seen: there is a greater fly nuisance near woods and farms. The medium which was indicated to capitalise on this fact was outdoor, since posters could be brought in rural areas near where housewives came in to shop. An intensive campaign was required for 1971, since two competitors had now appeared and more were expected.

The 1971 plan again used TV, starting with a heavy burst in May; the second burst was not required because posters ran until July (and in the event were allowed to over-run because demand on the medium was low and it was in the interests of the contractors to show that outdoor was effective). The poster design concentrated on one main product claim: the length of the product's life ('kills flies all summer long'). Posters were omitted from one area where TV was upweighted but they were used at double weight in another area and TV was reduced there. Magazines were used again.

The research carried out in 1971 was of greatest interest in evaluating the poster test. The results were again examined by weight of exposure to the other media. The now familiar relations between press and TV exposure were confirmed, but this time poster exposure seemed to be working in much the same way as the press had worked in 1969, i.e. posters added to recall of the advertising message and did so most among those only lightly exposed to television. Interestingly, the informants in the heavily posted area not only recalled the expected copy point (length of life) much better than in the non-posted area (about twice as many could remember the slogan); they also recalled more of the other points, those not on the poster. We seemed to be observing posters working by helping the *whole* of the television commercial and press advertising to be remembered.

The 1972 plan therefore increased the poster expenditure. It kept the other two media as well since research had confirmed the way the different media were operating. By now the number of competitive brands had risen to 14. In the event Vapona still clearly dominated the market in 1972; it had grown in size very rapidly and had retained the majority of the total sales. On the other hand keeping distribution and display was turning into a problem. It was decided that promotional money now had a role to play tactically with retailers. As a result the 1973 media budget was reduced and we were back, in media purchasing power, to the early days on the brand. It was known from research that awareness decays between the end of one season and the beginning of the next. Therefore we returned to the proven TV-press combination as the most effective way of stimulating awareness and turning it into sales.

This completes the case history as evidence of the value of continuous data, enabling us to learn from experience and to plot a course with some precision and success through difficult waters.

## 8 Econometric analysis

'The essential role of econometrics is the estimation and testing of economic models. The first step is the specification of the model in mathematical form. . . . Next we must assemble appropriate and relevant data. . . . We use the data to estimate the parameters of the model and finally we carry out tests on the estimated model to judge whether it constitutes a sufficiently realistic picture. . . .' So we are introduced to what sounds a straightforward procedure in a standard text on econometric methods [12.14]. Often the necessarily abbreviated description by an analyst of a particular application also sounds straightforward. But a look at later chapters in the standard textbook, or a few searching questions of the analyst, will reveal that we are dealing with an art. Multivariate statistics applied in this area require assumptions, checks and comparisons with other information and are not a sausage machine. Both in the selection of the model and in the jump from associations to the statement that A caused B the analyst is often on very thin ice.

It is therefore impossible to give a compressed example of such a venture which communicates as much about the techniques as was possible in the earlier examples. A more general review is given at the beginning of Chapter 15. But the area is potentially so fruitful that it is worth trying to communicate what actually happened in a particular case.

We follow Johnston's four steps. The objective was to evaluate what advertising did for a particular brand — but to look at several brands competing in the same market so as to get comparisons. The criteria were an attitude measure, called here 'awareness', and sales.

The model assumed we would be able to explain sales movements by two factors, which the advertiser more or less controlled, i.e. the price to the consumer (which varied as a result of deals and promotions) and television advertising. In practice other factors may also be used as explanatory or 'independent' variables such as the weather (especially for seasonal products), out of stock percentages and so on.

The specification of the model was in three stages. First, could advertising explain awareness? Second, could price and awareness explain sales, or third, did price and advertising explain sales better?

The assumptions about the relation between advertising and awareness were:

1   There is a base level to which awareness drops when there is no medium-term advertising effect; the level depends on the long-term results of advertising, other brand activity, survey error and so on.

2   An advertising burst contributes to a 'stock' of advertising which then decays. The size of the contribution depends on the weight or size of the burst and on its creative effectiveness. The decay pattern is roughly that a constant proportion of the stock is lost in each period.

3   Awareness at any time is linearly related to the stock of advertising at that time.

This model is a simple one; many more complications are introduced in some methods. However it contains the key ideas of response and decay.

The second step is to assemble data. Here awareness came from a continuous tracking study, sales from the Television Consumer Audit and advertising data from JICTAR since this was a product field advertised almost entirely on television. Also from TCA come approximate price data (the value sold divided by the volume or weight or number of units). The measurements of all these variables cause particular problems, but let us assume here that we now have satisfactory data for all brands on sales shares, awareness, relative prices and TVRs.

The first model requires estimation of three parameters at least: base level, decay rate and slope of the response. The last two items may in fact have more complex formulations with several parameters each. We could get into the questions of threshold, diminishing returns, whether the decay falls back to the initial level and so on. We then need calculations which give values for these parameters. Several methods exist: there is always an estimating procedure to give some results. The results must then be incorporated in a test of the model. How much of the variation in awareness is accounted for by the model? In this case it was possible to explain 70 or 80 per cent for most brands. This is a satisfactory level, given the small number of parameters. Did the model predict the values of later observations? In this case it did for most brands, but for one gave consistent underestimates. It was found that a new commercial was being used for this brand — leading to the conclusion that the new commercial was more effective in creating awareness. Were the parameters precisely determined? No, in this case different decay rates could not be clearly distinguished: a 'best' fit could be given but a range on either side had to be allowed for.

The most important tests of all now begin. Not statistical tests but very practical ones. Do the results, i.e. the estimates of the parameters, make sense? That is, are they consistent with other data about these brands' advertising? Are they actionable, that is, have we learned something which changes our recommendations for advertising? It is here that the statistician who has built the model has to make way for the decision maker who uses this input with much else. In this case we already knew, from the averages of awareness, which brands scored overall well or badly and we were able to draw broad conclusions about the advertising. What was not clear from the averages was how much of the awareness was base level (did we mind falling to this level?), how much was the slope as a reaction to advertising stock (were we growing at a satisfactory rate in relation to our advertising spend?) and how much was due to the level of spend itself (previously hard to separate

237

from creative content but which could now be distinguished). Thus we learned how the advertising contributed to awareness and what was likely to happen at different levels of spend.

Having completed the first model we moved on to the second and third, which have the same form, e.g. how do price and advertising affect sales? Previously we had only one explanatory variable (advertising) now we have two.

The steps look exactly the same. The model is now a bivariate regression rather than a regression on a single variable. The statistical estimation of the parameters looks no more difficult to the terminal user than before. But in fact a possibility has entered which makes the whole procedure more complicated. The simple statistical approach assumes that our two explanatory variables are independent – and in practice they are often not. Price may be – and in this case for our brand was – associated with advertising (we had advertised most when the price was low). It is easy to see that if the correlation between price and advertising were exact we could never be sure whether it was low prices or high advertising which caused high sales. Even when correlation is not perfect 'it becomes very difficult, if not impossible, to disentangle the relative influences of the variables' [12.14].

Thus it was possible to calculate a price elasticity for our brand – 1 per cent drop in relative price seemed to be associated with a 2 per cent rise in volume sales share and so a 1 per cent rise in sterling share. But we could not be sure whether this was reliable or how much of an overestimate it could be. Plotting the data – always a wise precaution – showed that even the effect of price was by no means clear (the correlation coefficient was only about 0.6), that is, a price reduction was not always associated with a sales rise.

Similar sums with awareness as an explanatory variable instead of TVRs gave comparable results but with less good fits, indicating that awareness was correlated with sales but that advertising probably worked in additional ways.

Thus the latter part of the analysis led to tentative conclusions only. The data could not clearly differentiate between the effects of price and of advertising. The benefits of price reduction, while not well defined, nevertheless did not look very attractive: variable costs went up two per cent for an income increase of a maximum of one per cent, assuming all the cost of lower prices to the retailer were passed on, which is doubtful. Profit would certainly be less if variable costs were more than half the manufacturer's sales price. Advertising was shown to work on awareness; we learned about decay which could help in scheduling.

The complexities of multivariate data can be much greater than is shown in this example, but the types of problem are at least demonstrated here. So are the benefits which can emerge from a thorough and cautious analysis (help on pricing, creative effectiveness assessment, scheduling — even budgeting).

## CONCLUSIONS

There are many ways of measuring what an advertising campaign has achieved. They are not cheap — in cash or in the time and people required to apply them. But making advertising accountable has many benefits, in clearer objectives and so better work, in justifying the advertising budget and above all in learning from experience.

As an absolute minimum, data on the total market and our brand's position in it should be collected; the change in our situation compared with competitors may be illuminating, as explained in Chapter 8. However, this historical data is in many cases inadequate to justify the money spent in advertising and never provides diagnostic material: it does not tell us how or why the changes we observe are taking place. For this we need normal market research data, which is often collected for other purposes. With a little care and sometimes little extra expense we can increase the value of these surveys. We can add questions to measure explicitly whether our advertising objectives have been met. We can add media questions to study the effect of advertising and even of different media. We may be able to build in simple experiments. The main object is to plan next year's campaign with better information than we have now.

# 13 IS RESEARCH TRUSTWORTHY?

*An introduction for the non-specialist into some of the methods by which research is carried out. A discussion on how far research can be trusted. How to commission and evaluate research.*

The media department relies partly on tradition and fashion and partly on fact — which nearly always means research. But not all research results or interpretations *are* facts. So the dependence is necessary but uneasy. It is not possible to describe how advertising reaches people without using the results of research. The buyer's skill — especially on TV — cannot be evaluated without it. The previous chapter has shown that the effectiveness of a campaign cannot be judged without research. In the compost of cost, commonsense and research from which media decisions spring, research is sometimes the dominant factor.

At the same time research is a job for a specialist and this book is not about how to do research. There is a gap between the practising researcher and the inexpert user which it is important to fill. Dangers and misuses can be pointed out. Some of the distrust, misunderstanding, mystique and overselling can be removed. So in this chapter the principal methods used in media research are outlined and a suggestion made on how to approach the results.

# FACTS – OR FICTION

The results of research are usually considered as 'hard' data – reliable, accurate facts. It is easy to forget that even the hardest data comes from rather imperfect methods. An example is the statement: '24 per cent of housewives who buy X regularly also read publication Y'. 'Buying' and 'reading' are easily thought of as observations like an auditor's report on so many copies sold. But there are no 'buyers' or 'readers' for media men: there are only people who answer questions which result in them being classified in this way. The researcher does not watch someone reading, but asks a question like 'How many issues of the *Daily Mirror* have you read or looked at recently?'

Research techniques themselves are the subject to controversy. For example, they nearly all depend on people's memories, which are notoriously fallible [13.1]. When their reports are compared with verifiable facts (sales claims with actual sales, for instance) researchers are delighted if they are within a few per cent of the real answers. As Stendhal remarked 'It is terrifying to think how much research is needed to determine the truth of even the most unimportant fact'.

It is therefore possible that some marketing decisions are wrong? That products are launched, publications fail, or advertising is placed on incorrect information? It is very likely that mistakes are made. Research *is* fallible. It is reasonable to see imperfections in research and to be somewhat cynical about the results. But it would be a bad mistake not to use these imperfect results. The figures may not be perfectly accurate, but they do connect with reality. It is not necessary to trust implicitly in order to make use of it.

It is also foolish to dismiss research because it usually produces un-surprising results. In the majority of cases, research only confirms what is already known. It does, however, provide numerical data which can be put to good use. And sometimes research surprises the user into a fresh and more accurate view of the world

The alternatives to using research are usually even less reliable. That oracle, the managing director's wife, does not always know best. The way of life of most advertising people is untypical. Especially on their own subject, agency men are unlike the rest of the population. A survey in my agency revealed that the average executive there watched TV for only a little over an hour an evening – and for only a third of this time was he watching ITV. So he saw ITV for only three hours a week, compared with the average housewife's 16 hours. And he is more selective –

and apt to think either that others are like him or that ordinary people sit numbly in front of the set all evening. Research can disprove such common misconceptions.

## COMMISSIONING RESEARCH

The major jobs in media research have already been briefly described in Chapters 4, 5 and 6. Most of these are commissioned by committees representing the industry as a whole. In these cases, and even for much of the research commissioned directly by media owners, the results are made available to all the people who want to use them. They become the common language or currency between buyer and seller.

It is desirable that both sides agree on the value of this currency. The agency and advertiser pay the TV contractor's or magazine publisher's bill partly because the number of viewers or readers is said to be so many. When the buyer is suspicious about the goods, negotiations become painful. The result is that much media research tends to be stereotyped and to develop at the pace of the slowest user. It is done not so much to find out, as is a manufacturer's or agency's private research, as to verify what is already accepted and to quantify small changes. There are pieces of work which are imaginative, and which find something new, but these are exceptions. The bulk of the work is routine head-counting.

Most research work is put out to independent specialist firms. This guarantees that the findings are unbiased since no research company will prejudice its reputation for honesty. It also ensures that maintenance of high technical standards. The Market Research Society publishes a directory [13.2] of research organisations. The Society does not have corporate members: it is the professional body to which individual practitioners belong. The directory lists firms which have at least one full member of the Society on their staff; it gives a brief description of the services each firm offers and a short guide to the commissioning of research.

Choosing a research company is hard because the standards used in the work are difficult to verify but have a major effect on costs. The two main points to check are the quality of the research officer who is actually directing the research and the quality of training and supervision of the interviewers who are asking the questions. There is continual dispute on the role of the researcher in marketing problems: on the one hand he might restrict himself to carrying out the field-work and reporting, which is relatively cheap; on the other he might play a major part in problem analysis, research design and the interpretation of the results, which is expensive.

The Incorporated Society of British Advertisers keeps for its members a directory of research companies. It has published a useful summary [13.3] of the standards which research companies should follow. This suggests the headings under which the user should assess the research companies he might use. It gives guidance on getting quotations, methods of delivery of the results, payment and general servicing. It also gives in full the standards which individual members of The Market Research Society follow. These set the code of professional conduct for the research business. It gives the code of standards for the Association of Market Survey Organisation as well. This is a voluntary association of market research companies rather than of individuals. The two standards are very similar.

To the user of research standards on reporting are particularly important. Reproduced below is part of The Market Research Society Code.

*Standards in reporting on sample survey results*

Every report of a sample survey should contain an explanation of the following points:

1    For whom, and by whom, the sample was conducted.
2    The objects of the sample survey.
3    General description of the universe covered, i.e. the people who are represented in the sample.
4    The size and nature of the sample and description of any weighting methods: where applicable, the planned sample as well as the number of interviews achieved.
5    The time at which the fieldwork was done.
6    A description of the method by which the information was collected, i.e. whether by personal interview, mail interview, mechanical recording device or by some other method.
7    Adequate descriptions of field staff and any control methods used.

The main body of every report of a sample survey should contain:

1    Questionnaire.
2    Geographical distribution of interviews.
3    Factual findings.
4    Bases of percentages.

The publication of media survey results should meet all these points. The most important headings are the size and nature of the sample, the method by which the information was collected and the questionnaire. Without these, any interpretation of the findings is worthless.

Further useful information on do's and don'ts in media research can be gleaned from the IPA and ISBA appraisals of published research circulated to their members, from the IPA/ISBA leaflet on the subject and from other sources [13.4].

Market research is a business in its own right. The value of commissioned research, i.e. put out to a research agency, was £55 million in 1977. The Market Research Society then had about 2,400 members. The two largest companies, Nielsen and AGB, operate principally continuous, syndicated services. The five largest companies doing ad hoc work are British Market Research Bureau, Marplan, National Opinion Polls, Research Bureau and Research Services.


## BASIC METHODS OF CONSUMER RESEARCH

*Personal interviews*

The classical method of consumer research is the personal interview with a pre-planned questionnaire. A trained and experienced interviewer can quickly establish the right relationship with an informant: formal and yet friendly. The interviewer has to record the answers to short, carefully phrased questions. As many of the answers as possible are coded in advance. There is no discussion: the interviewer should not take sides.

Very few subjects are impossible to treat in an interview. A considerable amount of information can be collected. In fact, the hardest part of an interview is ending it. People take trouble to help the interviewer. They enjoy being asked their opinions and having attention paid to them. For many, it breaks the monotony of the day. Some methods of collecting information need a payment or other inducement to the informant but this is not necessary for a single interview.

244

As well as asking questions directly, the interviewer may show cards to the informant with words or pictures on them. She may carry publications or samples of a product. She may ask to see packs or the contents of a shopping basket. She may ask some of the questions only if the informant has passed certain screening questions. She may give parts of the questionnaire to the informant to complete; she may leave these, or a diary of some kind, to be completed later.

There are many different ways of asking questions [13.5]. For example:

1   *Direct*, e.g. 'Have you had a holiday away from home during the last 12 months?'
2   *About the household rather than the informant*, e.g. 'Is there a television set in this home?'
3   *Recall*, e.g. 'I would like you to say when you last read or looked at a copy of . . . ?'
4   *Using a numerical scale*, e.g. 'In an average month how often do you see issues of . . . ?'
5   *Using a picture scale*, e.g. 'Which of these pictures best shows about how much you usually see by the time you finish with a copy of . . . ?'

*Self-completion*

The interviewer may ask the informant to complete part of the questionnaire personally during the interview, rather than writing down what the informant says. Or she may leave behind a questionnaire to be filled in and collect it later or ask for it to be mailed back.

Or we may carry out the whole survey by post. This approach has the advantage that it puts less pressure on the informant, who works at her own speed and in private. Much longer questionnaires, like the Target Group Index, can be completed. On the other hand, the informant may get careless because no one seems to be checking her answers and she may even get someone else to do the job (which may not be a serious defect if the questions relate to the household and the daughter or husband is helping). The response rate can be low, though incentives to the informant help here, and then non-representativeness becomes a problem. Non-literates obviously cannot take part and generally the older and less educated reply less. But postal methods are obviously cheaper than personal interviews and their use is growing.

*Panels*

The interviewer may return later to the same informant, so that she gets information about changes over times. Or she may ask the informant to join a panel of informants all of whom complete a diary or do some similar task. The information may belong to this panel for a few weeks or for years. A panel kept in existence for years needs replenishing as people drop out.

The proportion of people willing to join a panel is naturally lower than those prepared to submit to a single interview. Sometimes this raises doubts whether these people are typical. There is some evidence that a bias can enter in this way. For example, people who do not view much TV may be less ready to record TV viewing though this is a bias which can be allowed for. In some important areas like product purchase, panels have been found to give very accurate results.

Panels are already used considerably in investigations of both products and media. There are probably additional uses still to be discovered [13.6]. The panel of most direct concern to agencies is the JICTAR measurement of TV viewing described in Chapter 4.

*Other methods*

Formal questionnaires and diaries applied in interviews and to panels do not exhaust the research armoury. Interviews may be conducted by psychologists or special trained interviewers, with less reliance on a questionnaire – so-called depth interviews. Or several people may be encouraged to talk together about a subject – group discussions. Films or other advertisements may be shown in a theatre. Or people may be observed in situations as normal as possible: in a waiting-room for example where their reading of magazines is filmed. Or one person in a household may record the behaviour of others. Or magazines left in the household may have been prepared with spots of glue which, when broken, show whether pages have been opened.

Questionnaires can also be inserted in a publication to sample its readers. The method is cheap but obviously biased towards first readers and the proportion returned is often dangerously low [13.7].

In this country, compared with the US, the telephone is little used for interviewing. Nearly 40 per cent of households do not have their own phone. So it is uncertain whether a representative sample can be drawn this way [13.8].

## FOUR QUESTIONS ABOUT A RESEARCH REPORT

Four questions now follow which the user of research may ask when faced with a research report. The first three are recommended. They should prevent even the non-technical user from being taken in by bad research.

### 1 Is the sample representative?

Research tells us about the habits and views only of the people actually interviewed. These have been drawn or sampled by some procedure from a larger group. If the sampling procedure is a satisfactory one, the informants may be taken as representative of this group – but of this group only. We should not extrapolate from these to other people who are not represented.

One example of this danger has just been given: questionnaires inserted in a publication which are returned are not likely to represent later readers. A reading and noting check on a weekly carried out two or three days after publication will not tell us about readers who have the magazine passed on to them. Postal subscribers to a magazine (who may easily be contacted by post) are different from purchasers at bookstalls. People who fill in coupons or write to a magazine are unlikely to be representative of all readers. There is American evidence that homes accepting a meter in their TV set view differently from others, though British data indicate that the difference here, if any, must be small.

A common objective is to get a sample which represents the whole population. The classical method is carried out in two stages; first areas are selected at random and then a list of people is taken from the local Electoral Register (registers covering the whole country are actually available in London). Attempts are made to include in interviews those people not on the register, e.g. the recently moved and those under 18 on the qualifying date. The interviewer calls back if necessary several times at the given addresses in her attempts to interview the selected individuals. This is called a pre-selected sample, i.e. selected before the interviewer approaches the informant, or a random sample. It is a method that usually gives a representative sample as long as the proportion of people who elude the interview is not too large and the number of areas or sampling points is high. One weakness is that it can under-represent those away from home a lot. The National Readership

Survey uses this method and the research contractor succeeded in 1974 in interviewing 74 per cent of named individuals and 78 per cent of the other selected people, which is about the same as five years ago though it has been claimed that success rates are falling [13.9].

A cheaper method, because it saves interviewers' time, is the quota sample. This is often adequate. The interviewer picks the sample herself from people she finds at home, at work or in the street. She is given certain restrictions on the informants by age, sex, etc. (this is her quota) to ensure that she does not simply interview those people who are immediately available but who are therefore unlikely to be representative. A method in-between the random and quota methods is the random walk, where the interviewer follows rules for going down streets and picking doors to knock on.

There are other methods of sampling. The first people an interviewer meets in the street, or those who accept an invitation to see a film show in the evening, or to a neighbour's house for a cup of tea and a group discussion are not completely typical but may be sufficiently so for certain purposes. Other ways may be less satisfactory. The advertiser's employees, for example, will not usually give typical results in a test of a new product.

## 2 Does the informant understand the questions?

With all research techniques (except observation) we rely on answers given by the informant. Why should these be true? Does the informant even understand the questions?

The informant does not give the same careful attention to the answers as we do. Nor does the informant necessarily attach the same meanings to words as do specialists. Just because an answer is given is no guarantee that the question was understood, only that it was a stimulus of some kind. People are quite ready to express opinions, even on subjects about which they know nothing. But it is usually supposed it is more trouble for the informants to make up an answer than to tell the truth. In fact most people go to some pains to reply as honestly as they know how.

People do however want to please the interviewer, to treat the interview as a puzzle, to give the answer which they think is expected. For example, a survey [13.10] on the furniture preferred in waiting rooms indicated that modern Scandinavian styles should be provided. Actual tests showed that the majority chose familiar, chintzy settings. Informants also find it hard to remember the trivial actions which interest us so much. They think something happened last week when it was really two or three weeks ago. They repeat what they usually do or what they think they ought to have done rather than what they actually did. So although people are willing to answer questions, their desire to be helpful is itself a problem. Whenever possible, their answers should be checked with the facts. Of course, no checks are possible on answers about awareness, understanding or attitudes.

We should examine carefully the wording of the questions and the context in which they are asked — for example BBC TV ratings are obtained by interviewers who announce themselves as from the BBC; could this influence the answers people give? Useful ways of seeing how the questions look to an informant is to complete a questionnaire yourself, to apply it in an actual interview or to watch an interviewer at work. These are salutary reminders of the gritty world which neat tables of results make it easy to forget.

In one interview [13.11] housewives were asked '5 per cent of the people in this country are illiterate. Does this mean that the number of illiterate people is 1 in 5, 1 in 10, 1 in 20, 5 out of 10 or 9 out of 10?' As many as 31 per cent gave the wrong answer, and another 6 per cent said they didn't know — yet how often it is assumed that informants can cope with more complex matters than this. It is also easy to be deluded into thinking that everyone is involved with a subject which you yourself find fascinating, but the housewife knows little and cares less about some subjects which concern the advertiser greatly. Note also that very heavy repetition in the press and on TV (about politicians, for instance) has little effect on those who are not interested.


### 3    Are the conclusions substantiated?

This question goes beyond techniques. It covers the action which may be recommended as a result of the research. It reminds us that scrupulous standards in carrying out the work are not enough if what follows is not relevant. The results must be presented as simply and as honestly as possible. Selection of one's best points is a temptation to all salesmen; media representatives using research data are no exception. There is therefore always a possibility that the conclusions in a research report select, suppress and exaggerate. In this situation buyers need an appraisal of the research by their own experts. This is one of the jobs of a researcher in an agency.

Most users of research do not go through or even see all the tabulations produced. They rely on the written report and a few key tables. When the work has been put out to a research firm, usually this company will write the technical report. To this an interpretative gloss may be added by the sponsors of the research. The factual description (by the research firm) and the sales pitch (by the sponsors) should be clearly separated.

There are two very common kinds of confusion against which we should be particularly on our guard: drowning in jargon and mixing up association with causation. Jargon is rife in research as in all specialist activities. It has the effect of isolating and magnifying the subject being investigated. A researcher does not talk about the television in the living room or lounge, he talks about the set in the viewing room. The room thereby becomes a room for viewing. At once the other ways the room is used fade into significance: it is over-looked that people are talking, children do homework, meals are being eaten. It is easy to assume after that that people see and even pay attention to all the commercials shown during the time they are rated as viewing. Real life is not quite like that and commonsense is needed to remind us of this fact.

'A West German store's recent sales survey showed that girls with scarlet nails sell more, and get fewer complaints, than their colleagues with natural nails' [13.12]. It would be easy to conclude that painted nails caused more sales — and this is the kind of conclusion which many research reports draw. But perhaps it was the more attractive girls who painted their nails — and whom the store also put at the best-selling counters?

'A humble study was done in 1967 of 391 members of Princeton University, class of 1942. It was revealed that those who took one drink a day had a median income of $18,500. The income of those who took four or more drinks per day, however, was $27,500' [13.13]. Can you conclude that there is a pleasant route to increase your income?

Finally, a more complex and more typical example. In the US some TV stations, but not all, broadcast editorial comments, taking sides as newspapers do on controversial issues. Do viewers like this? Opinions differ between areas where editorials *are* broadcast and where they are not [13.14] — see Table 28. Where editorials are broadcast, people feel

Table 28

| Informants believe TV stations should broadcast editorials | Editorials broadcast | Editorials not broadcast |
|---|---|---|
| Yes | 75% | 51% |
| No | 18% | 38% |
| Don't know | 7% | 11% |
| | 100% | 100% |

more favourably about this approach. It may be concluded that the broadcasts themselves make people feel better: 'It seems clear that people have become more favourable towards editorialising as they have seen it practised'. This interpretation may well be correct. But it is also possible that in areas where opinion was favourable the TV stations therefore decided to carry editorial, while where it was less favourable they decided not to. Or perhaps there was an underlying cause: in some area, or for old-established stations, the climate of opinion both favoured editorial comment and suggested to stations that they should carry it.


*4 Is the sample big enough?*

The first question asked by unqualified people about a piece of research is often whether the size of the sample justifies the conclusions. But this point is very much less important that the accuracy of the answers and the representativeness of the sample. The question is in fact not re-commended unless we are down below 50 informants. For some purposes, e.g. qualitative work to give a feel for how people react to a magazine or an advertisement, a dozen is an adequate sample. It is, of course, the actual size of the sample which matters, i.e. 100 informants or 1000, and not the sampling fraction which is often very small (1000 informants nationally is only 1 in every 40,000 adults).

The theory of statistics helps to determine the precision of the con-clusion which can be drawn from samples of different sizes. The theory cannot be applied straightforwardly; even the market researcher's 'random' sample is not completely random as demanded by the simple theory. This can be allowed for as is shown, for example, in an appendix to the National Readership Survey tables. The 'design factor' which has to be applied to the actual number of interviews to get the equivalent number of completely random interviews is in this case 2; that is, 15,000 interviews have equivalent precision to a completely random sample of 7500. Other sample designs have even worse design factors.

One useful result from theory shows how statistical error decreases as sample size gets larger. Doubling the size of sample means that precision is increased only 1.4 times. This is because the standard deviation of any result, or the standard error attached to it, is divided by the square root of the sample size. The cost of doubling the sample is not quite to double the cost of the research, for planning, analysis and reporting costs do not increase in proportion. But we do not get value for money in terms of greater precision when bigger samples are drawn. And after all, research is not done to establish eternal truths but to improve commercial actions which themselves have a limited cost benefit. Therefore sample sizes are often smaller than statisticians would like.

We should not be overawed by statistical significance testing. There are people who like to see classical significance tests being applied to every survey result, and who pay no attention to findings which are not 'significant' in this sense. This can lead to the loss of valuable information. Data can sometimes be a reasonable guide for action without dismissing every doubt. As Mrs Dashwood asked (in *Sense and Sensibility*): 'Are no probabilities to be accepted, merely because they are not certainties?' We usually have the job of making decisions, not of ensuring beyond reasonable doubt that an observed result would be substantiated in a very large sample.

A justifiable desire for large samples does not come from a wish for precision and significance but from the need to examine small groups within the main sample. Do women read the publication differently from men? Do heavy TV viewers have different buying habits? Are those who bought promoted packs different from other buyers? Such questions soon decimate the total sample size. When there are 50 informants or less to be examined the dangers of misinterpretation of numerical results become very high.

# 14 DEFINING THE TARGET

*Different ways in which informants may be
classified in research into markets and into
media habits. A discussion on the definition
of the target for advertising. Ways in which data
on products and on media can be combined and
used.*

In the last chapter, most of the research referred to was about the audience of different media. We now start from a different point, the target or people we want to reach and influence by our advertising. What can research do to help choose and describe them?

The choice of the target is part of the overall campaign strategy and involves people other than the media man and principles outside the scope of this book. For example, there is a marketing element in it: are there enough people in the target to make the campaign economic? Is the target definition consistent with all the other aspects of the marketing plan, such as distribution and price? There is also a creative aspect: do the people writing the advertisements really understand the target, so that they can write sympathetically and convincingly to them? Because these requirements have to be met, the definition of the target is often not in a form that fits exactly any of those available in the data the media man is used to working with.

Thus a simple and common target definition like 'all housewives' or 'all men' present no problems in the use of media research: we can analyse the National Readership Survey or select the appropriate data in the JICTAR reports. At the same time, the campaign may not be very pointed or individual because the creative people do not have much to get their teeth into.

When a more specific target is agreed, like 'heavy users of shampoos' or 'men who do most of the maintenance on their cars' then the creatives often get a clearer understanding of their task and can write more convincingly. The media man may however have a more difficult task. For some such definitions there may be appropriate data on the target's media exposure but for many targets there is nothing exact. Compromise and approximation are then necessary. This is the area we now explore, by listing the main categories of classification available.

## DEMOGRAPHIC CLASSIFICATIONS

The usual way in which people are described in surveys or in panels is by demographic classifications. The four most often used are:

1   *Sex.* Under this heading it is normal to include as a classification *housewives*, i.e. those responsible for household catering; some of these are men but male housewives are often excluded. Another category is *other women* meaning women who are not housewives.
2   *Age.* Age groups are usually broad, such as 15–24, 25–34 and so on.
3   *Social grade.* People are normally given the grade of the head of their household, which is based on occupation. A simple description of social grades is given in the References [14.1].
4   *Region.* ITV regions are used most often when TV or mixed schedules are being planned.

### Product-demographic data

The results of a survey about a product are usually tabulated by demographic breakdowns. For example, of the 18,350,000 housewives in the country, the Target Group Index in 1974 estimated that 27.7 per cent or 5,083,000 used ground coffee. When the different social grades were looked at separately, the figures were as shown in Table 29. This

Table 29

| Grade | All housewives | Ground coffee users |
|-------|----------------|---------------------|
| AB    | 2,000,000      | 1,099,000           |
| C1    | 4,059,000      | 1,420,000           |
| C2    | 5,580,000      | 1,293,000           |
| DE    | 6,711,000      | 1,271,000           |

is *product-demographic* data and can be presented in various ways. For example, we can express the second column of figures as percentages of the first, and obtain the *penetration* of ground coffee usage within social grade. In this analysis the percentages do *not* usually add up to 100 and their (weighted) average is the penetration among the whole population (Table 30). This must not be confused with the *profile* of ground coffee users: in an analysis of the profile of a group the percentages must add up to 100 (Table 31).

Finally the profile can be compared with the profile of the whole population of housewives, to construct an index of *selectivity* which shows the relative importance of each social grade. It is exactly the same to divide each of the penetration figures above by the average penetration (Table 32).

Although each of the last three tables has been derived from the same initial table, they describe the market in rather different ways. The *penetration* data tells us what proportion of each social grade use ground coffee: over half the AB's but a third of this proportion, under 20 per cent, of the DE's. The *selectivity* indices show the same aspect as a comparison with the average: an AB housewife is twice as likely as the average to use ground coffee, a DE only two-thirds as likely. The *profile* data however reminds us that there are many fewer AB's than DE's generally, so there are actually more DE housewives than AB's making up the ground coffee market, in fact each social grade contributes about a quarter. All this is very loosely summed up by saying the ground coffee market is upgrade.

Table 30

| Grade | Penetration of ground coffee usage, % |
|-------|---------------------------------------|
| AB | 55.0 |
| C1 | 35.0 |
| C2 | 23.2 |
| DE | 18.9 |
| | 27.7 All housewives |

Table 31

| Grade | Percentage of ground coffee users in each grade |
|-------|--------------------------------------------------|
| AB | 21.6 |
| C1 | 28.0 |
| C2 | 25.4 |
| DE | 25.0 |

Table 32

| Grade | Selectivity of social grade for ground coffee usage |
|-------|------------------------------------------------------|
| AB | 1.98 |
| C1 | 1.26 |
| C2 | 0.84 |
| DE | 0.67 |

*Media – demographic data*

Similarly we can report media audiences with demographic breakdowns. Continuing with the 1974 TGI data we find the housewife readerships shown in Table 33. The same sort of figures for penetration, profile and selectivity could be calculated for a publication as for product usage. We can see for example that *Weekend* has a lower proportion of ABC1 readers (24 per cent) than *Radio Times* (42 per cent).

Partly because the lower social grades generally figure less prominently in target definitions, a publication with an upgrade profile can charge more for its average reader than one with a downgrade profile. For example, a full page in the *Radio Times* costs £6100 and

## Table 33 HOUSEWIFE READERSHIPS, 000s

| Grade | Weekend | Radio Times |
|-------|---------|-------------|
| AB    | 90      | 820         |
| C1    | 360     | 1290        |
| C2    | 700     | 1290        |
| DE    | 750     | 1540        |
| TOTAL | 1900    | 4940        |

gives a housewife cost per thousand of 124p; *Weekend* charges £2080 which is only 109p per thousand. The difference in overall cost per thousand is not large: 11 per cent.


### DEMOGRAPHIC DEFINITION OF THE TARGET

When the target for advertising is defined it is common to do so demographically. This often appeals to commonsense and also enables us to make use of the demographic information in both the product and the media data. A simple definition may be used like 'all housewives' or 'AB men' or weights may be attached to different groups to reflect their importance. The procedure is described in more detail in Chapter 15.

To continue the ground coffee example, we could evaluate publications to reach users by taking either

1   Their *total* housewife readership,
2   *OR* their ABC1 housewife readerships, on the grounds that these social grades are above average users of the product.
3   *OR* their *weighted* housewife readerships; we do this by multiplying their social grade profiles by the percentage of ground coffee users within each grade, as given above; we could similarly use the selectivity indices. Thus we take into account that an AB housewife is three times as valuable to us as a DE housewife.

By these methods we obtain three different audience sizes. We need not be disturbed that the *actual* sizes of these differ according to the target definition we take; it is obvious why this is happening. What matters is their *relative* sizes, especially when we take cost into account and calculate the cost per thousand in each case. Table 34 completes

257

these calculations. We would conclude from the ABC1 housewife figures that *Weekend* was quite expensive for reaching upgrade housewives; it would have to cut its rate by nearly 40 per cent to compete with the *Radio Times*. This is a very different conclusion from that indicated by the overall costs of the two publications.

However when we use the full demographic weighting we return much nearer parity. This is because we do now allot some value to the lower social grade readers in which *Weekend* is relatively strong. The rate would now have to be cut by only 5 per cent to equal the *Radio Times*.

This way of linking the target definition and the evaluation of media is so familiar — and usually so sensible — that it may come as a surprise to realise it is a makeshift. The demographic link is used mainly because it is there and not because it has been demonstrated to be the most efficient way of evaluating media to reach particular targets. It must be assumed to use this link that any associations which might exist between belonging to the target and reading various publications do not invalidate the simple weighting calculation.

It is not difficult to see why demographic classifications are sometimes poor descriptions of the real targets which interest advertisers. It is a truism that society is now more fluid. Previously rigid classifications are now less useful. Social grade in particular has become less helpful as a predictor of the products to which expendable income is directed. There are now more working women, more independent teenagers, more men who help in the home.

For these reasons the simple assumptions made in many demographic targetting decisions may be over-simple. We supposed above that to sell ground coffee we needed only to reach housewives; they may well buy

Table 34

| | All housewives | | ABC1 housewives | | Weighted housewives | |
|---|---|---|---|---|---|---|
| | '000 | C/000 | '000 | C/000 | '000 | C/000 |
| *Weekend* | 1900 | 109p | 450 | 462p | 480 | 433p |
| *Radio Times* | 4940 | 124p | 2110 | 289p | 1500 | 408p |

most of the product but they are not the only buyers and they may be influenced by others in their households. These people should be certain cases be allotted their due importance when targetting.

A survey by IPC Newspapers in 1973 [14.2] found that a third of housewives said their husband went with them 'for a fairly large amount of food shopping'. Half as many said the husband went along once a week or more. The same survey showed that for half their shampoo purchases the wife 'knows what brand he likes' and for a quarter he 'would mind if she bought a different brand'. Children also have their say.

It has therefore been suggested that instead of targetting on individuals and collecting data about them we should be studying households as a unit. The *Daily Mirror* in 1972 [14.3] gave data on the expenditure and purchasing intentions for a wide range of products together with readership of publications by the household. One of the differences from most research (where only one individual is interviewed from a household) was that it was possible to define households where the head and/or the housewife had read a particular paper yesterday, or where any adult has done so. For example, the *Daily Mirror/Record* was read by

| | |
|---|---|
| the housewife | in 30 per cent of the sample, |
| the head of household | 36 per cent |
| head and/or housewife | 39 per cent |
| any adult | 42 per cent |

## OTHER DEFINITIONS OF THE TARGET

If a demographic definition of a target is not always enough, what should be added to it or replace it? There is no general answer to this question. Such a definition is an integral part of the marketing strategy for a particular product, so the answers are as varied as product situations. The advertising task may be to keep existing users loyal. Or people who have not yet tried the product may have to be persuaded to do so. Or those with a favourable attitude to the product who do not buy it often may be asked to buy more.

The definitions just suggested are examples of the use of product information about individuals as a target definition. The most common of these definitions is 'heavy users' or 'heavy buyers'. It is usually more worthwhile to advertise to a woman who buys two packs a week than to a woman who buys one pack a month. However this is not the case if the object of advertising is to extend the use of the product, i.e. to persuade the light or non-buyer to buy more, when the reverse would be true.

Heavy users are a relatively small group for expensive products. For example, in the US nearly 90 per cent of all air trips are bought by less than a tenth of all men. But a similar, though less marked, skewness applies to products bought by 'everyone'. For some commonly bought products, 50 to 80 per cent of purchases are made by 20 to 30 per cent of all housewives.

Attempts have been made to find simple discriminators other than demographics which effectively determine a target. Possessing certain household durables may be a characteristic which makes people more likely to buy others [14.4]. Psychological classifications have also been suggested; it has been found that housewives' attitudes to economy or their conservative habits in shopping can be used to identify those who will be repeat buyers of a new product [14.5].


## PRODUCT-MEDIA DATA

If a target is defined in other terms than demographic, then the standard media data cannot usually be used; the National Readership Survey does not classify informants by areas of interest or psychological orientation; the JICTAR TV panels do not report product purchase. Nevertheless there are some sources of data where product purchase or attitudes to products *are* measured on the same informants as media exposure. This is *product-media* data. It is one form of *single-source* data, i.e. where information is obtained from the same informants about two or more characteristics of interest.

The Target Group Index [14.6] is the most widely used source of product-media data. This first went into the field in 1968 and has been published annually since then. The data source is a long self-completion questionnaire returned by 25,000 adults (of fifteen years old or over). Some 400 products or services and 2500 brands are covered; the same informants answer questions about their reading and viewing.

The TGI was preceded overseas by the TEM system [14.7] in Sweden and the Brand Rating Index [14.8] in the US. In the UK its forerunner was the All-Media and Product Survey [14.9], designed as an experiment to test various techniques and to evaluate the usefulness of single-source data. This survey was carried out in 1966-67 and consisted of some 7000 interviews with a long questionnaire plus diaries on television and cinema exposure kept by a proportion of informants. The surveys carried out by IPC and already referred to are also examples of product-media data. Of course media owners are particularly ready to provide this sort of data when otherwise the assumption made in agencies would be that their readers are not particularly useful targets for advertising. For example, the *Daily Mirror* was concerned to show the proportion of cars bought by *Mirror* readers. In 1971 the *Mirror* reader was more likely than an *Express* reader to be a purchaser of a low price car (although the reverse was true for high priced cars).

We conclude the ground coffee example by using the Target Group Index data directly: we evaluate the two publications by the number of their readers who are ground coffee users (Table 35). We now see figures rather different from those which the demographic approximations suggested. As is usual, the approximations give results that are closer to reality than the overall readerships; but also as is usual [14.10], the apparently more refined calculation (weighted readership taking all social grades into account) was no real improvement on the cruder one (taking simply ABC1s). We would now expect *Weekend* to have to cut its rate by nearly 20 per cent to have the same cost per thousand in the target as the *Radio Times*.

We have just seen methods that suggest in turn that *Weekend* is a little cheaper than the *Radio Times*, that it is a lot more expensive, only a little more expensive and finally 20 per cent more expensive. The differences demonstrate that when we evaluate a medium by its cost in reaching the target it can make quite a difference how we define this target.

There are four other ways of getting product-media data:

*1    Product questions on media surveys.* Though a survey is intended primarily to measure media exposure it may include a few questions about products. The special interest questions on the National Readership Survey are the best-known example of this. The target can be defined as 'car-owners who buy most of the petrol' or 'people who went abroad last year on a packaged holiday'. The reading habits of these groups can be examined directly without using any demographic linkage. Such surveys rarely carry more than a few product questions since media measurement takes up most of the interview. The target

## Table 35  GROUND COFFEE
## HOUSEWIFE USERS

|  | '000 | C/000 |
|---|---|---|
| *Weekend* | 450 | 460p |
| *Radio Times* | 1650 | 371p |

definitions obtained are therefore of use to only exceptional advertisers.

*2  Media questions on product surveys.* Many advertisers already commission their own surveys into their markets. These may describe the market factually — who buys, which brand they buy, who consumes and so on. Or they may investigate attitudes and beliefs. Or they may study the penetration and influence of advertising: recall and awareness of advertising proportions for example.

By a simple step and at a small additional cost, the value of these surveys can sometimes be doubled: media questions can be added. We have used this technique in surveys for holiday travel for BEA, batteries for Exide [14.11], Vapona [14.12], confectionery for Cadburys, analgesics for Miles Laboratories and many others.

One problem in private work of this kind is that the levels of exposure to media found in the survey are bound to be slightly different from accepted industry figures. The placing of the media questions in a different questionnaire from the standard, using different interviews, the time of year — all these cause differences. A solution to this is to ask the media questions about frequency of reading or viewing, not about average-issue readership or last night's TV viewing. Probabilities of exposure, interpreting these frequency claims, can then be chosen, so that their relative levels *and* the total reading and viewing figures are consistent with industry data. This device does not alter practical decisions but removes a possible source of confusion.

*3  Panels.* Because members of a panel can be interviewed repeatedly, or will themselves fill in a series of diaries or questionnaires on different subjects, a panel informant can give a great deal of information. The Attwood Consumer Panel is primarily concerned with housewive purchases but has pioneered the provision of product-media data. The Television Consumer Audit which expanded to national coverage in 1968 collects at intervals television viewing data by seven-day aided recall and press readership, as well as measuring household purchases.

*4    Marriage.* It is also possible to construct a single source by marrying together informants from two separate surveys or panels, i.e. the individuals are arranged in pairs, one from each survey. Then data from one individual is transferred to the other. From then on the second individual is treated as though he had given the answers the first actually gave. We carried out our first marriage [14.13] between NRS individuals and JICTAR panel members in 1965. The so-called Expanded TGI was introduced by Times Newspapers and Computer Projects (see the example below); this marries JICTAR data to the TGI. The marriage of data is particularly a French interest [14.14]; the method has been used also in the US and in Germany. Marriage is an expedient, i.e. it is inherently less trustworthy than single-source data, but may be used in the absence of single-source data. It is still uncertain whether it introduces serious errors in wrongly associating the characteristics of informants.

## The uses of product-media data

The improved definition of a target offered by the product aspects of product-media data can be put forward as the justification for collecting such data. This definition can be used in agency decisions at two stages before the campaign; at the outline planning stage when broad media choice is settled, or at the detailed scheduling and buying stage. It is important to keep these two uses separate, since one may be justified and the other not. There is also a use for such data after the campaign.

*1    Broad media choice.* When it is being decided how much money should be allocated to a medium – or whether to use it at all – it should be known how much our real target is exposed to it. The amount may be more, less or about the same as the demographic group normally used instead of the target. That is, its selectivity index may be above, below or about 100. For example, if we want to reach heavy tea-drinkers it may be useful to know that they watch commercial television more than the average housewife. It will therefore not take as much money to reach tea-drinkers on TV as often as all housewives. The effect of this information on planning a multi-media campaign may be to use less TV than would otherwise be thought necessary.

Sometimes a high selectivity index for a medium suggests that less be spent there – as in the example just given. Sometimes it suggests that a product be advertised on a medium which otherwise looks too expensive. For example, the cost of a cinema campaign to reach girls who use a lot of make-up is less than appears from its cost to reach all girls of a comparable age: the girls who go often to the cinema include a disproportionately large number of those who make-up heavily.

*2    Scheduling and buying.* There may be sufficiently detailed associations between the target and individual vehicles to make product-media data useful in drawing up and buying a detailed schedule. Does ITV during pub opening hours reach men who are draught beer drinkers? Are so many petrol buyers out in their cars on Saturday afternoons that this time should be avoided by the buyer? It is unlikely that for most targets product-media data will alter the normal evaluation of days and times on television [14.15]. TV is so much a mass medium that the cheapest time to reach heavy buyers of any product is likely to be also the cheapest time anyway.

The press is more likely to be selective. The evaluation of individual publications is therefore more likely to be altered by having product-media data. It is quite common [14.10] that the selectivity index of a publication can be as high as 140 or as low as 70.

*3    Post-campaign evaluation.* The purpose of linking directly product and media information in a survey carried out after a campaign is so that those who have been exposed to the campaign can be identified and examined separately. Several examples of such data were mentioned in Chapter 12 and more follow in Chapter 17. The analysis of such data can be extremely complex [14.16] or very simple. Here is one straightforward example from the Attwood Consumer Panel [14.17]. A short burst of press advertising was used for an established food brand. Informants were classified by whether they were heavy, medium or light readers of the publications used. The purchases of each group in

Table 36

|  | Exposure to the campaign | | |
|---|---|---|---|
|  | Heavy | Medium | Light and none |
| Index for sales change | 109 | 108 | 86 |

the 12 weeks after the campaign were compared with those in the 12 weeks before the campaign (see Table 36). Overall sales had increased. This analysis made it clear that the increase was entirely among those with some exposure to the campaign, while sales actually fell among those who had little or no exposure.

*Controversy about product-media data*

Although product-media data has the uses listed, it is still not standard, in the sense that the major industry media data sources include very little product information. This is despite the advantages it has in removing the inefficiency inherent in demographic targeting. To use a demographic target definition when it is not the real target can only introduce error in the valuation of media. It is also convenient not to have to employ complex demographic weightings. Further, when single-source data is used by the account executive, market planner and media man a source of possible confusion is removed. They can all use the same target definition and all agree on the same figures. This consistency creates greater confidence and teamwork than the use of separate retail audit, consumer research and media research data all perhaps with different definitions and producing slightly different figures.

An additional advantage to the user of a product survey who has added his own media questions is that he can choose which media, particularly which publications, are included. He is not limited to those in the industry data.

Against these benefits are set some practical objections:

1   *Problems in research methodology.* The technical difficulty with single-source data is that it may demand more information from an informant than is normally collected. It is impractical simply to add existing data-collection methods together and apply all of them to each informant. Other methods produce results which are different from the ones we are used to. For example, Attwood Consumer Panel readerships differ slightly from those of the NRS and single-interview product purchase results differ from those of the Attwood Consumer Panel, though the latter difficulty may not be serious [14.18].

2   *Samples might become too small.* To reduce the target from

housewives to heavy buyers will reduce the sample size from which the media figures are derived; the reduction could be to one quarter or less. The precision of the data is then correspondingly halved or worse. Some of the apparent changes suggested by a direct definition of the target may be illusory: the data may be too imprecise to use. The alternative is that a much larger and more expensive research job may be necessary.

3  *Any change in the industry system must be slow.* Obviously private product-media surveys do not raise problems of re-organisation. But the amalgamation of existing industry services and the provision of new industry product-media data would involve major decisions. There is not sufficient evidence yet that this upheaval is feasible, or even desirable, but there is a strong case for examining this possibility carefully. More than one proposal [14.19] on the integration of the planning of industry research has been written. The most relevant (first) paper referred to sets out the advantages expected from a review of the present systems for collecting data. It does not put forward a firm alternative specification but recommends a feasibility study and an objective for future planning of industry research.

4  *Will media decisions be changed?* The most serious objection to the collection of product-media data is that it may be a nuisance to do and still not change pre-campaign media decisions. The imperfections of the demographic link are admitted, but they may in practice be unimportant. There is confusion here between planning (where single-source data would probably have more effect) and buying (where it probably has less).
This question can be answered only by the examination of data. No theoretical answer is possible. Several studies [14.10, 14.15, 14.19] based on Attwood, TCA or AMPS data have been published. Most work done so far has been on mass-market products and on media where the effects of having product-media data may be smallest. There would be more fragmented targets and more specialised media where the effects are greater.

My opinion, formed from the data looked at so far, is that having product-media data can cause changes in post-campaign evaluation; it can cause some changes in broad planning, probably minimum changes in TV buying, and only small changes in press buying. The effect of product-media data on the evaluation of different publications is real enough, but it is generally smaller than the range of their cost-effectiveness. In other words, the publications with the highest number of relevant readers per pound are usually the same whether 'relevant' is defined by a demographic group or in product terms. There are exceptions: sometimes small but genuine improvements could be caused in advertising schedules. And even small improvements could be worth paying for as well as being critical to the publications involved.

## LINKS THROUGH QUALITATIVE DATA

We have now seen three broad levels of target definition. The most straightforward case is when the genuine target description agrees with a definition in the standard media data. This happens less often than is supposed, but for convenience is often made to happen. The second case is when, with a little trouble (for example, using TGI or special survey data) the two can be made to coincide. In the third case the definitions in the media data only approximate the true ones. Qualitative data and judgement must then be used to refine the crude arthmetic. We must distinguish those refinements that are intended to make more accurate estimates of the numbers of *readers or viewers* in the real target from those which are about the *effectiveness* of advertising in one medium rather than another.

As an example of the third case, we may for our media analyses have to turn 'mums who really put their children first' into 'mothers of children 5-15' and ignore the qualification 'put their children first'. However we might feel that the readers of *Family Circle* or *Good Housekeeping*, by the very fact they choose these publications, are more likely to be in our real target than mothers who read *Weekend* or *TV Times*. In other words, just as the link of product with media information can change an evaluation based on demographics alone, we might improve media choice further if we could link on such qualitative aspects.

Before media men became so reliant on research (or perhaps before advertisers insisted so much on numerical justification) this factor was frequently used, and admitted to be judgement. Some publications 'felt right', no matter what the figures said.

Research attempts to substantiate this effectiveness element by describing how people use media, how they talk about different publications and what qualities they attribute to them. The techniques can be observation, direct questioning, group discussion, numerical scaling or finding out the Life Styles of the audiences. The problem is to decide whether an agreement between the qualitative description of the target, e.g. 'put their children first', and of the medium is already taken into account in the cruder readership-in-the-target calculation; on this difficulty there is more discussion in Chapter 17.

For day-to-day work in an agency, the practical action to take is to ensure that the definition used in media analysis is as close as we can get to the real targets. When the working definition results in lists of cover and cost efficiencies, we must remember these are not absolutes if the definition was approximate. Qualitative or 'soft' data and judgement may then reasonably modify the arithmetical ranking. To measure the qualitative aspects in any way — both in the target and in the readers' and viewers' characteristics and attitudes — will give insights and also improves our decisions.

## MEDIA-MEDIA DATA

Most of the sources mentioned so far collect data from the same individual on more than one type of medium. The main industry sources however concentrate on only one medium each; JICTAR informants have given some data on readership but this is not readily available to users, NRS informants give information about radio, cinema and ITV but only in the broadest terms.

With media-media data a campaign in two media can be examined in detail. For example, publications can be chosen which add most to the cover of a TV schedule — or alternatively those which duplicate highly with ITV viewing. After a campaign it is possible to isolate the people exposed to one medium but not the other, people who were exposed to both media and so on. This can help to show how the different media work, comparatively and together.

The main purpose of the Expanded TGI data [14.20] is to allow detailed TV schedules and press schedules to be studied together. The common unit is opportunities-to-see. It is possible to show how non and light ITV viewers get improved exposure from a mixed schedule, compared with a pure TV schedule. In one example, for a schedule spending £250,000 to reach canned beer drinkers, it was calculated that for a small drop of OTS on the heaviest viewers improvements were affected on all the other groups — see Table 37. We can see in these numbers

Table 37  GROSS OPPORTUNITIES TO SEE

| ITV viewing | All TV | Mixed TV and press |
|---|---|---|
| Non | 0 | 500 |
| Light | 500 | 1070 |
| Light-medium | 590 | 910 |
| Medium | 930 | 1120 |
| Medium-heavy | 1360 | 1390 |
| Heavy | 2110 | 1900 |

that the all-TV campaign gives fewer overall OTS; in other words TV has in this case a higher cost per thousand. In fact the same budget bought either 990 TV OTS or 780 from TV and 420 from press (using 13″ by 5 columns or the equivalent). How these two media compare in effectiveness, what is the effect of the move when competitors' advertising is considered and so on are points of judgement which the analysis cannot answer. But at least the data is on a relevant target and the complexities of viewing and reading relationships have been taken into account.

# 15 MARKET AND MEDIA MODELS

*This chapter is for the non-technical planner or advertiser who is intrigued but baffled by econometrics and modelling generally, and the models used in schedule evaluation in particular.*

## Econometrics

In the 60s and early 70s 'models' in media meant mainly the help given by computers in evaluating and constructing schedules, nearly always in the press. That particular application is discussed in the second part of this chapter.

In the mid-70s other models were publicised, often under the general name of the econometric approach. Their application falls into two areas. First, the analysis of historical data covering marketing facts (e.g. brand shares, brands' prices) as well as media (e.g. what advertising each brand had). In Chapter 12, Example 8 summarised an application. Second, once a particular model has been constructed and accepted, or when general rules have emerged, we can use the approach to evaluate different courses of action. These range from pricing, below-line spending and media budgeting to detailed comment on possible allocations of budget, both over time and over regions. These two last uses were commented on in Chapters 8 and 9.

Having seen the way this approach enters into media planning it is time to comment on the approach itself. One particular part of it, the measurement of response, is dealt with in the next chapter. Here the subject is the general handling of numbers used this way to summarise, evaluate and improve campaign effectiveness.

It is necessary to remind the reader that we are now looking at only one description of advertising. This way of representing markets and marketing activity is at the macro level, and is done by relatively few numerical measures. These include the main financial decisions, such as the amount spent on advertising or its measured exposure, e.g. TVRs, price relative to other brands, sales and so on. But, instead of money or TVRs we may on the other hand study advertising objectives and the actual advertisements. As well as sales we may measure attitudes, brand positioning and so on. Or we can get into finer detail on sales, brand-switching data from panels for example. Finally at the micro level we can study individuals, as we do in advertising development.

There is therefore a whole range of ways of studying the reaction of the market to our advertising decisions. These ways are rarely used together and may even make incompatible assumptions. Eventually some reconciliation may be possible (see, for example, the record of the 1976 MRS seminar on this subject [15.1]). But normally we use one set of beliefs and techniques at one end of the range, others elsewhere.

To study the macro level is attractive for two reasons: it encompasses the final objective (sales) and the major decisions about money; also, statistical techniques are available which claim to find the relationships between the variables — subject to certain assumptions all too rarely spelled out and sometimes not met.

This approach is potentially a major aid to budgeting and media planning decisions, but the reader should be warned that work in the other, more detailed areas indicated above is not replaced by this broad statistical approach.

The models used at the macro level cannot explain *why* and so cannot lead by themselves to understanding or qualitative improvement.

The approach is not new; the principal route is through multivariate statistics, especially regression, which is a well-documented discipline. The techniques have however become much more accessible in the last few years, packages of programs being available through terminals.

Nor is the application to marketing new. Some work in the UK was done in the 60s, though publications then and in the early 70s were not much noticed [15.2]. In the US there was an earlier start and too wide

271

a range of application to summarise here, both in analyses of specific markets (the names of Palda, Kottler, Bass, Parsons and Clarke will be familiar to specialists) and in the development of general models available commercially [15.3].

However the subject attracted most attention in the UK when Callaghan OHerlihey opened shop [15.14]. He not only made large claims and argued his case convincingly, but he tailored his service to a specific and important area: the allocation of the TV budget. He also correctly argued for testing as well as analysis and certainly has satisfied clients [15.5]. His methods have stimulated discussion [15.6]. Other analysts are currently active too, both in agencies and at advertisers, either publicly advocating the econometric approach, such as Michael Stewart at Beecham, or practising it, but considering the results too valuable to publish.

Reaction to these developments include blind faith, bewilderment and backwoodsmanship. More informed comment has centred on two points. One is the danger that the models are incomplete or may recommend extreme action in extrapolated situations.

We can also have difficulty in choosing between models, or between parameters in a model, even thought the action then recommended is likely to change drastically. The method of estimation is insensitive, but the outcome is very sensitive. Another danger is that advertising might have long-term effects, i.e. over years, which models based on short-term measures, e.g. over weeks or months, are not designed to catch. There is no doubt that short-term response and decay exist, and can be measured both on consumer measures [15.7] and on sales. The question is whether other effects are produced which are either undetected by the techniques, e.g. actual levels or trends may be removed in the analysis but are the most valuable effect, or are outside the range of observation, e.g. sales fall two or more years later after advertising has dropped, or are too small to be noticed in the analysis. On the last point Stephen King [15.8] gave an example of a major image change in Oxo over ten years, which nevertheless averaged only 0.13 per cent improvement a month, hard to detect among other short-term changes. The subject remains a battlefield [15.9].

Having summarised too briefly a complex and advanced subject, it may seem strange to spend time on two aspects of a simpler one — the evaluation of the frequency distribution of exposures produced by a press schedule and the value attributed to each number of exposures (in Chapter 16). The easier problem is however important in its own

272

right — schedule evaluations are in frequent use — and the detail which is more easily grasped here illuminates principles which apply in more complicated cases.


## A NOTE ON COMPUTERS

The computer is only a store for numbers and letters and an adding machine. But it works so fast and impeccably that it has revolutionised the business and scientific worlds. In a book about media planning its clerical function is uncontroversial and will not be discussed after the next paragraph. Nor is its use in survey analysis included. Note finally that I write 'the' computer: we are not concerned here with the differences between machines, languages or programs. The user need not know in detail how results have been achieved.

The computer is in the agency — or available to it at a bureau — because it can carry out so efficiently a variety of accounting and record-keeping tasks. As an example of its administrative capability, consider television buying — similar systems exist for the press. When the buyer has agreed with a contractor to buy a particular spot, he writes down, or inputs at a terminal, only a few details. There are a large number of such records: each £1 million spent in TV means over 1000 spots, and each may be moved several times as the TV situation changes and campaign plans are altered. The computer printer then produces the order sent to the contractor, updates the records of money committed for this advertiser and with this station; it produces on request a summary of buys on each station. After transmission it checks the eventual invoice and, by comparing the bookings with JICTAR data, summarises buying performance. This frees the buyer for more rewarding work. All media owners face similar data processing problems, and computers are used by them in much the same way. It would be pleasant to believe that eventually the industry might move to an integrated clerical system. At present one computer writes an order, the ordinary post carries the message and another computer acknowledges it. But although centralised processing would bring economies and the idea has been in the air for years [15.10] the problems of implementation look insuperable.

But clerical work is not what is meant by 'the computer in media'. This phrase usually means helping the planning and buying decisions — or even taking them out of human hands. Most early attempts to harness the computer for this purpose were largely made by experts outside the media department who drastically over-simplified the real difficulties. The power of media models was at first exaggerated. Media men who were expected to apply their output quickly lost faith in them as their shortcomings became clear. Overselling, misunderstandings and resentment were created. But the claims made for computers are now more moderate, the models they employ are less mysterious and more realistic.

The essence of employing a computer to help in media decisions is the use of a model. A model means that a real activity is partially represented by equations. These stand for, or are a model of, what is actually taking place. It is an approach much used by operational researchers [15.11]. So a media model means a way of representing, by numbers, the way people read, watch television, are exposed to advertisements, buy products and so on.

A model need not involve a computer — it may be applied by someone using only paper and pencil. Some models in the media area are of this type. But with very few exceptions media models are so tedious to work through that a computer is the only way to do so. Purists in the meaning of the words may object, but in practice 'computer' and 'model' have become virtually synonymous to many people. The computer is difficult to program and the mathematics in some media models is formidable; but to the everyday user this is irrelevant. Computer output should be no harder to use than a table in a research document.


## THE WEAK POINT OF A MODEL

Since numbers enter so lavishly into both the construction and justification of media schedules it is natural to expect help from the computer. As we shall see, there are parts of the media problem where it easily surpasses the human planner. Other parts however, as we shall also see, have resisted the modelling approach. Before getting into the details of both cases, I shall try to explain the nature of the difficulty and the point at which the media model is weakest. It is the same point where most numerical research is suspect: where it tackles a situation essentially qualitative.

One of the challenges of media selection is that it requires the mixture or simultaneous evaluation of both 'hard' and 'soft' data.

These apparently simple words have proved beyond the capacity for definition of the best brains of the business. They were the subject of a three-day workshop organised by ADMAP in 1972 and the papers given there are recommended reading. Crudely, hard data describes events or facts which are naturally numerical and where the numbers used are generally accepted as accurate. The cost of time or space is a hard, realisable fact. The way media reach people can usually be taken as hard data, for example when the industry research data is accepted by both buyer and seller. But much more is involved in a good media plan than these numbers. The factors on which judgement has to be exercised, where the experience and beliefs of two people may genuinely differ, the qualitative aspects − all these are soft data. There are different degrees of softness, depending on the amount of relevant experience available. Some aspects of the problem might almost be quantified by research; others would defy any reasonable research budget. In general, soft data is extraordinarily difficult to express in numbers.

But expressing these qualitative factors in numbers *is* exactly what we have to do if the computer is to take them into account. Numbers are the only language the computer can manipulate. We *can* of course get the numbers. We can ask people who have a feeling that a large space size is needed, 'How much more effect will that have?' If people say the target is ABs but C1s have some value we can ask, 'What is the value of a C1 compared with an AB?' Some people are very reluctant to reply at all to such questions but others can be made to give answers. Even when we have the numbers, we cannot always be sure that it is sensible to manipulate them in exactly the same way as pounds sterling or percentages. In fact there is evidence that models get confused between qualitative media weights and probabilities [15.12]. The model then becomes a 'dosage' model instead of counting exposures and we are in unmapped territory.

We return again to qualitative factors in Chapter 17, having given this warning that their use in media models is controversial, some would say impossible. This has not helped us in our dilemma, which is how best to combine the computer's undeniable efficiency in handling the hard data with the soft data which is equally undeniably essential to the solution. One crude but effective method is to ignore the qualitative aspects and solve the numbers problem. This is in fact often done, especially in television, where apparent cost-efficiency dominates most other considerations. Another method is to justify intuitive solutions by judgement alone, and ignore research. In fact the method recommended, which is expanded below, is to enter only reasonably hard data into the media model and then to use the model as only one route in reaching a decision.

Some people hold 'science' in such reverence that they treat the computer output from a media model as though engraved on tablets of stone. But the results of modelling are only the logical implication of assumptions and guesses – which are imperfect. Therefore output should be inspected with caution; there should be a comparison with common-sense before the answers are used. If the computer is used to construct – or to assess – a schedule the answer should not be treated as an order.

This point applies to models generally. It is so important that I emphasise it in the following diagrams. Figure 11 outlines the procedure followed by sensible decision-makers who do not have an explicit model available for the process they are controlling.

Figure 12 shows an unrealistic procedure. Many people mistakenly think a model is always used in this way – and indeed this is how it is sometimes misused. Here, the solution to the model is uncritically applied. Because the problem has been reduced and over-simplified in order to make a model of it, the solution may not be the correct one for the real problem.

The correct procedure is shown in Figure 13. Both the preceding paths are followed. The solution of the model is just one of the factors entering the discussion or contemplation which should take place before action is agreed. In media terms, schedule assessments may be put on to the planner's desk, but he should look at them with all the other data and considerations in his mind at the same time.


## AN EXAMPLE OF USING SOFT DATA

Details of the media model are given below, but before discussing it I give an example of the procedure just outlined in order to make clear what all this discussion means in practice. The example also shows the attitude I suggest is adopted to media models.

Suppose a planner wants to reach housewives with a press schedule and is undecided whether colour should be used. The creative team can produce mono or colour advertisements; they believe the colour versions have more impact, but are ready to discuss whether this advantage outweighs the other factors. The planner agrees with the buyer two

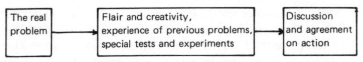

Figure 11

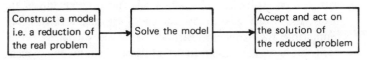

Figure 12

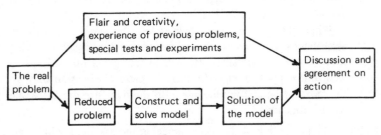

Figure 13

different schedules. One uses colour and is therefore drawn from a shorter list of publications; one uses black and white only, includes more publications and gives a higher frequency. The planner now wants schedule analyses of the two schedules before recommending which to use. The computer is to report how each schedule reaches housewives.

1 Before sending the schedules for analysis the planner decides that his criterion will be 'reading an issue', that is, the output will tell him how many housewives read none of the issue used, how many read just one, just two and so on.

The planner then looks at the two resulting frequency distributions. He notes how much cover ('reading at least one issue') each schedule gives. How many read very few issues (say, just one or two)? What is the average frequency for a housewife who is covered? How many read a lot of issues (perhaps ten or more)? He weighs up this information with other considerations: Will the ads attract attention? What will their overall effect be? How will

277

their performance match up to the overall campaign objectives? What result can be expected from seeing just a few or many? With the rest of his team, he reaches a view balancing both aspects of the problem and makes his recommendation.

2    The planner might however decide on a different definition of his input. He might say, 'In my view the impact of a mono ad will be only half that of a colour ad. Please weight down the black and white ads to 50 per cent.' He might further say, 'Summarise the frequency distributions for me. We believe people need to have four impressions at least. Tell me how many housewives will get four or more impressions.' In other words, the planner is this time using a media weight and a response function. He has decided in advance on numerical values to express his judgement.

What the planner now gets from the computer will be essentially two numbers, the percentages of housewives receiving four or more impressions. He will in fact get a full analysis as well, but suppose he ignores this and bases his decision only on the two numbers. The schedule with the highest score is the one he recommends.

Much of the promotion of the media model in the past decade has been to encourage planners to take the second of these two routes. But on the whole it is not much used. People are more at ease with the first approach. They accept the improvement the model gives when it is used with uncontroversial measures (issue-reading cover, the frequency distribution). They dislike putting a number on the value of a colour page, even though they are in effect doing the same thing when they combine the frequency distribution and type of ad. They do not want to decide in advance the value of receiving one impression, or four, or many.

## THE MEDIA MODEL

There is no general agreement on 'the' media model: there are different ways of handling media data in the computer. Nevertheless these ways have much in common and what is now described is widely accepted. The differences between models are not elaborated here: general reviews are available [15.13]. Nor is there agreement on a common language to describe the parts of the model. The designers of different systems have made up a variety of technical terms. I use one set of terms in this book, but the reader must be prepared to meet elsewhere the same words meaning other things and other words for the same things.

This is not a detailed, technical explanation of the media model. Even users of the model do not have to have complete information about all its specifications; the ordinary advertising man needs only reassurance that this specification is reasonable and a very general grasp of how it is applied.

The description given here is all in press terms. The data source most used is the National Readership Survey. In TV we quite often carry out schedule analysis and the method is actually much the same as the media model described here. It was outlined in Chapter 4; no one thinks of this as using a model. It is also possible to use mixed-media data, either collected for the purpose or married from two sources. As explained in the previous chapter, a press-TV data bank is currently available which is based on the Target Group Index and JICTAR data.

The details of how a media model service is obtained are not given here. Some are batch processed, that is, the problem is specified, usually on special input forms, and taken to the computer firm. It is treated as one of its jobs in rotation, and the results returned after one or two days. Other services are on-line, i.e. the user needs a computer terminal and inputs his problem direct to the computer, which has the necessary data already stored and returns the results virtually simultaneously.

The research data used is as follows:

*Individuals*

The central point of the media model is that it handles individuals; it does not average out the data before it starts. The computer processes thousands of individual records, not just a few figures in a table. All the complexity of the interrelations between readership and other consumer characteristics are retained; so are the duplications between the readership of one publication and of another.

There is admittedly a whole group of media models which do not take this approach. Rather than dealing with individuals, they handle averages and approximations to the resulting impression distribution on the target. The Metheringham (secret) formula is the most widely used of these. A formula approach is perfectly legitimate — it certainly cuts computer time, even to the point where no computer is needed, and it may be sufficiently accurate. But its results should be checked against the more exact individual method to ensure that the assumptions and simplifications made are not too damaging.

## Classification and weighting of individuals

The data about each individual gives her classification, by demographic and other measures, as discussed in Chapter 14. In addition, each individual may start with a sampling weight and the scale factor or sampling fraction must be known.

## Exposure to media

Obviously the survey must have measured how these individuals are exposed to media. The National Readership Survey for example is basically about frequency of reading, as explained in Chapter 5, though average issue data is also given.

To go further we have to know what kind of problem the model is to be applied to and in each application we have to determine the details of that particular problem. There are three classical applications of the model: evaluating individual publications for a particular target, evaluating given schedules and constructing schedules.

## 1 VALUED IMPRESSIONS PER POUND

The concept of VIPs (Valued Impressions per Pound) was introduced in Chapter 10. The job of the VIP program is to assess the values for a particular campaign of a long list of possible publications. Three factors have to be taken into account.

1 *Target definition.* The value to the advertiser of reaching each person in the basic data has first to be specified, i.e. the target has to be defined. This can be simply a filtering process; these people (for example housewives) are the ones the advertiser is interested in − all others are of no interest. The computer is instructed to examine the classification of each individual in

turn. If the individual is not in the target population then he is simply passed over and no more account is taken of him.

Different values may also be attached to different sorts of people. Housewives with children may be considered the prime target, but housewives without children are not to be disregarded. The computer can weight these two groups differently: housewives with children are accepted with the individual sampling weight they already have, but housewives without children have this weight reduced to, say, 60 per cent of its original value. This is called attaching weights of 100 and 60, respectively. We may weight by several different characteristics, not just with and without children but also by social grade and region for example. The different weights involved for each individual are multiplied together to produce the final target weight.

In defining the target, care must be taken not to double-weight. People in social grade E, for example, have fewer children than average in the household because this grade consists mostly of retired people. An analysis of the target by social grade and by the presence of children may show both social grade E and households without children to be of less importance than average — but a multiplication of these two small weights will produce one which is much too small. Rather than the multiplicative method just described for determining the final target weights, some models state the final weight for each possible combination of the characteristics used. This is called interlaced weighting.

2 *Realistic costs.* The cost expected for each combination of advertisement and publication to be evaluated must be estimated or taken over from the rate card.

3 *Media weights and impressions.* We already have for each individual the probability of reading an issue. It is normal to carry out the analysis on this data alone. The result is of course stated in terms of reading issues. But we may choose to go further than this. A media weight can be defined for each publication, and the computer will multiply the original probability for each publication by this weight. When the media weight is chosen to be spread traffic, for example, the result of multiplying this into the issue-reading probability is the chance that the individual will see an average spread.

The basic unit in the analysis has a different meaning depending on the media weight used; a word is needed for such a unit. I use the word 'impression' for the event described by the media weight used. Thus if no media weights are employed and the data is about issue reading, receiving an impression is simply reading an issue. If spread traffic is employed then receiving an impression is seeing a spread. The original probability in the data has now been replaced by a new one: the probability of receiving an impression.

The definitions both of a media weight and of the probability of reading as given above depend only on the publication and on the individual's frequency claim. It is possible however to use different values for different types of people, to allow for example, for men readers having different habits from women.

## Calculation of VIPs

Next the computer has to determine the cost-effectiveness of one insertion in each publication. It goes through each individual in turn, calculating the final target weight and the probability of receiving an impression for each publication to be evaluated. The product of these two, when summed over all individuals, is the number of readers (taking the target definition into account) in the survey data used, times the media weight. When this is multiplied by the scale factor and divided by cost we get the weighted or valued number of impressions delivered by the publication for every pound spent in it. Hence the definition already given in Chapter 10:

$$VIP = \frac{\text{Readers (or viewers) in target x Media weight}}{\text{Cost}}$$

During these steps the computer can carry out two other useful calculations. It can work out the average issue cover of each publication, i.e. its weighted readership as a percentage of the total target weight. It can also analyse the target definition by specified breakdowns. For example, if the target is housewives with children the analysis can find how many of these live in different regions or are in different age groups. The computer can give the results in the original order the publications were input, and it can sort them into the VIP order, where the highest VIP or most cost-efficient publication is given first. The results can also be given graphically, the VIPs being shown as a bar-chart or plotted against cover. A VIP analysis is a useful screening of a long list of possible publications: we see quickly and accurately which are the most valuable publications for our purpose.

A similar calculation can be made by hand for simple target definitions from normal readership tables. In fact it is sometimes useful to estimate VIPs even when readerships are not available, multiplying circulation figures by estimated readers per copy.

## 2 SCHEDULE ANALYSIS

The central application of the media model is the analysis of a schedule. This is a description of what happens when a schedule of advertisements actually appears. The object is to say whom the schedule reaches, how often, whether this schedule is better than that one and so on. I now outline how the model does this.

Suppose that the schedule to be analysed has been defined – so many insertions in each of the publications used. We first have to decide how each individual in turn is exposed to these insertions, knowing his probability of receiving an impression from each one.

The result is described by what I call the impression distribution for this individual. That is, the chance that he receives no impressions from the schedule, the chance he receives just one impression, just two and so on. Usually this is given both in its frequency and 'at least' or cumulative form. The details of this calculation are not given here. Models vary in the way they determine the impression distribution for an individual. It is still uncertain whether the differences matter (probably not very much) and how they compare with reality [15.4]. Sometimes models do not find the whole distribution, but calculate only cover and the expected number of impressions. Some find the distribution once and for all, recording for each individual not a probability of reading an issue but a set of ones and zeros representing whether each of a number of issues was read or not. Some calculate the distribution exactly – according to the assumptions made – others by an approximation.

With the calculation of the impression distribution the assessment of the schedule is completed as far as it affects this individual. The computer goes on to the next individual, and then the next. As each one is processed the impression distributions are cumulated, weighted by the target weights. The final result is the distribution of impressions which the schedule produces on the whole target. Two facts about this distribution are specially important: its non-cover (the proportion of the target receiving no impressions) and its average frequency (the expected or mean number of impressions received).

In 1969 and in 1978 the Media Research Group tested different computer services for evaluating press schedules [15.15]. The conclusion in 1969 was that there was 'encouraging uniformity' in the results of the three methods examined. In 1978 three simulation and three formula-based programs were available. The differences in the results were usually small, but for large schedules the formula models could give cover five or even more points above the simulation models. The two approaches should not be mixed, nor probably should different services, in evaluating schedules. These results aroused some controversy.

*Response function and effectiveness*

We now can if we wish express our judgement about the relative value to the advertiser of an individual receiving one, two, three and so on impressions. This is the response function: it is a set of numbers which is used to evaluate the impression distribution. It specifies what sort of schedule is thought best. Is it one with high cover and are later, additional impressions not very useful? Or are repeated impressions very important and cover matters relatively little? The subject of response functions is complicated and Chapter 16 is devoted to it.

The response function is used to turn the impression distribution into a single figure which sums up our evaluation of the schedule. Each term of the distribution is weighted by the corresponding number in the response function and these products are added up. The result is defined to be the effectiveness of the schedule. This figure can be used to compare two schedules and to decide which is preferable.

*Extensions of schedule analysis*

Instead of analysing one schedule only, the computer may be instructed to analyse many schedules one after the other. In an all-combinations analysis, the computer works out all possible combinations of, say, one, two and three insertions in one publication with one, two or three insertions in another, and gives results about each resulting schedule. The user gets a quick guide to the performance of many different schedules. Or the computer may analyse different additions to or deletions from the schedule. This shows how a given schedule can be improved.

# 3 SCHEDULE CONSTRUCTION

More complex than schedule analysis — but intimately linked with it — is the use of the model to construct or write a media schedule. This requires some of the same input as schedule analysis — target definition, media weights and the response function. We need also, as for a VIP analysis, the cost to be paid for each insertion. For this job the budget is also required.

The most common method used to construct a schedule (though others exist) is in steps. At each step the computer investigates in turn what would happen if an insertion were added (or several insertions, as previously decided) in each publication. The computer has to be told the largest number of insertions which would be taken in each publication. Each possibility results in a new schedule. There are, therefore, a considerable number of schedule analyses to be carried out in a schedule construction, so it is common to approximate at each stage and to use calculation or formulae rather than simulation; hence the attraction of Metheringham's method or the formula in IPC's Mediasched. Each possible addition means an increase in schedule effectiveness. Each increase in effectiveness costs a known amount. The addition with the best marginal rate of return (increase in effectiveness per pound spent) is the one selected. This completes a single step. The whole procedure is repeated again and again until the budget is all spent. A major advantage of the stepwise method is that it shows the effect of budget changes — at least in the terms the analysis is done. It becomes clear how cover or effectiveness increases as more and more of the budget is spent.

Sometimes this procedure is called hill-climbing — from the following analogy. Suppose you are in the mountains and you want to climb to the top of the highest peak. But suppose also you cannot see where this peak is: all you know is the direction which has the steepest slope upwards from where you are standing. You take a step in this direction — and then search again for the steepest slope. Often this method will in fact take you very close to the highest peak — the hill-climbing

285

technique is quite efficient. It is possible that there is a valley between you and the real summit so you do not reach it — you finish at a local peak because the method is not far-sighted enough to take you down into the valley in order to climb higher eventually. However evidence is accumulating that the surfaces investigated in media problems are quite well-behaved: no case has been published of such a valley existing in a real application.

Schedule-building methods are sometimes called optimisations, meaning that the results are actually the best possible schedules which could be written for the given budgets. However the methods do not necessarily produce the best schedule and it is better to use the word 'construction' than 'optimisation' to avoid the implication that we actually have the best possible solution. It is likely that the result is close to the best; even though individual publications may seem to come on or off the schedule rather arbitrarily during schedule constructions, the effectiveness of schedules produced by different construction methods are probably close to each other. Usually they are higher than hand-written schedules but not by a great deal. The surfaces are not only well-behaved but rather flat near their peaks. Construction methods are open to hypothetical objections, but in practice are quite efficient within their stated limitations. It is these limitations which are important, much more so than the intricacies of the mathematics.

The Media Research Group also investigated construction models [15.16]. The same four services were asked to produce schedules for two different specifications. Seven human planners also wrote schedules, some of them using computer aids for evaluating publications or hand-written schedules.

While the resulting schedules *looked* very different, especially the hand-written ones, they all gave very similar overall results according to a computer evaluation. The main conclusion was therefore that 'in a normal planning situation, manual schedules have a good chance of producing a schedule as good as that from a computer, provided sufficient time is available to go through the calculations, and that a good media planner is available to work on the problem'.

## MORE COMPLEX MODELS

In the US, models have been constructed that are more complex than the version discussed here. They take into account additional factors in the media problem. One well-known model, MEDIAC, for example included by 1971 [15.17]:

The distribution of exposures over time.
Seasonality, in sales potentials and media audiences.
Forgetting by the people exposed to advertising.
The effect on total market size of total advertising.
Competitive media exposures.

However, even when all these and further complexities are built in, improved decisions are not assured and certain defects are inherent. For example, the media data used is often out of date and, though forecasts can be used to modify it, new publications or other major changes are hard to include. Side effects, like the result on the trade of using a particular medium, are not allowed for. As already pointed out, some essential qualitative factors and the response function are hard to quantify. It is salutary to return to the factors listed in Chapter 7 and to note those which the model has difficulty in coping with. A better understanding of these factors would give greater improvement than increasing the complexity of the model.

## THE ADVANTAGES OF MODELLING

### Some results are accepted

Some of the results of using a model are identical with those generally accepted as useful, though the computer may get the results more easily. To find the cover of a schedule in the conventional sense is a job which counter-sorters can carry out on punched cards. Working out the average number of impressions produced by the schedule can be done on a desk calculator. These procedures are so familiar that most people, incorrectly, do not think of a model being involved.

### Some data could not be handled otherwise

There is far more information in media data than can be extracted manually. Now we can carry out in minutes more calculations than most media men made in a lifetime. We have the opportunity to squeeze existing data harder and to use new data which would otherwise be beyond our grasp. For example, the frequency data on the National Readership Survey cannot be analysed at the individual level without a computer. The benefits of thinking about people rather than formulae, of working on the full complexity of individual data rather than on averages, are comparable with those of the decimal number system rather than Roman numerals. The difference between the two expressions 23 and XXIII is a difference of kind.

*We can easily look at a wider range*

Without the computer to do VIPs for us we limit our choice. We may decide first to use, say, quality newspapers in a press schedule. Popular newspapers may be thought to offer a poor environment for the advertising. Next, we might consider which quality papers to use. But by taking the decisions in this order we never look at the possibility of an admittedly lower quality paper being used because of its relatively much lower cost.

*The model can surprise – and help – us*

In media planning, uncertainties are such that we often do not know which course of action is best. And unaided commonsense on its own cannot grasp simultaneously the many factors involved. A really long list of alternative publications, their duplications, target weightings, the response function and so on – all this is incredibly complex. Sometimes the model throws a fresh and helpful light on the problem. Although it only reflects our own assumptions, the output from the computer can be unexpected. Without it being accepted as infallible, it may tip the balance.

An example already given may help to make this point. When a TV schedule is analysed, as described in Chapter 4, a figure is given for its cover and so the average number of opportunities to see for those cover can be calculated. Typically, for a schedule of 400 TVRs on housewives, these figures would be:

Cover  81%     Average OTS  4.9

We know that only a proportion of those with an opportunity to see are actually present during the commercial — say 80 per cent. What is the effect of allowing for presence in such a schedule analysis? This is not an easy question to answer. A moment's reflection tells us that the average number of presences will be about 80 per cent of the previous average OTS — not exactly, because the definition of 'covered' will change. But how will this change? We need the computer to give us the full OTS frequency distribution and then a further model |[15.18] to indicate the presence distribution. The answer actually turns out to be:

Presence cover    78%        Average presences    4.1

We now see that cover is very little changed by the assumptions we have made, though frequency seems a lot less.

This example is typical: the use of media weights generally changes ideas about a schedule's effect. The average number of impressions an individual is thought to receive is altered in direct proportion to the average weight used. The number of individuals receiving a large number of impressions is drastically reduced. The first analysis was not actually wrong, but it could mislead. People not familiar with media research are apt to look on '4.9 opportunities to see' as if this described exposure to an advertisement — but it has just been shown that a more realistic figure for this is only 4.1. This use of media weights is recommended. I make this recommendation even though the media model admittedly does not cope very accurately with advertisement exposure or impression distributions — the assumptions which have to be made are not fully justified. Nevertheless the results are nearer reality than when the basic data is used on its own.


## The discipline of a checklist

It is a commonplace that defining the problem is often the hardest part of solving it. A model forces the user to be specific and consistent. Since we cannot use the media model without defining the target population, the kind of schedule required and so on, these definitions have to be written down and agreed. This in itself is a benefit. It is worth keeping a computer in a corner just to ask it well-thought out questions — even if it were never to answer them.

### The media model is educational

It is easier to explain some aspects of media analysis and media planning when a model is being used. Its logical structure is not difficult to grasp, carefully planned computer output is easily read, and the media planner is helped to explain what he is doing to the advertiser, others in the agency and trainees in his own department.


### Weaknesses are uncovered

Of course, the media model and soft data are subject to reservations and should be improved — but so should the only other method: judgement. Most media men tend to be complacent and conservative. It is a salutary shock to see how little is known.


### Sensitivity analyses are possible

A working model can be used to find out how sensitive decisions are to various factors in the input. This shows whether a particular factor is important (it has a big effect on the output and changing it would alter decisions) or relatively unimportant (because it has a small effect). Such a comparison is called a sensitivity analysis. This may be used to stop irrelevant arguments about soft data by indicating whether the subject of the argument really matters.


## THE DANGERS OF MODELLING

Why then is the media model not more widely accepted and used? The reasons are more serious than that a computer system is costly. There are in fact reasons for not using a model at all.


### The model is incomplete and mechanistic

Pascal pointed out that 'experts are used to reaching decisions intuitively and instantly. When you show them propositions they cannot understand, all definitions and sterile principles, they are astonished and disgusted'. The advertising business naturally attracts quick, intuitive thinkers. They must have had experience of dozens of problems similar to the one on which the media model might be applied — and they have solved the previous problems successfully without a model. Their authority and experience seem to be questioned. It offends them to reduce the variety which actually exists to the apparent simplicity of a media model. They wonder whether a few summary statistics about a schedule can efficiently represent its value. They see writ large the imperfections and assumptions.

Of course, one answer to this objection is that the decisions reached by these executives often beg the same questions as they put to model-users. They are apt to make as many assumptions and guesses as those they object to. They solved their problems before in the sense that the advertiser agreed to their schedule, not in the sense that their schedules were proved to be the best. The model-user cannot prove either that his solution is the best, but he can point to a carefully thought-through reason for it.

People out of sympathy with the modelling approach are often better off not using it. The model may confuse or mislead them because their attempts to adjust to it interfere with their practical, sensible abilities. They fail to combine their qualities with those of the model. This disadvantage can be overcome only by education, by starting with the use of the model in its simplest, least controversial applications, by ensuring that people and not the computer have the last word.


## Will the mad scientist take over?

If a commonsense media man abdicates to the computer because he is awed or baffled, it is possible that a mad scientist might take over the media work. He might be a model-builder who is more interested in techniques than in the realities of the media world. He enjoys tinkering with the clockwork and forgets the assumptions. His output might be uncritically accepted. The safeguard against this is again education — this time of the model-builder. Technologists have to be made aware that their models are not fully adequate descriptions of reality. Unscientific but experienced people may on occasion rightly reject their recommendations.

*A shotgun with telescopic sights*

It is sometimes objected that advertising is so crude a process that overmuch precision is out of place. Why bother with complex data and computers, if at the end the agency is going to buy television or popular newspapers? The plea is that money should be spent on creative research or more advertisements rather than on media research and analysis.

The only reply to these objections is to weigh the expected gains against the cost of better media research and better processing of this data. I believe the balance comes down on the credit side. An improvement of only 1 or 2 per cent in advertising efficiency would pay for all current media research and computer work.

*Does a model interfere with rate negotiation?*

When buyers get to work, two contradictory objections are sometimes made about the use of models. The first is that the negotiation of rates, positions, etc. wipes out the effects of scientific planning. What is the use of all that precision, it is asked, if the buyer could get six insertions for the price of five from a publication not included in the computer's schedule? The second objection is that no negotiation will in practice be undertaken since buyers will stick to the rates used earlier in the model.

The answer to these objections is that realistic rates should be used in the model. But surprises and unforeseen opportunities are inevitable. The buyer should take advantage of these. Indeed the model can be used to show what price a publication must come down to in order to compete effectively with publications on the schedule, which is a direct help to buyers. Usually the changes suggested during buying in the press are relatively small and there is no need to return to the model for re-evaluation. In TV the buyer should have as much freedom as possible.

To sum up, the dangers of using the media model are real. It is genuine controversy that is still heard about the application of the computer to help media decisions. But the computer is here to stay because the benefits of the model far outweigh the disadvantages. We should approach the computer with caution, but expecting to be helped.

# 16 RESPONSE FUNCTIONS

*This chapter is for those interested in research.
When a media model is used, the objectives of
the advertising campaign should be stated in
numerical form. These numbers describe the
response expected from individuals exposed to
the advertising. Case histories indicate what
shape the response function might be and show
how difficult it is to measure response.
Nevertheless, a recommendation is made on
the way to use a response function.*

## DIFFERENT DEFINITIONS OF RESPONSE

The response functions described here are the ones used in the media models of the last chapter. They are not the only specification of response which can be used in marketing, so before going into detail on this particular application it is necessary to distinguish the various uses of this concept. Too often they are not separated and ideas and terms from one are transferred uncritically to another.

The basic problem is to relate advertising (spend, stock, exposures etc.), which is the cause, and its effect (sales, awareness, etc.).

In determining budgets and in allocation over areas, the basic variable is money (though TVRs may be used in the analysis) and the result is considered among the whole population (the country, the whole of the TV region concerned, etc.). It is assumed that once the money is fixed at any particular level, the rest of the media plan is then drawn up in the best way. For example, when a region has got its allocation, the timing of the advertising is then sensibly determined.

When analysing historical data and when allocation over time is concerned, the independent variable cannot be just the advertising in each period, but we must consider (even if rejecting it) the influence of past advertising. The rate of decay of the planned advertising will also matter. Some people introduce this element of carry-over into budget determination and allocation over areas too. Thus the variable is the *stock* of advertising, allowing for decay. The effect is still over the whole population considered.

In the media (press scheduling) model the budget is fixed and time is not allowed to enter. The variable is the amount of advertising an individual receives. The result is not on the whole population but only on that particular group (which is largely self-selected, e.g. heavy viewers).

Thus our basic idea of response can be interpreted in three broad ways:

| Application | Independent variable | Dependent variable among |
|---|---|---|
| Budget determination, Regional allocation | Spend, TVRs | Population |
| Historical analysis, Time allocation | Ad stock | Population |
| Press schedule Evaluation | Ad exposures | Exposure groups |

## RESPONSE IN SCHEDULE EVALUATION

In the rest of this chapter we consider only the last of these definitions of response, the purpose being to evaluate the frequency distribution resulting from a schedule. What shape should the function be? How has the response been measured?

Using response functions is far from a universal practice: most decisions about schedules are taken after analysing them but not applying a response function. Balancing cover against repetition has always been a critical planning decision. Various criteria for schedules are used, for example 'effective' cover, e.g. at four opportunities to see rather than one, 'impression' cover (the percentage seeing at least one advertisement rather than reading at least one issue) and cost-per-thousand. These are all in fact ways of stating different response functions. Such a function is only a method of discussing the problem of schedule evaluation and not a new solution to this problem. Discussing the problem explicitly has the usual advantages of the modelling approach.

In addition there are two reasons for studying response functions. The less compelling, but nevertheless serious, reason is that a construction model absolutely requires the function if it is to be used at all. There must be an operating rule for one schedule or frequency distribution to be preferred to another. The second reason is that in measuring response we are turning back to the proper or fundamental study in advertising research: Did the advertisement work? Admittedly the question does not here require an *absolute* answer (so many sales were made or defended) but it does get a *relative* one (a few exposures did this much compared with many exposures).

## THE RESPONSE FUNCTION

A response function is a set of numbers defining the relative value to the advertiser of an individual in his target population receiving one, two . . . and so on advertising impressions. The definition just given is for a *cumulative* response function. That is, after an individual has received so many impressions, his total or cumulated response is so much. It is the meaning recommended for general use. It has been called the value of $r$ exposures. We have to distinguish carefully between cumulative response and the corresponding *additional* response

Table 38

| Impressions | 0 | 1 | 2 | 3 | 4 | 5 | 6 | 7 | 8 |
|---|---|---|---|---|---|---|---|---|---|
| Cumulative response | 0 | 50 | 75 | 90 | 100 | 100 | 100 | 100 | 100 |
| Additional response | 0 | 50 | 25 | 15 | 10 | 0 | 0 | 0 | 0 |

function. The function can be stated in either form and one implies the other. The additional response is the added value given by each separate, additional impression. It has been called the value of the $r$th exposure. It is the difference between each individual term in the cumulative function. Conversely the cumulative function is obtained by adding in succession the terms in the additional function.

An example of a response function given in both forms is shown in Table 38.

*Standardisation*

When 100 is taken as the highest value attained by the response function, each term is a percentage of the maximum value. This convenient standardisation can be achieved if the function is not originally given in this way by adding or subtracting a constant from each term and then multiplying by a constant. It has been proved [16.1] that such a transformation leaves unaltered the choice of the more effective of any two schedules. However the *relative* effectiveness figures of the two schedules may then be changed. We cannot say one schedule is much more effective' or 'very little more effective' unless the response function is on a scale with some absolute meaning.

The convention that 100 is the maximum value reached by response has this apparent difficulty — it does not seem to allow for cases where cumulative response increases in theory without limit. The difficulty is in practice easily overcome by picking on a number of impressions which cannot be exceeded in the campaign in question, and taking the response to this number to be 100. For example, if we are considering three alternative schedules of 12, 13 and 21 insertions it is clear that no individual can receive 25 impressions or more. We can therefore call 100 the cumulative response to 25 impressions and adjust the other terms to match.

How is the word 'value' in the definition itself to be defined? A universal answer cannot be given to this question. The objectives of the campaign must be taken into account; value must be defined anew for each application; the creative objective and treatment must be taken into account.

'Impressions' have been used above as the basic units against which response is measured. The definition used for impressions has a bearing on the response function. For example, suppose a step function (defined below) at four impressions is agreed when an issue-reading is taken as an impression. That is, an individual is counted as effectively covered when he has read four issues. Now suppose the definition of impression is changed to page exposure. The response function cannot be left as a step function at four impressions: four page exposures is more than four issue readings.

## DIFFICULTIES IN USING RESPONSE FUNCTIONS

### 1 Conflicting objectives

Although a single function is to be used, it is rare that a campaign has a single objective. It may have long-term benefits, e.g. to make the product name more salient, as well as short-term, e.g. to increase understanding of a particular product advantage. It may be intended to benefit other brands (umbrella advertising or total market increase) as well as the one named on the advertisements. There may be different objectives within one advertisement (several consumer benefits are stated, some more assimilable than others) and different objectives between advertisements in the same campaign. The same campaign may have launch requirements (wide cover) and long-term requirements (repetition). In practice it is necessary to decide on the most important media objective and on one response function. Or to analyse different parts of a schedule separately.

### 2 Individuals

The definition refers to 'individuals in the target population' as if they were all identical. Of course this is not true. The target contains individuals with a very wide spectrum of knowledge and prejudices about the product; they have different degrees of interest in it and likelihoods of being persuaded by advertising. It is possible to imagine them each having their own personal response. Can all this be represented by a single function?

It would not be difficult to adapt present practice if knowledge about relevant breakdowns became available. Information about response could be collected about, say, housewives separately from other women, or users from non-users, and a different function could then be used for each. Some US models already do this. In the absence of this knowledge, it seems reasonable to use the approximation of having one function. In any case, individual functions might genuinely resolve themselves into a single one. For example, suppose it was known for each person the number of impressions at which advertising 'worked', that is she became aware, or changed her attitude. (This assumption is, of course, for discussion purposes only – it is certainly an over-simplification.) Then it would be possible to state the proportion of the target who had been effectively exposed at each number of impressions, which is equivalent to a single function.

## 3   Time effects

The first way in which time enters this problem is in the duration of the campaign being considered. The relative values in a response function may alter considerably if we are considering either a period of a week or a whole year's sustained campaign. The length of the campaign or of the part of it being evaluated should be explicitly brought into the determination of a response function.

The point just made is only the beginning of the complication which time causes. The spacing of impressions also matters. There is a difference between one insertion a month and twelve insertions in one week followed by fifty-one weeks without advertising. As already stated, some US media models do allow for decay, but this has not been applied in the UK. This effect certainly has to be borne in mind in designing and evaluating field research. The media research data necessary to give as a routine the distribution of press impression over time, or decay effects, have not yet been developed. Current practice is therefore forced first to determine the number of insertions in each vehicle and then, in a separate operation, to spread these over the period of the campaign.

## 4   Competitors

The analysis of research results should distinguish the effect of our advertising from other causes of change. One reason results will be disturbed is competitors' activities: one impression from our campaign on a person who sees no competitive advertising may do more good than four impressions on a person who sees forty competitive advertisements. A flat response function discovered in post-campaign analysis may not mean that later advertisements are wasted — only that the people who see many of our advertisements also see many of the competitors' and perhaps the response of these people would have fallen unless they had seen a lot of ours. This is a common trap which has led many people to conclude wrongly that advertising has been over-exposed. In at least one case reducing this defensive advertising has led to sales losses.

The media model and the definition of response given above are in this sense again incomplete. A model could be constructed which does not analyse just our schedule, but also the competitors'. A response function might not be dependent only on impressions from our advertising but perhaps on the share of our advertising out of the total an individual receives.

## 5 · The heavily exposed

It is also likely that people exposed to many advertisements differ from those who exposed to few in other ways than seeing our competitors' ads. On TV, for example, the heavily exposed may pay less attention to the set than the more selective viewers. Our advertising is competing not only with other ads but with the stream of programmes which reduces its impact. The people themselves are also different, e.g. older and less educated, and may need more repetition.

The difficulties in using response functions are rather dismaying. The problems of time, of competition and of getting any valid measurement in the field are daunting. But the reasons for using a model at all still apply. In particular, the response function may be treated simply as a useful working tool. That is, no actual relationship between impressions and response is assumed — the response function is just part of the method of schedule analysis or construction which is expected to lead to better schedules. The criterion here for 'better' is not sought in the function itself, but in inspection of the schedules resulting from the system.

It is my experience that the response function is not the most sensitive factor in media decisions. Over the range in which the function is usually thought to lie, very different media decisions are unlikely. Qualitative factors, especially the inter-media choice, are in my opinion, much more critical.

## FOUR THEORETICAL RESPONSE FUNCTIONS

It is possible to use response functions but to avoid discussion of theoretical functions. Experimental results could be used in their raw numerical form, but this is not usually possible because appropriate results are rarely available. Numbers can also be used specified intuitively without reference to any mathematical function; this is indeed the most frequent method. The specification itself is likely to be assisted by a theoretical investigation, for without an understanding of the effect of different shapes of response function it is all too easy to commit howlers with media models. A further advantage of a theoretical review is that it offers a family of functions or a standard kit. Each number of the family is specified by a number or parameter. General rules about the effect of this parameter emerge. Statements can be made about a range of functions by specifying the values of the parameter applicable.

### 1  Linear response

By a linear response is meant a straight line through the origin, reaching 100 at some number of impressions beyond the largest number the schedule being considered could produce. A useful form of this function takes the value 1 at one impression, 2 at two and so on. When this is the case, effectiveness is simply the average number of impressions on the target population. The mean of the impression distribution is often the single most important fact about it. Other slopes of a linear function give other values for effectiveness, but are as already stated completely equivalent as aids to choosing the best schedule:

1    Total impressions.
2    Total impressions per pound, given on dividing the last figure by schedule cost. This is the inverse of cost per thousand.

## 2  Step function response

Step function response means that the value of cumulative response is 0 for zero, one, two . . . impressions up to some critical number of impressions where the value jumps to 100. It stays at that value for larger numbers of impressions. When the critical number is one, the result when effectiveness is calculated is simply cover. This is unlikely to correspond to the way advertising 'works' in any real sense, but the concept has its uses, as witness the wide-spread acceptance of '4 plus' in the analysis of TV schedules. The 'at least' distribution in a schedule analysis is equivalent to every possible different step function being used and gives more information.


## 3  S-shaped response

The S-shape (see Figure 14) is often put forward as the obvious shape for a response function. This shows low response at the beginning, gradually increasing to a steep slope, i.e. concave at small numbers of impressions, then flattening off again, i.e. convex at large numbers of

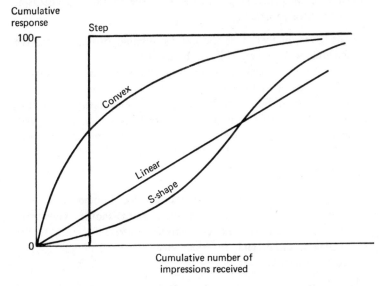

Figure 14

impressions. Two arguments are advanced in support of this shape, both of which are now examined. One is an appeal to intuition, the other claims that the shape leads to a concentrated impression distribution when it is used to construct or select schedules.

The intuitive argument takes the following line. Advertising 'clearly' does not have an effect at a small number of impressions — there 'must' be a threshold which has to be passed before the effect is detectable. Equally response 'ought to' level off somewhere. This argument is appealing and the S-shape has been the one most often used. But the intuitive argument is pure speculation. We are free to conclude from the examination of the data summarised below that thresholds, a low effectiveness at a small number of impressions and the rest of it are rarely if ever supported by evidence. S-shaped functions may well exist, but if so let the data be produced. 'The choice of the sigmoid curve ... seems to be many a mathematician's assumption of the nature of advertising response, but it is never validated. Usually it is asserted as the "curve of learning" in spite of the fact that experimental psychologists have been unable to find such a typical curve' [16.3].

The claim that an S-shaped response function leads to desirable impression distributions is more serious. The function is not being used here as a summary of the way advertising works, but solely as a tool in a schedule construction procedure. Then the argument proceeds as in the next three paragraphs:

> The given budget fixes the average number of impressions the schedule will deliver. This can be determined from average costs: for example typical costs are so much a thousand, so £100,000 will buy so many impressions.
>
> The impression distribution shows how many individuals receive less than this number and are therefore under-exposed, and how many receive more which are wasted. If we could reduce the tail or right end of this distribution and instead increase exposure to those who now receive too few impressions, then effectiveness would be improved.
>
> Therefore both *less* than the average number and *more* than the average number of impressions should have small additional response: the cumulative response function should be flat at either end but steep near the ideal number — in a word, S-shaped.

The first error in this argument is to treat the average number of impressions as fixed. Different schedules for the same budget can produce different means: indeed this is the field of manœuvre for the buyer. Moving one individual up from a low to a higher number of impressions does not always imply some other individual being correspondingly reduced.

The second and more serious error is to suppose that an S-shaped curve necessarily leads to the desired evaluation of an impression distribution. There is no logical connection between a reduction in spread being thought beneficial and the S-shape. Just because we 'want people to receive four impressions' say, there is no need to make the *additional* response at four higher than at two or three. It is only necessary that the cumulative response be higher at four. The last of the three paragraphs above in which the argument is put forward in fact contains a *non sequitur*.

If the major part of the impression distribution occurs over the concave part of the response function a larger variance may be credited with high effectiveness — the opposite to the desired effect. And if the mean of the impression distribution is exactly at the point of inflection, and the function is symmetrical, then moving one individual from the right of the distribution towards the mean, and another from the left towards the mean, would in fact leave effectiveness unaltered.


## 4   Convex and geometric response functions

The right hand end of an S-shaped response function is convex, i.e. each additional impression causes a smaller additional response than the one before. This is the shape which research indicates usually applies. And a convex function favours the concentration of the impression distribution which is usually thought desirable. It is sometimes thought that a convex function forces high cover when used in schedule construction. Because the first impression on an individual has higher effectiveness per pound than the total of five impressions, for example, it looks as though the first insertion in a new publication will always be preferred to the fifth insertion in a publication already carrying four. This is fallacious. When the media model compares an insertion in a new publication and in one already used, it does not use only the fact that some readers of the new publication will be reached for the first time and so have high additional response. It takes into account also the cost of this insertion. It is only if the two publications cost the same that the new publication will automatically be used. In practice costs differ and it is overall cost-effectiveness which dominates the decision. Thus a convex function does not necessarily lead to high cover. In fact a very gently curving convex function will lead to a short schedule with low cover.

The geometric response function is a particular convex function. It is easy to apply in practice and it has been found to fit many real examples. It is therefore the shape I recommend for general use [16.1]. The geometric function is defined by a parameter $f$, which is the value of the first impression (compared with total response). It is also possible to look on $f$ as the proportion of people not yet effectively covered who are so covered at the next impression. Or it can be defined by $r = 1 - f$, which is the ratio of the value of any impression (except the first) compared with the preceding one. Additional response is a geometric series, which is why the function is given this name. Both $f$ and $r$ must lie between 0 and 1 inclusive.

For those who like analogies, the concept behind the geometric response function can be put in the following concrete form. Suppose consumers are like a tank of water, and their attitude to your product is expressed by the temperature of the water. Advertising impressions are like injecting jets of steam into the water: this raises the temperature. If the tank is lagged, the temperature will rise by successively smaller known steps at each injection until their attitude reaches a saturation level: the water is boiling.

The geometric response function covers a wide range of possibilities. As $f$ approaches 0 it gets nearer to a linear response. At $f = 1$ it is equivalent to cover. Between the two there is a complete range to choose from, determined by the single parameter $f$. One way of choosing $f$ is to fit the geometric function to observed data [16.1]. Since this is seldom possible I advise the selection of one of the following verbal descriptions of the media objective, i.e. the compromise required between cover and repetition. Before doing so you should remind yourself:

1    What time period is being considered: over a short burst high repetition cannot be expected?
2    What definition of impressions is being used: if it is only issue-reading or TV rating more than one impression may be needed before the advertisement is seen at all?

Cover is all-important. This is the percentage (of the people we want to reach) who receive at least one impression. Only the first impression on an individual matters. $f = 1.0$

Cover is very important indeed. When an individual has had one impression he is more than half-way to getting all that can be expected from the schedule. When he has had two impressions he can get little more. $f = 0.7$

Cover is important. At one or two impressions an individual is about half-way to total response; when he has had five impressions he has little more to gain. $f = 0.4$

Both cover and repetition matter. At three impressions an individual is about half-way to total response; at seven impressions he has little more to gain. $f = 0.2$

Repetition is important. At six or seven impressions an individual is only half-way to total response; it takes over twenty impressions before the advertising has achieved nearly all its effect. $f = 0.1$

Only total impressions on an individual, or cost per thousand, matter. Cover is ignored. $f = 0.0$

## THE MEASUREMENT OF RESPONSE FUNCTIONS

I distinguish six different methods that can be used to measure response functions in the field. Brief descriptions of each follow with examples and comments.

### 1 Coupon return analyses

This method cannot be recommended as a way of assessing all campaigns. Coupon returns are rarely a valid measure of the overall effect of advertising. It is easy to imagine an individual who stops cutting coupons after one or two sights of an advertisement, but who is still positively affected by later impressions. Conversely, some people cut coupons who are of no interest to the advertiser. Nevertheless there are cases where the effect of an insertion is genuinely measured by the number of coupons returned — or better, by the number of sales traceable to the coupons returned. Where such evidence is reliable it can be analysed to answer questions about saturation, decay, publication effectiveness or media weight, creative content, advertisement size — and the response function.

My agency has advertised for several years a durable for which sales are entirely due to coupons returned. It has been found that for well-spaced insertions (four to nine weeks) in a single publication, response to each insertion there is roughly constant. There is no evidence that early insertions are any less useful than the average, i.e. that a threshold exists, or that saturation is reached. A linear response function is appropriate in this case. This of course implies that a short schedule is preferred, using only those publications proven to have high cost-effectiveness. Experiments are run all the time to check that effectiveness in other publications is still lower than in those already used. In practice it is not possible to do what the model suggests — to put all the money into the single most effective publication — because the model would break down and returns would diminish if insertions were very closely spaced over time.

## 2  Single interviews

Suppose that it is possible to measure in an interview with an individual after the campaign whether its main objective has been achieved, for example, whether she correctly recalls a particular copy point. Suppose also that questions are asked in this interview about media exposure, from which it is possible to deduce how much the informant has been exposed to our campaign, as suggested in Chapter 14.

In one case [16.4] informants were asked if they were aware of a particular brand P which had just been launched. Their TV viewing habits were also investigated by aided recall, from which they were classified into six groups: those who saw just one, those who saw two or three and so on. A reasonable geometric response function could be drawn relating awareness of brand P to impressions received. This study also investigated awareness of another brand Q in the same product field. And this was also associated with impressions received from brand P commercials. A geometric function would be drawn for this relation too. But the commercials for brand P can hardly have increased awareness of Q.

306

This horrid example shows that it is as well to be wary of the conclusions drawn from this research method. A casual relation is not proven by this type of association. The data may be contaminated by some third factor such as watching a lot of television, or having children in the household. Nevertheless this method cannot be completely ruled out. The results are quite cheaply obtained, may be correct and in my experience are a considerable help in understanding what advertising is doing.

Sometimes the casual hypothesis seems easier to accept than the existence of a third associated factor. This is the case with a French survey [16.5] which determined how often people visited the cinema during the time a certain commercial was being screened. They were also asked to name the brand advertised. A clear geometric function linked the two measures.

In other cases the effect of the third factor can be estimated and removed. This was done in one of my agency's research projects for BEA (now British Airways). We measured awareness of Silver Wing Holidays — and also of two other airlines. All three responses were plotted against exposure to a BEA TV and press schedule. Awareness was related geometrically to impressions in all three cases, but the relation was much flatter for the two other airlines. We assumed that the latter relation was not causal, but was due to living in London and the South, where more travellers live and where travel advertising is concentrated. This amount of association was subtracted from BEA awareness; what remained was a relationship which could be taken as causal. This information indicated the kind of schedule to buy in future. It was also possible to separate the effect of TV exposures from press exposures and so to estimate which was the more effective medium in this case.

It is possible to compare the response for different brands and so to compare the effectiveness of the advertising for each. In a study for Cadburys in my agency the awareness of advertising and claimed purchase was established for five different brands. Again there were media questions on the survey. All the brands were advertised on television and it was possible to compare the responses with informants' exposure to ITV. For four of the brands, plausible geometric response functions emerged, consistent with what was already known about the success of the brands. But for one brand, claimed purchase showed hardly any connection with exposure, though knowledge of the advertising was high and closely related to exposure. It was concluded that for this brand the advertising message was being transmitted efficiently but that its sales effectiveness through TV was weaker than for other brands. If money were to be moved out of TV, this brand was the first candidate. The result was to agree on tests for this brand in two other media: cinema and women's magazines.

## 3 Double interviews

This name is given to techniques in which data are collected in two interviews separated in time by the campaign. They may be interviews with the same informants or with different informants. This method can uncover casual relationships without a third factor intervening. Provided the measurements made are genuinely of advertisement effectiveness double interviews are recommended.

An example of repeated information obtained from the same informants is given by the TEM model in Sweden. Its application has been described [16.6] to petrol-buying behaviour and the Esso Tiger campaign. This used a heavy newspaper schedule. Motorists could be described by their mean number of opportunities to see; for each exposure group the percentage change in frequency of visits to an Esso station was ascertained. It was found that the lightly exposed (up to 30 opportunities to see) made fewer visits than before the campaign — presumably due to competitors' advertising and other natural causes. But the heavily exposed (70 and more opportunities to see) clearly increased their number of visits to Esso stations. The relation appeared to be a linear response.

## 4 Experiments

The method used most frequently to investigate response is a classical weight test experiment. Two or more groups of individuals are matched in all respects except their advertising exposure, which is deliberately set at different levels. While this is indisputably valid (although difficult enough) as a weight test, its extension to response measurement is risky. In normal practice, the individuals who are heavily exposed to advertising and to whom the upper end of the response function is applied are not identical with those lightly exposed: they are precisely those who are heavily exposed to all advertising. It is dangerous to assume that these people will react like those in the weight test. Normal experimentation is for this reason not an ideal method for measuring response. However, the advantage of the experimental approach is the certainty that what is observed has been caused by advertising. This is such an important point that no one could advise against the use of experiments. Used with care, the results of experiments are valuable.

Experiments can be carried out in the laboratory, under semi-real conditions or with complete realism. Examples of all three now follow.

In one laboratory test [16.7] a van parked in shopping centre was fitted with a cinema-type screen. Informants were shown a film interrupted by commercial slides and then completed a questionnaire which also included advertisements. Coupons were given out which could be redeemed on purchase of goods, so checking not only questionnaire responses but actual sales. This method is obviously not normal exposure since advertisements were shown up to six times in one session, but it showed interesting differences by type of product and by measure. For example recall climbed quite sharply, reaching 80 or 90 per cent after six exposures in a classical geometric shape, while stated purchase intention grew more slowly, in roughly linear form.

In another test, advertisements were mailed to women at weekly or at four-weekly intervals [16.8]. Recall was measured by a telephone interview. Response climbed twice as fast for the weekly mailing and reached a higher peak, but recall was found to decay more quickly than with the four-weekly mailings so that total awareness-weeks were less.

One of the most thorough tests ever made of the effect of advertising was carried out using a local newspaper in the US [16.9]. In this experiment two products were launched: Chicken Sara Lee and Lestare Bleach. They were supported by an advertisement repeated each week. In different areas of the town, by splitting the run and distribution, the advertising was terminated after four, eight or twelve weeks and in another quarter of the town no advertising appeared. Perhaps the most important measurement made seemed to follow a linear response. This was the difference between the proportion who bought the product after one, two . . . insertions had appeared in the areas covered by advertising and the proportion in the control area where slower sales growth occurred without advertising. Other indirect measures of response (recall, changed attitudes) seemed to be geometric in shape.

## 5   Observation

Another method of looking at response is simply to observe the results of a campaign (by sales or by indirect research methods) over time. In this case impressions on individuals are not studied — only the overall result. Decay over time now becomes an important factor. A good example has been published [16.10] for the launch of a confectionery product in the UK over two years. It is doubtful whether this technique can be used to study response, but it does produce much useful information in other fields.


## 6   Study of individual behaviour

The most promising method of all is also the most complicated and raises many further problems of its own. The method starts from detailed records of individual behaviour: media exposure, product purchase and other relevant characteristics. From these records a detailed and dynamic model of advertising effect can perhaps be built up [16.11]. What happens to people who see more of our advertising than competitors'? Do they buy a higher proportion of our brand? Are the purchases related to the amount of advertising exposure? How are changes in our brand share — or a stationary share — made up of individual increases and losses? How do other marketing factors (price, display, promotion . . .) also affect sales?

Such data might be used to construct a marketing model of individual media and marketing behaviour. This is a formidable task, for which the analysis techniques scarcely exist at present. Computer technology is probably adequate, and the data collection problems look soluble. It has been suggested [16.12] that the most important long term use of an integrated industry research system will lie in providing such data.


## CONCLUSION

Response is a critical part of the media model, yet little is known about it. If response were better understood, if we were more confident about the relationship between advertising expenditure and sales results, then many problems would be resolved for the media man, indeed for everyone in advertising. If advertising is ever to be a science it has a long way to go. At present it is a craft which can be improved by our being explicit, consistent and sharing our experience.

# 17 BEYOND COST PER THOUSAND

*This chapter is about the factors that should influence media choice in addition to cost per thousand in the target. The different elements or possible media weights, and the research about them, are briefly described. A way of approaching the problem of broad media choice in particular cases is suggested.*

In the last three chapters the approach to media choice has been based on numbers. The final chapter in this book should correct an impression which the reader may have formed, that media planning is exclusively about numbers and the media model. There is more to media choice than picking off the top of a VIP list and I now try to explain what the missing dimension is. Intuition is important here, but research can still correct and guide it. It is as possible to be systematic about qualities as about arithmetic. It is important to be so, for this is where the major media decisions are made, the choice of the main medium for example.

Although the term 'qualitative factors' may imply vagueness or a second-order correction, we bring the usual practical criterion into this discussion: does each factor considered mean that a pound spent in *this* medium produces or defends more sales than in *that* one? It is only the difficulty of measurement, the fact that we are handling soft data (see Chapter 15), which makes each factor non-numerical. Its ultimate effect is a hard, measurable one.

Why then *is* it not measured and turned into numbers? For the same reasons as set out before, in Chapters 2 and 12 for example. We are usually uncertain which is the appropriate intermediate measure to use (causing awareness, changing attitudes etc) because we do not really know how advertising works. Even to do small-scale pre-campaign tests is costly, slow and rarely done. To do a full-scale test is usually prohibitively expensive and does not always give usable results. To generalise from other examples may be dangerous. At each end of this range of alternatives we face different problems: the 'realistic' test may fail to detect the factor we are looking for; as we move to more specific, smaller-scale, laboratory-type tests where we are fairly sure of diagnostic results then we lose realism. For example, we have to expose the advertisement forcefully; also, research makes people rationalise and talk explicitly about habits and reactions which normally they hardly notice in themselves so we cannot be sure their statements accurately reflect their normal behaviour.

Another introductory point is that no *general* evaluation is possible. There is no conclusion such as 'TV is better than newspapers': we have to know *for what.* The media brief in each case should have provided the context for our judgement: we need to know who the target is, what the creative objectives are, even how the creative team would use the medium under discussion. In other words, we are preparing to help a *particular* decision, not to pass an overall judgement.

How soft data and commonsense enter into this decision, and how they contrast and combine with hard data has been discussed in several papers [17.1, 17.2, 17.3]. Frankly, little progress has been made. There are perhaps fewer misunderstandings and less over-simplification than there were five or ten years ago, but there has been no real improvement. The problem of main medium choice has been with us for many years, though in the past decade, with the TV/Press battle growing more explicit, all that has become clearer is how ill-informed we are. Ron Critchley's review [17.4] gives eleven successive quotations on this subject, between 1960 and 1973, which might almost be interchangeable.

It is however possible to classify the various elements which enter into the decision. One good review [17.5] listed 59 papers in its bibliography. No such lists or summaries can be comprehensive. It is worth distinguishing three types:

313

1   *Broad qualitative factors.* The agency takes its broad media decisions early in media planning. The choice of the basic medium, often TV versus Press, is the most important decision but gets very little help from research. These decisions nearly always have to be made by overall judgement, not by the quantification of research and a media model. Where help is most needed, the model is weakest.

2   *Finer qualitative factors.* The planner and buyer find themselves spending more time on the more refined qualitative factors. These affect mainly the intra-medium decisions: the choice of publications within a group, discussions about TV buying criteria etc. There is more research here though the amount at risk must be less. Does the editorial environment provide a suitable background for the advertising? Does the advertisement reproduce well in this publication? Do people read the publication in a hurry or at leisure? Is there particular sympathy between the publication and our target? It is possible to imagine all these factors being quantified, though as will be shown this is a difficult task. The subject is nearly always treated in press terms — including here — because this is where media owners have spent most research money and where the differences are more manageable.

3   *Quantifiable factors.* Finally there are factors which it would seem entirely natural to research and then to express as numbers. Does the medium select or attract a greater proportion of the target than can be detected in the basic data? Is a publication's readership increasing? Is the advertisement seen there on more than one occasion? Such questions could be researched but are rarely thought to be worth the time or trouble.

## A PRACTICAL APPROACH

Having introduced the subject and indicated its different elements, I now suggest how in practice it should be approached. There is one essential first step, then the problem is broken into three parts and finally these three are combined.

314

It is essential to clear out of the way how many people in the target are exposed to each medium we are considering. Sometimes this initial step is confused with some of the factors discussed below, but the fact that one publication contains among its readers a higher proportion of the target should already have been taken into account and must not be considered again as an additional reason for using it.

However, if the data used are out of date or not appropriate, we may have to adjust the basic figures, either by a numerical factor or just by specifying a reason for preferring an apparently more expensive medium.

It is often pointed out that data refer to the past, whereas the schedule being planned will appear in the future. Readerships are usually regarded as static, but there are many gradual movements and some striking gains and losses. Television on the other hand is admitted to be dynamic, but forecasting ratings is difficult. An unsatisfactory aspect of thinking of the press as static is that this underplays the advantages of the tactical timing of insertions. Special features and other known circulation boosters can be used in much the same way as advance programme information is used for TV, but whilst the TV buyer's performance can be evaluated and rewarded, the press buyer's efforts become submerged in the average. To build readership predictions into the system is a logical way of overcoming the problem at the planning stage and an obvious improvement on historical data.

The other side of the coin is when the data does not include an appropriate target definition. This was discussed in Chapter 14. A *selectivity* factor evaluates the kind of reader a vehicle selects or attracts — beyond the normal classifications available in industry data. This is often confused with the *environment* factor described below, but which concerns whether an advertisement is more effective in a particular context. Here we are just head-counting; some publications may select just the sort of people the advertising is directed to, and do this because of their editorial approach. For example *Mother* and *Practical Motorist* could attract the right readers for a baby food or a car fitting, respectively. A look at the advertising carried by such specialist publications shows this factor at work. The points made in Chapter 14 are summarised again here. We may have defined direct, appropriate targets (buyers of baby food or of car fittings) but these definitions are not in the basic data. We may therefore try to adjust the available readerships to take into account this characteristic. It is possible to investigate this factor by analysing data in which both kinds of definition have been included. This investigation has indeed been carried out [17.6]. The conclusions are:

1    A direct target definition, e.g. heavy buyers of a product category, can lead to a different evaluation of vehicles from a crude or indirect definition, e.g. all housewives. This is quite common in the press. It is rare in television, though an exception is the effect of regions, where the value of a TV area may not be adequately described by, for example, housewife audience data.

2    Very detailed demographic weightings derived from the composition of the real target and applied to the basic data do not seem to improve evaluations over the use of simple demographics.

3    The sizes of such differences as have been found have not been large, in relation to differences in cost per thousand. It *is* worth making use of this factor in media decisions, but its effect on publication choice is not usually a major one.

4    This situation may change, because we may discover ways of defining potential prospects which are more relevant than those used now — perhaps publications differ in the number of such prospects they attract. Or media themselves may become more precise — perhaps more of them will be conceived editorially as attractive to a deliberately limited, but valuable, type of reader.

We now assume that all this has been done, so we have a realistic cost per thousand in the real target as the first step in our evaluation of different media or vehicles. We need also to know the cover of the medium, the way it duplicates with other media etc. but these are not to the point here. When inter-media comparisons are being made we should also get as near as possible to comparability between media, e.g. a presence factor should be included for TV. All this information is often misleadingly called 'cost-efficiency': it is not about overall efficiency, only about the exposure of advertising.

*Understanding the target*

We should know about the target: who they are and what appeals to them. A great deal of research in the advertising agency is directed to these questions. Most of it is to help the creative department: the more

316

you know about the target, the easier it is to write relevant advertisements. Hence work on how the target uses the product, what they think about it and how it meets their needs, both latent and explicit. More broadly, work may be done on what the target is like, where their priorities lie, how they choose to spend their time and money, their interests and opinions. But having this information can help media choice too. Just as the advertisement can be made more appealing, the media choice can be made more sympathetic; advertisement and medium can work together.

## Creative objectives

It is essential in each particular choice situation to know what the advertising has to *do*. Is it to convey information, to change an image, to make a brand name more familiar or what? This is what makes the particular case unique.

## Understanding the medium

Under this broad heading come the individual factors listed below. In a sense, the whole of this book is about this subject. It covers what the media actually contain (news, stories, entertainment...), how they are distributed and used, what sort of people choose them and what they think of them. Each of these may contribute to the appropriateness of a medium to do an advertising job — the difficulty is knowing what is especially relevant to this problem *and* is not already included in cost per thousand in the target.

## Combining target, objectives and medium

The final modification to basic costs comes when we consider together the last three factors. How will *this* group of people be made to feel *that* by advertising in each particular medium?

# CREATIVE OPPORTUNITY

Without any doubt, the most significant qualitative factor is the use the creative team will make of each medium. This outweighs all the detailed research analyses. It also takes us outside the scope of this book, for we do not discuss here the various creative approaches which might be taken, how they might be tested or evaluated and how eventually the seal of approval will be put on the way the team design the advertisements. Media planning in its widest sense includes an understanding of this process; it includes sympathy and genuine cooperation with the creative department; it means encouraging creative directors to think widely about media so that a real choice is made (not 'any medium as long as it's television').

Good case histories go some way to explaining the creative influence on media choice. Understanding human nature does a lot more. It is always worth reading or listening to what creative people say about the different media (for a good recent example see [17.7]). It is also worth including probes about media in the same qualitative pre-research which is primarily to help the creative people.

It is not possible to be specific here about the qualities of each medium that a creative man will find most stimulating or relevant in each case. But it is relevant to summarise how he will instinctively react to the suggestion of each medium type.

## Television

This is seen to impose itself on the viewer, to demand attention and creative awareness even for low-interest products. It has of course sound and movement, so it can draw on all the emotional strengths and associations of music and the human voice. It can add warmth, excitement, style. It can demonstrate the product. It can tell a story or a joke. It can create mood, personality and image for the brand. It is also, to be frank, fashionable in creative circles.

## Cinema

This is inevitably compared with television. The effect is heightened by the big screen, the better quality of sound and picture. There is a sense of occasion or extravagance and a greater expectation that you will be entertained. There can be more attention, more intimacy. The large audience can however actively puncture the mood if the commercial is inappropriate.

## Newspapers

These are for *news:* information, announcements and realism. But like all press, they are for detail, for long copy, for the facts and figures people will want to refer to, for coupons. The reader's attention has to be caught, but once attracted it is assumed he will work through the advertisement.

## Magazines

More leisured, more specialist, reasoned and sensible advertising is appropriate here. The mood of advice, of information-giving, of confidence-creation, of woman talking to woman is welcomed. There is style which can be borrowed and used.

## Outdoor

These advertisements are glimpsed but often ignored. So they have to be short, startling, simple, memorable. Colour is useful for pack recognition. Essentially it is a reminder medium: high in frequency of exposure, low in detail of content. It can give a brand the look of a confident big spender.

## Radio

Few creative people at the time of writing work happily in the radio medium. Often it is again seen as a reminder, usually of a TV campaign. It is for news, music, jingles, DJ-style humour and to indulge wild ideas.

Clearly this list is incomplete and over-simple. But it should help to explain how a creative man, faced with the task of achieving *this,* finds *that* medium the obvious one. I am advocating that the planner learns how creative people evaluate media opportunities. He can discard his pocket calculator and rate cards more easily than most creatives can pick them up. Indeed non-researchers trying to use research can be embarrassing: here is a competent radio performer trying to sell independent radio: 'If you're hitting a million people every day of the week, seven days a week for four weeks, for the cost of two television spots, it's got to work out better in the long run. And there's an interesting figure which was dug up by Simmons in America, showing radio recall is 38 per cent more than television'. Has it *'got* to work out better' — does the same apply to the much higher frequency of outdoor? Are cover and ratings confused here? 'Dug up' is an evocative phrase, perhaps reminiscent of diamond mining, but what was Simmons measuring? Is recall the object? — and so on.

The choice that is most often debated is between television and the press, especially women's magazines. Despite the case histories reported in Chapter 12, no generalisations on their relative effectiveness as advertising vehicles can be made safely. The reader who is faced with this decision is advised to consider seperately:

1   The basic cost and cover calculations.
2   The need to get the attention of the target, bearing in mind the long hours in front on the TV set of the average viewer (see Chapter 4) and what we know of the mechanics of scanning and reading (Chapter 5).
3   Once attention has been gained, the kind of communication we want to achieve. The following remarks by a distinguished user of both media [17.8] are helpful:

> 'Television is an admirable medium for exposition in several ways: powerful and immediate to the eye, able to take the spectator bodily into the places and processes that are described, and conversational enough to make him conscious that what he witnesses are not events but the actions of people . . . Unlike a lecture or a printed book, television is not directed to crowds. It is addressed to two or three people in a room, as a conversation face to face . . . The printed book has one added freedom beyond this: it is not remorselessly bound to the forward direction of time, as any spoken discourse is. The reader can do what the

viewer and listener cannot, which is to pause and reflect, turn the pages back and the argument over, compare one fact with another and, in general, appreciate the detail of evidence without being distracted by it.'

## INDIVIDUAL FACTORS

In this section I expand further on a point mentioned above: understanding the medium.

### Content analysis

This may be formal, e.g. a breakdown of TV programmes or of a magazine by subject, or much more usually the impression gained by casual inspection. Even if very brief, this direct exposure is essential. The media man *must* be familiar with the tools of his trade.

### Reproduction

There can be no dispute about the wide differences between different printing methods and therefore different qualities of reproduction. This is not a matter of only experts being able to distinguish the different standards: anyone can tell. See-through, coarse screening, poor paper, flat colours and the rest are certainly distinguishable. At the extreme it is reasonable that they drag down the effect on the consumer, although IPC have some evidence to the contrary [17.9]. There is of course the well-known difficulty of interpreting laboratory tests meaningfully, i.e. with reference to sales effectiveness. It is also obvious that for some products there is believed to be an exceptional need for high standards: recipe advertising, fashion and cosmetics for example. It is therefore quite normal to insist on using only those publications where printing standards are sufficiently high. Or at least to down-weight publications with lower standards, though they may because of low cost still be used. In a similar way, television may be less suitable when points of detail are central in the advertising.

The advertiser often forgets that the reader does not compare the reproduction in one publication with that in another, as specialists do:

she sees the advertisement in the context of the editorial in the publication she has by definition chosen to read. It is only her viewpoint which counts — provided that we can succeed in communicating what we want. The fine detail of beautiful hair may not reproduce from a photograph on cheap newsprint, but a line drawing may achieve the same effect, or the lack of detail may not matter as much as experts think. But agencies continue, perhaps irrationally, to down-weight severely the cheaper publications, not only because of their own perhaps irrelevant standards but also because of the effect on the trade (in the widest sense). If agency men and advertising managers say 'We can't possibly show the pack at that standard of reproduction' it is likely that retailers, supermarket management and even the advertiser's own salesmen would say 'Well, X is slipping if they allow that sort of advertising.' Such a reaction could do more harm than any loss of efficiency with consumers. Conversely, some publications with high standards get business as a show case for the advertising and not for their effect on consumers.

*Page size*

This point is closely related to the last. A small page may be 'too small to carry the creative message', or a large page may be 'so unwieldy the reader can't take in the whole page'. It is important to distinguish this factor from noting or page traffic scores. Such scores describe whether a page or part of a page is seen, read and so on. The present point is about the creative use made of the page and the effect of this on the reader.

There is no doubt that a large page used properly can carry more detailed copy than a small page or part of a page. Amateurs and experts would agree. But the effect on the reader is not so easily discussed. After all, apparent size is a function of distance from the page.

The changes in 1973-4 to a smaller page size by the *Daily Mail*, *Evening News* and *Sunday People* were accompanied by the argument that, as long as the copy could be accommodated, the tabloid size is as effective as the broadsheet (it also allows more solus positions and reduces confusion on the page).

This point is in the tradition of the classical 'square-root' rule, which says that when you double a space size or TV commercial length you increase its effectiveness by the square root of two (about 1.4) and so on in proportion. There is evidence of recall and noting increasing in this way — and, of course, linear dimensions on a page, e.g. the diagonal of the space size, increase like this. It would follow that, since cost increases roughly in proportion to the area of the advertisement in the press, or length in TV, the effectiveness per pound spent *falls* by the square root of two when the size is doubled. Thus ad size should be only as big as is essential to contain the message. The argument begs many questions, e.g. is recall the best measure of effectiveness?) but contains more than a grain of truth. There is also no doubt that, as Bill Gregory has argued persuasively, the smaller page size is more economical for the media owner and so indirectly for the advertiser.

## Readers per copy

Some publications have only two or three readers on average to every copy; others have five, six or more. It is natural to ask whether some of the later readers are worthwhile. It is suggested that the person who buys the issue has a special relation with it; she trusts it more and reads it more carefully, though this is disputed. Some people argue that publications with high numbers of readers per copy should be downweighted.

Readers per copy is a useful description of how much a publication circulates. It can also be used to provide a readership estimate: the latest circulation figure or estimate multiplied by the average number of readers per copy in recent years. But the danger of double-weighting appears again when readers per copy is used as a weight: is the less thorough reading of the later readers already reflected in the advertisement exposure factor used? It is important to consider whether this exposure factor is derived from all readers — or only from early readers, which is often the case.

## Exposure occasions

Reading a publication on more than one day may be simply a function of size of publication and length of publication interval. A thick publication published monthly is likely to have its reading spread over more days than a daily which is seldom looked at the day after publication. There is little surprising here or which is not reflected in spread traffic. But looking at a page on more than one day or several times a day is a different matter. This is not measured by spread traffic, which counts only whether a spread was ever looked at.

There is evidence [17.10] that for some publications there can be several separate occasions on which the advertisement may be exposed. There is so far no independent authentication of advertisement exposure on later occasions of looking at the page. Could it be that the eye then 'knows' it has seen the page and goes almost straight for the item sought for? In other words, is a second occasion not an independent advertisement exposure? Commonsense — and some *Reader's Digest* work — suggests that the second occasion is largely independent, does have value to the advertiser and should therefore be taken into account. There is however little comparative data so it is hard to take account of this factor in practice. It is a concept which may well be investigated further.

*In-home exposure*

It is commonly thought that one of the advantages television has over press is that it often transmits messages to several members of the family at the same time and in their own home. With no conscious attempt at togetherness the family can discuss the relevance of products to their lives. If a child says 'I'd like to try that' as a new product is flashed on to the screen, his mother has an added incentive to buy.

With some publications the same argument is sometimes advanced. It seems unlikely that reading is as communal an activity as watching television or that the effect of relaxed reading in the home is much more than is already detected by spread traffic or other intensity measures. Care must always be taken not to allow for the same effect twice, i.e. double-weighting.

*Time spent reading*

The point was made above that some publications are looked at on more than one day or on more than one occasion. Readers can also give an estimate for the total amount of time they spend with a publication. There is no doubt that there are differences here between publications; the *Radio Times* for example [17.10] showed average claims of 3 minutes per page in 'yesterday's' reading of the *Sunday Express,* 2.3 minutes for the *Daily Mirror.* The actual figures are open to doubt, since questioning on any one topic is apt to make informants exaggerate its importance. But the relative values are not surprising.

My feeling about this measure is that it could again lead to double-weighting. Time spent may add nothing to spread traffic. Obviously the more thorough readers (with high spread traffic) are likely to spend longer with the publication than less thorough readers. What is required is their likelihood of being exposed to the advertisement, which spread traffic measures directly.

Page size and publication size have a direct but often overlooked effect. The *Sunday Express,* in the example quoted above, might demand more time than the *Daily Mirror* simply because there is more to read on the page. This does not prove that it gives more or less of an opportunity to be intrigued by the advertising.


*Readers' descriptions of media*

I give this title because the factor has been most investigated to distinguish publications, but it applied to other media too. The point is to investigate how the publication is seen by its readers and to extend this to the likely reception of advertising in it. The method may be formal [17.11] by scaling answers to questions like 'Do you agree it helps you pick up useful information?' or 'Is it an escape from real life?'; or it may be very loose, [17.12] reporting for example the informant's own words in answer to an open-ended question: 'Well, personally, I like my own little Woman's Weekly....it's cosy, it's a chatty book'.

I do not know of any examples where campaigns planned with the use of such information have been reported to be very different or more successful. It is likely to help creative people most, to indicate to them what people use the publications for and so to help them write more appropriate copy. At a fundamental level, it helps us to see what people get from media and so may be used to help develop creative concepts which are in tune with peoples' needs; for example most advertising is probably not informative enough.

## More quantitative data about readers

Normally, all we know about the readers (or those exposed to other media) is that they *are* readers (and since they have chosen a particular publication we know something about them), their demographics and that so many of them are in the target. The other data about them (whether they have a car, a telephone, a bank account, etc.) is usually employed numerically only to decide whether they are in our target. But media owners are often careful to tell us a lot about their audience which can add depth to understanding them. Even if we are not advertising cars, the fact that unusually many readers bought new cars gives us a feeling about it which may make us prefer this publication.

## Life style

Beyond demographics and possessions, we may have measurements of readers' activities, interests and opinions [17.13]. In the same way as the last factor, this can give us a better understanding of the difference between readers of publications or audiences to TV programmes. There is no doubt these differences do exist in both the US [17.14] and UK. Even publications which content analysis shows to be very similar (like *Time* and *Newsweek* in the US or some women's magazines in the UK) attract different sort of people simply because of their editorial approach. Qualities are at work here that are more appropriate to literary criticism than to conventional media research.

An example may make this clear. Suppose we are considering the *Radio Times*, the *Sunday Times Colour Magazine* and *Punch* for a women's schedule. Demographic data tell us a lot about the women who read these publications. They all tend to be upgrade, most for the colour magazine, least for the *Radio Times*. The *Radio Times* reader is of average age; both the magazine and the *Punch* reader are younger. The last two have in fact very similar profiles. But we do not get from such data a clear idea of what these groups of women are *like*. What is makes them choose these publications and may make them appropriate for our campaign?

Table 39 gives three statements [17.15] and the percentages agreeing with each. This makes it clear that in these respects (and of course many more statements are available for comparison) *Radio Times* readers have opinions close to the average. The colour magazine readers look more sceptical, liberal and ready to try new things. *Punch* readers differ from in being more nationalistic, but are even more progressive and experimental.

Rather like readers' descriptions of media, such data has not been much used in media planning. It is not generally available; even the quantified data of the previous factor *is* accessible but rarely employed for this purpose. The way it can be brought in is obviously to see whether our target or our creative objective are specially sympathetic with different publications. If we are selling food by using recipe advertising, to take an obvious example, the data above could be enlightening. When the information is additional to readership in the target it can be helpful. It is also of course useful in other media applications [17.16], editorial policy or designing new publications (*TV Life* is an example), or explaining to the trade what the readers are like (the *Financial Times* has used Life Style in this way). (For a broader view, see [17.17]).

Outside the UK, there are examples of pyschographic data put to use more formally in media selection. In Germany, for example, the data provided by magazine owners often includes a pyschographic section completed by informants who have also answered questions on products and on their readership. Thus the example given in Chapter 14, 'mums who put their children first' might be explicitly available in the data; so might 'mums who buy tinned vegetables and who put their children first'. Then this target group's readership can be examined directly, without fear of double counting. In France there are experiments on the addition of Life Style scales to standard readership

## Table 39

|  | All women % | Radio Times % | ST Col Mag % | Punch % |
|---|---|---|---|---|
| British workmanship is of a high standard | 49 | 45 | 37 | 56 |
| Sex outside marriage is wrong | 53 | 53 | 41 | 34 |
| I often experiment with new recipes | 62 | 67 | 74 | 82 |

research. But in the UK and US this method has not become publicly available [17.17].

*Editorial environment*

In addition to the effect that the editorial approach has on the selection of the publication by certain readers, does the surrounding editorial and even the name of the publication add to the message?

This question may apply to a publication as a whole, or it may be used to distinguish one part of a publication from another, in addition to page traffic differences. One part, e.g. the cookery section, may be thought preferable for a particular type of advertising, e.g. food advertising. The same question may be asked about different times and programmes on television. Perhaps the time of day affects the atmosphere in which the advertisement is seen. Such programmes are favourites: people are attentive to them; others are viewed in a desultory way.

The theory behind these considerations is that the consumer is considered to approach the advertising in a more acceptable frame of mind because the editorial approach prepares him to receive the advertising message. Some of its authority or character rubs off on the advertising. The advertising gains from being seen in the right company. This factor is important in many current press decisions; in my opinion too much is made of it. It is discussed on television but extremely rarely applied.

There is no doubt that the population as a whole thinks of publications as having more or less authority, having more or less knowledge on special subjects, or being more suitable for certain purposes. This does not prove that these attitudes carry over into advertising effect. One publication which has attempted to attack this tradition is the *TV Times* [17.18] before its relaunch in the autumn of 1968. Its research can be summarised as suggesting that editorial rub-off on advertising effectiveness either does not exist or is so slight as not to be a serious factor.

In this situation it is hard to defend some of the figures people use for the effect of editorial environment. The concept is attractive to common sense but the absence of evidence is disturbing. Its value must depend on the advertising objective (for brand saliency or pack recognition, for example, it cannot be very serious). In my opinion

328

there is little evidence in favour of using environment as a media weight.

There is certainly evidence that to associate different publications with an advertisement can have an effect. This has been demonstrated both in the US and UK [17.19]. The direction of the effect is the obvious one, that the more authoritative name lends credibility; the same girl can be thought smarter in *Nova* but more fun to be with in *Woman;* a floor-covering can score higher on some dimensions when it is known to have appeared in *Ideal Home* than in a Sunday colour magazine. It is speculative to extend this to the normal reading situation. Again, we are really learning about the character of the publication; extension to advertising effectiveness is difficult and no large body of data comparing media is available.

*Case histories*

This is just to repeat the point made in Chapter 12, that case histories where two media are tested against each other are the only way to get satisfactory information on how they compare overall and in practice.

## MEDIA WEIGHTS

The subject we are discussing can also be called 'media weights'. If our object is to put *numbers* on the values we find, then these are the weights we are looking for. A definition of a media weight is a factor that influences media selection additional to cost and to readership or viewing in the target population as determined by basic media research data. As already explained, it is now rare that we try to be precise in this way and it is not recommended that such weights be input into the media model which then may become a 'dosage' model. For when a qualitative weight is used (colour has this much more impact, reproduction there must be weighted down) then the previous simple definition of an impression has been confused. An impression is not now as easy to understand as 'being exposed to an advertisement'; it is something like 'being effectively exposed' or 'having seen the best advertisement in the most suitable publication'. The result of monochrome advertising or less good reproduction is to move a consumer far up a scale of advertising dosage received.

The dosage model is not accepted practice, though it is reasonable that it be used. It can be illuminating and lead to practical action. It can suggest useful advances in advertising theory which themselves can be tested separately. It allows sensitivity analysis to be done. It is a decision tool. In other words, it has all the advantages of a theoretical model. I sympathise with those who use it. But the model has not been verified; it may well be wrong; it is not easy to understand. I sympathise also with those who do not trust it.

The dosage model just described still treats weights as probabilities; the impression distribution is still in whole numbers: there is no such thing as half an impression. Sometimes another type of dosage model is discussed [17.20] in which the qualitative factors are applied separately from advertisement exposure and a continuous scale of impressions is used. A person exposed to one advertisement with a weight of one half is said to receive half an impression. Little is known about such continuous models; the probability method and a discrete impression distribution are at present recommended.

There is no novelty in the objectives of weighting. Weights can also be called the use of common sense, experience, flair or judgement. Every advertising schedule has been constructed with the use of media weights in this sense. The old-style media man always operated with a generally understood basis of 'good practice', received wisdom and a pile of well-thumbed publications under his arm. It is the numerical form of weighting which is new. The arrival of large-scale media research implied that explicit weights would be required and computers dramatised this need. It then came to be realised that schedules constructed from issue-reading data only were unacceptable on commonsense grounds. Basic media research on its own is not enough for constructing good schedules. Media research offers a valuable aid if combined with other information. Incomplete in itself, it can be brought closer to reality. It is this combination or bringing closer which is the function of media weights.

Modifications to the basic research data, whether inexplicit or expressed in numbers, are an essential part of media planning. Perhaps research will eventually improve to the point where media weights are unnecessary; we may eventually see the operation of a new Gresham's Law: 'Good research drives out media weights' — but this is not yet on the horizon.

The use of media weights is a sign of dissatisfaction with the research measurements and an attempt to bring industry data closer

330

to reality. Media weights are a bridge between this data and the real world, between the computer and experience. The bridge is fragile and a temporary structure. It will get shorter as the data improves and the gap to be bridged gets smaller. It will get more solid as more is learned about advertising. If we start media planning from the research data — and most of us do — it is fatal not to try to cross to the other side.

One way in which numbers are, however, helpful arises at the VIP stage. If we work out the relative cost per thousand of each medium we can be helped in our choice by turning on its head the obvious question. We do not ask, say, 'What numerical value do you put on a 30-second commercial being seen and on a full page in colour in a magazine?' Instead we say, 'For reaching the target a full page in colour costs only three-quarters as much as a 30-second (or, we can buy four pages seen for every three TV commercials): do you think the extra cost of TV is worthwhile?' It is much easier to answer the second question than the first, and the reply is all we need to know.

This is recommended rather than the classical use of media weights, which is to estimate them first, calculate VIPs and then consider the result of these calculations. This combination of soft data with hard makes it clear that the decision should depend on both, but estimating in this area requires a special skill and the results should not be taken over-seriously.

The old-fashioned method was to consider only one medium or type of publication as feasible, but otherwise to ignore qualitative factors. A publication was either 'in' — and then judged only on comparatively objective factors — or 'out'. This is of course equivalent to using media weights of one or zero only, which is unnecessarily crude. And the defect of this method is that it considers the two kinds of data separately. It may reject cheap opportunities just because they are also of lower quality.

How big do weights have to be to matter? Or to put in another way, what is the range of cost per thousand in the target? This varies of course from case to case. But generally the range is quite wide and so small differences in weights or in subjective evaluations do not make much difference to schedule effectiveness. Ranges of two to one or even three or one over ten or twenty publications are common.

The media owner takes a different attitude. First, he may be just on or just off the schedule because of the media weight or valuation his publication is allotted. Second, how many times has a cheap cost-per-thousand publication been dismissed as 'unsuitable' — without this criterion being clearly stated, let alone investigated? Other publications are almost as automatically added to schedules on non-quantified grounds.

## CONCLUSION

The subjects of qualitative factors and media weights make a fitting conclusion to this book. The phrases themselves suggest a paradox. They are about *qualities:* aspects of media on which research has not provided conclusive answers and probably never will. But the words 'factors' and 'weights' imply *numbers* and a logical, detached approach.

Using *both* sorts of data resolves the contradiction; *how* to do this cannot be taught easily but is the essence of the planner's job. He must be rigorous wherever he can. He must be sympathetic and intuitive where he cannot measure.

# *APPENDICES*

MEDIA BRIEFING
MEDIA EVALUATION
MEDIA PLAN
UPDATING ADVERTISING EXPENDITURE

The checklists in Appendices 1-3 are based on a checklist discussed at the ESOMAR Seminar on Media Planning (May 1969) and published by S. Broadbent and D. Phillips, 'An agency media checklist', *ADMAP* (July 1969).

# 1 MEDIA BRIEFING

1   *Team*                                           (Chapter 7)

Who are the people in the agency working on this campaign?


2   *Product, competition and objectives*            (Chapter 7)

What is the product, its uses, pack, price, method of distribution,
    level of distribution, type of outlet and seasonal rate of
    consumption?
What are competitive products (details as for our own
    product)?
Does the product category rule out any medium?
What is the recent product sales and advertising history, including
    media effectiveness measurements?

What is a similar history for competitors?

What is the product and client company position relative to competitive products and companies?

What are the marketing, advertising and communication objectives and strategy?

3    *Budget* ,                                             (Chapter 8)

Is there a media budget (excluding production costs) and, if so, what is it?

If there is a budget, does it break down separately for theme, scheme and trade advertising?

Can provision be made for tactical reserves?

Does the advertiser qualify for additional discounts from other products?

What degree of flexibility is there in the budget?

Or is there to be a recommendation to be made on the budget?
a    What can the product afford?
b    What is the advertising task and what will this cost?
c    What are competitors spending?
d    What has been learned about the return from advertising expenditure?

4    *Timetable*                                             (Chapter 7)

When will the campaign start?

When will it finish?

What are the relevant cancellation and copy dates?

Do these rule out any medium?

When will firm decisions be made on commercial length, colour etc?

When is the media plan to be presented?

When will the advertiser's approval be obtained?

What are promotional plans/sales cycles?

What is the advertiser's budget year?

5    *Target*                                    (Chapters 7 and 14)

Who is the advertising aimed at? What is the demographic profile
of the target market? What else do we know about them?
Is this target definition contained in the data to be used in
planning? In buying? In post-campaign evaluation? If not,
what definition should be used?


6    *Regionality*                                      (Chapter 9)

How are sales, or outlets, or expansion opportunities distributed
over the country?
How should advertising be spread over regions?


7    *Seasonality*                                      (Chapter 9)

How should advertising be spread over the weeks or months of
the campaign? Within this, should advertising be evenly spread
or in bursts?
Are special days or times important? How much more valuable
are they?


8    *Creative*                                        (Chapter 17)

What are the communication objectives in terms of type of
communication, e.g. demonstration, mood, etc.?
What are the creative possibilities arising from the communication
objectives, and how do the media available compare in creative
potential related to the communication objectives?
What values, and for what reasons, do the creatives initially
attach to these media:
    TV
    Daily and Sunday Newspapers
    Weekly and Monthly magazines
    Outdoor
    Cinema
    Radio

Others?
What are the creatives' first thoughts about commercial lengths, sizes, colour, bleed, special positions, etc.?

9    *Media objectives*                    (Chapters 7, 10 and 16)

What value have repetition and domination of the target as against cover of the target?
What is the initial evaluation of matching or avoiding competitors?

10    *Research*                           (Chapters 12 and 14)

What market or creative research is planned?
What pre- or post-campaign evaluation is planned?
Can media evaluation be built into these jobs?

11    *Initial contact with media*         (Chapter 10)

Do we already have options?
What is the availability situation — does this rule out any medium?
Have we the authority to place options? To make firm bookings?
If not, when will authority be needed? Obtained?
Can media be told about the product? The campaign? If not, when can they be told?

# 2   MEDIA EVALUATION

Which media are feasible on objective grounds, given the type of product, timetable, availability situation, regionality requirements?

What data is available on the past performance of the different media?
What qualitative or other factors should be taken into account as well as the cost of exposing advertisements to the target?
What is the effect of media choice expected to be on the trade?
Are there other services offered by media which would be useful?

What is the outcome of discussions with creatives about the different media?

Has full use been made of marketing flexibility in the media timing plan to ensure optimum use of media availabilities?

Is there sufficient flexibility in the timing plan to ensure maximum value through negotiations with media owners?

Have media owners representatives been contacted to establish minimum rates and maximum value obtainable, for selected media, and for possible alternatives?

3    *Cost per thousand in the target*        (Chapters 14 and 15)

What cover of the target do different media give?

What are the costs of exposing advertisements in each medium given the target definition and realistic costs?

4    *Media choice*        (Chapter 10)

What is to be the main medium (*is* there to be a main medium)?

What would be the result of spending all the budget in the main medium?

Would it weaken the campaign seriously to spend less?

Would a campaign in this medium alone leave serious gaps?

Should other media groups be used — at what level of expenditure?

What criteria are to be used in constructing schedules?

# 3　MEDIA PLAN

1　*Description*　　　　　　　　　　　　　(Chapter 10)

Advertiser, product, timing and brief description of the campaign.
Author of plan and date.

2　*Media brief*

Marketing and advertising or communication strategies.
Budget (excluding production).
Target definition and regional requirements.
Seasonal requirements.

3　*Media recommendations*

Media objectives and strategy.
Reasons for the choice of the main medium, for other media if
　used, and comments on the media rejected.
Allocation of the budget by medium, by commercial length
　or size, by region and by time.
Buying objectives and criteria.
Outline schedules and their predicted performance.
Media research or evaluation work planned.

# 4 UPDATING ADVERTISING EXPENDITURE

The key figures for advertising expenditure are given in the Advertising Association's annual survey, published in the journal *Advertising* in the summer of each year and further commented on in the autumn (the two parts of this review are reprinted together and can be obtained from the AA). These are generally net figures, i.e. discounts and deals are deducted. The AA total includes production costs, which do not of course benefit media owners, and also includes some types of press advertising (financial, classified, trade and technical) which are not normally handled by major agencies. The figures are therefore rearranged, in Table A2, which separates the mainstream expenditure studied in this book. This has grown less rapidly than the AA total. In particular, classified (which I exclude) has more than doubled in the last five years (from £150 million to £327 million) and TV production expenditure has doubled while display advertising in the Press and TV airtime revenue have each risen by less than two-thirds.

342

More frequent and up-to-date advertising expenditure figures are published by MEAL, but these figures are gross, i.e. at rate card and without excluding deals. The ITCA's net revenue is published monthly; when it is compared with the rate card ITV turnover the average discount can be deduced: a sensitive indicator of the state of the TV market (see Chapter 3).

Consumers' Expenditure (more relevant than the Gross National Product which includes industrial spending) and the Retail Price Index can be extracted from the Monthly Digest of Statistics.

The reader can update from these sources the figures shown in Tables A1-A3, which indicate the overall changes in the economy and in advertising expenditure.

Table A.1

| Year | Consumers' expenditure, £m, at current prices | Annual average, Retail Price Index (Jan 1974 = 100) | Annual percentage change in RPI, from col. (3) |
|------|------|------|------|
| (1) | (2) | (3) | (4) |
| 1968 | 27,331 | 65.2 | +5 |
| 1969 | 28,951 | 68.7 | +6 |
| 1970 | 31,365 | 73.1 | +6 |
| 1971 | 35,265 | 80.0 | +8 |
| 1972 | 39,785 | 85.7 | +7 |
| 1973 | 45,072 | 93.5 | +9 |
| 1974 | 51,811 | 108.5 | +16 |
| 1975 | 63,333 | 134.8 | +24 |
| 1976 | 73,424 | 156.5 | +16 |
| 1977 | 83,204 | 182.0 | +12 |
| 1978 | | | |

Table A.2 ADVERTISING EXPENDITURE (ADVERTISING ASSOCIATION BASIS, £m)

| Medium | 1968 | 1973 | 1977 | 19 | 19 | 19 |
|---|---|---|---|---|---|---|
| PRESS:Display advertising: | | | | | | |
| National newspapers | 68 | 104 | 177 | | | |
| Regional newspapers | 52 | 101 | 164 | | | |
| Mags and periodicals | 46 | 65 | 108 | | | |
| Others | 4 | 6 | 11 | | | |
| TOTAL DISPLAY IN PRESS | 170 | 276 | 460 | | | |
| PRESS:Non-display: | | | | | | |
| Financial | 10 | 16 | 19 | | | |
| Classified | 98 | 213 | 327 | | | |
| Trade and technical | 46 | 73 | 133 | | | |
| TOTAL PRODUCTION | 23 | 46 | 73 | | | |
| TELEVISION: | | | | | | |
| Transmission charges | 118 | 189 | 353 | | | |
| Production | 11 | 21 | 45 | | | |
| OUTDOOR (Poster & Transport) | 20 | 31 | 54 | | | |
| CINEMA | 6 | 7 | 9 | | | |
| RADIO | 1 | 2 | 26 | | | |
| TOTAL DISPLAY ADVERTISING IN MEDIA | 315 | 505 | 902 | | | |
| TOTAL OTHER EXPENDITURE | 188 | 369 | 597 | | | |
| ADVERTISING ASSOCIATION TOTAL | 504 | 874 | 1499 | | | |

Table A.3

| Year | Ad expenditure from Table A.2, £m | | Ad expenditure as % of Consumers' Expenditure, from (2), (3), and Table A.1 | | Display advertising in media | |
|------|-----------|---------------------------------|-------|-------------------------------|-------------------------------------------------------------------------|-------------------------------|
| | AA total | Display advertising in media | AA total | Display advertising in media | Indexed by Jan 1974 RPI: (3) Table A.3 divided by (3) from Table A.1 | Annual real growth rate, %, from (6) |
| (1) | (2) | (3) | (4) | (5) | (6) | (7) |
| 1968 | 504 | 315 | 1.85 | 1.15 | 480 | – |
| 1969 | 544 | 329 | 1.89 | 1.14 | 480 | – 1 |
| 1970 | 554 | 326 | 1.77 | 1.04 | 450 | – 7 |
| 1971 | 591 | 355 | 1.71 | 1.02 | 440 | 0 |
| 1972 | 708 | 418 | 1.80 | 1.06 | 490 | +10 |
| 1973 | 874 | 505 | 1.95 | 1.13 | 540 | +11 |
| 1974 | 900 | 504 | 1.76 | 0.98 | 465 | –14 |
| 1975 | 967 | 572 | 1.53 | 0.90 | 424 | –9 |
| 1976 | 1188 | 721 | 1.62 | 0.99 | 461 | –9 |
| 1977 | 1499 | 902 | 1.80 | 1.08 | 496 | +8 |
| 1978 | | | | | | |

# REFERENCES

## 1  A GAME FOR FOUR PLAYERS

An overview, largely from the advertisers' side, is given by S.H. Kennedy and D. R. Corkindale, *Managing the Advertising Process,* Saxon House (1976).

1.1    S.M.Britt, S.C.Adams and A.S.Miller, 'How many advertising exposures per day?', *Journal of Advertising Research* (December 1972).


## 2  HOW DOES ADVERTISING WORK?

2.1    *The Market Researcher Looks at the Way that Advertising Works,* ESOMAR Seminar (1967).

2.2    J.A.P.Treasure, 'The volatile consumer', *ADMAP* (June 1973).

2.3    R.Colley, *Defining Advertising Goals for Measured Advertising Results,* Association of National Advertisers, New York (1961).

2.4 The five ways were stated by James Webb Young, a Professor at Chicago in his book, *How to Become an Advertising Man*; they are commented on by John Treasure in the JWT booklet, *How Advertising Works,* collected in 1974.

2.5 A.S.C.Ehrenberg, 'Repetitive advertising and the consumer', *Journal of Advertising Research* (April 1974).


## 3  MONEY-GO-ROUND

3.1 D.S.Lees, 'An economist looks at advertising', *Advertising Quarterly* (Summer 1968). Professor Lees directed the Economists Advisory Study Group which produced *The Economics of Advertising,* Advertising Association (1967).
A useful summary of the controversy about advertising expenditure appears in: D.S.Dunbar, 'The politics of the economics of advertising', *Journal of Advertising Research* (March 1968).

3.2 Expenditures are analysed at card rates by MEAL (Media Expenditure Analysis Limited). Further details of advertising by individual advertisers in individual media, with a range of summaries by product group, by medium and so on, are available from MEAL.

3.3 The figures given in the table are estimates for 1977, based on the Family Expenditure Survey 1963-1973 and on the breakdown of advertising by product group in *Advertising* (Summer 1978).

3.4 Both these lists are from J. Walter Thomson/MEAL.

3.5 D.Ogilvy, *Confessions of an Advertising Man,* Longmans (1964).

3.6 For updating see the IPA's annual statistical report, *How Much, How Many.*

3.7 This breakdown is based on estimates made by the Advertising Association; *Advertising* publishes annually the AA Figures. See the Appendices. See also a key paper on this subject: J. Treasure, *The Real Cost of Advertising,* IAA Congress (1965).

3.8 A.M.Fisher and J.D.Wightman, 'Do we take the right media decisions?', *ADMAP* (December 1968).

# 4 TELEVISION

The annual handbooks of the BBC and IBA, plus the various JICTAR publications, including the monthly *Directors' Report,* are essential for up-to-date detail. A summary of the major events up to 1974 was given by *ADMAP* (March, 1974).

4.1 Lord Aylestone, *Financial Times* (July 1968).

4.2 Methods of estimating frequency distributions have a long history. The most recent paper was in 1974: B.Murray and S.Broadbent, 'Introducing presence into TV planning', *ADMAP* (April 1974). This described the construction of a conventional guide *and* the introduction of a presence factor. Before this, R.Hulks and S.G.Thomas, 'PREFACE', *ibid.* (December 1973), traced the development of various predictive models and outlined their own method which gave an estimate not only of cover but of the whole frequency distribution.
The guide most commonly in use is AGB's: see A.Fawley and E.Fairclough, 'The prediction of coverage and four plus coverage for television schedules', *ibid.* (February 1972). This replaced the Television Audience Measurment guide: G.Cleaver and G.Warren, 'Guides to coverage and frequency', *ibid.* (April 1966).

4.3 *Comparison Survey of Audience Composition Techniques,* TAM (1961).
See also S.F.Buck, R.Sherwood and W.A.Twyman, *Operating Effective Panels for TV Audience Measurement,* ESOMAR (1973) and [4.6].

4.4ı See, for example, A.S.C.Ehrenberg and W.A.Twyman, 'On measuring television audiences', *Journal of the Royal Statistical Society,* Series A (1967).
More details are given in the Technical Reports produced for JICTAR by ASKE Research Limited.
See also G.J. Goodhart, A.S.C. Ehrenberg and M.A. Collins, *The Television Audience: patterns of viewing,* Saxon House (1975).

4.5 W.A.Twyman, *Attention and the Measurement of Media Exposure for Press and the Television,* ESOMAR (1972). This has a 27-item bibliography.
Two later studies have been carried out by BMRB on TV audience presence research. The first, for the IPA and ISBA, was

reported in 1968; the second, for JICTAR, in 1976.
Earlier work had been carried out by LPE, J. Walter Thompson, Research Bureau and TAM between 1961 and 1967; references are given in the paper above.

4.6     M.M.Brown, 'Attitudes to programmes and the effect on commercials, *ADMAP* (January 1967).
T.Corlett and D.Richardson, 'TV Attention – a further step', *ibid.* (September 1970).

4.7     I.R.Haldane, *Measuring Television Audience Reactions,* MRS Conference (1970).
See also the four papers on TV viewing in *Journal of the Market Research Society* (January 1969).

4.8     R.Beeson, 'But I happen to like Charles Laughton in newspaper stories', *ADMAP* (January 1973).

# 5 THE PRESS

5.1     *British Rate and Data* (BRAD) is published monthly by Maclean-Hunter Limited. It lists publications (and other media) with circulation, cover price, rate card, copy and cancellation requirements and other details.

5.2     See, for example: J.Caffyn, *Experimental Intermedia Studies,* MRS Conference (1969).
R.C.Grass and W.H.Wallace, 'Advertising communication: print v. TV', *Journal of Advertising Research* (October 1974).
S.Bauer, *et al., Advertising in America: The Consumer View,* Graduate School of Business Research, Harvard University (1968).
There is more on this subject in the section on Intensity of Reading.

5.3     The most recent Royal Commission on the Press published its report in July, 1977 (and incidentally cost £¾ million). Other official sources are:
*The National Newspaper Industry: a Survey*, The Economist Intelligence Unit (1966).
*Costs and Revenue of National Daily Newspapers*, National Board for Prices and Incomes, Report No. 43, HMSO (1967).
*Costs and Revenue of National Newspapers*, National Board for Prices and Incomes, Report No. 141, HMSO (1970).

The Department of Trades Business Monitor publishes revenue information based on industry returns.

5.4  *Behind the headlines – the business of the British Press,* Harry Henry (Editor), Associated Business Press, (1978).

5.5  The most general recent review is J.R.Adams, *Media Planning,* Business Books (1971), but also recommended are IPC's *Sociological Monographs,* especially numbers 9, 10 and 11, published in 1974 and about the audience, content and use made of the mass media, especially the press.
A fresh view on national daily newspapers was given by Mintel in May 1973 and a summary of the virtues of newspaper advertising in P.Bostock, 'Read all about it!', *JWT* (1974).

5.6  National Readership Survey reports are published six-monthly (usually March and September) by JICNARS. Each volume covers the previous twelve months and so is based on about 30,000 interviews. The introduction and appendices to the published volumes give a clear explanation of the purpose and techniques of the survey. As well as national publications, the main regional evening newspapers are included.
The NRS records publication changes and circulations (from the ABC) as well as being a source of demographic and product information, e.g. the proportion of housewives who are working, adults who have a telephone in their households. The raw data is also available, e.g. as computer tape, and special analyses can be carried out by several bureaux (see the booklet on *Post Survey Information Service,* JICNARS).
Note that although the survey is called 'national' it excludes Ulster and those living north of the Caledonian Canal.
The IPA has published a series of booklets commenting on the NRS findings and related matters. Those of most general interest were: W.D.McClelland, *Readership Profiles of Mass Media,* No.2 (1963); J.M.Caffyn, *Qualitative Aspects of Readership Data,* No.3 (1964); M.A.Abrams, *Education, Social Class and Reading of Newspapers and Magazines,* No.5 (1966). But these are now out of date and except for D.Monk, *Social Grading on the NRS* (Fourth edition, 1978), mainly technical, nothing of wide application has been published recently. Instead, specialist areas have been covered (the differences between the surveys of 1967 and 1968, the effects of variability between interviews) including the critical studies of intensity of reading referred to below.

5.7 D.Aitchison, 'The Economics of Newspaper Advertising', *ADMAP*, (December 1974).

5.8 See, for example, the 1978 Evening Newspaper Advertising Bureau's qualitative readership survey, based on a sample of 12,000, and investigating attitudes as well as readership.

5.9 W.S.MacDonald, 'Impact of evening newspapers', *World Press News* (6 October 1967).

5.10 See, for example, M.MacDonald, 'The specialist press looks like a trackless forest, *Advertiser's Wekely* (21 October 1966). J.Clemens, 'Research and the trade and technical press', *ADMAP* (July/August 1966).

5.11 After an acrimonious period when different sources were available the situation (in 1978) has settled down: the National Businessman Readership Survey (NBRC) is sponsored by over a dozen media owners. The survey follows broadly NRS lines but with a different sample and classifications.

5.12 The Press Council publish an annual report, *The Press and the People,* concerned with complaints about advertising, but which also contains some useful figures and articles.

5.13 R.Hulks, 'Landmarks in media research, Part 2, The Press, *ADMAP* (July 1974).
The anti-research point of view, though eccentric, should not be forgotten. See W.S.Blair, 'The case against magazine audience measures, *Journal of Advertising Research* (April 1974).

5.14 The reference is to W. Langschmidt, *'Reliability of response in readership research'*, South African Advertising Research Foundation (1978). Pioneer work on monthlies was done by W. A. Belson, *Studies in Readership*, Business Publications (1962). This reported that intensive interviews recalled additional reading of monthlies which the NRS interview had not uncovered. The technique has since been changed but the problem has not gone away.

5.15 See The Thompson Gold Medal Papers (1962).

5.16 B.Allt, 'The Daily Mirror behaviour and opinions study', *ADMAP* (September 1972).
See also B.Allt, 'Page traffic, spread traffic and editorial reading in the Daily Mirror', *ibid.* (July/August 1971).

5.17 R.Fletcher and B.Mabey, 'Reading and noting revived!', *ibid.* (December 1971).

5.18    D.Phillips, 'Presence in front of advertisements', *ibid.* (May 1969).

D.H.Phillips, 'Current developments in the measurement of exposure to print and television advertisements, *ibid.* (March 1970).

See also the Thomson Gold Medal papers (1965) and P.I.Jones, 'Intensity of reading data – some experimental evidence', *ADMAP* (June 1968).

5.19    The quotation is from Tom Corlett's introduction to *The Measurement of Page and Advertisement Exposure – A Review of Progress by the ARC*, by W.A.Twyman for the ARC (May 1973), and refers to *Page and Advertisement Readership Studies: Report of an Experimental Study* by BMRB for the ARC (September 1969).

5.20    *Reader Categorisation Study: Indirect Measures of Exposure to Contents of Publications,* JICNARS (May 1972).

5.21    H.A.Smith and N.Webb, *How do Women Use Advertisements?,* MRS Conference (1974).

5.22    H.A.Smith, 'A breath of fresh air', *ADMAP* (June 1974). This describes the Evaluative Assessment Service of IPC Magazines for 1973. The work continues and illuminating case histories are now available.

5.23    See for example the papers at the ESOMAR Seminar, *Editorial Research in the Publishing Industry,* Verona (1974), and R.A.Roberts-Miller and N.Spackman, 'Research for publishers', *European Research* (March 1973).


# 6   OTHER MEDIA

The main facts about the outdoor medium are given in *Guide to Outdoor Advertising,* ISBA (1974), and from the various selling organisations mentioned. Earlier research is dealt with in B.D.Copland, *A Review of Poster Research,* Business Publications (1963).

6.1    W.Horwood, 'The poster people settle for peace after the battle', *Campaign* (9 June 1972).

6.2    F.Monkman, 'Structure of the outdoor industry in 1973', *ADMAP* (May 1973).

J.Billett, 'The future of the outdoor medium', *ibid.* (June 1974).

6.3   *The Size and Nature of the Poster Audience: Study II*, Mills and Rockleys Limited (1955). Study I was as early as 1949.

6.4   *The IPA Poster Surveys, 1961-1962*, IPA (1964).

6.5   *Poster Audience Surveys (An Investigation into Poster Campaign Audiences Based on Surveys in Ipswich and the West Midlands Conurbation*, JICPAS (1964).
*Newport Survey*, JICPAS (1969).

6.6   D.Needham, J.Andrews and D.Monk, 'The Gallaher/AAPB poster study of London and Leeds', *ADMAP* (September 1974).

6.7   J.A. Pounds and M.A. Newman, 'The poster audience model'; *ADMAP* (May 1976).

6.8   M.A.Kemp, *Exposure to Posters – Some New Developments*, British Poster Advertising Association Conference (1967).

6.9   A Survey of the Audience for Advertising on the Outside of the Red London Bus; London Transport Advertising (1967). See also *Report on an Inquiry into the Recall of Bus Side versus a 16-sheet Poster*, BET Federation Limited (1969).

6.10  Bulletin Board Survey, *Bertie the Bassett Hound Research Programme*, More O'Ferrall Limited (November 1967).

6.11  G.Consterdine, 'Increasing the audience to cinema commercials', *ADMAP* (October 1972).

6.12  P.Sharp, 'Whatever you thought about the commercial radio audience in London, you were probably wrong', *Broadcast* (20 July 1973).

6.13  A. Twyman, 'The state of radio research', *ADMAP* (August, 1976).

6.14  S. Mand, 'Radio – ready for the day of reckoning?', *ibid.* (October 1977).

6.15  *The Direct Mail Advertiser's Yearbook, 1968/1969*, British Direct Mail Advertising Association.

6.16  N.Scott-Barbour and A.Capper, 'Why in-store TV-failed', *Advertiser's Weekly* (31 January 1969).

6.17  T.E.R.Bray, 'Evaluation of background advertising – a case study', *ADMAP* (December 1973).

6.18  H.Thomson, 'About those other media', *Marketing* (December 1973).

## 7    BRIEFING THE MEDIA MAN

7.1    G.W.Ballington,'A professional society?', *ADMAP*
(September 1974).
7.2    There has been much discussion about the way agencies are
structured and the way in which the media decision is taken.
There is general agreement that the broad choice between
types of media is most important and much of the recent
published work is concerned with this. See, for example,
M.Chapman, 'Deciding on media: the agency role in the 1970s',
*ADMAP* (November 1969).
S.King, 'Inter-media decisions', *ibid.* (October 1969).
J.Billet, 'The changing world of the media planner', *ibid.*
(October 1970).
R.Rimmer, 'The fantasy world of the media planner', *ibid.*
(December 1970).
J.Chaplin, 'The rise and rise of Ron Rimmer', *ibid.*
(January 1971).


## 8    HOW MUCH TO SPEND?

The determination of the advertising appropriation is the subject of a
large number of articles and chapters in books on marketing.
A general review is given in *Setting Advertising Appropriations,* IPA
(1978); additional material and recent references are given in G. Eva,
'Why the research contribution to the establishment of the advertising
budget is misdirected', *ADMAP* (September 1978) but for a more
optimistic American viewpoint see M. McNiven, 'Cost effectiveness in
budgeting', *ibid.* (October 1978). Useful general descriptions are given
in: *The Advertising Budget – Preparation, Administration and Control,*
Association of National Advertisers, New York (1967). R.H. Campbell
*Measuring the Sales and Profit Results of Advertising,* Association of
National Advertisers, New York (1969); D. Berdy, 'Everything you've
always wanted to know about advertising – but thought you couldn't',
*ADMAP* (January 1975).

8.1    J.Bensman, 'The advertising man in New York', in *Media
Sociology,* edited by J.Tunstall, Constable (1970).
8.2    Nielsen – A.C.Nielsen Company Limited – a service auditing

retailer sales, mainly in the food, drug, pharmaceutical, tobacco and confectionery fields.

Attwood — The Attwood Consumer Panel (4000 households), Attwood Statistics Limited.

TCA — Television Consumer Audit (5600 households). This is a service sponsored by seven TV contractors and administered by the TCA Management Committee. Research is carried out by Audits of Great Britain Limited.

8.3   'The struggle for brand leadership', *Nielsen Researcher*, (July-August 1972).

8.4   The most recent example of this method of analysis is J.O.Peckham, *Marketing Advertising Patterns*, ESOMAR (1974).

8.5   S. Broadbent, 'Americans prove that it pays to look before you leap', *Marketing Week* (25 August 1978).

8.6   For example, three case histories were published, by A.R. Wolfe, C. Channon and G. De Groot, on ICI, the Midland Bank and Hoechst, at the ESOMAR Seminar *'The Business of Advertising'* (June 1978).

8.7   P.G.C.Hudson, *The Setting of Advertising Appropriations in Mail Order,* Marketing Society Study Group Report No.4, *On Setting Advertising Appropriations* (1967).

8.8   E.J.Ornstein, *Mail Order Marketing,* Gower Press (1970).

8.9   H.D.Wolfe, J.K.Brown and G.C.Thompson, *Measuring Advertising Results*, National Industrial Conference Board (1962).

# 9   WHEN — AND WHERE?

9.1   A. Roberts and S. Prentice, 'Burst *vs* continuous advertising', *ADMAP* (April 1978).

9.2   H.A. Zielske, 'The remembering and forgetting of advertising', *J. of Marketing* (January 1959).

9.3   C.P. McDonald, 'What is the short-term effect of advertising?', ESOMAR Congress (1970) and *ADMAP* (November 1970).

9.4   A description of the TV buyer from the contractor's point of view, as well as comments on budget allocation: H.Henry, 'Cost-per-thousand: holy cow or true yardstick?', *ADMAP* (September 1971).

9.5    J.Hamilton, 'The small station', *ibid.* (June 1968).

9.6    For general comments on allocation models see S. Broadbent, 'Spending the TV budget: allocation models', *ADMAP* (January 1978). In the same issue, D. Bloom, 'Area allocation system for advertising money (AASAM) and see also J. Adams 'A system of optimising regional budget allocation (SORBA)', *ADMAP* (December 1977).

## 10   THE MEDIA PLAN

10.1    *The Inter-media Decision.* Media Circle, Research Sub-Committee (October 1973).

10.2    J.R.Adams, *Media Planning,* Business Books (1971). This is published on behalf of the Institute of Practitioners in Advertising, succeeding John Hobson's *The Selection of Advertising Media* which was first issued in 1955 and of which the fifth edition came out in 1968. Both books are well worth reading, the former in full, the latter to get the flavour of traditional practice (but not the descriptions of the media which are now out of date).

10.3    For further examples of papers on planning, especially the part played by creative people, see as well as the above:
*The Creative Influence, ADMAP* Workshop 3, especially the papers by Boll, Burdus, Chapman, Ephron and King.
For a modern view of the creation of advertisements see D.Bernstein, *Creative Advertising,* Longman, (1974) and *What Advertising Is,* edited by M.Smelt, Pelham (1972).
See also:
R.Harris, 'Media strategy', *ADMAP* (February 1969).
B.Jones, 'Using market research', *ibid.* (March 1971).
T.Corlett, 'Using media research — perspectives from "Campaign Planning" ', *ibid.* (April 1971).
J.R.Adams, 'What is the media problem?', *ibid.* (April 1971).

## 11   BUYING

For a view of agency operations from the media owner's viewpoint, see M.P.Davis, *Handbook for Media Representatives,* Business Books (1967).

11.1　This example uses Attwood Consumer Panel Data (1966) and is part of the case history given in S.Broadbent and P.B.Mooney, *Can Informant Claims on Product Purchase Made at an Interview be used for Media Planning?*, ESOMAR (1968).

11.2　A.S.C.Ehrenberg and W.A.Twyman, 'On measuring television audiences', *Journal of the Royal Statistical Society*, Series A (1967).

## 12　WAS IT WORTH IT?

Deciding whether advertising money was well spent is the subject of many articles and books, and even more unpublished research reports. More is in fact available than is generally realised. As well as the examples referred to in the chapter, some useful advice is given in the UK references following.

D. Bloom and T. Twyman, 'The impact of economic change on the evaluation of advertising campaigns', Market Research Society Conference (1978).
D.R. Corkindale and S.H. Kennedy, *Measuring the effect of advertising*, Saxon House (1975).
S.King, *Advertising Effectiveness Research – A Short Bibliography*, IPA Forum (January 1969).
A collection of examples is given in J.R.Adams, 'Testing media schedules', *ADMAP* (January 1967) and in J.R.Adams, *Media Planning*, Business Books (1971).
D.Bloom, 'The Measurement of advertising results', *ADMAP* (April 1973).
E.J.Davis, *Experimental Marketing*, Nelson, 1970.
G.C.Draper, 'The measurement of travel advertising effectiveness', *Advertiser's Weekly* (26 November 1965).
P.J.Edwards, *British Cases in Marketing*, Business Books (March 1969).
D.W.Martin, 'Efficiency, dynamics and their measurement in media planning', *ADMAP* (July 1969).

Government Departments have been outstanding in their contribution, for example:

M.Arnott and E.Rodknight, *Public Policy and Measuring the 'Open-ended Situation'*, ESOMAR (1974).

G.E.Levens and E.Rodknight, *The Application of Research in the Planning and Evaluation of Road Safety Publicity,* ESOMAR (1973).
J.P.Morris, *Road Safety Publicity,* AA (1972).
J.Thayer, *Research and Information Programmes to Change Social Behaviour,* ESOMAR (1973).
B. Lee and J. Samuels, 'The evaluation of the drink and drive advertising campaigns', *ADMAP* (October 1978).

Internationally, the following collections are recommended:
R.H.Campbell, *Measuring the Sales and Profit Results of Advertising,* ANA (1969).
M.Mayer, *The Intelligent Man's Guide to Sales Measures of Advertising,* ARF (1965).
J.J.Wheatley (Editor), *Measuring Advertising Effectiveness,* AMA (1969).

An ESOMAR Seminar concentrated on the part played by research in a series of case-histories: *From Market Research to Advertising Strategy and Vice-versa* (1973).

12.1  *Measuring Advertising Results,* National Industrial Conference Board (1962).
12.2  R.A.Critchley, *Television and Media Effect,* BBTA (1974).
      This is a broad review of what is known about the effectiveness of television communication, especially in comparison with the Press and with reference to advertising. It is compressed (165 references are summarised in 127 pages), written mainly for technicians, draws no over-simple conclusions and is a unique and useful work. While it is relevant to several different parts of this book, for this chapter two of its chapters are particularly important: Chapter 4 is about the principles of researching media effects and about what to measure; Chapter 6 is a collection of case histories, from the US and UK, including controlled experiments and the measurement of 'natural' campaigns, and involving TV alone, Press alone and both.
12.3  M.Bird, *Comments,* ESOMAR Seminar (title above) (1973).
12.4  R.P.Bucci, 'Erroneous recall of media', *Journal of Advertising Research* (1973).
12.5  'Birds eye-view of advertising, 1973', *Women's Market,* IPC, No.25 (1974).
12.6  *A Study of the Long-term Consequences of Below-the-line*

*Activity,* AGB for the Management Committee of the TCA
(November 1970).
*Consumer Response to Promotional Activity,* AGB for the
Management Committee of the TCA (October 1971).

12.7   *A Selection of Case Histories,* BBTA (March 1972).

12.8   *BBTA Bulletin (June 1968).*

12.9   J.A.Burdus, 'An intermedia comparison: television and women's
magazines', *ADMAP* (November 1969).

12.10  'General Foods: a major advertiser tests the effectiveness of
general magazines and television', *ibid.* (April 1970).

12.11  G.Smith, 'How GM measures ad effectiveness', *Printers' Ink*
(14 May 1965).
F.A.C.Wardenburg and C.K.Raymond, *One Company's
Approach to Measuring Advertising Effectiveness.* Fourth
Annual Conference, ARF (1958).

12.12  S.Segnit and S.Broadbent, 'Area tests and consumer surveys
to measure advertising', *ADMAP* (November 1970), and also
in the ESOMAR Conference of that year, gives more details
of this case history up to analysis of the 1969 results and also
general comments on area tests and the use of media questions
added to product surveys.

12.13  J. Johnston, *Econometric Methods,* McGraw-Hill (Second
edition, 1972).


# 13   IS RESEARCH TRUSTWORTHY?

For a general introduction and reference book to market research
methods see: R.M.Worcester, *Consumer Market Research Handbook,*
McGraw-Hill (Second edition, 1978). This contains 26 chapters by
different experts, including a section on media research which covers
print, TV, radio, cinema and outdoor.

13.1   M.R.C.Lovell and J.M.Lannon, *Difficulties with Recall,*
ESOMAR (1967).

13.2   *Organisations Providing Market Research Services in Great
Britain,* MRS (published annually).

13.3   *Appraising Market Research Agencies,* ISBA (1974).

13.4   *Appraisals of Published Survey Results,* IPA/ISBA (1966).

See also: *Criteria for Marketing and Advertising Research,*
ARF (1953).

13.5  S.B.Payne, *The Art of Asking Questions,* Princeton University
Press (1951).

13.6  The Thomson Gold Medal Papers for 1966 were on the subject
of panels in media research. The papers were reviewed by Edward
Harden in *ADMAP* (June 1967).
See also, J.Parfitt, 'The use of consumer panels in media research',
*ADMAP* (October 1965).

13.7  R.A.Roberts-Miller, 'In-paper surveys .... better than nothing?',
*ibid.* (February 1972).

13.8  D.Miln, D.Stewart-Hunter and L.Marchant, *The Telephone
in Consumer Research,* ESOMAR (1974).

13.9  P.B.Hodgson, 'Factors affecting response rates in market research
surveys', *ESOMAR* (1974).

13.10  E.Ackroyd, 'What the consumer really wants', *MRS Newsletter*
(January 1969).

13.11  J.Treasure, *A Second Survey of Market Research in Great
Britain,* MRS Conference (1966).

13.12  *Weekend* (3 July 1968).

13.13  R.H.Ostheimer, 'Towards 1984 – markets', *ADMAP* (November
1968).

13.14  *Emerging Profiles of Television and Other Mass Media, 1959-
1967,* Roper Research Associates (1967).


## 14  DEFINING THE TARGET

14.1  The table below is from the *National Readership Survey* (1977)
The income column gives a range in which roughly half the
people lie. This uses the informant's statement of the head of
household's income (not the total household's) *after* deducting
income tax, national insurance and pension payments. The
realtionship between grade and income is complex.

14.2  B.Allt, *Husbands and Wives and Food Purchasing,* IPC
Newspapers (1973).
See also M.R.C.Lovell, R.Meadows and B.Rampley, *Inter-
household Influence on Housewife Purchases,* Thompson Gold
Medal Paper (1968).

14.3  *The Daily Mirror Household Readership, Income and Consump-*

*tion Study,* IPC (1972).

14.4　D.A.Brown and S.F.Buck, 'An exciting approach to forecasting sales of consumer durables', *Advertiser's Weekly* (22 April 1966)

14.5　J.H.Parfitt, *The Use of Panels for the Collection of Readership and Other Media Data.* Thomson Gold Medal Papers (1966).

14.6　There is a much fuller description of the TGI and of other standard sources in A. Twyman, *A view of consumer research sources for products and media,* IPA (1976).
　　　On the TGI specifically, the two key references are:
　　　C. Minter, *Can Advertising and Media Planning be Improved by the Use of Single Source Data?* ESOMAR (1970), and C.Minter, *The TGI: Understanding Changes in the Market,* ESOMAR Seminar, Estoril (1973).
　　　R. Hulks, 'Things we should all know about the TGI', *ADMAP* (November 1977).
　　　But there are other papers of interest; like many innovations, the TGI passed slowly through the stages of resentment and scepticism to become an accepted working tool and was even exported to the US.

14.7　J.Cerha, *Selective Mass Communication,* Stockholm (1967).

14.8　N.Garfinkle, 'The brand rating index', *ADMAP* (November 1967).

14.9　The design and objectives of AMPS were set out in S.Broadbent, 'A new type of media research, all-media and product survey', *Advertiser's Weekly* (10 December 1965).
　　　More details are given in the Technical Report and in G.Consterdine, 'All-media and product survey', *ADMAP* (September 1966).

14.10　S.Broadbent, 'How selective are media in reaching target groups?', *Advertiser's Weekly* (1 and 8 December 1967). *The Importance of Product Purchasing Behaviour in Relation to Readership,* Five Agencies Study Group Report No.2 (March 1968).

14.11　S.Segnit and K.Fletcher, 'Exide 1967 – a case history of media planning', *ADMAP* (April 1968).

14.12　S.Segnit and S.Broadbent, 'Area tests and consumer surveys to measure advertising', *ibid.* (November 1970).

14.13　E.M.L.Beale, S.Broadbent and P.A.B.Hughes, 'A computer assessment of media schedules', *OR Quarterly* (December 1966).

14.14　J.M.Agostini, 'The marriage of data from various surveys: an expedient or a unique way to make progress?', *ADMAP* (October 1967).

Table  RELATIONSHIP BETWEEN GRADE AND INCOME

| Social grade | | Head of household | | % of adults |
|---|---|---|---|---|
| | | Occupation | Net income, £ p.a. | |
| A | Upper middle class | Higher managerial, administrative or professional | 4000–5000+ | 3 |
| B | Middle class | Intermediate managerial, administrative or professional | 3000–5000 | 13 |
| C1 | Lower middle class | Supervisory or clerical, and junior managerial, administrative or professional | 2000–3000 | 22 |
| C2 | Skilled working class | Skilled manual workers | 2000–3000 | 31 |
| D | Working class | Semi- and unskilled | 1650–2500 | 22 |
| E | Those at lowest levels of subsistence | State pensioners or widows (no other earner), casual or low-grade workers | 650–850 | 9 |

14.15 The following reports examined the effect of using product-media data:

*The Importance of Product Purchasing Behaviour in Relation to ITV Viewing Patterns.* Five Agencies Study Group Report No.1 (1967).

W.A.Twyman, *Do Housewife Product Purchasing Groups View Differently from All Housewives?* All-media and Product Survey Agencies Committee (1968).

W.A.Twyman, *How the AMPS Survey was used by its Subscribers.* All-media and Product Survey Agencies Committee (1969).

14.16 C.D.P.McDonald, *Relationships between Advertising Exposure and Purchasing Behaviour,* MRS Conference (1969).

14.17 J.Parfitt and I.McGloughlin, 'The use of consumer panels in the evaluation of promotional and advertising expenditures', *ADMAP* (December 1968).

14.18 J.Parfitt, *How Accurately Can Product Purchasing Behaviour be Measured by Recall at a Single Interview?,* ESOMAR (1967). Further investigation of this subject was reported in S.Broadbent and P.B.Mooney, *Can Informant Claims on Product Purchase Made at an Interview be Used for Media Planning?* , ESOMAR (1968).

14.19 *The Case for Integrating Media and Product Research,* IPA, Occasional Paper 19 (1967).

There has been considerable discussion – and even a whole Market Research Society seminar – on the subject of collecting product data and media data from the same people. See for example:

W.A.Twyman, Some Reflections on the MRS Seminar *Problems in Integrating Media and Product Research,* Commentary (April 1968).

A.M.Fisher, 'Integrated product and media research – model or monster', *ADMAP* (May 1970).

B.Hedges, 'Market segmentation and media', *ibid.* (May 1970).

Most recently: S.Broadbent, 'A strategy for media research', *ibid.* (May 1975)

An analysis of the classifications currently in use and a proposal (which has not been followed up) for how to choose these classifications was given in S.Broadbent and P.Masson, 'Informant classification in media and product surveys', *ibid.* (January 1969). The following discussion of informant classification is also helpful:

364

J.Agostini, 'New criteria for classifying informants in market research and media surveys, *ibid.* (June 1969), but its main proposal, asking people what they are interested in, has not so far proved to be very constructive though analysis of the French data has been extensive, see for example:
A.Biecheler and J.Brousse, *A Global Study of Criteria Used in Media Knowledge,* Esomar (1974).
Another general approach is given in W.A.Belson, *The Best Method of Classifying Informants in Media Studies,* Thomson Gold Medal (1963).


## 15    MARKET AND MEDIA MODELS

15.1    T. Twyman, 'The proof of advertising value', *ADMAP* (April 1977).
See also T. Corlett, 'How can we monitor the influence of advertising campaigns on consumers' purchasing behaviour?', *MRS Conference* (1977).

15.2    For example, both industry and private analyses: J.M. Samuels, *The Effect of Advertising on Sales and Brand Shares,* Advertising Association (1970).
M.L. Vidale and H.B. Wolfe, 'An OR study of sales response to advertising', *OR Quarterly* (1957).
A. Kitchener and D. Rowland, 'Models of a consumer product market', *ibid.* (1971).

15.3    For example, the Hendry approach which is outlined by M. Starr, 'The Hendry system', ESOMAR Seminar, Noordwijk (1975) and that developed by Rao: A. Rao and J. Adams, 'The measurement and meaning of marketing inputs', MRS Conference (1977).

15.4    For example,   C.OHerlihey, 'How marketing must become a profit centre', *ADMAP* (June and August 1976), 'How to make half a million from (almost) nothing', *ibid.* (July 1977) and 'Why econometrics can make advertising and marketing scientific', *ibid.* (October 1978).

15.5    J. Branton, 'The Bowater-Scott approach to media planning', *ibid.* (January 1978).

15.6    T. Corlett, 'Anyone for econometrics?', *ibid.* (August 1978) and subsequent papers.

15.7 For example the following three references span nearly twenty years:

H.A. Zielske, 'The remembering and forgetting of advertising', *Journal of Marketing* (January, 1969).

R.D. Wells, 'An empirical model of television advertising awareness', *JMRS* (October 1975).

W. Moran, 'When to run, when to stop and flight', *ANA Workshop* (1977).

15.8 S. King, 'Improving advertising decisions', *ADMAP* (April 1978).

15.9 D. Bloom, 'Consumer behaviour and the timing of advertising effects', *ibid.* (September 1976).

M.J. Stewart, 'The long-term effects of econometrics', *ibid.* (February 1978).

T. Twyman, 'Are long-term effects possible or measurable', ESOMAR Seminar, Barcelona (1978).

15.10 A.Norelli, *A Review of Experience in the United States, Computers in Advertising,* IPA (1965).

15.11 For a general introduction to the OR approach see P.Rivett, *Concepts of Operational Research,* New Thinkers Library, Watt (1968).

P.Rivett and R.L.Ackoff, *A Manager's Guide to Operational Research,* John Wiley (1963).

For recent reviews of general model applications see:

P.Sampson, *Consumer Behaviour Prediction and the Modelling Approach,* ESOMAR (1974).

J.D.W.Stewart and J.Blanchard, *Research for Decisions: How Models Can Help,* ESOMAR (1974).

15.12 R.Carpenter, 'Some aspects of the use of media weights in press scheduling', *ADMAP* (April 1969).

15.13 S.Broadbent, *Media Planning and Computers by 1970,* Thomson Silver Medal Paper (1965).

D.H.Gensch, 'Computer models in advertising media selection', *Journal of Market Research* (November 1968).

M.M.Brown, 'Media selection models compared and contrasted, *ADMAP* (November 1968).

D.H.Gensch, 'Advertising Models in Advertising Media Planning', Elsevier (1973) describes adequately the position up to about 1970 but since then the picture has somewhat altered – see the review of Gensch's book in *ADMAP* (November 1973).

15.14 For a comparison of a calculated impression distribution with panel results see M.Marc, 'Combining simulation and panel data to obtain reach and frequency', *Journal of Advertising Research* (June 1968).

15.15 Media Research Group, 'Media model comparisons', *ADMAP* (March 1969).
Media Research Group, 'Press schedule evaluation', *ibid.* (April 1978; June 1978).

15.16 Media ResearchGroup, 'Media model comparison – an investigation into computerised press schedule construction models', *ADMAP* (September 1970).

15.17 L.L.Lodish, 'Considering competition in media planning', *Management Science* (February 1971).

15.18 S.Broadbent and B.Murray, 'Introducing presence into TV planning', *ADMAP* (April 1974).


## 16 RESPONSE FUNCTIONS

This chapter draws heavily on:

16.1 S.Broadbent and S.Segnit, *Response Functions in Media Planning,* Thomson Silver Medal Paper (1967).

16.2 M.M.Brown, 'Time: a missing dimension in schedule optimisation', *ADMAP* (June 1967).

16.3 C.R.Wasson, 'Real models in advertising, or phony games?', *Journal of Marketing* (April 1963).

16.4 D.M.Monk, 'Some aspects of advertising research', *The Statistician* (March 1963).

16.5 A. Morgensztern, *How to Determine the Optimum Screening Frequency of a Movie Commercial,* ESOMAR (1967).

16.6 J.Cerha, 'Why the smiling tiger did not sell in Sweden', *ADMAP* (June 1967).

16.7 M.L.Ray and A.G.Sawyer, 'Repetition in media models: a laboratory technique', *Journal of Market Research* (February 1971).

16.8 H.A.Zielske, 'The remembering and forgetting of advertising', *Journal of Marketing* (January 1959).

16.9 J.B.Stewart, *Repetitive Advertising in Newspapers,* Harvard (1964).

16.10 R.D.Godwin and B.Thorogood, *The Integration of Advertising Research,* ESOMAR Seminar (1967).

16.11 T. Joyce, *What Do We Know About the Way that Advertising Works?,* ESOMAR Seminar (1967).

C.D.P.MacDonald, *Relationships Between Advertising Exposure and Purchasing Behaviour,* MRS Conference (1969).

16.12 S.Broadbent and S.Segnit, *Integrated Media Research and Systems,* ESOMAR (1967).

Other relevant case histories appear in:

M.Mayer, *The Intelligent Man's Guide to Sales Measures in Advertising, ARF (1965).*

N.Steinberg, *Une Méthode de Prévision de la Pénétration Publicitaire,* IREP Seminar (1966).

*Preliminary Bibliography on the Effects of Repetition of Advertisements* (96 references) ARF (1967).

NICB, *Measuring Advertising Results* (1962).

Various Authors, ARF Fourth Annual Conference (1958).

R.Carpenter, 'Response functions-problems and limitations', *ADMAP* (March 1968).


## 17  BEYOND COST PER THOUSAND

17.1 This chapter draws on S.Broadbent and S.Segnit, *Beyond Cost per Thousand – An Examination of Media Weights,* Thomson Silver Medal Paper (1968) and on the same authors 'Factors influencing media selection', *ADMAP* (February 1969).

17.2 R.Jones, *Don't Be Daft About Soft Data,* Thomson Gold Medal Paper (1971).

R.Jones, 'Number-crunching and the unmeasured contribution', *ADMAP* (February 1973).

17.3 The need for caution in using the media numbers on their own has been strongly expressed by Leo Bogart, 'Mass advertising: the message, not the measure', *Harvard Business Review* (September – October, 1976) and by Al Ries, 'Military guide to media planning', *Media Decisions* (February 1977).

17.4 R.A.Critchley, *Television and Media Effect,* BBTA (1974). The reference is to pages 12-15. His Chapter 5 is particularly relevant to this chapter. This reviews the qualities of the different media, how they are seen and how advertisements in them are exposed. The book has already been commented on in the references to Chapter 12.

17.5 M.Marc and J.Durand, *Le choix entre les medias,* ESOMAR (1971).

17.6 S.Broadbent, 'How selective are media in reaching target groups?', *Advertiser's Weekly* (1 and 8 December 1967).
Five Agencies Study Group, Reports No.1 (1967) and No.2 (1968).
W.A.Twyman, *Some Reflections on the MRS Seminar on Integration,* Commentary (April 1968).

17.7 D.Bernstein, *Creative Advertising,* Longman (1974) — see on this point his Chapter 27.

17.8 J.Bronowski, *The Ascent of Man,* BBC (1973).
See also E.W.Whitley, 'The media mix: some considerations', *ADMAP* (January 1975).

17.9 *A Study of the Effects of Printing Quality on Readers' Perceptions of Magazine Advertisements,* Communication Research Limited for IPC Magazines Limited (February 1974).

17.10 'Page traffic and page frequency of three leading publications', *Radio Times* (1965).

17.11 A pioneer study in this area and one whose technique has not been improved on is 'A measured study of women's weekly magazines', *Woman* (1964).

17.12 D.Richardson, *Measuring the Role of Media in People's Lives,* Thomson Gold Medal (1971).
T.Corlett, J.Lannon and D.Richardson, 'The use of media', *ADMAP* (January 1972).

17.13 S.Segnit and S.Broadbent, *Life Style Research,* European Research (ESOMAR), (1973).

17.14 D.J.Tigert, 'Life style analysis as a basis for media selection', Chapter 7 in *Life Style and Psychographics,* edited by W.D. Wells, American Marketing Association (1974).

17.15 *British Life Styles, 1972,* Leo Burnett, London.

17.16 R.Mitchelmore, 'Using Life Style research', *ADMAP* (May 1974).
R.Adams, 'Psychographics in media planning', *Media International* (October 1974).

17.17 S. Broadbent, *Psychographics in media selection,* Jours de France Award (1977).

17.18 'Qualitative media assessments', *TV Times* (1967).

17.19   A.Smith, 'The presenter effect, or does the medium affect the message?, *ADMAP* (February 1972).

17.20   R.C.Carpenter, 'Some aspects of the use of media weights in press scheduling', *ibid.* (April and May 1969).

# INDEX

**Suzanne Wright** lives in England with her husband and two children. When she's not spending time with her family, she's writing, reading or doing her version of housework – sweeping the house with a look.

She's worked in a pharmaceutical company, at a Disney Store, at a primary school as a voluntary teaching assistant, at the RSCPA and has a First Class Honours degree in Psychology and Identity Studies.

As to her interests, she enjoys reading, writing, reading, writing (sort of eat, sleep, write, repeat), spending time with her family, movie nights with her sisters and playing with her two Bengal kittens.

### To connect with Suzanne online:
Website: http://www.suzannewright.co.uk
Facebook: https://www.facebook.com/suzannewrightfanpage

Suzanne Wright

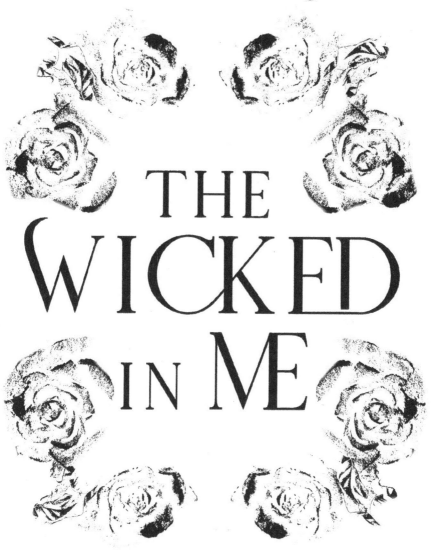

# THE
# WICKED
## IN ME

PIATKUS

PIATKUS

First published in Great Britain in 2023 by Piatkus

1 3 5 7 9 10 8 6 4 2

A CIP catalogue record for this book
is available from the British Library.

HB ISBN: 978-0-349-43454-4
TPB: 978-0-349-43455-1

Typeset in Garamond by M Rules

Printed and bound in Great Britain by Clays Ltd, Elcograf S.p.A.

Papers used by Piatkus are from well-managed forests
and other responsible sources.

Piatkus
An imprint of
Little, Brown Book Group
Carmelite House
50 Victoria Embankment
London EC4Y 0DZ

An Hachette UK Company
www.hachette.co.uk

www.littlebrown.co.uk

*For J, thank you for listening to all my ramblings when I'm having my mind-mapping buzz sessions out loud*

# Chapter One

Adopting a stone-cold poker face, Wynter Dellavale struggled to process the disbelief that crawled over her skin. When she'd opened the door to find her Priestess on the doorstep while their coven lingered at the front gate, she'd thought maybe Esther was calling on her to join them all for a late-night ritual or something. But *this* . . . no, it couldn't actually be happening. Nu-uh.

Planting her feet, Wynter folded her arms. "This is some kind of messed-up joke, right? Like, you know, humor but sort of . . . not?"

"This isn't something I would ever joke about." Esther clasped her hands in front of her, the image of elegance. "We have no choice. A new coven will be selected by one of the ruling Aeons in three days' time. There is no chance of it being us if we have a weak link. For us, you are that."

Anger bubbled up, hot and sharp. Wynter felt a cold smile slowly curve one side of her mouth.

The Priestess tensed. Well, Wynter wasn't exactly known for being a placid, sweet, touchy-feely person. More of a bitey-scratchy girl, really. Her mother used to joke that Wynter came out of the womb flipping the finger and snarling at anyone who dared cuddle her.

"I can be described as a lot of things, but not weak," said Wynter.

"In terms of power, no. But having a witch whose magick has been tainted . . . that is a weakness in the coven."

*Tainted.* She hated that word. People had been tossing it at her for most of her life. "Wasn't it you who always told me to rise above my limitations and make them work for me? That they'd only be

1

an obstacle if I allowed it?" The woman's advice had often carried a condescending note, but still.

"Yes, I believe in not permitting obstacles to block our path. And that is what you are, Wynter. An obstacle to this coven's future prospects. You would have been forced to leave when you turned sixteen if our prior Priestess had not been your grandmother. Agnes could never bring herself to cast you out, but I must. When we moved to this town eighteen years ago, we did it for one reason only—we hoped to eventually serve the Aeons directly. If that means snipping off any weaknesses, so be it."

The pitiless words were as sharp and cutting as any scalpel. Personally, Wynter didn't see what would be so amazing about living among the primordial beings in the underground utopia beneath the picturesque town of Aeon. Oh sure, you'd be privy to their secrets and, given they were the first civilization—yeah, as in Adam and Eve—they no doubt had a whole lot of interesting knowledge to pass on. It was considered an honor to serve them, just as it was considered an honor to be chosen to descend to their subterranean city.

There were a few things Wynter wasn't so comfortable with, though. Like how only the residents of said city were able to go down there and weren't allowed to speak of it to those who lived in the town. Like how the Aeons demanded the respect and devotion that was worthy of deities.

Though they possessed a godly arrogance, they weren't deities at all. They also weren't human. Referred to as Aeons merely due to being long-term natives of this place, they were incredibly secretive immortals who wielded impressive power.

"This is not merely *my* wish," Esther added. "I speak for the majority."

Wynter scanned the swarm of coven members near the gate. Rafe, the mentor she had to thank for all the training she'd received over the years, was notably absent. As for the others . . . many averted their eyes or shifted uncomfortably. Others raised their chin or sniffed. And it was clear that none were going to speak up for her.

Hurt sliced her gut like a jagged blade. She hadn't done a single thing to deserve them turning their backs on her. Not. One.

The coven wasn't alone. A few mages were among them, and said mages glared daggers at her. They'd pestered Agnes to cast her out after 'the incident' when Wynter was ten. It didn't matter that Wynter had been the true victim. Two teenage mages had died that night, and that was *all* they cared about.

Her coven had protected her from the angry families of those teenage boys over the years, but only because her grandmother had ordered it. With the exception of Agnes and Rafe, no one had comforted her after her ordeal, because they'd been too freaked out by the aftermath. They'd emotionally pulled away from her little by little over the years. And now they apparently wanted the Aeons to banish her just as they'd once banished her mother.

Wynter barely resisted snarling. "My magick might not be as 'wholesome' as yours, Esther, but I've proven my worth over and over." She'd trained harder than anyone else, she'd mastered every skill necessary, she'd done everything expected of her.

Esther flicked her eyes upward in exasperation. "Wynter—"

"There isn't one person more dedicated to this coven's welfare than me." Purely because it had been her mother's greatest wish for the Moonstar coven to descend to the underground city; a dream Davina had given up in order to protect Wynter. In return, Wynter had vowed to herself that she would repay her mother by making that dream a reality.

It seemed like she might just have to break that vow.

Esther sighed. "Let us not drag this out. There is no point. My decision is final, I won't change it. Once the banishment has been made official, Wagner will drive you to the border." Her eyes briefly slid to the were-jackal who stepped out of the crowd—one of the town's keepers.

He always looked so dignified. Always flashed gracious smiles.

Always addressed people so politely. But there was a darkness in those pale-blue eyes. It made that *thing* inside Wynter stir. A thing that had been her constant companion since she was just ten. A thing she'd kept secret purely to survive.

Wagner had come for Davina all those years ago when she'd been exiled. Back then, as he'd lingered on the sidelines, he'd made Wynter think of a hyena waiting to pounce on whatever scraps were left by other predators. He had that same look about him now.

Wynter flexed her fingers. "You get that this isn't a small thing, Esther, right? It's not just that I'll have nowhere to go—that I'll be out there alone with no family, or protection, or coven—I'll also have *no memories*. I won't even know who I am."

That was the thing about Aeon. If you ever left, your memories were taken from you—it was one of the prices to pay for the privilege of living in such a place of power and safety, though Wynter suspected that the Aeons simply didn't want outsiders to know much about the town. If it hadn't been for this 'price,' she'd have left years ago to reunite herself with her mother.

Wynter had begged Davina to take her with her when she was exiled, but her mother had insisted she stay—probably because she knew that Wagner was a big enough asshole to dump them in separate places so they'd each be alone, even if only to punish Davina for always rejecting his advances.

"Taking your memories would be a kindness," said Esther. "Surely you would wish to forget some of the things that happened to you here."

"A *kindness* would be for you to not make me suffer for something I have no control over." It wasn't like she'd *wanted* her magick to turn dark. Death always left a mark. And so her magick could no longer heal, calm, create or comfort. But it could all too easily kill, burn, infect, and destroy.

Esther let out a weary 'you're being dramatic' sigh. "This is not about making you suffer. It's not about *you* at all. I am Priestess; I have to do what is best for this coven."

Recalling something her grandmother had said to her on her deathbed, Wynter couldn't help wondering if Agnes had seen this coming . . .

*Home isn't really a house, you know, Wynter. It is a place where we feel safe and accepted and content—it could be a building, a piece of land, a group of people, or at a particular person's side. You'll find your home eventually, I promise.*

Wynter understood why her grandmother wouldn't have forewarned her that the coven might pull this shit. Agnes had liked to see the best in people, liked to hope that they would make the right decision in the end—even her bitchy successor.

Wynter shook her head at Esther. "You're making a huge mistake."

The Priestess blinked. "Is that a threat?"

"It's a fact." There were things that Esther didn't know. Things that only Wynter and Davina had known. Things that Agnes had guessed at but hadn't shared with others.

Esther rolled her eyes. "If you say so. Now have some dignity and endure this without causing a scene. Don't make this any more difficult than it has to be."

What, like Wynter was overreacting by not being breezy about having *her memory wiped*? It wouldn't be so bad if she was only being forced to leave, but she'd essentially also have her identity taken from her, because she wouldn't even remember her own damn name.

"Maybe you'll get lucky and find your mother," Wagner chipped in. "Of course . . . you won't *know* she's your mother, just as she would not recognize you. Very sad, really." He sounded so sincere, but she heard the subtle taunt there.

Wynter sniffed at him. "Try to be quiet, Wagner; the adults are talking right now."

There was a snort of laughter from someone in the crowd.

His face went red, and his eyes glittered with a promise of retribution. "You won't be feeling so cocky when Lailah arrives. She's on her way."

5

Wynter's insides seized. If an Aeon was ready to make the banishment official, it meant that the decision had already been okayed by that oh-so mysterious race. As such, appealing to them to overturn the Moonstar coven's decision would get her nowhere.

The crowd stirred as a familiar male witch shoved his way to the front. "What the hell is going on here?" Rafe took in the scene, and realization dawned on him fast. He cast Esther a hard look. "Tell me you're not—"

"Do not interfere," she ordered, her tone clipped. "This has to be done."

His mouth set into a flat line. "You said you wouldn't do this. You assured Agnes that you wouldn't do this."

"I told a dying woman what she needed to hear in order to pass peacefully," said Esther. "That is all."

As the two witches began to argue, Wagner leaned into Wynter and said, "Such a shame that you will have to leave. The mages don't think so. In fact, they have promised me many things in return for sending a ... message to you once we've left the boundaries of Aeon. They want you to pay for what you did to those boys. Understandable, I suppose."

Wynter's eyes slammed on him, her stomach twisting at the cruel intent there. She didn't fear him. No, she could handle this motherfucker in her sleep. But after Lailah was done with her, there'd be a short period of time in which Wynter would be utterly vulnerable. Maybe he'd take advantage of that, or maybe he only meant to scare her. Hopefully it was the latter, because he wouldn't hesitate to oblige the mages.

A sudden silence fell, and Wynter looked to see none other than Lailah elegantly strolling toward the house. There were five generations of Aeons. They'd mysteriously ceased procreating after that, and they'd never shared why ... just as they hadn't shared why they rarely left their city during daytime hours, or how they could put themselves in a state of Rest that could last centuries.

Lailah was part of the second generation. The tall, beautiful brunette also ruled Aeon alongside Adam, her consort Abel—yeah, it turned out that he hadn't been killed by Cain after all—and her brother Saul. They were a council of sorts.

She was very powerful. Very detached. Very *other*.

All of the Aeons who Wynter had come across were like that, really. They weren't old-fashioned as one might expect, but nor were they *in the now*. As if, having seen so many eras come and go, they'd somehow become removed from the flow of time.

Lailah lifted a brow at Esther. "Has it been done?"

"I have cast her out of the coven, yes," the bitch replied.

Rafe turned to Lailah. "Please don't do this—"

"Quiet." The Aeon's voice lashed him like a whip ... just as Abel's had lashed Wynter when she'd begged him not to exile her mother. Lailah turned to her, a cool smile touching her mouth. "Hello, Whitney."

*Jesus Christ.* "It's Wynter." But the Aeons ... it was as if they didn't really *see* people. They might glance at you. Might even glare at you. But, to them, you were no more unremarkable than any other mortal.

Wynter supposed it was a little like if a wasp got into your house. You might curse at it, you might want it gone, you might even be wary of it, but you wouldn't look at it as an individual with its own wants, needs, and motivations—it was just a wasp, the same as any other wasp.

"Wynter, then," said Lailah, not looking even a little sheepish. "It matters not. You will need to choose a new name soon, since you will not remember your own. Trust me, this won't hurt. I will simply take your memories, place you into a peaceful sleep, and then Wagner will drive you to the border."

Wynter felt her breathing begin to pick up. "I haven't done anything wrong. It isn't my fault that my magick is different."

"No," agreed Lailah, "it was your mother who shamed the coven."

"She didn't shame *anyone*."

Lailah's face hardened. "She used forbidden magick to bring

7

you back from the dead, knowing it was unnatural and that one should not interfere with fate; knowing it would twist and warp your magick."

Wynter was about to spit out that, no, actually, Davina had done no such thing and that something else had brought Wynter back. But then a familiar otherworldly breeze ruffled over her, one that carried a gentle warning.

Lailah frowned and glanced around, her extraordinary golden eyes narrowing. After a few moments, she seemed to shrug off the slight disturbance in the air. "As I was saying, what your mother did *was* shameful, whether you wish to face it or not. It was a selfish decision on her part. You have paid for it most of your life. Where was the point in what she did?"

"Where was justice when two teenage boys killed me?" Wynter shot back.

Lailah's smile was brittle. "You took care of that yourself, did you not?"

Sort of. Wynter hadn't been behind the wheel at the time. She had no clue what exactly went down; she only knew of the aftermath.

Lailah laid her hand on Wynter's head. "Do not think of this as an ending. Think of it as an opportunity to have a fresh start."

The *thing* inside Wynter stirred, uneasy. Well, at least it was paying attention. It didn't always seem present. As if it slept a lot or just saw no need to concern itself with anything unless the circumstances warranted its attention or intervention.

She thought about unleashing it on these people here, but that unnatural breeze returned, carrying that same warning—one that the entity within Wynter automatically heeded.

Squinting, Lailah again looked around, taking a more thorough scan of their surroundings this time. She exchanged a look with Wagner, who merely shrugged. Turning back to Wynter, she elegantly flapped her hand. There was some sort of weird suction from the ground. A suction that locked Wynter's feet in place with such force she swayed.

*Fuck.*

There'd be no running. Not that she'd have gotten far. Instinct almost had her calling to the sword she'd bound to her magick, which enabled her to conjure it whenever necessary. But she was massively outnumbered right now, and she didn't doubt that the blade would be easily wrestled from her grip. It might even then be turned on her. She'd rather have her memories scrambled than be impaled on a sword.

Staring at Lailah, Wynter lifted her chin slightly and said, "If you do this, there'll be consequences." It seemed only fair to warn her.

Lailah looked the height of amused. "Excuse me?"

"You don't have to take my word for it. But you should."

Wagner snickered. "Strange little thing, isn't she?"

"Strange indeed." Lailah looked at Esther. "What is her full name?"

Well, of course she'd forgotten it.

"Wynter Dellavale," Esther replied, her expression one of pure resolve.

Lailah nodded. "Wynter Dellavale, you are officially banished from Aeon. May your new life be plentiful."

*May your new life be plentiful?* Like the woman gave a damn? What a load of absolute shit.

Wynter opened her mouth to call the Aeon on her crap, but then an unnatural lethargy snaked through her. It was thick. Heavy. Drugging. It sucked every bit of energy and enthusiasm from her body like a goddamn hoover.

Her vision blurred. Her senses dulled. Her face went slack. She felt both light as a feather and heavy as dead weight at the same time.

She tried fighting the exhaustion. Tried digging deep for the strength to move. But her eyelids drifted shut and her body slumped. Strong arms caught her. *Wagner.* The suction beneath her feet faded away.

"I got her." He unceremoniously tossed Wynter over his shoulder and then strode away.

She was braced for sleep to pull her under ... but it didn't. She was wide a-damn-wake, lethargic but not at all sleepy. More, her memories weren't fading or fracturing. No, they were still clear and intact. Hope blossomed in her belly—

She inwardly flinched as blobs of wetness hit her when Wagner shrugged through the crowd. People were *spitting* on her. No doubt the mages. She heard "good riddance" and "should be dead" and something like "finally some justice."

*Assholes.*

Rafe yelled out protests, pleading with Lailah to undo what she'd done.

The backs of Wynter's eyes burned. He was the only father figure she'd ever known. He wasn't aware of all her secrets, but he'd known she was ... different, somehow, from other witches. Still, he'd said nothing of it to others.

No quitter, Wynter fought to open her eyes as Wagner carried her further away. But there was no lifting her eyelids. They didn't even flutter. She tried moving her fingers instead, but they didn't so much as twitch.

She was, essentially, a prisoner inside her own body. And this wasn't even the first time it had happened. She'd been this helpless once before, paralyzed by magick as two thirteen-year-old boys had some "fun."

Her heart pounded as the awful memories crowded her. Feet slamming into her ribs. The taste of mud as it was shoved into her mouth. The feel of pebbles jammed up her nose. The smell of urine as it splattered over her head like a warm stream. A scorching, blazing heat against the soles of her feet. Lances of pain as a blade sank deep into her flesh over and over. And then, finally, the feel of a knife slicing across her neck.

The lethal move hadn't killed her quickly—that seemed to only happen in movies. The boys had watched while she'd faded away. Until they got bored and thrust the blade into the side of her throat.

Rafe, seeming to sense how important it was to her that she

*never* be that powerless to protect herself again, had taught her everything from fencing to magickal combat. Sadly, none of that helped her now.

Still, Wynter had no intention of accepting defeat. No, she went back to battling the exhaustion. She'd get out of this situation somehow. She would. Really. She had managed to stay awake and keep her memories—those had to be good signs.

Hinges creaked, and then she was flung on a cushioned surface. The good ole musty car smell hit her hard. He'd dumped her on the rear seat of his vehicle, she realized . . . just as he had Davina back when she'd been exiled.

It wasn't long before hinges again creaked. Moments later, the car shook as his weight settled into it. The engine sputtered to life, and light-hearted whistling filled the air as he drove off.

Inside her head, Wynter growled in frustration as she battled to fight off the paralysis that had overtaken her. Those battles never came to anything, never—

"I know you're awake, Wynter," he said, making her pulse spike. "I know you still have all your memories, too. You're probably marveling over that. You may feel it's some sort of victory."

Yes, actually, she did. Or she *had* until that familiar taunting note entered his voice.

"I'll tell you the truth of what's coming. You see . . . none of the exiled are ever really put to sleep. None ever lose their memories. And none are ever driven to the border."

She paused her internal battle. Wait, what?

"No one ever really leaves this town alive, Wynter. An Aeon only seeks to daze and immobilize the outcasts, nothing more. Keepers such as me then drive to the falls and toss the exiled over the cliff. That's what happened to your mother. Yes, she's dead. Has been for a *long* time."

Her heart sank. She wanted to tell herself he was lying, wanted to believe he was just trying to mess with her head, but the ring of truth in his voice couldn't be ignored. Grief was like a jagged knife in her chest, sawing deep. It felt as if said chest slumped in on itself as she silently screamed with rage and devastation.

Her mother had done *nothing* to deserve being cast out. Not one thing. But she'd pled guilty to the accusation that she'd used forbidden magick, because she'd known that the truth would condemn Wynter. Davina had, in sum, given her life to save Wynter's ... only she hadn't known that would be the *real* price. Not until this motherfucker killed her.

Wynter was pretty sure she'd never hated anyone as much as she did him in that very moment—not even the teenager boys who'd once taken her life as if it were their right.

"Drowning is a harsh sentence, if you ask me," said Wagner. "Especially when a person's immobilized. You can't do a damn thing while water floods your nostrils, pours down your throat, and enters your lungs. But the Aeons, well, they have their traditions, and they like them."

Panic thudding through her, she dug deep for the strength to shake off the power holding her in place, but its grip wasn't weakening under her struggles. Calling for her sword didn't work either. *Nothing* worked.

*Fuck, fuck, fuck.*

"You know, the mages would like me to rape you," he said ever so casually.

Wynter inwardly froze.

"I won't, of course. I'm not an animal. But I have nothing against their second request. They want me to kill you *before* I throw you over the cliff. Want me to dismember you, in fact, just as you dismembered those boys with your magick when you took their lives. Hey, you might get a laugh out of this—they also want a ... souvenir, shall we say. An eyeball, to be precise. Seems a little morbid to me, but I'm not one to judge. I've never actually gouged out an eye before. It could be fun." He chuckled. "Scared yet?"

A little, which was why her heart was slamming frantically against her ribcage like it was trying to find a way out. She could wipe the floor with Wagner in an instant, *but not if she couldn't move.* It was hard to concentrate on fighting the restrictive power when more and more flashbacks slapped her hard.

She'd been far more afraid as a child after those boys had lured her to the woods. As she'd lay there powerless, swamped by fear and pain and rage, she'd inwardly cried for her mother. She'd told herself that Davina would find her ... but she hadn't. So Wynter had reached out to Nyx, the deity her coven worshipped, begging Her for help. But it wasn't Nyx who came. It was another deity, and She hadn't been entirely clear on what granting Wynter help would fully entail when She made an offer.

Wynter snapped out of her thoughts as the car slowed to a stop. The engine shut off, and then Wagner was out of the vehicle. She didn't think it was possible for her heart to gallop any faster, but it actually picked up speed.

Hands soon roughly grabbed her and snatched her out of the car. "I'll bet you've been trying your hardest to move, haven't you? I'm pretty sure they all do. They never succeed." He threw her over his shoulder once more. "Really, Wynter, you had to know this day would come. You were living on borrowed time. You should have died years ago, when fate intended it. You shouldn't have returned."

No, she shouldn't have. More, after coming back, she shouldn't have *stayed* alive for as long as she had. That wasn't how it worked. But *fuck* if she cared what he thought.

As he walked further and further while her body remained limp and useless, she screamed in her head. Screamed and screamed and *screamed* with fury.

She could hear the roar of the waterfall in the distance. That roaring got closer and closer until it was almost deafening. She again fought the power holding her captive, and she again failed to free herself. Goddammit, she was *not* going to die at this bastard's hands.

Finally, Wagner halted and then dumped her on the hard

ground. "There we are. Better. Now . . . do I take the eye before or *after* I kill you?" He hummed, rolling her onto her back. "Before, I think."

Her eyes still closed, Wynter silently hissed as she sensed him kneel over her . . . just as one of the boys once had. Right then, she screamed at Wagner to get the fuck away from her, but of course those words never escaped her mouth.

"Hmm, I'd rather have you looking at me while we do this. It's not as gratifying when I don't get to witness a person's pain in their eyes." He pried open her eyelids and smiled down at her. "Well, hello there." He held up his knife. "Like it?"

A breeze whispered over her in a gentle, encouraging caress. The entity inside her shoved closer to the surface until it stared out at him through one of her eyes. Black inky ribbons partially obstructed her vision as they slithered over said eye.

He stilled, his brows snapping together. "What the . . ."

Silently praying to the deity for strength, she again struggled to *move, move, move.* Her heartbeat stuttered as two of her fingers jerked. That was all she needed.

Wynter dug those fingers into the ground and thrust her rage and magick deep into the earth. Pure silence fell, as if nature itself had sucked in a breath, and then the ground began to quiver.

Wagner's eyes widened as the immediate landscape altered. Trees began to crack and blacken. Leaves started to wither. Flowers slowly dried up or wilted while bushes began to thin and decay.

He looked down at her. "What's happening? What are you doing?"

One side of her face began to burn, and his gaze dropped to where she knew a metallic blue mark would now glisten. A distinctive mark that very rarely showed itself. A mark that would tell him she was Favored by a particular deity.

Realization dawning on him, he paled and scrambled to get away from her.

Now that she could move her fingers, her other muscles began to unlock. Her hands were soon free of the paralytic power. Then her arms, neck, head, upper body, legs.

It was like moving through sludge, but Wynter finally managed to sit upright. She cricked her neck, exhaling a long sigh.

Wagner stared at her, shaking his head, his lips trembling. "I . . . I don't understand. This isn't possible. You don't . . ."

"Drink blood or eat flesh to survive? No, no, I don't. Never needed to, thankfully. That would have sucked. Or *I'd* have sucked, if blood had been involved. Whichever."

He shook his head wildly. "That's . . . no, no, it's not possible. Your heart beats, I can *hear* it. Nothing that She brings back is really alive. And it never exists for long."

"I really can't clear up the confusion for you. I don't have all the answers. The deity doesn't tell me much, and She can be kind of cryptic. When She offered to send a monster after those boys, She didn't specify that I'd be its host."

Wynter was no longer merely a witch. She was *more.* A vessel for something not of this world. And, as such, she'd become a monster in her own right.

She'd only seen her entity once. When Wynter's soul had landed in the netherworld—the realm that was effectively purgatory for the souls of preternatural beings—the deity and the monster had been waiting there for her. The deity had sent them out of the netherworld together and into Wynter's then-dead body, reviving it that easily. The entity had taken control in an instant, torn the boys apart, and then just as quickly retreated.

The monster was . . . well, monstrous. Neither male nor female, it was as hideous and horrifying as any nightmare. What she remembered most of all were its bottomless black eyes. There was no being that she could compare it to, because it was simply too foreign. And as black tendrils began to creep over her second eyeball, she knew it was about to take her over.

Wagner must have sensed it too, because he tensed as if to flee.

"You can run if you want," said Wynter, "but it will find you. It'll catch you. Shred you. It'll feast on your fear, drink in your screams, and relish your pain. That's kind of what it does. What it craves, even. After all, it exists only to wreak vengeance. And me? I'm more than happy to let it go wreak."

The monster lunged to the surface, and her vision went black.

# Chapter Two

## Six months later

Driving along the unpaved roads that cut through a labyrinth of tall, weathered trees, Wynter felt her hands flex on the steering wheel. "This could be a bad idea. A really, really bad idea."

Riding shotgun, Delilah tossed her a sideways glance. "You said that when we ate at that Indian restaurant with the dodgy reviews last night. That turned out okay. No one got the shits."

"I don't know about that," Xavier piped up from the backseat, his nose wrinkling as he cast the sleeping female on his left a brief look. "Anabel's been farting past herself, and some of those farts sounded wet."

"Shh," said the elderly woman on his right, her face in her book. "This is finally starting to get good." In other words, it was a sex scene. Hattie read erotic books like it was her job—the filthier the better, in her opinion.

If there was one thing Wynter wouldn't have expected when she set off alone, it was that she'd pick up some 'strays' while on the run. But after she'd saved herself and a bunch of captives from bounty hunters—yes, the Aeons had put a price on Wynter's head after she fled—four of said captives had decided it would be good for them all to stick together.

At first, she'd protested, but then it had occurred to Wynter that it would be better for her to travel in a group. Like her, they were witches. The people on her ass were looking for a lone witch, not what would appear to be a coven. And if the hunters did find her again, well, it wouldn't be bad for her to have some backup. Especially from a bunch of beings who had a streak of crazy in them.

Things hadn't been easy since the day she'd fled Aeon. She'd expected the Aeons to send someone to do the job that Wagner had failed to do, of course. The first hunter had tried to kill her. So had the second. But after that, they'd began to come for her in groups. None of those groups tried to end her, though. They'd all wanted to return her to Aeon. They'd even come equipped with *tranquilizer* guns. According to the bounty hunters who'd almost captured her, the Aeons now wanted her alive.

She could guess why.

What she needed was a place to go where they wouldn't dare venture. A place run by people who took in fugitives and who wouldn't be afraid of the Aeons.

There was only one such place she could think of—Devil's Cradle. Also referred to by many as 'the Home of Monsters.'

It was founded by seven beings—quite simply referred to as the Ancients—who were banished from Aeon a millennia ago after a war broke out between the immortals. A war that came about after Cain, Azazel, Lilith, Seth, Inanna, Ishtar, and Dantalion sold their souls to Satan in exchange for power. As you do.

Or so the story went, anyway. Wynter wasn't so quick to believe anything the Aeons claimed.

The Ancients been given many titles, including the Soulless Ones and the Seven Judges of the Underworld. Neither of which were comforting. The Aeons had only referred to them as 'the Condemned.'

She'd learned plenty about the Ancients since going on the run. They lived in an underground city beneath the town. Like the Aeons, they didn't procreate, rarely ventured outside during daylight hours, and were able to put themselves in a state of deep Rest.

Not all people believed that the Ancients truly threw their lot in with Satan, but it *was* confirmed that—unlike the Aeons—they could grant various things in exchange for other people's souls.

Power, beauty, fame, fortune, good health, longevity. Anyone who struck deals with them were considered their property and bore the mark of whichever Ancient they subsequently served.

Cain appeared to be the most feared. The Aeons had only ever spoken of him in hushed whispers. He'd apparently led the rebellion all those years ago, and he was considered by many to be the most powerful of the seven Ancients.

In spite of all the rumors, her little crew was *all* for her plan to move to Devil's Cradle. They were tired of being on the run. But in Wynter's opinion, there were worse things. Like being executed because an Ancient felt bored. It was said that they weren't sane in the truest sense of the word. Some people also described them as fickle and cruel, so it was a relief for many that the Ancients seemed to have no interest in leaving their corner of the globe.

Wynter squirmed slightly in her seat. "I just hope I'm not leading us to our deaths."

"I don't think we'll have a problem being accepted there," said Xavier, running his fingers through his tousled brown hair—which was often the closest thing he did to combing it, yet it always looked purposely styled. Just the same, he rarely exercised, yet his body was lean and solid.

"We might not even be granted an audience with an Ancient," said Wynter. "They don't always agree to see people. And when they do, they're not always in the mood to be helpful."

"We have no Plan B, though," Delilah pointed out.

"*I* proposed a Plan B," said Xavier.

Swerving in her seat to look at him, Delilah frowned. "Bombing Aeon was not a realistic plan. For starters, we don't *have* explosives—"

"That could be remedied," he told her.

"I'm not seeing how."

"You have so little faith in me."

"It's hard to have faith in a chronic liar."

Wynter's lips twitched. He would in fact lie about *anything*, including his very own name. Also, if he didn't like someone, his answer to the problem was to kill them. Really, it was little wonder he had a price on his head. She suspected that his struggle with scruples came from having been raised in a coven that practiced the dark arts. He'd left, wanting to go his own way, and now followed the right-hand path. Mostly.

Delilah sighed and then faced the front. Bracing her elbow against the car door, the Latina started plucking at the short, tight curls that framed her stunning face. All long legs and smooth olive skin, she snagged attention wherever she went. "I still think you should tell the Ancients that you were exiled from Aeon, Wyn. Having that in common with them might help."

Wynter shook her head. "For all I know, they have a loose alliance with the Aeons. It's unlikely, but it isn't impossible. Of course, it's more probable that they despise the people of Aeon. But if so, that could extend to me even though I've been banished. I'm not taking any chances."

If she'd thought that the Ancients would demand her personal information, she wouldn't have chosen to head there. But she wasn't worried that she'd be asked to part with any of her secrets. Another attractive thing about Devil's Cradle was that no one cared where you came from, what brought you there, or what happened in your life before you arrived. Everyone got to start afresh.

"What do you think the price will be to live there?" asked Delilah.

Wynter puffed out a breath. "I don't know, but I don't doubt that it'll be hefty." Just as there had been a big price to pay for being accepted into Aeon. "But if we can't pay it, well, no harm done. We can leave and take our chances alone."

The problem was ... she suspected she wouldn't survive long if she did. The Aeons would just keep sending people after her, and the groups they sent would just keep getting bigger. Wynter might be a monster of sorts, but she wouldn't be able to fight the Aeons and their people alone.

Finally, the trees around her thinned out. She drove onto a vast prairie land. And as she spotted the badland-type landscape beyond it, she knew she was close to the town.

A few days' drive from here, Aeon was a beautiful place with all its lush land. But as Wynter looked at all the cliffs, crooks, hills, and multi-colored tall, rock spires in the distance up ahead, she found herself more in awe of this place than she'd ever been of her old home. There was a surreal, haunting, primal beauty to all the stark, untamed, rugged landscape here.

She'd half-expected to come up against some kind of shield before getting this far, or to at least be stopped at an outpost and forced to state her purpose. But there were no magickal wards, no forcefields, no border control of any sort.

As she continued to follow the dirt road that cut through the prairie and led to the base of the rocky terrain, she kept a careful lookout for signs of life. But there were no guards stationed anywhere, and no one seemed to be patrolling the area.

And then she got it.

A smile curved her mouth. They didn't stop potential enemies from entering the town, because they believed in letting their prey come to them. It was a trap, really. Any enemies would arrogantly stroll into the heart of the Ancients' territory . . . and then they'd be taken out.

Cocky, but smart.

Reaching the end of the prairie, she drove through crannies, under arches, and then shot through a short tunnel. Exiting it, she felt her lips hitch up. Oh, they'd arrived.

"Looks like a cross between a military compound and a coastal town," said Delilah, leaning forward slightly.

Houses of various shapes, sizes, and colors bordered a pretty plaza. Beyond them were warehouses, pastureland, and utility structures. Trees, shrubs, lakes, and steep mountains lay on the outskirts, almost framing the town.

There was no shortage of people hanging around, even at this late hour. A few meandered along the plaza's cobbled paths. Others stood outside houses or bars or other establishments. One particular group was gathered around a bonfire, laughing and drinking.

Since no particular place shouted, *You'll find an Ancient here*, she pulled up at the curb and asked one resident where she should be looking. Even as he eyed her warily, he easily gave her directions to "the Ancients' base," which was apparently some kind of stately building.

Wynter thanked him and drove on. "I half-expected him to be rude or not answer. I mean, everyone we spoke to about this place was clear that the people here aren't all that friendly toward outsiders." Maybe he hadn't been an ass because he'd once been in their position.

"Ooh, I see a herbalist store," said Delilah. "I wonder if they're hiring."

Wynter slid her a frown. "Uh, not sure that'd be the best place of work for you."

Delilah's back snapped straight. "I am *a master* with herbs."

"Undeniable," said Wynter. "But you like many of your concoctions to have horrific side effects."

"Only if I don't like the personality or intention of the customer who buys them."

Delilah had once made a living from selling forbidden concoctions on the black market. But they always had 'side effects.' So, for instance, a guy looking for a date-rape potion would suddenly find himself suffering from a case of penile necrosis even if he hadn't himself ingested the concoction. In short, the magick backfired.

"I like to be a vessel for karma," Delilah added, lifting one shoulder in an unapologetic shrug.

"But your old customers didn't, and so came the backlash. I suspect there'll be people *here* you won't like. I don't want to have to kill someone because they threatened you."

"Aw, you'd do that for me? You're such a good Priestess. I just *love* our coven."

Wynter's hands tightened on the steering wheel. "I am *not* a Priestess."

"Every coven has to have one," said Delilah, her eyes dancing.

Which was why Wynter had firmly decided that . . . "This is *not* a coven." But Delilah persisted with this shit just to irritate her. "All I'm saying is that we'll struggle to keep a low profile if you're mutating the bodies of people you dislike."

As she pulled up outside tall iron gates that surrounded a dark, gothic, three-story Victorian manor, Wynter let out a low whistle. The building was as impressive as it was imposing. Slate multi-faceted roof. Towers and turrets. Decorative trimming. Wrought-iron balconies. Wide wrap-around porch. Stained glass in the door and arched windows.

"Some base," said Xavier, shifting forward in his seat.

Yanking up her metaphorical bootstraps, Wynter reached out of the open car window and pressed the intercom button on the security post.

After a few moments, there was a crackle of static. "Can I help you?" a rough voice asked.

"I'd like to talk to an Ancient, if possible," she said, not bothering with chit-chat.

"About?"

"Applying for residency."

There was a long moment of silence, and then a buzzer sounded. The gates slowly swung open.

"So far, so good." Her pulse beating faster than she'd have liked, Wynter drove up the long driveway and parked behind one of the few cars that sat outside the manor. "Xavier, wake Anabel." Wynter slid out of the vehicle and opened the rear door for Hattie.

Holding up her book, the old woman pointed at a page. "Girl, what's anilingus?"

Wynter felt her head jerk back. "What are you reading?"

"Erotica at its finest," Hattie replied.

Wynter waved her hand, not sure she wanted to explain the concept of rim jobs to an old woman. "We'll talk about this later."

Hattie awkwardly exited the car, looking all stiff and frail. It was a total act. She wasn't quite as harmless as she liked to appear. That said, you were safe with the darling woman as long as you didn't attack her or marry her. She'd killed every one of her husbands. She was the group's very own black widow.

Rubbing nervously at her arm, Anabel crossed to Wynter and the others, looking upon the manor with sheer dread. But then, pretty much everything made the blonde nervous. She was most in her element when in the kitchen making potions, where she wasn't required to interact with anyone. "So this is where we die," she said, her voice solemn.

Delilah sighed. "You say that almost wherever we go. We're not going to—*oh my God, what is that smell?*"

Anabel lifted her chin. "Farting is a normal bodily function."

"Not if it smells like something died up your ass."

"I don't handle ethnic food well."

Wafting his hand, Xavier grimaced. "Just please don't unload anymore of those farts until we're away from the Ancient."

Anabel sniffed. "You're all so dramatic."

Delilah snickered. "You'd know all about that, Miss *So This is Where We Die.*"

The blonde pointed at her nape. "I can feel death's breath on the back of my neck. I know that feeling all too well. And maybe if *you* remembered all *your* past deaths, you'd be a little more understanding."

Groaning, Wynter raised a hand. "All right, let's stop there."

Anabel often saw her potential demise everywhere—the paranoia came from her soul's ability to retain memories and skills from past lives. When you recalled every death, you also remembered just how easily life could be snatched right from under you.

None of the crew were entirely sure if she was in fact the reincarnation of Bloody Mary or if she simply believed it because she'd experimented on herself with one too many of her potions over the years. Whatever the case, if you called for Mary, Anabel's demeanor would change in an instant and she'd happily kill anything standing in her path.

"In case you've all forgotten, we have somewhere we need to be." Wynter exhaled heavily. "Fingers crossed this goes well."

She walked to the porch, unable to fully admire the ornate trim work and gingerbread cutouts while her gut was in knots. A lot rode on whatever happened next. As Delilah had pointed out, they had no Plan B.

Reaching the door, Wynter pressed the bell. Close-up, she could see that the stained-glass pane depicted mythical scenes of some sort. Nice work.

Finally, the door opened. She'd expected a butler. The dude in front of her was rugged and masculine with an outlaw-warrior vibe. *Gargoyle*, she sensed. He wasn't Wynter's type, but he was definitely hot.

Patting her faded red hair, Hattie smiled up at him. "You look just like the highlander on the cover of a book I read recently. Do *you* know what anilingus is?"

Wynter felt her eyes drift closed. Unfuckingreal. It didn't help that Xavier had choked on a laugh, or that a silently chuckling Delilah was leaning against Wynter as if unable to support her own weight.

Clearing her throat, Wynter opened her eyes and cast the man in front of her an apologetic smile. "Just pretend they're not there. I often do."

He grunted, moved aside, and waved them in with a sweep of his arm.

Stepping into a very grand hallway, she saw that the Old World feel continued inside the manor with its high, vaulted ceilings, carved columns, ornate lighting, imperial staircase, and decorative moldings. *Wow.*

"All of you wait here," the gargoyle instructed.

Wynter nodded and watched him stalk away, wondering just which of the Ancients she'd find herself facing. She then turned to Hattie. "Haven't we told you not to ask strangers sex-related questions?"

"I just want to know what this anilingus thing is," said Hattie, all innocence. "He was a strapping man, so I'm sure he's popular with the ladies—he seemed like a good source of information." She pointed at the page of her book again. "I'm thinking it's possibly back-door finger-fun."

Back-door finger fun? Seriously?

"More like tongue-fun," said Xavier, a smirk playing around the edges of his mouth.

Hattie's hazel eyes went wide. "Ooh, really? My, my, my. Do people wear tongue protection when they do that?"

Wynter sighed and scrubbed a hand down her face. They were all whacked. Every one of them.

*

"You're serious, aren't you?"

Cain flicked a look at Azazel and reminded him, "I rarely joke."

"I thought you were just in a bad mood because you had to fire one of your aides. I know you have no patience for conducting interviews."

Cain sighed and crossed to the vintage liquor cabinet. "Firing him was probably an overreaction on my part, but my mind isn't in a good place right now. I've been awake too long. I haven't Rested in over five centuries, and I'm feeling the sting of it."

Azazel sat on the sofa. "I sensed that you were struggling; I just wasn't sure how badly."

Cain poured whiskey into a tumbler. "The numbness wasn't so bad for a time, because things pierced it here and there, but that very rarely happens now. And that's the problem. It's emotion that makes a person feel alive."

When you'd lived so long that you'd experienced the same emotions over and over and over and over—anger, sadness, grief—they eventually lost their power over you. And when you no longer experienced the feelings that made people hesitate to hurt others, like empathy or remorse, it left you capable of many things.

Azazel thrust his hand through his dark hair and gave a solemn nod. "We've all hit that stage at some point where you start seeking other ways to make you feel alive. Adrenaline rushes. Doling out pain. Receiving pain."

"And it's never long before those things lose their shine, because boredom is our constant and closest companion." Cain knocked back some of his drink. "I've stopped wanting things. The only thing I really crave is retribution—that never goes away, never will. But other than that? There's nothing." When there was nothing you wanted, you were just drifting, floating, aimless. "And now there are times when my mood goes black. It's not anger. It's not rage. It's a dark state of mind, and I don't like the thoughts I have when those moods take me. I need to click the reboot option."

No more than two of the seven Ancients ever Rested at a time. The sisters, Inanna and Ishtar, had chosen to Rest three centuries ago. Ishtar had woken early, which meant Cain could now sleep if he wished.

"If that's what you need, I'm behind you." Azazel cocked his head, his blue eyes sharpening. "You ever worry that one day we'll wake and find that the Rest didn't do shit for us?"

Considering it had been an eternally long time since it had made him feel truly refreshed ... "Yes. When we were first banished, I swore vengeance would one day be ours. I didn't think we'd still be trapped in this place so many years later."

"You've given up hope that we'll ever be free?"

"No. I never will. But essentially being caged is wearing on us all, isn't it? That's why our Rests are becoming less and less rest*ful*." People thought that Cain and the other Ancients stayed in Devil's Cradle by choice. In truth, they were stuck here, courtesy of the Aeons. "But we can't open this invisible prison unless we kill the four who created it, and it's impossible to do that when they won't step foot on this land."

"At least we can take comfort in knowing they'll hate that we still live. The Aeons were sure we'd all lose our shit on being confined and that we'd then turn on each other. They underestimated us on so many levels. They probably have no idea how prepared we are for war."

"All the preparations mean nothing if we can't make them bring that war to us. We have no way to take it to them."

Azazel swept his hand down a face that females everywhere sighed over. He'd been described by more than one woman as having the look of an avenging angel—which might be why he'd been mistaken by humans for a fallen-angel-turned-demon.

"I kept thinking that, annoyed we still live, they'd come to finish us off at some point," said Azazel. "Particularly you. With the exception of your mother, they hate that you've ever breathed."

More, they upheld that Cain had no place on—or beneath, as it were—this Earth. In his opinion, he had as much of a right to exist as anyone else. He understood why the Aeons felt differently. He simply didn't agree. "I thought they'd come to rescue Seth, given how convinced they are that I brainwashed him into joining our side."

Azazel snorted. "They don't know your brother half as well as they think they do." He briefly glanced out of the window, adding, "He'll be disappointed that you plan to Rest awhile, but he'll understand."

"I don't intend to Rest for another few months. I have to settle several matters beforehand. You'll all have permission to wake me early if a situation warrants it." Cain sank onto the other velvet sofa. "You know, you didn't tell me what brought you here."

Azazel's eyes lit up. "Ah, well, I heard something you're going to find *very* interesting. It'll put a smile on your face like nothing else can."

"Go on."

Azazel paused, no doubt for effect. "The land of Aeon appears to be perishing."

Cain blinked. "Perishing?"

"It's as if some sort of wasting disease has settled over the town. It appeared six months ago, and it's eating away at the land, drying up the water sources, and poisoning the fruit and vegetables that grow there. Not sure if it has also spread to the city beneath it—our source still has no access to that part. But just the thought that the same blight could be there . . ." Azazel's mouth curved into a shit-eating grin. "Yeah, I like it."

"Your source must have been fucking with you. The Aeons can effortlessly combat environmental decay—they're masters of elemental power, after all."

"Oh, they've tried to fight the outbreak every step of the way." Azazel stretched out his long legs. "But whatever's afflicting the land hasn't responded to their attempts in any way. It keeps steadily spreading, no matter what they do."

Frowning, Cain shook his head. "That makes no sense."

"But it *does* make me smile. You want to as well. You know you do. Go on."

"If the land was really contaminated—"

"My source swore it was true. He seems fucking terrified. I'm not surprised, because the decay isn't even the worst of it."

"How so?"

"People are getting sick."

All right, now Cain *knew* the guy's source was talking shit. "No way am I buying that."

"It's happening, I'm telling you. Only the mortals have been affected, though. I heard it's like the black plague on steroids."

"Come on, Azazel, the healers there are some of the best in the world."

"Which is why no one has died. *Yet.* I mean, think what will happen if the healers run out of steam."

Cain took another swig of his whiskey. "You're not even a little skeptical?"

"I was at first, but my source isn't that *good* an actor. His fear was real."

"You sure it's not that you'd simply love for it to be true?"

Azazel hummed. "Maybe. Can't deny that I'd like the prissy Aeons to suffer for what they've done. They're oh-so proud of their land. Those who don't live in the underground city might not realize that it features the biblical Garden of Eden, but *we* know. And we also know that any damage to their pride and joy would hit them where it hurt. Infecting it ..." Again, Azazel grinned. "Someone should have thought of it sooner. It's a fucking genius way to piss those assholes off."

*If* it wasn't pure bullshit.

"Strange that no one's come here accusing us of being responsible for it. We were always their scapegoats. I would have thought they'd blame us right off the mark for something like that."

"Assuming it's actually happening ... they'd blame us, but they wouldn't contact us. They wouldn't want us to know we'd succeeded in what they believed we'd attempted to do."

"Ah, true." Azazel draped his arms over the back of the sofa. "Well, my source had no theories for what could be causing the decay or the plague. He said nothing had happened recently that could be connected to it. A keeper seems to have run off with an exiled resident at around the same time that the problems began, but that's it. I wonder if they're sick too or if they've had a lucky escape from whatever's running rampant through Aeon."

"They won't be so lucky when hunters track them down." Those hunters liked their prey to die *hard.*

"Considering most of the people in the town are kind of preoccupied with the blight and pestilence, I doubt the rogues are anyone's priority."

The door swung open, and Cain's younger brother stalked inside, the image of agitation.

Cain eyed Seth as he took another sip of his drink. "You all right?"

He grunted, planting his hands on his hips.

"Let me guess," began Azazel. "Ishtar."

"I don't know what bothers me more," said Seth. "That she's

playing stupid games again, or that she thinks they're going to work." His amber eyes narrowed at the expression that crossed Azazel's face. "Wait, *you* thought they might work?"

"She's exceptionally good at getting under your skin," Azazel defended. "Ishtar knows you too well. She knows what buttons to push. And you're a sickeningly forgiving person."

Yes, but Seth was ... different from the other Ancients. Good. Noble. And brave enough to side with Cain and the others while the rest of their family fought them head-on and drove them out of their own home.

"I *do* forgive her," Seth confirmed, slumping onto the sofa beside Cain. "But when I forgave her, I also let her go and chose to move on. I wasn't pining for her while she was Resting. It's been centuries since I've touched her. She talks like it was last week. That's when she's not flirting with Solomon in the hope of getting a reaction out of me," Seth added, referring to a mage in her service who'd never gotten along with Seth.

Cain braced his glass on his thigh. "She's probably hoping you'll both compete for her." Anyone who didn't know Ishtar would think she was a typical attention junkie. She *did* love to be admired and fawned over, but it wasn't about attention. It was about power. She craved the feeling of power she got from having others yearn for and fight over her.

Seth looked at him. "She came onto you as well, didn't she?"

Cain only nodded. He hadn't slept with Ishtar in over eight centuries and yet, like with Seth, she'd spoken of their time together as if it had been recent.

Azazel linked his fingers behind his head. "Well, she didn't hit on me."

"She would have done if you didn't loathe her," said Seth.

Azazel's brow creased. "I don't hate her. I just like to pretend she's dead."

Seth sighed. "I have to say, that sounds like hate to me."

Azazel gave an indifferent shrug. "It's a weird point of pride for her that she's had two brothers, you know. It's like she thinks you two broke some kind of bro-code for her."

Holding back a snort, Cain downed more of his whiskey. In truth, Seth had spoken with him before getting involved with Ishtar, wanting to be sure that Cain would be fine with it. Cain's only worry had been that she'd shit all over Seth.

"Really, I brought all this on myself." Seth skimmed a hand over his close-cropped, dark-blond hair. "I saw how she was with Cain; I ignored the red flags. But it was like with Lilith and Dantalion. When they were together, Lilith came across as a shrew, but it was simply that they didn't *fit*. They weren't good for each other."

"You were good for Ishtar," Cain told him as he returned to the liquor cabinet to top up his glass. "You're steady. Patient. You're the kind of man she needs. But Ishtar's more about what she wants than what she needs." That had always been her problem.

"Yeah." Seth let out a long sigh. "So, what were you two talking about? Anything interesting?"

Azazel beamed. "Actually, it's fucking *fascinating*."

Seth blinked. "Oh? What?"

The clock chimed, and Azazel softly swore. "Gotta go. Walk with me, I'll tell you everything," he said to Seth. The two stood upright as Azazel began, "So I spoke to my source at Aeon—"

A knock came at the door.

"Yes?" Cain called out.

Maxim stepped inside the parlor. "There's a coven here requesting to see an Ancient. They want residency."

"All right," said Cain. "Bring them to me."

# Chapter Three

Hearing footfalls, Wynter turned away from the painting she'd been admiring to see the gargoyle coming toward her.

He swept his gaze over her and the others. "Follow me."

Wynter raised an *Are you ready for this?* brow at her crew, who all nodded. "Let me do the talking, please." Because Christ knew what kind of shit they'd blurt out, and they did *not* need to be offending an Ancient.

Trailing after their guide, she asked, "Who has agreed to see us?"

"Cain," he replied.

Her heartbeat stuttered. *Not* the best news, considering he'd been described as a mental sadist, but it was better than being turned away.

Wynter passed through many ornamental arches and glanced into various rooms, noting several people lingering around.

Rolling back her shoulders, she fixed a placid look on her face. Innocuous, staid, uninteresting—*that* was what she was going for. Wynter wanted to fade into the background and draw as little attention as possible while here. She wanted to be simply another resident, wanted to come across as a mere run-of-the-mill witch.

Finally, her guide halted near a mahogany door and wrapped his knuckles on it. A deep voice bid them to enter. Following the gargoyle into the room, Wynter almost blinked in surprise. She'd expected a simple office. It was a parlor. Gothic and elegant, it had antique Victorian furnishings, thick red drapes, a large stone fireplace, Persian rugs—

Sharp, hooded eyes clashed with hers, so serpent-like in their intensity that it tripped every one of her inner danger alarms. At the same time, though, her body perversely perked up. And she couldn't really judge it for that.

Long and lean and supremely male, this man was perfect in form. His face looked carved from stone, all sharp angles and hard lines like an uncut jewel. His short, smooth hair was the color of obsidian, and he had the kind of full, carnal mouth that made a girl wonder just what he could do with it. His eyes were definitely his best feature, though—they were dark and almost ... lustrous, like two black pearls.

So this was Cain ... The originator of murder, the ancestor of envy, the quintessential personification of sin.

Someone could have warned her that he was also built to compel and seduce.

He stood tall and straight with his shoulders back and his feet planted—the image of self-possession. The long-sleeved tee he wore stretched tight across a delightfully toned chest. He'd shoved the sleeves up to his elbows, revealing ancient-looking tattoos. Even his forearms were toned, like those of a drummer.

"The coven I mentioned," the gargoyle said to him.

Cain lifted a glass tumbler from a liquor cabinet. "So I see." His voice was a deep, rumbly, *I'll talk dirty to you all night long* kind of sexy that made her think *very* filthy thoughts. "You can leave now, Maxim."

The guy obligingly breezed out of the room.

Cain took a swig of his drink, his gaze sweeping over the others, who'd all fanned out behind her. His eyes then once more locked with hers, unapologetically direct.

Her pulse skittered as his long legs began to cover the space between them. He moved with the sinuous grace of a tiger on the hunt, each step slow and precise, like he was callously savoring every fluid stride that took him closer to his prey. Damn, he had an explicit, sexy *rawness* to him. An edge. Not a devil-may-care edge; no, the edge of an apex predator who knew he was the penultimate alpha male and wouldn't hesitate to slit your throat if you stepped a foot wrong. And she was entirely unprepared for how much that revved her engines.

Silently cursing her unruly hormones, she kept her expression blank, trying and failing not to admire the muscles bunching and flexing beneath his shirt. While her combat-trained mind instinctively plotted all kinds of potential pre-emptive strikes just in case he moved to hurt her, the entity inside her blinked and lifted its head. It went on high alert, but she sensed no panic from it. It didn't feel threatened or vulnerable. She wasn't sure if it could feel fear.

Finally, Cain came to a stop in front of her, so close she could feel his body heat. He gave her a lazy, head-to-toe perusal. An electric awareness snapped the air taut as little sparks seemed to spring from her to him. Not liking that visceral chemistry or the damn fluttering in her stomach, she fought the frown that tried tugging at her brow.

Towering over her, he watched her. Studied her. Missed nothing. "I am Cain. And you must be . . . ?"

She gave him a respectful dip of the chin and said, "Wynter."

"Wynter," he echoed, swirling his tumbler. "Pretty name."

"It is, isn't it?" said Delilah, remaining slightly behind Wynter. "Perfect for a Priestess."

Wynter felt her lips thin.

"So you're a coven?" asked Cain.

Since they no longer needed to pose as one, Wynter shook her head. "No, we're—"

"The Bloodrose Coven." Delilah reached past Wynter and handed him *a fucking business card.*

Wynter whirled on her. "What in the hell? When did you get— you know what, we'll talk about this later." She quickly introduced the others, thankful they remained quiet.

Cain inclined his head at them, a ghost of a smile now touching one corner of his mouth. It didn't soften his expression or relax Wynter's nerves. Something told her he'd still wear that hint of a smile while caning your fingers.

"Drink?" he offered.

"No, thanks." She'd rather keep her wits about her.

The others also politely turned down his offer.

He gestured at one of the sofas. "Sit." An instruction, not an invitation. It wasn't spoken rudely, just in an expectant, no-nonsense tone that told her this was a man used to being in power.

He was also undoubtedly used to being obeyed ... so it would probably be best *not* to spend a lot of time around him, because Wynter had a will of her own and wasn't afraid to use it. That wouldn't help with her whole 'innocuous' act.

She sat in the center of the couch he'd indicated and then crossed one leg over the other. Anabel and Hattie sat either side of her while Delilah and Xavier each claimed an armrest.

Cain sank onto the sofa opposite them and took another swig of his drink. "Maxim tells me you came to apply for residency."

Wynter nodded. "That's right."

"I won't ask where you're originally from or why you'd choose to move to Devil's Cradle—that's your business. But I do need to be certain that you're all fully aware of the realities of this town." He balanced his glass on his thigh. "It was founded by myself and the other Ancients, all of whom live beneath the surface. There are rules, and everyone is expected to obey them. Punishments tend to be severe. Still, fights often break out. It can be difficult for several breeds of preternatural to coexist in a small town."

"The population seems bigger than I thought it would be."

"Oh, Devil's Cradle is home to many creatures. Some merely come here because they haven't been accepted anywhere else. I'm talking hybrids, misfits, cursed beings, or those with mutations. We also have species hiding out because they've been hunted near to extinction. Then there are the others, and most are the definition of unsavory. Outcasts, criminals, crazies. They have prices on their heads or are fleeing from persecution." He idly tapped his finger on his glass. "Every single resident has one thing in common—they're desperate for safety."

A little like Wynter and her crew, then.

"If you become one of us, the Ancients here will protect and shelter you. We will never give you up to anyone who may come for you, we will never ostracize you, we will never hold you accountable for anything you did before coming here. *But* there'll be a price."

"Will there be any exceptions to the whole 'not giving us up to anyone who'd come looking for us' thing?" asked Xavier.

"No," replied Cain. "We protect our own. You must understand, though, that this isn't a fanciful sanctuary. It's not some quiet, peaceful haven. Jungle law is very much prevalent here. If you can each hold your own, or at least find good allies, you shouldn't find yourselves constantly challenged. Going lone wolf—or lone coven, as it were—would be a mistake, especially if you're people who generally shy away from duels."

Wynter wouldn't hesitate to cross swords with anyone who'd think to challenge her. Ordinarily. Here, though, she wanted to keep her head down. Which would be hard to do when the people on this sofa with her were freaking insane. She was about to once more repeat that they weren't actually a coven, but then Cain spoke again.

"Are you all still interested in becoming residents here?"

"Yes," replied Wynter, and the others answered in the affirmative.

"Like I said before, there's a price," he warned.

And she could guess what it was. "Our memories would be stolen from us if we ever decided to leave?"

"No, we are not interested in erasing people's identities. Although it should be noted that, on leaving, the memories of your time here will become fuzzy and soon after fade."

That wasn't so terrible, since it wasn't like she'd forget her entire life. "Okay, so what's the price?"

"Unless, or until, you officially leave Devil's Cradle for good"— he took another drink from his glass and then tipped it their way— "your souls would partially belong to me."

\*

37

Cain watched as Wynter went very still. The others exchanged uneasy looks but didn't speak, clearly content to let her take the lead. To look at her, no one would think she was Priestess of a coven. Nothing about her screamed 'authority.'

Average height and slender as a rake, she didn't appear in the least bit threatening. Her posture was both self-protective and submissive. She kept making nervous little gestures—biting her lip, twirling her ankle, swallowing hard.

It would be so easy to dismiss her as any sort of threat, *but . . .* there was the noiseless stealth with which she moved. And her quicksilver eyes—sharp, piercing, framed by thick dark lashes— had done a predatory sweep of the room like a leopard on the hunt when she'd first entered. It had snatched his inner creature's total attention.

She also met Cain's gaze easily. Not boldly, not in challenge, but she was utterly focused on him. And he knew she was watching for a sign that he'd attack. He knew she was ready to counter any move he might make. It almost made him smile.

Knowing that she'd strike without hesitation if he should prove a lethal threat stirred his blood in a way he wouldn't have expected. The creature inside him liked it just the same. Liked her.

They also both sensed that there was something *off* about this little witch. Cain couldn't put his finger on what it was about her that raised a red flag in his mind, or why his monster didn't look upon her as prey. It saw another predator, which was why it had been watching her as intently as she watched Cain.

He stared directly into her eyes, wishing he could see inside her head. No amount of staring made her squirm in discomfort or falter with her act. Her nerves were rock steady. Wynter wasn't a slave to her emotions, no, she was their fucking master. He respected that.

It was possible she was purposely giving off a *nothing to see here, move along* vibe because she simply wanted to fly under the radar. If so, that wouldn't work. No one who looked like her would ever go unnoticed.

She was fucking beautiful with those unusual eyes, the heavy lower lip, her high cheekbones, and all that glorious dark hair that hung down her back straight as rain. But her attractiveness was only a small part of her draw. The way she carried herself, the steel in her spine, the sharpness in her eyes, the magick that hummed around her like an aura of electricity—all of it came together in a very pretty package. And he wanted her.

She gave her head a little shake. "We'd each have to sell you our soul?"

"No. But you would have to submit partial ownership of it over to me."

"In what way is that different? I don't really understand."

"When someone signs their soul over to me in exchange for something it means that, no matter where they are in the world, they owe me their compliance. They are chattel, essentially. Puppets on a string, even. If I ever tug on those strings, they have to do as I bid. Each of you, however, would not be under my control as I would only have partial rights to your soul. But you would owe me respect, loyalty, and be in my service for as long as you're residents here."

"Why you specifically? Why not all seven Ancients?"

"We would all have authority over the five of you, of course. But the other Ancients would not hold such rights merely because it is not *them* making you the offer. Had another Ancient been on duty here tonight and had you accepted their offer, you would all have been in *their* service."

She gave a slow nod of understanding.

"So . . . is this a price you're all willing to pay?"

She glanced at each of her coven members. For long moments, they silently seemed to hem and haw but, eventually, one by one nodded.

Wynter turned back to Cain. "The issue here is . . . I don't know if you'd actually *want* partial ownership of my soul."

He felt his brows flit together. "Why is that?"

She shrugged. "It's undead."

Cain stared at her for long seconds, taken off-guard—something that very rarely happened. He leaned forward and, careful not to spill his drink, braced his elbows on his thighs. "When did you die?"

"When I was a child. As you no doubt know, magick can do all sorts of things, even bring people back from the dead."

"I've heard that those with undead souls never feel real satisfaction. Is that true?"

"Yes. It's like there's a ... detachment there. No taste or smell or sensation fully gratifies us, so we exist in a kind of limbo. But it beats being dead."

"Yes, I suppose it does." He felt a slight stirring in his mind—one he hadn't felt in so long he almost didn't recognize it for what it was: fascination. "I've never touched an undead soul before."

She double-blinked. "You can ... touch souls?"

"If I'm granted partial or full rights to them, yes."

"So if we agreed to your condition, you could touch our souls? What would that mean for us?"

"It wouldn't allow me access to your thoughts or feelings, if that is what you're wondering. But with one touch, I would have a general idea of your character merely because the soul is the foundation blocks of a person. Additionally, I'd know if you died."

Her eyes narrowed ever so slightly. "Could you also cause us pain?"

He nodded. "There's nothing more sensitive than the soul."

"So, in essence, we'd be completely vulnerable to you?"

"Yes." And where it concerned Wynter, the dark heart of him liked the idea of that. "You would all also wear my mark on your palm. A brand that declares you're under my protection and in my service. Every resident is marked by whatever Ancient claims rights to their soul."

"How do we know you really intend to give those rights back to us when we leave?"

"You don't trust me?"

"Not even a little. No offense."

He felt his mouth quirk. Oh, he liked this little witch. And he'd definitely have her. "None taken. You needn't worry. I'll be as bound to the terms of the verbal contract as you."

"What *exactly* are the terms?"

"There's no fine print, Wynter. The agreement would be simple: For as long as you're a resident of Devil's Cradle, your soul will partially belong to me, and so you will owe me your loyalty and respect while also being in my service. In return, I will ensure you have shelter and protection from insiders or outsiders—no exceptions. The same will go for the rest of your coven if they agree."

"Just to be clear, we're not a coven," said Wynter, though her thoughts were mostly centered around his 'terms.' She'd known the price would be hefty; she hadn't known it would be *this* high. She'd heard that Aeons refrained from attempting to plant temporary spies here. She could now guess why.

Giving up some rights to her soul held no appeal, but neither did leaving Devil's Cradle. Her gut told her that *this* was where she needed to be. And it wasn't like she couldn't reclaim those rights. If she decided she wanted them back, she could just up and leave, couldn't she?

There was nothing in that agreement he'd mentioned that said he'd be privy to her secrets. He clearly hadn't sensed the entity she hosted—an entity that was totally chill right now and close to dozing again—so that was good. And since her monster wasn't bound to her soul, he wouldn't 'feel' it on touching said soul. In sum, she'd be able to keep him in the dark.

If accepting Cain's offer was a bad idea, she'd have received some sort of warning from the deity who'd branded her by now—She was seemingly full of opinions and often interfered with this or that.

The thing that most encouraged Wynter to accept his offer was that this dude was most *definitely* a match for the Aeons. He wouldn't tremble in his boots if they tracked her to Devil's Cradle. More, he'd be bound to protect Wynter from them.

But none of that meant anything if her crew weren't on board with this, though she doubted they'd turn Cain's offer down. They simply weren't sane enough to be as wary as they should.

She glanced at each of them and lifted one brow. "Well?"

Delilah lifted one hand. "I'm in."

"Same here," said Xavier.

"I'm tired of running," began Hattie. "I'm too old to keep doing it. I want to plant my derrière somewhere. This place is as good as any."

When Anabel didn't speak, Wynter gave her a gentle nudge and asked, "What about you?"

Anabel gave her a shaky smile. "We all have to die somewhere, so . . . yeah, whatever."

Wynter shook her head. *So morbid.* Cutting her gaze back to Cain, she said, "All right, then; it looks like we're staying."

His eyes glinting with a dark satisfaction she didn't quite understand, he held his hand out to her. "Then we have a deal?"

Wynter shook his hand. "We have a deal."

A swish of power curled around their joined hands, warm and binding. At the same time, there was a curious shifting sensation in her chest. More lines of blazing pain whizzed along her palm, as if something was being carved into the skin wickedly fast.

She flipped over her hand to find a large 'C' on her palm that curved around a triangle that had a snake threaded through it. The mark was a little red and raw, like a laser had mere seconds ago gone to work on her flesh. The burn had faded though, so she guessed the redness would soon also vanish.

As he went through the same branding process with the others, she traced the mark on her palm carefully, marveling at how she felt no different than before despite apparently only now possessing partial rights to her soul. There was no sense of being shackled or owned or anything.

Done, Cain drained his glass and then smoothly rose to his feet. "Now I'll have Maxim get you all settled. He'll find you a place to live. He'll also explain the rules and just why it would be a bad idea for you to ignore them. I'm hoping I won't have to ever speak to you under other . . . more unpleasant circumstances."

Wynter stood, and the others followed suit. "We won't be breaking rules or making waves or anything like that."

"Glad to hear it. I treat my own well. Until they displease me." He paused, looking at her intently. "So don't displease me, Wynter."

# Chapter Four

M axim ushered them into an office not far away from the parlor. Wynter glanced around the room. It was clean, masculine, and spacious. A little soulless, though, since it lacked any personal touches. The wood-paneled walls matched the hardwood flooring and sturdy office desk. Filing cabinets lined the wall. Above them were shelves on which folders and books were neatly stacked side by side.

Maxim took the chair behind the desk. "I don't need background information, but I do need your forenames. Surnames aren't required."

Xavier cleared his throat. "It is good to meet you," he said in a thick French accent. "I am Andre."

Wynter sighed. "No, you're not. Nor are you French."

He only chuckled, the weirdo.

"You'll have to excuse Xavier; he means nothing by it," Hattie said to Maxim, hunching her shoulders and shuffling forward, playing the frail card hard. Of course, Maxim fell for it and was quick to help her into a seat, unaware that she ogled his ass and blew it a kiss when he turned away. "I'm Hattie," she added. "By the way, I found out what anil—"

"Okay, so this here is Delilah," Wynter quickly cut in. "And over there is Anabel. I'm Wynter."

Back in his seat, Maxim scribbled down the names. "You have a choice to make. You can live on the surface of the town, or you can live in the underground city among the Ancients."

Wynter frowned. "People don't have to, like, *earn* their way down there somehow?"

"No, that's not how it works. Where you'll reside is simply a matter of preference."

Huh. Well, how about that. "What's it like down there?"

His brow smoothed out, and a hint of warmth entered his eyes. "Like nothing you'll have ever seen before. It's no more peaceful than it is up here, though."

Maybe not, but being below ground would be extra security. If anyone from Aeon came looking for some sign of Wynter, they'd never get down there to check. The rest of the crew must have had the same thought, because they all voted for living in the subterranean city.

"To be clear, there are no apartment buildings down there," said Maxim. "There are only houses, and no one has a house to themselves. There are dwellings with enough rooms to accommodate you all, however. Most were extended so that covens and packs etc. could stick together."

"Good, we'd want to share a place anyway," said Delilah. "We'd all especially want to live with Wynter. Being away from our Priestess makes us uncomfortable."

Wynter shot her a hard look. "Woman, I swear if you don't stop this shit *I will cut you.*"

Grinning, Delilah totally ignored that and slapped one of her damn business cards on the desk. "The Bloodrose Coven at your service," she told Maxim.

*For fuck's sake.*

His brow creased, he thanked her and placed the card in a drawer. "Now ..." He opened a thick-ass file that seemed to hold records of some sort. "If I remember rightly, there are two houses in the city vacant that are large enough to accommodate five people," he said, leafing through the pages before landing on a particular one. "Yes, there are, in fact, two. The problem is ... they're both vacant for a reason."

Wynter folded her arms. "Which is?"

"Mostly, it's about their location." Bracing his elbows on the desk, he interlinked his fingers. "Like calls to like, so vampires gravitate toward vampires, mages gravitate toward mages, etc., etc. Nests and conclaves and so on have formed. It's only natural. Some species prefer to congregate in the same area. Several courts of fey, for instance, can share territory with no issue. But other species, such as lycans or were-beasts, do not do so well with living very close to *other* packs. They don't wish to share their turf with their own kind."

Understanding how territorial those particular species were, Wynter nodded.

"The first empty residence is actually in a very peaceful neighborhood. The problem? You would be the only people in it who are not fey. And while fey can live among each other peacefully, they tend to drive out other types of preternatural using just about any means necessary.

"As for the other residence . . . that house plus both the front and back yards are the only slices of territory that separates two packs of lycans. Every other home on that particular street is occupied by them. And these two packs argue frequently. There's usually no physical fighting, merely bickering. But it can get loud and tedious, as I'm sure you can imagine."

Delilah frowned. "Neither house sounds like a winner. But, personally, I'd rather deal with childish lycans than the damn fey."

Hattie hummed in agreement. "Fey are tricksters right down to the bone."

"They'll pull all kinds of shit in their efforts to drive us out," said Xavier.

Wynter looked at Anabel, who was doodling circles on her inner elbow with her fingertip. "What about you, Anabel? Fey, or lycans?"

"I'll go with lycans," she replied. "Statistically speaking, they're less likely to kill us."

Barely resisting the urge to roll her eyes, Wynter turned back to Maxim. "We'll go with the latter option, then."

"I'm not surprised," he said. "Few like to live among the fey unless they are fey themselves. Now, nobody is required to pay rent or bills, but they are required to buy their own food and possessions. To adequately support your coven, I would say that at least two of you will need to work."

Hattie let out a self-depreciating laugh. "I don't think my frail old bones could take another day of work."

Wynter snorted. There wasn't a damn thing wrong with Hattie's bones or any other part of her. The woman would probably outlive them all. But Maxim, totally sucked in by Hattie's act, gave her a gentle smile and assured her that her coven would no doubt support her decision.

Delilah looked at Wynter and rolled her eyes.

"There are various job openings in both the town and the city," said Maxim. "If any of you struggle to find employment, however, let me know and I'll see what I can do. Sometimes shop owners are willing to let people purchase something in trade, but most prefer cash."

Wynter twisted her mouth. "I don't suppose you have a blacksmith's shop, do you?"

He blinked. "We have several, actually. There's a smithy who could use an extra set of hands, but he probably wouldn't hire you because he *likes* to be able to moan that he and his assistant are overworked. They call him Grouch for a reason."

"I could at least ask him, right?" said Wynter. "If he says no, he says no."

"There's no harm in it. I'll point out where the shop is when we're beneath the town. Don't be surprised or take it personally if Grouch turns you away."

Pausing, Maxim tapped his fingers on the desk. "Now for the rules you'll live by as long as you reside in Devil's Cradle. It's not a long, complicated list. Most of it is pure common sense. No stealing, no assault, no breaking and entering, no stepping into the home of an Ancient unless you're invited. People are allowed to challenge other residents to duels, but there will be no fights to the death unless it has been first cleared by the Ancient by whom they were marked.

Except for in instances of self-defense, murder is the one thing that is not tolerated unless approval has been granted. Is that understood?"

Each of them nodded.

"Excellent. I'm sure you have general questions. I can answer them while I escort you to your new home. First, are there any bags or other possessions that you need to retrieve from your car?"

"Yes," replied Wynter. "What do I do with the car?"

He pushed to his feet. "I will drive it to the vehicle storage warehouse for you later. In case you're wondering where that is, it's the warehouse closest to the river. You can access it any time." He crossed to the filing cabinet and, after a quick rummage through it, pulled out several sets of keys. "For your new home," he explained as he gave them each a set. "Now for your bags . . ."

After they'd grabbed their luggage from the trunk, Wynter handed him her car keys so he could later drive it to the storage unit. They then followed him back into the manor, through the long halls, and over to a door near the office. He opened said door, revealing a large elevator. It had glass walls, but all you could presently see out of them was the elevator shaft.

They all stepped inside, and Maxim hit the down button.

As the elevator smoothly descended, she found herself wondering if the entrance to the underworld at Aeon was similar. No one ever spoke of it with those who hadn't been 'chosen' to live beneath the town. The Aeons acted like there was something sacred about the simple downward journey from the surface. Wynter had never particularly understood it.

She blinked as they descended out of the shaft. Glancing out of the glass wall of the still-moving elevator, she felt her mouth drop open as she took in the view. Holy *shit*. The place was huge. So much bigger than she'd expected. It seemed to go on for miles, in fact.

It was nothing like the surface. No, this place was very much a modernized medieval city. There were timber-framed houses with wattle walls, cottages with thatched rooves, whimsical rustic dwellings, and enchanting towers. Some homes seemed to have been built into hills—you could just make out the windows and doors. Many had a real fairy-tale feel.

She could also see a number of small castles scattered around the city that were spaced well apart. More, beautiful canals interweaved through the city, Venice-style. Beyond all the buildings and the well-kept park were forests, rivers, mounds, and caverns.

"Well, fuck me," breathed Hattie, making Xavier snicker.

"The artificial moonlight is created by the Ancients' power, as you've probably guessed," said Maxim as Wynter glanced up at the cavernous ceiling and the aqua-blue stalactites that hung from it. "During the daytime, it's artificial sunlight."

Delilah looked at him. "Are the Ancients really weakened by sunlight? It's a theory floating around."

"There are many theories about the Ancients," Maxim replied carefully. "Few are accurate."

Finally, the elevator came to a stop inside a stone tower. There was no *ping*. The doors merely glided open. They all stepped out and headed for the exit in front of them.

"There's little technology here," Maxim went on. "No internet or Wi-Fi. No cell phones or computers."

Outside, Wynter chuckled as a cool wind ruffled her hair. "Artificial breezes, huh?"

"Yes," replied Maxim. "There's even snow at Christmas. The sunlight gives off warmth. On some days, the temperature is reasonably high. On other days, it's cooler. But it's never too hot or too cold. You'll hear sound effects at times. Birds chirping. Owls hooting. Even thunder, though a storm never follows. You're wondering how all that is possible. The short answer? Power."

God, this was *so* cool.

They walked along cobbled paths, bypassing residents, most of whom moved with purpose as they carried things back and forth. Some were hanging greeneries on the front of their homes.

"The place is busier than usual because everyone's getting ready for the festivities," said Maxim.

"What festivities?" asked Hattie.

"Ancients can enter a coma-like Rest for centuries at a time, if they so please," said Maxim. "One recently woke from a long one. Ishtar. It's tradition for the waking of an Ancient to be honored by the other Ancients. Each will throw some sort of celebration for her at some point in the next month. The first will take place in two evenings' time. All residents will be invited."

"Are any other Ancients currently Resting?" asked Xavier.

Maxim dipped his chin as he replied, "One. Inanna. She's Ishtar's sister."

They fell silent as they turned a corner. Again, people were striding purposefully around. Most gave Wynter and her crew the side-eye. She didn't react. She was too busy taking everything in. It was honestly like walking through a fairy-tale book. She internally squealed in delight on seeing an actual gingerbread house.

"I noticed there are no cars down here," said Hattie. "I'm guessing people walk or use the canal boats."

His eyes on the crowd outside a tavern up ahead, Maxim nodded. "Some also go by horseback, but the horses are used more for recreational activities than for travel."

Admiring the stained-glass windows of a house that had the look of a cute little country hideout, Wynter asked, "Where do the Ancients live?"

"Each has their own small Keep," replied Maxim.

Delilah frowned. "Keep? You're talking about the small castles that are spread around the city?"

"Yes." Maxim paused as bursts of riotous laughter came out of the tavern's open windows. "The Ancients don't live alone. Their own personal hirelings reside with them."

Hattie looked up at Maxim. "Do you live at Cain's Keep, then?"

"Yes. I'm one of his aides. He has several." Maxim gave each of them a pointed look. "As I said before, you must never attempt to walk into a Keep unless you're invited. The baileys outside them, however, are open to everyone."

"Okay," said Delilah. "So, we've met Cain. What are the other Ancients like?"

Maxim hesitated. "Azazel is like Cain in some ways—hard, commanding, a predator in every respect. He is not quite as serious, though. Azazel smirks often, as if he knows something you don't . . . but if you look close enough, you will see that he's not as entertained as he is removed.

"I've never met Inanna—she went to sleep three hundred years ago. I've heard she is as beautiful as Ishtar, who does not seem to be the most tolerant of people from what I have so far observed. Lilith is equally beautiful and surprisingly not vain about it.

"Dantalion—who, as with Azazel, mythology mistakenly claims is a demon—is more solitary than the other Ancients and seems to prefer his own company.

"Last but not least is Seth, Cain's younger brother. He is softer than the others. Smiles and laughs more."

Pausing, Maxim pointed to a castle not so far away. "That's Cain's Keep." He told them a little about it but quickly rounded up the conversation when he stopped outside a charming cottage that boasted angular lattice windows, a thatched roof, a heavy wooden door, and looked like some kind of magical retreat. "Here's your new home."

Wynter felt a smile build inside her. Oh, this would do her just nicely. It was *gorgeous.*

"If Grouch does grant you a position, Wynter, you won't be far from your place of work," said Maxim. "His blacksmith's shop is located in Cain's bailey."

So the cottage was both fantastical and conveniently located. Fabulous.

Once they'd headed up the path, Wynter used her new key to unlock the front door. It scraped the floor as she pushed it open. Walking inside the living area, she found herself charmed all over again. Curved walls. Wooden beams. Arched, brick fireplace. Columns that were in fact tree trunks. After everyone placed their luggage on the floor near the front door, they began exploring.

Delilah oohed and aahed in the living area while Hattie shuffled into the country-style kitchen to check it out. Xavier and Anabel raced upstairs, wanting first dibs on the bedrooms.

Maxim assured Wynter he'd return her car keys to her soon, wished her a goodnight, and then left.

Delilah turned to her, beaming. "How amazing is this place? Can you believe we live here? I mean, I would have been good with any home—I'm tired of sleeping in our car or motels. But ... we actually live *here*."

Hattie padded back into the living room, the frail-old-woman act firmly gone. "That kitchen is mine, girls. Let it be known that I will cut a bitch up if anyone uses that room without cleaning up after themselves."

Delilah snickered, saluting her. "We hear you, Gangster Granny."

Hattie sniffed. "Now someone needs to get the tins of soup out of my bag before my stomach eats itself."

After they'd eaten a light dinner, they wandered around the cottage, exploring every nook and cranny. The place was a lot bigger than it looked from the outside, mostly due to the extension at the rear of the property. Hattie claimed the downstairs bedroom, saying her 'bad back' couldn't handle the stairs. Anabel called dibs on the attic, so the three main bedrooms were left to Wynter, Delilah, and Xavier.

Wynter's room overlooked the cozy backyard. Like the other bedrooms, it was pretty basic, but it was also bright and clean. A simple lamp sat on the nightstand that was the same cherrywood as the drawers and triple wardrobe. Bare shelves lined the cream walls. Bulky square pillows were perched on the upholstered corner chair. The double bed had a simple white coverlet and pillow cases, and it called her name *big time*.

There was also an adjoined bathroom, but as there were no towels she'd have to skip the shower. She was way too tired to unpack, so Wynter only pulled three things from her duffel before plonking it on the floor—a tank top, a pair of shorts, and the sword that was tucked comfortably in its sheath. Once in her pjs, she carefully placed the sword in the closet . . . which was roundabout the time Delilah came into the room with a burning bundle of herbs.

"I won't be able to sleep until the entire cottage has been cleansed," said Delilah, gently waving smoke into the air. "I want all the negative energy gone."

Wynter said nothing as the woman did her thing. She knew that Delilah would cleanse every room, every corner, every cupboard, every closet door. "I'd offer to bless the thresholds of the house, but I'm guessing you beat me to it."

"You guessed right. Hattie swept away all the cobwebs, dust, and leaves. I tell ya, that woman has more brooms than she does clothes." A few minutes later, Delilah announced that she was done, adding, "Sweet dreams, Priestess."

Wynter sighed. "Is there no way at all to make you stop?"

"None whatsoever." Delilah shot her a bright smile and breezed out of the room.

Wynter simply shook her head. Though her crew drove her nuts at times, she couldn't imagine not having them in her life. It was crazy to think that if she hadn't been caught by a specific group of bounty hunters, she probably would never have met her crew.

Wynter switched off the light and then slid under the thick coverlet, her mind going back to the day the aforementioned hunters had nabbed her . . .

*

*Wynter slowly began to wake as a breeze lightly whispered over her face. It was cool. Refreshing. Otherworldly. And laced with a healthy dose of you need to wake up.*

*Frowning weakly at the throbbing ache in her temples, Wynter licked her dry mouth. God, she felt sick as a dog. Not to mention super groggy.*

*And hot. Really hot.*

*Her monster, on the other hand, was furious.*

Furious?

*She forced her heavy eyelids open and found herself staring at a caged lightbulb that hung from a plain ceiling. She shifted her arms and—*

Ow. *Her right elbow jabbed something hard. A cement wall, she realized. One on which names, dates, and profanities had been carved.*

*Springs creaked as she pushed up from the thin, saggy mattress on which she'd been sprawled. Wynter felt her sensitive stomach pitch. She was gonna hurl at some point for sure.*

*As she took in the rest of her surroundings, her worries of vomiting took a back seat. She was in a small, cramped, dimly lit space bordered by iron bars. Aside from the bed, the only piece of furniture was the dingy metal toilet on the other side of the cell.*

*Yeah. A cell. She was in a goddamn cell.*

*And as she looked beyond it, she realized there was a whole row of them—most were empty, but not all. It wasn't an official prison, though. It seemed more like someone had converted some sort of basement into a jail. Which would explain the lack of windows.*

*Since the last thing she remembered was being pursued by bounty hunters armed with tranquilizer guns, it didn't take a genius to work out that they'd managed to snatch her. The tranqs were no doubt responsible for her headache and nausea.*

*An otherworldly breeze angrily swooshed around the cell but didn't unlock the door for her. That could only mean that there was a system in place—magickal or otherwise—that would trip an alarm in the event of an escape. The deity wouldn't trigger an alarm that would have hunters bearing down on Wynter until she'd shaken off the grogginess.*

*Weirdly, her connection to her magick felt weak. It was hard to verbalize, but it was sort of like when your arm went numb and you couldn't properly move it. She suspected that she'd be able to call on her magick, but not use it fast or efficiently. Which could be due to the drugs or some kind of spell, she wasn't sure.*

*Her monster shoved at her, wanting control; wanting the blood of its captors.* Yeah, me too. *While the deity calmed it with a mere brush* of air, Wynter silently assured the entity that she'd let it have its way when the right moment came along.

She pushed off the bed. Her belly rolled so viciously she balked. Ugh. "The drug they use is a son of a bitch, right?"

Wynter tracked the unfamiliar male voice to the cell on her left. Although the lighting was crap, she made out a good-looking guy with an unkempt mop of brown hair crouched on the hard floor. "You could say that," she said. It didn't help that the scents of rust, iron, sweat, and must hung in the air. Or that said air was hot, stale, and stifling.

He gestured at himself with his thumb. "The name's Clay."

For some reason, she wasn't so sure she believed him. "If you say so. Is that blood you're using?" she asked, realizing he was drawing symbols on the floor. Satanic symbols.

He held up a palm that sported a wicked slice. "Don't worry, it's my own."

"You're attempting to call on a demon?"

"Asmodeus hasn't let me down yet."

She didn't know what concerned her more. That he seemed so breezy at the idea of calling on a hell-bound demon to possess him, or that he'd clearly done it before. But all she said was, "All right."

Looking into the cell on her right, Wynter saw a beautiful Latina sitting on the bed lotus style, her eyes closed, her palms exposed.

"That's Delilah," 'Clay' told her. "She sometimes goes into meditative states to talk to her dead ancestor. She's apparently gonna ask Annis for advice."

"Annis?"

He smiled. "As in the Black Annis, yeah."

Wynter only blinked. Annis had earned her ominous title through her extensive use of blood magick and the many dark deeds she'd committed. Wynter therefore couldn't imagine why anyone would ask the dead witch for advice of any kind, but whatever.

Hoping to walk off the effects of the drug, Wynter did a few slow laps of her cell, examining every inch of it. Runes were etched into each iron bar. Magick-nulling ruins, she realized. More were etched into the wall and cement floor. Which meant that a captive could blast the cell with magick all they wanted—it would do no damage.

"You won't be here much longer," said 'Clay.' "I heard some mutterings earlier about how they're taking you to Aeon once their money's wired through."

"They won't be taking me anywhere. Dead people can't do anything." She expected him to let out a skeptical snort, but he instead eyed her with interest.

"My name's actually Xavier," he said.

"Wynter," she offered, planting her butt on the bed, beginning to feel somewhat better now that—

There was a loud plop further along the row of cells.

Someone gagged. "Jesus, Anabel, how in God's name can your shit smell that bad?" complained a female voice hoarse with age.

"I've been eating tasteless goop for days," a younger female voice defended. "What else is it gonna smell like?"

Knowing the stench would soon make its way to her, Wynter inwardly groaned.

A hoarse huff. "When you're not dropping bombs in that toilet you're crying or talking to yourself," groused the old woman. "I'm trying to grieve over here."

Another plop and then . . . "Well if you'd died on death row in a past life, you wouldn't be coping well with being locked up either. And if you miss your husband so much then maybe you shouldn't have killed him. No, don't say you didn't, Hattie. I heard the bounty hunters talking about it."

"You're no more innocent than I am, girl. I heard you went on a killing spree."

"That wasn't me. Well . . . it was. But it wasn't. My body is responsible. As is a particular part of my soul. But I am totally innocent."

Okay, that made not one bit of sense to Wynter.

Hinges creaked somewhere up ahead as a door swung open, and a wide beam of light sliced through the 'jail.'

*Silence instantly fell. Wynter went very still, her system going on high alert, her monster slinking even closer to her skin.*

*More creaks sounded as heavy footfalls descended a small set of stairs. Then more footfalls. And more.*

*"Christ, it reeks in here," a male griped.*

*Before long, heavy footsteps echoed along the stone walkway. Then three burly figures dressed all in black came into view. Wynter recognized them from earlier.*

*They halted on reaching her cell. The one who was armed with a tranquilizer gun smirked at her and let his gun clang along the iron bars.*

*The tallest of the trio pointed at her. "You. Up. Time to leave."*

*"I'd rather not use another dart on you, but I will if you try anything," the armed hunter warned. "It's up to you how this goes."*

*She slowly slipped off the bed and crossed to the door, her monster coiled to lunge.*

*The third hunter pressed the pad of his thumb against the lock. There was a loud buzz and then a horrible grating sound as the mechanical cell door slid open. He then clapped once and said, "Let's get moving, the people of Aeon don't like to be kept waiting and . . ." He frowned. "I think you've got something in your eye. Both eyes. It's . . . what the hell?"*

*Wynter felt her mouth curl. "This is probably gonna hurt a lot."*

\*

Her world had then gone black as her monster took over. When it had retreated, she'd found herself standing in the walkway with the remains of the bounty hunters lying at her feet. The deity had been swirling around her, Her otherworldly laugh bouncing off the walls and ringing with power.

More, Wynter had been covered in blood and gore, which was the norm for when she shifted back to her own form. Her monster tended to make a mess of itself in its bid to maim and eat its prey, and the shifting process was so abrupt and forceful that its 'mess' would blast outward, only to ricochet back onto Wynter's body.

As such, if asked, she would have said that the other captives would be terrified of her.

And she would have been wrong.

All four had been plastered against the door of their cell, their eyes wide, their mouths open, but they'd been more fascinated than anything else—even a naturally nervous Anabel.

It was after Wynter had busted open each cell to free them that Delilah shocked the hell out of her by declaring they should all go on the run together. The others had nodded, eager. That was when Wynter began to realize that none of them were entirely sane . . .

\*

*Knocking bits of bone and brain matter from her tee to the floor, Wynter took in each smiling face. "You can't be serious."*

*"My ancestor told me I'd live if I followed you," Delilah told her. "I plan on living. Ergo . . ."*

*Hattie began plucking gory clumps from Wynter's hair. "I think it's a good idea for us to band together. We'll be harder to track that way."*

*"And there's safety in numbers," added Xavier.*

*Anabel nodded. "I like safety. I like that my chances of survival will significantly increase if I'm part of a group that not only includes you but a deity."*

*"You guys all know what I am, right?" Wynter asked them. "You saw what just happened? You know I have people on my ass?"*

*Xavier waved that way. "We all have people on our asses. That's why it makes sense for us to combine forces. You're uber powerful, sure, but you still got caught. It'll be good for you to have us watching your back."*

\*

They'd been doing that for her ever since.

Wynter did the same for them. Although, honestly, she hadn't needed to save them from bounty hunters anywhere near as many times as she'd needed to save them from themselves. All things considered, though, she probably should have seen that coming.

# Chapter Five

Washed, dressed, and feeling refreshed after the best night's sleep she'd had in a while, Wynter headed downstairs and into the kitchen the next morning. She was immediately hit by the scents of eggs, toast, and fresh coffee.

Both Xavier and Anabel sat at the barn-wood dining table, digging into their food.

Delilah was leaning out of the window that overlooked the backyard. "*Hattie*," she yelled, all accusatory. "You said you'd given up smoking."

"I have!" Hattie claimed from outside.

"Woman, I can smell the weed."

"That's for the pain."

"The pain of what?"

"Fucking cliffhangers."

Huffing, Delilah straightened and shut the window. "Oh, morning, Priestess."

"Stop that." Wynter had no sooner taken a seat at the table than a mug of coffee and a plate of food was put in front of her. "Hmm, thanks. Where'd you get the eggs and stuff?"

"I woke up early and went on a mini grocery grab," said Delilah.

Xavier bit into his cream cheese bagel, and his eyelids drooped. "*Damn* I need more of these in my life."

Spooning her oatmeal, Anabel wrinkled her nose at him. "I have no idea how you can eat cream cheese. It's just *ew*."

A line formed between his brows. "You're constantly testing your own potions—some of which smell like armpits—but you can't handle cream cheese?"

"It's the devil's work."

He rolled his eyes. "You say that about everything you don't like."

Wynter frowned when Delilah joined them at the table with only a cup of tea. "You're not eating?"

"Already ate," replied Delilah. "I was hangry earlier, so I figured it'd be better for everyone if I filled my stomach there and then."

Considering the woman would argue with you over absolutely anything when operating on an empty stomach, Wynter would have to agree with her.

As she dug into her breakfast, she looked around the kitchen and noticed that Delilah had also made time to unpack her cauldron, mortar, and pestle. Glass jars of herbs, ground roots, seeds, and powders were set near them. Her homemade medicinal tea mixtures were no doubt tucked in a cupboard somewhere, along with her bottles of this and that.

Wynter suspected that Delilah had hurried to set her own bits and bobs around the kitchen because she'd wanted to claim a small area before Anabel had the chance to do the same. The blonde's cauldron, tools, and the typical ingredients she used for the potions were nowhere in sight, but they'd no doubt be neatly set at the other side of the kitchen before the day was over.

Delilah sipped her drink. "So, is anyone regretting that they've surrendered some rights to their soul? Please say no, because I really like this place. I don't want to leave."

Anabel shrugged one shoulder. "I haven't had a freak-out yet, but it'll eventually happen. Still, I won't ask to leave."

"Me neither," said Xavier around a mouthful of bagel.

"I don't like not being the *only* proud owner of my soul, but the situation isn't bothering me half as much as I thought it would," said Wynter. "Maybe it's because I know it isn't permanent and that I could reclaim those rights at any time."

"Why do you think the Ancients insist on that particular price tag?" asked Xavier. "Do you think owning rights to souls increases their power, or do you think it's a scare tactic meant to keep people in line?"

"No clue," replied Wynter. "It might be a bit of both."

"What do we think of Cain?" asked Delilah. "My opinion? He's hot as fuck. Man, I'd like me some of that *if* he wasn't one seriously scary dude. I was expecting 'scary,' after all Wynter told me about the Aeons and all the rumors we heard about the Ancients, but Cain still ruffled my fur."

"My hackles rose just the same," said Xavier.

Delilah slid her gaze to Wynter. "We gonna talk about how he eye-fucked you?"

Nope, not at all. Casually forking some scrambled eggs, Wynter said, "There was no eye-fucking."

Xavier grinned. "Oh, there was. I'm not sure that's a good thing, given he's an Ancient, but you definitely had his attention. You once warned me that the Aeons were very removed and didn't really *see* mortals. I didn't get what you meant until we walked into that parlor yesterday. Cain's the same."

Pausing, Xavier gestured at himself, Anabel, and Delilah as he added, "He saw us, spoke to us, listened to us, but he didn't focus on us anymore than he'd have focused on a speck of dust. We didn't really register on his radar. You, however . . . *you* he saw."

Unease settled in Wynter's gut. Not merely because she had an Ancient's attention, but because part of her stupidly liked it. Hey, she'd have to be dead not to be attracted to Cain. But he was everything she *shouldn't* want in a guy—dark, dangerous, pitiless. Sadly, her hormones didn't give a crap about that.

Anabel bit her lip. "Do you think he might have sensed that you're not simply a witch?"

"If he did, he doesn't know exactly *what* I am," said Wynter. "He'd have turned me away if that were the case. Or killed me. Whichever." She paused. "On a whole other note, we need to go job hunting."

Delilah looked at the wall clock. "Yes, we do. And soon."

Anabel cringed, her fingers flexing. "I-I don't know if I can. There are so many people, and I haven't been able to mentally map the place out yet. I want some time to settle in first."

Wynter touched her arm. "That's fine. You can watch over Hattie and keep her out of trouble." She frowned at the sound of voices yelling outside.

Anabel froze, her eyes widening. "Who's that?"

Wynter sighed. "Seems like our dear neighbors aren't opposed to screaming at each other first thing in the morning."

Delilah slipped off her chair and walked into the living room. "They also apparently aren't opposed to having a standoff outside our front gate. They've noticed me watching them and don't even care. Assholes."

"I'd rather not make enemies of two lycan packs, so we're going to have to handle this the smart way." Wynter looked at Anabel. "Do you have enough ingredients to get working on some potions that might help?"

The blonde nodded. "I brought plenty in my bag."

The back door opened with a creak, and Hattie padded inside. "What's with the shouting?"

"Lycans are arguing outside," Delilah explained, returning to the kitchen.

Hattie *hmph*ed. "An old woman should be able to enjoy a joint in peace. The damn book wrecked me, ending on a cliffhanger like that. And the heroine forgave the hero *far* too easily, in my opinion. She should have made him plead for forgiveness. I like a good, long grovel." She hefted herself onto a chair. "All my husbands groveled."

Delilah shot her a look. "Was this before or during the slow, excruciating deaths they endured courtesy of the 'special teas' you gave them?"

"During, mostly," Hattie replied.

Wynter smiled, shaking her head. It was hard to believe that the sweet, fragile-looking woman had ever harmed a single soul. "Well, let's go job hunting."

When she walked out of the house soon after, the lycans had stopped arguing but were standing in their own front yards exchanging snarls. Their predatory gazes shot to Wynter, Delilah, and Xavier—none of whom did anything more than spare them cursory glances. Wynter would deal with the lycans later. For now, she had more important shit to do.

She wished the others good luck on their job-hunting adventures and then made her way toward Cain's Keep, enjoying the feel of the artificial sun's warmth on her skin. She couldn't see much of the Keep, thanks to the stone, fortified walls that surrounded both it and the bailey. Stark and imposing, the walls had integrated bastions and watch towers.

Plenty of people passed her; none so much as tipped their chin her way. They merely stared, openly curious. She didn't get the sense that they were being rude. It was more like they were reserving judgment for the time being. Well, all right.

She walked through the arched opening in the stark walls and then found herself in the bailey. A courtyard lay in the center. Workshops, barns, and stables were on the right. Some sort of quarters were situated on the left, along with a brewery, a bakehouse, and—*aha*—the blacksmith's shop.

Ahead of it all sat the Keep. Unlike the curtain wall, it was constructed of black, medieval stone. Tall and intimidating, it loomed above all. Stained-glass windows—some small and square, some narrow and rectangular—dotted the stone edifice. It might have looked grim and gothic if each stone didn't shimmer with power.

The sight was as impressive as the dude who called it his home.

She wasn't gonna think about him, though. Getting her mind back on track, she crossed to the blacksmith's shop. It was small and hot, and the air was thick with the scents of molten iron and coal. Workbenches, forges, and other large equipment were scattered around. There were tools just . . . *everywhere.*

One side of the shop was wall-to-wall with weaponry—small, big, modern, medieval. Her mouth fell open. There was everything she could think of. Cutlasses, brass knuckles, claymores, long-swords, pickaxes, hatchets, crossbows, sledgehammers, javelins—it was all there.

God, she thought she might come.

Rafe would *love* the collection. He'd made her learn how to dodge and even snatch weapons before he'd ever allowed her to use one. As a child, she'd had to seize a dagger from him over and over and over in the space of an hour.

Studying the weapons in front of her, she didn't notice any runes or flecks of power ground into the blades. None were enchanted, then. Something she could easily change.

"Who are you?" a gruff voice demanded.

She turned to see a stout male glaring at her like she'd pissed in his shoes. Well, this was off to a good start.

The monster inside her raised its head slightly and eyed him carefully. Like her, it sensed that he was a berserker—an elite preternatural warrior whose race was all but extinct. Still, her monster wasn't intimidated; it settled back down, intending to merely observe.

"Wynter," she finally replied. "I'm guessing you're Grouch." She held out her hand. He only sneered at it.

"What do you want, witch?"

She lowered her arm. "A job. Here."

"Here?" He burst out laughing, scratching his belly. "If you tell me you're a smithy, you're nothing but a liar. You ain't got the muscle for it."

"I'm not a smithy, but I can improve your weapons. Make them . . . unique."

A broad-shouldered female who bore a slight resemblance to him strolled into the shop. "Pop, Dina says she ain't got . . . Who the fuck is this bitch?"

Oh, these two were simply charming.

He laughed again. "You won't believe this, Annette. Winifred over here wants to work for us. Says she can improve our weaponry."

The female let out a derisive snort. "We don't need no witch working for us. There's a strip club up on the surface. Why don't you go see if they're hiring?" With that, they both turned away, dismissing her. Annette headed to one of the workbenches while Grouch crossed to the forge.

Wynter sighed long and loud. "Hmm. Such a shame you want to lose custom. But hey, I get it if you're overworked. It happens."

Grouch's head snapped up. "Lose custom? You threatening to hex my shop?"

She frowned. "Who said anything about hexing?"

He grabbed a sword hanging from a peg and advanced on her fast, pointing it at her chin. "Witch, you fucking *dare*—" He jerked back as she conjured her own sword and blocked his move. His face went slack as his eyes landed on her weapon. "What in the love of God?"

Annette sidled up to him, staring at the sword. "Is that . . . ?"

"Black glass? Yes." Wynter angled it so that the light danced along its length. "There's nothing delicate about it, though. It's more durable than iron and sharper than any blade."

Grouch licked his lips. "I'll buy it from ya."

"It's not for sale," said Wynter.

"What are those runes on it?" asked Annette.

Wynter gave her a hard smile. "Don't you worry about those." She 'sent' her sword back to its sheath in the cottage. "You two have a good day now." She strode off. *Fuck them.* There were other blacksmith shops. She could try those. She would.

She did.

And each time, it went almost as badly as it did with Grouch. There was laughing and sneering and an outright refusal to hear what she meant by 'improving' their weapons.

Figuring *any* job would do, she sought out others and talked to several shop managers. All turned her away. And she concluded that there really were too many assholes in this world.

It wasn't merely that they'd been rude. It was that they'd once been in her position. They'd once been newcomers here, looking for work. People had obviously taken a chance on them, and yet they wouldn't give another newcomer that same chance.

Wynter headed to the surface of the town and searched for work there. She found none. She did, however, realize that someone was following her. The feeling hit her mere milliseconds before a very familiar breeze fluttered over her in warning.

Wynter didn't look back. She continued to walk casually along the path of the plaza. She stopped near the mouth of an alley, feigning being lost, and then began to walk down the aforementioned alley in search of an exit.

She'd reached the large barbed fence at the rear of it when she heard the heel of a shoe scuffing the pavement. She turned and found herself facing a bulky male with a mean scar slicing diagonally from his hairline to an eyebrow.

She jutted out her chin, going for belligerent. "Problem?"

He smirked. "Not anymore. I've been looking for you for some time. And now I have you."

The monster within her woke from its slumber and studied their enemy. Wynter would rather not free it here. Anyone could walk past the alley and see too much—she couldn't risk that. Sending it telepathic images, she showed it what she had in mind for this asshole, knowing from past experience that the bloodthirsty entity was occasionally happy to watch.

As he took a step toward her, she said, "I'm not going anywhere with you."

"Oh, you think I'm here to collect on the bounty? I am. Kind of. You see, you're wanted alive. But a mage has offered me yet more money to instead kill you. I'll never turn down more cash."

Irritation surged through her. She really should have executed the families of her killers *long* ago.

"He also wants me to make it hurt." Wicked fast, the male witch raised his hand and let out a gust of magick that sliced at her skin, sharp as a scalpel.

*Fucking ow.* Ignoring the pain, Wynter struck with her own magick. Toxic and scorching hot, it lashed his face and neck, leaving deep welts that sizzled like meat on a grill.

He retaliated fast while chanting under his breath, blasting her with blue fire. She jerked back, but the cold flames seared her lips and chin. Oh, this fucker was *going down.*

She whacked him with a heavy surge of magick that sent him colliding into a dumpster. Even as he slid to the floor, he hit her with blue fire again, but he hadn't moved fast enough—she'd already called to her sword and angled it just right so that the blade deflected the flames.

Then she was on him.

She could have made this quick, but . . . *nah.* She jammed her thumb against a bleeding welt on his face and sent a dart of magick straight into his bloodstream.

He cried out as an inky blackness slicked its way up his veins. His skin paled and softened at first, looking almost papery. But soon, it became red and swollen and veiny. He cursed in shock and pain as blood blisters formed over his body; some burst, giving off a cloying rank smell.

What happened next . . . yeah, it'd make anyone queasy. His flesh began to blacken. Dry up. Peel. Decay. The rotting magick ate at his body, including his lips, making his mouth look like an obscene hole in his face. His teeth cracked and crumbled, and two of his withered extremities fell off.

The otherworldly breeze that had earlier carried a warning now danced over Wynter's skin, humming with approval. Similarly, the monster within her settled once more, satisfied with how she'd handled the situation.

Just as the inky blackness in his veins reached the witch's scalp, his eyes darted to the side of her now-burning face and widened almost comically.

Knowing her mark was visible, Wynter gave him a bright smile. "Yeah, you went and *fucked up.* I could have killed you quickly but, as you can now see, making people hurt . . . well, it's what I'm built for." And so she waited for the life to fade from his eyes before she sliced off his head.

\*

Walking up the path toward the cottage a short while later, Wynter puffed out a breath. Dealing with the male witch had been . . . well, fun, to be honest. But it hadn't exactly improved her day, considering she'd failed to find work. Figuring the job-seeking was a waste of time, she'd decided to head home after using one of Anabel's nifty potions to disintegrate the witch's body. Wynter had used a separate potion to heal her wounds.

The blonde insisted on them carrying 'evidence ridding potions,' paranoid that death would come for them any moment and that they'd need to cover their asses. It was at times like this when Wynter was glad of it.

Strolling into the cottage, she found both Delilah and Xavier slouched on the plush sofa. "Any luck?"

Delilah pulled a face. "Nu-uh. I went to all the herbalist stores. None of the witches want an outsider working for them, and they were seriously snarky. I almost had to smack a bitch down."

Xavier rubbed at his nape. "The witches I spoke to were just as reluctant to hire an outsider. I asked about the job opening in a bar on the surface, but the mage who ran it said I'd have to join his conclave—apparently, they'll take in any magick user."

Delilah pulled at her curls. "I tried applying for other jobs—waitressing, bartending, stuff like that. No joy. People were like, 'We don't know you or the Priestess who'd vouch for you, so no.'"

"Some said the same to me," said Xavier. "Hell, I couldn't even get a position as a stable hand unless I'd agree to work three months for free while they 'got to know me.'"

"You know about horses?" asked Delilah.

His face softened. "Used to have one back when I was a kid."

"Really?"

"No, not really."

Delilah flapped her arms. "Then why say it? Why lie?"

"Maybe I just like to hear myself speak."

Wynter sank into the armchair. "I had no luck finding employment either, and I'm not getting the sense that that will change anytime soon. So ... I guess we could each do what we usually do to make money. Only this time, we join together and start an official business. We could run the whole thing from home, since we now have a permanent base."

Xavier sat up straighter. "Now that's an idea."

Delilah nodded. "Hattie and Anabel would be up for it. Especially since it means they won't have to leave the cottage."

"Some of the local business owners might not be too happy," began Xavier, "but since a lot of them were rude as fuck to me today, I can't say I care."

No, neither could Wynter. Mentally running through everything they'd need, she asked him, "Do you still have that tent you often held your tarot readings in?"

His mouth curved. "I do. I could pitch it in the yard whenever I do readings." He dabbled in cartomancy, and he was damn good at it. It was the one time you could guarantee he wouldn't lie to you. "Where would you do your thing?"

She twisted her mouth. "The shed in the backyard might work. Anyone know if it's empty?"

"Never checked." Xavier stood. "Let's go find out."

Outside, they pulled open the wooden shed door. Dust motes danced in the air, and the scents of rust, dirt, and sun-warmed wood greeted her. She ignored all that and studied the building. It wasn't too small or cramped, which was good. It also wasn't in bad condition.

Yes, she could use this. It would need a good clean, of course, but Anabel could whip up a brew that was better than any bleach. First, though, Wynter would need to empty the shed. That wouldn't take long, since only the most basic backyard tools were stuffed inside it.

Before she got started on all that, though ... "We need to run this plan by the others and make sure we're right in thinking that they'll both be up for this," she said, turning back to the cottage.

"They'll be up for it," said Xavier, following her. "You know ... I don't have to stick with just card readings."

Sensing where this was going, Wynter shook her head. "No."

He frowned. "People like talking to the dead. They pay good money for it."

"No." Because, while Xavier had mastered the ability to communicate with spirits, he needed to use a conduit to speak with them. And that conduit was always a corpse. "We're not storing dead bodies in our yard."

"Why not? They don't smell that bad."

"Ugh, *yeah*, they do. Also, they freak people out. And the lycans will whine like babies, since their enhanced sense of smell will be tortured by the stench. So, no mediumship."

He huffed. "Fine."

"And no holding false seances either."

"Oh, come on."

Halting, Wynter turned to face him with a sigh. "Remember we talked about right and wrong? Well, conning people into thinking you're communicating with their loved ones is *not* anyone's definition of 'right.'"

"My clients always walk away happy. Isn't that what's important?"

"No, Xavier, it's not." She jabbed a finger toward him. "No seances." With that, she headed into the cottage via the back door.

In the kitchen, she gathered them all together and ran the plan past Hattie and Anabel. Both were up for it. Anabel loved the idea of hanging in the kitchen all day doing what she did best and, in the process, being able to avoid people. Hattie adored feeding others and hearing they enjoyed her food. Mostly, though, she loved the idea of making her own money so she could feed her book addiction.

Wynter turned to Delilah. "Make a list of all the ingredients you guys are going to need. Then I'll need you to go shopping."

Delilah's lips curved. "Shopping is one of the things I do best."

"First, well, you should know that a male witch just tried to kill me."

"A male witch just tried to *what*?"

*

Although he heard footfalls approaching, Cain didn't look up and wait for his visitor to come into view. He kept his gaze fixed on the sleek black serpent that slowly slithered along the ground near his feet, its unblinking eyes locked on him.

Maxim cleared his throat. "I'm sorry to intrude, Sire, I know you did not wish to be disturbed. But the oracle wishes to speak with you. She says it's important."

Cain felt his lips begin to flatten. "How important?" Because Demetria's definition of that particular word didn't always cohere with his own.

"She insisted you will want to hear this."

Inwardly sighing, Cain finally looked up. "Then I suppose you should escort her to me."

The aide hesitated. "She doesn't like the garden, Sire. The snakes make her nervous."

"I know."

Maxim's lips quirked and he shook his head. "I'm not sure I'll ever understand why you find people's fear so amusing." He turned on his heel and disappeared down the twisting path.

Careful not to step on the serpent now slinking around his feet, Cain crossed to the wrought-iron bench and sat. A white satin moth fluttered past him and settled on the moss-covered wall ruin. Fatal mistake. He could see the head of yet another snake peeking through the wall's arched, glassless window; it hadn't failed to notice the insect.

Cain cricked his neck, his mood a little less black than it had been when he first entered the garden. There had been no trigger for the change in his mood. But, then, there never was. It simply happened.

And he'd known it would be best for him to not be around others until the dark cloud passed.

The sooner he hit the reboot button, the better. But not until all his ducks were in a row. And definitely not until he'd coaxed Wynter into his bed. It wasn't as if he could afford to wait. Being mortal, she'd no longer be alive when he next woke. The thought . . . it bothered him.

He'd never envied mortals their short lifespan. No, they had their own version of immortality—their souls returned again and again. Cain's kind? Once they were dead, they were dead. And since he had no wish to quite simply cease to exist, he didn't begrudge the curses of immortality. Especially when Resting gave him a much needed reprieve whenever necessary. The aftermath could be annoying, though—waking to new faces, catching up on all he'd missed, seeing so many changes around him. It could be disorientating.

Well, disoriented was far better than the dark state of mind he continually found himself in lately. Being here helped. Few people ever bothered him when he was in his garden. Mostly because the place wasn't exactly safe. Nor was it all that welcoming.

A lot of people didn't understand how he could relax here. Personally, he didn't understand why bright, attractive gardens were considered peaceful. But then, people tended to equate beauty with *goodness* when, in truth, the two didn't always go together.

Soon, Maxim reappeared with the oracle in tow. The tall, Hispanic woman was one of the residents who'd sold her soul to Cain. It was longevity she'd craved, terrified of aging; hating each wrinkle that already lined her face. Really, the red mark on her cheek detracted from the blemishes. It was a mark that said she was Favored by a particular deity. In her case, it was Nemesis. Any witches Favored by Her would receive precognitive visions from the deity, hence why they were referred to as oracles.

Right then, Demetria's brown gaze nervously darted around. A delicate shudder rushed down her spine as she spotted a python dangling from a thick tree branch.

Cain felt a smile warm his chest. If she had any clue what lived inside him, she would not find those serpents so terrifying in comparison.

Sliding her eyes to him, she bowed slightly. "Sire."

"Demetria," he greeted. "What brings you here? For your sake, I hope it truly is as important as you insinuated."

"It is, I assure you of that." She waited until Maxim had left before moving closer and adding, "Something ... something is wrong."

"Wrong how?"

"My gift is failing me." She twiddled her fingers. "I *feel* that something is coming. I cannot tell if it is good or bad. I see *nothing*."

He felt his eyes narrow. "Nothing at all?"

"No. That never happens when there is such urgency behind a feeling I have. A vision always accompanies it." A shaky breath left her. "I consulted the bones. The reading confirmed that my gut is correct. But still, I see nothing. I believe I am being blocked."

"By someone here?"

"I do not believe it is a person. More like a presence. A power. It is jamming the frequency of my gift. Purposely."

He twisted his mouth. He hadn't sensed any such presence. But then, if something was powerful enough to block an oracle, it was powerful enough to remain undetected. "When was the last time you had a vision of any sort?"

"Six days ago. It was nothing consequential."

"And this feeling you got that something was coming ... when did that hit you?"

"Yesterday morning. I didn't report it to you straight away because I had hoped a vision would come to me if I waited. But it didn't." She sighed. "Being unable to see what lies ahead ... it feels like I have been cut off from a part of myself. I worry that Nemesis has forsaken me."

"I doubt it's anything as dramatic as that. If it was, you would no longer have that mark on your face."

74

"I tried reaching out to Her. She did not respond to my calls."

Cain shrugged. "Deities tend to do as they please." He pursed his lips. "We'll keep an eye on the situation. It's all we really can do."

Swallowing, she nodded. "I will let you know if . . ." She trailed off at the sound of Maxim's muted voice and the click-clacking of heels along the paving stones.

Cain barely resisted the urge to grind his teeth. He knew the rhythm of that walk. Knew exactly who was coming. And he wasn't in the mood to deal with them.

Mere moments later, Ishtar sauntered into view, a furious Maxim close behind her.

She beamed at Cain. "Such a lovely afternoon, isn't it?" She spared Demetria a disinterested glance.

Recognizing the female Ancient's voice, the monster inside Cain opened one eye. At one time, it might have perked up in interest. Now, utterly indifferent to her presence, it allowed its eyelid to once more drift shut.

His cheeks red, Maxim looked at him. "I'm sorry, Sire, I explained that you had company but—"

"It is not you who needs to apologize," Cain told him, a thread of menace in his voice.

Ishtar let out an airy chuckle. "I merely saw no reason why I couldn't announce my own arrival. It seems silly when I've spent so much time here over the eras."

No, she'd intruded because she'd wanted to know who his 'company' was and if said company was female. "You will apologize to Maxim."

Ishtar stared at Cain for a long moment. "You are not serious."

"Oh, I'm very serious. You don't get to be dismissive toward my hirelings. You don't get to make their jobs difficult. You will treat them with respect, or you will not come here at all. Now, apologize to Maxim."

Twin flags of red stained her cheeks as her cornflower-blue eyes bore into Cain, hard as diamonds. There was the smallest hint of arousal in their depths. She hated when he made any demands of her, but a part of her got off on it. Which was an annoyance for him, since he didn't wish to have such an effect on her.

"Do it now, or leave," he said.

Ishtar gave the aide a sickly sweet mockery of a smile. "I am so very, very sorry, Maximus. Yes, yes, that isn't actually your name, but it suits you so much better than Maxim. Or Maxie could work, if you're open to that."

As apologies went, that was probably the best Maxim would get, even if there wasn't a droplet of sincerity in it.

Demetria cleared her throat. "I will take my leave, Sire." She inclined her head at Ishtar, who didn't deign her a glance.

"Maxim will escort you out." Once the two had disappeared down the path, Cain cut his gaze to Ishtar, his jaw hardening. "You go too far."

"And *you* used to be more fun," she shot back. She bent slightly, making her blonde ringlets tumble forward, as she smiled at a snake that zipped through the long grass. Cain inwardly snorted. If she thought she was subtle in her attempt to flash her cleavage, she was wrong.

She returned her focus to him. "You are obviously in a frightful mood, so I will not bother staying long. I came to see if perhaps you would like to escort me to the festivities tomorrow evening."

"No, I wouldn't."

She frowned. "Whyever not? It would give us a chance to catch up. We haven't spoken much since I woke. We have arrived at events together before."

"That was a very long time ago."

"A time when we were . . . close, yes."

They'd never really been 'close.' Not in an emotional sense, at least. Neither had ever cared for the other. What brought them together had been simple: He'd been attracted to the untamed passion for life she'd once had, and she'd enjoyed that he didn't fall all over himself to please her the way so many other men did.

The trouble was that Ishtar wasn't interested in an equal partnership, and Cain wasn't interested in being a mere consort who obeyed her every directive. In that sense, their on-and-off relationship had been more of a battle for dominance. But it had given them both a reprieve from the relentless boredom that plagued every Ancient. For a while, anyway. He'd soon tired of it. Of her. Of things always ending the same way.

"It's not a time in my life that I intend to repeat," he told her. "I've been clear on that."

"'Rude' is what you have been. And unnecessarily so." She came closer, swaying her hips. "I have been asleep for over three centuries. Surely you missed me just a little."

He sighed. "If you need someone to shine your ego, I suggest you find Solomon."

She made a face. "He gives me my own way in everything. He does not push back or demand to be counted. Not like you. You always challenged me. I need that in a man. Need someone who is my equal."

Cain gave her a bored look. "Do you really think I'm going to fall for this? It's not like I fell for it last time you came to me swearing that you wanted a true partnership." He'd almost laughed, recognizing it for the lie that it was.

"I *do* want us to be equals, I just do not know how to have a relationship like that. You could show me—"

"Why are you pushing this when there are dozens of men out there who'll tell you exactly what you want to hear?"

"Because they do not *know* me. You might look down on me in some ways, but at least you know me. See me. Sometimes we just need to be seen. And you . . . you are the first person I thought of when I woke. The person I most looked forward to talking with. But you won't even make time for me. You won't even give us a chance."

"And what would be the point, Ishtar? You like to be seen. Until you don't. Until you want to pretend you're not riddled with flaws and vulnerabilities like everyone else, and so you then lash out at the people closest to you to drive them away. I'm not signing up for that."

"All I ever wanted—"

"Was me on a leash, just like the souls you own," he finished. "That's never going to happen."

She studied him hard. "You are different than you were before I chose to Rest. You hear everything I am saying, but you are not touched by it, are you? It's not even that you don't care, it's that you *can't*." She swallowed. "I remember that stage. Emotion often just slips right off you. It does not always take hold." She took a step toward him. "You can talk to me, you know." She sighed when he didn't speak. "But you won't, will you?"

No. She'd never been someone he confided in. Not even when they shared a bed.

"Have you ever really trusted anyone, Cain?"

"Yes." Very few of those people hadn't let him down.

Sorrow lined her face. "But I am not one of them, am I?"

"I'm not buying the oh-so sad act. You don't trust me any more than I trust you."

Her face went hard in an instant. "Fine." She notched up her pointed chin. "If you change your mind about tomorrow evening, I will be at home."

Yeah, and if he turned up to escort her anywhere, she'd sniff at him and declare that she'd already procured someone else to accompany her.

She flounced off, putting extra sway in her hips.

Unmoved, he looked away.

Maxim reappeared, his lips thin. "Again, Sire, I'm sorry that Ishtar—"

Cain waved off the unnecessary apology. "It's fine, Maxim." He stretched out his legs. "Tell me ... where's my new witch? The Priestess who insists she isn't a Priestess."

He blinked. "The Bloodrose coven moved into the cottage between the quarreling lycan packs, Sire. I heard ..."

Cain arched a brow. "Yes?"

Maxim briefly averted his gaze. "Grouch has announced to one and all that she intends to hex his shop."

"Hex his shop?"

"He refused to hire her, and she apparently made it clear that he would lose custom. I don't believe she'd do as he claims, though," Maxim quickly added.

"No, she's smarter than that," Cain agreed. A hex would have not only the berserkers turning on her but the town's population reluctant to trust her. Wynter didn't strike him as a person who'd recklessly make enemies or isolate her coven.

"She probably meant to do exactly what she's done—rile him."

"Perhaps." Cain paused. "I wouldn't have expected her to seek a job at a blacksmith's shop."

"Having spent twenty minutes with Wynter and her coven, I would say they're the type of people who will do many things we won't expect."

"My gut would agree with you on that." Cain pushed to his feet. "Bring her to me, Maxim."

The aide stilled. "You're not ... you're not going to discipline her, are you?"

"No, I don't believe Grouch's claims." Cain felt a smile tug at his mouth. "But *she* doesn't know that, does she?"

# Chapter Six

Nibbling on her lower lip, Anabel handed Wynter a box of vials. "Are you *sure* you wouldn't rather give them something lethal?"

"They're being loud, not threatening," said Wynter.

Anabel looked toward the living room window that gave them a clear view of their quarreling neighbors. "But they have claws and fangs and can shift into monstrous beasts."

"What's your point?"

"They could kill you. They could *kill us all.*" She rubbed at her throat. "They've probably already planned our murders step by step. Being torn apart is *not* a fun way to die, trust me. I once died during a wolf attack. Lycans are even bigger and deadlier than full-blooded wolves."

"You were attacked by a wolf?"

"It was rabid. My guards didn't even do anything to help me. Personally, I think they let me die on purpose because they hated my father." Anabel's nose wrinkled. "He tended to fly into murderous rages. Even killed my brother while caught up in one. And launching the Massacre of Novgorod didn't do his rep any favors."

"The Massacre of—Wait, are you talking about Ivan the Terrible?"

"Well . . . I just called him Papa."

Wynter gave her head a little shake. "Okay. Well. Thanks for sharing." She tightened her grip on the box of vials. "I'll be back in half an hour. Don't worry, everything will be fine."

Outside, Wynter casually walked down the path toward the gate. She was totally ignored by the two males yelling in each other's face while several lycans fanned out behind each of them. She'd heard enough of their disputes to know that the tallest was Diego and the other was Elias. They were also both Alphas.

Wynter tutted. "Now boys, is all that shouting really necessary?"

Diego snarled at her, his fists clenched. "This ain't your business. Go toddle back inside."

"Now that wasn't nice."

"*I'm* not nice."

"I'm thinking she already noticed that, asshole," snarked Elias. He might be shorter than the other Alpha, but he was more powerfully built.

Opening the gate, Wynter began, "What I'm wondering is ... why do you argue amongst yourselves so much when, in doing so, you're giving the vampires what they want? I mean, they hate that you outnumber them, right? It suits them that you're all at each other's throats."

"I don't care what does or doesn't suit them fuckers," Diego sneered.

She hummed. "I don't think that's true. I don't see *how* you could really be so indifferent to them. I've heard what derogatory stuff they say about lycans. Their kind hunted yours at one time, right? Their sharper senses were your downfall. There was even a period when they captured, brainwashed, and used a bunch of you as their guards. That's why they still call your kind their bitches. And don't they still tease you for having weaker senses?"

Diego's nostrils flared. "There a point to this conversation?"

"Yes. You see, I can help you. One of my crew, Anabel, is *extremely* talented when it comes to potions. She makes all sorts of weird and wonderful brews. She'll actually be selling them as of tomorrow. Some will be designed for demons, some for vamps, some for your kind etc., etc." Wynter pulled a vial of green liquid out of the box. "This baby here can sharpen lycan senses."

Elias snorted. "Bullshit."

"No bullshit," she said. "The effect wouldn't be permanent, of course. It would last about three months. Either of you guys want this free sample?"

Diego gave her a brittle smile. "My parents warned me not to accept potions from strangers."

"It isn't poisoned or anything. Here, I'll prove it." Wynter pulled off the small cork and took a sip of the minty concoction. Of course, nothing happened. "There. See. All good."

"Did it work?" Elias asked.

"On me? No. This is designed to work strictly on lycans." She looked from one Alpha to the other, a challenge in her eyes. "So, which of you wants to try it? I guess this is where we find out who's the biggest, baddest Alpha around—"

Diego snatched the vial and knocked back the potion. For a few moments, he merely stood there, clearly dubious. Then his back snapped straight, he blinked rapidly, and shook his head hard. The tension slipped from his body, and his eyes widened. "*Fuck.*"

Wynter smiled. "My girl's good, huh?" She took another from the box and offered it to Elias, who didn't hesitate to accept and drink the potion.

His physical reaction was much the same as Diego's. "Jesus Christ."

"You can call those freebies," she told them. "Like I said, the effects will last about three months. You want more after that? Well, I can be persuaded to sell them to your two packs at a discount, what with us being neighbors and all. I can even be persuaded to ensure that Anabel doesn't create a sense-sharpening potion for vampires. That way, you'll have an edge on them."

Diego narrowed his eyes. "And what do you want in return?"

She shrugged. "It's really pretty simple. Stop arguing outside my home. I realize that neither of you want to cross the other's territorial lines and that this strip of land here is the only neutral ground between your turfs, but it's also *my home* now. And Anabel . . . she can be a little jumpy. Most things make her nervous. Including all the yelling. If you keep that up, she'll stop making those babies. And who could blame her for that?"

Elias twisted his mouth. "We'd get a discount, and she'd agree not to make potions like this for the vamps?"

Wynter dipped her chin. "Yup."

Elias finally nodded. "We're gonna want more of those."

One of the lycans behind Elias sidled up to him. "It's *that* good?"

"It's *that* good," Elias confirmed.

"As I said, they'll be on sale as of tomorrow." She cut her gaze to a female near Diego. "Nice nail art. I'll bet it comes right off after you shift, though, right?"

"Obviously," she said, though not *too* rudely.

"Another of my crew whips up her own bespelled cosmetics and stuff," Wynter told her. "She makes nail polish that will not only actually stay on when you shift but still be perfectly intact when you shift back."

Her lips parted. "You're shitting me."

Wynter smiled. "Nope. She made it for herself. She can shape-shift, so if you see a small black cat with painted claws, that'll be Delilah." Really, Delilah could shift into a cat of *any* size, but she mostly used the form of a domestic cat ... unless deep in battle. "She'll be selling her products tomorrow, too."

"Where?"

"Here. Baked goods will also be up for purchase, thanks to Hattie. Xavier's *the best* at tarot card readings, if you're interested in those. And me? Well, if you have a weapon you'd like to be made a little more ... interesting than it already is, bring it to me. We'll be running a sort of one-stop-shop. You should check it out. Now, I gotta go, I have some more free samples to give out. You all enjoy the rest of your day."

Wynter sought out leaders of several species—minus those who'd refused to employ her or her crew—and offered them free samples of potions that would appeal to them, telling them all about the upcoming one-stop shop. Each interaction went pretty well, since the leaders all tried the samples and were impressed by the effects.

The box of vials empty, she headed back home. She was approaching the corner of her street when she noticed Maxim.

Spotting her, he altered his course and made a beeline for her. "Priestess."

"Wynter is fine. How are you, Maxim?"

"I'm well, thank you. Cain would like to see you."

Being sent for like this couldn't be good. But even as her stomach sank, her hormones perversely fanned themselves.

"Follow me," Maxim added. "I'll escort you to him."

Trying not to feel like she was walking the damn plank, she trailed after him as he led her through the bailey and toward the Keep. Curiosity dimmed her nervousness. She'd wondered just what it would be like inside. Wondered what sort of home would appeal to someone like Cain.

Passing two guards, she and Maxim strode through the thick wooden doors. As they walked through the arched halls of the castle, she saw that it was a fusion of both the old and the new. She wouldn't have thought the two styles would go well together, but it somehow worked.

Even with the modern amenities and state-of-the-art features, the place still had an Old World feel with the carved columns, ornamental arches, beautiful flooring, and the domed, frescoed ceilings. The Keep also boasted an impressive collection of paintings, sculptures, ceramics, and other artwork.

Maxim led her outside, across a courtyard, and through tall iron gates that made her think of a cemetery. "Stay on the path. It's important."

"Okay." She trailed behind him once more, and then they were in a garden that was like no garden she'd *ever* seen before. It was gothic and brooding.

Flowers were everywhere in shades of black, scarlet red, and burgundy, including Black Dahlia and Bleeding Heart Dicentra. There were also some night-blooming plants that she knew would glow and give off intoxicating scents after dark.

She recognized some ancient herbs that were often used in forbidden magick spells. There were also lots of vines on the wall ruins that were scattered around. It wasn't until one of the vines moved that she realized not all *were* vines. Some were snakes.

Choosing to ignore that little nugget, she continued admiring her surroundings as she wandered down the twisted path. She particularly liked the moss-covered urns and gargoyles that bordered a bog-like pond. A complicated rockery caught her eye, and she realized that all the rocks were actually skull-shaped.

Finally, she and Maxim reached a little nook. Seated on a wrought-iron bench, Cain locked his dark eyes on her. Her insides again did that twisting thing, and warmth bloomed low. The damn immortal stirred up everything feminine inside her.

It wasn't only his looks that did it for her. She was self-aware enough to know that what really rung her bell was that Cain wore power. *Embodied* it. It was in the depths of his eyes, the timbre of his voice, every single sensual move he made. And, well, she'd always had a weakness for dangerous men. It would no doubt one day be her downfall.

Her inner monster eyed him but didn't move. Not quite hiding from him, but wanting to watch him without being sensed . . . like a tiger might observe its prey from the underbrush.

"The Bloodrose Priestess, as you requested," said Maxim.

She felt her eyelid twitch. "Really, Wynter is fine."

Cain nodded at him. "Thank you, Maxim."

The aide left the way he'd come, and then she and the Ancient were alone. Apart from the many serpents nearby, that was.

"This place is amazing," she said.

Cain tilted his head. "Most don't use the word 'amazing' when they describe my garden."

"Then they're not really seeing it." They were probably too

distracted by the obvious danger, because many of the snakes here were highly venomous.

He hummed. "How are you liking Devil's Cradle so far?"

"It has exceeded my expectations."

He stared at her intently and ... Gah, she didn't like it. Nor did she like the way her skin heated or her hormones were playing fucking hopscotch. Not much rattled Wynter, but this chemistry spooked the shit out of her. It made her feel vulnerable and off-balance.

He sort of ... uncurled as he stood, sensuous as the snakes surrounding him, and prowled toward her. She cursed her pulse for quickening, for responding to all that latent strength and contained power. She felt both threatened and turned on at the same time. So much sexual tension thickened the air she was surprised it didn't hurt to breathe it in.

His nostrils flared as he stood before her. "I like the smell of your magick. Jasmine and black pepper. It hums with chaos. So much potential for destruction." His gaze flitted over her face, broody and far too perceptive. "You like the taste of all that darkness, don't you?"

To be truthful, yes, she did. She liked what she could do. She liked how easily she could do it.

"Would you remove death's mark from your magick if you could?"

She licked the inside of her lower lip. "Anyone would if they could, right?"

His mouth hitched up. "Such an evasive answer. You're rather fond of giving those." He paused. "So, you threatened to hex Grouch's shop?"

Blinking, she almost drew back. "I didn't threaten him in any way. He *accused* me of meaning to hex his shop."

"Hmm, not according to him."

"He's really saying that?"

"To all who'll stand still long enough to listen," Cain confirmed.

"Knowing it would eventually get back to you, and that you'd summon me to deal with it, right?" *Motherfucker.*

She was *not* getting punished for something she didn't do. But that might well happen, and she might have to grin and bear it, because she couldn't leave this place yet. The problem was ... she didn't believe the entity inside her would stand for that shit.

Really, she wasn't so sure that she'd successfully manage it either. It wasn't in her nature to stand down, admit defeat, or allow herself to be intimidated—hence why she again held his gaze steadily.

"Ah, there's that hunter stare again," he said, an almost imperceptible note of amusement in his tone. Like she was a puppy barking at a Rottweiler stupidly thinking she stood a chance against it.

"The what stare?"

He twirled a strand of her hair around his finger. It wasn't a flirtatious move—she sensed that right off. No, there was a challenging glint in his eyes. He was testing her, pushing her, trying to make her uncomfortable.

"When we last spoke, you watched me with the stare of a hunter," he said. "You saw the level of danger in front of you, but you remained calm. Collected. At ease. You're doing it again now. And like last time, you're also ready to lunge at a moment's notice. Even knowing that I'm far more powerful than you, you'd still strike first if you thought I meant you harm, wouldn't you?"

"I have no idea why that makes you smile." And damn if that smile didn't make her best parts tingle.

"You won't need to act in your own defense today, little witch. You said you didn't threaten Grouch. I believe you. After all, you wouldn't lie to me, would you?" His gaze dipped to her mouth, which promptly dried up.

Why yes, yes, she would lie to him if it was necessary. But she couldn't admit that, so she gave him a different truth that *sort* of answered his question. "I own my shit. If I had made any such threat, I wouldn't have denied it."

"No?"

"No."

Cain studied the witch's face, caught the glimmer of secrets in her eyes. "Hmm, I'm not sure I believe that." Oh, she might very well be a person who would confess to and take responsibility for her actions, but he didn't doubt for a moment that she'd bullshit him if she felt the situation warranted it. She was fearless enough to take that risk—he knew that from the glimpse he'd gotten of the core of her being.

"I like your soul," he said. "I've never before touched one that has so much to give. It beats with grit, inner strength, guts, and drive. It isn't stained with foul emotions like so many I own or have rights to. It might be undead, but it's not a flickering candle that's close to burning out. It's a roaring fire. Black fire."

"You talk about it like it's a pretty, shiny new toy."

Hmm, maybe he did. Cain liked to collect rare things—art, books, objects. He'd never had rights to an undead soul before, nor one that held so much promise. "I'm sure it'll be a fun toy to play with."

She frowned. "What does that mean?"

Oh, she'd find out soon enough.

"There's nothing special about my soul," she said. "I'd bet most of them are 'roaring fires.' You have people coming to you all the time to make deals, so you're used to seeing the souls of those who are greedy or envious or chronically dissatisfied. You've forgotten that there's more to people than that."

"Not all those who bargain their soul do so for selfish reasons. Some wish to save the life of a loved one, find safety for those they care for, or perhaps locate a person who has gone missing from their lives. Desperation is a powerful feeling. It can make a person do all sorts of things they'd never otherwise do."

Biting her lip, she conceded his point with an incline of her head.

Seeing her teeth digging into that fleshy lower lip, he was tempted to tug it free with his thumb and then replace her teeth with his own. His body tightened at the thought.

It felt good to really *want* something. More, it felt good to feel that there'd be some satisfaction in having it. After eons of nothing being out of your reach, you ceased to yearn for things with any true intensity because there was no real gratification to be had from always getting what you desired. But Wynter . . . he fucking burned for her.

And he would have her.

He'd need to be careful with this one, though. She was sharp. Too sharp. He had more secrets than he knew what to do with.

"Do you ever get people asking to have their soul returned to them?" she asked.

"Yes. Some find that whatever they sold their soul for wasn't quite as gratifying as they'd expected. That particularly happens with fame. Once they tire of its price, they come crawling back to me looking to wangle out of their contract, fairly oozing regret. A wasteful emotion, really."

"You don't have any regrets at all?"

"They tend to eat at a person. If you're going to live an eternally long life, you can't afford to have regrets. They'd drive you insane."

"Some might say you are insane."

He felt his mouth twitch. "Oh, they might. They do. They may even be right."

"You don't sound too concerned about that."

He chuckled. "On an entirely different note . . . the sole male in your coven, is he your lover?"

A line formed between her brows, and she shook her head.

Satisfied gripped his gut. "Good."

"Is it?"

"Yes. I don't like it when things are in my way."

Wynter stilled as the implications of that sank in. Her body was totally up for dancing the horizontal tango with him. But nothing about that would be wise.

He moved closer, boldly pushing into her personal space. "Just so there are no misunderstandings, I want you. I want your taste in my mouth. I want my cock in your body. I want my fingers in your mind."

"My mind?" she echoed.

"When you've lived as long as I have, very little can surprise you. Even less can pique your interest. People become too easy for you to read. Too predictable to be entertaining. But you . . . you're difficult to get a handle on. Even now, nothing in your expression is telling me what you're thinking. It's incredibly frustrating. I want to be up here," he added, tapping her temple.

Yeah, well, she didn't want him up there. As for spending a night in his bed . . . that idea held *way* too much appeal for her liking. She embraced her sexuality; she wasn't afraid to explore or admit to her desires—there was a certain power in that, really. But this wasn't a man who'd quite simply fuck her. He was far too dominant, far too used to control, for it to be that simple. "I'm not interested in warming your bed."

"You're interested. Oh, you don't look it. I don't see any trace of arousal on your face." He very gently tapped her cheek with his finger. "But I can read your body much better than I can read your expressions. You let people see only what you want them to see, don't you? It makes me wonder what else you're hiding."

She was hiding that she'd reached the unfortunate conclusion that she was fucked in the head. Wynter wasn't used to being at a disadvantage. Her magick was a force that was almost as dark and deadly as the monster inside her—both those things made her very good at killing. Plus, she was trained to take down any breed of preternatural, and she was confident in her ability to take care of herself.

But as she stood in front of this immortal, she knew that none of it meant anything. He could overpower her in an instant. And that only made her want him more. So it was official—she was indeed fucked in the goddamn head.

"You'll be attending the festivities tomorrow evening, yes?"
She nodded. "Yes."

"Good. We'll talk more about this, then. Or maybe we'll skip the talking."

She went still as something seemed to *stroke* over her very being. Something old and dark and powerful. And the sensation . . . it was like nothing she'd ever before experienced. It was as if every nerve-ending went up in flames. Little bumps swept over her skin, and cold fingers danced down her spine.

Cain hummed. "I'd wondered if your soul might be unresponsive, what with it being undead, but it isn't. Far from it. When we last talked, you asked if my being able to touch your soul meant I could cause you pain. I can. But I can also make you come harder than you ever have in your life. There's nothing more sensitive than the soul. It's just one big erogenous zone." He gave her a pointed look. "Think on that." He turned his back on her—a silent dismissal.

Shaken in more ways than one, she took the hint and left, following the winding, twisting path. She didn't speak as Maxim escorted her out of the Keep, her thoughts a massive jumble.

She'd known Cain wanted her, so his declaration hadn't come as some great shock. It hadn't been entirely expected, though, either. When a being was as *other* as Cain, you couldn't really 'expect' anything of them.

Damn, she still felt a little tingly from when he'd stroked her soul. Stroked. Her. Soul.

Now that she knew *exactly* what he'd meant by how sensitive a person's soul was, she was hoping there'd never be a time that he'd decide to demonstrate what kind of intense physical pain he could now inflict on her.

*I can also make you come harder than you ever have in your life.*

Well, she wasn't going to think about that.

After crossing the bailey, she headed straight home. Her entire crew was scattered around the living room, drinking tea and looking a little drained. They were no doubt tired from how hard they'd worked to get prepped for their 'shop' opening tomorrow. Not that it was stopping Delilah and Anabel from sniping at each other.

"What's going on?" asked Wynter.

"*She*"—Anabel jabbed a finger in Delilah's direction— "is

blaming me for the wolf attack I told you about. She's saying it was *my* fault that I died that day."

"If you hadn't stepped foot on his territory, it wouldn't have happened," said Delilah. "You could have stayed away. But oh no. You pulled a Little Red Riding Hood, and you paid the price. Simple."

Anabel's lips parted. "Paid the price? I was eight years old. Have some compassion."

"It interferes with my choices."

"It *should*. Maybe if you let it, you wouldn't have started brewing your precious karma potions and then you wouldn't have a bounty on your head."

"I don't know what you all have against my acting on behalf of karma. My family's been doing it since our line first began. It's in my blood, and I'm proud of it."

"I don't know how you can possibly be proud of being a descendant of the Black Annis, even if it does mean you can shapeshift into a monstrous saber-toothed cat. That crone was *evil*."

"She was brilliant."

"She ate children."

"Well, we don't talk about that."

Wynter lifted a hand. "All right, just stop. I shouldn't need to point out that this conversation is heading nowhere." She blew out a breath.

Xavier studied her. "You look kind of flustered. What's wrong?"

"Nothing," said Wynter. "Just annoyed with Grouch."

"The blacksmith who pointed a sword at your neck?" he asked.

She nodded. "One and the same. He's telling everyone that I'm going to hex his shop. It got back to Cain, who then had Maxim escort me to him."

"You went to see Cain?"

"Not willingly."

Xavier studied her face and then grinned. "He made a play, didn't he?"

Damn the perceptive bastard. "No—"

"He did." Xavier let out a teasing chuckle. "I doubt he even believed Grouch. He wanted you there so he could hit on you."

Delilah leaned forward in her seat. "Xavier's right, isn't he?"

Wynter grunted.

Anabel rubbed at her arm. "This isn't good. Not at all. What are you going to do?"

Wynter knew what she *should* do—stay the hell away from this person who could possibly ferret out her secrets. Besides, she didn't want to be an immortal's toy. But ... he'd like the chase. She saw that in him. Saw that he wouldn't easily give up. And she couldn't delude herself into believing that she'd manage to hold out against him.

Would it be better to give in, enjoy one night, and then move on? Maybe. She really didn't know.

"I'll tell ya what you're gonna do, Wyn," began Delilah. "You're gonna let yourself have this. Gonna let yourself have him, to be more exact."

"Del—"

"You need to get laid, okay. Let him do the laying. I'm thinking he'll be good at it."

"Let's just—"

"No, no hemming and hawing. Trust your Aunty Delilah, this is what you need. It's what your body needs. Tomorrow, you're going to primp yourself up and choose an outfit that flashes some camel toe—"

"*And* I'm walking away now," said Wynter, spinning on her heel.

"What's camel toe?" asked Hattie.

Xavier burst out laughing.

# Chapter Seven

Wynter hadn't expected to have so many customers their first morning. Many probably came by purely out of curiosity, but few people left empty-handed—buying potions, baked goods, and bespelled cosmetics via the open living room window. It was Delilah who handled the transactions, leaving Hattie and Anabel able to stay in the kitchen.

Sat in his tent in the front yard, Xavier also got a lot of custom. Wynter spent the first hour keeping an eye on things, wanting to be sure all was going smoothly. She was about to head off to the shed when a male demon, bored waiting for his partner to choose from Delilah's selection, abruptly asked Wynter, "So what do you do?"

She tilted her head. "Do you have a weapon of any sort on your person?"

His tongue flicked out to touch his upper lip. "Yeah."

"Then follow me and I'll show you." She led him into the shed, which was now clean and pretty bare apart from a workbench and two stools.

He frowned at the selection of small bottles on the shelf. "What are all those?"

"Some are reversal potions, some are healing potions," she replied. "So, what do you have?"

He pulled out an athame so sharp and shiny it almost made her drool.

"Nice." She place it on a workbench. "I can do various things to weapons to give them an 'edge,' shall we say. The enchantments serve as distractions. They give you a way to mess with your opponent's head. I'll make this one a surprise. If you don't like it, I can undo it."

He nodded. "All right."

Her old coven hadn't liked her using her magick much, but even they had welcomed this particular service. In fact, most of the townspeople had—particularly the keepers.

Wynter hovered her hand above the blade and called to her magick. Dark with an ultraviolent undertone, it shimmered in the air like waves of heat as it reached out like vaporous, outstretched fingers.

"Whoa." He moved closer, watching as said vaporous fingers sank into the metal, heating and empowering it. Runes glittered and sparked as they appeared along the blade. And then it was done. He studied the runes. "I don't recognize them."

"Because you don't possess dark magick as I do." She lifted the athame. "All right, to show you what this baby can do, I'll unfortunately have to prick you with it—or you can do it to yourself, whatever."

He took the athame from her. "Why?"

"The runes will cause an illusion, but it will only work on whoever the blade wounds. Others won't experience or be able to witness it." She grabbed a reversal potion from the shelf and handed it to him. "This will undo it."

"All right." He lightly stabbed the pad of his thumb with his blade, making blood bead to the surface. Mere moments later, he reared back, staring at his hand in horror. Caught up in the illusion only he could see, he jerked and cursed, his hand beginning to tremble.

She tapped the vial he held. "Drink."

He swiftly knocked back the reversal potion and then shuddered with a cough. He flexed his hand, studying it from every angle. "Sweet Jesus, that was a mind fuck. I thought I'd stabbed right through my thumb. There was blood everywhere and the wound just kept growing and growing until my thumb was hanging from my hand by a string of skin. The pain was unreal."

"My illusions are strong enough to fool *all* the senses. They create panic and confusion. The runes on your blade will make your opponent believe that their wounds are infinitely worse than they truly are. Even if they suspect it's an illusion, they'll still be distracted, especially by the pain."

"How long will the illusion last?"

"Approximately twenty minutes."

He stared at Wynter, his eyes sparkling with interest. "That's . . . I've never seen anyone do anything like that."

She smiled. "Pretty cool, huh? Be sure to spread the word."

Shortly before lunchtime, he returned with several of his lair who wanted their own weapons to be enchanted. They weren't her only customers. Others came—partially out of genuine interest, and partially because they didn't want people with enchanted weapons having an edge over *them*.

Later, after the 'store' was closed and the entire crew was then sat around the kitchen table, Xavier poured their profits onto the surface while Delilah scribbled down the items or services they'd taken in trade. Hattie's 'space cakes' had been highly popular, as were Anabel's potions that enabled people to see past fey glamor.

"I'd say that was what you'd call a successful day," said Wynter.

"And it's only the beginning, darlin'," noted Hattie, stroking a crystal serving platter they'd been given as payment—one she'd been quick to claim for herself.

Lots of witchy stuff had been offered in trade, including candles, plants, and incense burners. Wynter had chosen some items for herself, as had the others.

"How long do you think it will be before local business owners get in a snit?" asked Anabel.

"Considering we're stealing business from the bakeries, the herbalist stores, the cosmetic shops, the blacksmith shops, and the diviners . . . I'd say not long," replied Wynter.

The blacksmiths wouldn't suffer a dramatic loss, since she couldn't create weapons, but there would be *some* loss because people wouldn't need to renew their blades when they could simply ask her to jazz them up. They'd also be reluctant to part with their enchanted weaponry, so they wouldn't be in a rush to replace them—she'd seen that for herself back when she lived at Aeon.

Pushing her old home out of her mind, she said, "Well, we'd better start getting ready for tonight's festivities."

Delilah nodded. "The parade part sounds a little boring, since everyone's required to stand around waiting for their turn to wave when Ishtar's float goes by. But I'm looking forward to the feast. There's supposed to be some music and dancing ... *and* there's a rumor that things will get a little, shall we say, raw at one point. Don't know if it's true or not. But if a mist builds up and people start getting down and dirty, fully expect Cain to make a move right there. Oh, and don't forget to show some camel—"

"Jesus, Del, do you have no shame?" demanded Wynter while Hattie cackled.

"Not when I wanna get laid," replied Delilah. "I also want *you* to get laid. It's been too long. We fix that tonight."

Shaking her head, Wynter turned to Xavier. "Any chance you could help me cart my new stuff upstairs?"

"Sure," he easily agreed.

Anabel and Delilah also helped, so it only took one trip to move everything upstairs. The trio then left, leaving Wynter to properly 'nest.' She set her African violet plant on the windowsill, arranged some candles around the room, and laid her astrological-themed throw over her armchair. She then placed her books on the shelf, which looked great bordered by her brand-new raven bookends. Only then did she unpack her suitcase and spruce up the décor with her collection of crystals. She'd add other things as she went along.

Done, she helped the rest of her crew carry their new things to their bedrooms and then returned to her own so she could get ready for tonight's event. She chose one of her favorite dresses—made of black sheer lace, the racy number barely hid her underwear and ended just beneath her knees. The latter would no doubt disappoint Delilah.

Descending the stairs a short while later, she found the others gathered around the living area, which now also had some personal touches with the crescent moon mirror, triangular wall vases of fig and ivy, triple moon trunk, pretty throw pillows, and the Moon tarot card rug.

"Everyone ready?" she asked.

Anabel shrank in her seat. "Is it really compulsory for the entire town to attend?"

Xavier nodded, standing. "Ishtar will allegedly take it as an insult if not everyone is there to celebrate that she's woken."

Anabel frowned. "But it doesn't make any sense. You said celebrations are held in the village hall. Everyone can't possibly fit in there."

"No," he agreed, grinning, "but they can all fit in the huge arena that's apparently located deep in the woods. And I, for one, am looking forward to seeing it."

\*

Perched on top of the highest of the underground city's three towers, Cain skimmed his gaze along the residents who were waiting for the parade to start. Standing shoulder to shoulder, most lined the streets. Others hung out of windows or sat on roofs.

Aides walked around handing out streamers or balloons—most of which were taken reluctantly. There was no real excitement on the faces of the people below. They might be glad to have another Ancient awake as it was more protection for Devil's Cradle, but they didn't seem to like that they had to stand around and essentially pay homage to Ishtar like she was some sort of goddess. But then, Ishtar saw herself as such.

Hearing footfalls, Cain glanced behind him to see Azazel and

Seth approaching. The other Ancients would join them soon—it was tradition for them to situate themselves at the main tower during parades or similar events.

Azazel scratched the back of his head. "I just saw a coyote wearing mascara."

Cain did a double-take. "A coyote?"

"Yeah. Turns out that the new coven in town is selling bespelled cosmetics that aren't disturbed by the shifting process."

Cain felt his brows flick up. "Innovative idea."

"I heard that the Priestess is a pretty little thing," said Seth, coming to stand on Cain's other side.

"She is," Cain confirmed. "She's also off-limits."

Seth's mouth kicked up. "Is she now? For how long?"

"Until I say differently." Cain spied Wynter and her coven in the crowd. She was shaking her head at Hattie, who was pointing her finger at the page of an open book. Beside them, both Xavier and Delilah laughed. Anabel, however, huddled close to Wynter, nervously eyeing the crowds as if she expected someone to suddenly lunge at her.

"Fair enough," said Azazel. "But you might want to find a way to make that clear to one and all, because from what I heard, she's picked up a few admirers."

Cain had anticipated that, which was why . . . "It'll be made clear tonight." No one would dare touch her after that.

"Be ready for Ishtar's reaction," said Azazel. "She won't like that someone else has your attention, and she's never careful with your toys."

"Wynter wears my mark on her palm. Not even Ishtar will disrespect that."

"She won't *physically* hurt your witch, no. But there are other ways to hurt someone or make their life difficult."

"There are. And I know how to make Ishtar's life difficult. She's well aware of that. It'll make her hesitate to play games."

"'Hesitate' being the key word," Seth cut in. "So if you want the

Priestess for more than one night, you'd better hope that Wynter has staying power, or Ishtar will succeed in making her think you're more trouble than you're worth."

"Which you are," Azazel quipped.

Cain couldn't deny it. "Yes, but Wynter doesn't know that yet."

Azazel snorted. "By the way, I spoke to my source again. The deterioration is still rampant in Aeon, and people are still getting sick." When Seth let out a skeptical sound, Azazel looked at him. "You're still not buying it?"

Seth shrugged. "I find it difficult to believe that decay and illness is prevalent in such a place of power."

"Why?" asked Azazel. "There's a whole other kind of rot there. Metaphorically speaking."

"And you think that perhaps the universe decided it was time that the land reflected that?"

"Maybe. Stranger things have happened."

Hearing the clicking of heels, Cain turned to see Lilith heading their way with Dantalion not far behind her. They all exchanged brief greetings.

Seth tilted his head at Dantalion. "When I heard you would throw the first celebration, I hadn't for a moment expected you to suggest a parade."

"I didn't," said Dantalion, rubbing the dust of stubble that was as blond as his short hair. "Ishtar insisted on it being a prelude to the celebration. You can't be surprised. Having everyone wave and smile at her as she goes by in a carriage is exactly the sort of thing she'd enjoy."

Lilith locked her vivid green gaze on Seth. "I had thought she would want you sitting beside her."

"She suggested it this morning. I said no." Seth's eyes slid to Cain. "She complained that I was as obstinate and awkward as my brother, which made me wonder if she'd made that same suggestion to you."

"She wanted me to escort her to the celebration," said Cain.

Lilith let out a derisive sound and flicked her long, red hair over her shoulder. "In other words, she wanted you both fawning all over her." She studied the crowd. "Has anyone noticed that the fey seem to be in a foul mood?"

"As of today, there are potions available in the city that allow people to see past fey glamor," said Azazel.

Lilith blinked. "Oh. Well, they'll hate that. They're forever tricking people."

Azazel looked at Cain. "Your witch's coven is responsible for that as well as—"

Marching band music cut through the air.

Seth sighed. "It's starting."

Surrounded by dance troupes, stilt walkers, and a uniformed marching band, a horse-drawn carriage exited the bailey of Ishtar's Keep.

"Doesn't do anything by halves, does she?" muttered Dantalion.

People clapped, waved, smiled, and whistled as the carriage went by. Most of those wide smiles were forced, but Cain doubted Ishtar would notice. She was too caught up in the personal power she gained from being the focus of so much attention.

Sticks beat on drums. Horse hooves clip-clopped. Balloons popped. Leaders called out to their dance troupes.

"Hey," began Azazel, "what do you think all these people would do if they knew the truth about the Ancients?"

"Run," said Dantalion. "I think they'd all run."

*

Wynter obligingly smiled as the horse-drawn carriage passed by. Ishtar was as beautiful as Maxim had said. Presently, she looked high as a kite. The Ancient was clearly *loving* this. Personally, Wynter couldn't see any appeal in it, but to each their own.

Once the parade was finally over, several aides led the crowds through the woods and over to an open-air arena. It truly was huge, just as Xavier had said. Spectacular, too. It made her think of the Colosseum in Rome.

Everyone filed inside and—guided by ushers—filled the many spectator rows. Tray tables were attached to the back of each seat much like on airplanes. No sooner had Wynter and her crew sat down than Anabel had whipped out a vial of antibacterial potion and cleaned her own tray.

The Ancients were the last to take their seats, claiming the VIP area directly opposite of where Wynter and her coven were situated. Flanked by Seth and Azazel, Cain was quick to spot her. One corner of his mouth kicked up. His eyes bore into her own, gleaming with both promise and challenge.

Even as her mouth went dry and warmth bloomed inside her, Wynter slipped on her poker face, intent on ensuring he didn't sense the effect he had on her. That only made his smile widen.

Ishtar rose to her feet, the image of grace. "Thank you all for coming." Power swirled through the air, carrying her voice to every guest. "And thank you, Dantalion, for the time and effort you invested in celebrating my return."

The male Ancient nodded, looking bored.

Ishtar went on to make a little speech, but Wynter barely heard it. Well, it was hard to focus when she could *feel* Cain's eyes on her. She wouldn't look at him. She wouldn't. She wouldn't.

She did.

And the heated glance he speared her with went straight to her freaking womb. She shot him a narrow-eyed look and turned away, relieved her cheeks didn't flush.

Finally, Ishtar quieted, smiling as applause rang out. Music filled the air again, and then the entertainers who'd surrounded her carriage during the parade trickled onto the performance space below. The artists danced and sang and entertained, and the spectators clapped and swayed and sang along.

It wasn't until the interval that food and drinks were served.

Which was about the same time that Anabel started panting like an exhausted racehorse.

Lifting her corn on the cob, Delilah frowned. "What's with all the heavy breathing?"

"He keeps looking at me," said Anabel, her eyes wide. "Why does he keep looking at me?"

Wynter tracked her gaze. One of their lycan Alpha neighbors, Diego, was blatantly staring at the blonde, his lips curved.

Delilah smirked. "Girl, you got yourself an admirer."

Anabel began rubbing her temples. "Oh God, oh God, he wants to eat me."

Delilah snickered. "Eat your pussy, maybe."

Hattie cackled and patted the blonde's arm. "You should really let him, dear. He might even be up for some anil—"

"*Please* stop saying that word," begged Anabel. She turned to Wynter. "How do you do it?"

"What?" asked Wynter, cutting into her steak.

"Stay so calm and chill when you know a guy is watching you," replied Anabel. "Don't say you haven't noticed Cain staring at you. You totally have."

Wynter sniffed. "He's trying to make me squirm with that unblinking stare."

"He's also fucking you with it," said Xavier. "And he's not being subtle. People have taken notice. I'm thinking he's doing it so publicly to send a message."

Yeah, she was thinking the same thing. And she wasn't sure if she liked it or hated it.

Soon, the dirty dishware and leftover food was collected and taken away. The performers then reappeared. Some did a short dance routine while the band set up shop in the corner of the large space. Once they were done, a stilt walker grabbed a mic and invited people to 'come on down.' The band began to play, and the stilt walker belted out song after song.

Some guests left the spectator section and headed to the

performance space, which soon became a makeshift dance floor. Others were content to remain in their seats, still clapping and singing along. Wynter and her crew did the latter . . . until Delilah drained her drink and jumped to her feet as she said, "Here's where we go dance and show all the boys what we got."

Anabel grimaced. "I'm going to nix that and—no, Del, *I don't want to, you can't make me.*"

"True, I can't. But if we leave you alone, that lycan Alpha is gonna come over and—"

Anabel shot to her feet, glowering. "This is some fucking bullshit right here."

Delilah just snickered.

All five of them made their way to the 'dance floor.' Hattie brought out her best moves, none of which were ladylike. Delilah mimicked every move, egging the old woman on. Wynter and Xavier stayed close to Anabel, who slowly but surely thawed out until she was *owning* that dance floor.

Wynter blinked as the lights dimmed low and mist began to haze the air.

Delilah grinned. "And this is where it hopefully gets good."

Anabel actually whooped, having lost her inhibitions somewhere along the line, and kept on dancing to the thumping music.

The mist became thicker and thicker and thicker, until Wynter could no longer see her crew. It didn't help that it was dark and—

Hands clamped on her hips as someone plastered their front to her back. Warm lips touched her ear. "There you are."

Her heart slammed into her ribcage, and she inhaled sharply. She knew that voice. *Cain.* His breath stirred the little hairs on her ear, making a delicate shudder run through her.

"You knew I'd come for you, didn't you?" His hands slid down her outer thighs to snake beneath her dress. "And you knew what would happen when I did." He dragged his fingertips up her inner thighs, digging them into her skin, dragging her dress upward as he did so. "You want this. Don't you?"

Wynter reached back and slipped her hand between them. She cupped his dick and, finding it delightfully hard and thick, gave it a squeeze. "That answer your question?"

He growled and bit into her neck, ghosting his fingers over her panties. "I don't know what it is about you ... but I want to mark you the fuck up. Your skin. Your pussy. Your very soul."

Pleasure *swept* over her being like a firm, warm, electrically charged hand. Her back arched, and she sucked in a breath. Jesus *Christ*. It was like being touched ... *everywhere*.

Static danced over her skin and raised the hairs on her flesh as her body came alive. Her nipples throbbed, her muscles flexed, her nerve-endings turned hypersensitive, and her pussy clenched as if full ... only she'd never been more acutely aware of how empty she was.

"Maybe I'll feel less possessive after I've come deep inside you," he said. "I guess we'll soon see."

She thrust her hips toward the fingers still doing featherlight brushes over her panties. "Cain." A breath stuttered out of her as one hand snaked around her throat. Her lips tingled as his thumb swept over them. She bit the digit, and his cock pulsed against her palm.

"I'm not just going to fuck you, sweet witch. I'm going to ruin you. Corrupt you. Consume you." His tongue traced the shell of her ear. "You'll break. You'll cry. You'll feel like you're mine."

An electric wave of pleasure once more swept over her soul, snatching the breath from her lungs. Wynter's head flew back. God, her skin was suddenly like one giant hot spot. She'd never felt so sensitive *in her life*. Ever. Her buzzing nerve-endings *screamed* to be touched, stroked, scratched—

Another surge of pleasure. And another. And another. And another.

She lost herself. Lost all awareness of everything around her, except for him; for the hand collaring her throat and anchoring her to the world.

She was ... she was a *mess*. All she could think about was finding her release. Nothing else mattered. Nothing.

She trembled, she whimpered, she arched, she *burned*. Her mind, body, and soul were strung so tight it would take one pinch of her nipple. One. She'd explode like never before. But he didn't give her that. He kept on delivering caress after caress to her soul—each one hot and electric.

She couldn't take it. She couldn't. It was unbearably, painfully intense. Too consuming, too devastating. An overload of sensation that just wouldn't—

She broke. Exactly like he'd said she would.

Wynter thought she screamed, but she wasn't sure. The pleasure hit her with the force of an avalanche and ripped her apart, making her vision darken around the edges. She was honestly surprised she didn't pass out.

She leaned back against Cain, her legs trembling, her breaths sawing at her throat. Tears trailed down her face. Well, he'd told her she'd cry, hadn't he?

That whole soul-gasm thing had more than primed her on a physical level, and she was rearing. To. *Fuck*. She squeezed his cock. "Please tell me you have a condom."

"I don't need one. Ancients can't carry STDs. Nor can we procreate." Cain licked up one tear with his tongue, and his inner creature memorized the taste. It liked her this way—soft, vulnerable, needy. He turned her to face him, drinking in the dazed look she wore, and gripped her jaw. "I want you to come for me again. This time, you'll be stuffed full of cock when you do."

He brought his mouth crashing down on hers and sank his tongue inside. Moaning, she thrust her hand into his hair while he tore open his fly and freed his throbbing dick.

He hoisted her up, constructed a wall of pure power behind her, and slammed her against it. She gasped as he effortlessly tore off her panties, clueless as to how strong he truly was. He inched the head of his cock inside her, stretching her open, gritting his teeth as her inner muscles rippled around him.

"You know what you're going to do for me, don't you?"

"What?" she whispered.

"Anything I want." He slammed her down on his cock. "Everything I want." He took two fistfuls of her ass. "Any *time* I want." Before she could protest, he sent out a little wave of power, letting it vibrate against her skin. "This won't be the last time I have you, Wynter. Not even close."

He fucked her hard, knowing she needed it, knowing her body would be craving it. She held tight, angling her hips to take him as deep as he wanted to go. And he wanted to go *deep*. "Fuck, you feel good."

All around them, there were moans and cries of pleasure coming from the people hidden by the mist. They mingled with his grunts and her whispered demands for him to move harder, faster.

Growling, he gave her what she needed. "Pull your breasts out of your dress, play with them for me."

She didn't hesitate, clearly not at all shy. Her hands weren't gentle as she palmed and squeezed the full globes, or as she pinched and twisted her nipples. She liked it rough, and she owned it without shame. He liked that.

He adjusted his angle slightly, and she let out a hoarse cry that seemed to call to the monster inside him. It unfurled, edgy with a possessiveness it wasn't used to feeling. It shoved at Cain in demand, and he knew what it wanted. He knew that, far from being done with her, the creature also wasn't prepared to share her.

Sensing that Cain would resist, it slinked closer to the surface. *Shit.* If his monster took control, if it fucked her . . . Cain couldn't allow that. There'd be no guarantee that she'd live through it, for starters.

He let the creature sense his acquiescence, satisfied when it settled.

"Cain," she breathed, her pussy fluttering and tightening around his cock.

He snarled. "That's it, come." He raked his teeth over the side of her face, drawn to that spot in a way he couldn't explain, and she all but detonated in his arms.

He slapped his hand over her lower stomach as he gave his creature what it wanted, but she was so out of it she didn't feel a thread of power *push* its way inside her.

She slumped, her orgasm fading, and he gripped her ass tighter as he hammered into her harder and faster. Finally, he exploded, jets of come bursting out of him as a powerful release thundered through his body and seemed to shoot up his cock.

Boneless, Wynter looked at him through opaque eyes, the image of sated. Gripped by the sight of her mouth all red and swollen, he kissed her softly, needing another taste, swallowing her sigh of pleasure.

She didn't realize anything was different. But she would. Soon. And he had a feeling he'd find himself on the receiving end of one of her hunter stares when she did.

Perversely, he was looking forward to it.

# Chapter Eight

Entering the kitchen the next morning, Wynter blinked at Anabel. "Why are you walking funny?"

A laugh bubbled out of Delilah, who put a hand to her stomach as she leaned forward in her chair. "Oh God, my ribs are hurting like hell."

Her cheeks crimson, Anabel glared at the other witch. "Probably because you won't stop laughing despite your promise."

Delilah lifted her cup. "I'm not laughing, I'm chuckling."

"It's the same thing." Anabel plopped herself on a chair and moodily dragged it along the floor as she scooted forward.

Delilah looked at Wynter. "Anabel and Diego had some fun in the mist last night, and it turns out he has a *beast* of a cock."

"Oh, I see." Wynter hadn't spoken to either Anabel or Hattie last night, since both had left the arena before her. They'd been tucked up in bed when she'd returned.

"At first, when I saw her waddling like a goddamn penguin, I thought she'd taken him up the ass."

"That thing in his pants will *never* get near my ass," declared Anabel.

Beside the blonde, Xavier patted her arm in comfort—a gesture that was totally spoiled by the way his shoulders shook in silent laughter.

Having grabbed a Danish pastry and poured herself a coffee, Wynter settled at the table. "Where's Hattie?"

Xavier gestured at the backyard. "Enjoying her early morning joint."

Eyeing Wynter, Anabel tilted her head and said, "You know, I kind of expected you to be walking bowlegged, since Cain had made it clear with his gaze alone that you were going to get royally fucked."

Delilah smiled. "From the little she told me and Xavier last night, she *was* royally fucked. I had a feeling the dude would bring plenty of game to the table. I do love to be right."

Anabel tore off a piece of her croissant, her gaze on Wynter. "Does sex ever really leave you feeling satisfied? I mean, food doesn't. Sleep doesn't. So it made me wonder."

"Usually, no," replied Wynter. "Even if I come, I don't feel fully sated. But last night was different. He stroked my soul and, *Jesus*, it was more intense than anything I've ever felt in my life." And she wasn't as happy about that as she'd like to be because, seriously, what guy could live up to that? How could she not compare any future sexytimes with what happened last night?

Delilah's eyes lit up. "Oh, now that sounds intriguing. The sidhe I fucked last night had some amazing tricks, but soul-touching wasn't one of them."

"Being bitten by a vampire was an interesting experience," said Xavier, his mouth curving.

"One you'd repeat?" asked Anabel.

"Maybe," he said. "I might have gotten more than simply bitten if Elias from next door hadn't interfered to be a dick. He came over, acting all flirty with me—even suggested a threesome with him and his boyfriend. It was obvious he was only trying to put her off. I don't get why he'd do that."

"Lycans are more territorial than any other preternatural species," said Wynter. "Our lycan neighbors will feel they have a minor claim to us five, what with us living so close to them. That in and of itself will make them act a little territorial at times, not to mention protective."

"Wait, *that's* why Diego made a move on me?" asked Anabel.

"No, I'm sure he likes you," said Wynter. "But I also think he acted fast because he felt a little proprietary and didn't want others to beat him to it." She looked at Xavier. "I think another reason Elias interfered is that lycans hate vamps. He wouldn't want 'the enemy' touching any of us."

"That's his problem," said Xavier. "He has no right to make it mine."

"Agreed. I'll have a chat with him if he doesn't let up."

"No need, I can deal with him just fine."

Wynter narrowed her eyes. "You're *not* killing him."

"We all have the right to cut toxic people from our lives."

"That doesn't mean ending their existence. Besides, he's not a toxic influence; he just annoyed you."

"Well, I don't like him."

"*Still* not a reason to end his existence. No, I'm done discussing it. Let's move on and talk about something else. *Any* subject will do."

Delilah raised her hand. "I have a question. Do you think there'll be a repeat of what happened with you and Cain?"

There was no denying that staying clear of the Ancient would be for the best, but Wynter knew herself well enough to know that . . . "If he made another move, I probably wouldn't resist."

The kitchen door slowly opened, and then Hattie shuffled inside, muttering something under her breath.

Anabel frowned. "Something wrong?"

"I can't find my copy of *Fifty Shades*," replied Hattie, sitting on the only empty chair at the table. "It has to be here somewhere."

"I thought you preferred the movie anyway," said Anabel.

"Only because that Jamie actor is a dish." A dreamy smile took over Hattie's face. "I would *love* to meet him, you know."

"You would?"

"Oh yes, I'd love to talk to him."

"About what?"

Hattie hesitated. "Well, I don't know, I'd just love to talk to him. Wouldn't you?"

Anabel's nose wrinkled. "No, not really."

"Why not?" demanded Hattie, seeming offended on his behalf.

"I don't even like talking to people I *do* know. I have absolutely no desire to strike up a conversation with a perfect stranger."

"He's not a stranger. You know who he is."

"I know his name and his occupation. I also know that the guy who used to sell me herbs was called Horatio."

Xavier snickered and chugged down the last of his coffee. "She makes a good point, Hattie. Which doesn't happen often." Ignoring Anabel's scowl, he cocked his head and said, "I can hear voices outside. Seems like people are already gathering at the gate. We ready to open our shop, people?"

There was a round of yeses, and then everyone got moving.

The day went well. More potions were sold, more bespelled cosmetics were purchased, and more baked goods flew off the metaphorical shelves. Xavier's custom also picked up, and Wynter had plenty of people appear with weaponry.

Since many customers paid in trade, the fridge and kitchen cupboards were soon packed with food. Bags of toiletries, household accessories, and clothing were also handed over.

At the end of the workday, Wynter and her crew ate dinner and, like yesterday, distributed the 'goods' they'd been given in trade. They then set up a corner altar in the living room, adding a number of items such as an athame, candles, a bell, and a small cauldron.

They also added a few touches to their front yard, including a welcome mat and some hanging baskets overflowing with fern. Following that, they worked as a team to add some live plants to the backyard for Delilah and Anabel's concoctions. There was mint, lavender, foxglove, and heather but to name a few.

Looking forward to trying her new green-tea scented shower gel, Wynter was soon stood under the hot spray in her private bathroom. Her thoughts—just as they'd annoyingly often done throughout the day—strayed to Cain; strayed to what they'd shared in the mist.

Christ, she'd *never* been fucked like that. And she wasn't only talking about the whole soul-gasm part of the night. The proprietary way he'd touched her, the forceful thrusts with which he'd taken her, the punishing grip on her ass, the words he'd spoken in that goddamn sex voice . . . The bastard had ruined her, just as he'd promised he would.

As the memories flickered through her mind, she found her hand drifting down her body. Her eyelids drifted shut as she touched herself—rubbing her clit, stroking her slit, circling the entrance of her pussy. She dipped her fingers inside . . . or tried to. She couldn't. *Couldn't.* Like there was a barrier there or something. One she couldn't internally feel, but one that nonetheless stopped her fingers from sliding inside.

Realization hit her, and her mouth dropped open. *That motherfucker.*

\*

Cain was deep in discussion with one of his aides when a knock came at the door of the solar room. "Yes?" he called out.

Maxim entered. "You said I was only to disturb you if there was an emergency or if a particular visitor arrived. In this instance, it is the latter. What would you like me to do?"

Cain felt his lips hitch up. This could be fun. "Send her in."

After Maxim left, Cain dismissed his other aide and then draped one arm over the back of the sofa as he waited impatiently for his witch to appear. His creature reared up, eager to see her.

Maxim soon escorted her into the room. To Cain's disappointment, her poker face was firmly in place. He doubted it would be too hard to crack the mask, though.

"Leave us," he told his aide, who then nodded and walked out.

Her chin inched up. "I think there's something you forgot to tell me," she said, her voice carefully even.

Cain pursed his lips. "No, I don't believe so." He was terribly impressed when she didn't so much as narrow her eyes. Letting his gaze roam over her, he said, "You're wearing too many clothes. Take them off. I didn't get to strip you bare last night. I want to see every inch of you. Show me."

"*Or* you could explain what the hell you did to me."

"I did a lot of things to you," he reminded her, pitching his voice low and deep. "You'll have to be more specific."

"You know *exactly* what I'm talking about."

Cain arched a brow. "I do?"

"Yeah, you do."

"There are just so many things you could be referring to. At least give me a hint."

Finally, the poker face crumbled. Her stunning eyes flared, and that edible mouth tightened. More, she pinned him with one of her trademark hunter stares that thickened his blood and enticed his inner creature.

She set her hands on her hips. "You're gonna play dumb now? Really?"

Smiling, he stood. "No. I just want to hear you tell me how you came to discover what I'd done." He covered the ground between them in three fluid strides. "Did you try to get yourself off? Hmm?" It couldn't have been that someone else did it. After he'd publicly made his interest in her so abundantly clear, no one would have dared touch her that way.

She folded her arms. "Tell me what exactly you did."

"Simply ensured that the only person whose tongue, fingers, and cock you can take inside you are mine."

Her lips parted. "Seriously? You *seriously* did that?"

"Yes, I did."

"And you don't think that's wrong, not to mention messed up?"

"No. No, I don't."

"Jesus, you're on dope, aren't you? There's no other way you'd pull a stunt like this and think it was acceptable."

He tipped his head to the side. "I strike you as someone who cares what's acceptable?"

"After this, no, no, you don't. You need to undo what you did."

"Why?"

Her brows snapped together. "What do you mean why? Because it's not normal."

"To you, maybe not." He lightly tapped her cheek with his finger. "But don't judge me by the standards of mortals, Wynter." In truth, what he'd done was perfectly normal for his kind when they were possessive. But there was no way he could tell her that.

"And how would *you* feel if ... you know what, scrap that. Something tells me that empathy isn't your thing. But come on, Cain, not only did you insert some kind of barrier inside me, you didn't even think to tell me. Why not? Why, *knowing* it would make me even more pissed about the situation, did you decide to leave me to find out on my own?"

"Truthfully?" Cain hooked his arm around her waist and pulled her flush against him. "Because fucking with your pretty little head makes me hard." And while pressed firmly against him, she was able to feel the evidence of that.

Long moments went by as she simply stared at him. "You know, someone mentioned you were a mental sadist. I thought they were joking."

"No, 'mental sadist' fits. And you're still wearing too many clothes. I told you, I want them off."

"What *I* want is for you to undo what you did."

He smoothed one hand down her back and palmed her ass. "I don't think it bothers you quite as much as you'd like me to believe it does. A part of you gets off on what I've done; on knowing I'd go so far to make sure no one else can have you."

"And that part of me is as mentally sadistic as you, so I discount everything it wants and feels."

He chuckled. "You've surprised me yet again, little witch. I expected you to deny it. In fact—" He cut off as knuckles rapped on the door. "Yes?"

Maxim stepped inside, his expression apologetic. "Sorry to disturb you, but Seth would like to see you. He says it's very important."

Sighing, Cain stepped away from Wynter. "I'll be back in a moment. Wait here for me. Don't leave."

"Oh, you don't have to worry that I'll go anywhere." She gave him a look that said she wouldn't be moving from that very spot until he'd done as she ordered. Something he absolutely could not do—his creature wasn't ready to let her go yet; it would take the matter into its own hands if Cain refused to ensure it had what it wanted.

Putting the matter aside for now, Cain crossed to his aide. "Where is my brother?"

"The manor," replied Maxim. "He said you'll find him in the main parlor."

Cain headed upstairs to his chamber and over to the life-size mirror. He splayed his hand on the glass, and it instantly turned to rippling black water. He stepped through it and, utterly dry, stepped out of an identical mirror in one of the manor's bedrooms.

He made his way downstairs and into the main parlor, not bothering to first knock on the door.

Sitting on one of the sofas with his aide at his back, Seth tipped his chin at Cain. "Hello, brother. I'll be with you shortly. Although you're welcome to stay and hear their story." He gestured at the two men seated on the opposite sofa. "This here is Ed and Artie. They're bounty hunters."

Not yet sure why Seth was acting as though he hadn't called for him to come, Cain chose to play along. "Is that so? And just what would they be doing here?"

"Me and Ed were hired by people from Aeon," the one who had to be Artie said. "They sent us after a witch. They want her brought back alive."

"We've been on her trail for a while," said Ed. "We caught up to her once. She killed two of our group. And I mean *eviscerated* them. She got better at covering her tracks after that, but we've been at this a long time. We managed to track her down."

Cain looked from one male to the other. "I'm guessing you believe she's here."

"We do," Ed confirmed. "It makes sense that she'd come here. You offer sanctuary to people on the run."

"If you know we offer sanctuary to such people," began Seth, "you must also know we don't give them up."

Artie gave a slow nod. "We do know that. But we figured if we explained that the Aeons want her, you might be inclined to hand her over. I mean, they were once your people until ..." *Until you lost to them in a war*, he didn't add but left implied.

Seth looked at Cain. "Her name is ..." Trailing off, he cut his gaze to Artie. "What did you say it was again?"

"Wynter Dellavale," the bounty hunter replied.

Everything inside Cain went very still, including his monster. He didn't allow his expression to alter, not yet certain he wanted the hunters to be aware that she was a resident here.

Now understanding why Seth had called for him, Cain asked, "Why do the Aeons want her?"

"We don't know," said Ed. "They didn't say. At first, they wanted her dead. But that changed. They didn't explain why."

"I got the impression they want her badly," Artie added. "Look, we asked to speak with an Ancient because we know better than to touch the property of one without first seeking permission."

Cain raised a brow. "Did you believe that wish would be granted?"

Artie sighed. "I heard that Ancients sometimes grant that permission, depending on the circumstances."

"We do indeed. As for this particular circumstance ..." The way Cain saw it, he had two choices. Deny she was here, or make it clear that she was under his protection and that any hunters who came for her would die—that would make the price on her head invalid. People from Aeon might come for her, but that would be something he'd welcome.

Cain chose the latter option. "This is what you're going to do. You're going to leave Devil's Cradle. You're going to spread the word that Wynter Dellavale is in my service and under my protection;

that I will kill anyone who tries cashing in on the bounty. And, no matter what the people of Aeon offer you, you will cease trying to capture her. You may, however, pass on her location to them. If they want her, they'll have to come get her."

Artie nodded. "We'll pass on that message."

Once Seth's aide guided them out of the parlor, Cain turned to his brother. "Azazel's source informed him that a witch was recently exiled from Aeon. I hadn't suspected it was Wynter—she came here as part of a coven. Although, to be fair, she never once claimed they were a coven." In fact, she'd repeatedly told him that they weren't. "The others made that claim."

Seth twisted his mouth. "Why do you think the Aeons want her?"

"We won't know unless we ask her. She's currently in my Keep, so I suggest we do exactly that."

They'd taken no more than three steps out of the room when they saw Azazel heading their way. The Ancient frowned. "There a problem?"

"We'll explain on the way," Cain told him.

*

Wynter handed the broadsword back to Maxim, who studied its brand-spanking new runes with utter fascination.

"And this enchantment will work on anyone the blade slices?" he asked.

"Yes, including you, so be careful," she advised. "You wouldn't *truly* be itching all over, but you'd think that you were, so you'd scratch and scratch and scratch—it's not only distracting, it's maddening. But it will stop after twenty minutes or so."

"That's . . . I'm impressed. Very." He carefully sheathed his sword. "Thank you, Wynter."

"No, thank *you*," she said as he handed her payment.

She'd no sooner stuffed the cash in her pocket than a gentle breeze swirled around her ankles and traveled up her legs, fairly humming with warning. It wasn't a warning of danger, though. More like a heads-up that she needed to be prepared.

The solar room door opened, and Cain stalked inside. He wasn't alone. Seth and Azazel followed him into the room. And as all three men honed in on her, their expressions hard and intense, she suspected that at least *one* of her secrets were out.

*Hell.*

Maxim briefly greeted them before breezing out of the solar and abandoning her.

Cain stepped toward her, his bottomless eyes settled on her with a mind-melting focus that—even right then, despite the circumstances—did *far* too interesting things to her hormones. "Wynter, this is Azazel and my brother, Seth."

Azazel squinted. "The Priestess of the Bloodrose Coven, right?" It felt like a trick question.

"No. My crew says that shit to wind me up." She returned her gaze to Cain. "Well, I see you're busy, so I'll get going."

"There's no rush," he said, his voice smooth and casual, yet there was a firmness there that insisted she stay. "You might be interested to know why I was called away just now."

"Oh?"

"Bounty hunters requested an audience with an Ancient. They're looking for someone in particular."

Her insides seized. "Bounty hunters usually are."

"In this case, they're seeking a witch. A witch by the name of Wynter Dellavale. You. And they're seeking you on behalf of the people of Aeon."

"Yeah, so?"

He blinked. "You failed to mention that they wanted you when you came here looking for sanctuary."

"You said you weren't interested in what brought me or my crew here," she reminded him. "Are you going to hand me over to the bounty hunters?"

He gave her a pointed look. "You and I have a verbal contract, remember?"

"That doesn't answer my question."

He closed the small space between them, pinning her gaze with his own. "I sent them away, Wynter. I will send away anyone who comes for you, or I will kill them—one or the other." He stared at her like she was a puzzle he was desperate to solve. "Tell us why the Aeons want you."

It wasn't a request; it was a demand. And considering the Aeons might very well bring trouble to their door, she supposed it was only fair that the Ancients understood the situation. Not that she'd tell them *everything*. But then, they didn't need to know *everything*.

"They exiled me," she said.

"I know that much. But why?"

"My old coven lives in the town. Occasionally, people are 'chosen' to live among and directly serve the Aeons in the city below. In the opinion of the newly appointed Priestess, Esther, I was a weakness in the coven that would prevent them from being chosen, so they wanted me gone."

"Why did they consider you a weakness?" asked Azazel.

"Because my magick is dark," she replied. "Impure. Unworthy. Tainted. Or, at least, that's how they see it."

Azazel's brow lifted. "You don't?"

"No," she said. "Whether or not magick is bad depends on the intentions of the user."

He inclined his head. "True enough. I heard a witch was exiled but that the keeper who was meant to escort her to the border instead ran off with her. Was he killed by people on your trail?"

Just remembering that little shit stain made her nostrils flare. "Wagner didn't attempt to escort me to the border. The Aeons claim they steal the memories of exiled people, put them to sleep, and then have someone drive them out of there. I learned something when I was exiled. I learned that, in fact, they paralyze you with power so that you're easy for keepers to toss over the falls. The exiled are never truly banished. They're killed."

"But you escaped," said Cain.

"I escaped. And Wagner got what was coming to him in the process."

Cain's eyes drifted over her face. "Why do the Aeons want you so badly? It cannot possibly be merely because you murdered a keeper and fled."

She moved to a display table on which a potted plant sat. Wynter dug a finger into the soil and injected a thread of magick into it. Within mere seconds, the plant wilted, dried up, and decayed until it was utterly unsalvageable.

Cain regarded her with renewed interest. "You're the cause of the rot."

She slowly nodded. "I'm the cause of the rot."

# Chapter Nine

Shock. It was an emotion that Cain hadn't felt in a truly long time. So long, in fact, he almost hadn't recognized the feeling when it crashed into him.

There hadn't been even a millisecond where he had considered that Wynter might be responsible for the current fuckery going on at Aeon. He hadn't even been sure anything *was* truly going on there.

Cain found himself staring at her again, conceding to himself that he'd sincerely underestimated her. Oh, he'd known she was powerful. He'd known she was essentially an alpha playing at being an omega. But he wouldn't have guessed she could wield *that* level of power. No one would think it to look at her.

Seth scratched his head. "Don't take this the wrong way, Wynter, but how could one little witch infect the land that way?"

"I didn't infect it, I cursed it," she said. "There are ways to undo a curse, of course. But the methods are very intricate. You can't undo one by simply combating the *results*. The people of Aeon are no doubt trying to tackle the decay because they haven't yet realized the root of the problem. That's why curses are often so successful—people don't always immediately suspect that that's what they're dealing with, and so they don't take the right steps to counteract it."

She made the whole thing sound simple. Like hexing protected land was easy enough. It wasn't. Not at all. But then, maybe it wasn't as difficult for those who possessed dark magick.

Cain twisted his mouth. "So once the residents of Aeon realize it's a curse and treat it as such, they'll be able to undo it?"

She nodded.

"And to undo that, they'll have to end your life, right?" asked Azazel. "You wanted to cause destruction, and so only your own destruction will undo it. That's why witches rarely cast such curses, from what I heard."

"The cost is often considered too high, yes," she said.

"Not that I'm judging, because I think this is all fucking brilliant," Azazel went on, "but why retaliate to this extent? I know they essentially betrayed you on every level, but for you to be prepared to die just to get revenge ..."

Her eyes dulled, but then her expression shuttered ... as if she'd severed whatever connection she felt to the emotions rolling through her. "When I was a child, they exiled my mother. Or so I thought until the day they did the same to me, and I realized she was dead."

"Why did they exile her?" asked Seth.

She linked her fingers. "I died. Then I came back. The Aeons don't take kindly to the use of forbidden magick."

Azazel propped his hip against the wall. "How did you die?"

She looked down, her tongue poking the inside of her cheek. "When I was ten, two teenage boys lured me into the woods where they then paralyzed me with magick so they could have a little sadistic fun. They pissed on me. Spat in my eyes. Shoved sharp little stones up my nose. Tried making me choke on dirt. Stabbed me multiple times. Burned the soles of my feet with magick. Sliced my throat but then, bored of waiting for me to die, jammed the knife into the side of my throat."

Cain ground his teeth as anger bubbled up inside him. She'd recounted the incident so matter-of-factly, but her words were laced with the helplessness she'd felt back then. There was also a pure predatory rage there—it was subtle, but he heard it. So did his creature, which was at this very moment utterly enthralled by her.

She swallowed. "I felt *everything*, but I couldn't move. Couldn't scream. Couldn't cry out for help. So being paralyzed by power yet again made the 'exile' so much worse. Especially since the keeper intended to dismember me on behalf of the angry families of the boys who were executed after what they did to me—oh, *and* he meant to gouge out one of my eyes for them to have as a souvenir. To put it simply, I was in a blind fury."

"Anyone would have been." Cain crossed to her, unable to do anything else when she looked so very alone. "It would be safe to conclude that the Aeons believe you're behind the blight and intend to force you to fix it. They probably didn't suspect you at first, since it wouldn't initially seem like a magickal attack. But when the blight kept unnaturally spreading, they no doubt concluded that it had to be you who'd caused it, and now they want you to unravel what they will believe is a spell."

"That would explain why they went from wanting you dead to wanting you alive," Seth said to her.

Wynter's brow creased. "You didn't ask the bounty hunters?"

"We did," said Seth. "They don't know why the Aeons want you."

She eyed Cain closely. "It's possible that more hunters will come for me."

"It's unlikely, since I insisted that it be publicly known that you're in my service—people are highly reluctant to harm the property of an Ancient. It's a death sentence."

"I doubt that will stop residents of Aeon from coming for me, though—they'll be acting on orders from the Aeons; they won't dare ignore said orders. Hell, you may even be visited by the Aeons themselves. If you're not prepared to go up against them to keep me safe, I can understand that, but I'll need to leave."

She wasn't going anywhere. His creature would never allow it, even if Cain would. He put his face closer to hers. "I told you I wouldn't give you up. I meant it."

"But can you speak for the other Ancients when you say that?"

"Oh, they won't do the Aeons any favors. We loathe them even more than you do. The Aeons know that. So I doubt they would come for you *personally*. At least not initially. But they may send representatives."

Pausing, Cain took a moment to study her face. "I see you're skeptical that we'd protect you. I can understand why. I'll be honest, it's not *all* about you or our verbal contract. The fact is . . . *nothing* would please me and the other Ancients more than for Aeon to be uninhabitable. That was once our home, and they banished us much as they did you. For as long as you're alive, their land will continue to waste away, and their people will continue to fall ill. For those reasons alone, we will never let them harm you."

She glanced from him to Seth to Azazel. "You all want revenge, too."

Cain nodded. "And together, we'll get it."

"One question," Azazel said to her, raising his finger. "Will the curse only effect the surface of the town?"

"I can't say for sure, but it's possible that the city below will also suffer."

A grin spread across Azazel's face. "Best news I've heard in a long time. The other Ancients will be just as pleased to hear it."

The four of them talked a little while longer but then, tossing Cain a look that said they'd at some point revisit the reason she'd originally come to the Keep, Wynter left.

As the solar room door closed behind her, Azazel smiled. "I like that girl."

"You like what she did to Aeon," Seth corrected.

"Same thing." Azazel shook his head. "She really has no clue just how valuable she is to us. For the first time, we have something the Aeons want. We have a way to lure them here; a way to drag them into our path so we can kill them."

Cain nodded. "And in doing so, we'll finally destroy our cage."

"We need to tell the others," said Seth.

"We do." So Cain called them to the Keep, and soon every Ancient was sprawled around the solar. He brought them all up to speed, watching as they went from bored to enlivened.

Grinning, Dantalion said, "You know what I love most about this? The Aeons actually brought this on themselves. *They* exiled her. *They* sent hunters after her. *They* drove her here, serving the key to our freedom to us on a silver platter."

"Oh, the irony." Lilith's mouth curved. "It almost feels like fate or some higher power had a hand in this, doesn't it?"

"Or this is some trick," said Ishtar, her voice clipped. "She could be working for them. Could be a spy."

Lilith frowned. "That doesn't even make sense."

"She lived at Aeon for years; she was one of its people," said Ishtar. "She could *still* be one of them."

Seth shook his head. "I felt her hatred for the residents there. It all but hummed in the air. Plus, the Aeons long ago ceased attempting to plant spies here. They got tired of us always sniffing them out and sending the bodies back in pieces—they hated giving us those victories. Wynter is no spy."

"No, she's not," said Cain. "She's someone who needs to be protected at all costs—for her sake, and for ours."

Dantalion nodded and then sliced his gaze to a sulky-looking Ishtar. "If your ego is so fragile that you cannot bring yourself to protect a woman Cain fucked, you at least need to keep your distance from her."

Ishtar's face flamed. "Did I say I would hurt her? No. I merely said she could be a spy. I do not trust her."

"You don't *want* to trust her," Azazel corrected. "You want her to be a villain to justify your distaste for her. Fine. But leave her be."

Ishtar shot Cain a petulant look. "If I were you, I would stop sleeping with her. You'll only end up hurting her, and we do not need the 'key to our freedom', as Dantalion called her, turning against us."

Cain almost rolled his eyes. "I'll take that on board."

He had no intention whatsoever of keeping his hands off Wynter. His creature would put up a protest if he did. It currently regarded her as something it owned—how long that would last, Cain wasn't sure. Probably only a few days. A week at most, because the monster didn't prize her. It had never prized any of the women it very briefly considered its own. It had only 'claimed' them in its way because it didn't do well at sharing.

In that sense, it could definitely be said that the creature was as selfish as they came. But the fact was . . . it wasn't built to 'care.' Or treasure. Or protect. It was cold-blooded. Cruel. Insidious. And it was built to kill.

"How long do you think it will be before people from Aeon come to our doorstep?" asked Seth.

"Not long," predicted Dantalion. "The Aeons will send others in their place. They won't come here unless they absolutely have to."

"There is no saying that the Aeons will come at all," said Ishtar. "They will most likely continue sending others her way."

"Which is why it is imperative that we ensure she is protected," Lilith pointed out. "And we will."

A short time later, after the conversation came to an end, the Ancients began to trickle out of the solar.

Lingering, Seth said, "I take it you're no longer planning to Rest sometime soon."

"Definitely not," replied Cain.

Seth rubbed at his nape. "I didn't want to say anything in front of the others; I was worried Ishtar would twist my words. Don't take this the wrong way, but there's something not quite right about Wynter. Not in a negative sense, it's just . . . I can't explain it. To be fair, though, I've never before met someone who has an undead soul and possesses dark magick. It could simply be that."

It could be. But truthfully, Cain wasn't so sure. He'd suspected from the very beginning that there was much more to Wynter than there appeared to be. That suspicion had only grown. And while he didn't usually care to know the secrets of others, he was nothing close to indifferent where she was concerned.

He had no right to demand she part with her secrets when he was unable to part with his own. He could certainly try to figure it all out for himself, though. Yes, he could watch, observe, and study her. He'd solve the mystery of little Miss Dellavale eventually.

He'd also keep fucking her until he was no longer so greedy for everything she had to give.

Although his monster's possessiveness would fade fast, the creature nonetheless wouldn't object to Cain having her in his bed—it didn't particularly care how Cain chose to entertain himself. But until the possessiveness was gone, there was no way for him to undo what he'd done on his creature's behalf. And how the fuck could he explain that to her when he couldn't even admit to having a monster inside him?

*

Wynter was adjusting the position of her workbench when she sensed someone enter the shed the next day. Turning, she found that there were *two* someones.

*Well, if it isn't the berserkers.*

"What brings you here?" Seeing that they weren't holding weapons, she added, "You're clearly not potential customers."

Grouch folded his arms. "We're here to make you a proposition."

"A proposition?" she echoed.

"We were wary of hiring you when you first came to us," Annette told her. "Trusting strangers ain't our thing. Now that you've been in the city a few days, we've been able to see that you're no asshole. You're also good at what you do. We can agree to give you a chance."

Wynter looked from one berserker to the other. "A chance to what?"

"Work for us," said Grouch. "On a trial basis at first. We're talking minimum wage, but I'd say that's more than what you're earning per day right now."

Then he really had *no* idea how much custom she got. She might have been touched by the offer ... if he and his daughter weren't acting as if they were doing Wynter some grand, charitable favor for which she should get down on her knees and give thanks. They were very clearly expecting her to pounce on their offer and snap up this amazing opportunity.

She gave them a polite smile. "Thanks, but I'm good as I am."

Grouch stared at her for a long moment. Then he puffed up his chest, his brows snapping together. "You're not serious."

"Uh, I really am."

Annette perched her hands on her hips. "We're the best blacksmiths in this town."

"So I've heard," said Wynter. "You must be super proud."

"People come to us all the time looking for work," Annette added.

"I'd imagine they do," said Wynter. "Everyone wants to work with the best."

"Except you? What, you're bitter that we didn't hire you before?"

"Bitter? Not at all. I was disappointed initially, but I'm now glad you turned me down. If you hadn't, I might not have started this shop with my crew. It's doing pretty well."

Grouch glowered. "You're cutting into our profits."

Wynter shrugged. "That's just business. *You* cut into the profits of the other blacksmiths, but I'm guessing you're fine with it."

His nostrils flaring, he snapped his mouth shut.

"Look, I understand your issue," said Wynter. "People aren't so bothered about going to the best blacksmith or purchasing the best weapons, when they can buy something cheap and have it enchanted to improve it. They also don't need to buy a new weapon in order to have a different enchantment—I can change runes at any time. All this affects your business, I know.

"But I warned you that you'd lose custom. You didn't listen to me. You laughed at me, insulted me, pointed a sword at me. And then you lied that I was going to hex your shop so that I'd get in trouble with Cain. All that considered, did you really think I'd jump at your offer? Really?"

"So you *are* bitter," said Annette.

Wynter shook her head. "It's not bitterness. I simply have no reason to like you. I don't want to work for you. I don't want to work for anyone. Like I said, I'm good as I am. But thanks anyway. I appreciate the offer." Not really, but whatever.

Annette's face hardened. "You'll regret this."

Wynter pursed her lips. "I don't see how."

"People think you're all badass right now," said Annette. "They're forgetting what else dark magick can do. I'll be happy to remind them."

"Well, I wouldn't dream of getting in the way of your happiness, so . . ."

Annette's mouth tightened. "There's something else you're not considering. We're not the only business owners who aren't too fond of your little shop. Together, the group of us can cause you some serious aggravation."

"That would be a very big mistake," said a new voice.

Everyone momentarily froze, and then the rapidly paling berserkers spun to face the newcomer.

Annette took a step backwards and nervously wiped her hands on her thighs. "Cain, we . . . I mean, I—"

"No excuses, no lies." He took a slow, aggressive step toward the berserkers. "Now listen to me very carefully. Every person in this shed wears my mark. That alone should be enough reason for you to watch out for each other. I see that it isn't. So let me be very clear—if you make any trouble for Wynter, her coven, or her shop, you will pay for that in blood. Nobody fucks with what's mine and escapes punishment. Is that understood?"

"Yes," Grouch immediately blurted out while his daughter nodded.

"Good." Cain carelessly waved a hand. "Now get out of my sight."

The berserkers gave him a wide berth as they scurried around him and out of the shed.

Cain closed the door, his gaze fixed on Wynter. All the intensity in those unfathomable eyes hit her in her core.

"Pay for that in blood?" she repeated. "You don't think that's a little excessive? I mean, it's not like they threatened to kill me or anything."

"No, but they would have played games with you." He stalked toward her. "The only person who gets to mess with your head is me."

She felt her brow furrow. "I don't even know what to do with that comment." She didn't know what to do with him *in general.* "You're like no one I've ever met before."

He trailed his fingertip from the hollow beneath her ear all the way down her throat. "I could say the same to you. I'm not easy to intrigue. I'm even harder to shock. You managed to do both."

"Hmm, well, I appreciate you coming all the way here to take away that barrier thing."

"You think that's why I'm here?" he asked, his mouth kicking up in amusement. *Amusement.*

She felt her lips flatten. "It *should* be why you're here. I want whatever you put inside me gone."

"I'm only guarding what's mine. Is that so bad?"

"Since when am I yours?" And since when did her body get all tingly over the M word?

"Since I decided." He bit her lip before she could bark out a retort of any kind. "The barrier, as you call it, will fade on its own within a few days. Now, the reason I came here was to tell you not to make any plans for after tonight's celebration. You'll be coming home with me."

Bold bastard. "Oh, I will?"

"You will. Because you want to."

"So very sure of that, aren't you?"

"We can pretend I'm wrong, if you'd like. But you don't strike me as a game player, or as a person who has an issue with reaching out to take what they want."

Ordinarily, no, she didn't have such an issue. Nor did she play games. Life was too short for that shit—something she'd learned early. But this was . . . oh, who the hell was she kidding? Certainly not herself. The truth was that she had no intention of resisting him, whether it would be wise or not.

He stroked a hand down her hair. "I want to fuck you in my bed.

I want you to break for me again." He dipped his head and stared deep into her eyes. "You want the same thing. And so you'll come home with me later, won't you?"

Sniffing, she lifted an imperious brow. "I'll expect more than one orgasm."

One of his sexy-as-shit smiles surfaced. "I'd be disappointed if you didn't."

# Chapter Ten

"I prefer the seats we had last time," said Hattie as they waited for the celebration to begin. "They were comfier."

Anabel sighed. "They were exactly the same, simply in a different section of the arena. You're just moody because you had to come away from your book."

"The hero was about to declare his love for the heroine. It was about damn time. He hesitated for too long. How hard is it to admit that you love someone?" Hattie patted her hair. "I said it to all my husbands."

Anabel's brow puckered. "But did you actually mean it? I only ask because, well, you killed them. In cold blood."

"I warned them I don't handle betrayal well."

"I don't think they knew that meant you'd poison them."

"They did seem surprised when they were dying."

Beside Wynter, Xavier rolled his eyes before leaning toward her. "Cain is staring at you again," he said. "He's not the only one who's been sliding glances your way. Except she's not so much glancing as glaring."

Wynter felt her mouth flatten. "If you're referring to Ishtar then, yeah, I'm aware."

"I heard some whispers that she's been trying to seduce both Cain *and* Seth ever since she woke from her Rest," said Xavier.

Ignoring the way her gut twisted in what suspiciously felt like jealousy, Wynter frowned. "Is she imagining some kind of triad or something?"

He shrugged. "Actually, I thought maybe she had her eye firmly on one of them and was hoping that flirting with their brother would spur them to make a move on her. But it might be that she has her heart set on a triad. She seems like a person who'd get off big time on having two men worship her like that."

"She probably *could* have that kind of relationship. I've seen enough guys eat her up with their eyes." Cain wasn't one of them, though.

"But she doesn't seem to want the easily attainable ones. I suppose if you've lived as long as she has, you'd need challenges to keep the boredom at bay. And you'd *have* to keep the boredom at bay unless you wanted to go stir crazy."

Wynter nodded. Merely an hour of boredom could drive her insane. Eons of it would fuck with her mind for sure.

"How do you feel about the Ancients all knowing you were exiled from Aeon?"

"Now that I know for sure that they won't side with the Aeons, I'm not too worried about it. But ... I feel like there's something they're not telling me."

"Really? About what?"

"I don't know. I really don't. It's just ... you should have seen the way Azazel's eyes lit up when I told them everything. Seth seemed just as revved about how badly the Aeons want me. I don't think I've ever seen any Ancient or Aeon look like that. They're not easily moved by anything."

"How did Cain react?"

"He was a little more introspective than the other two, but I sensed some extreme satisfaction wafting from him. They're all loving that the Aeons want something they have."

Xavier's brows dipped. "There's a lot of bad blood between the two camps, right? Maybe it's simply that."

"Maybe," conceded Wynter, recalling Cain explaining their craving for revenge.

"What are you two whispering about?" demanded Anabel.

"Your weird foot fetish," replied Wynter, straight-faced.

Hattie frowned at the blonde. "You have a foot fetish?"

Anabel jerked back. "What? Ew, no."

Xavier chuckled.

Just then, Delilah plopped into the seat that she'd earlier vacated in order to use the bathroom. "Seems like I got here just in time," she said as Ishtar stood.

Like the previous night, the Ancient thanked everyone for coming and all that jazz. She also passed on her gratitude to Azazel for organizing this particular celebration, though said gratitude was stiffly spoken—something that seemed to amuse him. Wynter got the sense that the two Ancients didn't get along so well.

In no time at all, the action began. And it *was* action. Azazel had arranged for Olympic-like games to take place in the performance space. All were dangerous and death-defying, especially the crazy-ass chariot races. A lot of gasping and cursing came from the spectators.

During the interval, food and drinks were given out. Wynter barely tasted her meal, far too conscious of how closely she was being watched by both Cain and Ishtar. The other Ancients often looked Wynter's way as well ... as if it wasn't rude to idly observe someone like they were a damn zoo animal in a cage.

Finally, the interval was over. A lone male waltzed into the performance space. She'd never met him before, but there was something familiar about him.

"Does anyone know who that is?" she asked.

"His name is Bowen, he's one of Azazel's aides," replied Delilah. "He's a berserker."

And then it clicked. "He's *got* to be related to Grouch." Wynter would bet good money on it. "The resemblance is there."

Delilah's brow furrowed. "Grouch as in the smithy who pissed you off earlier?"

"Yeah, that Grouch."

"I *did* hear that he followed some of his relatives to Devil's Cradle. They didn't all seek refuge here at the same time."

"That would explain why he's in Azazel's service while Grouch and Annette are in Cain's." Wynter stilled as a rumble of power split through the air.

In the performance space, a portion of the floor shimmered and rippled. The sand dispersed, and a grating sound rang through the arena as a stone platform rose to the surface. Bordered by rope, it resembled a boxing ring.

Using a microphone, Bowen addressed the spectators as he said, "Now for our next event . . . This is the battle square. As you can no doubt see, there is magick embedded in the stone. It is spelled so that any injuries people receive while within the square will immediately heal. But the wounds will not *feel* healed to whoever receives them. More, the injuries will not *look* healed. In fact, they will seem so real and will hurt the 'injured' so much that it will play tricks on their mind. They will believe they are wounded, bleeding, weakening—maybe even dying."

Well, how delightful was that.

"The ropes are also spelled," he went on. "They contain any magick, energy, or power that's released within the square." He flicked his hand, and then a rack of swords came into view. They were all pretty basic—long, straight blades attached to a hilt. "So . . . do we have any volunteers?"

It was almost amusing how quickly people snapped up the opportunity to engage in a fight. No one particularly cared who their opponent was—they just wanted the release that came with violence.

The brawls probably shouldn't have been so entertaining, but they were. Especially whenever one of the fighters was someone who'd laughed when she asked for a job—then Wynter became *really* invested in the duels.

Pretty much everyone was disappointed when the stone platform returned to the sand. But then the weirdest thing happened. Power again rose in the air, and then a lengthy ditch appeared, stretching from one end of the performance space to the other. It was surrounded by ropes, just like the battle square.

"This here is the gauntlet," Bowen announced. "Like the square, it is spelled so that injuries immediately heal but don't *seem* healed. This time, we're not looking for volunteers. The participating groups will be chosen at random."

He paused as another male strode toward him holding a glass bowl. "The names of every pack, lair, nest, coven, etc. is inside this bowl. For whichever groups are chosen, the objective is for them to battle their way through the gauntlet. This will not be easy, since soldiers will soon fill the ditch. They will not be real soldiers, but they will look real, and they will move to kill.

"Any participants who 'die' will be spat out of the gauntlet while the remainder of their group continues to fight. Participants may shift shape, use weapons, fight with magick, use any preternatural ability, or even adopt a combination of all. Whichever group finishes the gauntlet in the fastest time will receive a cash prize."

Bowen dipped his hand into the bowl and pulled out a small, folded piece of paper. He then read out the name of a mage conclave. A demon lair was called out next. Then a fey court, and last but not least ... "The Bloodrose Coven."

*Motherfucker.*

Wynter exchanged solemn glances with her crew. Wonderful. Just wonderful.

Dutifully, they slid out of their row and began to make their way to the performance space.

Delilah sidled up to her. "Seems awful convenient that our coven was chosen when Bowen's related to a person who said you'd regret not taking the job they offered you."

Behind them, Xavier made a sound of agreement. "I'm thinking this is fixed."

"Cain threatened they'd pay if they fucked with me," said Wynter.

"Yeah, but berserkers are spiteful bastards," Delilah reminded her. "They don't know how to back down. And this isn't something that can be pinned on them, is it? Seems totally random. *Seems.*"

Finally, they all reached the performance space. At this point, several aides had joined Bowen. It was Maxim who indicated where Wynter and her crew would stand.

"This is your fault," she said to Delilah.

Frowning, Delilah put her hand to her chest. "How is it mine?"

"They couldn't have done this if you hadn't declared us a coven." Wynter felt Cain's eyes on her, but she didn't look up. She was *all* business right then. This was about her and the people under her protection, no one else.

The other participants all looked eager as hell to get going. They also seemed tremendously cocky, certain they had this in the bag.

The Shaman of the mage conclave gave Xavier a look of false sympathy. "You really should have taken us up on our offer and joined our conclave."

"I prefer to be on winning side," said Xavier, his voice even.

The fey Lord grinned. "Oh, now that's cute."

The Shaman shot the Lord a derisive look. "*You* lot have no chance of coming out on top either."

"Neither of your little tribes do," the demon Prime cut in. He didn't even *look* at Wynter or her crew, as if he'd discounted them as no threat.

Anabel turned to her, her mouth tight. "We can't allow any of those groups to win this." If there was one thing she disliked, it was being dismissed. Probably because she was fucking brilliant. "I know you wanted us all to keep a low profile, but we won't be doing ourselves any favors if we let these people believe they're right to underestimate us."

"I agree," said Xavier. "Respect is everything in a place like this. Fear? Even better."

Delilah nodded. "It'll mean people are less likely to bother us, and so you won't be forced to demonstrate how powerful you are to keep us safe."

"Which would be for the best," Hattie added.

Wynter sighed, knowing they were right. "Okay, we can give

it our all. Mostly. I can't let out my ... you know." Her monster couldn't be unleashed here and now.

Understanding, the others nodded.

"I know you're all about me sticking to the right-hand path," Xavier said to her, "but you can't get mad when I use magick to—"

"I won't," Wynter assured him, anticipating what he'd say. She cut her gaze to Anabel. "You're *sure* you want to be part of this fight? It will mean you'll have to take a mental backseat for a while."

"I know," the blonde assured her. "It's fine. Clearly these people here need to see that we're not easy targets."

Delilah leaned into her. "*And* you want Diego to see that you're badass."

Anabel frowned. "I'm not badass, I'm just the reincarnation of—"

"Whatever," Delilah interrupted, her hand up. "He'll be wowed, trust me."

"Bloodrose Coven, you're up first!" Bowen called out.

Of course they were.

Wynter led the way as they crossed to the berserker, who looked *far* too entertained at the moment.

Delilah promptly shifted into a sleek black cat, her pretty gold nail polish still intact. Bowen snickered at the dainty sight of her, and she shot him a look so cold Wynter could swear the air temperature cooled just a little.

Maxim appeared and cleared his throat, his brow creased in concern. "Um ... are you sure you want to do this, Hattie?"

The old woman patted his hand. "Don't you worry about me, dear. I'll be just fine." She shifted into a crow and then settled on his shoulder. He froze, looking adorably unsure what to do all of a sudden. Much like Delilah, she hadn't needed to strip off her clothes because she wasn't an actual shifter; it was her magick that forced the change.

Xavier conjured his rapier bone sword and swiped it through the air.

"What bone is that?" asked Maxim.

Xavier smirked. "Angel bone. This baby could cut through dragon scales like butter."

Wynter turned to Anabel, who'd conjured her broadsword. "You ready?"

The blonde nodded, standing tall. "Ready."

Wynter put her mouth near the blonde's ear and quietly sang the few select words that would call to the alleged part of her soul that liked to come out and play. "Mary, Mary, please come out."

Anabel did a slow blink, and then her eyes . . . they were the same pale blue, but now a hint of madness swirled in their depths. Her posture lost its stiffness, and she gazed around with avid interest, no doubt planning to stir some shit.

Wynter put a hand on her shoulder. "Stab to kill."

"They'll all fall," Anabel/Mary promised.

Anticipation thrumming through her blood, Wynter called to her own sword. It appeared in her hand, dark and shiny.

Bowen gave it a long look, surprised. "You may step into the ditch. Note that the gauntlet will not end until every one of you has crossed the finish line . . . assuming any of you will reach it. Remember, those that 'die' will be spat out." He jumped when Hattie squawked in his face, and a round of laughs came from the spectators.

Wynter exchanged determined looks with her crew. They each slid under the ropes and hopped down into the ditch. *Whoa.* She felt the power in the ground beneath her. The slight vibration purred against the soles of her shoes.

Her monster stirred, not quite sure it liked the situation. She tried communicating that all was fine and that this was a mere game. But the intensity of the foreign power unnerved it. A subtle breeze came, carrying a hint of assurance that eventually made her monster settle.

That was when the soldiers appeared.

There were dozens of them up ahead. Some held swords while others raised a hand that glowed with magick.

"Begin!" yelled Bowen.

The soldiers swarmed them *mega* fast.

Wynter and Xavier both whipped up their swords and parried the blow that came their way. Delilah lunged, shifting from a domestic cat to a huge monstrous feline and knocking a soldier down, digging her iron claws into his chest. Hattie raked her talons on the face of another soldier, making him stagger backwards and crash into his compatriots. Anabel/Mary . . . well, she just laughed like a loon and beheaded the nearest soldier.

The five of them battled their way through the gauntlet. Wynter, Xavier, and Anabel/Mary sliced, feinted, parried, ducked, and twisted. They moved fast. Fluid. Smooth. Flowed with the fight. Like it was a dance.

At the same time, the crow and cat pounced and bit and raked at the soldiers like savages. The two animals dodged swords, fists, and feet. While the cat also needed to evade any magickal blows, the crow had no such need. Any such hits bounced right off her and rebounded back at her attacker—Hattie negated magick with her very being whenever she was in her crow form.

Wynter impaled one soldier on her sword while Xavier slit the throat of another. The men collapsed to the floor. He knelt and slammed his hands on their stomachs as he began to chant. Their backs arched, their eyes flew open, and then they were up . . . running at the soldiers.

Her body balanced and her muscles loose, Wynter fought on. Like Xavier and Anabel/Mary, she also lashed out with her magick—dazing, burning, whipping, or knocking people down. Of course, she was careful not to go full throttle. She couldn't slam her foot down on the magickal pedal here and now.

The air whistled as the swords slashed through it again and again. Blades clanged. Voices cursed. Magick crackled. The cat roared. The crow shrieked and flapped its wings.

Wynter hissed as a blade caught her side. Jesus *fuck*. She didn't make the mistake of angrily lunging and thrusting her sword. She didn't need to anyway—he drew back as the crow dipped down and stabbed an eyeball with her beak, yanking it right out of the socket.

His cry of agony died an abrupt death as Anabel/Mary disemboweled him. The woman was in her element as she hacked through the soldiers, giggling and dancing and high-fiving thin air. Her newest victim, like most of the others, was soon back on his feet courtesy of Xavier and then joined their rapidly growing army.

It wasn't long before Wynter and her crew were approaching the finish line. Which was a goddamn relief, because the throbbing wound in her side was deep, and the blood loss was *not* helping matters.

The sight of the finish line seemed to fuel the others, because they charged with renewed vigor. The soldiers backed up under the pressure of the assault. One by one, they went down until only a single soldier remained. He hit the ground hard as Delilah landed on his chest with a roar. Wynter brought down her sword and sliced off his head . . . before promptly kicking it out of the ditch. It sailed through the air and landed at Bowen's feet, splattering the sand with blood. The head then winked out of existence.

Pure silence fell as everyone simply stared at Wynter and her crew. Then came the applause.

Panting and sweating, she turned to the others and said, "Let's get out of this goddamn ditch."

"Yeah, let's." Xavier severed whatever connection he had to the soldiers he'd raised from the dead, and they fell to the floor like sacks of spuds.

The moment she slid out from under the ropes, her wounds disappeared, her pain faded, and the blood and mess cleared from her skin and clothing. She glanced at the others, realizing it was the same for them . . . and that one of them was missing.

Wynter looked down into the ditch, sighing. Anabel/Mary had put the hilt of her sword to a dead soldier's mouth as if it were a microphone and was singing, "Man down, man down, man down."

Calling out 'Anabel' earned her no response, so Wynter shouted, "Mary, leave him."

The blonde's head snapped up. She looked about to object but then pouted. "Fine." She casually hacked off a soldier's leg as she made her way out of the ditch.

Back in her human form, Delilah smiled at her and said, "Night, night, Mary."

The key phrase made the blonde pout again. "No fair." Her blue eyes cleared so that they were once more normal, and Anabel went stiff as a board. "Is it over?" she asked, glancing around her.

"It's over," said Hattie, now human.

Anabel bit her lower lip. "She didn't drink anyone's blood again, did she? I don't taste any."

Xavier shook his head. "No, she didn't do it this time."

Hattie smiled. "That was fun. Haven't plucked eyes out in years. Nice to know I've still got it."

Wynter 'sent' her sword back to the cottage, and the others did the same with their weapons. Together, they all strode back to the start line of the gauntlet, sure to make eye-contact with the other participants.

Delilah smirked at them. "And that's how it's done."

The demon Prime looked at Wynter, his mouth curved. "Nice to know you're not a dainty, fragile princess who leaves the bulk of the fight to her knights."

Wynter gave him a bright smile. "Hope I can say the same for you."

He only laughed.

*All* interest, the Shaman tried catching Xavier's eyes. "Impressive, um . . ." He winced. "I'm sorry, what's your name again?"

"Seamus," Xavier said in an Irish accent, managing to look sincerely affronted that his 'name' had been forgotten. "Now feck off."

Inwardly shaking her head, Wynter met Bowen's shocked gaze head-on. "You know, there's a reason berserkers are low in number these days. It's that you all have a seriously bad habit of judging people by their appearance. It means you don't always see the danger coming. Which is bad, really. Even fucking rats sense danger coming."

His face darkened. "I—"

"Need to *really* rethink your idea to use me and my crew as 'entertainment' like we're a fucking joke," Wynter finished. "That's all." With that, she headed back to their spot.

Maxim stood there, fighting a grin. "Quite the dark horses, aren't you?"

Hattie beamed. "Indeed. And I'll be damn surprised if the other groups beat our time, because I know we were fast."

Wondering what she'd see, Wynter let herself look up and meet Cain's gaze. There was no shock. There was *pure* heat. Oh, she was gonna get fucked tonight all right.

*

The breath left Wynter's lungs as her back hit the wall. Then Cain's mouth was on hers, devouring her as his body caged hers. The man had wasted no time in getting her upstairs to his bedchamber when they arrived at the Keep, and now he was wasting no time in stripping her. Aggressively. Like having anything concealing her skin from him somehow offended him.

Her tee went first, then her bra. He swooped down and latched onto a nipple, suckling hard, while his hands tackled her fly. With a growl, he shoved down her jeans and panties, and she kicked them aside.

Planting his hand either side of her head, he pulled back a little and raked his gaze over her. Slowly. Thoroughly. As if it was his right. "Nice," he said, his eyes tracing one of the rune tattoos on her abdomen. She had many such tattoos here and there.

"Thanks. Now do me."

Holding her gaze, he closed his hand around her breast, blatantly proprietary. A darkness rippled behind his eyes . . . almost as if something else looked out at her for the briefest moment. Which had to be her imagination—

She hissed at the pinch to her nipple, the small pain shooting straight to her clit.

"You liked that," he sensed. "Good. Because tonight, you're gonna hurt for me a little."

She had no idea what that meant.

He effortlessly lifted her and carried her to the four poster bed. The chamber carried a hint of 'old.' Tapestries hung on the walls. Candles were scattered here and there. Long, draping curtains were positioned just right.

He lay her on the mattress. "Don't move." He shed his clothes. His body ... shit, it was a fucking masterpiece. A little too perfect. There was much hard, sleek, perfectly defined muscle to be seen. And Jesus, his tattoos were impressive. There were so many. Symbols, totems, runes, codes, and ancient writings that she didn't understand.

The perfect V of his hips was another *tick* in his 'hot' column. As was the thick oh-so long cock that she badly wanted to take for a ride again. It stood loud and proud and rock-hard, tapping his belly.

He knelt between her legs and pushed them wide apart. "Such a pretty pussy you have." He snaked his hands down her inner thighs and brushed his thumbs over her folds. "Sit up for me."

Um ... okay. She did as he asked, curious.

"Give me your hand. The one that wears my mark."

She held it out to him, surprised it wasn't trembling with the anticipation thrumming through her.

He took it and held it up, his eyes tracing the brand. She was about to ask why a snake was threaded through the triangle that sat within the C, but then he spoke.

"I like seeing my mark on you." He licked along the C, and Wynter nearly jumped out of her fucking skin. She stared at him, her eyes wide. Because that tongue ... she felt it licking her slit, warm and wet.

"Let's get you nice and slick, shall we?" He traced the C again.

Once more, she felt a tongue swipe between her folds. The

sensation was so much more intense than a physical touch, as if she was ten times more sensitive than usual. And oh God, it was amazing.

Wynter slapped her free hand on the mattress to support herself as his tongue did wicked, wicked things over and over and over. Honestly, she was so swept away by sensation she could have forgotten he was there if the bastard didn't begin taunting her with words between licks.

"I could do this anytime, anywhere," he rumbled. "Whether we were alone or surrounded by people."

She gasped as he lashed a particular spot—it was like a wet flick to her clit. He licked at the center of the mark over the little triangle, and she almost came off the fucking bed. It was like he'd stabbed his tongue deep inside her—something he did again and again, until she was so desperate to come she'd have done anything he asked. *Anything.* So it was terribly fortunate that the only thing he told her to do was come. Oh, she could do that.

Her head fell back as her orgasm washed over her, heating her skin and causing her inner muscles to ripple around mere air. Fuck, she needed to be filled. Badly.

Cain released her hand and slipped his finger deep into her pussy. "Soaking wet." He withdrew the digit and sucked it clean. "Lie back. Move your hair away from your face, I want nothing obstructing my view. That's it."

Staying on his knees, he gripped her thighs, raised her hips and tilted them to line up his cock with her entrance. "Come when you want." He thrust hard, *forcing* his way deep, stretching her without mercy.

She'd barely had a moment to register the sting when a warm, electric wave of pleasure washed over her soul, wrenching at her body so her back bowed almost violently. It was different this time. Held an edge. It was like when her scalp prickled from having her hair pulled, or like the burn from a hand coming down sharply on her ass—the pain complemented the pleasure and gave it a dark,

146

addictive feel. The sensation came again, *so fucking intense*, and she cried out.

"Shh, you can take it." He pulled back his hips and then slammed his cock home just as he sent another wave of pleasure/pain sweeping over her soul. "That's it, hurt for me."

Cain began powering into her hard and deep, just as he'd been aching to do since he'd watched her in that gauntlet. There was something very feral about Wynter Dellavale when she fought, and that appealed to him on a fiercely sexual level that was entirely primitive. Just the same, the predatory elegance with which she'd moved had intensified his monster's need to *own* her.

Driven by a similar insanely intense need to possess her, Cain took her with thrusts of his cock and strokes to her soul. He wanted her fucking addicted to him. To *this*. Wanted her to need him like she'd never needed anyone else. Wanted her to come back to him again and again, unable to help herself.

So he fucked and wrecked and dominated her—overwhelming her body and soul. He wanted her mind as well, greedy for every part of her. She was becoming an obsession and he knew it, but fuck if he could do anything about it.

She came hard, fracturing right before his eyes, so beautiful she gripped his gut. Not done with her yet, he kept going; kept brushing her soul with pleasure/pain while brutally hammering into her pussy. And then he sensed another orgasm building fast.

He growled. "That's it, break for me."

She screamed, her spine snapping straight, her inner muscles clenching his cock, her eyes wet with tears.

Cain groaned, slamming harder and faster. "Love it when you cry." He shoved deep and came so hard his vision went black for a second.

She was trembling beneath him, her eyes shut, her lips parted. He draped himself over her and brushed away a tear with his thumb. She didn't move. Didn't respond when he feathered soft kisses down the side of her face that he often found his gaze drifting to. And he quickly realized she'd passed out.

Cain felt his mouth curve. She'd be annoyed about that tomorrow, but he had no intention of waking her. Instead, he rolled onto his side and drew her close, surprised when he sensed that his creature planned to stay awake and watch over her.

# Chapter Eleven

Azazel leaned back against the wall of the solar room the next morning as he said, "Her story checks out. My source confirmed what she told us about her past, her mother, and why both were exiled."

Cain turned away from the window overlooking his garden. "You thought she was lying?"

"I expect everyone to lie to me, because I lie to everyone else. *Our kind* live a lie." Azazel frowned, pensive. "Plus, she has this unfamiliar vibe about her. I don't think she's all witch. Maybe she's a hybrid of some kind. She never mentioned her father. It could be that he isn't a witch. My source isn't sure who he is, only that he never came to Aeon with her old coven."

"Do the Aeons suspect she's responsible for the land's deterioration?"

"Yes, though they don't know how."

"Did you tell your source there's a curse at work?" If so, Cain would be pissed.

"No. That's a need-to-know thing. He doesn't need to know." Azazel tipped his head to the side. "So, you took her home with you last night."

"Yes, and I'd like to get back to her before she wakes up and disappears, so are we done?"

Blinking, Azazel pushed away from the wall. "Wait, she's still here?"

"Yes."

"Where?"

"My bedchamber."

Azazel squinted. "As in your personal chamber, or one of the rooms you use for women you bring home?"

"The first," Cain carelessly replied, going for aloof.

"Don't act like that's nothing, Cain. Our monsters don't easily accept other people in their den. *Especially* for an overnight stay. Your creature didn't fight you on it?"

"It likes having her where it can see her. Which is more about control than anything else. It wants to be able to see for itself that no other man is near her."

"So it's possessive of her?"

"It insisted on me plugging her."

Azazel's lips parted. "You're serious?"

"It isn't prepared to share her. If I hadn't done what it wanted, it would have done the deed itself. Then it probably would have ended up killing her, though not necessarily on purpose."

"Does she know she's been plugged?"

"She believes it's simply a barrier. Obviously, I can't explain the situation to her."

Azazel puffed out a breath. "I don't even know what to say. I can't relate at the fuck all to your situation. I know our monsters are territorial by nature, but mine has never wanted me to plug anyone. Is this normal for you?"

Far from it. "There have been times when mine has wanted me to plug other women, but it's never insisted on it before. So the most it has done is sulk for an hour when I refused to act on what it wanted. It's never been prepared to take the matter into its own hands before. I don't know what it is about her that has it acting out of character."

"It's not the only one acting out of character. As far as I know, you've only allowed one other woman to enter your personal chamber—that was Ishtar. That didn't end well. And I don't just mean your relationship with her."

No, he meant that Cain's creature had grown to feel so much

distaste for her that it had hated having a den she'd 'soiled.' That was how the monster had seen it. Cain had eventually had to switch chambers.

"If your creature decides it wants to keep Wynter—"

"It won't," said Cain. "In a few days, it'll be bored of her."

"But if it isn't, if it *does* want to keep her . . ."

"She's fucked," Cain finished with a sigh.

Azazel gave a slow nod. "Yeah, she's fucked."

\*

Walking through the stone corridors of the Keep, Wynter shook her head at herself. God, she'd actually passed out after sex. Like some kind of swooning maiden. How embarrassing.

Cain, being a person who seemed amused by other people's discomfort, would for sure find her embarrassment hilarious. As such, she'd been kind of relieved when she woke to find he was gone.

After she'd dragged on her clothes, she'd exited the chamber to find Maxim waiting outside. He'd informed her that Cain was in a meeting with another Ancient. She wondered if it was Ishtar but then shoved the matter out of her mind. It wasn't Wynter's business.

Cain apparently also hoped she'd wait for him to return. Nu-uh. She had shit to do. And the more time she spent around that beautiful bastard, the more threatened she felt as a woman. Because with the power he could wield over her body and soul—bringing her a pleasure that no other man ever had or ever could—he'd set up a craving in her.

After thanking Maxim for escorting her to the exit, she left the Keep and headed home.

She walked into the living room to find Delilah organizing her for-sale cosmetics near the window.

Taking in the sight of Wynter, Delilah smiled. "Well, well, well, *someone* looks awfully well fucked. Had a good night, Priestess?"

Wynter shot her a droll look. "Don't call me that."

Snickering, Delilah glanced toward the kitchen. "You got those potions ready yet, Anabel? Customers will be coming soon."

"I'm almost done!" Anabel shouted.

Delilah snorted. "You said that half an hour ago."

"You can't rush genius!"

Rolling her eyes, Delilah turned back to Wynter. "Quick warning, Anabel's all in a tizzy."

Wynter frowned. "Why?"

"Diego sent her flowers. He doesn't seem to have realized why Anabel switched from a Nervous Nelly to a bloodthirsty bitch in the gauntlet, but it would seem he's happy to roll with it. She isn't sure how to handle the attention or acceptance, though. Given Cain all but dragged you out of the arena while giving you sex eyes, I'm pretty confident in assuming that he wasn't put off by your vicious performance last night."

"Very good guess. In fact, he seemed to get off on it."

"I got that impression." Delilah sobered a little. "Think he'd be able to handle what you are?"

"He'd handle it. It's *the way* he'd handle it that's the problem."

"He doesn't strike me as a person who's easily fazed."

"It's not that I think he'll fear me, Del. I'm not even sure it's an emotion he *can* feel. But he'll want me dead all the same. Every single one of the Ancients will. At the very least, they'd toss me out of Devil's Cradle."

Delilah stood up a little straighter. "If they did, you wouldn't be heading off alone. We'd go with you."

"I wouldn't ask any of you to—"

"We'd go with you," she repeated, her voice hard. "Would you stay here if one of us was kicked out?"

"Fuck, no."

"Then you get it. Now let's—*Hattie,* you're not supposed to be reading right now, we've got stuff to do," Delilah called out, looking toward the kitchen yet again.

"I'm not reading," came Hattie's reply.

Delilah's lips thinned. "Woman, I can see you looking down at an open book."

"I'm just admiring the font."

"You're talking out of your ass is what you're doing," Wynter cut in, turning to look at her.

"Speaking of asses, there's an anal sex scene in here," said Hattie. "Why would he tell her to push out as he pushes in? That's risky business. I mean, she could fart."

Wynter closed her eyes. "I'm sorry, I can't have this conversation. Stop laughing, Del, it ain't funny. Now I have just enough time to go shower and change, I'll be back soon."

The day seemed to drag on, though Wynter couldn't explain why. It wasn't like it was a *bad* day. Plenty of customers came and went, and some products were so high in demand that Delilah had to take orders.

As usual, they were tired by the end of the workday. Hattie, though, was more chipper than usual as they ate a late dinner. A knock at the door had her hazel eyes going wide with excitement. "Oh, this could be him," she said, standing.

"Him? Who's him?" asked Wynter. "And why do you look all happy and flushed?"

"Hattie has a 'gentleman caller,'" explained Xavier, smiling.

"A fellow witch," she added, patting her hair.

"Don't worry, he's not trying to lure her away from us or anything," Xavier told Wynter. "He'd simply like to get to know her better."

There was no 'simply' when they were dealing with someone who handled betrayal and heartache by whipping up poisonous teas. "Just don't marry him, Hattie. That's all I ask." Providing there was no walk down the aisle, the guy should be safe.

Hattie waved that away and hurried out of the kitchen, humming to herself. When she returned, she didn't have a strange male at her side. No, it was Maxim.

Wynter blinked. "Oh, hey, Maxim."

His expression serious, he said, "Cain would like you to join him at the manor. Your old coven is here."

*Well, fuck me sideways.*

\*

Standing in the grand foyer with Azazel, Cain turned as he heard two sets of footfalls heading their way. And there was his witch. She looked remarkably calm and casual, given the situation. In fact, she seemed more interested in the décor than why she'd been called to the mansion. Which was probably why Maxim kept casting her curious glances.

Her eyes met Cain's and . . . no, there was still nothing there to suggest that she was feeling anything besides blasé. If he hadn't known how much the Moonstar coven had fucked her over, he might have bought her indifferent act. His creature, too, wasn't so convinced that she was fine—it knew exactly how good she was at showing people only what she wanted them to see.

"Right on time, little Priestess," said Cain, resisting the urge to touch her—that could wait.

She nodded at both him and Azazel. "Maxim says my old coven is here." She glanced around. "What room are they in?"

"They're outside," Cain told her. "After what they did to you, they're not welcome here. They were told to wait at the gates. I will go out there first to talk with them. You and Azazel will follow soon after."

She stared at him for a long moment, looking as though she might object, but then she briefly inclined her head. "All right."

"So careful to keep your expression neutral," he said. "I hope you don't have it in your head that I'm about to make a deal with these people. I've assured you that I will protect you. I meant it."

Not giving her a chance to respond, Cain stalked out of the manor and down the driveway. The iron gates swung open with a faint creak, but he didn't step out of them. None of the dozen witches moved forward. They stood very still, eyeing him warily.

Finally, the woman in the center gave him a placid smile, her lips trembling slightly. "Good evening. My name is Esther, Priestess of—"

"Yes, I heard," he said, sure to sound bored. "What do you want?"

She slowly inhaled, clasping her hands in front of her. "There is a rumor that a stray member of my coven is under your correction. I have come to take her home, where she belongs."

"Have you now?"

"Her name is Wynter Dellavale. I have it on good authority that she is here. If you would be so kind as to summon her—"

"No one would ever describe me as kind."

Someone from the slowly gathering crowd snickered, drawing the attention of the coven. These witches weren't the first people to come searching for an outcast, and they wouldn't be the last. The residents often enjoyed watching such people be turned away just as they were once turned away by those who mattered to them.

"What do you want with her?" Cain asked.

"To take her home, as I said," replied Esther. "She is ours."

Was she *fuck*. "Yours?" The word almost came out on a growl—a sound that would have come from Cain's creature. It really didn't like hearing another refer to Wynter as theirs. Like him, it wanted this bitch gone. "You didn't seem to feel that way when you chose to cast her out of your coven."

Esther licked her lips. "That was a mistake. We will make it up to her."

"Hmm now, see, this is my problem ... I don't believe you. I don't believe you give a whisper of a shit about Wynter. Of course, I don't expect you to admit that to someone whose protection she is under—it would be unwise of you, to say the least. What I do expect is for you to leave here without drama."

"But—"

"The bounty hunters *did* pass on my message to the Aeons, yes?"

Esther cleared her throat. "Yes. They claimed she is now your property. Your kind protects what belongs to them—I know that. But you have no real idea of who she is or what she is capable of. If you did, you would not be so eager to keep her at Devil's Cradle."

"I know everything I need to know."

"But Wynter is the source of that information, and she cannot be called a reliable source." Esther sniffed. "I'm sure she told you that her magick is tainted because she was killed as a child. That is a lie. Her death was an accident. She was not tortured as she claims. She invented that lie so that she would not be held responsible for what she did to the boys who accidentally ended her life. Ten years old, and she murdered two teenage boys. Hacked their bodies with that dark magick of hers."

"Sounds like my kind of girl," said Cain, hiding his surprise at the latter revelation. There was every chance that the Priestess was lying, of course. She'd certainly lied when claiming that Wynter's death had been an accident—he'd heard the note of deceit in her voice. But that note had been absent during her latter claim. He needed to have a talk with his little witch for sure. "I'm pretty sure I'd have done worse."

Esther's face tightened. "Her magick isn't merely dark, it is death itself. She has ruined the land at Aeon. You think she will not do the same to your town?"

"Since I don't intend to exile her as the Aeons did, no, I don't think she'll make any such attempt." Cain heaved a bored sigh. "I'd say we're done here."

"Protecting her would be a mistake," Esther blurted out.

He narrowed his eyes. "Now that almost sounded like a threat."

She swallowed, her eyes flickering nervously. "The Aeons asked me to pass on a message."

"This ought to be good," he muttered.

"They wish me to remind you that they gave you mercy all those years ago. They could have killed you; they didn't. You owe them for that, they said."

Anger coursed through him and put a rock in his gut. "Owe them?" he echoed, his tone silky smooth. "Do you hear that, Azazel? We owe them."

The porch floorboards creaked and then . . . "Yeah, I heard."

Esther's eyes flew to something behind Cain. "Ah, there you are. It is time to come home, Wynter."

"Aeon isn't my home," Wynter said, no inflection in her voice, as she and Azazel moved to flank Cain.

Esther's eyes flared. "It will be no one's home if you do not fix what you have done."

Wynter snorted. "You can't tell me that the big, bad Aeons are struggling to handle a little environmental erosion, surely."

She scanned the sea of faces, taking in the hard expressions, marveling at how—despite all they'd done—it still hurt that they'd so easily banded against her. But then, she'd been an outsider to them since she was ten years old. It was now simply official. Rafe's absence did lessen the sting slightly.

She cocked her head. "Did you know that the exiled are killed before they can even reach the border?"

Surprise rippled across many faces, including that of Esther.

"Ah, you didn't. Well, let me tell you . . . there's no memory-wipe process. They're paralyzed and then thrown over the falls."

"That is a lie," Esther insisted.

"No, it's not. The banished die."

"If that were true, you would not be alive."

"If it wasn't true, I'd have no memories. But I do. I live because I managed to escape Wagner." And then . . . well, she was pretty sure her monster ate most if not all of him, but that was a whole other story. That same monster was currently watching Esther closely, entertaining the many—and very creative—ways it would make her suffer.

Esther shook her head, dismissing Wynter's claims with ease, and said, "I have no time for this. I do not know what you did with that death magick of yours, but you need to come home and reverse whatever spell you cast."

Wynter pursed her lips. "Yeah, nah."

"You *will* return to Aeon, and you will do so *immediately*."

"It's like you've forgotten that you're not my Priestess anymore. Weird."

"Wynter—"

"The only way I'm leaving Devil's Cradle is if I have no choice but to go. And the only person who can force me to leave is Cain." Feeling like a cold fist was wrapped tight around her heart, Wynter met his dark, currently unreadable gaze. "Do you want me gone?" If he said yes, he was *so* dead.

His brow inched up, imperious. "You and I have a deal, remember?" He cut his eyes back to Esther. "Wynter stays here."

And the cold fist released her heart.

The Priestess gritted her teeth. "The Aeons—"

"—are not who you think they are," Cain told her. "Notice that they didn't come here themselves. This is a dangerous place. You are their people. But they insisted on *you* facing the danger, not them."

"This is unhallowed ground," said Esther. "They cannot step foot on it."

Cain felt his lips twitch. "Is that what they told you?"

Azazel chuckled. "Such story spinners."

Cain dismissively flicked a hand and half-turned away from the coven. "Return to your rotting home. Tell the Aeons that Wynter will remain here."

"You cannot possibly be willing to risk their wrath over this," Esther insisted. "She is a mere witch. No one important. Her magick is impure, twisted—"

"More powerful than yours, which I suspect is your real problem with Wynter," Cain finished.

Esther's mouth snapped shut. For a moment. "I implore you to reconsider—"

"No imploring," said Azazel. "This is tedious enough as it is."

Oh, Wynter couldn't have agreed more.

When the Priestess again went to protest, Cain clipped, "No, we are done. You will leave, or you will die. The choice is yours."

Esther clenched her fists. "She will ruin your town. She—"

"Leave, or die," Cain ordered.

Wynter crossed her metaphorical fingers that the bitch would be dumb enough to push him. But, her cheeks flushing, Esther pivoted on her heel and stalked away with her coven members in tow. *No such luck.*

The crowd who'd gathered smirked and poked at the witches, spouting taunting comments like, "That's it, run along."

Cain glanced from her to Azazel and then tipped his chin toward the manor. In silence, they headed inside.

Back in the foyer, Azazel turned to her. "Your old coven is a joke."

"You won't get an argument from me," said Wynter.

Looking deep into those quicksilver eyes, Cain tilted his head as he asked, "Was what Esther claimed about the teenagers true?"

Not even a flicker of emotion crossed Wynter's face. "That they accidentally took my life? No. That I took theirs? Yes. I did mention that they were executed."

"You didn't say that you were the one who performed the executions," Cain pointed out. It made him wonder what else she'd left out of her story.

"People always give me weird looks when they learn what happened to the boys," said Wynter. "And hey, I get it. But I don't like it. Surely there's stuff that you two haven't publicly shared because you know others will react in a way you won't like."

Unease tingled its way down Cain's spine. "What makes you think that?"

"You and the Aeons are all super secretive," she reminded him. "You let people draw their own conclusions, and you don't bother to confirm or deny any theories. It stands to reason that you simply feel some things are better left unsaid. And no, I'm not asking for clarification on that." She paused. "I would, however, like to know if you have any idea of who the Aeons might send next."

What she wanted was to change the subject, Cain thought. And he had to admit she was smooth at easing a conversation away from one topic and onto another. He wouldn't call her on it now, though. Not when he sensed that the scene outside hadn't been quite as easy for her as she'd like him to believe.

"I doubt they'll insist your old coven returns," he said. "But someone will come. Keepers, perhaps. The Aeons will only come if it's a last resort."

Wynter poked the inside of her cheek with her tongue. "Is there an Aeon who you'd hesitate to hurt? That might be who they'll send."

Cain exchanged a look with Azazel. "There's one, but they wouldn't send her."

"Why not?" asked Wynter.

"Because they prefer to keep she and I apart," replied Cain. "And they would expect me to keep her here, which wouldn't suit them."

Wynter's brow puckered for the *briefest* moment. "An ex of yours?"

"My mother."

Wynter slanted her head. "But she sided against you in the war, right?"

"It wasn't quite as simple as that."

She parted her lips as if to question him further, but whatever she saw on his face made her instead choose to hold back her words.

Azazel turned to Cain, claimed he had somewhere to be, and then excused himself.

Finally, Cain crossed to Wynter and allowed himself to touch her. He smoothed her hair over her shoulder and palmed the side of her neck. "It was hard for you. That scene."

She averted her gaze. "It shouldn't have been. It's not like I thought they cared about me or anything. I already knew I meant nothing to them."

"But you were hardly going to enjoy having a reminder of that, were you?"

"I suppose not," she muttered. "Can we talk about something other than those assholes?"

Since he would much prefer to see the strain gone from her face, he didn't push. "We can talk about how you were gone when I returned to my chamber this morning. I didn't like it." He bit her lip in punishment, and her pupils dilated. "You knew I wanted you to wait for me."

"I would have been late for work if I'd stayed."

He cupped her hips. "I would have made it worth it."

Her mouth curved. "Probably, but I'm not going to allow you and your magickal cock to blind me."

"Magickal?"

"I have responsibilities that I take seriously. And I know better than to give you your own way all the time in any case."

Cain slid his hands up her back. "If I had my own way when it comes to you, you would be tied to my bed all day every day, ready for whenever I want you."

"No, I really don't think you would. I mean, it would be pretty hard for me to use the bathroom, and I don't think you'd want me making a mess of your bed."

"Hmm, maybe I would instead put you in chains, then. Chains long enough that you could make it to the bathroom."

She frowned. "I don't like how serious you look right now. I gotta say, it's kind of freaking me out."

"I doubt many things truly freak you out, little witch." He kissed her softly, teasingly. "Come home with me."

"Hmm, what'll happen if I do?"

"I'll make it worth your while in orgasms."

"And soul-gasms?"

He felt his mouth quirk at the terminology. "Those, too."

She splayed her hands on his chest. "All right, I'm in."

# Chapter Twelve

Returning to the Keep after having a long meeting with Seth a few days later, Cain was met at the front entrance by Maxim. The aide informed him of a minor issue that had cropped up in his absence, adding, "Also, Ishtar arrived while you were with your brother. I explained that you might be a while, but she insisted on waiting for you. She is in the solar room."

Cain felt the corners of his eyes tighten. For the most part, she'd given him the cold shoulder since he first got involved with Wynter. Apparently that phase was over, but he didn't mistake that for Ishtar having shaken off her 'funk,' as Azazel called it. She pettily clung to the slightest of insults. To Ishtar, that he'd be sleeping with Wynter when he could instead be sharing a bed with her was an insult.

"Thank you, Maxim," he said.

Cain headed for the solar, intent on getting this over with before Wynter arrived. As per usual, she would turn up at some point within the next half hour. He wondered if Ishtar was aware of that; wondered if the Ancient hoped to annoy his witch by being present when she arrived. It was the kind of childish thing that Ishtar was apt to do.

Entering the solar, he found her sitting on the sofa, casually dressed, her legs tucked underneath her, her face a mask of uncertainty. He held back a frown, wondering at her game. And this *was* a game. Ishtar never showed vulnerability unless it suited her agenda. She certainly didn't dress in a simple get-up of jeans and a tee—that was more Wynter's style. He inwardly sighed, sincerely tired of the never-ending plays that Ishtar made.

"Does anyone in your service have the ability to resurface a person's lost memories?" she asked without bothering to greet him, as if too unsettled to waste time on formalities. "Since waking, I have noticed that there are many holes in my memories. As if they were suppressed during my Rest. I have already spoken with the other Ancients. They all said they know of no one who can help me."

His creature huffed at the feigned urgency in her voice. "If any in my service are capable of it, they haven't admitted to it," Cain replied simply. "But then, I don't ask about people's abilities."

Her hand fisted. "There has to be someone who can assist me with this."

"You haven't been awake long. You need to give it time."

"But my memories should feel less foggy at this point." She stared out of the window, exhaling a wistful sigh. "I wonder if Inanna will have the same problem. We will have to wake her soon, won't we?"

"Lilith plans to do it tonight."

Ishtar's gaze snapped to his, blazing. "And no one thought to tell me? Inanna is my *sister*."

"Lilith went to your Keep yesterday to speak to you," he calmly reminded her. "One of your aides told her that you were not receiving guests." If he had to guess, he'd say that Ishtar had been sulking after feeling slighted by the, in her opinion, 'boring' celebration Lilith threw for her that included poetry recitals and theatrical entertainment.

"She could have returned at another time to deliver her message."

Like Lilith had nothing better to do than chase after her? "She was no doubt waiting for you to contact her at your earliest convenience to ask what she'd wished to speak with you about."

Ishtar pulled a face. "Stop being so reasonable. There was a time you were never reasonable. We had such fun in those days," she added, injecting a sultry note into her voice. "But then you changed. Fired all manner of dramatic demands at me."

"Only you would think that someone was being dramatic by demanding to be treated as an equal."

Her mouth firmed. "You are not exactly in a position to judge. Your current toy is hardly your equal. I doubt you treat her as such." Ishtar examined her nails. "She fought well in the gauntlet. For a witch. I do hope she will partake in other such celebratory activities."

Cain went very still. "Do not even think to bring her into your games and put her in harm's way. I will not allow it. The other Ancients will not allow it. She is to be protected."

"So you say, yet you do not protect her from you or your monster," Ishtar sniped. "She is in danger every moment she is with you simply because you are what you are. Still, you keep her as your toy. That tells me you care nothing for her." She sniffed, a triumphant glint in her gaze. "Does she know that?"

Cain refrained from rolling his eyes at how eager she was to believe that Wynter meant nothing to him. "Why don't you ask what you really want to ask? I may answer. I may not."

Ishtar straightened her legs and planted her feet on the floor. "Is it true that she sleeps in your personal chamber when she is here?"

For fuck's sake. Did the woman really have nothing better to do than monitor his private life as best as she could? "I will not discuss the finer details of what is between myself and Wynter."

Ishtar barked a harsh laugh. "You think there is something *between* you? She doesn't even know you, Cain. You will have shown her only parts of you."

That wasn't something he could deny. It also wasn't something that he intended to confirm. The matter simply wasn't Ishtar's business.

"If she were to learn the truth, if she were to learn about your monster, she would leave you."

Said monster narrowed its eyes, in complete disagreement. That was the thing about the creature. It had no real sense of self-awareness. It didn't see itself *as* a monster.

It also didn't seem any less possessive of Wynter. Yet.

"You know I am right, Cain. She would *never* accept the real you.

She would never look past your secrets. So I hope your creature is as bored of her as I suspect it must be. Because if not and she chooses to leave you before you end things first, it *will* kill her for the insult."

"You judge my monster by the standards of your own. Mine does not possess an ego that, much like yours, cannot handle criticism, rejection, or abandonment."

Her face hardened, her fingers digging into the armrest. "You can be such a bastard."

"I can."

"But you are only being so testy right now because you know I am not wrong." Ishtar regally rose to her feet. "The witch would not accept you as you truly are, Cain. You are fooling yourself if you believe differently." With that, she stormed out of the room, leaving him alone with his thoughts . . . and those thoughts didn't take his mind anywhere good.

*

Adjusting her tee, Wynter was just about to say her goodbyes to her crew when a fist pounded on the front door of the cottage. Feeling her brows snap together, she walked into the living room. "Who the hell is that?"

Glancing out of the window, Xavier replied, "Uh, there's a bunch of demons in the front yard. One of them looks *seriously* pissed, and I think he might be holding a fireball in his hand. Could be hellfire," he mused, uncaring.

Her face solemn, Anabel sank further into the sofa and put a hand to her chest. "So this is how we die."

Wynter rolled her eyes.

"Delilah, get out here *now!*" a voice from outside bellowed.

They all looked through the archway that led into the kitchen. Delilah was currently muttering to herself while peppering ingredients into the steaming cauldron.

"Del!" Wynter called out. "We need you in here!"

Delilah cursed but hurried into the room. "What's wrong? Make it quick."

"Did you get on the wrong side of any demons lately?"

"Not that I'm aware of. Why?"

A fist once more pounded on the door.

Wynter sighed. "Hattie, keep an eye on the cauldron."

But the woman who was curled up in the armchair didn't even look up from her book.

"I'll do it," volunteered Anabel.

Wynter pointed at Delilah. "You come with me." She led the other witch to the front door and opened it wide, revealing eight males who were also local demons. The furious-looking one holding a fire ball had a bandage on his cheek.

"Is there a problem?" Wynter asked.

"Yeah." He jabbed a finger in Delilah's direction. "*Her.*"

Delilah put a hand on her hip. "What about me?"

"All I asked for was a potion to make my girl's tits bigger," he said, his nostrils flaring. "You told me to pour it on her breasts and lick off any excess liquid. I did. Only it didn't work, and shit got *fucked up.*"

Delilah folded her arms. "I warned you there might be side effects."

"Woman, I grew a third nipple. *On my face.*" He tore off the bandage and, yep, there it was.

"You can hardly notice it."

Wynter glanced over her shoulder at a smirking Xavier. "Get me a reversal potion, please."

"Sure thing," he chuckled.

Wynter shot her an 'I *know* I told you not to sell any karma potions' look, but Delilah was too busy arguing with the demon to notice. It was a wonder she hadn't gotten herself killed long before now.

Xavier reappeared, his eyes still bright with laughter. "Here."

"Thanks." Wynter took the vial and offered it to the demon. "Drink that. The nipple will vanish."

He jerked back, his hands raised. "You think I'm gonna drink anything else *she* made?"

"Actually, this is one of Anabel's brews. It's just a reversal potion. Look, take it or don't. The nipple will probably go away by itself in a few days anyway. So if you're happy to wait that long . . ."

His lips thinning, he snatched the vial and downed the contents; the effect was pretty much immediate. He looked at his lair members. "Has it gone?"

They all nodded or answered in the affirmative.

He rounded on Delilah. "That shit was—"

"Unfortunate," Wynter cut in. "I'm guessing you didn't tell your girl what the potion was meant to do."

He averted his gaze briefly. "Well, no."

"And that right there is the problem. Performing such magick on someone without their knowledge can backfire. Delilah *did* warn you there could be a price, correct?"

"Yes, but she didn't mention anything about third nipples."

"No one ever really knows what the cost will be. Look, I get why you're upset, but you're not at all blameless here. The potion wouldn't have backfired on you if you'd been honest with your girlfriend."

He sighed. "You realize I'll forever be known as the guy who once had a nipple on his face?"

"Another thing which is unfortunate," she said, hoping her words overrode Xavier's snicker. "In future, whether you purchase a potion like this from here or somewhere else, be upfront with the person you want the potion to work on. We said the same to a woman who was looking for a cock-lengthening brew—"

"You make cock-lengthening brews?" he asked, all his hostility slipping away.

"Me? No. But Delilah does."

"They only work for a few hours," Delilah told him. "It's kind of like Viagra, only it changes the size of your dick as well as enhances your libido for a short period."

He and his lair exchanged intrigued looks before he turned back to Delilah. "How much *are* these brews?"

Wynter inwardly snorted. *Men.* Figuring all was now well, she shot Delilah a 'We'll talk about this later' look and then turned to Xavier. "I'll leave you guys to handle this."

"We got it," he vowed, smiling. "You go see Cain."

That was the plan. It had become a routine—she worked, she ate with her crew, and then she spent the night in Cain's bed. Each time a voice in her head taunted that she was in danger of growing attached to the Ancient, Wynter pointedly ignored it.

Reaching the Keep, she greeted the aide at the entrance, who then escorted her upstairs to Cain's chamber. She found him standing near the window, sipping amber liquid from a tumbler.

"Sorry, I'm late," she said. "Had to avert a crisis." The hairs on her neck stood on end when his eyes met hers, utterly vacant. "What's wrong?"

He very slowly angled his head. "Why would you think something is wrong?" he asked, his voice flat.

"Because I'm not stupid." It was easy to tell that all the shutters were down right now. Still, she raised her hands and said, "We don't have to talk about it." She had no right to push him to share things with her, given that she wouldn't return the favor if he ever pushed too hard. "Just don't insult my intelligence by expecting me to believe you're not working through something in your head right now."

He let out a low hum. "What was the crisis you mentioned?" he asked, though he didn't sound particularly interested.

She plonked herself on a bulky chair. "To cut a long story short, Delilah pissed off a demon. He and a bunch of his lair turned up at the cottage looking for her. All is well, nothing happened; they were buying more potions when I left."

His gaze returned to the window. "It must be strange for demons to have to coexist with an entity that differs from them in many ways. There would surely be a struggle to find balance."

Her skin tingled, because there was something about the way he'd spoken ... as if he was fishing for something. Testing her, even. "I guess."

"Have you ever been around a demon when their inner entity surfaced and took control?"

"Quite a few times since coming here, yes. They're intrigued by dark magick. They like to ask questions about runes."

Cain's eyes bore into hers. "And you answer? As if they are a being in their own right?"

"Of course. They *are* a being in their own right. Just because something is the epitome of inhuman doesn't mean it should be feared or loathed or seen as 'less.' It's simply different. I'll only have a problem with such a being if it means me harm. Otherwise, I'm all about 'live and let live.'"

There was a flicker of ... something in the depths of his dark eyes, and then a warmth steadily filled them. "Come here."

That bedroom tone made her pulse spike. "I like this chair. It's comfortable."

"But it can't make you scream with pleasure."

"You do make a good point."

He set his glass down on the window shelf. "Come here."

Huffing, she pushed out of the chair. "It really is a good thing for you that you're a master orgasm deliverer," she began as she crossed to him, "or the whole demanding routine would *not* work for you."

His hands slid up her sides, over her breasts, and up to cup her neck. His eyes drifted over her face, glimmering with heat but also something else. Something she couldn't quite name.

Once more, her skin prickled. "Is this where you tell me we're done?" she asked.

"I should, for your sake. I'll never be good for you." It wasn't said with self-loathing. It was a mere statement of fact.

"Okay, let's be clear on something. I don't need someone to be good for me. *I* take care of me. I'm pretty good at it, actually. What I really don't need is someone giving me the brush off with a modified version of 'it's not you, it's me.' If you want this to be over, well, it's not like it'll be a shock. I figured you'd get bored fast."

"So did I, but I'm not bored. Nor do I want you to go anywhere. I simply wish to be transparent about this one thing—having me in your life will not make it better. That really is the most I can say."

Wynter had never thought he would be a positive contribution to her world . . . mostly because she hadn't expected him to be *any* kind of contribution. She would have originally thought that he'd have turned her away by now. She wasn't sure what to make of the fact that he hadn't. "Okay."

He dipped his head. "Never say you weren't warned." Then his mouth was on hers, feasting and consuming. Not taking her over, but *demanding* her participation; *demanding* she give as good as she got—which she did. He ended the kiss with a nip to her lip. "Make me one promise."

"What?"

"If there ever comes a time that you're so afraid of me you want to run, *don't* run."

She blinked. He'd said it as if running would be the absolute worst thing she could do in such a situation. Like it was a matter of life or death. Which confused the shit out of her. But then, so did many of the things he said.

Unable to imagine herself ever being so scared of him that she'd flee—something she generally never did in the face of danger—she nodded. "Okay, I promise."

His hand squeezed her nape. "Keep that promise." And then he was devouring her mouth again.

Soon, they were both naked and he was pinning her to the bed as he fucked her into the mattress. He took her hard and fast, pleasuring her soul and her body at the same time.

Afterwards, he drew her close. They talked a little about mundane things before finally drifting off.

A whispered voice came to her while she slept, coaxing her to follow. Wynter refused, burrowing deeper into the warm arms that held her. But the voice kept on whispering, kept insisting that she follow. She frowned, intent on ignoring it. Cold fingers ghosted over her face, demanding her attention but patient for a response.

More whispers, more coaxing, more cold fingers.

She clung to Cain, wanting to stay exactly where she was.

"Wynter!"

Again, she frowned. That was not a whisper, nor was it spoken by the same voice.

"Wynter, stop!"

Why were they yelling? Why was *Cain* yelling?

Fingers snapped around her upper arm, and she flipped her eyes open. Her breath caught. *The fuck?* She wasn't in bed anymore. She wasn't even in his chamber.

She knew that statue. Knew that bog-like pond. Knew the twisting path she stood on.

She was in Cain's garden, and the man in question was staring down at her.

"Wynter, what in the fuck are you doing out here?"

She blinked hard, shivering at the cool air. "I-I don't know." Licking her lips, she glanced around, her stomach twisting when she caught sight of lots of narrow, wriggly dudes on the ground.

He dragged in a ragged breath. "Listen to me, Wynter. You cannot come out here alone. Ever. It isn't safe."

"I didn't do it on purpose." She rubbed at her brow. "I must have been sleepwalking."

He heaved a sigh and curled an arm around her shoulders. "Let's get back inside."

She caught a glimpse of something just before she turned. A small temple of some sort. Maybe. She really didn't care because, hello, wriggly dudes with fangs.

She let Cain lead her back to the Keep, wishing the stone floor wasn't so damn cold beneath her bare feet. And then she remembered the voice that had come to her in her sleep. Remembered that it had wanted to show her something but hadn't been clear on what.

No, it had only been a dream. She'd been sleepwalking. She'd *definitely* been sleepwalking.

# Chapter Thirteen

As he, Seth, and Azazel waited in Inanna's drawing room the next afternoon for the other Ancients—including Inanna herself, who'd been woken by both Lilith and Ishtar—to arrive, Cain told the two males of the incident last night.

Azazel leaned forward in his seat. "She what?"

Cain lifted his brows. "I really need to repeat myself?"

"Yeah. Yeah, you do. Because she should be dead."

Cain flexed his fingers before splaying his hand on the sofa's armrest. "I'm aware of that." It was his creature, having woken from a light doze, who'd alerted him that she was gone. "When I realized she was in the garden, I expected to find her swarmed by so many snakes I'd barely see her." And he'd felt something he hadn't felt in a long time—panic.

"None of them harmed her?"

"No, not one of them even so much as touched her. Nor did they hiss in warning or get in her way. They just slithered along the path either side of her. If I didn't know any better, I'd have thought they were following her to protect her."

At the other end of the sofa, Seth shrugged. "Maybe they somehow sensed she was yours. They wouldn't harm anything that belongs to you. They *might* even go so far as to protect it."

Azazel's eyes narrowed. "You're sure she was sleepwalking?"

Cain felt his brow furrow. "What else would she have been doing out there?"

"I don't know," replied Azazel. "But you've got to admit it's weird that she'd go to the one place she'd find uncomfortable truths if she knew where to look. So I'm asking, are you certain she was sleepwalking?"

Cain thought back to last night. "She was moving like someone in a daze. Slow and awkward, not with purposeful strides. She only snapped out of it when I touched her, and then she looked freaked out. Wynter's got an amazing poker-face, but I don't think she was faking. She went pale. Started trembling. She seemed disoriented and confused."

Seth scratched at the side of his neck. "You don't think . . . No, there was no way he would have called out to a random witch even if he *was* awake."

"He isn't awake. I'd sense it if he was." Cain ran his tongue over the front of his teeth. "She's been to the garden before. She likes it. She isn't fussed by the snakes. It's not strange that she'd go sleep-walking to a place she likes. But you know what *is* strange?"

Azazel gave him a pointed look. "A lot of things are strange lately."

"Exactly," said Cain. "And it all started with Wynter's appearance. Yet, Demetria didn't see her coming. Nor did she foresee the appearance of Wynter's old coven, or that the Aeons would suddenly turn their attention our way. In fact, she's had no visions whatsoever since shortly before Wynter came here."

Seth blinked. "None?"

Cain shook his head. "Demetria came to me the day after Wynter moved here. She said that for a few days she'd had a gut feeling that something was coming, but that no vision had accompanied the feeling. I had another brief conversation with Demetria earlier. She still isn't having visions, and she still feels that she's being blocked."

Seth frowned. "Wynter can't be responsible for that."

"No," agreed Cain. "She's powerful, but she couldn't block any attempts that a deity might make to contact their Favored. Demetria maintains it is a 'presence' that is causing the interference."

Azazel's head twitched to the side. "What kind of presence?"

"She isn't sure," said Cain.

Azazel rubbed at his jaw. "A deity could do it."

"We'd sense the presence of a deity," said Seth.

"Only if they wanted us to."

"True enough," allowed Seth. "But why *wouldn't* they want us to?"

"That's the question, isn't it?" Azazel twisted his mouth, resettling his gaze on Cain. "I'm guessing you've had a good, long look at Wynter's body naked?"

"Every inch," Cain confirmed.

"She has no marks to declare that she's Favored by a deity?" asked Azazel.

Cain shook his head. "We wouldn't need to see a mark to know a deity had their eye on her. The Favored are easy to recognize. They're all the same. Arrogant. Overconfident. Superior. You'd think they were deities themselves the way they act. That isn't Wynter."

"No, it's not." Seth stretched his legs out in front of him. "I don't know her, but you can tell a lot about a person by the way *others* treat them. Each member of her coven seems to respect and care for her. They see her as their Priestess, even if she doesn't. They'd follow her anywhere."

"I haven't spent much time around them," said Cain. "Maxim has, however. He told me that they're more like a family—dysfunctional though it might be. There's no hierarchy, no politics, no power struggles. Wynter is more of a guiding, protective force than a leader demanding respect and obedience. The others might not be entirely sane, but she gives them room to be who they are."

"A person like that would make a good consort," Seth chipped in ever so casually. "Don't even try to tell me you haven't considered it."

Cain didn't object to having done so, because it would have been a lie. The idea of making her his consort had wormed its way into his head and seemed intent on staying there. He'd tried ignoring it, but it pushed for mental space often.

He'd never claimed someone as his consort before. He'd never been possessive enough of a woman to care to. Likewise, though his monster had taken a shine to certain females over the years, it had never had any solid interest in a woman. Until now.

"Seth's right," said Azazel. "You thought your creature would grow tired of her. But she's still sleeping in your personal chamber, which tells me you were wrong. Is it even beginning to lose interest in her?"

Cain pulled in a breath through his nose. "No. But that doesn't mean it won't at some point."

"It doesn't mean it will." Seth paused. "I don't think you're at risk of losing interest in her either. Around Wynter, you're different. As if she takes up so much of your focus that it doesn't leave room for any dark shit to come along and sweep you under."

Azazel nodded. "I'm guessing the black moods have stopped taking you, because you seem more ... balanced. Positive, even. And I know that'll be partly because our freedom seems close. But it's not *all* about that. She's good for you. So keep her." He said it as though she was a wallet he'd found and liked the look of.

Cain arched a brow. "Even though *I'm* not good for *her*?"

"Even though," said Azazel.

Cain briefly tipped his head to the side. "I did warn her I'm not."

"And?"

"And she didn't seem bothered by it." Which hadn't whatsoever surprised his monster—the creature didn't believe she had reason to be bothered, since it considered his and Cain's secrets to not truly be so bad. For the creature, it was simply their nature.

"So keep her," Azazel repeated. "Or at least give it some serious consideration."

Seth opened his mouth to speak, but then they heard voices coming.

Moments later, Lilith and Dantalion arrived. They briefly greeted Cain, Azazel, and Seth before returning to their conversation about whether humans served any real purpose. Shortly after that, Inanna and Ishtar entered, linking arms and smiling brightly at each other. Inanna was literally the only person Ishtar truly loved.

The sisters shared the same cornflower-blue eyes, pale blonde hair—though Inanna's was straight rather than curled like

Ishtar's—and highly feminine air. But Inanna carried herself with a regal grace unlike her sister, whose every move was sensual and aimed to seduce.

Each person greeted Inanna and welcomed her back.

"How do you feel?" Seth asked her as they all took seats around the room.

"Like I woke too early, but I could not have woken to better news," she replied. "If there is to be a war, I wish to be part of it." Her gaze slid to Cain. "Tell me about the witch. I understand you have spent much time with her."

There were many things he could say about Wynter. But he didn't want the other Ancients to know her as well as he did. He didn't wish to share her in even such a basic way. "What is it you wish to know?"

"Mostly, I want to be assured that she will not flee in terror if war breaks out."

"It's not in her nature to flee. It's in her nature to avenge." Cain loved that. "She harbors a deep hatred for the people of Aeon—so much so that she's prepared to pay the cost of the dark curse she placed upon the land."

"Yes, but Priestesses are generally happy to step back and have others do their dirty work."

"If you ask Wynter, she will tell you that she isn't a Priestess. She has no interest in a position of authority, only in protecting and guiding her 'crew,' as she refers to them. The coven is more like a family, which is as it should be. They are a tight group, and they fight like a well-oiled machine, but not so much with technique as with sheer ruthlessness."

Azazel nodded. "They went through the gauntlet, and they completed it in under a minute—beating every past and present record. Their focus wasn't to get to that finish line, or even to beat the times of others. They were *enjoying* what they did, and they kept moving forward so fast because they were eager to make the next kill."

Inanna's mouth curved. "I think I could like these people."

"From what I have heard and seen, they're not the sanest of individuals," said Dantalion. "But then, neither are we." He paused. "I agree with Cain. Wynter isn't someone who would flee. If anything, she would run toward a war. She would want blood. And her coven would be right behind her."

"Just because they were confident during the gauntlet does not mean they would be so confident on a battlefield," said Ishtar, her voice clipped. "The two circumstances are very different. During the gauntlet, they had the comfort of knowing they would not truly die."

Lilith let out a tired sigh. "Must you let your personal feelings about Wynter's involvement with Cain color your opinions about her?"

Ishtar's back snapped straight. "I have no feelings about their 'involvement' one way or the other."

"Of course you don't," said Lilith dryly. "My mistake."

"I merely think that—"

"Ishtar," Inanna cut in. She said no more. She simply looked at her sister, her eyes soft. But whatever silent message she passed on made Ishtar leave the room in a huff. Inanna was more of a maternal figure than a sisterly one. But then, they *had* been born a hundred years apart.

Inanna exhaled heavily. "I sometimes wonder how different she would be if our father had not made her feel so insignificant growing up. I wonder if she would have been happier in herself; if her own sense of self-worth would not only come from what others think of her; if total adoration would not be the only thing that made her feel complete."

"Not even pure adoration makes her feel complete for long, though," said Seth. "The effect is only ever temporary."

"Yes. It saddens me that my sister will never really know true happiness." Inanna returned her gaze to Cain. "Your witch will need to watch her back. In Ishtar's mind, you have chosen someone else over her. It reminds her too much of our father's rejection of her. He truly was a bastard," Inanna added in a low mutter. "I have warned her not to do anything stupid. We need Wynter alive, unharmed, and on our side. She assured me she would not do anything to risk changing any of that. But her fragile ego can often overrule her good sense."

Cain felt his face harden. "I'd advise you to ensure that she doesn't let that happen. Because if she harms Wynter, she will pay. And we both know how badly I could hurt her."

Inanna studied him closely. "The witch is not simply a bedmate to you." She gave a slow nod. "I will keep a close eye on Ishtar, but you should still keep a close watch on Wynter." She pushed to her feet. "Now I wish to get a few things done before the celebration tonight. You arranged it, Seth, correct?"

"I did," Seth confirmed.

She smiled. "Then I know it will not be tedious. Oh, and please do not throw any celebrations for me," she said, addressing every Ancient. "I know it is tradition, but I would much rather save it for when we are finally free of our cage and the Aeons are dead. Just the thought warms my black heart. They will regret what they did, but not quite as much as they will regret not ending our existence—that was the worst mistake they ever made."

*

"Can I kill him?"

Wynter sighed at Xavier. "No."

"Why not? He'd deserve it. You reap what you sow in this world."

"Explain how Elias could possibly deserve it. Without lying."

"So, what, you think it's fine that he keeps pestering me to have a threesome with him and his boyfriend?"

"I wouldn't say he's pestering you. I'd say he's so amused by how much his first offer annoyed and flustered you that he now keeps repeating his offer to mess with you. That's not a criminal activity."

Huffing, Xavier looked down at the arena's performance space, which was beginning to fill with entertainers now that the interval was over. "You're not even really listening to me."

"Of course I am," she told him. "But we've been over this. You can't kill a person simply because you don't like them. It's not a reason for someone to die."

"You choose to focus too much on logic."

"Well, aren't I strange," she said, her voice dry. She raised a hand when he went to argue. "No, you're not allowed to kill him. He's in the service of an Ancient, remember? They'll never permit you to end his life over such a trivial reason. Your request would only succeed in pissing off Elias's boyfriend and pack. And let's be honest, you don't actually dislike him. You're attracted to him and unhappy about it. For you, this situation is a very weird version of 'you only hit the one you love' thing."

Xavier glared at her. "I don't love him."

"No, but you're into him. Reluctantly. That's what this is all about."

"I'm not into him. He's a dick. He said I was a 'naughty little liar' and needed a Daddy to keep me in line."

"You *are* a bad little liar, and you *do* need someone to keep you in line."

"Again, you're choosing to focus on logic." He raised a finger. "And excuse me, I need no one. Except you, Delilah, Anabel, and Hattie."

"It's good to expand your circle."

Sitting on Wynter's other side, Delilah leaned in with a frown. "What're we talking about?"

"I want to kill Elias," Xavier declared. "Wynter says I can't."

Delilah's brow creased. "What's wrong with Elias?"

"He annoys the hell out of me," said Xavier. "He keeps coming to my tent for 'readings.' But then all he does is grill me. I had to tell him about my past just to get him off my back. Though I didn't tell him much except for how I originally came from Montana and that my parents were ranchers."

"You were born in Chicago," said Wynter. "And your parents were both teachers."

"I didn't say I told him *the truth* about my past."

Delilah rolled her eyes. "At least you're aware that you're bullshitting."

Yeah, that was the thing about Xavier. Unlike many chronic liars, he didn't believe his own tales. He didn't invent fictional pasts to avoid speaking of something painful. He didn't present different faces to different people because he was uncomfortable with who he truly was. Nope, it was simply his way of keeping people at arm's-length. The world tended not to trust liars or attempt to bond with them. That suited Xavier just fine.

When he *did* let people in, though, he wasn't a half-assed friend. He was loyal and protective and accepting.

Sensual music began to play as the performers resumed their show. Acrobats, dancers, jugglers, and illusionists showed off their talent, but it was no circus-like performance. Nope. There was a BDSM undertone to the whole thing. Artists dressed in leather or PVC. Whips, canes, handcuffs, and crops were mingled into the routines. It should have been weird, but it was actually quite fun and creative.

"You know," began Delilah, "given that the rumor-mill says Seth isn't fond of Ishtar, I figured he'd throw a celebration she'd be bored by. But look at her, she's *loving* this. So is that woman I'm guessing is the sister who rose from her Rest yesterday."

Wynter had noticed the new face. The woman was just as pretty as her irritating sister. Though the siblings were similar in looks, they each possessed a different 'air.' Ishtar came across as sultry whereas Inanna was more poised.

"Yeah," began Wynter, "I'm getting the sense that Ishtar respects talent, even if she doesn't necessarily respect people in general." She certainly liked seeing her sister happy and enter-tained. Ishtar seemingly wasn't quite as one-dimensional as she might come across.

"Plus, there's a sexual theme going on here," Delilah went on. "It could be interpreted as Seth flirting with her in a roundabout way."

"I'd agree, but look at how enthralled most people in this arena are."

Delilah glanced around. "Huh. He did this for the masses."

"That would be my guess," said Wynter. "Throwing something boring as a dig at Ishtar would have made everything about her. To me, this says he doesn't care enough about their past to bother with digs."

Delilah pursed her lips. "I never thought of it like that, but yeah, I see it now."

Feeling eyes on her, Wynter looked to see Cain staring right at her, his usual promise of sex glittering in his eyes. That easily, a jolt of need surged through her. It was like his ability to touch her all the way down to her soul—something nothing else had been able to truly do since before she died—had trained her very being to respond to him. Sometimes, it felt like her body *knew* he was the only thing that would ever make her feel that way; sometimes felt like it would always crave him.

"So ... how long are you going to ban me from selling karma potions?" asked Delilah.

Wynter looked at her. "Oh, for, like, ever."

"Why do you have to overreact?"

"I'm overreacting by wanting you to avoid activities that would put your life in jeopardy?" Wynter slammed up a hand. "No, I'm not going over all this again." She'd already reamed Delilah's ass over it this morning.

"Acting as conduits for karma is what my family has always done—all the way back to Annis."

"Who was a child killer and cannibal, so forgive me if I don't condone the 'path' she put your family line on. And let's be honest, none of you are truly interested in acting on behalf of karma. No, you all use that excuse to justify the crap you do to people."

"That's not true."

Wynter lifted her shoulders. "True or not, the situation we have here remains the same—you cannot keep selling those potions if you want to live a long life. The demon could have *killed* you, Del."

"But instead, he bought cock-lengthening potions. His girl sent me flowers for teaching him a lesson *and* improving her sex life. I provide a service to the community."

"Service my ass. And it might have worked out all right this time, but if there's a next time, you might not be so lucky. Plus, as you're already well aware, I'd rather we didn't make enemies here."

"Says the Priestess who pissed off berserkers, made a bitchy Ancient all green-eyed, and kicked a severed head at Azazel's aide."

"I'm not a Priestess."

"That's what you're gonna focus on right now? Really?"

*

Standing at the foot of his bed later that evening, Cain watched his cock disappear into Wynter's mouth again and again, riveted by the sight in a way he couldn't explain. Seeing her soft lips stretched tight around his shaft . . . it did something to him. Brought out a primitive satisfaction in him every single time.

The pleasure went beyond mere physical stimulation, because this wasn't just a convenient mouth. The woman propped up on her hands and knees on his bed wasn't simply a convenient body. Wynter was . . . more.

He tangled his fist in her hair as a dark wave of possessiveness rose up inside him. It was *too* dark. Dangerous. Unstable, even. But he did nothing to fight it.

She sucked harder, faster, and a growl rattled his chest.

"That fucking mouth," he gritted out. "*My* fucking mouth."

Her eyes snapped to his, glazed over with a hunger that gripped his balls.

"Hand," he demanded, holding out his own. "The one wearing my mark."

She hesitated, unsure.

"I won't let you fall. You know better than to think I would."

Careful not to lose her balance, she lifted one hand and gave it to him.

"I didn't tell you to stop sucking, did I?"

She shot him a narrow-eyed look but went back to sliding her lips up and down his shaft.

He pushed at the center of her palm, knowing it'd feel like he'd plunged his thumb into her pussy, and felt her breathing stutter around his cock. He did nothing other than that. He didn't want to make her come yet. He just wanted her to feel him everywhere. If he could have given her that same sensation in her ass, he would have.

She kept taking him in and out of her mouth, instinctively trying to throw her hips at the 'thumb' filling her, as if desperately needing the friction. Still, he didn't give it to her. He kept on enjoying the feel and sight of her swallowing him down again and again . . . until he fucking had to be inside her.

"Enough." Tightening his fist in her hair, he wrenched her head back and swept his thumb over her swollen lower lip. "Don't know what I love more. Seeing you suck me off, or feeling you do it. I could watch you swallow my dick for hours. But right now"—he tugged on her hair, urging her up to her knees and guiding her closer—"I want to bury my cock so deep inside you you'll never get it out."

Cain kissed her, licking his tongue inside her mouth, swallowing her little moan. He tapped her delectable ass and released her hair. "Turn around. I want you on your hands and knees again."

More than ready to be fucked, Wynter didn't hesitate to do as he'd asked. She arched into the hand that stroked its way from her nape to the base of her spine. That same hand dipped a finger inside her.

"Ready for me. Good."

She felt her lips part as the broad head of his cock slid inside her. Pleasure danced along her soul, as electric and consuming as ever . . .

but the touch was light. More like fingertips than a hand. It came again, and again, and again. The bliss was immense—making her body sing and ache for more—but each touch was too soft. Too slow . . . much like the cock lazily making its way into her pussy.

After another fluttering sweep of soul-deep pleasure, he was finally buried inside her to the hilt. And then he began to thrust. Gently. Carefully. So sluggishly it was agonizing. The waves of pleasure he delivered to her soul were just the same. Every featherlight wave was as amazing as it was *frustrating*.

Soon she was trembling, whimpering, dazed with sheer *want*. "Cain," she croaked.

"What do you want? Tell me, pretty witch."

She swallowed. "To break."

"Hmm, and how do you want me to touch your soul? Like this?" He sent out a firm wave of pure spine-tingling pleasure. "Or like this?" The second wave was a crackly charge of dark bliss that held a sting—and there was no hiding that her body responded more intensely to that.

He let out a low, velvety chuckle. "You like it when it hurts." Then he was slamming into her. Hard. Fast. Deep. Ruling and ruining her, just as he always did.

She floated, out of her mind with pleasure/pain as he subjected her to an overload of sensation. The drag and thrust of his cock, the bite of his fingertips, the slap of his balls, the surge after surge of darkly decadent pleasure to her soul that electrified her nerve-endings . . . It all flooded her body with endorphins and *totaled* her control so that she was an absolute slave to the moment.

Still pounding into her, Cain curled his body over hers and splayed one hand around her neck while the other gripped her hip a little too tight. He growled low into her ear, squeezing her throat. "I want my fingerprints all over you. I want them imprinted on your bones. I want them stamped on your fucking soul."

Another squeeze to her throat, and she shuddered as her orgasm came hurtling toward her.

"Look at me."

She twisted her head and met a pair of menacingly dark eyes just as her release *whipped* through her very being like a lightning rod, striking her from the inside out.

He groaned, his cock swelling. "Those fucking tears." He rammed harder into her pussy, bit into her shoulder, and exploded while her inner muscles milked him dry.

Finally, her orgasm faded, and she blinked away yet more tears as her breaths sawed in and out of her lungs. Jesus, he'd kill her one day.

"If I killed you, I wouldn't be able to fuck you anymore. People tend to frown on stuff like that."

Wynter snorted. She hadn't realized she'd spoken aloud. "Since when do you care what people do or don't frown upon?"

"Since never. But don't worry, your corpse would be safe with me. Necrophilia isn't my thing."

"That is a comfort."

"I had hoped it would be."

She let out yet another snort.

Once they'd both cleaned up in the bathroom, he helped her slip on one of his shirts and began to button it for her. This had become a 'thing.' Unlike him, Wynter didn't like to sleep naked. He didn't complain purely because she didn't fuss over his preference for her to wear either his tees or shirts for bed.

"Do you always insist on this?" she asked.

He briefly looked up from the button he was closing. "What?"

"That whoever sleeps in your bed also wears your stuff at the time?"

He drifted his gaze over her face. "No. I don't usually fuck women in my chamber, let alone put them in my clothes."

She blinked. "Oh." She wanted to ask why she was the exception, but that felt too much like fishing for compliments. And he'd only expect the same honesty in return—Wynter often fumbled when it came to talking about 'feelings.' But she could give him something.

"Well, um, I don't usually sleep in other guys' beds or wear their tees or shirts."

Satisfaction glittered in his eyes. "So we're even."

"Yeah. Yeah, we are."

# Chapter Fourteen

Setting down her chopsticks, Wynter briefly squeezed her eyes shut, hoping none of the other patrons were paying any attention to their conversation. "Hattie, can we talk about this later? Or maybe, like, never?"

Hattie let out a *pfft* sound. "Don't be all prudish, just tell me what it means. If I'm going to get back in the saddle again, I should know these things."

Xavier's mouth slowly curved into a wicked grin. "George is gonna get lucky, is he?" he asked, referring to the old woman's 'gentleman caller.'

"At some point, yes." Hattie notched up her chin, looking mighty pleased with herself. "He's a very nice man, and he's not past his prime yet. I don't want to embarrass myself by looking confused when he makes suggestions in bed."

Wynter massaged her temple. "I really don't think he'll suggest a spit roast."

Hattie's brow creased. "Why not?"

Jesus Christ, she was gonna have to say it, wasn't she? "It would mean he's also suggesting that you include a third party."

"Oh, I see. So would be it two men and one woman, or one man and two women?"

Wynter took a swig from her glass of water. "The first."

"I think I can guess where each man would position himself. Does the 'spit' part mean she's not supposed to swallow? I don't know why you're groaning at me, Wynter, it's a perfectly logical query."

"I hate to interrupt your *wacked* conversation but can we please leave soon?" Rubbing at her upper arms, Anabel glanced around the restaurant. Located on the surface of Devil's Cradle, it served supremely good ethnic food and was highly popular. "There are too many people here."

Hattie lifted her glass. "We said we'd come out and get some D, remember?"

Anabel did a double-take. "Dick?"

"Vitamin D." Hattie pointed at the sky. "From the sun."

"It's seven p.m.; the sun has set." Anabel again scanned the room, paranoid. "We *really* should go home. I'm telling you, we're not safe." She started clawing at her nape. "I can feel—"

Delilah pointed her chopsticks at the blonde. "Do *not* start harping on about death's breath again. I'd tell you to get a handle on your neurosis, but I don't see that ever being possible."

Anabel scowled. "I'm not neurotic."

"You believe death pants on your goddamn neck."

"Because it does!" Anabel looked at Xavier. "*You* believe me, don't you?"

"Of course I do," he assured her. "Now come on, girls, we're supposed to be relaxing. Chilling. Celebrating how good things are going for us right now." A charming smile graced his lips as a member of staff appeared to swipe the empty glasses. He looked at her nametag. "Mona," he drawled in a deeply Southern accent. "Pretty name. I'm Colton—" He cut off as a male hand landed on his shoulder.

"You telling lies again, boy?" asked Elias, amused.

Stiffening, Xavier twisted slightly in his chair to toss a glare at the Alpha standing behind him. "Don't call me 'boy.'"

"Your infractions are building up," Elias told him, lowering his voice. He bent and put his mouth to Xavier's ear. "But that's okay. Daddy won't mind paddling that ass."

Xavier stared at him like he was crazy. "You get high a lot, don't you? It explains so much."

Elias let out a rumbly chuckle, squeezed Xavier's shoulder, shot Wynter a subtle wink, and then stalked off with some of his pack members.

Xavier met Wynter's gaze. "Can I kill him now?"

Stifling a smile, she said, "He's just trying to unnerve you, stop letting him."

Hattie patted her chin. "I wonder if he's any good with a paddle. Do you think he really is a Daddy Dom? He doesn't strike me as the type to be interested in age-play."

"What do you know about age-play?" Delilah asked her.

"I read about it." Hattie sipped at her water. "I find the lifestyle fascinating. I can see the appeal in it."

Delilah tipped her head to the side. "You're thinking about being George's Little, are you?"

Hattie adjusted her blouse. "If he's partial to it, well, a person should try everything at least once. And, given my age, I'll be in diapers soon anyway."

"I tried the Little thing once," said Xavier.

Delilah lifted her brows. "Really?"

"No, not really," he replied.

She flapped her arms. "Then why say it?"

"Maybe your annoyance fills the empty spots inside me."

"People, can we go back to relaxing, please?" Wynter cut in.

It really shouldn't have been so difficult to do that, but with Anabel panicking, Delilah and Xavier bickering, and Hattie asking Wynter one uncomfortable question after another ... yeah, there was no 'chill' vibe at the table at all.

Wynter excused herself and headed to the restroom. She was just finished doing her business in a stall when an otherworldly breeze fluttered over her skin, humming with warning. She tensed, her pulse—

The stall door flew open, and a burst of magick—thick, cloggy, *dirty*—backhanded her. Pain exploded in her cheekbone, her vision swam, and the world spun around her. Oh, she was gonna hurl.

Her monster's head snapped up, and it would have taken control if that otherworldly breeze hadn't returned, ushering it to bide its time.

Dazed, Wynter would have fallen if strong hands hadn't caught her. Then she was being hauled out of the stall. A familiar male voice spoke to her. No, hissed words at her. She couldn't understand them. Couldn't focus. Couldn't really think.

She felt completely disconnected from the situation as the male huddled her against him like they were a couple, supporting her weight while walking out of the restroom and over to the side exit. She didn't *want* to walk alongside him, but her legs moved without direction. She didn't *want* to stay silent as he led her out of the door, but no words escaped her when she parted her lips.

Outside, he lifted her into a van and roughly dumped her on the vehicle floor before leaping into the van. Laying on her side, she saw someone further down the alley staring at her, looking stunned. *Grouch.*

Hope spiked in her chest, clearing away some of the fog in her mind. A smug little smirk twisted his mouth, and then he casually strolled through the side door of the nearby pub.

*That motherfucker.*

"Go!" ordered a voice, slamming the sliding door of the van closed, and then the driver peeled out of there.

Again, her monster went to rise in a fury. Again, the breeze urged it to wait.

*Fuck waiting.*

Wynter ground her teeth, anger coursing through her. Her 'daze' was wearing off now. She knew who'd taken her. Knew she was gonna rip off his cock and—

Hands rolled her onto her front, making her face scrape along the rough floor. *Ow.* Cuffs were snapped onto her wrists, and she felt power buzz against her skin. They were bespelled to keep her from using her magick, she realized. *Fuck.*

Again, hands roughly dragged and shoved until, finally, she

found herself plopped on her ass with her back pressed against the side of the van.

Squatted in front of her, the male who'd snatched her smiled. "Hello again, Wynter."

Blanking her expression, she stared at the man who looked so much like one of the boys who put her through hell. "Phineas."

Her monster stirred once more, impatient to act. She didn't really have a choice but to release it at some point. She couldn't use her magick, so there was only one way she was getting out of this situation. The monster would easily escape the cuffs. But it wouldn't move until the deity gave it Her permission.

"Your old coven thought you'd be hard to capture," he said, cocky. "Can't imagine why."

Darkness fell over them, and she knew they were now driving through the tunnel that led out of the town. She stilled as she heard the rumbling of more engines and the screeching of tires.

"Those three vehicles you're hearing aren't driven by people coming to save you," said Phineas. "Nah, they're filled with people from Aeon. Each vehicle will head off in a different direction, which means anyone who tries saving your ass will have four trails to follow."

Clever. Didn't matter, though. It was really all for nothing. Because neither he nor the driver would live much longer.

"People will realize you're gone soon, but they won't find it so easy to track you. *We're* going off-road and taking a little detour that'll make it simple to lose whoever might follow. We've been driving around these parts for days familiarizing ourselves with the territory."

Pausing, he cocked his head. "You're remarkably calm for someone who'll be delivered to the Aeons soon. They are pissed at you. Were you this calm when you killed my boy?"

"I don't remember."

"You think I believe you were really in some kind of shock-induced trance?" He sneered, his eyes blazing. "You killed him in cold blood."

Her monster most likely did—Wynter truly wasn't sure how it all went down. "That's kind of what he and his buddy did to me."

"And what does that matter? You're *nothing*. A mere witch from a weak-ass coven. You can't be easy prey and expect predators to not come sniffing around. That ain't how it works. My son . . . he was meant for great things. You took his future from him."

"He got overpowered by a ten year old girl, Phineas. Not so sure you can claim he was meant for greatness."

The mage clenched his fist and raised it, but he didn't slam it into her jaw as she'd expected. No, he just snickered like she was too pathetic to be worth the blow. "It was your dark magick that overpowered him. Not you."

"It wasn't dark until he did what he did. When you think about it, he instrumented his own destruction."

He squinted. "I'm going to enjoy watching you die. That'll have to wait a little while, though. The Aeons need you to fix your mess first."

"They can't even combat a little soil erosion, huh?"

"It's not mere soil erosion. And only dark magick can fight dark magick. The Aeons' power is too pure to counteract it."

She let out a scornful chuckle. "Now if it were true that their power is pure, said power would actually be the perfect antidote for the decay, wouldn't it? The Aeons aren't truly so lily-white on any level. But you've already figured that much out for yourself, haven't you? You knew Wagner would toss me over the falls."

"What did you do to him?"

"I'm not entirely sure what exactly happened to him. I just know he's dead." She stilled as a breeze touched her face in what felt like a 'right, you can reign fresh hell on the fuckers now' message. "He never had a chance to do your dirty work, if that's what you're wondering," she added, feeling her monster very slowly slink to the surface as it prepared itself to lunge.

"That's all right. I don't mind doing it myself. I won't be dipping my dick in you—not inside the woman who killed my son. But everything else? Yes, I'll enjoy doing ..." He trailed off, his lips parting as black inky ribbons began to crawl over her eyes. "What in the hell?"

"You shouldn't have come for me, Phineas. You see, this thing that lives inside me ... it *loathes* you. It always has. I managed to hold it back over the years, but only because I promised that it could one day tear you apart if the time was ever right. This moment, well, this feels kind of right. And I'd be a twat if I went back on my promise so, yeah, you and your friend are now gonna die." Her vision went black.

\*

"I want to be able to shift," said the male sitting opposite Cain in the parlor's manor. "My dragon ... I feel it inside me. I hate that it's trapped. I want to be able to shift."

Cain inwardly sighed. The majority of the time, those wanting to sell their soul requested something reasonable. Cliché, but reasonable—fame, fortune, power. But then there were those who really hadn't thought the situation through; who hadn't considered the downsides to having their desire granted. The male in front of him was one of those people.

"You have no real idea what you're asking," Cain told him. "Draconian mages were stripped of their ability to shift because they were too destructive. Once they turned dragon, the mage stayed in that form and lost their humanity."

"I don't believe that. It's just a story told to scare us. Dragon shifters—"

"Are different. You're a mage with the suppressed capability to shift. You do not have a separate entity inside you, whatever you might think. It is the *bestial magick* that is trapped. It has no personality, no wants, no likes, no dislikes. It is simply power. Once unleashed, it would destroy who you are. You would *become* a beast."

He licked his lips. "You're wrong. Look, I don't even care what will happen. It's my risk to take. I am offering my soul to you in payment."

"You haven't asked what exactly that would entail. It's not a small price to pay."

"It doesn't matter, I—"

The door sharply opened, and Maxim stepped inside, his expression grim. "I'm sorry to disturb you, Sire, but it's Wynter."

Cain was out of his seat in an instant, assuring himself with one touch to her soul that she was in fact alive. Stalking out of the room, he clipped, "Tell me."

"She disappeared from the ethnic restaurant above ground," Maxim explained. "An unfamiliar black van was seen speeding out of town, so people are concluding that she was taken. Her coven are in pursuit, but they're on foot; they asked someone to pass on the message to you. More of the townspeople have joined the search—"

Cain didn't wait to hear more. He used the enhanced speed of his kind to rush out of the manor, through the town, and up to the invisible border a short distance away from the tunnel that would take him out of town . . . if only he could fucking get to it.

Vehicle after vehicle drove through the tunnel fast. He knew the people inside them would search for Wynter. Meanwhile, all he could do was stand in that very spot. It was as far as he could go. Literally.

Anger rumbled through Cain like a thunderstorm, and his hands balled into tight fists. Wynter was gone. Taken. And there wasn't a single fucking thing he could personally do to bring her back. *Nothing.*

His creature went ballistic, thrashing inside him, wanting out; wanting to hunt and track and annihilate whoever took her. It took everything Cain had to contain the monster.

Azazel materialized at his side, his jaw hard as granite. "I heard what happened. She'll be found, Cain. Whoever kidnapped her won't get far with her. They don't know this land like our people do, they'll be caught."

Cain didn't speak. Couldn't. A roar had built in his chest. He knew it would escape him if he opened his mouth.

"She's not dead, right?" Azazel asked.

Cain only shook his head.

"Thought as much. In my opinion, her kidnapper won't kill her. If that was their intention, they would have done it there and then rather than snatch her."

But that brought Cain no comfort, because it meant they likely planned to take her to the Aeons, and those fuckers *would* eventually kill her if they got their hands on her. Azazel knew that as well as Cain did. If someone didn't get to her before—

Movement caught his eye. He watched as Delilah and Xavier walked out of the tunnel, their faces hard as stone.

"I didn't say it was your fault," Delilah said to him.

"Well, it feels like you're tossing the blame at my feet," clipped Xavier.

"That's not what I'm doing, I'm just saying I was distracted by you and Elias having yet another snarky encounter—that's on me. I should have been more alert. We *all* should have been. Instead, Hattie yanked out a small paperback and got lost in the story, and Anabel started having a meltdown like—"

"Hey, I warned you we weren't safe, but you wouldn't listen," ranted Anabel, walking out of the shadows of the tunnel . . . with a crow on her head and Wynter at her side.

Relief slammed into Cain, making him draw in a sharp breath. Then he frowned. She was covered in blood spatter, brain matter, and all manner of things. She should have looked a mess; should have seemed sheepish and awkward when she laid eyes on him. But no, she somehow managed to look regal as a queen.

"Hate motherfucking mages," spat Xavier.

"I hate them more when they're smart." Delilah looked from Cain to Azazel. "Bastards came in four vehicles and took off in different directions to confuse anyone who might follow. Hattie here flew around until she spotted a van that had crashed into a tree and then she led us to it. Wynter had already taken care of shit by then."

Wynter gave Cain a half smile ... like she hadn't just been kidnapped and evidently engaged in a battle of some sort. There were no cuts on her, no bruises, not a single injury. His creature settled slightly, but it wouldn't be happy until she was in their den.

Azazel cleared his throat, staring at her. "I think you have bone fragment in your hair."

Utterly dignified, Wynter swiped blood-soaked bangs away from her face. "It is highly possible." She went to walk past them.

Cain slid into her path. "What happened, Wynter? Who took you? And where the fuck are they?"

"Mages from Aeon came for me," she said. "They're probably dead by now."

"Probably dead? Why probably?"

She went to answer, but then the crow plucked brain matter from her shoulder and spat it on the ground. She offered the bird a smile of thanks and then both of them went to town on the bits of gore, dumping them on the ground.

"Long story," Delilah answered on Wynter's behalf. "She set them on fire."

Azazel blinked. "That wasn't a long story at all."

"It was more that Wynter set the van on fire while the mages were inside it," Anabel explained. "So, yeah, they're most likely goners at this point. The screaming *was* dying down as we left the scene."

"I still say we should have waited for them to take their last breaths," said Xavier.

Wynter rolled her eyes. "Only because you wanted to reanimate their bodies."

"And that would have been so terrible?" he asked.

"No," replied Wynter. "But you would have made them chase Anabel at some point. You always reach *that point*."

"She likes to feel death's breath on her neck."

Anabel whirled on him. "I don't *like* to feel it, I just do. It's a curse."

"It's a fucking delusion," he said.

She gasped. "You said you believed me."

"I lied. That's what I do."

# Chapter Fifteen

Wynter loved her crew. She did. And one of the things she loved most about them was that they could so quickly move on from an 'incident.' There was no clinging to panic. No insistence on dwelling on what *could* have happened. No letting such things get them down or spoil their day.

Another thing she loved? They were sneaky as hell.

Take now, for example. Oh, the little disputes they were having were genuine enough. But they were having them here and now for one reason only—to distract the two Ancients who no doubt had the kind of questions hovering on the tip of their tongue that Wynter wouldn't want to answer.

It was working.

Cain and Azazel were staring at the four oddly, as if her being covered in blood and gore was now a secondary matter. Yeah, she really did adore her crew.

Needing a shower in a major way, she proposed they all head home and began to walk. It looked like Cain might resume his line of questioning, but then Hattie shifted and—promptly back to acting like a frail old lady who could use a little help keeping steady as she walked—asked him if anal fisting was truly a thing because she just didn't see how an entire hand could fit up *anyone's* asshole. She wanted to know if he'd done it, if he'd been on the receiving end of it, if he'd tried 'back door fun' of any kind.

Wynter subtly exchanged an amused look with Delilah. God, Hattie was an absolute hoot.

There did come a point where Cain managed to break away from the conversation, but Xavier quickly distracted him with a child-hood story that was most likely pure bullshit.

Azazel . . . well, he didn't really require distractions. He was too focused on Anabel, undoubtedly wondering how someone so clearly nervous of the world around her could have performed so ruthlessly in the gauntlet.

They'd kept that whole thing about her supposedly being the reincarnation of Bloody Mary to themselves—Anabel rarely shared that little titbit with others.

Finally, they arrived at the manor. Her crew continued waving their crazy flag as they strolled through the building, took a down-ward ride in the elevator, and headed for their cottage. But when Wynter went to turn down the street that led to her home, Cain's hand slipped around her upper arm.

"Come," he said, trying to lead her toward the Keep.

"I need to shower and change."

"You can do that at my home," he said, a determined set to his jaw that told Wynter her time to evade his questions was over.

"I have no clothes there."

His eyes heated. "You won't need any."

He couldn't possibly be thinking about sex right now. She was a godawful mess. But then, Cain was turned on by the strangest shit.

"Anabel can pack a bag of your things for me to drop off at the Keep," said Azazel. "Can't you, Anabel?"

The blonde slid him a wide-eyed look. "Why are you talking to me? I don't like it."

His lips hitched up. "Now you're just hurting my feelings. That's mean. It's all right, though. I like mean."

"Then Delilah is your girl."

Delilah frowned. "Hey."

"Well, it's true, karma potion extraordinaire." Anabel pivoted on her heel and made a beeline for the cottage. The others followed, including Azazel.

Resigned, Wynter inwardly sighed as Cain guided her to the Keep.

Standing at the entrance, Maxim gave her an odd look as he took her in her appearance. "I'm hoping none of that blood is yours, Priestess."

"Not mine," she confirmed. "And seriously, call me Wynter."

He grunted. "It's good to see that you're back and well."

"Thank you," she said.

Soon, she and Cain arrived at his chamber. He pulled her straight into the attached bathroom and, carefully peeling her tee from her body, asked, "What exactly happened tonight? Don't think I didn't notice that your coven—"

"Crew," she corrected, kicking off her sneakers.

He sighed. "It's a coven, Wynter. Call it what it is."

"We're not having this conversation."

"That's fine, since we need to talk about the mages anyway." He unclipped her bra and dropped it on the floor near her tee. "Your *coven* did their best to keep me distracted so I wouldn't question you. I'm guessing they were worried you'd lose your emotional cool if you had to recount everything and so, knowing you wouldn't want to get upset in public, they bought you some time."

Wynter felt bad letting him believe that, but telling him the full truth wasn't an option. Still, she'd give him as much detail of what occurred as she could. She didn't want to lie to him any more than she absolutely had to.

"The event wasn't that traumatic," she said, shoving down her jeans and panties. "I was at the ethnic restaurant. A mage dragged me out of the bathroom, into the side alley, and then shoved me into a van." She peeled off her socks. "I was a little dazed because he'd hit me with some *real* dirty magick, so I didn't get a chance to fight."

Naked, she paused as Cain stripped off his own clothes because, yeah, that body could scatter anyone's thoughts. "The only other person in the vehicle was the driver. They both must have stupidly been convinced that I wasn't strong enough to overcome their magick, because the chattiest of the two was cocky as hell. I pretended I was as weak and helpless as they thought. Bided my time.

As soon as an opportunity came, I made my move." More specifi-cally, she'd freed her monster.

Together, she and Cain got rid of the last of the gore from her hair so the bits wouldn't clog the drain. He then turned on the hot spray of the shower and ushered her into the stall. Joining her, he said, "You didn't simply execute them, though. You used your magick to hack them into pieces and then let them burn. Why?"

"I didn't want a quick death for them." Apparently, neither had her monster, since it had torn into them without actually killing them. "Remember the boys that took it upon themselves to end my life when I was a kid?"

"How could I fucking forget?" He soaped her down, not in the least fazed by the blood.

"Their families made my life hell for years. They'd been pushing to have me exiled since I was a kid. You might remember I told you that the keeper who should have tossed me over the falls was asked by the father of one of the boys to make me suffer first."

Cain nodded. "He wanted the keeper to gouge out of one of your eyes."

"Yes. Phineas also wanted him to rape and dismember me."

His jaw hard, Cain squirted shampoo onto his hand. "Fucker."

"Phineas was one of the mages who came for me tonight. With the exception of rape, he planned to carry out the other deeds once the Aeons were done with me. In his view, his son hadn't done a damn thing wrong—I was nothing, my death was nothing. He wanted me to suffer." She shrugged. "I decided to return the favor."

"I'm glad you did," he said, washing her blood-matted hair, still not a tiny bit queasy. "He deserved worse."

Her monster was rather satisfied with that comment. Though it thought of him as part of Wynter's circle, she couldn't go as far as to say it liked Cain or cared to have his approval. But it did like hearing a compliment from a fellow predator. At that moment, it was close to dozing off, relaxed now that it had had its fun.

"The Aeons haven't yet realized there's a curse at work," she said.

"According to Phineas, they believe they're struggling to fight the blight because only dark magick can counter dark magick."

Cain snorted. "They know that it isn't true. They simply don't want others believing they're weak."

"I figured that."

Once they were done showering, Cain turned off the spray and stepped out of the stall. As he wrapped a soft towel around her, he asked, "What aren't you telling me?"

Oh, plenty of things. None of which she could share. Bar one. "There *is* something else."

"What?"

"Grouch saw me get taken. It turns out he didn't alert my crew or anyone else. He just waltzed into the Irish pub like he didn't have a care in the world."

Cain's eyes darkened to flint as rage all but pulsed in the air. A towel curled around his hips, he stalked out of the bathroom.

She followed, watching as he crossed to the internal phone.

He snatched it from the wall, pressed a button on the pad, and said, "Bring Grouch to the Keep. He may still be in the Irish pub above ground. If not, search for him until you find him. You know where to put him."

Fury coursing through him, Cain set down the phone. Twice the emotion had gripped him tonight, and he was struggling to let it pass. He wasn't used to feeling such a depth of extreme emotion. It left him edgy and tense. A crawling sensation kept sweeping over his skin. Skin that felt too tight.

It didn't fucking help that he knew Wynter was lying by omission.

He ground his teeth and rolled his shoulders. Turning to her, he found her standing very still, watching him closely. He crossed to her, drilling his gaze into hers, as if he might see something in the depths of her eyes that would give him answers.

"When I asked what you aren't telling me, I meant about yourself. But you knew that, didn't you?" He lowered his face to hers. "I'm not so easily sidetracked."

"You'll never tell me what skeletons are in your closet, Cain," she said, calm and nonjudgmental. "Why should I tell you about mine?"

All right, she had a point there. Which he intended to ignore on the basis that he didn't like it. "I want to know you. I want to know everything there is to know about you." He tapped her temple. "I want to know what goes on up here." He couldn't even explain where this insane urge to have explored every part of her—inside and out—came from.

"Right back at you. We're in the same boat here."

"Are we really?"

She tipped her head to the side. "You don't think so?"

"No, I don't. I'm renowned for my jealousy issues, though I was never actually jealous of Abel—that story was pure bullshit. But I don't like to share. It's not because I'm a possessive individual by nature. I'm simply selfish that way." Always had been. "With you, though, it's more than a mere refusal to share you. I want you to belong to me so completely that I own your every fucking thought."

He couldn't even say why. He couldn't explain it to himself, let alone her. He wouldn't have thought he was capable of experiencing that depth and intensity of possessiveness. He wasn't sure how he felt about the fact that he could. "Unless you can say the same, no, we're not in the same boat."

She sighed, giving him a look that said he wasn't very bright. "Cain, why do you think I've never given you shit for boldly and publicly marking your territory with just your gaze alone? Did you think it's because I'm a pushover? If so, you're wrong. The reason I didn't gripe about it is because I know that no one will touch you if they know you're involved with someone—they're aware you'd take it as an insult to both you *and* me. An insult that you would never tolerate."

Cain felt his eyes narrow. He hadn't thought she was in any way a pushover—far from it. He'd presumed that she'd decided to simply let his behavior fly over her head. In actual fact, his little witch had let it alone purely because it suited her.

"I've never been openly territorial of you because I really do expect you to at some point announce that you're bored and ready to move on," she said. "Really, it would be better for me to end it before you do—the whole thing will sting a lot less that way. But I haven't. I keep coming back here. Back to you. That should tell you something."

"You don't want us to be done, despite my warnings? Despite what you might have heard or assumed about me?"

"No, I don't want us to be done."

A dark satisfaction settled into his bones. But . . . "You shouldn't have said that."

Her brow furrowed. "Why not?"

Because his creature—liking her comment a little too much and, arrogant as the monster was, feeling that it was really only to be expected—would hold her to that.

He was saved from having to answer by the knock at the door. Opening it, he found one of his aides holding a bag of Wynter's possessions. Cain handed it to her, and they both quickly dressed. It was as she was dragging a brush through her wet hair that Maxim called using the internal phone line to declare that Grouch was in custody.

Cain turned to Wynter, intending to ask her to wait here, but she spoke before he had the chance.

"I want to be there while you deal with him."

His entire system rebelled at that. "No, Wynter, you don't."

She flicked up an imperious brow, dropping the easygoing act she pulled off so well. "Don't tell me what I do or don't want. Don't presume to know what I can and can't handle. I'm quite aware you're not going to simply slap him on the wrist. Have I ever given you reason to think I'd wish to spare someone who wronged me?"

Far from it. Her vengeful streak ran as deep as his own. "Then come. Observe. You should know what you're getting yourself into when it comes to me. If you don't like what you see, well, that's understandable. But you're not going anywhere, Wynter, so don't bother to run. I would just drag you back."

"You realize I'm not a doll or object that you can move around as you please, right? That I have a mind and free will and all that jazz?"

"I do realize that," he began as they started to make their way to the dungeon. "It's inconvenient at times, because it would be easier if I was in control of your every move."

She stared at him for a beat. "You're not even joking, are you?"

"No." He liked things a certain way, and he insisted on it being the case. But Wynter? She might come across as reasonably compliant, but he'd quickly learned that she followed her own rules, and he wasn't entirely sure what they were. She often made decisions he wouldn't have seen coming, or reacted in ways he wouldn't have expected.

Sometimes, it seemed to him as if she was on a path. As if she was focused on a goal he couldn't see.

Finally arriving at the door that led to the dungeon, Cain pushed it open. They descended the stairs, their footsteps echoing slightly. It wasn't often that he had prisoners here, because it wasn't often that anyone would dare anger him to such an extent. Which disappointed his creature, in all honesty, because it had a sadistic streak a mile wide. Not that Cain could judge.

Spotting Maxim standing outside a cell up ahead, Cain strode purposely along the narrow passageway with Wynter at his side, their heels scraping the stone floor as they passed several small cells and secure pits.

The candles within the lanterns flickered, casting shadows over the plentiful torture equipment—spiked beds, racks, iron maidens. There was also an array of torture instruments, such as barbed whips and rusted hooks. The scents of iron, stone, and rust laced the stale air.

He slid Wynter a sideways glance. She was taking everything in, but she didn't look appalled or apprehensive. Then again, she was wearing that damn poker face, so he had no real clue what was going on in her head.

Reaching Maxim, Cain nodded at the aide and then turned to

the cell. His captive stood very still, his wrists cuffed by long chains that were attached to the cell's cracked, stone wall. The berserker had his chin held high and his jaw set, but fear flickered like the flame of a candle in his eyes.

Cain slid open the cell door and strolled inside. "Well, this brings back memories, doesn't it? You've been here once before. You assured me that you wouldn't displease me again. And yet, here we are."

Grouch fired a nervous look at Wynter, who remained outside the cell. "Cain, I don't know what she told you—"

"Yes, you do," said Cain. "You're very aware of why you're here. What I really am struggling to understand . . . is why you would ignore that someone had taken what belongs to me. You may not like Wynter, but you know she's mine. Not merely in my service, but a woman I have a claim to.

"You knew I'd be beyond pissed that she was taken. Yet, you did nothing to help her. Nor did you alert anyone of what you saw. Now why would you want me to be pissed, Grouch?"

"I-I didn't know she was being kidnapped. The guy wasn't carrying her or dragging her. She was walking at his side, and she wasn't calling out for help."

Anger whipped through Wynter and shot to her extremities. "You *knew* something was wrong. You saw him dump me on the floor of the van. And you smirked like a smug piece of shit."

"*Smiled.* It was just a smile," he insisted.

Maxim grunted. "Yes, because you're so known for smiling."

Cain took a step toward the berserker, who snapped his mouth shut. "What don't I like? Tell me."

Grouch swallowed. "Lies or excuses."

"Lies and excuses. And yet, you fed me both last time you were here. You're doing it again right now when you're already in enough trouble as it is." Cain slanted his head. "Does that really seem wise to you?"

Wynter almost shivered at the menace threaded through each syllable. Her Ancient could be damn scary when he wanted to be.

She would genuinely hate to be on the end of that piercing, murderous glare.

Her monster was now wide awake, riveted by the action playing out in front of it, fairly salivating with anticipation as it waited for the berserker to be punished.

"Give me some honesty, Grouch," said Cain. "Show me you have *some* sense of self-preservation."

Grouch squeezed his eyes shut. "I didn't think you'd really care if she disappeared. She's just a woman who warms your bed."

"There you go again with the lies. You weren't thinking of whether or not I'd care. You were thinking about how her disappearance would suit *you* and your business. I warned you that if you made any trouble for Wynter, you'd pay for it in blood. She was in danger, and you did nothing. Which is even worse than if you'd tried sabotaging her business. You *knew* that. But you didn't care. Isn't that right?"

After a long moment, Grouch nodded. "Y-yes. I should have done something to help her or told someone what I saw," he conceded, his voice low. "Staying quiet was a shitty thing to do."

"Wynter might have died at the hands of her kidnappers. I'd say 'shitty' is an absolute understatement. Wouldn't you?"

"I would." Grouch glanced at her, sweat now beading his brow. "I'm sorry."

Wynter inwardly snorted. There was no *real* sincerity in that apology. Only stark fear.

"You're saying all the right things, Grouch. But I don't know if I believe you." Cain flicked his aide a glance. "What about you, Maxim?"

Arms folded, the gargoyle replied, "I think he's simply telling you what he thinks you want to hear."

Cain hummed. "So do I."

As did Wynter.

"It doesn't make any difference either way, really," said Cain. "Because the thing is ... I don't want to hear that you're sorry,

Grouch. I don't want to hear an honest confession. I just want to hear you scream."

Grouch sucked in a breath as his back arched like a brow. Then he screamed. Like *really* screamed—the sound rang with pain and terror. As if someone was flaying the skin from his bones and pouring acid over the wounds.

*Holy shit.*

He dropped to his knees so hard she'd be surprised if he hadn't shattered his kneecaps. Still making those bloodcurdling wails, he keeled over, his face scrunched up tight. She'd honestly never seen anyone look like they were in this much agony.

Cain was assaulting his soul, she knew. She was well aware of how pleasurable his touch could be when he reached out to her soul. Although she'd known that he could also cause her terrible pain, it wasn't really until now that she'd properly considered just how intensely unbearable any pain he delivered would be.

Ever so casually, Cain raised his hand and closed it tight.

The screams cut off, and Grouch began to choke. His teary eyes wide, he wheezed. Grabbed at his throat. Tried sucking in air.

He stared at Cain with a plea in his eyes ... and the immortal stared back at him, his gaze implacable—there was no anger there, no hint of temper, no glint of annoyance. And that made the whole thing so much more disturbing. Yet, she felt no pity for the berserker. He hadn't cared about what could have happened to her, so why should she give a damn what happened to him?

Finally, Cain uncurled his hand. Grouch collapsed to the ground, coughing and sucking in huge gulps of air.

"He's going to faint if he keeps breathing like that," said Maxim, somewhat dispassionate.

Cain pursed his lips. "Most likely." He narrowed his eyes. "I won't tell you not to fuck up like this again, Grouch. I don't need to. Because you'll never have the chance to repeat your mistake. No one who targets something that belongs to me ever does." He waved a dismissive hand. "Throw him in the snake pit."

Whistling, Maxim freed Grouch from the chains, fisted the back of the berserker's shirt, and then hauled him out of the cell and along the passageway.

Wynter managed not to tense when Cain's dark eyes slammed on her. She stayed very still and held his gaze steadily. She never ever let herself forget that she was in the company of an apex predator. But sometimes ... sometimes she failed to remember that him having access to her soul meant she was so very vulnerable to him.

His lips twitched. "Ah, there's that hunter stare yet again," he said, amusement lacing the words. "I find that I like it." He crossed to her, standing oh so close. "I'd never hurt you, pretty witch." Sobering, he added, "Still ... you'll never be utterly safe with me."

She swallowed. "I don't know what that means. But I do know I'm not looking for someone to wrap me up in cotton wool and keep me safe and protected, so there's that."

Plus, as few things could truly kill her, there was some part of Wynter that perversely liked being around a creature that was a true danger to her. It made her feel more alive. Which was probably twisted, but there it was. Hell, they were both twisted, really. What a pair they made.

# Chapter Sixteen

The cottage was rarely ever quiet. Especially in the morning when they were usually getting ready to open their homerun shop. But today was their day off. And since Delilah was in the bath, Hattie and Xavier were shopping, and Anabel was experimenting with potions in her bedroom, Wynter found herself alone in the kitchen and . . . yeah, the silence was almost eerie.

Still, it was kind of nice to be able to sit at the table drinking tea and be alone with her thoughts. So her mouth tightened when there was a gentle knock on the front door.

Wynter pushed away from the table, crossed the living area, and pulled open the door. She tensed as she took in the astonishingly beautiful blonde standing on her doorstep with a female aide at her side. *What in the hell . . . ?*

Ishtar gave her a soft, practiced smile. "Good morning, I hope I'm not interrupting anything."

Wynter highly doubted the woman would care if she was. The words were polite but empty.

"We've never officially met, have we?"

Careful to keep her expression neutral, Wynter said, "No, we haven't."

"I am Ishtar."

"Wynter."

She peered over Wynter's shoulder. "I do hope you don't rudely intend to leave me standing on the doorstep."

The Ancient wanted to enter her home? The same Ancient who'd glared at her several times? *Not funny, universe. Not funny.*

Unable to turn the woman away without insulting her, Wynter stepped aside and invited her to enter.

Ishtar instructed her aide to remain outside and then slowly strolled through the door and into the living area. She glanced around, unimpressed. "I sometimes forget how small these houses are. It must be frightfully inconvenient to have so little space. Why, you couldn't swing a cat in here."

Wynter really wouldn't want to swing a cat *anywhere*, but whatever. Her inner monster tilted its head, studying the visitor. It didn't want her in its domain. Didn't trust her near Wynter. But it remained calm, not getting the sense that the woman meant her physical harm. At least not today.

"Can I get you a drink? Tea? Coffee?" Cyanide?

"No, thank you." Ishtar gingerly sat on the armchair, her brow creasing in concern. "I heard about the attempted kidnapping. It must have been quite an upsetting experience for you."

Wynter sank onto the sofa. "You could say that." It wouldn't be true, but it could be said.

"You know people will keep coming on behalf of the Aeons, don't you? It will be never-ending. I am aware that Cain and the other Ancients believe that one of the Aeons will eventually come here. I am more of the opinion that they will continue sending others to do their dirty work. But if they do come here, you will need to be ready for what happens next."

"What does that mean?"

Ishtar smoothed a non-existent wrinkle out of her long, flowing skirt. "I know you are involved with Cain. I can see why you would be drawn to him at a time when your life is in such peril. He is, after all, more than a match for the people who would do you harm." She paused. "This is the first time we have ever had something that they want. And so, it is the first time we are in a position to barter with them for what *we* want. I cannot elaborate on that. Not without the full support of the other Ancients, and they would never grant it to me. What I mean to say ... is that you should brace yourself for what will feel like a betrayal."

Wynter's insides seized. "A betrayal?"

"I am sure it is easy to believe that you matter to Cain. He is good at making a woman believe that—it is something I know from experience. He is a master manipulator, which I can admit I admire. The people around him who are of use to him . . . they are simply pieces on his chessboard. He moves them to wherever he wants them. Each move he himself makes is practiced. Cunning. Calculated.

"And you . . . *you* he wishes to keep close, because you may gain him what he wants. As such, that is where he placed you on his board. If the Aeons offer him what he seeks in exchange for you, he *will* make that trade."

Wynter barely stopped her eyes from narrowing. Was Cain good at manipulation? She believed so. Would he use people however he pleased? Undoubtedly, since he didn't see many as relevant. But would he trade Wynter for something he wanted? *That* she didn't know. What she did know was that she couldn't trust this woman's intentions for even a second.

From her peripheral vision, Wynter sensed Delilah silently descend the stairs but didn't look her way. "Why are you telling me this?" she asked Ishtar.

"As I said, I know from experience how good he is at making a woman believe she means something to him. I bought it. I wish someone had warned me to keep my guard up. Then I would have been ready for that moment when he kicked me completely off his chessboard. That is the thing with Cain. He constantly replaces his pawns, because he tires of them so quickly." She paused at a bang upstairs.

Wynter inwardly sighed. Anabel and her fucking experiments. Wynter just hoped the woman hadn't set herself on fire again.

"Each new game comes with new pawns," Ishtar went on. "Right now, he is playing a game with the Aeons. Like it or not, you are a key piece on his board right now. But once you have served your purpose, he will kick you off it too."

Quite possibly. Wynter wasn't under the impression that she was important to Cain. He was possessive of her and seemed intent on keeping her around, but it didn't automatically follow that he felt any deeper emotions for her. She'd never allowed herself to think differently.

Still, she wasn't convinced he'd so callously set her aside. Or maybe she simply didn't want to consider it. "You really believe he'll hand me over to the Aeons if they make him the right offer?"

Ishtar gave her a sympathetic smile. "Darling girl, he has tunnel vision where this particular matter is concerned. They betrayed us all, but they have also deprived Cain of something his entire life. Some*one*, I should say. For a millennia, his whole focus has been on retrieving what should never have been taken from him. He has known you, what, a few weeks? Do you think he would truly turn down the opportunity to obtain what he's sought for so long *just* to ensure your safety? Especially when you are mortal and will die soon enough in any case?"

"What do you suggest I do?"

"There is nothing you really can do. Cain will not give you space. He will not move you to another square on his chessboard until he is ready. And there is no way to ensure he doesn't trade you if the opportunity arises. You would have no way to fight him.

"None of the other Ancients—not even myself—would wish to stand against him to help you. We want him to have what he seeks. Seth, though . . . Seth may help you. He has a good heart, unlike the rest of us. He would empathize with your situation. He is also the one person who Cain would not harm, so if Seth gave you sanctuary at his Keep, you would be free of Cain's clutches."

So, what, she wanted Wynter to pit one brother off against the other? Was that it? Or was it just a simple case that Ishtar wanted her away from Cain and figured that Seth was the one person who could keep them apart without there being any bloodshed?

Ugh, Wynter didn't have the patience for this. Deciding the best way to get the Ancient to leave would be to let her think this 'play' she was making had worked, Wynter said, "I suppose it's worth a shot."

Triumph very briefly flashed in Ishtar's eyes. Again, she gave Wynter a gentle smile. "All you can do is try. And you should. This is your life at stake. I know Cain is contracted to not give you up to anyone who may come for you, but there are loopholes. All he would have to do is return the rights to your soul, and he would no longer be obliged to do anything to protect you. Until then, he will indeed keep you safe. But only because you are of use to him."

Maybe, maybe not. But wanting this conversation over with, Wynter continued to play the part of the crushed female. "It's so hard to accept that he had me so fooled. He said so many sweet things to me. And he always insisted on me sleeping in his bed at night."

A hardness slid into Ishtar's expression at the latter comment, but it quickly melted away. "Of course he did. As I said, he wishes to keep you close."

Wynter groaned. "I feel so stupid."

"You are not stupid, dear girl. He is simply a very accomplished liar who reads people well. He senses what they'll need to hear, and he tells them those very things." Seemingly satisfied that her work was done, Ishtar rose. "Now I must go. I am sure I will see you at the festivities tonight. Do enjoy yourself. And best of luck with Seth. If anyone can keep you safe from Cain, it is him." The Ancient then breezed out of the cottage.

Delilah stepped into the doorway of the living area. "What in the world was that?"

"A play of some kind," Wynter replied. "Whether or not she's telling the truth about Cain being willing to hand me over to the Aeons at a later date, I don't know. But she did *not* come here out of any concern for me, so why else tell me all that?"

Delilah leaned against the doorjamb. "To shake any faith you might have in Cain? To make you distance yourself from him?"

"But *why*, though? I know she wants Cain, but she can't possibly view me as a true threat. She sees me as a mere mortal—weak, naïve, easily manipulated. She thinks *nothing* of mortals."

"Exactly. To her, you're nothing. And yet, you have him; she doesn't. That stabs her ego. It's all about how *she* feels."

"I guess. Still, this doesn't add up to me. I mean, she put a whole lot of effort into trying to make me believe that Cain will one day betray me. Why warn me, when she'd surely be finding it amusing that I'm being played? Why shorten her fun? Why not prefer to wait for the day where I get to see for myself that I'm nothing to him so she can laugh at my expense?"

Delilah frowned. "Maybe you're wrong in believing she doesn't see you as a threat. Something about your relationship with Cain unsettled her enough to inspire her uppity ass to come all the way here and sow some seeds of distrust." She paused. "Are you going to tell him about her impromptu visit?"

"Probably not. He wouldn't like it. I don't want the Ancients arguing among themselves at a time when their enemies could potentially arrive."

"You don't want to ask Cain about it? You don't want to find out if just maybe there *is* something they'll offer him in trade?"

"You think he'd really be upfront about it if there was?"

"I guess not, but it's worth asking. We need to know, Wyn. We need to be sure these people will truly keep you safe."

Wynter leaned forward in her seat. "You're now thinking it might be good for us to just cut and run."

"Yeah, I am."

"Maybe that's what she intended. Maybe that was the purpose of her little visit."

Delilah squinted. "Huh. Maybe."

"Look, I'm not going to dash out of here in a blind panic. For all we know, the Aeons have people watching Devil's Cradle. If I get the sense—or an otherworldly warning—that we need to leave, then that's what we'll do. At the moment, I'm not feeling that. And I have to consider that Ishtar could simply be playing mind games."

"Do you trust Cain to keep you safe?"

"At all costs? No. I don't trust that *any* of the Ancients will. But there is a strong chance that they'll back me, even though it would only be to piss off the Aeons."

"And if they don't back you?"

Wynter felt her face harden. "I'll wreak the kind of havoc they'll have never seen coming."

*

Okay, so she hadn't expected this when she walked into the arena. People weren't ushered into the spectator area. They were guided to the performance space, which had been made into a makeshift gambling area. There were blackjack tables, roulette wheels, craps tables, and roped-off poker games. There were also several stalls scattered around featuring carnival games such as Hoopla, Basketball, Ball and Bucket Toss, and Tin Can Alley. The battle square was once more exposed, and the people surrounding it took bets as others went head to head in the square.

The combination should have been weird, but it worked. There was something for everyone.

Hattie glanced around, excited. "All that's missing are male pole dancers. That would make my night complete."

Xavier snickered. "I don't think George would like watching you ogle other men. But hey, there's apparently gonna be some kind of Vegas-like show after everyone's eaten, so maybe they'll have some male strippers."

"We won't have to stay long, will we?" Anabel held her arms close to her sides. "It's bad enough that the place is packed with people. All the bunnies are making it hard to take a step without crushing something. And why are they wearing top hats? It's just weird."

Wynter turned to her with a sigh. "See, this is why we ask you not to experiment on yourself. There are no bunnies. Or top hats. You're hallucinating again."

A line dented Anabel's brow. "But they look so real. Are you sure?"

"As sure as I am that Bruce Willis was not hanging out in

our cottage earlier talking to you about herbs, despite what you insisted." That had been a weird half hour.

"He seemed so real." Anabel looked at her bare arms. "Just like this hideous rash."

"Oh no, that's real."

She stomped her foot. "Dammit."

Delilah gently elbowed the blonde. "Hey, on the upside, I don't think Diego will wanna touch you tonight."

Anabel brightened. "That's a good point. He'll give me space for sure." Her eyes narrowed in thought. "In fact ... " She let out an experimental cough loud enough to make a few people turn. Spotting the rash covering her face, neck, and arms, they understandably took a step back. Many preternaturals were immune to viruses, but not all.

She kept coughing and sniffling, clearly delighted that the crowd parted like the red sea. "I should really do this more often. I can't believe I didn't think of it before."

Delilah frowned. "You'd *willingly* look hideous just so people would give you a wide berth?"

Anabel sniffed. "Unlike you, I do not care what others think of my appearance. I reject vanity in all its forms."

Wynter sighed. "If you convince people you have a rash, they're going to worry that it's contagious, and then they won't come to our shop anymore."

Anabel looked at her for a long moment. "Xavier's right, you really do choose to focus too much on logic."

He smiled at the blonde. "*Thank* you."

Anabel looked off to the side, her mouth curving. "Ah, that's cute."

"What?" he asked.

"The pony."

He cleared his throat. "Not real."

"Shit."

"Ooh, I see George." Hattie pulled a little spray bottle out of her purse, squirted some of the contents into her mouth, and then dropped the small cannister back into the bag. "I'll catch up with you lot later." And off she went.

Xavier rubbed his hands. "All right, let's go waste our money."

Wandering from table to table and stall to stall, they pretty much did exactly that. Eventually, they made their way to the battle square, where they managed to win back a lot of the cash they'd lost, since they were pretty good at predicting which fighter would come out on top.

At one point, hands clamped on Wynter's hips, and a mouth grazed her temple. "Thought I might find you over here, little witch."

She smiled, her body perking up in all the best places. Although her earlier conversation with Ishtar had filled her with doubts, Wynter had chosen to shake them off. He'd given her no reason to believe he was using her, and she wasn't going to let Ishtar poison what they had unless, or until, proof of such a claim appeared. "I figured you'd be playing poker with the other Ancients or something."

"One game was enough." Cain hummed. "What a view."

Realizing he was looking at her cleavage, she rolled her eyes. *Typical boy.*

He nipped her earlobe. "Now I'm remembering the time I thrust my cock between your breasts until I came all over them," he whispered.

She swallowed at the memory, her hormones getting all stirred up. "You're mean to do this to me here."

He let out a wicked chuckle and, curling his arm around her waist, moved to her side. "Who did you place your money on?"

"The lamia. And I'm glad. She's totally wiping the floor with the vampire." The lamia continued to do exactly that, and victory was very soon hers. The crowd's winnings were handed out. Wynter happily accepted hers and pocketed the cash.

Just then, another Ancient sidled up to them and nodded. "Cain, Wynter."

"Hey, Azazel," she greeted simply.

His gaze cut to Anabel, and his brow creased. "What's with the rash?"

"I'm allergic to crowds." The blonde tilted her head. "Why are you wearing a tin foil hat?"

Xavier leaned into her. "Not real," he muttered.

She closed her eyes. "Dammit."

Delilah nudged Wynter, chuckling. "Get a look at Hattie staring at George's ass while he's tossing hoops at the bottles. I don't know how to feel about the fact that her sex life is currently better than mine."

"And mine," added Xavier.

"Only because you're set on fighting Elias and his boyfriend," Delilah pointed out. "A threesome would spice things up for sure."

Xavier narrowed his eyes. "You know as well as I do that Elias is just messing with me."

"That doesn't mean he wouldn't gladly fuck you."

Anabel's face softened, her eyes landing on her shoulder. "Aw, how beautiful. I love butterflies." She began uttering soft, non-intelligible sounds to the flying insect that only she could see. But then her brow puckered, and she glanced up at Xavier. "It's not real, is it?"

"Oh no, it's real," he assured her.

A sigh of relief slipped out of Anabel, and she smiled brightly. "Good. For a second there, I was worried I was embarrassing myself cooing over thin air." Shaking her head at herself, as if she'd been dumb to doubt her eyes, she went back to freaking serenading a non-existent butterfly.

Wynter shot Xavier a hard look, but before she could order the lying bastard to tell her the truth, Delilah leaned into Wynter and whispered, "We need to teach her a lesson or she's not gonna stop carelessly sampling her wares."

That was true enough.

Azazel turned to Wynter. "What is happening?" he asked quietly, glancing briefly at Anabel, who was putting her fingers to her shoulder and trying to coax the 'butterfly' to walk onto her hand.

"She experiments on herself with her potions," Wynter explained, her voice low. "There are often temporary after-effects. Hence the rash and hallucinations."

"And the edginess around people?"

"No, she's always like that." Feeling eyes on her, Wynter looked to see Ishtar staring at her. The Ancient looked from her to Cain, clearly confused. Wynter shrugged in a 'I'm just weak where he's concerned' gesture. It was better to keep up the naïve act.

Cain squeezed her hip. "We're leaving now."

She frowned. "We are? But there's a show coming up. And the usual feast."

"I know." He picked up her hand. "I'll feed you at the Keep, and I'll be sure to entertain you." He licked at the mark on her palm.

Her breath snagged in her throat as an invisible tongue swiped between her folds. "Bastard."

His gaze was lit with both humor and need. "I could make you come in front of all these people, if you'd prefer." He jabbed his tongue into the center of her palm.

She jumped, feeling as if the aforementioned tongue had sank into her pussy. "No, I damn well wouldn't."

"Then you'd better come with me, hadn't you?"

Anabel's head shot up, and she let out a sad sigh. "Ah, it's gone." Her eyes flitted from person to person, taking in their expressions. Whatever she saw made her face darken. She whirled on the male at her side. "*Xavier.*"

He bust a gut laughing, the shit.

# Chapter Seventeen

Cain snapped awake, his creature urgently shoving at his consciousness. He splayed a hand on the mattress beside him, finding only empty space.

Wynter was gone again.

Lifting his head, he looked toward the adjoined bathroom and called out her name. No response. *Fuck.*

Cain swiftly yanked on a pair of sweatpants and rushed out of the chamber. He'd locked the gates to his garden in case she did any more sleepwalking, so at least he didn't need to worry that she'd go traipsing through it again. On the off-chance that she'd headed there, he made his way to the first floor of the Keep and strode out of the rear doors. He exhaled heavily as he spotted her near the gates dressed in only his shirt. She was swaying slightly toward them, gently touching the iron bars with her forehead.

He moved to her side and looked at her face. She was staring straight ahead, her gaze unfocused.

Taking her arm, he gently turned her to face him, but she tried turning back to the gates. He had no idea why she kept coming here whenever she went sleepwalking, but he didn't like it. It made him feel far too uneasy.

She dug in her heels when he tried leading her away. The move was weak but determined.

He gripped her chin. "Wynter? Wynter?"

She blinked rapidly, and then the vacant glint faded from her eyes. She glanced around, her brows dipping. "What am I ... shit, I did it again?"

He nodded, slipping his arm around her shoulders. "Come on." He guided her back into the Keep and up to his chamber. Flicking the lock, he asked, "Were you dreaming about anything in particular?"

"Not that I can recall." She sat on the edge of the bed. "Did I say or do anything?"

He shook his head, walking toward her. "You just kept rocking back and forth on your heels, nudging the gates with your forehead. If they weren't secured shut with a padlock, you probably would have wandered through the garden again." And on this occasion, she might have been hurt. Sure, the snakes hadn't bothered her last time, but that could have been a one-off. "Sleepwalking isn't normal for you?"

She shook her head. "Listen, I can stop staying over if this is weirding you out too much."

Stood between her legs, Cain leaned over her, silently urging her to lay back. He placed a hand either side of her head and nuzzled her neck. "I like having you here."

"Does it make that much of a difference, considering we're both asleep?"

He straightened and smoothed his hands up her thighs, shoving up the shirt he'd put on her, baring her pussy to his view. Dancing his fingertips over her folds, he said, "I don't want you sleeping anywhere else."

She raised herself onto her elbows, her expression blank. "You don't trust me not to spend my nights with other men?"

Pausing in stroking her folds, he arched a brow. "Did I say that?"

"You haven't answered my question."

"Do I believe you'd let another man touch you, let alone sleep in your bed? No."

Placated, Wynter relaxed and glanced down at his hand. "Then do continue." Because things had been moving in a direction she very much liked.

The corner of his mouth kicked up. "I'd rather do this."

A hot lash of pain-edged bliss *struck* her soul like a flogger, making her jump with a gasp. "Fuck." He did it again. And again. And again. Until every part of her felt so *charged* it was like static flames skipped along her over-sensitized skin.

"Yes, take it for me," he said, flicking open the buttons on the shirt she wore.

Her back bowed as she was hit by yet another sharp lash to her soul. It was like being whipped by pleasure/pain. Sometimes the strikes were heavy and held a real bite. Others were more like the slap of a hand and left a stinging sensation in their wake.

He started off slow, but the tempo soon began to build, ramping up the tension coiling in her muscles. Jesus, her heart was *pounding.* Her breaths—so quick and shallow—repeatedly caught in her throat as lash after lash of darkly decadent sensation thrashed her very being.

Parting her now unbuttoned shirt, he said, "I think I'll leave this on you. I like fucking you while you're wearing my shirt."

A groan mixed with a sob as his hands closed over her breasts. She arched into his touch, her nipples so tight they hurt. Her pussy felt even more sensitive. Her clit pulsed, and her inner muscles contracted almost painfully. "Fuck me."

Dark eyes blazed into hers. "Not yet. I want you out of your mind with need."

She would have told him she was already there, but her thoughts scattered as soon as the 'whipping' recommenced.

More lashes, more pain, more pleasure.

Drowning in sensation, she felt . . . floaty. Weightless. Adrift. It was only his hands on her body that kept her aware of the physical world.

Her body gave up any pretense of belonging to her. In that moment, Cain truly owned it. Ruled it. Manipulated it to his liking. But then . . . didn't he always? It was impossible to hold some part of herself back when she felt him literally *everywhere.*

"No one else could ever make you feel this good," he said,

swiping the head of his dick through her folds and rubbing at her clit. "No one."

A hot, quivering bundle of sexual frustration, she stared up at him, wishing she could brand him cocky. But it wasn't arrogance; it was pure fact. "And you like that, don't you?" He was just enough of an asshole to find satisfaction in knowing that any man who might come after him would fail to measure up.

"Yes, I very much do," he easily admitted, his tone as dark as his gaze.

She lifted her hips to meet the broad tip of his cock, but he didn't push it inside her. "*Fuck me.*" Another electric lash to her soul had her all but bucking off the bed. "Cain, seriously." Her voice broke. Dammit, she was close to crying.

Draping himself over her once more, he licked at the corner of her mouth. "You're so desperate for my cock you'd do anything I asked right now, wouldn't you?" The question was rhetorical.

She couldn't even claim he was wrong, which would have been mortifying if there was any room in her system for anything but raw need. Her breath caught as he began to slowly sink inside her pussy, stretching her, stroking over hypersensitive nerve-endings.

He put his mouth to her ear. "I'm going to use you now. Brutally. Coldly. Like you're nothing but a toy. My favorite toy, but still just a thing that's here for my convenience. A thing that's sole purpose is to make me feel good. And you know what, baby? You're gonna get off on it."

Then he was moving inside her. No, *pounding*. Fucking in and out of her pussy as pitilessly as he'd promised, focused only on chasing his own orgasm.

He was so detached, so distant, so coolly remote ... like she truly had no purpose in his mind other than to make him come. At the same time, though, he once more thrashed her soul with lashes of darkly carnal sensations. So even as she felt utterly used and objectified, she knew he wasn't really so uncaring of her own pleasure.

"Do not come. I get to come first. Then you. Hmm, your pussy just rippled around my cock. You like it when I give you orders."

It was impossible to fight a blush right then. "No, I don't."

"Such a little liar." He thrust his hand into her hair and fisted it tight enough to make her scalp sting. "Little liars get punished."

She expected a spank of pain to her soul. Instead, it was a series of soft, velvety *flicks* of sensation. *Exquisite* sensation. But too feath-erlight to be anything but a tease. She shook her head, too desperate to come to bear more of that.

"Let's try this again."

"I liked it, okay! Now stop acting as if you even care that I lied. You're just being cruel because you can."

"Of course I am. I like fucking with your head." He kept callously ramming his cock deep, animalistic in the primitive, dispassionate way he sought his own release. "Such a pretty toy."

Another hot lash to her soul, quickly followed by another and another. She couldn't take anymore. She truly couldn't. "Cain," she whimpered, tears pooling in her eyes.

He groaned, slamming into her even harder, fisting her hair even tighter. His cock swelled as he said, "You come when I'm done." He pounded once, twice, three times. Then exploded. He kept on thrusting through his orgasm, filling her with one hot splash after another. "Now you."

A supernova wave of pure bliss swept over her soul . . . and she shattered. Screaming, shaking, scratching his back. The orgasm tore her to shreds, violent and blinding.

Finally, she sagged.

Fighting to catch his breath, Cain looked down at the trembling pile of pure sated woman beneath him. He thumbed away her tears and pressed a kiss to her jaw.

"Why do you like it when I cry?" she asked, her voice hoarse.

"One, I'm a sadistic bastard. Two, I like knowing you were so wrecked by pleasure that you simply couldn't take it."

His monster relished that they had that power over her; that they could reduce her to this. Relished that, strong though she may be in so many ways, she was vulnerable to them.

"I'm not keen on the way you're looking at me right now."

He slanted his head. "How am I looking at you?"

"Like . . . like a predator who's just taken down prey and feeling very pleased with itself. I'm no one's prey."

He bit back a smile. "I'll bear that in mind." To beings as powerful as him, everything and everyone was potential prey.

She sniffed. "Yeah, you do that."

Cain felt his mouth quirk. He still couldn't say what it was about her that had him so fucking obsessed with her. He couldn't understand why she brought out so many primitive instincts in him. He wasn't sure anyone had ever held his attention the way she did.

With other women, he'd gotten bored fast. Especially in bed. It wasn't a slight to them, he was simply so fucking jaded that everything—including sex—held a mundane edge.

With Wynter, it was different. Instead of tiring of the feel, scent, and taste of her, he only wanted more. He liked learning more and more about what got her off. Liked introducing her to new things and sensations. Liked the thought of eventually knowing her body better than anyone else ever had.

Realizing she'd fallen asleep, Cain smiled. She didn't once stir as he moved them further up the mattress and pulled the coverlet over them. His creature settled in, prepared to stay awake and watch over her, so Cain let himself drift off.

It felt like no more than an hour later when he woke to a gentle knock on the door. Light had crept around the edges of the curtains, so he knew it was morning.

As he'd expected, Maxim was on the other side of the door. The aide passed Cain a tray filled with food for both him and Wynter, as per usual. Maxim also relayed a surprising piece of news that made Cain lift his brows. His little witch had failed to pass on that herself.

He thanked the aide and then closed the door. Once he'd set

the tray on the table, he turned to the bed to see that Wynter was beginning to wake.

She groaned. "No, it can't be morning." She tried dragging the coverlet over her head, but the move was too lazy to work.

"It's morning. And I have a question for you."

She opened one eye. "Is it sex related?"

"No."

"Then it can wait." Her eyelid fell closed.

His lips twitched. "Maxim told me a little something just now." All he got in response was a disinterested hum. "I have to say, I'm confused as to why I had to hear this from him instead of you. Is there something you want to tell me?"

"Yes, but it's sex related, so it has nothing to do with your question and you won't want to hear about it."

Actually, he did want to hear about it and ... *Little minx.* He yanked the coverlet off her and spanked her ass. "That's for trying to distract me."

Yelping, she pouted at him. "It's not like it worked. You didn't need to slap me *that* hard."

"I know, but I wanted to."

She muttered something, but he only made out the word 'sadistic.'

He folded his arms. "Apparently, one of Ishtar's aides was seen standing in your front yard yesterday."

Wynter's eyes slid to the side. She sighed. "She did in fact grace me with her presence, as you've no doubt guessed."

Annoyance tightened his muscles. "And you hadn't planned to tell me?"

"I didn't want to cause trouble between you and the other Ancients. You all need to be on the same page right now, not fighting amongst yourselves. Plus, she didn't do anything major. She didn't threaten me, she wasn't rude, she wasn't even remotely unfriendly."

"What *did* she do? I noticed her watching us last night with an odd look on her face. Like she was struggling to understand what she was seeing. What kind of game did she attempt to play with you?"

"A game where she insisted *you're* the one playing a game with me." Wynter sat up in bed, his shirt parting slightly to reveal a strip of her front. "In short, she encouraged me not to trust you. She said you're keeping me close only because I might be of use to you, and that you'd give me up to the Aeons if they offered the right incentive. She also encouraged me to go to Seth for sanctuary."

*Son of a bitch.* "What did you say?"

"I pretended to believe her and said I'd think about going to your brother. Look, I don't fully trust you. I can't, just as you can't *possibly* fully trust me—we know too little about each other. But I don't believe you're playing me. If it turns out I'm wrong, well, I'm wrong. Then I'll hurt you."

"You're not wrong. And no, we can't invest true trust in each other when we have so many secrets between us. But you can trust that I won't betray you. Nor would I hand you over to the Aeons." Even if he was willing, his monster would never stand for it. "I will, however, deal with Ishtar."

"Don't do it on my account. I really can't take what she said personally when she doesn't even *know* me. She has it in her head that I'm this silly, naïve little girl who's totally taken in by you."

Cain felt his eyes narrow. "You like that she's put you in a box and believes she has you all figured out, because it means she won't look closer. You don't like people to look too close, do you, Wynter?"

"Neither do you."

That was something he couldn't argue with.

"What would have happened if I'd run to Seth?" she asked, tipping her head to one side. "I couldn't quite understand why Ishtar was encouraging me to do it."

Cain reached out and dragged Wynter close so that she knelt in front of him, her front pressed to his. "For me, it would have been a little like history repeating itself. When I lived at Aeon, there was a woman I briefly dated, though we termed it courting back then.

Abel had a 'thing' for her, though he didn't seem much interested in acting on it until I began courting her."

"I've only met him a couple of times, but I have to say, I really don't like him. Especially since he exiled my mother."

Cain gave her a comforting squeeze. "He's an asshole that way. You're not alone in so thoroughly disliking him."

Wynter settled her palms on the twin columns of his back. "So, what happened with you and the woman?"

"After she and I had an argument during which she declared we were done, she ran straight to Abel for comfort. I'm sure he expected me to confront him and demand he hand her over. After all, she and I had argued many times but reconciled. It wasn't a stretch to think that I might wish to reconcile with her yet again. But I didn't confront him, which I suspect is why he initially took her as his consort; he'd hoped to provoke me."

"Consort," she echoed. "Do you mean Lailah?"

"Yes, it was her. As you know, I'm a jealous bastard. But I felt none in that situation for two reasons. One, I'd tired of her dramatics. Two, I'm very unforgiving. The fact that she'd hoped to play me off against a brother I had no love for was something I could never have overlooked, so I didn't care where she was, what she was doing, or who she was doing it with.

"I can very easily cut someone out of my life if they wrong or betray me. It's like they were never part of it to begin with. Ishtar no doubt remembers the incident. She remembers how easily I turned away from Lailah and how I refused to later reconcile with her."

Realization flashed on Wynter's face. "So by telling me to run to Seth, she was hoping you'd then turn away from me in much the same way as you turned away from Lailah."

That would be Cain's guess. It wouldn't have worked, though. He'd have headed to Seth's Keep and dragged Wynter back to his own. And Seth, being nothing like Abel, would have helped Cain in easing Wynter's concerns rather than attempt to keep them apart.

"Sneaky, isn't she?"

"It's one of her many traits," said Cain.

"Well, thank you for telling me that story. You didn't have to. And just so you know, I'd never play one brother off against the other like that."

"I know. You are nothing like Lailah. In fact, you are unlike any woman I've ever met. You're a singular creature, Wynter. And very much all mine." Cain slipped one hand between them to possessively cup her breast. "It's a shame you can't wear my shirt to work."

She snorted. "Counting the amount of times you've touched me in public, I'd say it's already pretty clear to the people here that you consider me off-limits to anyone but you."

That didn't feel like enough, though. Nothing did. Maybe because so many things had been taken from him that his hold on her always felt precarious. Like she could slip through his fingers at any moment. There was really only one way to guarantee he could *always* keep her with him, but she'd never go for it.

His monster didn't believe that, though. It didn't see why she'd object to staying with them forever. Or why Cain would worry that she'd leave them if she learned the truth. Again, it was that lack of self-awareness at work.

"You're frowning all of a sudden," she said. "What's wrong?"

What was wrong? Nothing. Except that she'd so wholly and unknowingly snagged the interest of a creature that would absolutely terrify her.

Sometimes, Cain felt that Wynter nonetheless *could* truly accept him and the truth of what he was. Other times . . . other times he remembered he wasn't that fucking fortunate.

He could very easily turn his back on someone who rejected him, but he wasn't sure he could so effortlessly do that with Wynter. And that left him only one choice—never let her learn just what she shared a bed with.

# Chapter Eighteen

Doing a languid stretch, Wynter glanced at the shelf on the shed wall. She was almost all out of reversal potions. Again. Well, it had been a long day, and she'd had a tricky customer who'd asked her to edit the runes on his dagger four times before he'd been satisfied with the results.

She'd originally thought that people's interest in enchanting weapons would decrease once the novelty of it wore off. But she still had a steady stream of customers. Some even came with cutlery or jewelry. And once the shapeshifting beings learned that she could also put runes on claws, some had come seeking such a service.

The rest of her crew were doing just as well. Xavier, being such an expert at divination, had plenty of regular clients who liked to have weekly readings. Many people stopped by of a morning to pick up baked goods from Hattie. Anabel's potions practically flew off the shelves on a daily basis, since she had such a massive selection. And Delilah's cosmetics remained highly popular—particularly her gift sets.

In sum, their homerun shop was still doing well. Which still supremely irritated many of the local businesses. Some had had the downright gall to attempt to replicate both Anabel and Delilah's brews, though they'd had little success.

Still, both females were furious that others would try to steal their ideas and products. It had taken Wynter a good fifteen minutes to talk the nutcases out of cooking up their own improved versions of Molotov cocktails for Xavier—who'd happily volunteered his services—to sling through their windows . . . all while Hattie walked around demanding to know who'd hidden her copy of *Fifty Shades of Grey* because she still hadn't yet located it.

Wynter had managed to distract them by relaying Cain's response to Ishtar's visit. Delilah had crowed about being right that Ishtar's actions were motivated by both her hurt ego and how threatened she felt by Wynter's involvement with Cain. The crew felt uneasy on hearing that he hadn't addressed the claim Ishtar made that the Aeons had something he wanted. Wynter hadn't felt too great about it either, but *she* skirted shit all the time to preserve her own secrets, so she had no right to press him.

Her stomach rumbling, Wynter grabbed her empty mug and set of keys. It was time to lock up and—

An otherworldly breeze slammed into her body, vibrating with urgency and a warning of danger. She heard a heel scuff the floor a mere millisecond before pain lanced through her back and chest. Sucking in a sharp breath, she glanced down. Shock and panic zipped up her spine. *No.* No, that was *not* a sword sticking out of her body.

Except it was.

And it had penetrated her heart.

A hiss sounded in her ear. "That's for my father, you *bitch.*"

Agony scraped Wynter's insides like a serrated blade as the sword withdrew from her body. A hand roughly shoved her to the floor, and she was too damn weak to even throw out her hands to catch her weight. Her heartbeat pulsed in her ears—slow, erratic, faint.

Footfalls sounded, and then a male spat out a curse. "Annette, what have you done?"

*Bowen.*

"I did what I had to do," the woman claimed.

Wynter's heart stuttered to a stop, and darkness swallowed her.

*

Cain kept his expression blank as Ishtar swanned into Seth's drawing room with an overly bright smile on her face. Well, of course she was smiling, and of course said smile held a hint of smugness. Given that Seth had invited her here, she probably thought that his brother had 'come round' and wanted to revisit old times. She'd soon be disabused of that theory, because he was just as pissed as Cain about the shit she'd pulled with Wynter.

"Seth, darling," she all but sang. Her step faltered when she noticed Cain standing in front of the fireplace, but then her smile widened. "Well, hello, you. I get to have quality time with both brothers. How lovely." She elegantly lowered herself to the spot on the sofa beside Seth, her brow wrinkling at the hard look he wore. "Whatever has gotten into you?"

"Tell me something, Ishtar," said Cain, "did you really think that urging Wynter to run to Seth to seek refuge from me would work?"

Ishtar's smile melted away. "She told you, I see." The Ancient spoke as if Wynter was a petty child who ran off to tell tall tales to her parents.

"She chose to fairly give me the chance to speak in my own defense," said Cain, purposely vague. Any conversations he had with Wynter weren't Ishtar's business.

The Ancient's upper lip quivered. "And you fooled her into believing she matters to you."

Cain took a menacing step forward. "I told you to leave her be."

"You also insisted that she was under the protection of every Ancient. That therefore includes me. I did what was fair and just. You know that well. Or do you have it in your head that she doesn't deserve to be protected *from* you? From how you are toying with her affections to keep her close?"

"Don't claim you did anything but act in your own selfish, petty interests. You care nothing for Wynter's feelings. What is 'fair' to her has no relevance to you. You would not give a damn if I was 'toying with her affections.' Which I'm not."

Ishtar flapped a dismissive hand. "Anyone can see that you are using her. Except for her, apparently—she stupidly trusts your word. Well, if you are looking for an apology from me, you will not get one. Twist my actions if you must, but I did what I thought was right."

"Right for who?" Seth cut in. "You, I'm guessing. You certainly didn't do right by Cain or Wynter. And don't for one moment think we'll truly believe otherwise. Cain's not twisting your actions. *You* are. But then, I suspected you would. Gaslighting is something you seem to enjoy."

"Do not cast me into the role of 'villain,'" she said, her tone tart. "Pretend to care about the witch's itty bitty feelings if you wish. But if you truly did care, you would be hesitant about using her as bait to lure the Aeons here. You would be second-guessing your decision. You're not, though, are you? No. Face it, we are *all* using her to get what we want. She will realize that eventually, Cain. Then she will turn on you."

Wynter had been right, he realized. Ishtar viewed her as a silly, naïve girl. She didn't see that his little witch was as ruthless as they were. She didn't see that Wynter would find some satisfaction in being the bait that lured the Aeons to their death, considering they'd blessed the execution of her mother.

Oh, Wynter might not be so pleased that no one had shared this with her. But if there was one person who understood the need for secrets, it was her—she had plenty of her own. She wouldn't turn on him for holding certain things back from her.

"Does it not bother you that you're a person who'd find so much satisfaction in seeing Cain suffer in any way?" Seth asked Ishtar. "You weren't always so wrapped up in your own feelings that those of others rarely mattered to you. You've changed over time. You lost pieces of yourself somewhere along the way."

Ishtar's eyes glimmered with annoyance. "You like to think you are so much better than the rest of us, don't you?"

Seth's expression tightened. "Do not insinuate that my being different means I am not a true part of the circle. And do not think you can change the subject so easily, or that Cain and I don't have a right to our anger."

"You are both being dramatic and you know it."

"Dramatic? You urged Wynter to not only run from him but to run to *me*. You didn't care that it might have caused trouble between myself and Cain. You didn't care how it would have made him feel. You didn't care about anything but soothing your wounded ego. You want Wynter to reject him just as he rejected you. How much of a hypocrite does that make you, given you reject people all the time? You never care how those men feel about it. You'd never believe they have a right to be angry with you for turning them away."

"*Mortals,* I turn *mortals* away," she specified. "I made the mistake of getting a little too attached to one of them once-upon-a-time, as you may recall. I offered him immortality. He refused, and so I lost him. I had to watch him grow old with another. I will not put myself in that position again."

"On the surface, it sounds like a tragic love story in which you were an innocent victim," said Seth. "Maybe you did love him in your way. But if so, it was a selfish love. You hadn't offered to make him your consort. You wouldn't even consent to exclusivity. You expected him to be faithful to you, but you wouldn't offer him that same loyalty. The main reason you wanted him was that he was so desired by everyone in the city. You treated him poorly, like a mere shiny bauble, and you know it."

She looked from Seth to Cain, sneering. "As if either of *you* are better in how you treat your bedpartners. Neither of you agreed to exclusivity when I requested it."

"Because you wouldn't agree for that to be a two-way street," Seth reminded her. "I wasn't interested in offering you more commitment than you would offer me. I suspect the same applied with you and Cain. But I won't ask him for clarification on that because, again, you're simply trying to change the subject."

"No, this topic is very much related to Wynter." She glared at Cain, her chin jutting out. "You may treat her well, but you do it for the wrong reasons—to appease her, to keep her sweet, to give her a false picture of yourself."

"If you truly believed I held so little regard for her, you wouldn't care about my involvement with her," said Cain. "You see that she matters to me, and you don't like it."

Ishtar shook her head. "You may have fooled *her* into believing she is important to you, but you will not make *me* believe that."

"I don't care what you do or don't believe." Cain took yet another step closer to her. "All I want is to make one thing perfectly clear."

She rolled her eyes. "I'm to stay away from the witch, I suppose."

A growl built in Cain's throat. "Do not cross me on this, Ishtar. You will not hurt what's mine; I absolutely forbid it."

She pinned him with a furious glare. "What's *yours*?"

"Yes, mine. Wynter belongs to me."

"Your monster—"

"Would wipe your existence from this planet if you took her from it," he finished, his tone clipped. "I am not fucking around here, Ishtar. She is off-limits to you in every respect."

Her eyes hardened to stone. "Is that so?"

"Yes, it is. No more games, no more visits to her house, no more making this about you. I won't allow it. Work through whatever shit is going on in your head, and move on. If you don't, if you ever again try to fuck with her, I will return the favor. You know I don't make empty threats. Focus on your own life and stay out of mine."

Her face red, she slowly stood, the image of composure. She sauntered to the door and swung it open, but then her gaze flicked back to Cain. "Such a shame that mortals have a short lifespan, isn't it? Oh, I'm sure it feels long to them. But, really, their lives are over in a blink. You won't keep her for long, Cain. You won't want to. She appeals to you now, but it will not last. She will soon show signs of age that repulse you."

Seth exhaled heavily. "Ishtar—"

Ignoring him, she continued speaking to Cain. "I will not kill her because I need her alive if I am to get what I seek. But something will kill her eventually. Age, illness, an accident, an attack. Mortals are so fragile. Any number of things can erase them from this world, and it can happen at any moment. So be braced to lose her, because you will. And you will not get her back. An undead soul can return to a body only once. After that, it is game over. They never come back again."

*

*Fuuuuck, that hurt.*

Wynter hated dying. She really did. It never hurt any less. Temporarily landing in the netherworld wasn't much fun either—there was nothing pleasant about that place. But on returning, she'd always find that any wounds she'd suffered were healed. It always took a few minutes for her strength to fully return, though.

"What are you even doing here, Bowen?" a voice hissed. Ah, dear Annette. And she had company, it would seem.

Wynter had to give it to the woman, she'd taken her by surprise. It wasn't the first time Wynter had been impaled on a sword, but it was the first time someone had done it from behind.

"I saw you sneak out of the house with a damn sword," began Bowen, "I had a feeling you were coming here."

Remaining still while her body regained strength, Wynter lifted her eyelids just enough to peek at the berserkers who stood a few feet away. If it wasn't for the subtle breeze dancing over her skin in caution, her inner monster would have lunged at the little fuckers and ripped them apart by now.

Bowen thrust a hand through his hair. "You'll be the number one suspect when she's found dead. Dammit, Annette, you're smarter than this."

Wynter would have to disagree.

Annette's hand flexed around the hilt of her bloodstained sword. "My father is *dead.*"

"And, what ... you thought this would change that?" Bowen sniped.

"He deserved vengeance."

"So you plan to kill Cain as well?"

"You know I can't do that. But I can kill the little bitch who snitched on my dad and had him thrown *into a pit of snakes*, so I did."

Bowen looked at her like she was insane. "And you think Cain will let this go? You think you won't meet the same end?"

She snorted. "Like I'm dumb enough to stick around. I moved my car from the warehouse and left it outside the tunnel that leads to Devil's Cradle. A bag of my stuff is in the trunk."

"At least you have *some* plan in your head, even if it is pointless."

"Pointless?"

"Annette, you killed the property of an Ancient without permission ," he said slowly, as if talking to a child. "That leads to death every single time. You will be hunted for the rest of your days. Someone will eventually find you and drag you back here."

She gave her head a dismissive shake. "I know how to lie low."

"Doesn't matter. Your days are now officially numbered." He swore. "I can't believe you did this. You think this is what your father would have wanted? Really?"

She snapped her mouth shut and then shrugged. "What's done is done."

Groaning, he dug the heels of his hands into his eyes. "If Cain ever realizes I let you go, not even my being Azazel's aide will save my ass."

She tensed, her grip on her sword tightening. "Are you thinking of turning me in?"

He dropped his hands to his sides. "No, of course not. You're my damn niece. But you have officially fucked us both."

"He's right, you know," Wynter cut in, pushing to her feet, a little dizzy but otherwise fine.

Both berserkers gawked at her.

Annette's gaze dipped to the massive bloodstain on Wynter's tee. "You . . . there's no way you . . . I killed you, I know I did."

"Yeah, you did." Wynter cricked her neck. "I tend not to stay dead."

The assholes continued to quite simply stare at her, as if struggling to process the situation. Annette's hands soon began to tremble, and the color started to leave Bowen's face. Understandable, really. Even in the world of preternaturals, beings that didn't *stay dead* were considered fucking weird. Unnatural. Generally unwelcome.

Swallowing hard, Bowen backed toward the door.

A wind thick with rage swept around the room, slamming the shed door shut.

Wynter smiled at him. "I wouldn't bother trying to run. She won't let you leave."

Annette raised her sword and prepared herself to lunge. Wynter didn't get a chance to intervene. The hilt glowed red, and a sizzling sound filled the room. Annette dropped the weapon to the floor with a loud cry, shaking her blistering hand. A low, dark, otherworldly laugh bounced off the walls.

Bowen's fearful gaze darted around the shed. "What was ... who ... " He squeezed his eyes shut, clenching his fists. "What the fuck is happening here?"

Annette licked her lips, plastering herself against the wall behind her. "You need to let us go."

Wynter pursed her lips. "No, I really don't."

"You can't kill us," Bowen insisted. "If you do, you'll die—the Ancients who own the rights to our souls will see to that."

"Oh, I'm not planning to kill you," said Wynter. "But I need you both gone from here. I mean, I can't have you telling people that I came back to life. It's not the sort of thing people are comfortable hearing."

"We won't tell anybody, we swear," Bowen vowed, and his niece nodded frantically.

Wynter grimaced. "The thing is ... you're not exactly people whose word will mean shit to me. One of you killed me, and the other had no issues with abetting my killer. Plus, well, I'm feeling a little vengeful right now. The cool thing is I don't need to *kill* you to send you to the netherworld. I can open a path to that dimension and trap you both there for as long as I like. You'll be wandering through it with no chance of rebirth because you won't be truly dead."

Bowen blanched but shook his head. "You're lying."

"Nope." Wynter smiled. "An interesting thing about the netherworld . . . is that its timeline isn't parallel or even in sync with that of this dimension. A minute here can be like a *month* there, or even a year, or maybe a millisecond. Fascinating, right?"

Annette began to shake, scratching at the wall behind her.

"It ain't a nice place. All cold air and dark mists. It's almost impossible to see anything, but you can *hear* everything. Screams. Snarls. Growls. Roars. There's so much fear and pain. It's all about beating souls down as part of the purification process; breaking them and then building them back up to cleanse the soul of sin, making them fit to be reborn.

"Now, as you both won't *actually* be dead, you might be spared the pain—I really can't be sure. I *can* be sure that, in any event, the experience will be worse than whatever the Ancients might have put you through. That makes me feel better about what you two fucks just did."

Bowen's breaths began coming hard and fast. "You're lying, you can't really do that, you can't—"

The floor beneath them darkened and began to ripple like black water.

Annette whimpered. "No."

"Uh, *yeah*," said Wynter. "I'd tell you to just be glad I'm not going to kill you. But, as I think you've figured out, there really are worse things than death."

They sank into the water like hands had yanked them down, along with Annette's sword. Then the floor returned to normal.

Wynter exhaled heavily. Well, that had been unpleasant. And now it was time for damage control.

She left the shed and walked through the back door of the cottage. Anabel looked up from her cauldron and muttered a quick hey. Slicing vegetables, Hattie tossed Wynter an absent smile. At the table, both Delilah and Xavier offered her a brief nod.

Seconds later, they all froze. And then everyone's eyes snapped to her bloodstained tee.

"I need a rejuvenating potion, and one of your special bleach brews," Wynter said to a gaping Anabel.

"What in the world *happened*?" demanded Delilah.

Wynter lifted her shoulders. "I died. Again. Now, about those potions . . ."

Everyone started talking at once, firing questions at Wynter. She told them how Annette had attacked her from behind and stabbed right through her heart . . . at which point Hattie snatched the largest knife from the block and demanded, "Where's the little bitch?"

Wynter cleared her throat. "Um, the netherworld." Silence fell. "Well, I couldn't let them go blabbing, but I also couldn't kill them—"

"Wait, them?" interrupted Xavier.

"Oh, Bowen was here, too," Wynter explained. "He wasn't in on it, but he witnessed what happened and planned to do nothing about it. He intended to help her escape and cover for her. Look, I'm feeling super dizzy, and I have evidence to clean up, so can we maybe get—thank you, Anabel."

Wynter drank the rejuvenating brew while her crew cursed the berserkers to hell and back. Then, gratefully taking the cleansing potion from Anabel, Wynter returned to the shed and tossed the majority of it over both the pool of blood and the footprints left by both berserkers. Once the floor was completely clear, she dripped the last of the potion onto her tee. The rip remained, but the bloodstain vanished.

"People are going to notice they're missing," said Hattie as she and the others entered.

Wynter sighed. "I know. Sticking them in the netherworld was probably shitty, but I didn't know where else to hide them. And like I said, I couldn't kill them. This way, if Cain touches her soul or Azazel touches Bowen's, the Ancients will sense that they're alive."

"Which means no one will suspect foul play and, as such, not come knocking on our front door," said Xavier.

Wynter nodded. "Exactly. Annette actually packed a bag and had a car ready. She told Bowen she left it outside the tunnel. Maybe I could drive it off a cliff or something."

"I'll take care of that," said Delilah. "I can sneak out of the town as a cat. No one will spot me. People might assume that Bowen left with her."

"Possibly," said Wynter.

Glancing around, Anabel shuddered. "I can feel the rage in here. Your deity was pissed, huh? I'm surprised your monster didn't surface and go AWOL."

"The deity stayed its hand," Wynter explained.

Each time she felt herself dying, she wondered if it would be the one time that she didn't come back. But it was always as if something spat her back out of the netherworld. She'd appear there long enough to feel the mists brush her soul, hear broken screams, and catch a glimpse of this or that . . . and then she'd be back.

Was there anything that could kill her for good? Wynter really didn't know. She suspected that the Ancients could. They'd at the very least try if they learned what she strove so hard to hide. Which was one of the reasons why being around Cain so much wasn't smart. It was like flirting with death, in a way. She couldn't help herself, though. Or maybe she just didn't want to.

He drew her back to him so effortlessly, and it wasn't simply about sex. It was as if the darkness in him spoke to her own. Attracted it, even. It was hard to explain. But when she'd been involved with other males, she'd always felt like she didn't 'fit' with them. Felt that they were lightyears apart in terms of what sort of people they were.

Cain, though . . . he was someone who truly knew about

darkness. Someone who understood how vengeance could be such a driving force. Someone who made her *feel*. Really feel.

Fucked up though it might seem, she actually felt comfortable around him on some level. He was dangerous, yes, but so was she. He was capable of extreme cruelty, yes, but again so was she.

If anyone could understand her, if anyone could take her as she was, it would be him. And that was sort of comforting. So it was a real fucking shame that there might come a day when he actively tried to kill her.

# Chapter Nineteen

Striding up the path toward Wynter's cottage, Cain nodded at the lycans in the neighboring yard. Ever since the first night she'd slept in his bed, she hadn't slept anywhere else. She'd come to him every evening after dinner, and she'd eaten breakfast with him each morning before heading home. So when she hadn't turned up as usual that evening, he'd thought about sending Maxim to bring her to the Keep. But then Cain had reconsidered it, because summoning her felt . . . wrong. She wasn't a mere resident, she was his. So he'd made his way to her home to find out the reason for the delay.

He knocked on the door, which swung open moments later to reveal Xavier.

"Is Wynter here?" Cain asked.

He nodded, stepped away from the door, and indicated for Cain to follow him inside. Strolling through the living area, Cain noticed a black cat curled up on a footstool near the fire. A cat with hot pink nail polish on her claws and what looked like gold mascara on her whiskers. She opened one eye, regarded him carefully, and then shut said eye.

Walking into the kitchen, Cain found Wynter sat at the table, her head resting on the surface, her eyes closed. He frowned, not liking how pale and drained she looked. His creature stilled, just as uneasy. They'd never once seen her look fragile before.

Ishtar's words from earlier rushed back to Cain . . .

*Something will kill her eventually. Age, illness, an accident, an attack.*

Wynter had had a broken sleep the night before, so maybe it had simply taken its toll.

"She drifted off while eating," Xavier told him, switching a kettle on to boil, utterly at ease with turning his back on an Ancient—something people generally avoided doing. In fact, whenever Cain entered a house, its inhabitants usually became tense and wary and either stared at the floor or watched his every move. Anabel and Hattie? They gave him a single nod and then went back to their conversation.

Pointing at an open book, Hattie looked at Anabel. "All I'm saying is that, realistically, her cervix would be in ruins if she had a harem that large. Especially when one of them is an alien with an overgrown appendage."

Anabel briefly glanced away from a cauldron. "You're concerned about realism when you're reading a book about ETs with giant penises?"

"My first husband, bless his soul, was hung like a bull. My cervix took a *thrashing* during that marriage. If he'd been part of a harem, well, I can tell you right now that my ovaries would have been scrambled eggs. Anyway, back to my question—"

"No, not back to the question. We should forget about the question. We should *always* forget about your questions."

"I just want to know if it's some sort of kink I'm failing to understand." Hattie switched her gaze to Cain. "You're male, maybe you can help. Do you know why a man would decide to give a woman a facial during sex? I mean, all us ladies like using a rejuvenating mask now and then, but during intimate moments? No, I can't see the appeal in it."

Grabbing what looked like homemade tea balls out of a cupboard, Xavier snickered. "It's a euphemism."

Hattie's nose wrinkled. "For what?"

He stifled a smile. "It's when a man ... offloads on a woman's face."

Hattie gaped in horror. "He *pees* on her?"

"Yes."

Anabel's head snapped up. "No, it—Xavier, don't be an asshole."

Feeling his lips twitch, Cain took a seat at the table. He didn't think he'd ever met a group of people who were so different who yet fit together so well. Turning his attention to his witch, he glided his fingertips over her scalp. It was a few moments before her eyelids fluttered open.

Finally, she righted her head and blinked up at him. "Oh. You're here." There was no unwelcoming note in her voice, just pure confusion.

"You didn't come to me like you usually do," he said. "I came to see what was keeping you. I didn't expect to find you asleep."

She rubbed at her eyes and sat up. "I didn't mean to doze off."

"You look tired. And drained. And too pale for my liking."

"Flatterer." Wynter sighed. "Anabel, you're supposed to be using the test bowl," she called out without even looking in the direction of the blonde.

Anabel froze with a large wooden spoon halfway to her mouth. "I am. I did. A little something is missing. It's easier to tell what it is if I taste it."

Xavier gave the blonde a droll look. "It's also harder to keep pieces of your sanity if you keep using yourself as a trial subject."

Anabel rolled her eyes but dripped the potion into a bowl and tossed in some crushed herbs. A waft of blue smoke hit her in the face, and she cursed like a sailor between coughs.

Xavier walked to the table and set a steaming mug of tea in front of Wynter. "Here, this will perk you up."

She smiled at him, lifting the cup. "Thanks."

He slid his gaze to Cain. "She needs to get plenty of rest tonight."

Cain was impressed. Not even in the face of an Ancient did the male fail to speak up for his Priestess. Cain liked that. She deserved such a depth of loyalty. "I'll make sure she does."

Xavier gave a nod of satisfaction and then crossed to another cupboard, where he began pulling out jars.

Wynter glanced around. "Where's Delilah?"

"Chatting with Annis," replied Xavier.

Cain felt his brows knit. "Annis?"

"She's a descendant of the Black Annis," Wynter told him.

Cain blinked. "As in the witch version of the bogeyman?"

Wynter nodded. "Yup. Delilah goes into meditative states where she communicates with Annis. The ability to do so allegedly runs in the family."

"It doesn't concern you that your coven member is in contact with a highly sinister entity that was a literal scourge upon the Earth?"

"We're not a coven."

Cain felt his lips tip up. "Trust you to concentrate on that part of the question."

"We're very much a coven, no matter what you say," Xavier cut in before taking a bite of a sandwich.

Wynter frowned. "What are you making? That brown stuff looks like shit."

"It's a Snickers sandwich," said Xavier.

She slanted her head. "A, what?"

"You've never had one?" Xavier lifted a hand. "Oh, it will change your life. Put chocolate spread on one slice of bread, lather peanut butter spread on the other slice, and then slap them both together."

"Is there anything you won't put on a sandwich?"

"Not really. Now stop stalling and drink the tea. I know those mixes taste awful, but they work."

"I will, I will, just give me a sec."

As a yawn cracked her jaw, Cain swept her hair away from her face. "If you're too tired to traipse all the way to the Keep, we can stay here tonight, if you'd like."

There was a loud bang, and then a cloud of thick green smoke burst out of Anabel's bowl. "Mother*fucker*," the blonde cursed, waving her hand.

Wynter's eyelid twitched. "Your place works," she said to Cain. "I just need to throw some of my stuff in a bag."

"I'll come with you," he told her. "I want to see your room."

Her brow pinched. "Why?"

"Because."

She shrugged and then knocked back some of the tea. Tea she almost promptly spat out. "Jesus, it tastes like cat food."

"You've eaten cat food?"

"I'm not good at turning down dares."

He gave her a wolfish smile. "I'll bear that in mind."

She forcibly chugged down her tea, grimacing and shuddering. Finally done, she led Cain upstairs and into her bedroom. The space might not have an altar or pentagrams, but the décor clearly stated 'a witch lives here.'

"A lot of the stuff was given to us in trade," Wynter told him, noticing he was scanning the space. "The room was pretty basic originally." She put the back of her hand to her mouth as another yawn escaped her.

"I don't like that you seem so exhausted."

She blinked, her mouth curved. "Well, then maybe you shouldn't have fucked me in the middle of the night. Don't worry, the tea will kick in fast. Then it'll be like I've been downing energy drinks."

He watched as she pulled underwear out of her drawer. Another time, he might have rifled through her collection just to tease her. But his mood . . . it wasn't good. What Ishtar had said kept playing on his mind. Mortals *were* so very fragile. It *would* be all too easy for him to lose Wynter. And if he didn't manage to convince her to give up her mortality in order to stay with him, he'd lose her eventually. Maybe to death, or maybe even to a man who could give her what he couldn't—a family, normality, the promise of safety.

His creature would likely only give her up if she outright rejected it—the monster would be too pissed at her to want to keep her. But Cain couldn't tell her it even existed, which meant there'd be no rejection. And so the creature would continue to view her as belonging to it.

If another man touched her, it would want him dead. It would insist that Cain killed him, and Cain knew he was cruel enough to do it. He'd done much worse things over the years, and he'd tortured people for far less.

There was only one way he could grant her immortality—she'd have to agree to sell him her soul in return. He'd have to convince her to do it somehow. He just wasn't sure how yet.

"I spoke with Ishtar about the little visit she paid you," he said as Wynter packed her bag. "She won't be back here."

"Okay, good."

He narrowed his eyes at the skepticism in her tone. "You think I'm wrong?"

She hesitated, as if choosing her words carefully. "I think some people are a law unto themselves."

"I won't deny she's that. Nor can I claim that she hesitates to push people too hard—it would be a downright lie. But I made it clear that you're mine."

"That might have made things worse, if she's the jealous type. Plus, I'm not so sure she'd take your possessiveness seriously. In her mind, I'm a mere mortal who can't possibly have any real relevance to you. So, in my view, is there a chance she might ignore your warning and keep being a sneaky game-playing bitch? Yes."

Of course Wynter would think that. She had no idea just how serious his declaration would be taken by the other Ancients. "I don't believe she'll dare bother you again. She has plenty of reasons to heed me. And, to put it simply, she won't view you as worth being tortured for."

Wynter did a double-take. "You'd torture her if she kept on bugging me?"

"Yes."

"That's a little melodramatic, don't you think?"

"No."

Her brow creased, and then she nodded. "Oh, I see. It's not really about me, it's the principle of the thing. If she disrespects your wishes, she has to pay for it."

"That woman has disrespected my wishes more times than I can count. I've never bothered using any form of violence to repay her for the insult, because I've never managed to drum up enough emotional energy to care all that much about anything she does or doesn't do. But you . . . I won't have her play games with you."

"Only you get to fuck with my head, huh?"

"Exactly."

She chuckled and zipped up her duffel. "Did you always have that little weird sadistic streak, or does it come from being alive so long that it twists you in some ways?"

"Twists?" He settled his hands on her hips and drew her close. "You see immortality as a negative thing?"

"No, I think it would depend on the individual. It might suit some but not others."

"And would it suit you?" he asked, careful to keep his tone casual.

She pursed her lips. "I don't know. I'm not sure if I'd like who I'd eventually become. I mean, there have been several times through-out my life when something was important to me but, somewhere along the line, it lost its significance—maybe because I changed, grew bored of it, or took it for granted. If I was immortal, that would happen to me over and over and over. I wonder if there'd come a point when I wouldn't truly value anything anymore."

In that case, she didn't see herself clearly. "It's true that immor-tals change repeatedly, and so things that once mattered eventually no longer do. That's why it's important that an immortal is able to change and adapt—something I doubt you'd struggle with. If they become too rigid and unbending, they'll eventually grow to hate their life. Although some things cease to matter, it isn't a case that you come to value nothing at all."

"What kind of things do you yourself value?"

"Honesty. Loyalty. Strength. Honor. I see all those things in you." He gently flicked her hair over her shoulder, exposing her neck so he could kiss a path down her throat. "You wouldn't lose those qualities if you were immortal. They're too embedded in who you are. Sort of like your soul's foundation blocks. Everything you are is built on top of them." He scraped his teeth over her pulse, his stomach clenching at her little gasp. "Hmm, I think I should fuck you here before we leave."

"Do you?"

"Yes." He backed her into the bed. "Every time you walk into this room, I want you to remember what I did to you right here on this bed. I want you to remember that you're mine."

She snorted. "Like you ever let me forget. Now get your cock out and do me. I can feel my energy coming back, so it's gonna be hard for me to sleep tonight unless you can fuck the energy right back out of me."

He felt his mouth kick up. "That's a challenge I'm happy to accept."

*

"You know, I had it in my head that it'd be good to come to the surface for some fresh air," Delilah said, as they all wandered around the plaza the following evening. "But the air weirdly feels fresher in the underground city."

"It really does," agreed Wynter. Still, it was nice to occasionally stroll around the surface and have a little change of scenery. The main reason she insisted on it now and then, though, was that it was good for Anabel to leave the house. Her natural anxiety only worsened if she confined herself inside four walls for too long. And since the blonde currently needed to top up on supplies, Wynter had proposed a shopping trip.

As usual, Anabel was as edgy and hypervigilant as a soldier in a warzone. But rather than walk slowly and hesitantly, she moved with speed and purpose, clearly determined to get the whole thing over with so she could go home.

Wynter asked her, "What else is on the list?"

"We've bought everything other than the bottle of wine I need," said Anabel, who put all kinds of stuff into her potions so that they didn't taste disgusting.

Hattie gestured up ahead. "There's a liquor store over here."

"Excellent," said Anabel, who then led the way to the shop.

Inside, the blonde grabbed a grocery basket and wandered down the first aisle, scanning the various bottles that filled the floor-to-ceiling racks. Wynter and the others trailed behind her, acting as mules to carry whatever bottles she selected.

At one point, Xavier shoved the two he was holding at Delilah and then strolled over to a very pretty assistant who'd just descended a sliding ladder. "I do not think we have met," he said, his accent now distinctly Italian. He held out his hand. "Alessandro."

Flushing, the girl shook it. "Posy."

He grinned. "An unusual name, is it not?"

Wynter shook her head and turned away.

"So," began Delilah, eyeing her with a smirk, "I heard a few thuds and moans while I was meditating yesterday. Sounded like you and Cain had a whole lot of fun christening your bed. He strikes me as a man who's good with his hands. Am I right? I'm right, aren't I?"

He used *every* tool in his sexual arsenal exceptionally well, not merely his hands, but Wynter wasn't one to kiss and tell. "You'll just have to use your imagination."

"Oh, I do. Believe me. Any woman with a pulse would. But I need some details."

"No, you don't. You're simply being nosy."

"And you're simply being mean by giving me nothing."

Hattie gently nudged Wynter. "Why are you being so secretive? I never took you for a prude."

Wynter frowned. "I'm not a prude. I merely don't like to blab all about my sex life."

"Whyever not?" asked Hattie. "I do it all the time."

"And we often wish you didn't."

Delilah chuckled. "You do sometimes overshare, Hattie."

The old woman sniffed. "When you reach my age you don't

bother minding your words. Too much effort. I've never really had a problem talking openly about sex, though. Nobody should. It's nothing to be embarrassed about. One of my husbands, Herb, blushed every time I mentioned sex. He was boring in bed. But not in *other* women's beds—well, metaphorical beds. He usually had sex with them in his car. His excuse for cheating on me was that a man had to treat his wife like a lady and save his darker urges for prostitutes."

Delilah snorted. "Darker urges are the most fun."

Hattie let out a cackle. "I can't argue there. I'd have been happy to entertain those urges of his if he'd only given me the option."

"How did you find out he was cheating on you?"

"Same way I found out about my other husbands. I followed him in my crow form. Not one of them noticed. Not even Herb when I shit on his head."

Anabel turned to them. "Right, I'm done."

They all headed to the checkout desk, where Xavier caught up to them. Apparently in a gracious mood, he grabbed all four bags. As they left the store, he waved a little slip of paper and gave them a smug smile. "I got myself a date."

"As Xavier or *Alessandro*?" asked Hattie, trying and failing to replicate the accent he'd used when introducing himself to the assistant.

"Alessandro, of course. Playing the role of Italian stallion is always fun." He slid the paper into his back pocket. "I have some Italian blood in my heritage."

Delilah's brows lifted. "You do?"

"Nope, not even a little," he replied.

She flapped her arms. "Then why say it?"

"Maybe your indignation makes me feel energized."

The two bickered as they all left the plaza and began a leisurely walk to the manor. Wynter's step faltered as a light breeze fluttered over her skin, alerting her to ... something. Instinct made her glance at a wooded area not too far away.

Delilah nudged her with her elbow. "You okay?"

Wynter slowed to a halt. "Yes. And no."

"What does that mean?" asked Anabel.

"It means that someone—maybe even multiple someones—is hiding in those trees over there," said Wynter, rolling her shoulders. "I say we go find out why."

\*

Cain looked up from his plate as Azazel breezed into the dining room, his brow furrowed. Anyone else might have been sheepish about interrupting someone's dinner, but not Azazel. The Ancient had zero time for manners unless it suited him.

"Something wrong?" asked Cain.

"Wrong?" Azazel rubbed at his nape. "I'm not yet sure. But I'm certainly confused."

"About?"

"One of my aides, Bowen, is missing. No one has seen him since yesterday. I sent people to find him. One thought that maybe he was keeping Annette company, since both berserkers would be grieving her father, so he went to her house in search of him. Bowen wasn't there. Neither was she, and many of her possessions are gone."

Lowering his cutlery to his mostly empty plate, Cain poked the inside of his cheek with his tongue. "I knew she hadn't opened the blacksmith's shop today. I thought she was merely taking time off work to grieve." He lightly touched her soul. "She's definitely not dead. I feel her. But the connection is . . . weak."

Azazel nodded, taking the seat opposite. "My link to Bowen is just as weak. As if something is dulling it. I don't know what could possibly do that. In any case, it seems as though she not only left, she took him with her. His belongings aren't missing, but it could be that he caught her leaving and impulsively decided to go with her, or maybe he wasn't bothered about any of the shit he's left behind. Aside from the rights to his soul that I own, of course."

"The usual reason for a resident to sneakily leave is very simply that they did something they shouldn't have."

Azazel hummed. "Maybe Annette messed up somehow, or maybe after Grouch died she was scared she'd be next. Scared that you might decide to slit the throat of anyone who ever pissed Wynter off. Didn't you say that Annette and Grouch once threatened to ruin her business?"

Cain nodded. "I made it very clear that—"

A knock came at the door.

"Yes?" Cain called out.

Maxim stepped inside. "Sire, Dantalion sent an envoy with a message. Two male witches apparently appeared outside the gates of the manor. One claimed they needed to speak with both you and Wynter."

Cain felt the muscles in his arms and shoulders bunch. "Is that a fact? Who?"

"I'm not sure, he allegedly wouldn't say more than that," Maxim replied. "Dantalion granted them entry and placed them in the blue parlor. He thought you might like to be the one to question them."

The Ancient was right to presume so.

"It has to be people from Aeon, right?" asked Azazel.

"That would be my guess," said Cain. "Maxim, I need you to bring Wynter to the Keep. I'm not sure where exactly she is, but I have to consider that the male witches didn't come here alone; that they could be a distraction. If so, others will no doubt look for her. They'll jump at the chance to take her."

Maxim gave a curt nod. "I will find her."

"Also send some people to search the town for strangers. If any are found, detain them. They'll be permitted to leave providing they attack no one."

"Understood, Sire."

Satisfied, Cain made his way upstairs.

Following him, Azazel asked, "Did Wynter ever mention a male witch to you?"

"No." If either of the visitors turned out to be an ex-boyfriend of hers, they wouldn't be getting anywhere near her. Especially when it was highly likely that both males were here on behalf of the Aeons or, at the very least, her old coven.

Cain and Azazel used the chamber's mirror to quickly transport themselves to the manor. They then made their way to what had been branded the blue parlor due to the teal painted walls.

Dantalion sat at the piano, his fingers gliding deftly over the keys, playing "The Music of the Night" from *Phantom of the Opera*. He didn't stop when Cain entered. He barely even looked up, apparently already bored of the situation. His aide stood behind him, silent and still.

Cain settled his attention on the two men sitting stiffly on the sofa. They couldn't have been more opposite in terms of appearance. One was broad, dark, and heavily muscled. The other was lean and gangly with pale blond hair. "Just who might you both be?"

The burlier of the two met his gaze steadily, much like Wynter herself often did. "My name is Rafe," he replied. "This here is Griff. As you may have guessed, we were sent here by the Aeons." The man didn't seem at all happy about it.

Azazel walked behind the sofa. "For what purpose?"

Rafe didn't glance over his shoulder at the Ancient. "They want me to try to 'reason with Wynter' and appeal for her to come home."

Cain went very still. "Neither of you will be speaking with Wynter, and she will not be leaving with you either. She stays here."

"I figured you'd say that," said Rafe, seeming relieved. "I warned them you probably would, but they insisted that I ask. They thought maybe she'd agree to see me."

"Why you?"

"Aside from her mother and grandmother, I'm the only person in the coven who gave a damn about her. She was like a niece to me. So they sent me as a friendly face."

"Without an entourage?"

"We didn't request to be accompanied by one," said Rafe. "We were teleported to a spot just beyond the border. I don't believe others were teleported here after us, but I can't be sure. The Aeons would veto telling me such a thing as they wouldn't trust that I'd keep a promise not to warn Wynter."

"Well, now that we've established that you won't be granted an audience with *her*, tell me why you also asked to speak with me."

"Lailah wishes to have a one-to-one talk with you using Griff— he is a conduit."

The piano music abruptly cut off.

Cain barely refrained from lifting his brows in surprise at Rafe's declaration. Conduits were rare these days. They could provide a psychic space that allowed people in various locations to communicate. "Is that so?"

Griff swallowed nervously. "She's already there waiting."

Cain had guessed as much, considering she'd had to have touched Griff in order to project her consciousness to the psychic space.

"She said to tell you that you'll want to hear what she has to say," Griff added.

"Hmm." Cain gave both Azazel and Dantalion a brief look that warned them to pull him out of the conversation if need be, because what better way to take Cain off-guard than to drag his consciousness into a psychic space where he'd be oblivious to what went on outside of it?

Griff held out his hand, his fingers splayed. Cain pressed his fingertips to those of Griff, and then his surroundings altered in a flash.

# Chapter Twenty

Taking cover behind a cluster of trees, Wynter skimmed her gaze along the men stood around the clearing. She counted eleven, in total. There were all tall, armed, and powerfully built.

"Do you recognize any of them?" whispered Delilah.

"Yup," Wynter replied, her voice just as low. "They're keepers from Aeon." Even if she hadn't known each face, she'd have identified their origins by the distinctive insignia on their swords—most of which also sported runes, courtesy of her magick. Her monster easily recognized the men too and, not a fan of how they'd treated Wynter over the years, it was not at all happy about their presence.

Anabel sidled closer, hugging herself and biting her lip. "Keepers are like enforcers, right?"

"They're mostly executioners," said Wynter. "But they'll also act as enforcers, messengers, or bodyguards—whatever the Aeons want them to be."

"So minions, basically," Anabel surmised.

"Assholes, too. Especially the one with the crew cut and the scraggly beard. He used to harass the hell out of my mom. He acted like a real prick toward her when she refused to date him." Fort had also flashed Wynter several seriously creepy smiles over recent years, commenting on how she looked so much like Davina.

Xavier licked the front of his teeth. "It's a pretty small force, so I doubt they're here for war."

Wynter's thoughts exactly. "The Aeons won't have sent them here to start a battle. It would be senseless. Such a low number would never survive it."

"Oh, what a spectacular behind," Hattie whispered, ogling a keeper who'd bent over to wipe his boot.

Delilah gently bumped the old woman's shoulder with her own. "Not sure if you're paying attention to the conversation we're having here, but these are very bad men."

"Oh, I know," said Hattie with a small wave of her hand. "I do love a bad boy, though. Admit it, we all do."

Delilah frowned. "Not goddamn executioners, Hattie."

Xavier raised his hand for silence. "And we have yet another keeper, apparently."

It would seem so, because a burly male who Wynter also recognized stalked into the clearing. She felt the corners of her eyes tighten. "Cletus," she bit out.

Xavier's brows met. "I'm getting the feeling I should loathe Cletus. Why should I loathe him?"

"He likes to take from women what they don't want to give," she fudged.

Fort turned to fully face Cletus. "Well?"

"No sign of Wynter anywhere," replied Cletus. "I told you it'd be a waste of time. The Ancients will be keeping her in their underground city."

Fort rubbed at his bearded jaw. "Did you find a way to get down there?"

Cletus shook his head. "I'm not even sure where the entrance is."

Fort's brother and fellow asshole, Milos, propped his fists on his hips. "We could try and pay off a local to lure her out here to us."

Fort dismissed that idea with a puff of sound. "They won't do us any favors. Not for any amount of money. It's best that we lay low and remain undetected."

"We don't have to say we're from Aeon," said Milos. "We could claim to be bounty hunters or something."

"A lot of people here are probably on the run, so I doubt hunters would be welcome in a place like this." Fort scratched at his head. "Lailah did warn us it wouldn't be easy to find Wynter, so I don't think we need to worry that she'll lose her mind if we return without her. Not as long as we're successful at mapping out the town as best we can. She said she wants the location of every nook, every cranny, every blind spot."

Delilah softly cursed. "The Aeons are preparing to invade the town, huh?"

"Looks like it," said Wynter, listening as Fort barked orders to each of the keepers. "And these bastards are gonna simplify it for them. I can't say I'm down with that."

Xavier looked at her, his eyes bright. "Can we kill them?"

"It's that or let them run back home with information that we don't want the Aeons to possess so, yeah, we can kill them," said Wynter.

He flashed her a slow grin and conjured his sword. "Just what I wanted to hear."

Looking similarly pleased, Hattie and Delilah shifted into their animal forms. The crow settled on top of the monstrous cat, who flexed its iron claws. Both women could also fight with magick, but they preferred using their animal forms since it meant that their senses, reflexes, strength, and speed were enhanced.

Wynter lifted a brow at Anabel. "Are you joining the fight or waiting here?"

A sword materialized in the blonde's hand, which answered the question.

Wynter called to her own blade and then placed her mouth near Anabel's ear. "Mary, Mary, please come out," she quietly sang.

The blonde's demeanor changed in an instant, switching from nervous to eager as her eyes took on that familiar not-so-sane light.

"No drinking blood," Wynter told her.

Anabel/Mary nodded, a feral smile splitting her lips. "Understood."

Conscious that she couldn't allow her monster free rein right now, Wynter silently assured it that the keepers would die, relieved when it didn't push for supremacy.

"Fort's mine," Wynter told her crew. "Okay ... now." Pumped full of anticipation, she rushed out of the woods with the others at her heels.

Taken off-guard, it took the keepers a moment to react. But, highly trained as they were, they sprung to attention fast and raised their weapons.

She made a swift beeline for Fort, but freaking Cletus came at her from another angle, forcing her to turn to him. She blocked the sword that swung her way, and their blades clanged.

Sneering, he danced backwards. "I've been looking for you."

"Clearly not hard enough," she said. "I found you first."

They parried and thrust over and over. She didn't need to worry about the Ancients or townspeople watching her fight, so she didn't check her speed; didn't hold back magickly or otherwise. He staggered backwards under the pressure, unprepared for the rigor with which she flew at him. He fell on his butt, and she wasted no time in skewering him with her sword.

Milos came into view and sent balls of blue light sailing at her—one clipped her shoulder, the other smashed into her chest. Pretty they might be, but they also hit like a goddamn hammer, bruising her for sure.

She retaliated with her own magick, hurling dark smoky spiked orbs right at his fucking head—orbs he annoyingly managed to evade. Swords raised, they went at each other. They ducked and twisted and deflected, cursing and snarling.

Around her, her crew battled hard. Dead keepers were up and running, fighting the live keepers. Roars, cries, grunts, squawks, the clashing of steel, and the insanity-laced giggles of Anabel/Mary filled the air.

Wynter hissed as Milos's blade stabbed her smarting shoulder. His brows snapped together when the runes had no effect on her. Yeah, well, there was something he didn't know, and she saw no need to educate him about it.

Although a wet warmth pooled on her skin and soaked her tee, she didn't look at the wound. She kept swiping out with her sword, aiming for every weak spot, ensuring her every strike was precise.

He twisted his hips and kicked out at her stomach. Missed. Growled. Charged.

She ducked and came up on his side, thrusting her sword deep. He stumbled, his lips parting in both shock and pain, and then dropped to his knees. She swung her sword, beheading him . . . and smirked at Fort as she did so.

Screaming in fury at the death of his brother, Fort yanked his blade out of a reanimated keeper. He didn't look good. At all. Sweat beaded his forehead, and his tee sported several scarlet stains.

He rushed Wynter with another loud cry of anger, his nostrils flaring when she parried the blow. "You *bitch*," he said. "I'm going to enjoy this. I didn't get the privilege of tossing your thou-art-holier-than-thou mother over the falls. I'll pay that bitch back by impaling her daughter on my blade, and I'll avenge my brother in the doing of it."

Anger flooded her at the mention of her mother, but Wynter kept it in check. "You were honestly surprised she rejected you? Come on, Fort, you make ogres look good."

He lunged with a roar. His blows were precise and powerful. The tall bastard had a long reach, and he used it well. Sadly.

Knowing to go for his exposed legs, Wynter swung her hips and slammed the flat of her foot on his thigh, loving his subsequent grunt. The piece of shit waved his arm, sending a gust of magick at her. The weight of it sent her skidding back several feet, but she managed not to fall. Liking the surprise flickering in his eyes, she grinned and then lashed out with her magick.

Growling as deep welts sizzled to life on his face and neck, he retaliated with a swipe of his sword. She blocked it, and then they were at it again.

Around them, chaos raged on. But she could sense that the numbers of keepers had dropped. And beneath the sound of Anabel/Mary singing "Mighty Morphin Power Rangers"—whatever the fuck that was about—the distinctive noises of battle had dimmed.

Wind came at her again, belting her in the face and stealing her breath. She stayed on her feet, but it meant throwing out her arms to—

Pain blazed along her chest as the sword sliced through cloth and skin. "Motherfucker." His taunting laugh only fueled her anger. She struck at him with magick, and he cursed as whips of dark power zapped their way along the ground and crashed into him.

The bastard rallied fast and rushed her again, thrusting and parrying, his breathing rapid and shallow. He was running out of steam, and they both knew it. Maybe that was why he began to strike out wildly, desperately, like death itself was hot on his heels.

Well, it was.

When the opening she was waiting for finally came, she kicked out at his knee with a snarl. His leg buckled slightly, and she took advantage. Lunging forward, she thrust the sword deep into his gut, twisted it sharply, and then withdrew it. After a moment, he slumped to his front, dead. *Boom.*

Wynter glanced at her crew. Delilah and Hattie were back in their human forms, and both had suffered only minor wounds. Xavier looked like he'd been attacked by an alley cat, so he'd likely been hit with skinwalker magick or something.

Anabel/Mary was lying among the corpses that were sprawled on the grass with their eyes open wide and their clothes soaked with blood. She wasn't dead herself. She wasn't even severely injured. But she'd linked her fingers through that of a dead keeper and was chatting to him like they were a smitten, stargazing couple. But she snapped to alertness and sprung to her feet at the sound of people racing through the woods.

Tensing, Wynter spun to face the new threat. Not more keepers, she quickly realized. Nope, these were residents of the town—including Maxim. And as they took in the scene before them, their lips parted in surprise.

Wynter cleared her throat. "Don't mind us, we were just leaving."

\*

There was nothing pleasant nor unpleasant about the psychic space Cain found himself in. It was merely a rectangular room that was all white paint and gleaming white floor tiles. There were only two chairs. Lailah sat in one, her posture regal, her smile placid.

His creature eyed her with distaste. Even before she'd played a part in imprisoning Cain, it had never liked her. It saw only weakness when it looked at her. A hypocrite. A backstabber. A person who would do anything—fuck over anyone—to obtain what she wanted and get where she wanted to be.

In that sense, she and Abel deserved each other. Like often called to like, didn't it?

"I wasn't so sure you would agree to speak with me," she said, her voice soft. "We were once friends but, well, that was a long time ago."

Cain strode toward the empty chair that was positioned opposite her own. "A friend wouldn't have done any of the things you did, so I'd say that was the wrong choice of word."

Her smile dimmed. "You left us no choice when it came to the banishment."

Annoyance spiked through him. "Do not pin the blame for your actions on me. Own them. Or don't. But do not use me as your scapegoat."

Her eyes briefly slid to the side, and she rested her clasped hands on her lap. "I did not ask to speak with you so we could rehash the past. The present is my concern, and it should also be yours. This woman you have given sanctuary to . . . She is not what you think. Her old Priestess, Esther, told you that the land of Aeon is perishing, yes?"

Sitting, he gave a slow nod. "She did."

"Nothing has been able to fight the blight. It continues to spread like a cancer. More, our people are continuing to fall ill. If it wasn't for our healers, I suspect that many would be dead."

Cain said nothing. He simply stared at her, keeping his face blank.

"My people managed to find someone who, like Wynter

Dellavale, was brought back from the afterlife using forbidden magick. He examined the decay. He verified that, as we'd come to suspect, the land has been cursed."

Cain forced himself not to tense.

"We had hoped that the male witch would unravel the hex for us. He was not able to, however." She paused. "He said that his power was no match for it. That each attempt to snap the threads of the curse achieved only in stretching them—they bounced back into place like elastic every time."

Impressive. Unheard of—at least for Cain—but impressive.

"I asked how that could possibly be. He said that it wasn't simply dark magick at work. But he had no clue exactly what else *is* at work. He was certain of one thing, though. Her life-force is not tied to the curse. Her death would therefore not be enough to undo it."

Cain was so taken off-guard that he must have betrayed his surprise in some way, because Lailah nodded and said, "Yes, I think we now see what has become clear to me and the other Aeons— Whoever you are harboring is not merely a witch."

"You're only just figuring this out?" Cain had sensed that early on. He just had no actual clue what exactly Wynter was. "That was always your problem, Lailah. You never viewed mortals as a threat, so you paid no real attention to them."

Her mouth tightened for a mere moment. "When I exiled her, she warned me that there would be consequences. It was such a casual warning. Very matter-of-fact."

"And I'm sure you dismissed it."

"Having never demonstrated any great displays of power, she'd never given me any reason to assume I should heed her. It wasn't until it became clear that she is not a simple witch that I recalled how something else happened that day. There was a disturbance in the air that felt ... strange. Wrong. Alien. I cannot explain or adequately describe it."

"And you dismissed that as well," he guessed.

"I did," she admitted through gritted teeth. "Perhaps I was right to do so. Perhaps it was nothing. But perhaps it wasn't. What I am certain of is this: She broke my hold on her mind and body in order to fight one of our keepers and free herself. That is no easy thing. I do not know what exactly Wynter is, but if she was able to hex a place such as Aeon so thoroughly without tying her own life-force to that curse, we have to ask ourselves … What else can she do?"

That was indeed an excellent question. At this point, Cain had a great many questions for his oh-so secretive witch. "It seems that she might be more interesting to have around than I initially thought."

"Don't be a fool, Cain. If she can be a threat to Aeon, she can be a threat to Devil's Cradle. Perhaps even to you."

"You don't really believe the latter, but you're hoping I will. Why? What is it that you want?"

Her face hardened. "I would have thought that was obvious. I want you to surrender her to us. Return your rights to her soul, withdraw your protection. Send her back to Aeon with the conduit and her old coven member."

"Essentially, you wish me to do you a favor? No, Lailah, I'm not feeling motivated to do that."

"It would be in your best interests as well as ours. Wynter is a power we don't understand."

"You and the other Aeons are all about destroying what you don't understand," he said, his voice hardening. "If something doesn't fit neatly in a box, if you're not so sure you can effortlessly kill it, you reach the conclusion that it must therefore be eradicated."

She swallowed. "As I said before, I didn't request to speak with you so that we could revisit the past—"

"But there are so many parallels, aren't there? Curses, mysteries, secrets, deaths."

The fingers on her lap flexed. "Aeon was once your home. Would you truly see it rot away?"

He gave a casual, unbothered shrug. "I don't really see how it's my business."

"How can you not care that you have given sanctuary to someone who is clearly a dark power?"

"I've been described as a dark power plenty of times. Maybe you've forgotten, Lailah, but Devil's Cradle goes by another name—the Home of Monsters. What better place for her to live?"

"She knows there is bad history between the Aeons and the Ancients. She is using you. Relying on you to keep her safe. Depending on you to fight at her side if a battle ever began."

"Considering war again, are you?" Cain truly did hope so.

Lailah's eyelids dropped slightly. "She must be made to undo what she has done, or Aeon will be no more."

"You can relocate. It's not so hard. We all did it. It wasn't our choice, just as it won't be yours. And we weren't too pleased about it, just as you won't be. But sometimes things simply don't play out as we'd like them to."

"Is that what this is about for you? Revenge?"

"Of course."

She drew in a breath through her nose, and then her face softened into an expression she'd often worn in front of him many years ago. "Cain, please, think of—"

"Switched tactics quickly, didn't you? Don't bother playing that card, Lailah. I stopped giving a shit about you long ago."

She winced. "I didn't choose Abel over you, if that's what you think. It wasn't like that. I chose him because I couldn't be with you. Your creature would never have accepted me. It didn't like or trust me."

"And you later proved that it was right not to. Is this why I'm talking to only you rather than all four ruling Aeons? You all thought that I'd be more likely to agree to cooperate if there was a 'friendly face?'" Much like they'd thought sending a 'friendly face' to Wynter might help their cause. "Let me be very clear. This conversation was a waste of your time. I won't hand Wynter over to you."

Lailah's mouth went flat. "Perhaps we can come to an arrangement."

"No."

"Don't be so quick to disagree. You have not heard my offer yet." She seemed utterly convinced he'd fall all over himself to accept it. "Give us Wynter, and we will give you Eve in exchange."

"No."

Lailah's face went slack, and her eyes widened. "No?" she spluttered. "But she is your mother. You spent years demanding to see her."

"According to Adam, she didn't want to see me." Cain knew that wasn't true, though.

Lailah looked as if she might admit as much, but then she coughed. "That has changed in recent years. Eve misses both you and Seth. I know your brother would very much like to have her at his side. Let's not pretend you don't wish to make the trade. I know you do. You simply don't want to back down so easily."

"There will be no trade." He planned to retrieve his mother himself once he was free. "There is only one thing—one—that I want from you and the other Aeons. You already know what that is."

She averted her gaze. "We cannot grant you your freedom."

He hadn't thought for a moment that they would. Because they *knew* that he and the other Ancients would wreak vengeance. "Then we have nothing further to discuss."

"We have unless you want war. You would be foolish to take us on. You were powerful once, but being contained has weakened you all over time. None of you would stand a chance against any Aeon, let alone a group of them and whatever army they brought. Don't put us in this position, Cain. Don't force our hand. We have left you in peace."

He barely held back a snarl. "You left us in a cage. You hoped it would send us stir crazy and that we'd destroy each other. You left us to rot. Tell me why the fuck I shouldn't do the same to your precious land."

She inched up her chin. "Then you leave us no choice."

"There you go again pinning the blame for your actions on me. If you instigate a war, it will be your choice. It will also be your mistake. But then, you're good at making those, aren't you?" Without waiting for a response, he returned his consciousness to his body.

Cain blinked twice, bringing the room into focus. No one had left, and Maxim was now in the room. Cain flicked the males from Aeon a look and then told his aide, "Show them out."

Rafe slowly stood. "Will you truly protect Wynter? I know you're powerful. But will you eventually get tired of people coming for her? Will you one day give her up just to get the Aeons off your back? They'll kill her if you do. Maybe not right away, but eventually. And they'll make it hurt."

"Wynter isn't going anywhere," Cain told him. "And those bastards won't ever get their hands on her."

Rafe nodded, satisfied. "Tell her I said to take care of herself, and that I'm sorry I wasn't able to protect her from Esther's plans." He allowed Maxim to lead both him and Griff out of the room.

Dantalion dismissed his own aide and then turned back to Cain. "What did Lailah say?"

"Exactly what I thought she'd say," replied Cain. "She asked that I surrender Wynter to the custody of the Aeons."

Azazel's brows snapped together. "Why would she believe you would do that?"

"Apparently, given the destruction that Wynter has caused, I should consider her a danger to all of us and to our land."

Dantalion rolled his eyes. "Lailah is foolish if she thought that you'd be so easily manipulated. What else did she say?"

*Her life-force is not tied to the curse. Her death would therefore not be enough to undo it.*

Cain wouldn't mention that yet. He needed to speak to Wynter about it first. "She offered to give me Eve if we handed over Wynter in return."

Azazel frowned. "She actually thought you'd trade her for Eve? Seriously?"

"That makes no sense," said Dantalion. "Nor does her attempt to cajole you into handing over the witch. Why would we give up the only thing that will lure them here?"

"The Aeons apparently have it in their heads that we've weakened in power over the centuries—I chose not to correct her on that," said Cain. "They also believe we wouldn't want them to come here; that we'd feel we wouldn't stand a chance against them. In Lailah's eyes, I am simply being stubborn and spiteful. She has no idea that in threatening war she gave us exactly what we want."

Dantalion stilled. "So they will come?"

"They will have to," said Cain. "Their keepers won't stand a chance against us alone; they need the aid of Aeons if they are to kill us to get to Wynter."

A look of grim satisfaction came over Azazel's face. "Who exactly do you think will come? They won't all lead the army here."

"At least one of the ruling Aeons will have to lead them, but I doubt it will be Adam," said Dantalion. "He only gets his hands dirty if he absolutely has to. Abel is much the same, but he will at the very least send Lailah to do the deed for him. If so, Saul will be here even if only to protect her. She is most likely the only person he cares for."

Cain nodded. "They always did like fighting beside one another." The siblings were close, much like Abel and Seth had once been—and that was another reason Cain doubted that Abel would come. The Aeon wouldn't want to have a direct hand in Seth's death, because it was Cain who Abel held responsible for Seth's 'betrayal.'

Dantalion rubbed at his chin. "We need to call a meeting with the other Ancients and inform them what happened here. I'm happy to hold it at my Keep."

Cain and Azazel both nodded their assent.

When Maxim returned to the room moments later to inform Cain that the witches were being escorted out of town, Cain asked him, "Is Wynter at the Keep?"

Maxim grimaced. "Probably not, though she assured me that she would head there soon."

Cain stiffened. "Why are you pulling that face?"

The aide cleared his throat. "I found her, like you asked. She and her coven were in the woods near the lake." Maxim tugged at his collar. "They, um … they were standing over the dead bodies of several keepers from Aeon. Apparently they stumbled upon them."

Anger spiked through Cain, tightening his muscles and clenching his jaw.

Dantalion growled. "They dared send keepers here?"

"Was she hurt?" asked Cain.

"She had no lethal wounds," replied Maxim, "though, if the stains on her tee were anything to go by, her left shoulder and chest suffered bad injuries. She swore they would all be healed by Anabel's potions. Wynter also said she would meet you at the Keep once she'd showered and changed."

Azazel rubbed at his jaw. "Do you think Rafe and Griff knew that others had been sent?"

Cain shook his head, silently cursing the Aeons to hell and back.

"You're certain all the keepers are dead?" asked Azazel. "It would have been nice to have one or two to play with."

"Oh, they are definitely dead," Maxim told him.

Cain drew in a breath through his nose. "It's almost as if danger finds that coven wherever they go."

"Or as if Wynter's a magnet for it." Dantalion shrugged at Cain. "After all, she attracts you. You're probably the biggest danger there is."

That wasn't something that could be denied.

# Chapter Twenty-One

Entering his chamber a short while later, Cain found Wynter curled up on a chair reading a tattered paperback—casual, relaxed, at ease . . . like she hadn't earlier engaged in a battle.

Her head snapped up as she sensed him, no lines of stress on her face, no lingering anger at having fought for her life. "You're looking very fierce right now," she said, her brows lowering.

He was feeling fierce. Closing the distance between them, he said, "Stand."

Her eyes narrowed slightly, but she slowly set her book down on the bulky armrest and then just as slowly pushed out of her chair.

"I hear you ran into some keepers in the woods," said Cain, unable to keep the thread of ire out of his voice. He peeled off her tee and examined both her left shoulder and her chest. Whatever wounds she'd earlier sported were gone. The skin was completely unmarred.

"My injuries weren't too bad. Nothing Anabel's brews couldn't fix."

Cain's back teeth locked at the easy way she'd dismissed the wounds. "Yes, *this time*. Next time you might not be so lucky."

She frowned. "It wasn't luck. It was skill. And I'm not sure why you're mad at me, but shake it off. It's not like I *want* keepers on my ass. Or like I took on a whole squadron of them by myself. I had backup, and there weren't many to take down."

Irritation buzzed through Cain. He slid his hand up her chest to collar her throat while bunching his free hand in the hair at the back of her head. "Don't make light of this. Don't act as if the incident was a minor issue. An attack on you will *always* be far from minor to me, no matter how much backup you have." He paused, his nostrils flaring. "That's twice now I've been notified that you were targeted while I was none the wiser."

Her frown smoothing out, she played her fingers through his hair. "The protective routine shouldn't make me all tingly, should it?"

A ribbon of amusement unfurled inside him. "You know, most people get nervous when I'm pissed off."

"Most people don't have my perverse libido."

He let out a long breath and shook his head, releasing her. "The keepers weren't the only 'visitors' we had from Aeon today. Two males also came, though the parties seem to have traveled here separately. One was sent to convince you to come home—a male witch by the name of Rafe."

Her face brightened. "*Rafe* is here?"

A black jealousy threatened to rear up inside Cain, and his creature coiled as every muscle tightened. "This man means something to you?"

"Not in *that way*," she said with a shudder. "He's like family. I owe how well-trained I am to him. In which case, I also owe him my life ten times over. You didn't kill him, did you?"

"No, purely because I sensed that he didn't want you to return to Aeon. He asked me to tell you to take care of yourself, and to pass on an apology for his failure to alter Esther's plans."

"What? That's dumb, I don't hold him responsible."

"He seems to feel that he could have done more for you. I sent him and his conduit friend home. But not before I had a talk with Lailah via the conduit."

Wynter's eyes sharpened. "Interesting. What did you and Lailah talk about?"

"Several things. Mostly you. The Aeons have worked out that a curse is at the source of the environmental degradation."

"I figured they would eventually."

Cain studied her face carefully as he expanded, "Someone whose magick is dark like yours told them that your death wouldn't be enough to undo it; that more than dark magick weaved it."

Wynter didn't betray her emotions with even a *flicker* of a micro-expression. It was as impressive as it was frustrating.

"You said that only your destruction would end it."

"Uh, no, *Azazel* said that. Or presumed it, I should say. I simply never corrected him. And before you ride my ass about lying by omission, bear in mind that it will only make you a hypocrite—you do the omission thing, like, *all* the time."

Cain snapped his mouth shut. "If Azazel had *asked* if your life-force was tied to the hex, would you have answered him truthfully?"

"No, because he would have asked how it was otherwise possible for a mere witch to afflict protected land with such a curse."

"I'd already sensed that you aren't a mere witch." If she was surprised that he'd already reached that conclusion, she didn't show it. "What exactly are you?"

"What exactly are you?"

"I asked first."

"I'll answer if you will."

He sighed, having already expected that would be her response. Nothing could be easy with this woman. "I don't like that I had to find out the truth about this from *Lailah*. I don't like that there's so much about you I don't know."

Her expression went blank. "Does this mean you're done? That you want to end it?"

Cain frowned. "Fuck, no." He caught her face with his hands. "It will take time for you to trust me with all you hold inside—I know that. The same applies to me. But we'll get there eventually. Until then, well, I suspect neither of us are going to like the gaps in our knowledge of the other. I can complain about it even as I accept it."

Her shoulders relaxed. "All right. Did Lailah say anything else?"

Sliding his hands from Wynter's face to her neck, he replied, "She's finally worked out that you're not an everyday witch. She seems to feel that I should find you a 'concern.' A danger to Devil's Cradle. A 'dark power' that I can't afford to trust."

"And do you see me that way?"

He hiked up a brow. "Do you truly think I do?"

"No, but . . . I don't know, you're just looking at me differently right now. I've had people turn on me before because I don't fit the mold."

*Same here, baby.* "The Aeons don't like that they don't fully understand you. Nor do they like that they can't explain why you can do the things you do. For them, that's reason enough to want you dead. They have no real tolerance for things that are 'different.'" He settled his hands on her shoulders and gave them a little squeeze. "I'm not them, Wynter."

She gave a slow nod, a long breath slipping out of her.

"You warned Lailah that there would be consequences when she exiled you?"

"Yes."

"She said there was a foreign disturbance in the air that day."

"So she merely wanted to chat with you?"

Cain lowered his face to hers. "She wanted me to hand you over. I refused. So she then offered me something in exchange for you. I essentially told her to go fuck herself. Which means there'll be war."

"And that pleases you, doesn't it?"

"It does." He cocked his head. "Just how many things are you hiding from me?"

She licked her lower lip. "Probably not as many as you're hiding from me."

Probably not.

"When the Aeons come, I want to be part of the battle."

Cain almost barked a humorless laugh. "That isn't going to happen."

Her spine straightened. "Excuse me?"

"Wynter, I know you're powerful. I know you can fight with both sword and magick. But you wouldn't stand a chance against an Aeon."

"I'm not saying I'd go challenge one. But they won't come alone. They'll bring a massive force. I can be part of handling said force."

"You need to stay down here in the city, where you'll be safe."

She did a slow blink. "Please tell me you're joking. As you now know, my death won't undo the curse—"

"You say that like it therefore wouldn't matter if you ceased to exist. It would matter to me, Wynter. It would matter a fuck of a lot."

"I get it. I wouldn't want you to die either. But ask you to sit this fight out? No, I wouldn't do that. Don't ask it of me. I won't stay home twiddling my fingers while others battle a bunch of assholes that I brought to their town."

"You realize that every single one of their army will be ordered to take you? *You* will be their focus, Wynter. They'll kill whoever they need to kill just to get to you. And we both know you'd die before you let them take you. Why risk yourself that way?"

Her brow creased. "Why do you sound offended that I would?"

His lips flattening, he pulled her toward him using his grip on her shoulders, closing the small gap between them. "I want you to *want* to live, Wynter. I want you to value enough what we have that you'd at least want to live so we can see where this goes."

"So by being part of the battle, *you* don't value this? Is that what you're saying?"

He ground his teeth. "No."

"It's no different for me, so don't twist what I'm saying. You're uber powerful, sure. But you'll be up against beings that can actually kill you. Your life will be at risk. I don't hear you offering to stay home." She perched her hands on her hips. "Why, in your mind, should you get to face them but I don't? What did they do to you that makes your grudge so much more important than mine?"

He stared at her, touching his incisor with the tip of his tongue. "I will trust you with the answer to that . . . if you first tell me one thing honestly."

She folded her arms. "Go on."

He had a thousand questions he would love to fire at her, but she'd refuse to answer any that she wouldn't consider worth the trade of truths. In her position, he'd do same. So he settled on asking, "Who is your father? *What* is he?"

She blinked. "I don't actually know who he is. I never met him, and my mother didn't say much about him."

"Why not?"

"She was *not* a fan of his. All she ever said was that he was a witch and that I was better off not knowing him. She promised to tell me more when I was 'old enough to hear it,' but she didn't get that chance. I asked my grandmother and other members of the coven about him. Apparently, he was a one-night stand. When she told him she was pregnant, he wanted nothing to do with us. Davina didn't want to tell me that when I was so young, she worried it would hurt me."

That didn't explain *anything* for Cain. He didn't see how someone who wasn't a born hybrid could be so different from an average witch.

"Now it's your turn," she said. "Yes, I know my response didn't whatsoever satisfy you, but I did as you asked and answered your question. Now you need to live up to your end of the bargain."

Heaving a sigh, Cain sank into the armchair and patted his thighs. "Sit."

She straddled him and rested her hands on his shoulders.

He smoothed one hand up her back. "What do you know about the war that went on between the Ancients and the Aeons?"

She pursed her lips. "Not much. The Aeons were pretty vague about it. They just said a war broke out, your side lost, and they 'mercifully' let seven of you leave and make a home elsewhere."

The word 'mercifully' made his creature growl. "They lied. They didn't allow the survivors to live out of mercy, Wynter. It was supposed to be a punishment. A cruel one at that. We didn't settle here to make a new home. They put us here. We cannot leave the boundaries. It's essentially a cage."

Her jaw went slack. "Wow. I just thought you all preferred to stick to your little corner of the world."

"We probably would—the Earth as a whole doesn't hold much interest for us. We may be stuck in Devil's Cradle, but we have ways of peeking at the outside world and we're not impressed by what we've seen of it. Plus, we're not roamers, and we prefer to live in groups. But we still don't wish to be trapped." He ghosted his fingertips over her nape. "The Aeons believed we'd lose our minds and kill each other. They underestimated us. They've continued to do that for a long time." And more fool them.

"Your only way to get revenge is to make them step on your land ... except there was never a reason for them to come here," she mused.

Cain nodded. "Until now."

Wynter stared at him, biting her lip. Damn, this explained so much—how easily he'd promised to keep her safe, how unbothered he'd been by the prospect of the Aeons coming for her, how eager he and the other Ancients were for war.

He toyed with her hair. "Four Aeons were responsible for caging us. Only their deaths will open that cage."

"What four?"

"The ruling Aeons. Adam, Abel, Lailah, and Lailah's brother Saul."

"So they're more powerful than you and the other Ancients combined?" She wouldn't have thought so.

"No. We can't dismantle the cage ourselves, because they used our blood to enforce the power they used to construct the prison— essentially making us our own captors."

"Blood magick works a little like that. If you fuel the spell with the victim's blood, the victim can't undo it. They might as well have put the spell on themselves."

Cain swept a fingertip over her lower lip. "Lailah wronged you when she essentially sentenced you to death, just as Abel wronged your mother when he did the same to her. It is only natural that you would crave vengeance. But not even you can argue that my craving for vengeance runs far deeper than yours."

Hell no, she couldn't. Which was mega frustrating. She'd always known there was bad blood between the Ancients and the Aeons, but she hadn't expected his beef with them to be so profound. "I can't argue that, no," she admitted. "I won't try to. But I still intend to be part of the battle, Cain." She braced herself for an outburst, but he steadily stared back at her.

Finally, he shrugged. "If you're so determined, fine."

Oh, now that was way too easy. "I don't like how cooperative you're suddenly being. It's weird." She couldn't help but get the feeling that he'd come to some decision in his head that he didn't care to share. "If you're thinking of locking me in a room on the day of the battle, don't."

His brows lifted, and he pursed his lips in thought. "That's not a bad idea. You probably shouldn't have put it in my head."

"I mean it, Cain."

"I see that." He deftly flicked open the catch at the front of her bra. "Now tell me more about the incident in the woods."

"Hoping to distract me now, are you?"

"The conversation is getting us nowhere. It seems better to simply move on." He slid the cups of her bra aside and filled his hands with her breasts. "Or better yet ... we can forget talking." Warm and firm, his palms squeezed and plumped.

Maybe she should have insisted that they remain on topic, but what was the point? They weren't going to agree on the matter. And, well, this was *way* more fun. So she gave into the moment—arching into his touch, digging her nails into his shoulders, moaning as he nipped and licked at her mouth but didn't kiss her. *Asshole.*

Cain curled an arm around her waist and lifted her so that her breasts were level with his mouth. He latched onto her nipple and, mother of God, he sucked hard. So hard her inner muscles clenched and a pulse of pleasure shot to her clit.

Wynter thrust her fingers through his hair and scraped his scalp with her nails. He growled around her nipple, and the slight delicious vibration shocked a gasp out of her.

"Undo your shorts, I want you naked," said Cain, shedding her bra while kissing his way to her other nipple. And then the taut bud was in his mouth and, *hell*, the man had some serious game in the bedroom.

She undid her fly and pushed at her shorts and panties. It was Cain who gripped the waistbands and tugged them down to help her shuck off the clothes. Then she was naked. And hot. And damp. And more than ready for whatever soul-deep pleasure he had in mind.

"Cain," she breathed.

"You're going to ride me. You're going to fuck yourself on my cock while I watch. And you're not going to come until I allow it. Understood?"

Why that revved her engines instead of switching them off, she really couldn't say. She also didn't care to question it. "Yes."

"So very cooperative in bed." He cupped her pussy, blatantly possessive. "It is a shame you're not so cooperative outside of it."

"You'd get bored of me if I was."

Cain nearly barked a laugh at that ridiculous statement. "I could never find you boring, little witch. You fucking fascinate me even as you drive me insane with your secrets and stubbornness." He slipped one finger between her folds and dipped it inside her, a growl vibrating his chest. "Wet and ready for me."

Aching to be inside her, Cain tore open his fly, freed his cock, and then casually splayed his hands on the armrests. "Remember, you don't come until I allow it." Maddened by her refusal to sit out the fight, he needed this from her; needed to exert what control over her he could.

Wynter muttered something beneath her breath, but all he made out was "high-handed." She positioned herself above his cock and wasted no time in lowering herself over him. Her lips parting, she dug her fingertips into his shoulders as she slowly bore down until, finally, she'd taken every inch.

He closed his eyes for a moment, feeling his face smooth out. "Yeah, that's what I needed. That sweet pussy swallowing my cock."

She set a fast rhythm as she rode him hard. He didn't touch her. Didn't kiss her. Didn't pleasure her soul. He just watched her, occasionally urging her on, as she impaled herself on him over and over.

Feeling her inner muscles, he shot her a look of warning. "Not yet."

Sparks of anger flared in her eyes, but she held back her release.

"That's a good girl."

Mentally cursing him, she sank down on his cock again and again, so damn wet it was almost embarrassing. Every slice of his dick through her body built the tension inside her. Every whispered and often filthy praise was like a flick to her clit. Every look of carnal promise speared her womb, reminding her what was coming. It became harder and harder to stave off the release edging her way, and she was soon squeezing her eyes shut against the struggle.

"You did good, little witch. Now you can come."

She sucked in a breath as an avalanche of pleasure tumbled along her soul, electrifying her from the inside out. Her eyes snapped open, and her pace faltered. God, the level of sensation . . . There might as well have been thousands of tongues, mouths, teeth, fingers, and hands all over her. And her orgasm stole over her in a blind rush.

"My turn." Cain clamped his hands around her hips and began slamming her on his cock. He then pretty much flayed her soul with euphoria. He kept switching it up—a wave of pure bliss, a stroke of pleasure/pain, dark lashes of sensation.

Her lungs burned for air. Her heart pounded furiously in her chest. Her nerve-endings were on fire, sensitive to even the air itself.

Her mind became all fuzzy and foggy . . . until she felt disconnected from her body yet felt every single physical touch so much more acutely.

She wouldn't last. She couldn't. Wynter didn't even get the chance to warn Cain—her orgasm swallowed her whole. She burst, broke, imploded, screamed.

She was distantly aware of his fingertips biting into her hips as he slammed her harder onto his dick while punching up his hips to meet each downward thrust. A soft curse escaped him as the first hot rope of his come splashed her inner walls. His shaft throbbed and swelled as he fucked his orgasm into her body.

She slumped forward, panting like a damn racehorse. "I swear, giving up partial rights to my soul was worth it just for the soul-gasms."

Feeling his lips twitch, Cain swept a hand up her sleek back. "And to think I almost had Dantalion cover for me that day you came to the mansion looking for residency."

She lifted her head to meet his gaze. "You did?"

Cain nodded. "My mood was ... not good. I was tempted to retreat my garden for a few hours. If I had, it would have been him you made a deal with." Cain twisted his mouth. "It would not have been easy to convince him to give me his rights to your soul, but I'd have somehow managed it."

Her brows snapped together. "Wait, *give* them to you?"

Cain felt this brow arch. "You think I'd have allowed anyone else to own any rights to any part of you?"

Sitting up straighter, she gave her head a little shake. "I mean, how could he have given them to you?"

"Ancients can trade souls, or even the partial rights we hold to them. Dantalion doesn't have an undead soul in his collection, so he wouldn't have parted with half of yours easily no matter what person in my service I offered him in exchange."

"Wouldn't I have had some say in the matter?"

"No, because once you give up that half of your soul, you no longer have a say in what happens to it."

"You never mentioned that before."

"I figured it was obvious." Cain used his thumb to smooth away the line that furrowed her brow. "Don't worry, sweet witch, I'd never give away my rights to your soul. They will never belong to anyone but me."

She swallowed. "Even if this thing we have ends?"

"Even then. But it won't end. I won't let it. I thought I made that clear."

"You did," said Wynter, putting a placatory hand on his chest, not liking how his expression had hardened. "It's not that I doubt your honesty. It's just that, well, things don't always work out the way we want them to." It was a lesson she'd learned early.

"But sometimes they do. And this will."

He said it so simply, so resolutely, it made her chest ache. Though she believed he meant every word, she couldn't quite conjure up enough faith to also believe that her secrets would change nothing between them. "I hope you're right."

"I am. So often that it's irritating, according to Seth." His eyes flitted over her face, warm and intent. "Too beautiful for words."

"That was a nice thing to say. You're quite the looker, too. For an old guy."

Humor lit his eyes. "An old guy?"

"Well, you *do* predate the Bible."

"As does your soul. It has led many lives. And no, I cannot tell you about them—I have no access to such details. But I have enough knowledge of souls to sense that yours is very old."

"You're doing it again."

"What?"

"Using that weird tone when you talk about my soul. Like it's a shiny toy."

His lips quirking, Cain pressed a kiss to her neck. "I do enjoy playing with it. You enjoy it just as much. I'm planning to play with it some more while we shower."

Her body stirred. "I look forward to it. But I gotta warn you . . . it won't matter how many more monumental orgasms you give me tonight, or how sweet and complimentary you keep being, I'm still gonna be on the proverbial battlefield."

His hand gently delved into her hair and combed his fingers through it. "Understood," he said, sounding oh so agreeable.

She bit back a snort. She didn't doubt for a single moment that he'd try to keep her out of harm's way. Wynter wasn't too worried about it, though, because he had no way of truly confining her anywhere. He simply didn't know it yet.

# Chapter Twenty-Two

Bracing her elbows on the dining table, Wynter rubbed her temples. "Xavier, I can't keep doing this with you."

"You wouldn't have to if you'd only shove logic aside for a minute," he said, leaning forward in his seat. "In the grand scheme of things, what does it really matter if an Alpha lycan goes 'missing?'"

Wynter dropped her hands to the table. "It will matter to his pack. A lot."

"*Or* they'll be thrilled that someone else gets the chance to be Alpha. Did you ever think of that? I could be doing them a favor."

"A favor?" echoed Delilah in a mocking tone. "Really?" Stood at the stove with Anabel as they worked on a new batch of a particular potion, Delilah shook her head and gave him her back.

"Yes, really," clipped Xavier.

Wynter sighed. Getting through to the guy could sometimes be a trial. "As I've said before *several times*, whatever Ancient has rights to Elias's soul wouldn't be happy if anything happened to him. The Ancients don't take kindly to anyone screwing with their 'property.'"

He snorted. "That didn't stop you from trapping two berserkers in the netherworld."

Yeah, well, they weren't talking about Wynter.

"Ooh, we could toss Elias in there, too," he suggested, his eyes brightening.

"I only dumped Annette and Bowen there because they would otherwise have blabbed my secrets." Well, *that* and she'd wanted them to suffer some. "This situation you have with Elias is very different."

"He ruined my date, Wynter. He told her I'd lied about my name—"

"Well, you did."

"—that I wasn't really Italian—"

"Well, you're not."

"—and that I was a chronic liar whose word couldn't be trusted."

"You honestly disagree with that assessment?"

Xavier's mouth flattened. "You're supposed to be on my side."

She reached across the table and put her hand over his. "I'm *always* on your side. You're one of the best people I know, even if you do mix fact and fiction often. But you can't kill someone just because they annoy you."

"Why? I used to do it all the time."

"And that's why you have a price on your head. Look, I get that growing up practicing the dark arts means you still struggle with ethics at times. But if you truly mean to follow the right-hand path, you can't take detours from it whenever it suits you. If it's a life or death situation, fine. But this is not. You have to learn to handle mundane shit without resorting to acts like murder."

Shuffling past the table, Hattie paused long enough to say, "She's right, darlin'. Various people will wrong or upset you many times in your life. Killing them isn't the answer."

Xavier cast her look of disbelief. "Says the woman who poisoned each of her husbands."

"What does that have to do with anything?" asked Hattie, her brow wrinkling.

"It has *everything* to do with it," he insisted.

Hattie huffed and continued walking toward the living room. "You're just trying to shift the focus of the conversation onto me. I'm wise to your tricks, boy."

Cutting his gaze back to Wynter, he jabbed his thumb in the old woman's direction. "So it's okay to you that *she* killed in situations that weren't matters of self-defense?"

"No, it's not," replied Wynter. "But she did all that *before* becoming part of our crew—"

"Coven."

"—so I'm not holding her responsible for any of it, much like I don't hold the rest of you responsible for what you did in the past. It's the present and the future that count."

Anabel gave a little clap. "Well said."

Delilah raised her index finger. "Apart from when you referred to us as a crew. We're a coven. Get with the program already."

"Why do you have—?" Wynter cut off on hearing a knock at the front door. Sighing, she got to her feet. "I'll see who it is." On the other side of the door, she found one of the local dragon shifters. And he looked the image of devastation. "Jesus, is everything okay?" Wynter asked him.

He sniffled. "No. I need to speak with Delilah."

Her scalp prickled with unease. Praying this situation wasn't what she thought it was, Wynter said, "Um, okay. Del, you have a visitor!"

Moments later, Delilah appeared at her side and tipped her chin at the shifter. "Oh, hey."

"*Oh. Hey?*" He shook his head. "What did you do to me?"

Delilah blinked. "Excuse me?"

"That potion you gave me . . . All I wanted was my mate to be a little less butch."

Wynter closed her eyes. Oh, dear God.

"I did what you said—I swilled it in my mouth and then kissed her. The next thing I know, it's like I've been downing estrogen pills."

Delilah gave him a haughty look. "I warned you there might be side effects."

"Side effects? I've lost ten pounds, I'm growing boobs, my voice is getting all high, and I can't stop crying." His voice broke.

"Sounds rough. How awful for you."

"It *has* been rough." He wafted his hands as his eyes teared up. "I need this to be over."

Wynter slammed her gaze on Delilah. "I cannot believe you."

The woman gave her a look that was *all* innocence.

Anabel appeared and handed Wynter a reversal potion. "Here."

Taking it gratefully, Wynter held it out to the dragon shifter.

"Thank you," he all but sobbed. He knocked back the potion and closed his eyes. When he opened them again a few moments later, they were blazing with anger. He pointed a finger at Delilah. "You—"

"Will *happily* tell your mate that you not only find her 'too manly' for you but you actually asked for a potion to change her," said Delilah. "Would you like that?"

Panic rippled across his face.

Wynter held up a hand. "Look, I'm sorry for what happened to you. I truly am. But if you hadn't tried using magick on your mate without her knowledge, you wouldn't have suffered any side effects. Delilah informed you it wouldn't be a good idea, correct?"

He stiffly and reluctantly inclined his head. "Correct."

"But you took a chance. You paid the price. It's truly that simple. Now, I figure you've suffered enough, so I see no reason why your mate has to learn about this . . . so long as you walk away right now without insisting on making Delilah pay."

He averted his gaze, and moments of silence went by. Finally, he grunted. "Fine. But don't ever expect more custom from me." With that, he barged down the path and exited the yard, slamming the gate closed behind him.

Shutting the front door, Wynter whirled on Delilah. "You did it again? Seriously? I told you not to sell any more of those damn potions."

Delilah frowned. "Can I help it that karma chooses to flow through me to do its work?"

Wynter snorted. "Karma hasn't chosen you to do *shit*. This has nothing to do with balancing the scales of justice—"

"It is *absolutely* about justice. My family follows the teachings of Annis. I know you don't think much of her because of some of her . . . darker deeds, but she was strong and powerful and ballsy and beautiful."

Anabel frowned. "Didn't she have one eye, crooked teeth, and bluish skin?"

Delilah stared at the blonde for a long moment. "Beautiful on the *inside*."

Wynter scrubbed a hand down her face. "Look, I understand that you want to respect and honor the teachings of your ancestors—I don't like it, given one of them ate children, but I get it. However, what you're doing isn't okay, Del."

"You can't tell me that dude didn't deserve what happened to him. He talked like destiny had short-changed him by giving him a mate that wasn't very feminine."

"Which makes him an asshole, sure," Wynter allowed. "But he's an asshole who could *kill* you—that's my issue. Dragons can exhale fire."

Anabel let out a low whistle. "Wow, talk about death's breath—"

"No, I don't have the patience for your neurosis right now," snapped Del, whipping up her hand.

"I don't *have* a neurosis!"

"That's right. You have *several*."

Wynter swiped a hand through the air. "Both of you stop. Now listen to me, Del. I need you to stop selling those potions here. We're not on the move anymore. We're here to stay, and there are a whole lot of dangerous people in this place. Stop tempting them to kill you. God, between you and Xavier, it'll be a sheer miracle if our crew isn't wiped out at some point."

"Not crew, co—"

"And I'm done." Wynter went up to her room, packed an overnight bag, and then returned downstairs. "I'm heading out. Try not to do anything stupid while I'm gone."

Delilah saluted her. "Sure thing, Priestess."

"Don't do that."

"Cain must *rock* in bed for you to stay with him every night." Delilah grinned. "I'll bet he fucks like an animal. I'm right, aren't I? Come on, Wyn, be a sweetie and give us some details."

"Like I've told you before, you'll just have to use your imagination. Now I'm going. Behave. All of you."

Delilah blew her a kiss. "Later, Priestess."

"Stop it."

*

Gathered in Cain's ledger room, he and the other Ancients spent hours discussing battle plans, bouncing ideas back and forth until they finally settled on a particular course of action. It would involve every resident of Devil's Cradle. Most would be part of the battle. Others would be responsible for guarding the elevator that descended to the underground city in the unlikely event that any invaders managed to enter the mansion.

If the Aeons had the ability to collapse the town and crush the city below it, they would definitely do so. But the land above and below was too well-protected by power, just as Aeon itself was. As such, the Aeons would likely order their troops to do the next best thing—overrun the town like ants, search for the entrance to the city, and destroy both.

They'd fail.

The Ancients would make sure of it.

"We each need to pass on our plans to those in our service, ensuring they all know in advance exactly where they need to be and what they need to be doing when the Aeons finally make their move," said Cain.

He planned to convince Wynter to stay in the city and guard the lowest level of the elevator. How, he wasn't yet sure. His witch was a warrior right down to the bone.

Seth nodded. "We should not delay in that. The Aeons could strike at any time."

Ishtar sniffed. "I hope they do it soon. I tire of waiting."

Dantalion leaned back in his seat. "I predict that a great many of their troops will be mercenaries. After all, the Aeons will need to feel sure that they have large enough numbers to take on our population, but they're hardly likely to risk a large number of their *own* population even if they are certain of success."

"I agree." Azazel folded his arms. "More and more people in our service are arriving. They're prepared to fight alongside us, even if they don't much like it."

That was the thing about selling your soul. If the Ancient who owned it called on you for anything, you had no choice but to obey. But that wasn't something that the Ancients advertised, and any in their service were ordered to keep it quiet. As such, the Aeons wouldn't be prepared for outsiders to come and join the battle.

The Ancients hadn't called on *all* their people. Why? When they won the war—and they would—some invaders would scuttle back to Aeon with tales of what happened. The Ancients didn't want their enemies to know just how large a force they could build, or the Aeons who came to avenge the dead would bring an army big enough to overwhelm them.

"The healers need to be placed sporadically around the town during the battle," said Inanna. "They will not be asked to be fight, they can remain hidden, but they will need to be of help to any injured residents."

"Where will your new pet witch be?" Ishtar asked Cain. "Tucked up somewhere safe, I suppose." She tittered.

Unwilling to grant her the angry reaction she hoped for, Cain merely gave her a blank look and said, "You don't need to know my plans for Wynter. She's not your concern."

Ishtar stiffened. "On the contrary, she is the concern of every person in this room."

Inanna sighed at her sister. "Let us not do this."

"Do what?" Ishtar shrugged one shoulder, all innocence. "I asked a simple question."

Cain fired her a bored glance. "You asked a question you knew I wouldn't answer, and you did it so you'd have an excuse to whine and moan and complain."

Seth offered him a look of commiseration. "I suspect she's still sulking over what you said to her at my Keep."

"I am *not* sulking or whining or anything else," Ishtar upheld.

Lilith lifted her hands. "Can we please stop arguing amongst ourselves? It's not unusual at meetings, no, but any conflict between us right now is a weakness we can't afford."

Ishtar sniffed. "I am merely curious as to where Cain intends to place the witch."

"There's no reason for you to know where Wynter will be," he said.

"Oh, I see. You think I will send someone to kill her." Ishtar lifted her chin. "I prefer to do my own dirty work, as you well know. But I can understand why you would nonetheless take precautions. As I pointed out the other day, mortals are so very fragile. You will need to constantly take measures to ensure she is safe from the dangers of the world. I would personally find it both boring and tiring. It would be like supervising a child."

Cain only stared at her, keeping his expression blank.

Her mouth tightened in annoyance. "I wonder . . . has it occurred to you that she might have wangled her way into your bed so that you would protect her this way? In your position, I would have to ask myself if she was in fact using me. Even someone like you can be played. Just ask Azazel. Not even he was exempt from that."

Azazel's eyes flared. "Don't go there, Ishtar," he warned, his tone dark. "Not unless you want me to strike back."

"So sensitive," she mocked. "And there is nothing for you to strike back with in this matter. No man has ever played me."

"Sure they have," said Azazel, a cruel smirk touching his mouth. "They do it all the time. You think men *really* want to shower you with the unreasonable amount of attention they give you? You think it's pure adoration that makes them go that far? No, it's that they know you need that from them. They're doing what they have to do to worm their way into your bed. They simply want to get laid. That's why the attention eases off over time, Ishtar. Once they've had their fun, they cease making an effort."

Predictably, she lashed out with a small blast of pure power. Azazel sidestepped it easily with a snicker, the door behind him unexpectedly opened ... and the power wacked the person in the doorway.

Cain watched as Wynter sucked in a pained breath when the power punched into her body, roughly arching her spine until it cracked, and causing fine fractures to spiderweb across her flesh. Her mouth opened in a silent scream, every muscle tensing, every vein cording ... and then she collapsed to the floor. She lay there, her eyes open, unseeing. Vacant. Lifeless.

Behind her, Maxim leaned over her and touched her pulse. Swallowing, he looked up at Cain and shook his head.

Shock gripped Cain by the throat, scattering his thoughts, leaving him unable to process what had just happened. But then the monster inside him reared up in a blinding rage, driving the shock from his mind. Reality slammed into him like a fist to his gut and—that fast—a savage, explosive fury whipped through him, pulling his lips back in a snarl.

Blanching, Ishtar stared at him, shaking her head. "Cain, I didn't mean it. I didn't know she was here. I didn't kill her on purpose, I swear."

Inanna stepped in front of her sister. "It was an accident, Cain. The blast wasn't meant for the witch."

No, it wasn't. And yes, Ishtar had aimed for Azazel—who'd have no more than flinched at the impact. But the bitch was *gloating*. Cain could sense it. So could his monster, who wanted *out*, wanted to kill. Cain's skin rippled as the change began to—

"Ow," muttered Wynter.

He slammed his gaze on her, shock once more stealing his breath as she awkwardly sat upright. His monster stilled, not understanding what it was they were seeing.

At her side, Maxim gawked at her, looking lost.

Wynter's gaze went straight to Ishtar and narrowed dangerously. But that wasn't what made Cain's stomach drop. It was the black trails that began to slink over her eyeballs.

Wynter blinked rapidly and took a deep centering breath. And another. And another. Finally, the black ribbons gone from her eyes, she shot Ishtar a put-out look while pushing to her feet. "Well, that was uncalled for."

Cain could only stare at her. He might have wondered if Maxim had been wrong; if he'd mistakenly missed that her pulse was still beating. But the mark that had appeared on the side of her face told him a different story. It was one he'd recognize fucking anywhere. A metallic blue snake in the shape of an S, its mouth open wide near the corner of her eye.

The mark of Kali.

If the deity felt that the death of a witch was an injustice, Kali occasionally sent the witch back long enough to get their revenge. To aid them with that, She placed the soul of one of Her many netherworld creatures *inside* the witch's body—together, the two wreaked vengeance on those who'd caused the injustice.

Cain slowly crossed to Wynter, so many things now making sense. And yet, *nothing* made sense. Not really.

She met his gaze as steadily as always—no uncertainty, no nerves, no sheepishness despite the situation. Cain couldn't help but admire that.

He slanted his head. "How? How can you be . . . you? Revenants aren't even really people."

They didn't sleep. They weren't sane. They didn't have a heartbeat. They were literally undead witches that acted as a temporary vessel for something monstrous. Wynter might have an undead soul, but her body wasn't a walking corpse.

Lilith looked from Wynter to Cain. "You knew nothing of this?" she asked him.

"No." And he hated that he'd made the discovery *this way*. That it hadn't been a case of Wynter trusting him with her secret. That he'd had to watch her fucking die. "When did Kali make you a revenant?"

"When I was ten," Wynter replied.

"And yet you still live?" Ishtar shook her head, scoffing,

"Impossible. Absolutely impossible."

"Evidently not," said Dantalion, staring at Wynter with renewed interest. "You saw her monster try to surface, Ishtar. We all did."

Cain squinted at Wynter. "So it was Kali who brought you back after those boys killed you."

Wynter nodded.

Seth frowned. "You said your mother brought you back."

Wynter cut her gaze to him. "No, I said she was accused of, and exiled for, bringing me back using forbidden magick. I never said she actually did it."

Thinking back, Cain realized she was right. She'd let them make their own conclusions. And they had, not bothering to question her further.

"It was your monster who eviscerated your murderers," Azazel guessed, to which she nodded. "If your death was avenged, how is it that you're still here? It is only a need for vengeance that tethers a revenant's soul to this realm. After they attain it, both the witch and the monster return to the netherworld."

"All I know is that there's something Kali wants me to do for Her," Wynter told him. "She never said what. Or when. Or anything else. Only that I'd 'one day know.' She's never bothered to expand on that."

Even as Cain heard the ring of truth in Wynter's voice, he couldn't understand how she could be in the dark about so many things. But then, all things considered, it wasn't really all that unbelievable. He'd encountered deities before. They were cryptic beings who were so secretive they made the Ancients seem like open books. They'd think nothing of keeping even one of their Favored ignorant of any facts they didn't wish them to be aware of—and they'd see no real wrong in that.

Seth wandered closer, tracing her mark with his eyes. "How do you hide it? Why would you? And why would Kali allow it?"

"I don't conceal the mark; *She* does," Wynter replied. "And no, before you ask, I have no clue why. She makes it visible occasionally, when it seems to suit whatever purposes She has."

Cain's monster pressed more firmly against his skin, thoroughly enthralled by the mystery of their witch. "I've never seen you eat flesh or drink blood."

"Yeah, I don't do that," she said.

Azazel eyed her curiously. "How can the entity inside you survive without it?"

She shrugged. "I don't know; it just can."

Inanna folded her arms. "Why didn't you tell us what you are?"

"You know why," said Wynter. "You're all at the top of the power food chain. You don't have natural predators. You're not used to having people around you that could be a danger to you. Revenants can kill anything."

Why yes, they could. In truth, they could do many, *many* things—cause diseases, plagues, blight, misfortune, and physical defects but to name a few. They could also curse absolutely anything or anyone.

"That's why no one can fight the curse you placed on Aeon," Dantalion realized. "Does anyone there know what you are?"

Wynter shook her head. "Kali told me I mustn't tell, so I didn't."

Ishtar's eyes narrowed. "She didn't want us to know the truth either?"

"She said She'd reveal to you all that I was one of her Favored *if* She felt it necessary," Wynter told her. "It would appear that She felt it necessary."

"She *talks* to you?" Ishtar asked Wynter, her tone doubtful.

"Sometimes," Wynter replied.

"And what is it that She says to you?"

Wynter's expression shuttered. "Nothing you need to know."

Ishtar's face hardened. "I would have to disagree."

"Disagree all you want. I don't owe you explanations, and I won't give you any."

"You should if you wish to stay here. You cannot expect us to allow you to live among us when we do not fully understand what you are."

Wynter snorted. "That's rich coming from an Ancient. Everyone in Devil's Cradle is expected to accept that there are things we can't know about all of you."

"You are not an Ancient, so that rule does not apply to you. You will tell us what we want to know."

"Enough, Ishtar," Cain cut in, his rage still on a low simmer inside him.

Ishtar sliced her gaze to him. "You cannot tell me you are happy for her to hold back from us. We are due an explanation."

"She *has* explained," he pointed out. "It is not her fault that she does not possess all the answers."

"She knows more than what she says."

"Perhaps. But if Kali has ordered her to keep such things to herself, no amount of pressuring her will achieve anything." Not only would Wynter stand firm out of loyalty, but the deity would interfere as She saw fit. "Other than annoy Kali, that is."

Azazel nodded, staring at Ishtar. "And considering you've pissed Her off enough by killing one of Her Favored, I'd say that bitching at Wynter wouldn't be the best idea."

Ishtar frowned at him. "You are not concerned about what you've learned here?" She searched every face. "It bothers no one here that we have a revenant among us?"

"It was a shock, of course," said Seth. "A huge shock. It is not every day you meet a revenant, and I hadn't thought it was possible for one to be so ... different. But I don't feel a need to be concerned, no. Her being a revenant doesn't change anything. It doesn't negatively impact me. And the situation we have with the Aeons remains the same. It is them I intend to focus on. You should do the same."

"But, as she herself proclaimed, a revenant can kill anything," Ishtar reminded him. "Even us."

"Yes," he allowed, "but just because she *can* hurt us doesn't mean she *intends* to. Wynter is not our enemy."

"You don't know that. The Aeons could have sent her here."

"If she meant to kill us, she would have attempted it already."

"Agreed," Lilith interjected. "Wynter has had plenty of opportunities to end Cain's life, I'm sure, given they sleep in the same bed. Yet, he remains unharmed. She has made no overt moves on the rest of us either."

Ishtar's lips flattened. "You cannot tell me it is fine with you that she insists on being so mysterious."

"I see no need to hold her accountable for not being able to answer our questions," said Lilith. "Whether it's because she has no answers or because Kali forbids her from sharing certain things, the fact of the matter remains the same—it is out of Wynter's hands."

Ishtar's gaze danced from face to face, narrowing as it settled on Azazel. "You are uneasy with this."

Azazel sighed. "I am. I don't like that Kali seems to be working off-script and keeping the whys of that to Herself. But . . . do I care that Wynter's a revenant? No. Do I believe she's here on behalf of the Aeons? No. Do I see the point in getting het up about any of this? No."

Letting out a little growl, Ishtar whirled to face her sister. "Tell me at least *you* have concerns."

Inanna rubbed at her wrist. "I admit, I am not comfortable with how little we understand of Wynter. But it is senseless to hold what she is against her. And if we did that, it would make us too much like the Aeons themselves, who do not like or accept what they struggle to understand."

"Hear, hear," said Dantalion before moving his gaze to Ishtar. "And if your ego wasn't still smarting due to Wynter sharing Cain's bed, you would not stoop to their level. No, don't try claiming that this isn't about your ego. Most everything you do or say is about your ego. Let this moment here and now be an exception. If you would only look at the situation from my point of view, you would see we have reason to be pleased that there is a revenant among us."

"*Pleased?*" Ishtar echoed, her eyes bulging.

"It would seem that Kali has given us a weapon," said Dantalion. "We deserve our revenge, do we not? Nothing delivers vengeance quite like a revenant."

"Wynter isn't a weapon," Cain said to him, his voice hard.

His mouth curving, Dantalion raised his hands in a gesture of peace that had no real sincerity in it.

As it occurred to Cain that Wynter had been remarkably quiet for the past few minutes, he looked at her. Her arms folded, she was idly rocking back and forth on the balls of her feet, the image of bored ... even as that hunter stare tracked every person in the room.

Needing to be alone with her right now, Cain flicked his arm. "Everyone out. Except you," he said to Wynter. "You stay."

Ishtar gaped. "You cannot be serious. You still want her close after all you have just learned?"

His nostrils flaring, Cain stalked toward the bitch, liking the unease that flashed in her eyes. "You should be much nicer to Wynter. It is only the fact that she lives that means *you* live. If her death had been intentional, I would have destroyed you on the spot. Not even Inanna could have saved you."

Inanna gently pulled on her sister's arm. "Let us go. Now, before you do or say anything else that could well get you killed."

One by one, the Ancients filed out of the office.

Pinning Maxim with a look, Cain said, "You will say nothing of what you saw and heard here."

The aide nodded. "Understood, Sire." He gave Wynter a quick dip of the chin and then closed the door, giving her and Cain privacy.

She puffed out a breath. "That could have gone better." She let her arms fall to her sides. "Look, I'll understand if you're a little freaked out by all this. I admit, it's a lot to take in and—"

Cain delved his hands into her hair and pressed his forehead to hers. "I thought you were gone. It all happened so fast. You were fine, and then you weren't. Just like that. It took me a few seconds to process it. That delay in my response is the only reason Ishtar lives. She had struck out at Azazel and hit you accidentally. But that didn't matter to me right then. I couldn't think beyond the fact that you were dead." A revenant. His woman was a revenant. Who kept coming back to life. "Not much about you makes any sense."

"Tell me about it," she muttered.

"You truly don't know what Kali wants you to do for Her?"

"Truly. She didn't even tell me that much until I turned eighteen. Before then, I thought maybe I had a certain amount of lives. Like a cat. Because I came back to life after accidentally drowning when I was fourteen."

"You haven't pushed Kali for answers?"

"I asked Her for clarification once or twice, but She blew me off each time. I haven't bugged Her to tell me because it would only irritate Her. I'd rather not inspire Kali to get Herself a new sort-of-revenant who won't ask questions."

Cain studied her face closely. "There are some things you're not telling me, aren't there?"

"At Her insistence, yes. I have no choice in that."

Fucking deities. "Does your coven know what you are? And no, don't call them a crew."

Wynter rolled her eyes. "They know. They saw my monster in action when I was taken by the same bounty hunters that caught them."

"You freed them, and they chose to stay with you," he guessed.

"Yes. A seemingly bad idea, really. But none of them have a strong sense of self-preservation, which I'm sure has not escaped your notice."

No, it hadn't. "I caught a glimpse of your monster when you woke just now. I wonder what Kali put inside you. Nothing harmless, I'd imagine. Did it kill the keeper who was told to execute you?"

"Yup. I don't know exactly what it did to him, though. It's like I black out whenever the monster takes over. I can only try to piece together what happened."

"Guessing games are no fun." Cain knew that well—he'd been playing them since he first met her. "You've kept many, many things from me, little witch." He pressed a kiss to her throat. And another. And another. He scraped his teeth over her pulse, wanting to feel it beat against his mouth. "Hypocrite though it makes me, I find myself wanting to spank you for it." He palmed her ass and gave it a squeeze.

She blinked. "Are you . . . are you thinking about sex right now?"

He felt his mouth curve. "Do I find it strangely arousing that you could kill me if you so wished? Yes, I do." As did his monster. And they both needed to remind themselves that she was here, alive. "So I'd say it's time that I fucked you."

She gaped at him. "You can't honestly be serious."

"Oh, I'm very serious."

"But . . . you're supposed to be weirded out. Freaked. Put-off by the fact that I'm not even really alive—at least not in a natural way."

Cain almost snorted. She might be a revenant, but he was a *far* worse creature. In any case . . . "Nothing about you could put me off."

Her mouth bopped open and closed. She put her hands to her head. "I have no clue what to say to you right now."

He cupped her jaw. "Did you want me to be 'freaked,' as you put it?"

"Of course not."

"Then all is good." He took her mouth, swallowing anything else she might have said. "Get naked. Now."

Giving him a look that called him crazy, she nonetheless began to strip. "You need help. Like professional help."

"I warned you that you'd one day want to run from me. You told me it wouldn't happen. If you truly believe that there's nothing I could tell you about myself that would make you no longer want me, why can't the same apply to me when it comes to you?"

She stilled, her expression pensive.

"You don't have the same faith in me that you have in yourself?"

"It's not that, it's . . . ugh, you know what? Fine. If you say you're not freaked, I believe you. But I still say you need professional help."

"Noted. Now you're still not naked. Let's fix that."

# Chapter Twenty-Three

Silence fell in the cottage the next morning after Wynter dropped the "Unfortunately, the Ancients now know what I am" bomb on her crew. Sprawled around the living area, they shifted uncomfortably and exchanged glances.

"It goes without saying that this isn't good," said Anabel.

"I had no choice but to come clean. There was no way I could pretend I hadn't just died, or any way for me to hide Kali's mark." Cradling her cup with both hands, Wynter sipped at her tea. "I told myself when we first came here that I'd be able to keep the truth from the Ancients, but I knew deep down that they would likely find out sooner or later."

"I suspected they would too, but I was all for 'later.'" Anabel nervously rubbed at her shoulder. "At least we now know that an Ancient can't *permanently* kill you—I know you worried they could."

"I don't know for certain that they can't. Ishtar's strike wasn't meant to be fatal. It was more like a swat. An Ancient would have no more than winced. I freaking died. If one—or all of them combined—really put their back into it, they might well manage to wipe me out for good."

Hattie flicked her hand. "They'd be fools to harm one of Kali's Favored."

"That Ishtar woman is a *complete* fool," said Delilah. "I can totally see her doing something so stupid."

"Yeah, she's one spiteful little bitch," said Xavier, idly shuffling his tarot cards. He glanced at Wynter. "I'll bet she felt all smug when her power killed you. It meant you were not only dead but that she could cry 'accident.'"

"I think she was more furious that I came back from death than she was that I'm a not a mere witch. Although it will undoubtedly gall her that she can't brand me weak any longer." Wynter took another sip of her tea. "She pounced on my being a revenant, trying to use it to turn the others against me."

"Did it work?" asked Anabel.

"Not with Cain," replied Wynter. "It didn't seem to work with the rest either. They don't like that they have so many unanswered questions, but they don't seem to view me as a potential enemy. Still, I doubt they'll like being around me much."

Anabel nodded. "They don't have an 'edge' around you the way they do others; they can't say and do whatever they like to you with no fear of repercussions because you can actually kill them. They won't be used to that. It'll annoy them, if nothing else."

"They're mostly focused on the upcoming battle with the Aeons. My worry is that when the war has passed and they can give my being a revenant more mental space, they might suddenly share Ishtar's apparent concerns."

"They might," mused Xavier. "But if it looks like they're going to turn on you, we'll go before they have a chance to act on it. At the moment, I don't think there's a risk that they'll attempt to kill you. They need you to lure the Aeons here."

"Not necessarily," said Anabel. "Wynter has already succeeded in luring them here—it won't be long before they make their move. The Ancients don't need her alive at this point. It's not like they'd have to *prove* to the Aeons that she's safe and well."

Xavier pointed a finger at the blonde. "Now that's true. I didn't think of that."

Neither had Wynter. Hence the cold fingertips that trailed down her spine.

He cut his gaze to her. "Now that they know you're a revenant, they'll also know that your life-force isn't tied to the curse. They literally have no real reason to *want* you to live unless of course they don't object to your existence."

"Not true," Hattie objected. "Kali is an excellent deterrent. She would never stand for anyone hurting one of Her Favored. They know that well. I doubt even the Ancients would want to take on a deity. I'm not all that worried—Cain wouldn't allow any of the others to do Wynter harm. He's firmly ensnared."

Wynter frowned. "Ensnared?"

"Hooked. Enthralled. Bewitched." Hattie gave a firm nod. "He'll keep you safe. Or you'll kill him. One or the other. I'm leaning toward the first, though."

"I do agree that Cain wouldn't be party to anything that harmed you," Anabel told Wynter. "I don't know what he feels for you, but I do think he wouldn't turn on you. I also think he'd likely protect you from the other Ancients if necessary. Maybe that will be enough to stay their hands."

Delilah crossed one leg over the other. "We only have that comfort if Cain *truly* took the whole revenant thing as well as he seemed to. Do you think he did, Wyn?"

Considering he'd fucked Wynter on his dining table like he hadn't seen her in decades ... "Yeah, I do. I have no doubt he's a very accomplished liar, considering he's been keeping secrets for most of his life—and he's lived a very, very, *very* long life. But if he'd been creeped out or disgusted by what I am, I would have picked up on it. My monster would have sensed it, too."

Xavier's brows snapped together. "Why would Cain be disgusted?"

"Well, I *am* a revenant."

"But not a typical revenant," said Xavier, setting his tarot cards on the coffee table. "It's not like he's been banging a walking corpse. The only thing about you that's truly undead is your soul, and he already knew about that."

"True, but I'm not *naturally* alive. Kali's power brought me back, and it keeps me here. So it wouldn't have surprised me if he'd been a little freaked. He was more bothered by the fact that I'd died right there in front of him."

"Like I said, he's ensnared," said Hattie. "And I'll bet he's encountered far stranger things in his life than a revenant who's not a regular revenant—it would likely take a lot more than that to spook him. Which is a relief, since he has access to your soul and could cause you some serious pain."

Oh, indeed. Wynter would like to *think* that he would never hurt her, but she liked to think a lot of things. Such as that her crew would start valuing their own safety instead of constantly risking it.

She zeroed in on Hattie. "Speaking of pain . . . are you *sure* your eyes aren't sore? They're seriously bloodshot, and I don't think it's just because of the damn joint you smoked earlier."

Hattie waved away her concern. "They're fine. Really. I was up all night finishing a book, that's all. I couldn't put it down; it was a real page-turner. I wasn't crazy about the dolphin shifters, though." Her face scrunched up in distaste. "Dolphins are nasty creatures."

Delilah blinked. "Nasty?"

Hattie nodded. "They act all sweet and friendly, but they're sociopaths down to their fins."

"Kind of like you, then," said Delilah.

Hattie's brow wrinkled. "I don't have fins."

"But you *are* sociopathic."

"That doesn't make me a socio*path*. I feel empathy. Love. Remorse. I have a conscience."

Delilah arched up a brow. "The same conscience that saw no reason why you shouldn't kill any of your husbands?"

"They were crimes of passion."

"They were incidences of premeditated murder."

"Their *betrayals* were premeditated. They had full-blown affairs, every one of them." Hattie put a hand to her chest. "Broke my heart, they did."

"You know, most women in that situation just get divorced."

"I don't believe in divorce, it's a sin."

Delilah shook her head and mouthed, "Wow." She pushed to her feet. "And on that note, we'd better moving. We have a shop to open."

The day was both as busy and as normal as any other day. So it took Wynter by surprise when Cain strolled into her bedroom that evening while she was packing her duffel for yet another night at his Keep. He'd only ever turned up at the cottage once before, and that had been to find out why she was late. A quick look at her quirky wall-clock told her she wasn't running late tonight.

"Oh, hey."

"Such a gushing reception," he teased as he crossed to her, calm and predatory and far too sexy for her damn liking.

She snorted. "I'm not one to gush."

"Yes, I've noticed." He planted a soft kiss on her mouth and swept his hands up her arms. "I was passing your street. I decided to stop by."

She narrowed her eyes, skeptical. He never simply *stopped by*. And, considering how busy he was, she wouldn't have expected him to ever take the time to do so.

A sneaking suspicion slithered through her mind. "You came here to check that I wasn't packing all my stuff to hightail it out of Devil's Cradle, didn't you?"

After a brief moment, he inclined his head. "It occurred to me that you might prefer to leave now that your secret has been exposed to myself and the other Ancients." He twirled a strand of her hair around his finger. "Of course, I would have had to stop you."

Wynter fought a smile. He wouldn't find it so easy to detain her, but she'd let him think otherwise. "If I snuck off like that, I would have been leaving partial rights to my soul behind."

"You wouldn't be the first. People have done such a thing before. Mostly if they broke a rule and didn't wish to be held responsible for it. In fact, Bowen and Annette left without notice only recently—Azazel and I suspect they might have committed some crime. You've not noticed their absence?" Whatever he saw on her face made him squint. "What is it?" he asked.

Damn, this news probably wouldn't wash down well. "They didn't actually leave willingly." Far from it. "See, Annette killed me," she blurted out.

His brows snapped together. "Excuse me?"

"She came to the shed where I work and skewered me from behind with a sword."

His eyes flared, and his mouth set into a hard line. "Did she now? When?"

"Not long after you killed her father. Bowen rushed in, saw what happened, and talked of covering for her and ... well, I didn't like it much. So when I woke up, I dealt with them."

"I can still feel her soul; she's not dead."

"No, I, uh ..." Wynter rubbed at her earlobe. "I kind of stuck them in the netherworld."

Taking a moment to digest those words, Cain did a slow blink. His creature stilled, surprised. "The ... the netherworld?"

"I didn't know where else to put them," she burst out in her defense. "I couldn't kill them for obvious reasons. But they'd seen me rise from the dead, and I couldn't risk that they'd go blabbing about it. They're not exactly trustworthy people, and they wouldn't have done me any favors."

For long moments, Cain could only stare at her. His woman never failed to take him off-guard. Never. "How, exactly, did you put them in the netherworld?"

"I've been able to open a portal to it ever since I first became a revenant. I don't know if it comes with the revenant package or it's simply because my soul is undead and so I therefore have a connection to it."

Of all the scenarios he'd considered when he tried making sense of why he couldn't properly touch Annette's soul, this hadn't been one of them. His monster was thoroughly impressed by Wynter's ability. Cain, however, didn't like the thought of her having any such connection to a separate realm—it felt too much like she wasn't fully in *this* realm. "You made it look like she'd left?"

"It wasn't hard. She'd already packed up her stuff and stashed it in a car she'd parked outside of the town's boundary. It was just a matter of moving said car so it looked as if she headed off somewhere." Wynter bit her lip. "You mad?"

"At you for what you did to protect your secrets? No. Particularly since Annette took it upon herself to end your life, forfeiting her own. But I *am* angry. Angry that she dared put her hands on you. Angry that I didn't foresee she'd do such a thing. Angry that I'm only learning of it now." He didn't bother asking Wynter why she hadn't told him before today—the answer was obvious. "I will explain to Azazel about Bowen. He will understand; there'll be no reprisals."

"Bowen was one of his aides," she reminded him.

"Not a prized one. In any case, Azazel wouldn't punish you for protecting yourself. That was all you really did. And I wouldn't dare allow it if he tried, so there's that. Can you bring both berserkers back out of the netherworld?"

"Only if they haven't died there. A soul can't, obviously, but a living being can. I can go look, but it might not be so easy to find them—"

"Then leave them where they are." Cain didn't want her roaming around that realm when he'd have no way of getting to her if need be. He didn't trust that Kali wouldn't decide to keep Her there. "I would only seek to punish them anyway. They'll suffer plenty in their present location." He'd heard enough about the netherworld to know that there was nothing pleasant about it. "Are any other residents roaming there?"

"Nope, just them."

"You certainly keep things interesting, little witch. Just full of surprises, aren't you?" He cocked his head. "Did anyone at Aeon ever discover your secrets and find themselves subsequently dumped in the netherworld?"

"Only one. Nobody suspected I had anything to do with his 'disappearance,' thankfully. Being an absolute asshole who regularly beat up women, he had a whole host of enemies. It was believed that a relative of one of those women probably killed him. The investigation into his death went nowhere, though. The Aeons didn't pursue the matter. They don't care much what happens to the mortals there."

"What did he do to earn that fate?"

"He stumbled upon me covered in blood and gore after I let my monster chomp down some dude who tried raping me."

Cain felt his jaw harden as rage shot through him. "I see."

"No one ever traced that death back to me. The guy who tried raping me was actually a keeper. Aeon . . . it's not like here. You and the other Ancients all run a tight ship. Although there are plenty of rules at Aeon and a high number of keepers to enforce them, the Aeons themselves don't keep a close watch over 'mortal matters.' They don't oversee the activities of the keepers or make sure justice is always served. The keepers exploit that and get up to all sorts of shit, confident there'll be no repercussions."

"So our source often says."

Her brows lifted. "You have a spy there?"

"There isn't much he's able to tell us, since he has no access to the underground city, but he occasionally passes on helpful information."

"That's how you knew about the blight."

"Yes. I didn't believe it at first, or that people there could possibly be falling sick. But our source was adamant. And, according to Azazel, very afraid."

She twisted her mouth. "How come you need a source? You once said you have ways of getting glimpses of the world outside of Devil's Cradle. Can you not spy on Aeon that way?"

"No. The town is shielded from view by the Aeons' power, hence why it's never been detected by human satellites. It's just as shielded from preternatural surveillance. Devil's Cradle is similarly shielded by myself and the other Ancients."

"Speaking of the Aeons . . . you never told me what Lailah offered to give you in exchange for my life."

"You didn't ask."

"I didn't want to ask too many questions because it might have prompted you to do the same, and there was a lot that I wasn't ready to tell you back then."

He nodded, understanding, since he'd been in exactly the same boat. He still was, really. There was so much he could never tell her if he truly meant to keep her.

"But you know one of my secrets now," she went on. "That doesn't mean you owe it to me to tell me any of your own, but I was hoping you could at least tell me this."

Cain toyed with the ends of her hair. "Lailah offered to hand over Eve."

"Your mother? She's a captive at Aeon?"

"In a sense. She lives in comfort and is able to go about her daily life, but she has many restrictions and wouldn't be permitted to leave. As they say, a gilded cage is still a cage." Cain tensed when Wynter pressed herself against him, giving him a comfort that was as foreign to him as the offer of it. Forcing his muscles to relax, he curved his arms around her.

"Were you close to Eve?" she asked.

"No. I didn't have much of a relationship with her, but that was neither her fault nor mine. It is a very long story," he quickly added when he sensed she'd question him further on it. "One I will share with you some time. But not now."

Wynter looked like she might press him, but then she dipped her chin. "Okay. If she's a captive of sorts, is it because she sided with you in the war or something?"

"No. Eve's gilded cage was created long before then. Unlike the other Aeons, she didn't betray me or the other Ancients. She chose to stay neutral, all the while hoping everyone on both sides of the war would throw down their swords and wave a white flag."

"Out of optimism or naïvety?"

"The latter, mostly."

Wynter nibbled on her lower lip. "I guess I can understand why Lailah would think you'd jump at her offer."

"I will personally retrieve Eve once I'm free, providing she wishes to come here. Given that Aeon is wasting away, I'll be surprised if she doesn't."

"So this is what Ishtar meant when she said that the Aeons had something you want."

"Yes. But I don't believe that Ishtar truly thought I'd give you up to them in exchange for my mother or anything else. I think she simply wanted *you* to believe it might happen. Sowing seeds of distrust is a favorite game of hers."

"I have to say, I struggle to understand what it is about Ishtar that once appealed to you. Yeah, okay, she's beautiful. But she's also a pain in the ass."

He pursed his lips. "She didn't used to be so petty and vindictive. Those qualities crept up on her during our imprisonment. But she was always a person who needed to be the dominant figure in a relationship. I was never going to be a submissive partner. In that sense, we were each a challenge for the other. Challenges give you a reprieve from boredom."

Wynter sniffed. "I guess."

Cain bit back a smile at the slight note of jealousy in her voice. He didn't think his little witch would appreciate that he liked it. "I didn't care for her. She didn't care for me either."

"You sure about the latter? Because she seems intent on snagging you."

"Ishtar has a habit of wanting what she can't have. She pursues it because to actually obtain it would shine her ego and make her feel empowered."

"And a part of her doesn't like others playing with her old toys."

"There's a little of that, too." Cain stroked a hand over her sleek, dark hair. "She's no threat to what you and I have, Wynter. She never held even the slightest bit of appeal to me that you do."

"Did you put one of those barrier things inside her?"

He shook his head, watching as some of the starch slipped from his witch's shoulders. Once upon a time, his monster had wanted

Ishtar plugged, but it hadn't pushed Cain to do it, just as it hadn't attempted to take the matter into its own hands. And Ishtar had hated that his creature showed no real possessiveness toward her.

"You know, you said this barrier you put in me would fade. It hasn't."

He smiled. "And how would you know? Tried pleasuring yourself again, did you?"

She narrowed her eyes. "Actually, no, I simply decided to check. You thoroughly see to my needs, which means I don't have to do it myself nowadays."

"I intend to see to them again once we get to my Keep. Or . . . perhaps I could do that right here before we—" He cut off as a crash came from above them that was quickly followed by muffled feminine oaths. "What was that?"

"*Anabel, tell me you're not testing shit on yourself again!*" Xavier yelled from downstairs.

"*I knocked over a lamp, that's all!*" the blonde shouted.

"*You don't* have *a lamp!*"

Another crash, another female curse.

"*Dammit, Anabel, don't make me come up there!*"

"*Try it and I'll* fry *you!*"

Both continued to bicker loudly until a monstrous wild-cat roar split the air.

"*Christ Almighty, can a woman not read in peace?*" griped Hattie from the neighboring room.

Wynter swiped a hand down her face. "No, I'd rather we just head to your Keep now. I don't think you need to ask why."

He felt his mouth quirk. "No, I definitely don't."

# Chapter Twenty-Four

"It really is a *horrible* way to die, I'm telling you," said Anabel as she wiped down the kitchen table the following evening. "One of my worst and most traumatic experiences for sure. I still have nightmares about it."

Delilah paused in sweeping the kitchen floor. "What did you do to upset him so much?"

Anabel did a double-take. "What?"

"You must have done *something*. What was it? Did you insult him? Tease him? Criticize him? Flip him off?"

"He was a shark, Del. I really don't think any of those things would have bothered him all that much."

"They don't just savage people like that for no reason."

"Well, *I* didn't do anything wrong." Anabel scrubbed the table a little harder than necessary. "I was surfing, minding my own business."

"Likely story."

"It's not a story, it's the truth."

"Maybe he was rabid," suggested Hattie, drying the plate Wynter had just washed. "That disease can make an animal *crazy.*"

Wynter felt her nose wrinkle. "I don't think sharks can catch rabies."

"Wynter's right, they can't," said Xavier, taking the dry plate from Hattie and putting it away in the cupboard. "It's a mammalian disease."

Delilah looked at Anabel. "Then we're back to you provoking the shark."

"I did *not* provoke him," the blonde insisted. "I can't

315

believe you're blaming me *for my own death*. Where's the compassion? Where's the sympathy? Where's the distress you're supposed to feel?"

"Why would I be distressed?" Delilah went back to sweeping. "I didn't know you back then. You were a whole different person."

Hattie glanced at Anabel. "This does explain why you wouldn't watch *Jaws* with us at one of the motels we stayed it."

Anabel jutted out her chin. "The flashbacks are painful, all right? I see no need to worsen it for myself by—*stop it, Del, you're not funny!*"

But Delilah kept on humming the *Jaws* theme tune.

Wynter tossed the woman a look. "Leave her be."

"I just wanna know what she did to the shark," said Delilah.

Anabel slapped the cloth on the table. "I didn't do anything!"

Xavier put away yet another plate. "Relax, *I* believe you. Now if you were Del, I'd have a different opinion, because she's a fucking shit stirrer who could rile up even a nun. A shark would be no problem for her. She'd welcome the challenge."

Delilah glanced at him. "Coming from a fellow shit stirrer, that was an excellent compliment."

Anabel scowled at her. "He wasn't complimenting you; he was pointing out that you're wacked."

"Aw, don't be jealous that he likes me better. *Everyone* likes me better." Delilah shrugged. "You're just too neurotic for most people's tastes, sweetie. But don't beat yourself up about it; it's not your fault. Actually, scrap that, it's totally your fault, since you insist on using yourself as a test trial subject. I'm curious, did you do that during every life you led? Because it would explain a few things. Like why you'd stupidly taunt a shark."

"*I did not taunt him.*"

"Yeah, yeah."

Hattie cut in, "How old were you when it happened, Anabel?"

"Eighteen." The blonde sighed. "I always die young, and I always die hard. My hope is that I'll one day live to be a ripe old age but, given our present circumstances, I don't believe that'll happen in this lifetime."

Delilah gave her a soft smile. "We'll miss you when you're gone, if that helps."

Anabel fired her a glare. "It doesn't."

"Stop giving me hate eyes. You adore me really."

A snort. "What's there to adore?"

"Ooh, now that was bitchy. Is this how you behaved toward that poor shark?"

Anabel lunged at Delilah, but Xavier slid between them and ushered the blonde backwards as she growled, *"Just let me kill her, no one will care."*

Wynter arched a brow at a grinning Delilah. "This makes you happy? Really?"

"Really," Delilah confirmed.

God, the woman was a trial. "There are so many things wrong with you I don't know where to begin."

"Yeah, I hear that often," said Delilah, sounding awful smug about it.

Done washing the dishes, Wynter wiped her hands on a kitchen towel. "Apologize to Anabel."

Rolling her eyes, Delilah turned to the blonde. "I'm sorry I hurt your feelings."

Anabel set her fists on her hips. "Are you actually sorry, though? Ever? About anything?"

"It's rare, but it happens," said Delilah. "An empty apology still has meaning, though, right?"

"No," barked Anabel. "No, it really doesn't."

"Why not? It's the thought that counts. Isn't that how the saying goes?"

Wynter groaned. "I swear, you two could argue about anything. Like *literally* anything."

Anabel frowned. "We're not *that* bad."

"You both fought over a cushion this morning. *A cushion.*"

It had been exhausting watching them quibble like children. "There are two other fucking identical cushions in the same damn room."

"Well, I had it first," claimed Delilah ... which Anabel quickly denied, and so they began to argue yet again.

Wynter was about to break it up, but then an alarm began blaring loudly from outside. Everyone went quiet.

She'd been warned about the potential of an alarm going off sometime soon. According to Cain, there were plenty of scouts roaming the border to keep a lookout for the Aeons. Apparently, they were finally here. Or, at the very least, they were heading in the direction of the town.

Her gut rolling, Wynter swept her gaze along her crew, taking in their now-grim expressions. "You all sure you want to be part of this?"

"We're sure," said Anabel.

"There's no way you're going into any kind of battle without us," Delilah declared.

Xavier nodded. "We went over this earlier."

"Three times," Hattie chipped in.

Wynter raised her hands. "I was just checking."

"Are you planning to release your monster at any point?" Delilah asked her.

Wynter shook her head. "No. It doesn't distinguish friend from foe, and it wouldn't stay with you four to fight at your side. I'm not down with that. We're a team."

"We're a coven," Delilah corrected. "The *Bloodrose* coven. And you're our—"

"Don't make me hurt you right now."

"So touchy."

"Whatever. Now let's get moving."

\*

318

No sooner had Cain heard the alarm than he and the other Ancients, as pre-agreed, met in the manor's large foyer as they waited for Maxim to appear and relay the scouts' report. Around them, townspeople made their way to the exit, but no one stopped to ask anyone for guidance. They didn't need to. The aides had already relayed the Ancients' plans well in advance, so everyone knew what they should be doing and where they were supposed to be.

It took no longer than a minute for Maxim to appear at Cain's side, his face solemn.

Cain flicked a brow. "Well?"

"A very large army was teleported to a spot just beyond the southern end of the prairie land," replied Maxim. "It took several teleportation trips before all the troops were gathered. Enough troops to successfully take us out. They are on their way here, led by a small party. A woman appears to be fronting it." He rattled off a description of her.

"Lailah," said Cain.

"Being as misogynistic as they are, neither Adam nor Abel would allow her to lead them, so I think we can safely say that they aren't here." Dantalion sighed. "Unfortunate."

"Saul will probably be with her," said Seth. "He would have no problem following her lead. He's done it in the past." Seth cut his gaze to Maxim. "They're approaching from the southern side, you said?"

The aide dipped his chin. "It would seem that they don't intend to use the tunnel to enter the town, given that it's located on the opposite side."

"They would know that we will have people guarding the tunnel to make it difficult for them to invade the town," Seth pointed out. "The only other way to enter would be to clamber over the cliffs, which we suspected they might."

"We shall soon see if we were also right in suspecting that the Aeons will attack us from a distance rather than invade the town with their troops," said Dantalion.

"I will be sincerely surprised if they use a different tactic," said Cain. Lailah would be sure of her success, but she wouldn't give the Ancients even the slightest edge. If she remained beyond the border of the prison, it would prevent the Ancients from physically getting to the Aeons.

"I suppose we had better gather on the roof and wait for the army to appear," said Lilith.

The others murmured their agreement and followed her along the hallway. Cain lingered, needing to see Wynter one last time before the battle began. He didn't question the impulse. Didn't care to.

It wasn't long before he spotted her and her coven were making their way to the exit. All looked serious and battle-ready, even Hattie ... who now moved with grace and purpose as opposed to awkwardly shuffling forward the way she usually did. Not that he hadn't sensed that the 'bad back' routine was anything other than a farce.

Everything in him, including his monster, wanted to send Wynter back down below. If he'd thought it would get him anywhere, he would have done. But he'd already tried convincing her to remain underground after fucking them both raw last night. The conversation had gotten him nowhere. She'd calmly argued her right to be present for the battle and, essentially, talked him in circles.

He knew she'd be an asset. He couldn't deny that the strategies she suggested made sense. But although she was far more powerful than he ever could have imagined, it didn't make him feel any better about the fact that she'd be on the battlefield. She had a habit of rising from the dead, yes, but—despite how Kali seemingly had some purpose for Wynter—there was no guarantee she would always return from death.

He'd eventually relented as he knew that she'd fight with or without his blessing. And since Kali would likely free her if he attempted to keep her contained, that option was out. At least this way he would know exactly where she'd be at all times since, between the two of them, they'd agreed on the best place for her and her coven to situate themselves throughout the battle.

When she stopped before him, Cain collared her throat and kissed her hard, uncaring of their audience. "Stay alive. If you do die, make sure you come back to me."

She nodded, a battle-thirsty spark in her eyes that called to the creature inside him and made it want to bite her. "Be careful," she said, squeezing his upper arm. "And kill any Aeons extra hard for me."

That he'd be happy to do.

He gave Maxim a look that reminded him to stay close to her at all times. The aide nodded, his expression grave. Satisfied, Cain headed upstairs and ascended the staircase that led to the rooftop terrace. The cool evening breeze fanned over his skin. Thick, inky black clouds that carried a hint of purple blanketed the sky.

The other Ancients were spread out, facing the southern cliff, waiting for their enemies to arrive. Given that the manor was the tallest building they had, it made sense to plant themselves there.

Cain moved to stand between Azazel and Seth as he took in the scene below. The townspeople were swiftly moving into position. Some would stand in full view of the invaders. Others would remain hidden until the moment came when they needed to spring.

Wynter, her coven, and Maxim soon joined the rest of the aides and positioned themselves in front of the manor. One of the reasons Cain had agreed for her to act as the Ancients' line of defense was that she would then be where he could see her at all times. From this angle, he could glimpse the side of her face—she looked focused, determined, ready. Her mark wasn't visible, and he couldn't understand why Kali would hide it.

It was a shame that Kali wouldn't involve herself more fully to protect Wynter. 'Upgrading' people in this realm and occasionally guiding them was about as involved as a deity got, even when it came to their Favored.

By the time a scout signaled that the Aeons were close, the movement below had come to a stop. Everyone was ready.

Cain flexed his fingers, welcoming the feel of the adrenaline pumping through his veins. Anticipation was a live wire inside him. An anticipation his monster shared.

So long. They had waited so long for this battle. *Too* long.

He spared a glance at the other Ancients, sensing that they were equally amped up. Killing Lailah wouldn't be enough to take down the invisible cage that held them—all four of its creators would need to die for that to happen. But ending the life of at least one of the fuckers would be a joy all on its own. More, it would be enough to draw the other ruling Aeons here.

Soon, people began to plant themselves on the top of the cliff opposite. Cain recognized the first row of people as Aeons. Most were from the second and third generations, and all had partaken in the original war. They were also evidently being used as shields for Lailah and Saul, because the siblings came up behind them along with other Aeons.

"There's got to be, what, a dozen Aeons over there?" asked Azazel, a note of eagerness in his voice that said he was relishing the thought of obliterating them all.

"It appears so," replied Cain. "The scout told Maxim that the number of troops was large enough to take on our population, but it doesn't seem that large. Perhaps some have been told to situate themselves out of sight."

"Perhaps," said Dantalion. "How good of Lailah to bring along her brother. We now get to kill two of the ruling Aeons."

"Just as we expected, they are being careful not to cross the boundary and mean to attack us from outside our prison," commented Inanna. "How very brave and noble."

Lilith sniffed. "I'm rather insulted that they would send such a small force of Aeons."

It truly *was* a small force. Of course, so many Aeons against seven Ancients probably seemed like a hopeless situation to others. But there was a reason that the Aeons had had to cheat in order to defeat Cain and his people a millennia ago—the Aeons weren't as powerful. Which was something they'd always resented.

322

"You forget, Lilith, that they thought we'd weaken over time," said Dantalion.

"And they were wrong," said Ishtar. "Well, shall we get this party started or what?"

Battle adrenaline pumping through his blood, Cain used power to amplify his voice as he addressed the intruders. "You should not have come here."

There was a slight shift in the crowd on the cliff, and then ... "If you had not given us cause to do so, we would not have," said Lailah, lifting her chin. "We would have left you in peace. You brought this on yourselves."

"Do you never tire of pinning the blame for your actions on us?" asked Cain.

Azazel flicked him a look. "I'm thinking, no, they don't."

Lailah slid her gaze to him. "I have no idea why you're smiling, Azazel, but I shall enjoy wiping that smile from your face. Of course, it does not need to come to that. I will give you all one last chance to surrender the witch to us. Do it now."

As if she would genuinely walk away after hauling her ass all the way here. Lailah had come for a war. And she'd get one.

"Wynter stays with us," said Cain.

A troop hurried to Saul's side and spoke into his ear while pointing directly at Wynter. *Motherfucker.*

Saul grinned. "I see her, sister. She's directly in front of the manor."

Cain's gut clenched. He'd known that Wynter would be easily spotted from her position, but he still didn't like her being the focus of the Aeons. His creature rumbled an uneasy sound.

Lailah skimmed her gaze along the people in front of the manor and then finally settled it on Wynter. She smiled. "Ah, there you are. You and your dark magick have caused us much trouble, young witch. Perhaps you think it was clever of you to seek refuge here. You would be wrong. Because now all the people down there with you will be forced to fight to defend themselves and their home. Some will even die. Most will, I expect. That will be on you. *But*... such deaths can be prevented if you give yourself up now."

"No one here will buy that you will trot along back to Aeon without a fight if you're given what it is you seek," Cain said to Lailah.

The female Ancient shot him a glare. "We *will* take her, Cain. If it means killing you and the other Ancients first, so be it." Her gaze dropped back to Wynter, her mouth stretching into a taunting smile. "We do have one thing to thank you for, witch. All these lovely runes on many of our troops' weapons. How fitting that your own magick will be used against you and your people here."

A derisive snicker came from who might have been Xavier.

Faint flashes of red light came from several of the swords being held by the troops on the cliff. No, Cain, realized ... the *runes* had flashed red. And the people holding those weapons seemed to have no fucking clue why.

Cain glanced at Wynter just in time to see a smirk curve her mouth as she stared at Lailah.

Seth leaned toward him. "Did Wynter just ... deactivate the runes on those blades?"

"I think she did," said Cain. "She must have a failsafe in place so that no one can use her own enchantments against her."

"Do you think she'd planned for a day when her own people would turn their weapons on her like this?" asked Azazel.

"Maybe." One thing was for certain: His woman was full of surprises. And as Kali's mark gleamed to life on her face, he switched his gaze back to the intruders.

Lailah's lips parted. Saul went stiff as a board. The other Aeons and their troops shifted nervously.

"Are you sure you wish to tangle with one of Kali's Favored?" Lilith called out.

Lailah barked a laugh. "You cannot believe we would think that mark is real. I have seen revenants in my time. Wynter is no revenant." She swept her gaze along the line of Ancients. "No agreement can be reached here today, I am assuming?"

None of the Ancients replied.

"Then you leave us no choice," said Lailah, her voice grave.

Beside her, Saul gave some sort of signal, and their troops drew their weapons.

"If our town must fall, so will yours." She lifted her hands, and the water in the river rose high in a wave. A wave she sent rushing toward the manor.

\*

Wynter felt her entire face go slack as the river—the actual motherfucking river—sailed through the air. "Holy mother of God."

Xavier gaped. "What in the . . ."

Half turning to glance at the Ancients and hoping they did *something*, Wynter automatically tensed, bracing herself to get slammed by the gulf of water.

Power blasted out of Cain's hand and collided with the wave. The water disintegrated into mist that morphed and . . . buzzed? Then it was a massive swarm of locusts, and those locusts zoomed at the people on the cliff.

Perched on Wynter's shoulder as a crow, Hattie squawked in alarm.

"Yeah, no shit," said Xavier.

The swarm practically fucking *engulfed* the Aeons and their troops. People cried out and stumbled around. Hell, some even went tumbling off the cliff.

"Well, now," said Anabel/Mary, seemingly impressed.

Power lit the air directly above the swarm and cracked like a whip, causing it to disperse.

Her flushed face a mask of sheer unadulterated fury, Lailah struck with a bolt of lightning that zipped toward the Ancients.

Seth briskly repelled her strike . . . and then the two camps of immortals officially went to blows. Power traveled back and forth

325

in whips, blasts, winds, flames, and waves. Power so intense and potent that it charged the air like static.

"Damn," Wynter murmured in awe, resting a hand on the head of the huge monstrous cat that butted her leg in what seemed like a 'Are you seeing this shit?' question.

Someone on the cliff yelled out an order. A battle cry went up, and troops clambered down the cliff—some in human form, some in animal form. More, other troops began pouring out of hiding and speedily followed them.

"Here they come," said Xavier, twirling his sword by its hilt.

Tension bunching her muscles, Wynter idly flexed her grip on the hilt of her own blade, watching as the troops spilled onto the town. They weren't hesitant or cautious about invading unknown territory. No, they were bold and aggressive and cocky, seemingly sure that they held the upper hand. They attacked buildings as they ran, apparently intending to cause as much damage as death.

None of the residents moved to stop them. Everyone stayed in place, watching, waiting, readying themselves to act.

Her monster stirred dangerously as troops charged toward the manor. It wasn't so pleased with her plan for it to sit out the battle. In fact, it had tried to rise when Lailah pinned her attention on Wynter, but Kali had thankfully stayed its hand.

When the charging troops were no more than twenty feet away from the manor, the townspeople sprung at them from all sides. They leapt out of windows, rushed out of doors, or poured out of the forest—their aim to box in the troops and decimate them.

Wynter watched as sheer chaos unfolded up ahead of her. There were roars, growls, screams, battle cries, and the clanging of swords. Energy balls, orbs of fire, and flashes of magick lit up the darkness. Lycans and other shapeshifting creatures galloped around, lunging at troops and tearing into them with teeth and claws. Dragons took to the air and began blasting enemies with ice-cold breaths or white-hot flames.

It wasn't a case of packs, lairs, covens, conclaves, nests, courts, and hordes fighting individually. The townspeople all fought as one, along with the people who'd been called here to fight by the Ancients who owned their souls.

"It's becoming pretty clear that the troops weren't expecting such a resistance, let alone such a well-coordinated attack," said Wynter. "They're flapping."

"Maybe they thought a population made up of so many preternatural breeds couldn't possibly fight well together, given they often fight among themselves," mused Xavier. "If so, they were wrong. And they're realizing it far too late."

That wasn't leading anyone to retreat, though. On the contrary, in fact, the troops who'd evaded the attacking townspeople were almost on her and the rest of the people lined before the manor.

Feeling charged from head to toe, Wynter lifted her sword and angled it just right, conscious of Xavier and Anabel/Mary—who each stood either side of her—doing the same. Wynter licked her lips, ready and eager. "Get ready, people." It was just as Anabel/Mary began singing Queen's "Don't Stop Me Now" that a troop swung his sword at Wynter. She parried the blow and pitched her body forward to shove him back.

And so it began.

She twisted this way and that way as she struck at the asshole again and again. He didn't aim to kill but to incapacitate. She fought hard, refusing to give him the opening he needed. When the crow flew at his face, taking him off-guard, Wynter wasted no time in impaling him on her sword.

He'd no sooner dropped to the ground than another troop charged her, but he was swiftly taken down by the monstrous cat that made no bones about ripping out his throat.

More and more troops came forward. They knew Wynter, knew that her blade was enchanted, knew that their skin wasn't truly covered in insects. But the enchantment still distracted the fuck out of them, and she never hesitated to take advantage—slitting throats, puncturing hearts, slicing off heads.

She didn't only use her blade, she also struck out with her magick. This time, she didn't hold back power-wise. The toxic magick burned, infected, blistered, withered, and charred as it killed. Which meant that many of Xavier's reanimated corpses looked so absolutely *hideous* it was nauseating.

"Fuck," he spat as he accidentally bumped into her.

She stumbled slightly, and the bastard dueling with her lunged forward and almost accidentally severed her head clean off her neck. She jerked back out of reach, but the tip of his sword nonetheless slashed her face. *Motherfucking ow.*

He grinned at the wound, but his expression morphed into one of horror when Anabel/Mary hacked off his extended arm with a smile. The huge cat then pounced, finishing him off, while Anabel/Mary went back to singing—choosing Elton John's "I'm Still Standing" this time as she expertly swung her sword to slice and block.

Wynter swore as an overgrown coyote pretty much flew at her. One of Xavier's corpse-friends caught it, and both beast and zombie hit the ground hard. Together, Wynter and Xavier speared the coyote before it had the chance to rise.

"Our side definitely has the upper hand," he said before then beginning to chant as he reanimated the dead coyote.

Panting, Wynter took a moment to drink in her surroundings and found that she had to agree with him. Plenty of mangled bodies were sprawled on the ground, but most were invaders from Aeon.

Not all those fighting were engaged in close-up combat. Some covens and conclaves stood off to the side and attacked with magick. Some fey attacked with elemental power while others shot arrows coated in dust that she knew caused all kinds of shit, including confusion, memory loss, lethargy, muscle pain, sensory paralysis, and—

Another troop rushed her.

"Hell." Bracing herself, she slammed up her sword. Their blades clashed again and again as they fought with all they had.

It turned out that her opponent didn't 'have' enough.

She punched her sword into his gut and viciously twisted the blade before yanking it out. He dropped like a stone, and then she saw that the Moonstar coven wasn't too far behind him.

Ho, ho, ho, how fabulous.

# Chapter Twenty-Five

A warning from Esther had the nearby troops edging away from her coven to avoid any magickal blows, providing her a clear path to Wynter. It was very wise of the troops to move. Because this would get ugly—Wynter would make sure of it. She had a score to settle.

Taking a quick scan of the witches fanned out behind Esther, Wynter noticed there was no sign of Rafe. Either he'd found some way to sit out the battle or the coven had left him behind, not trusting that he would fully back them.

"Who the fuck is this bitch glaring at you?" asked Xavier, frowning as said bitch effortlessly destroyed the puppets he sent her way.

"That would be Esther," replied Wynter, not needing to elaborate. She'd already told her crew all about the Moonstar witches.

His eyes narrowing, Xavier twirled his sword. "I don't suppose you'll let me kill her, will you?"

"Nope, this one's mine." Once the Priestess came to a halt several feet away, Wynter smiled at her and said, "I can't tell you how delighted I am that you're here."

Esther jutted out her chin. "I cannot say I share that delight. I would have much preferred to never set eyes on you again." Her gaze slid to Kali's mark and she tittered, all haughtiness. "Did you really think that anyone would be fooled by that mark on your face? Foolish girl. Kali will not be pleased that you are falsely posing as one of Her Favored."

Wynter skimmed her gaze along each of the Moonstar coven members, sensing that none believed the mark was real.

Uninterested in proving anything to these people, she didn't respond to Esther's comment.

"You have made a series of bad decisions of late," said the Priestess. "I would advise you to break that habit, put down your sword, and come quietly."

Come quietly? "Oh, you're here to detain me?" Wynter couldn't help but smile. "You think you have it in you? Well, aren't you just adorable."

Xavier snickered.

Esther dismissed him with a glance. She hadn't paid any real attention to the cat, crow, or Anabel/Mary either. Well, underestimating people was kind of Esther's thing.

The Priestess squinted. "If you know what is good for you, Wynter, you will come without a fight."

"So you can hand me over to the Aeons? You'd really do that?" Wynter took in each face that stared back at her. "I mean, I can see why you'd stand aside while someone else captured me. You'd never go up against the Aeons even if you wanted to. But for you all to actually take it upon yourselves to do the deed, *knowing* the Aeons will put me through a serious amount of pain once they've gotten what they want from me . . . That's kind of cold of you, isn't it? I was one of you once."

Some *did* look uncomfortable with the situation. They might not have particularly cared about her, but they'd cared for Agnes— handing over the woman's granddaughter to beings who were fond of sadistic torture didn't sit right with them. Having Wynter exiled had been one thing. This was another.

"You stopped being one of us a long time ago," said Esther. "You were a stain on the coven for years. You defiled our town with your filthy magick. You afflicted a plague upon our people. You incited a war between the Aeons and the Ancients. The others from Aeon have looked upon our coven with utter contempt since you left. We have been scorned. Judged. Snubbed. And all for something that wasn't our fault."

"Then you've had a taste of how I felt for years after my magick turned dark, huh?"

Esther snapped her mouth shut.

As a little breeze swirled around Wynter's legs that carried a hint of derision, she said, "Kali's not a fan of you, you know. Neither is what She put inside me." The monster kept throwing her mean-ass snarls. "It would really like to end you. And I mean *really* like it. To be truthful, I'm kind of tempted to let it, since I know for sure it would rip you apart. But *I* want to be the one who sees you fall."

Esther scoffed. "You will not convince me you are a revenant. Nor will I believe you are a match for me. Your magick is not pure enough to take down a Priestess, Wynter."

"You're not the only Priestess here," Xavier said to her. "Wynter is ours, and I'd say she's a fuck of a lot better at the position than you are."

Anabel/Mary nodded while the cat and crow moved a little closer to Wynter.

Esther took in the sight of them and laughed. "A rag-tag group doesn't make a coven."

"A *family* makes a coven," said Wynter. "That was why Agnes despaired of what yours had become. It is no longer a family. It is a gathering of power-hungry people. There's no real loyalty among you. No true bonds. Hell, half of you don't even like each other. But my coven? We're everything you're not."

Xavier grinned. "You called us a coven," he whispered. "About fucking time."

"And you still haven't worked out what you should have long ago learned," Wynter went on, holding Esther's gaze. "No magick is pure. It's just power. *Your* magick might be able to do warm, fuzzy things like heal or create, but it can also kill. Where's the purity in that?"

Esther pressed her lips into a thin line. "It may interest you to know that Rafe is dead. Lailah snapped his neck."

Rage and grief blasted through Wynter, tightening every muscle.

Esther smirked and, God, Wynter wanted to fuck this bitch's shit up in the worst way. But rushing at her in anger . . . no, Wynter wouldn't do that. She wouldn't dishonor him by forgetting all he'd taught her. No, she'd avenge him by *applying* all he'd taught her—starting with boxing her rage away and focusing on getting the job done.

"It was his punishment for returning to Aeon without you," Esther added. "In that sense, his blood is on your hands. All you had to do was return and restore the town's health. But no. And now your precious mentor is no longer with us. Don't despair, though; the two of you will soon be reunited. Well, perhaps not 'soon.' Going by just how much you enraged the Aeons, they may well torture you for a very long time before finally killing you."

"Yeah, that's not going to happen. Your little attempt to detain me will fail, as will any attempt the rest of your army makes. But don't take my word for it. Give it your best shot. I'm thinking it'll be fun to watch you try."

While Esther made a sad attempt at smack talk, Wynter nodded along and quietly warned her coven, "Be ready. They'll attack hard, knowing they can heal me. They'll want to kill all of you purely to spite me."

Xavier cast her a sideways glance. "Are they going to attack from afar?" he asked, his voice too low to carry to the coven.

"Yes," Wynter replied. "And so are we."

"Oh," whined Anabel/Mary. "Using magick is *boring.* I want to slice off heads."

"We're way too outnumbered to go charging at them," Wynter pointed out.

"Some might charge at us," said Xavier. "A few are armed."

"No, they're there solely to protect Esther. They'll defend her from the other townspeople so that she and the rest of their coven can concentrate on blasting *us* with magick." It wasn't a coven made up of warrior witches. Most of them relied on magick alone, and they were powerful enough to be able to defeat opponents without getting up close and personal.

Wynter had an edge here, though. She knew each of them well. Knew their strengths and weaknesses. Knew how best to take each of them down.

Esther and her coven undoubtedly thought that they could boast having the same knowledge about Wynter. In truth, they knew very little about her magick. Something they'd soon discover.

Anabel/Mary sighed and stabbed her sword into a corpse. "I'm *tired* of just standing here. And I'm thirsty—"

"*No* drinking blood," Wynter ordered before, *so* done with Esther's smack talk, calling out, "Well, shall we get this over with?"

Cutting off her words, Esther gave her a courteous smile that held a hint of maliciousness. "That would suit me fine." She hissed something at the people flanking here, and they all then began to chant.

"Here we go," said Wynter.

A glittering mist of silver magick clogged the air and rushed at her. She could feel the compulsion that throbbed within it. The bitches thought to force her to drop her sword and follow them blindly.

Wynter waved a bored hand. Her own magick slashed through the air, dark and thick, slicing through the mist and severing the spell, causing the mist to dissipate.

Esther ceased chanting, shock written all over her face. The other Moonstar witches exchanged uneasy looks.

Wynter cast them a challenging smile. "You're gonna have to do better than that." She blasted them with a red-hot, toxic gust of magick that whipped their faces, leaving ugly, hissing welts. "Yeah, I was right. This *is* going to be fun."

\*

Adrenaline spiking through his bloodstream, Cain dodged yet another flaming spear, watching Lailah bare her teeth in frustration. Bites and stings dotted her bare flesh, and he'd bet they itched and throbbed like a mother.

Retaliating fast, he released a ball of power that exploded in the air as it neared the Aeons, the force of it making several stagger and causing minor fissures to appear in the cliff face.

The Aeons were doing exactly as he'd expected—they were repeatedly calling on the natural elements and sending out blasts of air, fire, water, and earth.

Good choice of 'weaponry,' really.

Such power was potent, and they were experts at wielding it. But Cain was an expert at *twisting* it. Which was something he did repeatedly. And so water became locusts. Winds became hornets. Sand became bees. Fire became tiger mosquitoes.

And he sent those little creatures right at the Aeons each time.

Witnessing the bastards squirm and wriggle and slap at themselves was nothing short of entertaining, particularly because the Aeons *knew* and hated that they looked ridiculous. Cain wasn't simply doing it to amuse himself and his creature, though. He wanted their fury, wanted to lure them into making mistakes.

It was working.

They no longer fought like a true squadron. They were each more focused on wiping away the taunting smirk that he purposely kept on his face. And so the number of Aeons was steadily dropping. Not fast enough for Cain's liking, though.

He would have preferred to focus on killing those shielding the siblings, but he couldn't afford to take his attention off Lailah and Saul for long—they were attacking too hard and fast, aiming to keep the Ancients preoccupied so that their backup could spring surprises on them. It was a technique they'd used during their last war. It had worked well then.

Cain was resolute that it wouldn't work so well now.

But he'd have to first help the other Ancients tire out Lailah and Saul, which wasn't proving easy.

"Watch out for those pulsing surges of energy that Saul's throwing," said Seth, a note of pain in his voice. "They hit like a fucking sledgehammer."

"I learned that the hard way," said Cain, once more warping a cloud of sand into a swarm of bees and siccing them on the Aeons. "My thigh is still partially numb from the hit." His leg had almost buckled under the force of it. "You okay?"

"I've got a broken rib for sure," replied Seth.

A female shriek of anger preceded a crack of power that dispersed the swarm of bees. Lailah sharply waved her arm, projecting a shower of rocks, pebbles, and crystals at the Ancients.

A massive gust of power rushed out of one of the Ancients and met the 'shower,' absorbing every fragment before they could make contact with anyone. *Dantalion*, Cain suspected.

Yelling something at the troops that Cain couldn't quite hear, Saul raised his arms, palms out ... and then crackling projectiles of fire whooshed toward the Ancients so damn fast all they could do was try to dodge them.

Cain hissed loudly as one brushed his arm, burning through cloth and grating off layers of skin. "Bastard." Before he had a moment to retaliate, a large wave of ash formed into a cloud of bats—a signature move of Lilith's—and promptly flew at the Aeons. She chuckled when the immortals flapped their arms at the creatures and cried out in alarm. But that laugh turned into a harsh expletive when Saul sent yet more projectiles their way wickedly fast.

Clenching his fists, Cain readied himself to dodge the projectiles, but they didn't aim at him or the other Ancients. No, they blasted the manor. It was a pointless move, since the building was warded against any and all attacks. But, unaware of that, Saul continued to blast the manor.

Cain spared Azazel a quick glance. "Cover me while I focus on Saul."

As Saul relentlessly attacked the manor, Cain took advantage of his distraction—striking with orbs, beams, and waves of pure power.

Instead of retaliating, Saul used the element of air to 'jump' from spot to spot in an attempt to evade any 'blows' ... perhaps thinking that Cain was attacking him so hard to distract him from destroying the manor.

Again, Cain took advantage, striking repeatedly; drawing blood, slamming flesh hard enough to bruise, bombarding the Aeon with blinding pain.

With a roar, Saul locked his gaze on him. Maybe feeling forced to defend himself or maybe finally realizing that attempting to damage the manor would get him nowhere, the Aeon sent out a wave of water that swiftly turned to ice as it whooshed through the air.

Cain slammed the block of ice with enough power to knock it off-course, sending it crashing into the river below. He smirked at Saul, goading—

A female cry of outrage sounded. *Ishtar.* Familiar pulses of power then shot toward the first line of Aeons and yanked at their shadows, causing said Aeons to fall on their asses and slide toward the edge of the cliff . . . exposing the two ruling Aeons they'd been shielding. A gust of Azazel's power rammed into the two siblings, knocking them down like skittles, scraping at their flesh like claws.

Saul called on air to relocate him fast while Lailah slammed her hand on the ground. Most of the fallen Aeons skidded to a halt, but a few tumbled off the cliff with cries of terror. As Lailah joined those shielding her in leaping to her feet with a snarl, Cain drank in the fear that briefly flickered across her face.

"She's finally realized that she's in deep shit," said Azazel.

Cain nodded. "Took her long enough."

Power again began whipping back and forth as the two sides went back to exchanging pitiless blows.

\*

A line of white flames thundered to life, seeming to spurt out of the ground in front of the chanting Moonstar witches. Hissing and spitting, those flames raced toward Wynter and her coven, their heat *searing.*

"Not today, Satan." Anabel/Mary tossed a glass vial on the ground, and a large billow of crimson smoke rose up in the air and put out the flames in an instant. "Lovely."

"Hattie, Delilah—go at them from the rear," ordered Wynter, her words coming fast. "Xavier, send some of your corpses to attack the coven from all angles. Let's keep their attention divided."

"You got it," he told her, crouching down to touch the nearest dead bodies.

It was as bird and feline slinked off that balls of fiery magick sailed at Wynter. She repelled them with her blade, sending them whooshing back toward the people who'd tossed them.

The two covens then went head to head.

Each blow of magick on both sides was merciless. Cloth ripped or burned. Skin tore or blistered. Blood pooled or splattered. Bones snapped or cracked. Glass shattered as Anabel/Mary tossed potion after potion that negated and blocked magickal hits.

Being attacked from all sides, the Moonstar witches had their hands too full for them all to be able to focus entirely on Wynter, Xavier, and Anabel/Mary. But neither Esther nor the witches flanking her once allowed themselves to be distracted.

Yeah, well, neither did Wynter or the coven members at her sides. They all countered the attacks with both sword and magick, pouncing on any opening to retaliate. Shelving any pain, she lashed out again and again, loving how her enemies floundered at the intensity of her magick. Meanwhile, one crimson gust after another poured out of Anabel/Mary's palms, and Xavier sent out surges of magick that reeked of death.

Above them all, power thundered through the air as the Ancients and Aeons continued trading blows. But Wynter didn't have time to follow the battle going on above her. She didn't even allow herself to think much on it. She had her own battle to focus—

Wynter swore as a wave of magick hit her so hard that the force sent her stumbling backwards. "Fucker." She struck again, sending sparks of dark magick whipping along the ground.

The Moonstar witches backpedaled, trying to avoid the snapping, crackling whips. They failed. The magick lashed their flesh, leaving open sores that gaped.

"Feel the burn," said Anabel/Mary.

Well, it was only fair. Wynter sported a fair number of wounds, courtesy of the scalding hot white orbs the other coven kept tossing at her—more of which then came flying her way. She slammed up her sword to deflect them just as Anabel/Mary threw yet another vial. It smashed a foot away from the other coven, its contents splashing their flesh. No, *corroding* their flesh.

"Acid." Wynter smiled. "Nice."

Chanting, a glaring Esther emitted another glittering mist. Wynter once more used her magick to hack through it and dissolve the spell.

Esther snarled. "Yield, Wynter. Your little group will die here if you don't."

"Looks like the ones dying are *your* people." Wynter sent out another surge of magick. The surge swirled and morphed as it sailed toward her old coven, becoming red and black ashes that stuck to the skin of whatever witch they hit. More importantly, the ashes melted into any open wounds, wrenching cries and hisses and winces out of the witches.

Horrendous blisters soon began to pebble on the flesh of the aforementioned witches, including Esther. Those blisters burst and bled and sizzled, making the little skanks freak the fuck out.

"What in the name of . . ." Esther trailed off, striking out harder, absolutely panicked. That panic only increased when she realized that an inky blackness was spreading through her veins. The other witches who were similarly affected kept glancing at their Priestess even as they fought, looking for reassurance, maybe?

Well, they'd find none.

Soon enough, as the magick began to eat at their bodies, their skin began to blacken. Sag. Peel. Decay.

Teeth fell out. Hair thinned. Lips shriveled. Muscle wasted away. Extremities withered and became stumps.

"Damn, Wyn," said Xavier, grinning. "This is ... sickening. I love it."

Wynter lifted her hand and paused the magick that was rotting Esther's body before it could reach her brain. At this point, the Priestess looked both hideous and pitiful. Which was just absolutely wonderful.

Esther tried backing up, almost falling over the dead witches behind her. The coven's number had steadily dropped until only a few were left standing, and Wynter doubted the woman had even noticed.

Wynter eyed her from head to toe. "Now your appearance matches the monster you are within. And I'd say you'll fit in just fine with the other monsters you'll meet where you're going." Wynter psychically tapped into her connection with the netherworld. The ground beneath Esther darkened and rippled like fluid. "I told you I wanted to be the one to see you *fall*, right?" Then the Priestess dropped with a scream.

*

Cain sucked in a pained breath as a heavy, white-hot bolt of light crashed into him, burning like a firebrand. The Aeons were now fighting harder, redoubling their efforts to take down the Ancients, no longer resorting to only using elemental power. But he and the other Ancients were hitting them just as hard and fast, giving no quarter. Hence why Cain then whipped the invaders with power, slashing their flesh and sending some sprawling to the ground ... giving Seth time to rise after being knocked off his own feet by a strike from Lailah.

Cain had sensed several of the Ancients fall at one point or another, but none were down for long from what he could tell. It was hard to be certain. Aside from Seth and Azazel—who Cain could see in his peripheral vision—he had no way to check on the others. Not without turning his attention from the Aeons, which he couldn't afford to do. But although he'd heard the occasional cry or grunt of pain, he had no sense that any of the other Ancients were badly injured.

Now that the Aeons were scared and weakened by both injuries and exhaustion, Cain and the Ancients were no longer concentrating too much on Lailah and Saul. They instead made a point of taking out the siblings' backup one by one. But each time someone shielding them fell, another Aeon was quick to replace—

Cain spat out a string of curses as razor-sharp power pierced and snipped at his flesh like scissors. "Fucker." He launched a ball of plasma that smashed into the legs of an Aeon, exploding on impact, *destroying* said limbs. Cain's creature hummed its pleasure. Plasma was its favorite weapon, but Cain didn't often toss it, despite how deadly it was—the orbs didn't move as swiftly as others so were easily blocked.

Seth swore as spheres of blinding light zoomed through the air like bullets. "Christ, they're fast." He moved swiftly, emitting a wave of repellent power, but not fast enough to deflect every sphere.

Two wacked into Cain and, *Jesus*, they packed a punch. A punch made of iron that singed flesh like molten lava.

Another sphere must have crashed into Inanna, because she spat, "Bastards." Then she was launching power grenades at the Aeons, who scrambled to deflect them.

Cain took advantage of their distraction, forming a vortex of power that zipped toward them. Its magnetic force sucked several off the cliff but Lailah acted fast, lifting her hands, causing massive wings of white air to appear. Said wings flapped hard, destroying the spiral and hitting the Ancients with a surge of wind that almost knocked Cain clean off his feet even though he'd braced himself for impact.

No one had time to retaliate, because the Aeons struck again swiftly, splattering the Ancients with blobs of mud. Cain hissed as the weird fucking dirt ate at his skin.

"It's like goddamn acid," Azazel ground out.

Worse, smoke rose from the mud, rushed up Cain's nostrils, and entered his lungs, eating at the oxygen there like a sponge.

He stood very still as he purged the toxic smoke out of his system fast, growling as power sliced and stabbed him like a fucking immaterial blade. He assumed the other Ancients were forced to do the same . . . which was most likely why Saul chose that moment to act.

Silver shockwaves *rocketed* toward the Ancients. One smacked into Azazel, sending him zooming backwards. Another hit Cain, causing him to stagger into his brother—which, inadvertently, knocked Seth out of range of a third shockwave.

Free of the effects of the mud, Cain righted himself just as Azazel returned to his side.

"Fucking hate shockwaves," Cain heard Dantalion growl, and then pulses of near-nuclear energy crashed into several Aeons, killing two. Only one rushed to replace the living shields . . . and it seemed to be right at that moment that Lailah and Saul finally realized how dramatically their numbers had dropped.

Lailah let out a cry of fury and emitted an omnidirectional wave of gas that shimmered in the air.

Cain didn't even want to know what that gas would do. He let out a gust of darkness that formed a giant smoky hand with skeletal fingers. Said hand hit the wave and sent it ricocheting back to the Aeons, who bowled over coughing as they fought the effects of the gas.

Taking instant advantage, the Ancients attacked as one—launching missiles of glass shards, zapping bodies with electric tenacles, hurling orbs of power that cleaved and bisected whatever they touched. The latter took out the two Aeons who stood in front of Lailah . . . providing a clear path to the bitch.

She screeched as a shower of glass shards buried themselves in her skin, which was exactly when Cain launched a ball of plasma that crashed into her head. Her mouth dropped open in a silent scream as she arched violently . . . and her skull exploded like a bomb.

A roar of grief rumbled out of a severely injured Saul, who tried reaching for the remains of his sister but was quickly hauled off by two surviving Aeons. The three disappeared out of sight, as did the many others on the cliff.

"Death by plasma ball to the head," said Azazel. "I bet she never thought she'd go out that way."

"My, my, my, the rats are all fleeing the metaphorical sinking shit fast," Lilith observed.

Tracking her gaze, Cain noticed that the troops who'd invaded the town were retreating quickly. He wasn't sure if someone had called the troops back or if they were taking it upon themselves to scamper after watching their leader fall, but they were sure high-tailing it out of there in a hurry.

They were also being pursued by many of the residents, who were battering their numbers fast. The Ancients helped, zapping troop after troop with power. Some managed to escape, but Cain didn't care. He wanted some to return to Aeon and relay what had happened here; wanted the other Aeons to not only be pissed but scared.

His gaze quickly sought out Wynter, scanning the line of—*there*. She was facing off against Esther . . . who promptly disappeared into the ground like it was water. *The fuck?*

The rest of the Moonstar coven was quickly dispatched, at which point Wynter rolled her shoulders and blew out a breath. Either she felt the weight of his gaze or merely wanted to check on him, because she twisted to look up at the manor roof. Cain took an easy breath as he saw that she was fine. Oh, she was covered in blood spatter, minor wounds, and bruises, but she was otherwise okay.

His creature was too wound up to be settled by that. It wanted her close. Now.

Anabel started poking at Xavier's forehead with what appeared to be a severed finger. Wynter whispered something into the ear of the blonde, who then tensed. And dropped the finger with a squeal.

"So," began Inanna, "how long do we think it will be before more Aeons come?"

343

"Hopefully not long," said Dantalion. "I'm not sure who will lead them. Maybe Saul. Maybe Abel. Maybe Adam. Maybe all of them. I believe we can be certain of one thing—whoever comes will bring a bigger army, and they'll be better prepared for us."

"They'll still all die," said Cain.

The other Ancients nodded. Because no other scenario was acceptable unless they wanted to remain caged forever.

# Chapter Twenty-Six

"Do you have any intention of freeing Esther from the netherworld at any point?"

Humming as Cain drifted his fingers through her hair, Wynter replied, "At present, no. I'd like her to suffer some, and I feel no need to go traipsing through the place in search of her. But I might later change my mind, you never know." They'd been talking for a while as they lay in bed, exchanging stories of their personal battles during the war. "Are you sure you don't want me to free Annette and Bowen?"

"There's no real point. Both will be killed for committing what was effectively treason, so neither avenue involves mercy." He stroked over her arm, where she'd earlier been wounded. Anabel's healing brews had worked wonders, as usual, so there wasn't a single scratch on Wynter now.

"Was it difficult to hold back your monster during the battle?" he asked.

"No, because it won't disobey Kali—She has a great deal of influence over it. Thankfully. But it certainly wasn't pleased that it couldn't 'play.' I couldn't have let it out, though. It would have killed anything in its path, including my own coven."

"So you're finally admitting it's a coven."

Wynter narrowed her eyes at his teasing smile. "*Anyway* . . . how long do you think it will take to repair all the damage to the town?"

"We have a lot of people here to work on it, so hopefully not long."

"But there'll later be more damage, won't there? When other Aeons come, I mean. You do think they will, right?"

"Some will come, yes. Saul will certainly be one of them as he'll wish to avenge his sister. Considering she was Abel's consort, he should technically want to do the same. I'm not sure if they had a tight relationship, though. People claim consorts for all sorts of reasons. It doesn't always mean that they value that person."

"Lailah and Abel never *seemed* close to me. And I heard that their relationship was an on-and-off thing that involved a lot of conflict and drama. They weren't faithful to each other either, or maybe they simply weren't exclusive—I don't really know. But if he kept reinstating her as his consort, she had to have meant something to him, right? Then again, if that was the case, he would have either been at her side tonight *or* he would have sent someone else to lead the army in her place. I wouldn't have wanted *you* to partake in a battle without me, even if I thought said battle would be easy to win."

Cain's face softened slightly. "Yeah?"

"Yeah."

He squeezed the side of her neck. "Same goes. So, I'd say we can conclude that Abel didn't feel as strongly for Lailah as another person would for their consort. He might still wish to get even with us. However, he wouldn't wish to be part of a battle that would mean fighting against Seth—they were once very close. But I suppose it is worth considering that Seth fought against Abel's consort tonight, so perhaps that will be enough for Abel to turn on him. We shall have to wait and see."

"Would it bother you to go to war with Abel?"

"No. He was never really a brother to me."

Wynter worried her lower lip. "Did you really once try to kill him?"

"Yes. But that's a story for another time."

*So mysterious.* "I'll want to hear it," she cautioned.

"You will eventually."

"If you didn't kill him all those years ago, why are you known as the originator of murder?"

346

"Oh, people had killed others before I was born. I was by no means the first person to attempt to, or successfully commit, murder. But I was the first to target a brother. And that's the end of that story for tonight." He combed his fingers through her hair again. "Right now, you need to sleep. We both do."

Cain held her close, something he'd gotten so used to that he wasn't sure he'd be able to sleep without her right there next to him. He hadn't known her long, no, but he'd walked the Earth long enough to be certain that what he felt for her was no temporary attraction; that what they had was worth keeping. Protecting. Nurturing.

He'd never had someone like Wynter in his life before. It was almost like she'd been designed to intrigue, attract, and enchant him. He'd be a fool to let her go ... but if he meant to keep her permanently, he'd need to one day be honest with her.

There were so many things she didn't know about him. So many things he would like to think she could accept, but he simply couldn't be sure. He did know one thing. He would only tell her when he felt sure she wasn't going anywhere; that she'd feel too attached to Cain to leave him; that she'd feel he was worth the trouble his creature would give her.

It would likely take time for her to get to that point. Cynical as he was, a part of him doubted that she really ever would. But he had to hope that part of him was wrong, because he had absolutely no idea how he'd give her up. And he didn't believe that his monster would let him anyway.

Closing his eyes, Cain forced his mind to rest. Sleep took him fairly fast, but his creature later woke him abruptly. And, sure enough, Wynter was gone again. Cain called out her name, softly cursing when he received no response. He jumped out of bed and dragged on a pair of sweatpants, making a mental note that locking the door to his chamber wouldn't be enough to keep her from wandering out of it in her sleep.

Just as he'd expected, he found her stiffly walking toward the gates to his garden. He sighed. He really had no idea what it was about the garden that—

He stopped breathing and stumbled to a halt. Because the padlock dropped to the fucking ground, and the iron gates creaked open in welcome. She hadn't even *touched* them.

*What. The. Fuck?*

Wynter walked into the garden, slow and mechanical.

"Wynter!" He hurried toward her, but instinct made him slow to a stop. This clearly wasn't a simple case of her being subconsciously drawn here in her sleep. Not if the gates had opened for her like that. Something else was at work. Something had to be leading her here somehow. He wouldn't find out what was going on if he woke her and took her back inside the Keep.

So, instead, he trailed behind her, remaining close to ensure that the snakes did her no harm. But, like the last time she came sleepwalking here, they didn't even try. They simply followed her, rustling the long grass either side of the path. Protecting her? Drawn by her? He didn't know.

The cool artificial breeze ruffled her hair and the long tee that he'd earlier slipped on her simply because he liked the look of her in his clothes. She didn't shiver or otherwise react. Didn't jump or jerk at the sounds of crickets or the frogs croaking. She just kept moving forward.

Soon, they neared the temple. Fuck, he couldn't let her go in there. He was about to reach forward and cuff her arm with his hand, but then she stopped right at the base of the stone steps.

He sidled up to her and studied her face. She was staring up at the temple, unseeing.

"I know what you hide here."

The hairs on his arms stood on end. The words had come from her mouth, but it wasn't Wynter's voice. It was thicker. Rang with power. *Deity.*

"Kali," he greeted through gritted teeth, not bothering to bow or any such shit. Should he have showed some respect? Yes. But this being was *inside* his witch, and he didn't fucking like it. His creature was *furious*. "So it's you who keeps leading her out here."

"No. Something else draws her to this place."

He wasn't buying that. "Hmm."

Kali laughed, meeting his eyes. "I sense you do not like that I am using her body. She is more mine than she is yours, darkling."

The latter word startled him so much he could only blink. He hadn't heard it in a long time. It was an affectionate term often used to describe the children of his kind. Not that it had ever been used on him before—affection hadn't been a big part of his upbringing.

Since he hadn't been a child in a very long time, he didn't appreciate *Her* using it, but he wasn't about to rise to the deity's attempt to provoke him for fun.

"You need not worry for Wynter," said Kali. "I mean her no harm. I also mean you no harm. We have similar goals, you and I."

"Goals," he echoed. "Are you planning to use Wynter to reach those goals? Is that why you didn't make her an average revenant? Is that why you keep sending her back to this realm?"

"You will have answers to your many questions in due course, when the time is right. Now is not that time."

He narrowed his eyes. "Why are we having this conversation?"

"As I said, we have similar goals. So I will caution you to be prepared for betrayal. It may happen, it may not, but be on the lookout for it all the same—that is all I can say on the matter." She paused. "I will tolerate your presence in my witch's life, but that will change if you attempt to interfere in my plans. Is that understood?"

*Tolerate* his presence? Like She had some fucking say in the matter?

"One more thing, darkling. If you prove unworthy of Wynter, if you betray or hurt her . . . you will bring sheer hell upon yourself. And by that, I do not mean *I* will avenge the slight. I will not need to. Wynter will do that herself, and she will not be merciful. So heed my warning. There will not be another."

The deity seemed to burst out of Wynter, because her eyes closed and her body fell forward. He caught Wynter's limp form and lifted her easily. For a long moment, he stared down at her, struggling to sort through what he'd just learned from Kali, unsure if he could truly believe all She'd said—deities lied when it suited them. They only ever interfered in matters on this realm when they had their own agenda. And Kali . . . she'd never been one to have productive agendas. *Fuck.*

\*

Sitting across from Cain the next morning at the small table in his chamber, Wynter felt a frown tug at her brow. "Why are you looking at me weird? You've been doing it all morning."

"You were sleepwalking again last night." He lifted his cup of coffee. "You went back to the garden."

Wynter inwardly groaned and tossed the last of her bagel into her mouth. "Was I banging my forehead on the gates again like a weirdo?"

"No," he replied, his face blank. "They opened for you. The padlock fell right off. And then I had a little chat with Kali."

Wynter could only gawk at him. "What?"

"She spoke to me through you."

*Well, fuck me sideways.* Wynter leaned forward in her seat. "What exactly did She say?" Instead of replying, he patted his lap in invitation. In a hurry to hear more, she quickly accepted said invitation.

Cain adjusted her position so that she straddled him. "On top of cautioning me to be on my best behavior where you're concerned, Kali wanted to warn me that I may soon be betrayed."

"Betrayed? By who?"

"She didn't say." He paused, smoothing his hand up Wynter's thigh. "She was very vague in pretty much everything She said. It was very frustrating."

"Yeah, I know how that feels," she muttered. "She's drip-fed me information ever since She marked me and sent me back to this realm."

"How has that not driven you crazy?"

"I got used to it, I guess. And what can I really do about it? She's a deity, Cain. They do what they want when they want." Wynter clasped her hands behind his nape. "I'd rather not make Her mad by griping about it, since She could probably drag my soul back to the netherworld whenever She felt like it."

And that bothered him far too much. He simply wasn't sure what he could do about it yet. Cain dipped his head and pressed a suckling kiss to her throat. "I didn't like seeing Her in your body. And I really don't like that She feels you're more Hers than you are mine—yeah, that was what She said." He bit down hard enough to leave a mark on her throat. "She couldn't be more mistaken."

"And you couldn't be more possessive. Which brings me neatly to a matter that I'm not good with. The barrier is still there. You said it would go by itself, but it hasn't."

His mouth curved. "You tried finger-fucking yourself again?"

She pointed at him. "Don't try to wander off the subject. Why is the barrier still there? Don't you trust me not to betray you?"

Hearing the note of hurt in her voice, Cain might have felt shitty … if he hadn't also sensed that she was playing him. He shot her a narrow-eyed look that made her snort. "It isn't a sign of distrust." He whipped the shirt off her body. "You know that. I've already explained why I did it." Though he hadn't been entirely truthful, since he couldn't yet tell her about his creature.

"So you're not going to remove it?"

He had no way to remove it without provoking his creature to personally replace it, but she didn't need to know that. Holding her against him, he stood and crossed to the bed. "No." Laying her down gently on the mattress, he bent over her to lick and nip at her neck. "It does you no harm, does it?"

"That's not the point."

"Then what is?"

"It shouldn't be there!"

"You can bitch about it all you want, I've told you before, I know it doesn't bother you as much as you'd like me to believe it does."

She huffed. "Fine." She delved her hand into his sweatpants, pulled his cock free, and fisted it tight. "Let's make this even, though, shall we?"

He raised his head as an odd vibration ran up his hardening shaft followed quickly by a strange sensation ... as if cold mesh encased his cock. "What are you doing, little witch?"

She gave him a smug grin and folded her arms just as the sensation faded away. "I cursed you."

"You did, what?"

"I cursed you so that if you trying sleeping with another woman while we're together, your dick will wither and rot. Why the fuck are you smiling?"

A number of reasons. One, no one else would ever have *dared* do such a thing. Two, he would never have seen it coming. Three, that she was so possessive of him made things more balanced. Four ... "Your vengeful streak really does run as deep as mine." *That* he really liked. "But then, it's what revenants are built for, isn't it? To avenge."

She frowned. "This isn't me being vengeful."

"Ah, I see. You're trying to turn me on."

"What? No, you weirdo. It's supposed to bother you enough that you'll remove the barrier in exchange for me removing the curse."

"There's no need for you to do that." Lifting her hips toward him, he went back to teasing her neck with his tongue and teeth. "I would never be so much as tempted to betray you, so the fact that you've cursed me ... well, it's moot."

"Moot? Are you kidding me?" She gasped when he ground his cock against her clit. "You really are *unbelievably* fucking twisted if this is revving your engines."

He hummed. "I like that you're so possessive."

"This isn't about possessiveness."

Cain sent a surge of pain/pleasure sweeping over her soul that had her arching right off the bed. "Admit it, you don't want to remove the curse. You're just as fucking insane as I am." He lashed her soul yet again. "Definitely made for me," he added, watching her nipples tighten, her skin flush, and little bumps sweep across her flesh.

He put his mouth to her ear and let out a low growl. "I'm going to wreck you again. I'm going to make you break for me." He pressed a kiss to the pulse now beating frantically in her neck. "Love it when you break."

Exploring her body with his hands, he repeatedly whipped her soul with pleasure/pain—sometimes he kept his lashings firm, sometimes he made them featherlight, constantly switching things up so she wouldn't know what to expect.

She scratched at his shoulders, her pupils blown. He knew her nerve-endings would feel raw and supersensitized. Knew her breasts would be aching, her pussy would be damp, and her body would be crying out for release.

He knelt between her thighs and hooked her legs over the crooks of his elbows. "I think it's time I put my cock where it belongs," he said, lining the broad head up with her opening. "Inside you."

He thrust hard, driving his dick deep as he lashed her soul yet again. She came apart with a scream, her inner muscles clenching and spasming. He slowly fucked her through her orgasm, sinking in and out too lazily for another release to build inside her just yet.

Cain planted one palm on the mattress beside her head. "Hand," he said when the aftershocks from her orgasm slipped away. "I want the one I marked."

She held it out to him, swallowing hard.

He cuffed her wrist and held her palm up to his mouth. Still thrusting slow and easy, he traced the C of his mark with his tongue, smiling when she jolted, knowing it would feel like his tongue had licked at her slit. He traced and flicked and danced his tongue over the C again and again, adding the occasional whip of pleasure/pain to her soul when she least expected it.

He wanted her to feel off-balance. Utterly possessed. Like her body wasn't her own but *his*. His to pleasure, rule, ruin, corrupt, play with—whatever he wanted, whenever he wanted.

Upping the pace of his thrusts, he kept licking at his mark while also teasing her soul. "You crave this, don't you?" he said, a growl edging into his voice. "You crave what I do to you, crave the pleasure and the pain and everything in between."

She licked her lips. "Which is what you want."

"Of course it is." If sex was the only way he could tie her to him for now, then he'd use it. "It's only fair." He dropped her hand so he could grip her thigh tight. "I crave you."

Wynter's breath stuttered as he began pounding into her body, stuffing her full again and again. More electric waves of bliss swept over her soul. The dark pleasure nipped like teeth, scratched like nails, and burned like sharp but light slaps.

And she wanted more.

He gave it to her, showering her soul with waves and lashes and featherlight flicks all while slamming his cock hard and deep into her pussy. Raw need carved into his face, he glanced down at where their bodies were joined. "Look how well you take me."

It was hard to keep her eyes open when this insanely good out-of-body pleasure was wracking her very being. There was so much sensation, internal and external, she had no idea how her brain could possibly compute it all. No idea how the organ hadn't short-circuited for at least a mere moment.

Trembling and panting, she soon ended up in that space where she floated, anchored only by the scent and feel of the man dominating her body, mind, and soul. He'd warned her from the very beginning that he wanted that extent of power over her. Well, he had it. And she wondered if he knew it yet.

A mess of chemicals and tension and so much overwhelming

pleasure/plain she could barely breathe with it, she dragged her nails along his back as her release slinked toward her. "Cain ..." God, she was *so close.*

He switched his angle, rubbing against her clit with each pounding thrust. "Now be a good girl and break for me."

One abrupt lash to her soul was all it took. She choked on a scream as her orgasm snapped through her—intense, blinding, explosive. She shook and arched and cried.

Cain growled and licked at the corner of her eye. "*Fuck.*" He rode her with hard, feral digs of his thickening cock before finally exploding inside her.

When her thoughts were no longer scattered to the wind and she could finally talk again, she said, "I have to say, I've grown rather fond of your cock."

A low, rumbly chuckle vibrated against her neck. "I gathered that when you possessively cursed it."

Wynter frowned as the memory rushed back to her. It had been a spur of the moment thing, and she'd thought it would be enough to get him to remove the barrier ... because she'd forgotten for a minute that he was a total fucking nutcase. "I still can't believe you don't care. I mean, it's a *curse.*"

He lifted his head, smiling. "You know ... humans often talk about the Curse of Cain. In truth, it holds a metaphorical meaning. But now? Now the term really does apply. And if anyone asks, I get to tell them that my woman is so possessive—"

"You don't get to tell them *anything.*"

"Are you embarrassed that you cursed my dick? Because it really doesn't mind."

God, he was *nuts.* She was tempted to quite simply undo the curse despite that he wasn't going to be cooperative, but maybe he was expecting that. Maybe he was calling her bluff. Well, she wasn't so easily manipulated. "What about the metaphorical Curse of Cain thingy, what is it?"

He hummed, flicking her nose with his. "Add it to the list of things I'll tell you one day. And when I do, you have to remember that promise you once made me."

"That I wouldn't run when I realized why I'm not totally safe with you?"

He gave a slow nod. "That one."

She couldn't even complain that he was holding back, since she was doing the same to him. Still, she might have made a snippy comment out of frustration if it wasn't for the grave look on his face. He truly did believe there was a high chance that she'd not only want to leave him but would literally flee. "I'm not easily spooked."

"I know, I'm counting on that. Because I get the feeling that chaining you to the bedpost to keep you here won't be as easy as I originally thought."

She did a slow blink. "You really weren't kidding when you first mentioned putting me in chains, were you?"

"Snapping an iron cuff closed around your wrists will just be so much easier than tying complicated knots."

"I'm struggling to decide what to do with that comment. But then, I think most people would."

He pursed his lips in thought. "Yeah, they probably would."

"You know, we always tend to have seriously weird conversations right after sex."

"You have likely had far stranger conversations with your coven, and probably at far stranger times."

The thing was ... the man wasn't wrong.

# Acknowledgements

Thank you so much to my family—I spend a lot of time in my head, but you encourage and support me anyway. I love you all for it.

I want to also say a huge thanks my PA, Melissa. I don't think I'd get through signings and release blitzes without you. Especially since you remind me to breathe.

I'd like to say a mega-big thank you to the team at Piatkus, particularly my editor Anna Boatman. I brag all the time about how I have the best publishing team an author could ever ask for. Thank you for that!

Also, thank you so very much to all my amazing readers for taking a chance on this book. I hope you enjoyed THE WICKED IN ME.

And thanks a bunch to my characters—they wrote this story themselves, I just watched what happened in my head and then typed it.

Take care,

S :)